Vital Records
of the Town of
Plymouth

An authorized facsimile reproduction of
records published serially 1901-1935 in
The Mayflower Descendant

With Added Index of Persons
by

Col. Leonard H. Smith Jr.

CLEARFIELD

Originally published serially in
The Mayflower Descendant
Plymouth, Massachusetts, 1901–1935

Added Index of Persons
Copyright © 1989 by Leonard H. Smith, Jr.
All Rights Reserved.

Indexed edition reprinted for
Clearfield Company, Inc. by
Genealogical Publishing Co., Inc.
Baltimore, Maryland
1992, 1999

International Standard Book Number: 0-8063-4841-0

CONTENTS

Preface 5
Historical Data 6
Vol. 1 (1899) 7
Vol. 2 (1900) 17
Vol. 3 (1901) 28
Vol. 4 (1902) 33
Vol. 5 (1903) 37
Vol. 7 (1905) 40
Vol. 12 (1910) 44
Vol. 13 (1911) 51
Vol. 14 (1912) 68
Vol. 15 (1913) 83
Vol. 16 (1914) 97
Vol. 17 (1915) 110
Vol. 18 (1916) 119
Vol. 19 (1917) 135
Vol. 20 (1918) 142
Vol. 21 (1919) 145
Vol. 22 (1920) 152
Vol. 23 (1921) 161
Vol. 24 (1922) 166
Vol. 25 (1923) 170
Vol. 26 (1924) 176
Vol. 27 (1925) 185
Vol. 28 (1930) 189
Vol. 29 (1931) 192
Vol. 30 (1932) 196
Vol. 31 (1933) 203
Vol. 32 (1934) 211
Vol. 33 (1935) 216
Vol. 34 (1937) 221
Index of Names 223

PREFACE

In 1899 the Society of Mayflower Descendants in Massachusetts began printing in its quarterly, *The Mayflower Descendant,* the vital records of the town of Plymouth, Mass., as they had been literally transcribed from the original records by George Robert Bowman. The printing continued, irregularly, until the demise of the publication in 1937. Unfortunately the printing of the transcript was not completed. (*The Mayflower Descendant* was revived in 1985.)

This volume is a facsimile reproduction of the Plymouth town records which were published, with the addition of a name index.

The major work in this index was done several years ago (which, incidentally, is the reason the pagination begins with the title page instead of the text) but was suspended on the recommendation of a member of the staff at one of the nation's well-known institutions with the comment that the vital records of Plymouth were in the process of being published elsewhere, by an agency with which I instantly realized I could not hope to compete. However, that publication has never reached the market.

The consolidation of the Plymouth records from 29 different volumes of an elusive source into this single volume will, it is hoped, be of value to a great many researchers.

I owe a debt of thanks to Norma Helen Smith and Dorothy Marvelle Boyer for many hours of proof-reading.

HISTORICAL DATA
Relating to Counties, Cities and Towns in Massachusetts
by
Paul Guzzi, Secretary
Commonwealth of Massachusetts

[Note: Different printings show different Secretary's names.]

Plymouth, Plymouth County.
The first entry appearing in "Plimouth's Great Book of Deeds of Lands Enrolled" is dated 1620.

- 1670 June 7*   Bounds between Plymouth and Sandwich as established Jan. 19,* 1663 ordered to be recorded.
- 1707 June 4*   Part established as Plympton.
- 1726 June 16*   Part known as the "North Precinct" established as Kingston.
- 1729 July 10*   Part called the plantation of "Agawam" included in the new town of Wareham.
- 1827 Jan. 20   Part annexed to Wareham.

*The asterisk (*) as used in this pamphlet [i.e. *Historical Data*], means Old Style or according to the Julian Calendar. The present calendar, the Gregorian or New Style, was adopted by an Act of Parliament of Great Britain. It was ordered that September 3, 1752, should become September 14 and that the legal year should commence with the first of January, instead of March 25, beginning January 1, 1752.

To change Old Style to New Style add 10 days to a 17th century date and 11 to an 18th century date.

THE MAYFLOWER DESCENDANT

A Quarterly Magazine

OF

Pilgrim Genealogy and History

1899

———

VOLUME I

———

BOSTON
PUBLISHED BY THE
MASSACHUSETTS SOCIETY OF MAYFLOWER DESCENDANTS
1899

PLYMOUTH BIRTHS, MARRIAGES AND DEATHS.

Literally transcribed from the Original Records at Plymouth, Mass.,
By GEORGE ERNEST BOWMAN.

On the title page of the oldest book is written, in a very bold hand:

    PLIMOUTH TOWNE BOOK
    FOR BIRTHS MARRIAGES
        AND BURIALS
        ANO DOMINIE
           1699
        THOMAS FAUNCE
         TOWNE CLERK

On the back of this leaf is written:

on ye 3^d Day of June 1715, The Metinghouse at plimouth was mu[*worn*] The Thunder

Plymouth Births, Marriages and Deaths.

on The 4th day of ffebruary 1722-3 was a Dreadfull [worn] Raised the Tide 3 or 4 foot higher Then had ben kno[worn]

The next page seems, from its earlier date, to have been the original title page. It has the following inscription:

PLIMOUTH TOWNE
BOOKE
ANO DOMINE 1696-7
FOR BIRTHS BURIALS
AND MARRIAGES
PER THOMAS FFAUNCE
TOWNE CLERKE

These three pages contain also much scribbling in various hands.

The numbering of the pages begins with that on the back of the second title page. The third leaf, containing the second and third pages, is missing. The original paging is indicated by numerals enclosed in brackets, and inserted before the first word of each page.

[p. 1]

The Children of Mr. John Co[*]ton pastore of the of plimouth and of mistres Joanna Cotton his wife

1 John borne at guilford in Conecticut Colony August [*]]th
2 Elizebeth Borne att guilford August the 6th 1663
3 Sarah borne att Marthins vinyard January the 17th 1665
   She dyed at guilford September the 8th 1669
4 Bowland borne at plimouth december the 27th 1667.
5 Sarah borne at plimouth Aprill ye 5th 1670
6 Maria borne at plimouth January the 14th 1671
7 A Son borne at plimouth September the 28th 1674
   he dyed the day following September the 29th
8 Josiah borne at bostorn September the 10th 1675
   he dyed at plimouth January 9th 1676.
9 Samuel borne February 10th 1677 :
   he dyed at plimouth December the 23th 1682
10 Josiah borne at plimouth January the 8th 1679

*Worn.

11 Theophilos borne at plimouth May the 5th 1682 Abraham Peirce son of Abraham Peirce & Rebeckah his w[*] was born January 1638. Deceased January 1718 †

Mehitabel Nelson born April the 5th 1670

[Pages 2 and 3 are missing]

[p. 4]

The Children off Eliazur Downham and Bathshaba his Wif[*]
1 Eliazur borne the 15th day of Janaway 1682
2 Nathannell borne the 20th day of March 1685 Decasd feb[*] †
3 Mercy borne the 10th day of december 1686
4 Israil born october 1789 ‡
5 Elisha born in August 1692
6 Josiah born June 1794 ‡
7 Barshua born Aprill 26 1696
8 Susannah born in June 1698
9 Joshua born April first 1701

The Children of John Cobb and martha Cobb his Wife
1 John Borne the 24th of august 1662
2 patience borne the 10th of august 1668
3 Ebenezor borne the 9th day august 1671
4 Elisha Borne the 3th of aprill 1679
5 James Borne the 20th of July 1682

The Children of Thomas Clerk and Rebeckah his Wife
1 Suzannah Borne the 21 day feburay 1684
2 Thomas Borne the 25th day of desember 1685

The Children of Thomas Clarke & Elizabeth Clarke his wife
Josiah Born on the 15th of december 1690
Eliazebeth born 12 day of July 1692
Rebeckah born June ye 2d 1694

The Children of The above Named Thomas Clark & Susanah his Wife
1 Annah born January 24 1700
2 Abigall born on the 9th of december 1701
3 Sarah born february 10 170 4/3

*Worn.
† The birth and death were both entered at the same time.
‡ These are plainly mistakes of the town Clerk for 1689 and 1694.

John atwood Son to Nathaniell atwood and Mary his wife
1 was born the first day of may 1684
2 Elizabeth born the 24th of Aprill 1687 deceased March 30 169[*]
3 Joannah born the 27th of february 1689 deceased March 30 169[*]
4 Mary borne on the 26 of aprill 1691
5 Nathaniell borne on the 3d of october 1693
6 Isaac born on the 29 december 1695
7 Barnabus born on the 1 day of January 169$\frac{7}{8}$
8 Joannah born June 8th 1700

[p. 5]
The Chldren of Nathaniell Southworth & Desier his Wif
1 Constant borne the 12th day of august 1674
2 Mary Born the 3d day of aprill 1676 Decea^d being y^e wife of Jo: Rider Feb^{ry} 2nd 1757
3 Ichabod born Aboute the midle of march 1678
4 Nathaniell born the 18th day of may 1684

The Children of Elkanah Cushman and Elizabeth his wife
1 Elkanah born the 15th day of September 1678
2 Jams born the 20th of october 1679
3 Jabes born the 28th of december 1681 died the may following 1682

The Children of Elkanah Cushman and Martha his Wife
1 Allerton born the 21th day of November 1683
2 Elizabeth born the 17th day of Janawary 1685
3 Josiah born the 21th of March 168$\frac{7}{8}$
Mehittable borne october the 8th 1693

The Children of Joseph ffaunce and Juduth his Wife
1 hannah born the 12th of Jun 1678
2 Mary born the 2 day of June 1681
3 John born the 3 day of december 1683
4 mercy born the 30th of June 1686 Shee dyed the 26 of Aprill 1687
5 Mehittale born May 27th 1689
6 Joseph borne May 21 1693
7 Eliazar born ffebruary 6 169$\frac{5}{6}$

*Worn.

8 Thomas born July 15 1698
9 Benjamin born february 17th 1703 : deseased June 28th 1704

[p. 6]
The Chil of Abraham Jacson Junor and Margareat his wif[*]
1 Abraham borne the 9th day december 1686
2 Samuel Borne August y^e 15th 1689
3 Sarah Borne february y^e 14th 1691 Deseased May 4th 16[*]
4 Israiel Borne December 11th 1693
5 Lidia Borne March ye 22^d 1696
6 Seth Borne June ye 7th 1698

The Children of Edward Doty Senior and Sarah his Wife
1 Edward born the 20th of May 1664
2 Sarah born the 9th day of June 1666
3 John born the 4th day of august 1668
4 Mary & martha born the 9th day of July 1671
5
6 Elizabeth born the 22 of december 1673
7 patience born the 7th of July 1676
8 mercy born the 6th of febuaway 1678 Shee dyed the last day of november 1682
9 Samuel born the 17th of may 1681
10 mercy born the 23 of September 1684
11 Benjamin Born the 30th of may 1689

The Children of Gorg bonan Junor and Elizabeth his w[*]
1 Elizabeth born the 18th day of June 1684
2 Samuell born the 15th day of october 1686 he deceaced the 9th day of January 1686
4 Ruth borne the 29th december 1688
5 Ann born November 28 1690
6 Sarah born July 27 1693
7 Lidiah born october 20 1696
8 Ebonazar born march 3^d 1699
9 Suzannah born April 25 1702

The Child of Thomas Doty and Mary his wife
Hannah Doty was born December 1675

*Worn.

Plymouth Births, Marriages and Deaths.

The Child of Jerusha Finney, daught^r of Robert Finney Lydia Finney, Born Decemb^r 8. 1747.

The Child of Elizabeth Wood Widdow Mary Wood, Born Jan^{ry} 12. 1744/5

[p. 7]

The Children of Isaak Lobdell and Sarah lobdell his Wife
1 a daughter born the 13th of february 1680 Shee dyed the 22th of the Same month
2 Sarah : born the 27th of September 1682
3 Martha : Born the 24th of february 1684 She died the 13th of aprill 1686
4 Samuell born the 17th day of february 1686 : 87

The Children of John Doty & Elizabeth his Wife
1 John Born the 24th of August 1658
2 Edward Born the 28th of June 1671
3 Jacob Born the 27th of May 1673
4 Elizabeth Born the 10th of ffebruary 1675/6
5 Isaac Born the 25th of october 1678
6 Samuell Born the Last of Januawary 1682
7 Elisha Born the 13th of July 1686
8 Josiah borne in october 1689
9 Martha borne in october 1692

The Children of John Rickard Juno^r & mary Rickard his wife
1 John born the last of february 1679
2 Mercy born the 3th day of february 1682
3 John born the 3th day of february 1684
4 Ester borne the first of aprill 1691
James Born september 25 [or 26^h] 1696 *

[p. 8]

The Children of Josiah Morton and of Suzannah Morton his Wife
1 Suzannah born the first day of ffebruary 1686 Shee dyed the first day of March 1687
2 Josiah born the 13th of Aprill 1688

* Between Ester and James space was left for two more names.

Plymouth Births, Marriages and Deaths. 145

3 Suzannah born the first day of september 1690
4 Henerey born on the 7th day of January 1692 he deceased in Novem 1697

The Children John Briant Junor & Sarah Briant his Wife
1 John Born the first of September 1678
2 Jams born the 26th of July 1682
3 Ruth born the 26th of September 1685
4 Sarah born the 28th of february 1688
5 Joanah born on the 13th of november 1690
6 George born on the 3^d of desember 1693

The Children of John Gray and Joanah his wife Edward Borne the 21 day of September 1687. he dyed the 20th of february 1687–88
Mary born the 7th of december 1688. desceased on the 17th of March 1703
Ann Born the 5th of Agust 1691
desire borne on the first day of desember 169[*] Shee deceased on the 6th of december 1695
Joannah born the 29th of January 1696/7
Samuel Born on the 23^d of desember 1701/2
Marcey born on the 4th of february 1703/4

[p. 9]

The Children of John Churchill and Rebeckah Churchill his: Wife
1 Elizabeth Borne the 7th day of october 1687
2 Rebeckah borne August 29th 1689
3 John borne december 20th 1691
4 Sarah borne ffebruary 10th 1695
5 Hannah borne february 27th of Aprill 1697

The Children of John Sturtevant and hannah Stirtevant his Wife
1 hannah Borne the tenth day of Aprill 1687. on A Sabbath day att 4 Clock afternone

The Child of John King and Hannah King his Wife Amariah King was born March 4. 1752. was Born in Plymouth—

* Worn.

William Green Sone to William Gren
and Elizabeth his wife was born the 24th of April 1684

[p. 10]

The Children of John Mordow and Lidiah Mordow his Wife
1 John Borne the 13th of december 1687 he dyed the 8th of Januawary 1687
2 : Jonat borne the 3d of febraary 1689 deceased April 24th 1697
3 : John Borne June the 8th 1691
4 : James Borne June 13th 1693 at 3 of the clock in the afterno[*] : he deceased March the 11th 1693/4
5 : Robert born on the 14 of March 1697/8 he deceased July 28: 1699
6 : Robert born october 8th 1699 he deceased 7 weks after
7 James born January 14 1694/5 att 11 Clock at Night
8 Thomas borne on the 19 of november 1701 att 8 Clock at nigh[*]

The Children of John Drew and hannah Drew his Wife
1 Elizabeth borne the 5th day of february 1673
2 John borne the 29th of August 1676
3 Samuel borne the 21 of february 1678
4 Thomas borne the 1 day of may 1681
5 Nicolus borne about the middle of october 1684
6 Lemuell borne August the 4th 1687

The Children of James Easdell, & Rebeckah his wife
1.
2. } [No names were entered.]
3.

The Children of Samuel Garner and Suzannah his wife
1 Samuel borne September the 27th 1683
2 Nathaniel borne September the 10th 1685
3 Suzannah born the 10th of September 1687
   She dyed the first of september 1689

[p. 11]

*Worn.

Plymouth Births, Marriages and Deaths.

The Children of Thomas ffaunce and Jean his Wife
1 patience borne the 7th of november 1673 [She Marry'd Eph'm Kempton & Died at Dartmouth Aged 105 year 6 months & 5 Days.*]
2 John borne the 19th of September 1678
3 Martha borne the 16th of December 1680
4 pricilah borne the 20th of August 1684
5 Thomas borne the 18th of May 1687
6 Joannah borne the 24th of June 1689
7 Jean born the 18th of November 1692

The Children of Ephraim Morton and hannah his wife
1 hannah borne november the 7th 1677
2 Ephraim borne october the 31th 1678
3 John borne July 20th 1680
4 Joseph borne March the 4th 1683
5 Ebenezur borne Aprill the 11th 1685

The Children of Nathaniel Holmes and Mersey his Wife
1 Elisha borne the 19th of April 1670
2 Mersy borne the 10th of September 1673
3 Nathaniel borne the 10th of november 1676
4 Sarah borne the 2 of october 1680
5 John borne the 17th of April 1682
6 Elizabeth borne the 25th of April 1686
7 Eliazur holmes borne the 16th october 1688
   Deceas'd Aug'st 21st 1754*

[p. 12]

The Children of John Bradford and Mersey his Wife
1 John borne the 29th of december 1675
2 Alse borne the 28th of January 1677
3 Abigal borne the 10th of december 1679
4 Mersy borne the 20th of december 1681
5 Samuel borne the 23th of december 1683
6 pricilla borne the 10th of March 1686
7 Wiliam borne the 15th of April 1688

The Children of William Churchill and lidiah his Wife
1 William borne on the 2 day of August 1685

*This entry is in a modern hand.

148

2 Samuel borne on the 15th day of Aprill 1688
3 James borne on the 21th of September 1690
4 lidiah born on ye 17 of Aprill 1699
5 Josiah born August 21 1702

(To be continued.)

PLYMOUTH BIRTHS, MARRIAGES AND DEATHS.

(Continued from page 148.)

[p. 13] The Children of m^er William Clarke and of mrs: Hannah Clarke his Wife

Sarah born the 19th of June 1678
William born the 7th of June 1682
Nathaniel born the first day of June 1684
Samuel born the 8th of december 1687   Decea^sd Ap. 2nd 1763
The Child of M^er William Clark and Mrs Abia Clarke his wife
Hannah Borne August 2^d 1697

The Children of Eleazer Churchell & Mary his Wife †

1. Hannah Churchell born
2. Joannah Churchell born
3. Abigail Churchell born
4. Eleazer Churchell born
5. Stephen Churchell born Feb^ry 1684-5
6. Jedidah Churchell born
7. Mary Churchell born
8. Elkanah Churchell born
9. Nath^ll Churchell born
10. Josiah Churchell born
11. Jonathan Churchell born

The Children of Samuel Lucos & patience Lucos his Wife

1 John Borne on the 24th of January 168⁷⁄₈ deceased January 31st 169⁶⁄₇
2 Joseph Borne on the 26th ‡ october 1689
3 William Borne on the 19th of october 1692
Patience Borne on the 2^d of January 1696

The Children of John dotey senior and Sarah dotey his wife

1 Sarah Borne on the 19th of february 169⁵⁄₆
2 patience born on the 3^d of July 1697
3 desire born on ye 19th of Aprill 1699

* The 4 was written over a 3.
† This family was entered in the same hand as that of Ebenezer and Marcy Churchell on the next page.
‡ The 6 was written over a 4.

[p. 14] The Children of William Harlow Junior and of lidiah his Wife

1 Elizabeth born in the 3^d Weke of february 1683
2 Thomas born the 17th of march 1686
3 A daughter born the 5th of february 1687 Shee dyed the 5th of march following 168⁷⁄₈

The Children of Ebenezer Churchell & Marcy his Wife

1. Ebenezer Churchell Born, June 20th. 1749
2. Branch Churchell Born, Decemb^r 17. 1751
3. Bethiah Churchell Born, Septr. 13. 1753   Decea^d Decr. 28th 1753
4. Bethiah Churchell Born Novr. 24th 1754
5. Rebeckah Churchell Born Novr 1. 1756   Decea^sd. Aug^st. 12th 1760.
6. Marcy Churchell Born April 19th. 1759   Decea^sd. Sept. 9. 1760
7. George Churchell Born April. 18th. 1761.
8. Marcy Churchell Born Novr. ye 10th 1763

The Children of Samuel dunham Junior & mary his Wif(eeern)

1 Samuel borne the 19th of July 1681
2 Wiliam born the 2^d of february 1684
3 Mary born the 13th of october 1687
4 Ebenezer born the 24th of february 169½
5 Nathaniell born the 12th of May 1698

The Children of thomas Lazell and Mary his Wife

1 Elizabeth borne the 17th of november 1687
2 Joshua borne the 18th february 168⁸⁄₉
3 Thomas borne Aprill 28th 1691
4 Mary borne on the 3^d day of march 1693
5 Hannah Born the 18th of august 1696
6 Sarah Born on the 14th of March 1699
7 John born August 9th 1701

[p. 15] The Children of Eleazar Ring and mary Ring his Wife

1 Eleazar Borne The 7th of November 1688. he dyed on the 3^d of december 1688.
2 Andrew born on the 14th of November 1689

3 phebe born on the 26th of January 1691
4 Samuel born on the 12th of March 1694
5 Andrew born ye 28th of March 1696
6 deborah born on the 10th of July 1698
7 Mary borne on the 9 of December 1700
8 Jonathan born on ye 23d of December 1702
9 Suzannah born on ye 9th of Aprill 1705
10 Elkanan born on ye the 19th of octobor 1706

The Children of James Warren and of Sarah Warren his Wife

1 John Borne the 27th of November 1688 he deceased the first of March 1689
2 Edward borne on the 14th of September 1690 he deceased on the 28th day of february 1690 or 91
3 Sarah borne the 27th of May 1692
4 Alse borne on the 3d of September 1695
5 Patience borne on the 13 of January 1698/9
6 James borne Aprill the 14th 1700 Deceas'd July 1757
7 Hope borne august 2th 1702 died May 3. 1728
8 Marcy born on the 21 of March 1705/4
9 Mary born January 14 1707 Deceas'd Febry 4th 1795
10 Elizabeth borne on the 17 January 1710/11 died Novr 5. 1744

[p. 16] The Children of Josiah ffinney and Elizabeth his Wife

1 Josiah borne the 29 January 1687/8 he deceased September the 19th 1696
2 Elizabeth borne on the 8th of february 1690
3 Robert borne october 21th 1693
4 pricila born on ye 9th of March 1693/4
5 Josiah born on ye 9th of october 1698
6 John born on ye 13th of december 1701
7 phebee born on the 21 of ffebruary 1705/4
8 Joshua born on ye 20 of July 1708

The Children of Elaxander Cannedy and Elizabeth his wif(worn)

1 hannah borne the 27th of September 1678
2 Elizabeth borne the 6th of Agust 1682
3 Jean born the 19th of Aprill 1685

4 William borne the 8th of march 1689
5 Sarah borne November ye 11th 1693
6 Annable born May 8th 1698
7 John born the 23 April 1703

The Children of Robert barrows and Lydiah his Wife

1 Elisha borne the 19 of march 1686 he deceased on the 19th of January 1689 or 90
2 Robert borne on the 8th of November 1689
3 Thankfull born desember 8th 1692
4 Elisha born on the 16th of June 1695
5 Thomas born on the 14th of february 1697
6 Lidiah born on the 19th of march 1699

[p. 17] The Children of William Shirtlif and of Suzannah Shirtlef his Wife

Jabiz born the 22d of Aprill 1684
Thomas born the 16th of March 1687
William born the 4th of Aprill 1689
John born About the middle of June 1693
Barnabas born the 17th of March 1695/6
Ichabod borne November the 8th 1697
Elizabeth Shurtlif born May 28 1699
Mary born december 22d 1700
Sarah born June 8th 1702

The Children of John Morton & phebe his Wife

1 Joannah born some time in february in the yeare 1682
2 phebe born on the 7th of July 1685

The Children of John Morton and Mary his Wife

1 Mary born on the 15th of desember 1689
2 hannah Born on the first of September 1694
3 John borne About the Middle of June 1693
4 Ebenazar born october 19th 1696
5 Deborah born on The 15th day of September 1698
6 persis born November 27th 1700

The Children of Leiut John Bryant & of Abigail Bryant his Wife.

1 Mary Born September ye 11th 1666

Plymouth Births, Marriages and Deaths.

2 Hannah Born December ye 2d 1668
3 Bethiah Born July ye 125 1670
4 Samuel Born february ye 3d 1673
5 Jonathan Born March ye 23 1677
6 Abigaill Borne December 30th 1682
7 Beniamin Borne December 16th 1688

[p. 18] The Children Isaac Cushman and Rebekah Cushman his Wife

1 Rebekah born on the 30th of November 1678
2 Isaac born on the 15th of November 1676 this should have ben first set dow(*worn*)
3 Mary born on the 12th of october 1682
4 Sarah born on the 17th of april 1684
5 Icabod born october 30th 1686
6 fear born March the 10th 1689

The Children of John Nelson and Lidiah Nelson his Wife

1 Samuel born on the 4th of July 1683
2 Joanah born on the 9th of may 1689

The Children of John. Nelson & patience Nelson his Wife

1 Liddiah borne february ye 5th 169¾
2 Sarah borne May the 5th 1695 Deceasd Janry 25th 1767 ye Widdo of Thos Spoon(*worn*)

The Children of Samuel Rider & Lidiah Rider his Wife

1 hannah borne June ye 1 1680 Deceasd June 29th 1763 ye Widdow of Jere Jack(*worn*)
2 Sarah borne on the 26th March 1682. Dyed Novr 19. 1778 *w of Joshua Bramhall**
3 William borne on the 18th of June 1684
4 Lidiah borne october 11th 1686 *w of Elisha Cobb**
5 Samuel borne on the 26 July 1688
6 Elizabeth borne on the 26th March 1690 She deceased on the 11th of december 1695
7 Joseph born in ye Middle of July 1691
8 Benjamine born in June 1693
9 Mary born on the 10 of october 1694
10 Elizabeth born on ye 16 of March 1695

* The entries in italics are in a very modern hand.

Plymouth Births, Marriages and Deaths.

11 Josiah born about the Middle of May 1696
12 Abigaiel born on ye 29 of January 1700

[p. 19] The Children of Samuel Recard and Rebekah Rickard his Wife

1 Rebekah born on the 9th of february 169⁰⁄₉₁
2 hannah born the 25th of September 1693

The Children of Robert Harlow Junr & Jean his Wife

1 Sarah Harlow born April 6th 1751. Deceasd April ye 27th 1754
2 Jean Harlow born July 19. 1753
3 Robert Harlow born July 14. 1755
4 Sarah Harlow born Decr 12. 1757

The Children of Stephen Bryant & Mehittabel Bryant his Wife

1 Stephen Born on the first day of May 1684
2 daved Born on the 16th of february 1687
3 William born on the 22d of february 169½
4 hannah born
5 Ichabod born on ye 5th of July 1699
6 Timothy born on ye 25th of August 1702

Abigaill Ransom the daughter of Robert Ransom Junior and Ann his

1 Wife was Born on the 7th day of June 1691
2 Robert born on ye 15th of September 1695
3 Lidiah born on ye 26 of ffebruary 1700
4 Ebenazar born on ye 6th of September 1702
5 Mary born on ye 9th of June 1705

The Children of Thomas Bumpas & Marcy his Wife

2 Joanna Bumpas born June 23rd 1752.
1 A Son not named born April 26. 1751 & Dyed the Same day
3 Samuel Bumpas born March 14. 1754. Deceased May 5th 1755
4 A Daughter Born, Named Marcy, May. 2. 1756. Deceased May 6. 1756.

[p. 20] The Children of Eliazar Cushman and Elizabeth Cushman his Wife

212   *Plymouth Births, Marriages and Deaths.*

1 Lidiah borne the 13th of december 1687
2 John born on the 13th of August 1690
(3 *deborah born on the 10th of July 1698*)*

The Children of Phineas Swift & Rebeckah his Wife
1 Jedidah Swift born June 5. 1753.
2 Abiah Swift born March 7. 1756.

The Children of John Pratt & of Margeret his Wife
1 Benijah borne on the 8th of desember 1686 deceased december 4th 90
2 Ebenazar born on the 29th of Aprill 1688
3 Joannah born on the 26th of october 1690
4 Benijah born May the 6th 1692 deceased August 12th 1692
5 Samuel born september 12th 1693
6 John born March 10th: 1696
7 A daughter born November 17th 1697 deceased december 3d 169(*worn*)
8 Margeret born July 29th 1700
9 Patience born December ye 4: 1701
10 Thomas born September 23d 1703
11 Mehittable born february 24 1705

The Children of Robert Bartlet and Sarah his Wife
1 hannah borne february 21th 1691
2 Thomas borne february the 9th 1693¾
3 John born Aprill ye 13th 1696
4 A son borne february ye 16 1698 he deceased february 20th 169(*worn*)
5 Sarah borne Aprill 9th 1699
6 James born on the 7th of August 1701 Deceased Janury 13 1722-23
7 Joseph born ffebruary 22d 1703¼
8 Elizabeth born March 2d 1705/6
9 William born August 2d 1709 Deceased March 24 1710
10 Ebenazar born Desember 5th 1710
11 Robert born Aprill 30 1713
12 Samuel born Desember 9th 1715

(*To be continued.*)

* This entry has been erased.

16

THE MAYFLOWER DESCENDANT

A Quarterly Magazine

OF

Pilgrim Genealogy and History

1900

VOLUME II

BOSTON
PUBLISHED BY THE
MASSACHUSETTS SOCIETY OF MAYFLOWER DESCENDANTS
1900

PLYMOUTH BIRTHS, MARRIAGES AND DEATHS.

(Continued from Vol. I, p. 212.)

[p. 21] The Children of Nathaniel Harlow and Abigal his Wife
1 Abigall born the 27th of January 169$\frac{2}{3}$
2 Nathaniel borne the 27th of february 169$\frac{5}{6}$
3 James borne the 1 of August 1698

The Children of Samuel Harlow and priscilla his Wife
1 Rebekah born the 27 of february 1678

The Children of Samuel Harlow and hannah his wife
1 John born desember 19th 1685
2 hannah born November 15th 1689
3 Samuel born August 14th 1690
4 William born July 26th 1692

Plymouth Births, Marriages and Deaths.

5 Eliazer born Aprill 18th 1694
6 pricillia borne october 3d 1695

The Children of John Carver, & Grace his Wife.

1 Sarah Carver born July 25, 1749
2 Lemuel Carver born Dec'r 6. 1751

The Children of Jonathan Mory Junior and hannah his Wife

1 Benjamin born November the 10th 1690
2 Maria born on the 22d of September 1692
3 Mary born on the 18th of September 1694 Descaaed november 23d 1715
4 Thankfull Borne the last weeke in March 1695/6
5 Jonathan borne August 1699
6 Relyance born on the 6 of June 1702
7 Curnelios born on ye 2d of May 1706
8 Josep born January 19 1710 7 clock afternone

[p. 22] The Children of Joseph Bartlet Junior and lidiah bartlet his Wife (She m Jo. Holmes 1705)

1 Joseph Borne May ye 15th 1693
2 Samuel Borne on the 29th of august 1696 Deceas'd Mar: 25th 1759
3 Lidiah Borne on the 1 of January 1697/8. Deceas'd May 29. 1742
4 Beniamin Born the 9th day of octtober 1699
5 Sarah born The 24th day of March 170 2/3

The Children of Richard Cooper and hannah Cooper his Wife (He d 1724)

1 Sarah Born November ye 4th 1693
2 Isaac Borne october 10th 1695 he deceased the 9th of March 1503/4
3 John Borne on the 12 of december 1697
4 Elizabeth born on the last day of March 1700

The Children of Samuel Bradford and hannah Bradford his wif (worn)

1 hannah Born on the 14th of february 1689
2 Girshum Born on the 21 of desember 1691
3 Peris born desember 28 1694
4 Elizabeth born on the 15th of desember 1696
5 Jerusha born on the 10th of March 1699
6 Welthe Bradford May 15th 1702
7 Gamaliel Bradford May 18th 1704

The Children of Elias Trask, and Abigail his Wife.

1 Abigal Trask, born, July 1. 1746.

Plymouth Births, Marriages and Deaths.

2 John Trask, born, May 14. 1751.
3 Samuel Trask, born, Dec'r 27. 1753.

[p. 23] The Child of Samel Waterman and Marsey Waterman his Wife

1 Annah borne december 7th 1693

The Children of Samuell Waterman & of Bethiah his Wife

2 Samuel born September ye 23 1703
3 John born January ye 12. 1704
4 Hannah born on ye 13th of March 170 5/6

The Children of Edmund Tilson and of Elizabeth Tilson his Wife

1 John Born on the 19th of November 1692
2 Edmund Born on the 2d of March 1693/4
3 Joanna Born october ye 9th 1696
4 Mary born April ye 14th 1668
5 Eliazebeth born May ye 6th 1700
6 A Child born february ye 10th 1702 Deseass'd february ye 21. 170 (worn)
7 An born June 12th 1703
8 Ruth born february 5th 1705

The Children of John Rickard Senior and of Mary his Wife

1 Marcy borne october 27th 1677
2 lidiah borne december 12th 1681 *
3 John borne desember 29 1681
4 Joseph borne on the 7th of february 1683
5 Marcy borne May 14th 1687
6 Joannah borne September 22d 1691
7 Abigaiel borne the 22d of May 1694
8 Rebeckah born the 3d day of January 1699

[p. 24] The Children of Ebenazar Cobb and Marcey his Wife

1 Ebenazar born on the 22d of March 1694
2 Mercy born January 6th 1695/6 deceased March 23d 1697
3 Nathaniel born the 20th of february 1698
4 hannah born ffebruary 27th 1699
5 Sarah born on the 15th of Aprill 1702
6 Marcy born January first 170 4/5
7 Nathan born January 14th 170 6/7
8 John born May ye 30th 1709
9 Mary born october ye 13 1711
10 Elizabeth born March 30 1714
11 Job born ffebruary 28th 1717
12 Rolon born on ye 30th of october 1719

* This is plainly a mistake of the Town Clerk.

Plymouth Births, Marriages and Deaths.

The Children of John ffoster and hannah his Wife
1 Hannah Born July 25th 1694
2 Sarah Born on the 16th of Aprill 1696 Marcy Born
4 John Born November 7th 1699
5 Thomas born on ye 19th of March 1705
6 Ichabod born on ye 7th of ffebruary 170 7/8 he Deceased on ye 8:th of augst
  Gershom born March 2d 1708/9
7 Nathaniel born June 6th 1711
8 Seth born Aprill 16 1713

The Children of Ephraim Coole and of Rebekah Coole his Wife
1 Ephraim born february 3 1691
2 Samuel born September 17th 1694
3 Rebeckah born August 7th 1696
4 Mary born July 27 1698
5 Dorothy born ffebruary 3d 1701
6 James born on the 14 of November 1705
7 Samuel born on the 2d of April 1709

[p. 25] The Children of John Barnes and Mary his Wife
1 John born on the 26th day of June 1694
2 Hannah born on the 8th of January 169 5/6
3 William born on The 19 of october 1697   Died July 23 1714
4 Seth born on the 25th of August 1699
5 Mary born on the 8 of february 1701
6 Jonathan born on the 16 of Desember 1703 died in 1748
7 Thankfull born october 23 1705
8 Elizabeth March 15 1707
9 lidiah born Desember 4th 1713

The Children of Nathaniel Thomas and Mary Thomas his wife
1 Nathaniel born the 27th of May 1695 he deceased Aprill 5th 1699
2 John borne the 21 of october 1696
3 Nathaniel born on the 24th day of June 1700
4 Joseph born November 11th 1702
5 Mary born on ye 15 of July 1709 Deceased aprill 3d 1714

(wor)dren of Samuel Cornish and Suzannah Cornish his Wife
1 Samuel Borne on the 15th day of July 1694
2 Abigail Born october 24 1696.   Deceased May 31th 1724.
3 Josiah borne the 24 of february 1698
4 Joseph born on the 4th of february 1702

5 Benjamin born on the 13th 170 3/4 february
6 Thomas born the 23d of January 170 5/6
7 James born on ye 8th of June 1711
8 Naomy borne in ye year 1710 & Deceased in November 17:10

(*To be continued.*)

PLYMOUTH BIRTHS, MARRIAGES AND DEATHS.

(Continued from page 21.)

[p. 26] The Children of John Clarke and Rebeka his Wife
1 James born on the 12th of March 169$\frac{5}{6}$
2 Abigall born on the last of July 1698
3 John born on the first day of September 1701
4 Joseph born on the 26th of January 170$\frac{3}{4}$
5 Mary born on y^e 12 of January 171$\frac{1}{2}$

Plymouth Births, Marriages and Deaths.

The Children of frances Lebaron and Mary his Wife
1 James borne on the 23d of may 1696
2 Lazaros borne on the 26 day of december 1698 Decesd Sept 3. 1773
3 ffrances born on the 13th of June 1701

The Children of Joseph Stirtevant anna his wife
1 Joseph Born September 4th 1695
2 David born on The 11th of June 1697
3 Annah born aprill 20th 1699
4 Jonathan born March 1702
5 Ephraim born ffebruary 5th 1704
6 Mary born Novemb 3d 1708

[p. 27] The Child of Ebenezer Norcut, & Susanna, his Wife
Elizabeth Norcut born August 20th 1745.

The Children of William Ring and hanah Ring his w(orn)
1 deborah borne January 24 1695. She deceased May 29 1696
2 Hanah borne the 26 of May 1697
3 William was born on the 25th of July 1699
4 Elizebeth born on the 15th of ffebruary 1701
5 Eliazar born on the 16th of January 1704/5
6 Deborah Ring born on ye 5th of ffebruary 1708

The Children of Ebenezer holmes & phebe holmes his w(orn)
1 Ebenazer borne october the 9th 1696
2 Elizebeth born August 18th 1699

The Children of Thomas Spooner Junr & Deborah his Wife
Nathaniel Spooner Born, March 8th 1747/8
Anna Spooner Born, March 8. 1747/8
   Are Twins.

[p. 28] The Children of Benjamen Eaton & Mary Faton his Wife
1 William borne on the 1 of June 1691
2 Hannah borne on the 10th of ffebruary 1692
3 Jabiz borne on the 8th of ffebruary 1693
4 Sarah borne on the 20th of october 1695
5 John borne on the 6th of october 1697

The Child of Sarah Kempton
Abigail Kempton alias Abigail Thomas. Born Sept 11th 1747

The Children of Richard Seers & Bathshua Sers his Wife
Silas borne on the 23d of August 1697
Seth born on the 18th of March 1699
Mary born on the 3d of ffebruary 1703/4

James born on ye 22d of June 1705
John born about ye middle of November 1707

The Child of William Prat, and Mary his Wife
Ruth Prat, Born in Plymouth, Monday October ye 1st 1745.

The Children of James Barnebe & Joanah his Wife
1 James borne on the 1 day of March 1698
2 Elizabeth on the 18th of August 16*
3 Ambross born on ye 20th of Aprill 1706

The Children of Isaac Harlow, and Jerusha his wife
1. Rebeckah Harlow born Octr 21. 1750.   Decesd
2. Isaac Harlow, born, March 9. 1753   Decesd
3. Bette Harlow, born, Janry 18. 1755.
4th Willm Harlow, born, May 3rd 1757
5 Jerusha Harlow born August 8th 1759
6 Rebeckah Harlow Born Jany 4. 1762
7 Deborah Harlow Born Novembr 3rd 1764
8 Lemuel Harlow Born Novr 30th 1768

[p. 29] The Children of Abiall Shirtlef & Lidiah Shirtlef his Wife
1 James born on the 16th of November 1696   Deceasd Sept. 17th 1766
2 Elizebeth born on the 6th of desember 1698
3 Lidiah born the 28th of ffebruary 1700/1
4 david born the first of June 1703
5 Hannah born July 31 1705
6 John born november 8th 1707
7 Benjamin born April 17 1710
8 Wiliam September 8th 1713
9 Joseph born January 22d 1704/5
10 Abiall born october 23d 1717 Decd June 1778

The Children of Beniamin Warren & hanah Waren his Wife
1 Beniamin born on the 15th day of March 1698   Deceased
2 Abigial born on the 9th of May 1700
3 hannah born on ye first of March 1704
4 Nathaniel born on ye 20th of July 1706
5 Benjamin born on the 10 of aprill 1709
6 Pricila born on the 12 of agust 1712
7 Patience born october 27th 1715

The Child of Captain Benjamin Warren Esther Warren. his Wife
1 Joseph born September 4 : 1717
Marcy born May 15 1721

*This entry has been erased

Plymouth Births, Marriages and Deaths.

The Children of Caleb Lorein and Lidiah his Wife
1 Caleb borne on the 7th of June 1697
2 hanah born on the 1 day of august 1698
3 Ignatious born the 27th of december 1699
4 policarpos born in January 1701
5 Caleb born on the 2d of october 1704
   John*
   Thomas*

[p. 30] The Children of Edmond Weston & Rebeckah his Wife
1 Nathan born february ye 8th 1688
2 Zachariah born desember the 16 1690
3 Rebeckah born July the 31 1693
4 John born July 27th 1695
5 Edmond born october 2¦ 1697

The Children of Nathaniel Howland & Martha howland his wife
1 Joseph Borne on the 8th of May 1699
2 Mary borne on the 15th of february 170¾
3 Nathaniel borne the 9th day of June 1705
4 Joseph born on the 28th Day of August 1708

The Children of David bozworth & Marsy his Wife
1 david borne The 21th of May 1699
2 Jonathan borne on the 16th of february 170½
3 Nehemiah born March 15th 1702
4 hannah born June 24. 1705

[p. 31] The Children of Stephen Barnabe & Ruth barna(be) his Wife
1 Lidiah Was borne September the 4th 1697
2 Ruth born Jully 12th 1699
3 Elizabeth born Desember 5th 1701
4 Timothy born on ye 15th of Aprill 1706
5 hannah born December 5th 1709

The Child of Stephen Barnebe & Judeth his wife
Joseph Barnebe born April 3. 1712

The Children of Nathaniel holmes Junr & Joana holmes his Wife
1 Nathaniel borne September 13th 1699
2 James borne Desember 27 1700
3 Bathshabe borne Desember 18 1703
4 Sarah borne aprill 10 1707   Deceased March 11th 1715
5 Barnabas borne Desember 17 1710
6 Zeffaniah borne January 16th 17½½

*These two names are in a modern hand.

7 Joanna born october 7 1715
8 Ephram born ffebruary 14 17⅛

The Children of Jacob Cook & Lidiah Cooke his Wife
1 William born on the 5th of october 1683
2 Lidiah born on the 18th of May 1685
3 Rebekah born on the 19th of November 1688
4 Jacob born on the 16th of June 1691
5 Margarett born on the 3d of November 1695
6 Josiah born on the 14th of May 1699
7–8 John & Damores born May 23d 1703

(To be continued.)

PLYMOUTH BIRTHS, MARRIAGES AND DEATHS.

(Continued from page 81.)

[p. 32]   The Children of George Barrows & patience his Wife
1 Moses Born on the 14th of february 169⅞
2 George Born March 11 1698
  Samuel B*

The Children of John doty Junior & Mehittaball doty his wif
   (worn)
1 Mehitteball born November 4th 1694
2 Edward born the first of November 1697
3 John† born february 5th 1700
4 Sarah born october 14 1707
5 Suzannah born April 20 1710
6 lidiah born february 10th 171 12/13

The Children of Joshua Mors & Eliazebeth Mors his W(worn)
1 Joshua borne September 12th 1699
2 Elizabeth born on ye 8th of october 1701
3 Edward born on the 25th of July 1704
4 Joseph born on the 29th of December 1706
5 Newberrey born on ye 28 of July 1709
6 Abigail born on ye 22d of September 1711
7 TheoDoros Born August 20th 1714

[p. 33]   The Child of Mr Thomas Lorein and Mrs Deborah
     Lorein his Wife
1 Thomas born on the 4th day of february 1700

* This entry was not completed.
† This has been altered into "Jacob" in a different hand and ink.

Plymouth Births, Marriages and Deaths.

The Child of Abner Silvester, and Jedidah his Wife
Nath[ll] Silvester born October y[e] 22. 1749.

The Children of Abner Silvester, and Abigail his Wife
1 Caleb Silvester Born December 16th 1754   Deceas[d] July 5th 1756
2 Abner Silvester Born Aug[st] 1. 1756

The Child of David Shepard & of Rebekah Shepard his Wife
1 David born on the 4th day of february 1700
2 Rebecah born on y[e] 12th of Aprill 1702
3 Prudence born the 26 of March 170$\frac{4}{5}$
4 a son born March 24 176–7*   Deceased aprill 170$\frac{6}{7}$
5 Ruth born february 22 1708
6 A son born June y[e] 8 : 1713   Deceased on y[e] 26 of June 1713
7 Abigal born on y[e] first Day of September 1715

The Children of Jeduthan Robbins & hannah Robbins his wife
1 Jeduthan born Aprill 23[d] 1694
2 hesther born on the 4 of June 1695   deceased
3 John born on the 21 of May 1696
4 Nicolos born on the 25th of January 1698
5 perses born on the 27th of November 1699
6 Hannah born Aprill 1702
7 Elizabeth born March 1708
   Lemuel †
   Abigail †
   Mehitabel †

[p. 34]   The Children of James Winslow and Mary Winslow his Wife
1 Seth born March y[e] 7th 169$\frac{8}{9}$
2 Mary born March y[e] Last 170$\frac{0}{1}$

Isaac Lothrop Esq[r] born June 23th 1673.   Deceased Sept[r] 7. 1743

The Children of Isaac Lothrop & Elizabeth his wife
1 A daughter born the 28th of october 1699 deceased November 19th 1699
2 Maltiah born June 29 day Ano Dom 1701   Deceas[d] July 6th 1771
3 Elizabeth born on the 15th of Aprill 1705   Deceas[d] Nov[r] 1. 1745.
4 Isaac born on the 13th of ffebruary 1707   Deceas[d] April 26. 1750

* 1706-7.
† These names are in a modern hand.

The Children of John Woshborn & lidiah Woshborn his Wife
1 John born on the 19th of Aprill 1699
2 Ichabod born on the 7th of february 170$\frac{0}{1}$
3 Marsey born on the 21 of Aprill 1702
4 Elisha born November y[e] 5, 1703
5 Ephraim born on y[e] 6th of June 1705
6 Barnabas born feburey 12 170$\frac{6}{7}$
7 Jabiz born Aprill 10 1708
8 Eben born Agust 18 1709
9 Thankfull born february 24 17$\frac{14}{15}$

[p. 35]   The Children of Nathaniel holmes & Ellinor holmes his Wife
1 Marsey born on the 26th of december 1701
2 Nathaniel born on the : 1 : of March 1702
3 Joshua born on the 11th of June 1705
4 Patience born November 14 1707
5 Elener born March 15th 1709
6 Joseph born Novem[r] 8th 1712
7 Benjamin Born ffebruary 13th 1715
8 Richard born Desember 26 1718
9 Meletiah born April 7th 1720.

The Children of Ebenazer Eatton & Hanah Eaton his Wife
1 Ebenezer born September 17th 1702
2 Benjamin born November 23[d] 1704
3 Marsey born March 15th 170$\frac{6}{7}$
4 Elisha born october 11th 1708
5 Gidian born on the 5th of ffebruary 17$\frac{11}{12}$
6 Joanna born y[e] 29th of Aprill 1716

The Children of Benjamin Curtice & Mary Curtice his Wife
1 Mary born desember 8th 1701
2 Benjamin Curtice born on the 10 of october 1704

The Children of Josiah Torrey & Marcy his Wife.
1. Marcy Torrey Born Jan[ry] 8th 1752.
2. Joseph Torrey Born Aug[st] 8. 1754.

[p. 36]   The Children of Ephraime Kempton & pattience Kempton His Wife
1. Ephraime Born Fabruary The 9th 170$\frac{8}{9}$
2. Thomas born on the 20th of february 170$\frac{4}{5}$
3. William born on y[e] 3[d] of August 1707
4. Joanna born jully y[e] 22 1710.

The Children of Eleazer Elles & Deborah his Wife
1. Zilpa Elles Born August 5th 1747
2. Barnabas Elles Born, Dec[r] 9. 1749

166

3. Je* Elles Born, July 15. 1751
4. Abigail Elles Born, Nov 24. 1753
5. Deborah Elles Born, May 15. 1756.
6. Molly Elles, Born March 17th 1758.
7 Pelham Elles, Born Feby ye 3d 1761
8 William Elles, Born April 20th 1764.

The Children of Richard Eaverson & of Eliazebeth Eaverson His Wi(fe)

1 Richard Eaverson born November 10th 1700
2 Ephraime Eaverson born September ye 1. 1702
3 Ebenazar born on the 14th of Aprill 1705

The Children of John Eastland and of Mary Eastland His Wife

1 Zeruiah born December ye 8th 1703
2 Joseph born on the 12th of November 1705
3 Elizabeth born 31 January 1708
4 Marey born November first 1710 Deceased November 13th 17(worn)
5 hannah born ffebruary : 13 : 17$\frac{11}{12}$ Decesed Desembe 2d 1717
6 Jean born September 15 1715 Decased December 18th 1717
7 Joshuah born on ye 13th of April 1718 Deceased July 25 1719
8 Mary born on ye 3d Day of March 1720

(To be continued.)

---

*This name is very badly blotted, but appears to be Jesse.

PLYMOUTH BIRTHS, MARRIAGES AND DEATHS.

(Continued from page 166.)

[Vol. I, p. 37] The Children of Jacob Michell & of Rebekah his Wife

1: Suzanah borne January y̆e 15th 1702/3
2: Rebeckah born on the 19th of october 1704
5: Lidia born June 20th 1710
6: Noah born September 16 : 1712
7: Isaac born January 20 1714/5
8: Sarah born April 29 : 1717
9: Elizabeth born April 27 1722
3 * Seth Michel born March 16. 1705/6
4 * Mary Michel born March 7. 1707/8

The Children of Joseph: Warren & Mehittabl Warren his Wife
1 Joseph born on the 17th of January 1694
2 pricila Waren born on the 15th of June 1696

The Children of Isaac Dotty and of Martha Dotty his Wife
1 Eliazebeth born on ye 24 day of April 1704
2 Jeane Born on ye 10th of November 1706
3 Isaac born on ye 30 of March 1709
4 Rebeckah born on ye 10 of March 1711
5 Neriah born on the 8th March 1713/4
6 Jabez born January first 1716
7 Hope born November 11th 1718   She Deceased April 5th 1720

* In the margin is written "Should have been Entred before."

8 Ichabd born on ye 13th Day of January at four oClock in the Morning
9 and Mary born on ye Same Day at 2 a clock in ye after none in ye year 1720/21

The Child of John Holmes & Experiance Holmes his Wife
1 Samuel born November : 21 : 1704

[p. 38] The Children of Mr Thomas Little and of Mrs Mary Little his Wife
1 Thomas borne att Marshfeild September ye 20th 1701 died at Marthas Vineyard in 1744
2 Isaac borne att plimouth May ye 18th 1704 died at Plimton in June 1755
3 Mayhew born febry 6. 1706/7 deceased June 22. 1735 a Jemaco Mary born July 26. 1709 died Mar. 1 1755
George born April 11. 1712 deceased in the fall of ye year lost at Sea in the year 1729

The Children of John Churchell Jun. & of Desire Churchell his Wif(e)
1 Priscilla Born ye 27th Day of November 1701
2 Samuell Born ye 8th Day of March 1704/5
3 Sarah born on ye 25 of april 1706
4 Phebe born on ye 8 of october 1708
5 Rebeca born Desembe 11th 1713

The Children of Samll King Junior and of Bethia King his Wife.
1 Joanah Borne octtober ye 8th 1697
2 Sarah Borne March ye 25th 1698/9
3 Rebekah Borne June ye 2th 1700
4 Samuel Borne June ye 24th 1702

The Children of John May Junr & Bathshua his Wife
1 Anna May Born Febry 20th 1746/7. Deceasd Sepr ye 12. 1778
2 Bathshua May Born Febry 19th 1748/9.

[p. 39] The Child of Jeremiah Jacson & hanah Jacson his Wife
1 Thomas Jacson borne on the first day of march 1704/5

The Children of Martin Wright, & Sarah his Wife
1 A Son Still born   1750
2 Joseph Wright Born Septr 5th 1751.
Sarah Wright Born June 12th 1759

The Children of Joseph Finney & Marsey Finney his wife
1 Alse born on the first of April 1694
2 John born on the 17th of desember 1696
3 Mary born on the 5th of May 1700

Plymouth Births, Marriages and Deaths.

The Children of Elkanath Cushman Junior & hesther his Wife
1 Elizabeth born on ye fifth of desember 1703
2 Elkanan born on ye 10th of July 1706
3 James born August 29th 1709

The Child of John Torrey & Mary his Wife
Haviland Torrey Born July 20th 1752.   Ent'd in the New Book Page 65

[p. 40] The Children of Robert Waterman & Mary Waterman his Wife
1 Isaac born on the 10th of May 1703
2 Josiah born on ye 5th of March 170⁴/₅

The Children of James Thomas, & Abigail his Wife
2 Jonathan Thomas Born June 1. 1752. Deceased Dec'r 22nd 1754
1. James Thomas Born January 25th 1751. Deceased Nov't ye 10th 1751.
3. Priscilla Thomas Born July ye 26th 1754.   Deceased Dec'r ye 9th 1754

The Children of Benjamin Bartlett and Sarah bartlet his wife.
1 Nathaniel born on the 21 of July 1703
2 Jonathan born on the 24th of January 170⁴/₅
3 Benjamin born on ye 23 of January 170⁶/₇
4 Joseph born on ye 27th Day of March 170⁸/₉
5 hannah born on ye 14 of february 1710.11
6 Sarah born on ye last Day of January 1713

The Children of Isaac Cushman Junior & Sarah Cushman his Wif(e)
1 Phebe born on the 14th of March 1703
2 Alse born on the 26th of June 1705

The Children of Silvanus Bramhall, & Mary his Wife
1. Joshua Bramhall Born, April 27. 1736.
2. Sarah Bramhall Born, Sep't 28. 1737
3. Silvanus Bramhall Born, July 24. 1739
4. Nehemiah Bramhall Born April 20. 1741.   Deceased
5. Joseph Bramhall Born, Jan'y 30. 1742/3
6. George Bramhall Born, April 3. 1745
7. Mary Bramhall Born July 20. 1746.   Deceased
8. Lydia Bramhall Born March 1. 1748.   Deceased
9. Cornelius Bramhall Born May 7. 1749
10. Mary Bramhall Born June 14. 1751.

[p. 41] The Child of Abiall ffullar & Annis ffuller his Wife
1 John born the 25th of february 170⁴/₅

The Children of Amariah Harlow. & Lois his Wife
1. Amariah Harlow Born March 22. 1746/7
2. Lois Harlow Born March 9. 1748/9

The Children of ffrances Adams & Mary his wife
1 Mary born on the 10th of November 1704
2 Jemimah born on ye 12th Day of January 170⁶/₇
3 Thomas born on ye 5th of May 1709
4 ffrances born September 27 1711   died at Jamaica in 1752
5 John born June : 14 : 1714
6 Richard born January 170⁴/₅

The Children of henery Sanders & Ann Sanders his Wife
1 Annah born on the 20th of october 1701
2 Sarah born the 14th of february 1703
3 Abigaiel born the (*) of March 1705
Jonathan Sanders Borne Nov'r 17 1713

[p. 42] The Children Adam Jones & Mary Jones his Wife
1 Marcey borne on ye 21 of June 1703
2 Remember born : on the 8th day of July 1705

The Children of Benjamin King, & Bettey his Wife
1 Bettey King born Aug'st 29. 1751.
2 Rebeckah King born March 1. 1753
3 Benjamin King born March 19. 1758.
4 Susannah King born June 15th 1769

The Children of Ebenazer burges & Marsey burgas his Wife
1 Elizabeth born on the 25th of January 1702
2 Samuel born on the 8th of March 1703
3 Thankfull born on ye 19th day of october 1704
Nathaniel born april 7th 1706   Deceased. December 21. 1723.
Ebenazer born November 28 1707
Benjamin born July 9th 1709
Mary born July 14 1712
Jabez born January 15th 1717   Deceased September 9th 1723

The Child of Joseph ashley & Elizabeth Ashley his Wife
1 Thomas Born on the 21th of ffebruary 1704

The Children of Zephaniah Morton & Jerusha his Wife
1 Zephaniah Morton Born March 12: 1748/9.
2 George Morton Born Dec'r 27. 1750
3 Eleazer Morton Born April 6. 1753.
4 Sarah Morton Born Dec'r 20. 1755.
5 William Morton. Born. Oct'r 10. 1757.
Rebecca Morton born April 1st 1760

(To be continued.)

---

* Doubtful. Is either 10th or 16th

THE MAYFLOWER DESCENDANT

A Quarterly Magazine

OF

Pilgrim Genealogy and History

1901

VOLUME III

BOSTON
PUBLISHED BY THE
MASSACHUSETTS SOCIETY OF MAYFLOWER DESCENDANTS
1901

PLYMOUTH BIRTHS, MARRIAGES AND DEATHS.

(Continued from Vol. II, p. 227.)

[Vol. I, p. 43] The Children of Joseph Silvester & hannah Silvester his Wife

1 Sollomon born July 9th 1690
2 hannah born on ye 15th of march 1692
3 Joseph born on ye 23d of June 1695
4 Marsey born on the 29th of September 1697
5 Thankfull born on ye 21 of September 1703

The Children of Thomas Holmes & Joannah his Wife
1 Joannah born on the 10th of october 1697
2 Jemima born 25th of february 170⁴⁄₅
3 Thomas Born on the 3d of March 170⁸⁄₉
4 Abner Born on ye 24th of March 1712

The Children of Thomas Morton & Martha Morton his Wife
1 Thomas born on the 12th day of february 1700 *
2 lidiah born on the 15th of November 1702
3 lemuell born on the 21 of october 1704   Deceasd
4 Sarah born July 6 1706
5 Nathaniel born on ye 2d of october 1710
6 Mary born on ye 30th of Agust 1712

The Children of Joseph Allyn and Mary Allyn his Wife
Elizabeth Born September ye 29–1700
Mary Born November The 10–1702

[p. 44] The Children of John Gibbs Juner & Hesther his Wife
1 Joshua born on the 20th of december 1690
2 Marcey born on the 21 of January 1695
3 Jane born on the 13th of March 1697
4 John born on the 16th of ffebruary 1699
5 hannah born on the 24th of ffebruary 1701
6 Exsperiance born on ye 19th of ffebruary 1703

The Children of Caleb Shareman & Rebeckah his Wife
1 Young Shareman Born June 6. 1746.
2 Ring Shareman Born Decr 17. 1749.
3 Hannah Shareman Born Octr 27. 1751.
4 Sarah Shareman Born June 27th 1753
5 Elizabeth Sherman Born July 1st 1755

The Children of Ephraim Morton Juner & hannah Morton his Wife
1 Samuel born on the 2d of January 1698/9
2 Elkanah born on the last of october 1702
3 Benjamin born on the first of october 1705
4 Elisha born January 15th 17¹⁄₁₁

* Above the year has been written 99 in a different hand.

5 Curnelios born Agust 18 1713
6 Ebenazar born on ye 25th of November 1715

The Children of Joseph Churchill & Sarah Churchill his Wife
1 John born on the 3d of July 1678
2 Margeret born in october 1684
3 barnabas born on ye 3d of July 1686
4 Joseph born in January 1692

The Children of Paul Doten and Ruth his Wife
1 Paul Doten born July 13th 1750.   Deceasd Decr 1774
2 Ruth Doten, born May 18. 1752.   Deceasd June 24th 1791
3 Bathsheba Doten born July 10th 1756
4 Lydia. Doten born July 12th 1758
5 Susannah Doten born Octr 11 1764 at Liverpool in Noviscotia
Mr Paul Doten the parent aboves deceasd Janry 1777
Mrs Ruth Doten the parent aboves deceasd March 1785

[p. 45] The Children of Manasses Morton & Mary Morton his Wife
1 Elizabeth born ye 10th of July 1704
2 Zeffaniah born on ye 6th of January 1707

The Children of Silas Morton, & Martha his Wife
1 Hannah Morton born Augst 17. 1749.
2 Silas. Morton. Born July 10th 1752
3 Timothey Morton. Born Augst 30th 1754
4 Martha. Morton. Born Sept 21st 1757
5 Job. Morton. Borne June 29th 1760
6 Olever. Morton. Borne Sept 5th 1763
7 Thomas Morton. Born Octr 21st 1765
8 Ezra. Morton. Born Janry 21st 1768
9 Hannah Morton. Born Augst 13th 1770
   Lemuel Morton. Born Febry 23rd 1775

The Child of Stephen Totman & dorithy his Wife
1 Elkanan born September 3d 1703
2 Thomas born November 15 1705
3 Lidiah born July 11 1708
4 Stephen born March : 4 : 1711

The Children of Eliazar Rickard & Sarah Rickard his Wife
1 Sarah born the 26th of desember 1688
2 Judyth born the first of ffebruary 1701
3 lidiah born the 15th of August 1704

The Children of William Elles Junr & Patience his Wife
1 Thomas Elles born Sept 26. 1744.
2 Betty Elles born Augst 10. 1748.
3 Lydia Elles born May 20. 1750
4 Mary Elles born May 14. 1753.   Deceasd

[p. 46] The Children of Josiah Rickard & Rebecah Rickard his Wife
1 Giles born on ye 14 of october 1700

Plymouth Births, Marriages and Deaths.

2 Benjamin born on ye 20th of february 1702
3 Josiah born on the 21 of october 1703

The Children of Samuel fuller & Marcey fuller his Wife
1 Nathaniel born in ye year 1687 on ye 14th of November
2 Samuel born on the 30 of August 1689
3 William born on ye 14th of february 1691 Who deceased August 26 1692
4 Seth born on the 30th of August 1692
5 Benjamine born on the 7th of march 1696
6 Ebenazar born on the 24th of March 1695
7 Elizabeth born on the 30th of March 1697
8 John born on ye 19th of December 1698
9 Jabez born sometime in the begining of June 1701
10 Marcey born on the 3d of october 1702
11 James born on the 27th of february 1704

The Children of Elkanah Churchell Junr & Susannah his Wife
1 Susanah Churchell Born June 16. 1749.
2 Maria Churchell Born, October. 17. 1751.
3 Elkanah Churchell Born, August 8th 1754
4 Jabez Churchill Born, October 2nd 1756
5 Andrew Churchill Born Janury 20th 1758
6 Abigail Churchill Born July 14th 1760
7 Andrew Churchill Born Janry 7th 1763

The Children of Daniel Ramsden & Sarah his Wife
1 Samuel born on the 5th of June 1690
2 Joseph born on the 15th of August 1693
3 benjamin born ye first day of June 1699
4 hannah born on the 28 day of September 1700

[p. 47] The Children of Eliazar pratt & hannah his Wife
1 hannah born on ye fortenth of May 1699
2 David born on the 6th of July 1702

The Children of Ichabod Bartlett Junr & Hannah his Wife
1 Ichabod Bartlett Born April 26th 1754.
2 Hannah Bartlett Born April 23rd 1756
3 Jerusha Bartlett, Born March 5th 1758
4 Mercy Bartlett Born Sept 1st 1765

The Children of John Eaverson
1 James born: on ye 5th of January 1703
2 Marcey born the 30 of Janawary 1705

The Children of Seth Luce, and Hannah his Wife
1 Ann Luce born May. 6. 1741.   Deceasd Janry 30th 1757.   New Stile
2 Ephraim Luce, born Novr 21: 1742.
3 Seth Luce born. Augst 18. 1744
4 Ebenezer Luce born Janry 12. 1746/7
5 Crosbey Luce, born June 5. 1749.
6 Hannah Luce Born Augst 28. 1751
7 Elizabeth Luce Born Febry 27. 1754
8 Deborah Luce Born May 27. 1756

The Children of John bryant Junior & Mary his Wife
1 James born on the 27 of August 1702
2 Ebenazar born on the 14th of March 1705

The Children of Samuel Rickard & Rebeckah his Wife
1 Bethyah born on ye 15 of october 1698
2 Henery born on the 4th of februry 1700
3 Mary born on ye 8th of Aprill 1702
4 Elkanan born on ye 7th of June 1704

(*To be continued.*)

PLYMOUTH BIRTHS, MARRIAGES AND DEATHS.

(Continued from page 15.)

[Vol. I, p. 48] The Children of Samuel Bryant & Joannah bryant his Wife
1 Samuel born on y^e 14 of May 1699
2 Joannah born on y^e first of March 170$\frac{3}{4}$
3 Abigaiel born July 5th 1703

The Children of Josiah Bradford ; & Hannah his Wife
William Bradford, Born Octr 30th 1749.
Hannah Bradford, Born July 9. 1751.
Josiah Bradford, Born Feb^{ry} 7. 1754.

The Children of Jonathan Bryant & Margerey his Wife
1 Rebeckah born december 6th 1702
2 pricila born september 3^d 1705 *
3 Marcy born on ye 19th of August 1705 *

* The dates are so given in the original.

Plymouth Births, Marriages and Deaths.

The Children of Robertt Ransom & of Anna his Wife *

1 Robert born September ye 15. 1695
2 Lidiah born february ye 26 1700.
3 Ebenezer born September ye 6th 1702
4 Mary born June ye 9th 1705.

The Children of Amariah Churchell & Eliz^a his Wife

1 Caleb Churchell borne May 15th 1747. Deceas^d
2 Eliazebeth Churchell born Feb^{ry} 1. 1748/9. Deceas^d Mar: 31. 1749
3. Amariah Churchell born April 12. 1750
4 Faith Churchell Born March 13th 1753
5. Elisabeth Churchell Born March 21. 1755
6 Lucy Churchill born Jan^{ury} 3rd 1757
7 Mary Churchill Born Octob^r 3rd 1758
8 Mendell Churchell Born July 27th 1760
9 Solomon Churchill Born July 27th 1762

[p. 49] **The Children of Bennony Shaw and of (‡) his Wife**

1 Lidiah born November ye 2^d 1697
2 John born May ye 3^d 1699
3 Mary born January ye 16th 1700
4 Margarett born : June 28th 1701
5 Elknath born November 2^d 1703.
6 Mosses born Jun^e 28th 1704.

The Children of Eliazer Morttion and of Rebekah his Wife

1 Eliazer borne January ye 8th 1693.
2 Ann Borne May ye 19 1694
3 Nathaniel born August 24 1695
4 Rebekah born April 9th 1703.

The Children of John Polland and of Lidia Poland his Wife

1 John born January ye 20th 1702.
2 Eliazebeth borne May ye 26 1703.
3 Mary Polden born February 28th 1706
4 William Polden born March 12th 1708. Deceased June 9th 1725
5 Lydia Polden born April 20th 1710
6 Thomas Polden born April 12th 1712
7 Hannah Polden born May 9th 1719
8 Benjamin Polden born July 12th 1721
9 Thankfull Polden born October. 9th 1725
10 William Polden born August 17th 1727

[p. 50] **The children of Isaac Samson & lidiah Samson his Wife**

1 Isaac born on the 18 of Aprill 1688
2 Jonathan born on ye 9th of ffebruary 1609 ‡
3 Josiah born on ye 5th of June 1692
4 lidiah born on ye 22 of April 1694
5 Ephraim born on ye 8th of May 1698

* See Mayflower Descendant, I: 211, for another child.
† No name was entered.
‡ This is plainly a mistake for 1689.

6 Peleg born on ye 12 of November 1700
7 Pricila born on ye 12 of November 1700
8 Barnabas born on the 12 of ffebruary 1704‡

The Children of Eliazar Roggers & of Ruhamah his Wife

1 Elizabeth born on the 15 of october 1698
2. Thomas born october 8th 1701
3. hannah born ffebruary 26th 1703
4 Experiance born April 28th 1707
5 Eleazar born october 2^d 1710*
6 Abijah born August 4th 1714
7 Willis born April 22^d 1711*   Deceased May 27 1713
8 Moriah born october 21st 1716   Deceased Janary 27 1723/24
9 Ruth born —— —— Deceased Aprill 18 1720

The Child of Nehemiah Stirtevant & (*Ruth Sampson m 1703*). †
1 Curnelios Sturtevant was born on ye 10 of November 1704

The Children of Samuell Totman & Experience Totman his Wife

1. Joshua Totman Born May. 4. 1727.   Deceas^d June 1727
2. Sam^{ll} Totman Born Novr 17. 1729.
3. Deborah Totman Born at North Yarmouth. Mar: 23. 1731/2
4. Hannah Totman Born at North Yarmouth, July 23. 1734.
5. Joshua Totman Born at North Yarmouth. Octr 14. 1737.
6. Experience Totman born Novr 7. 1740.   Dec^d Jan^{ry}. 1740/1.
7 Experience Totman born Jan^{ry} 19. 1743/4

[p. 51] **The Children of Jonathan Shaw & Mehittabel his Wife**

1 Jonathan born on the first of Aprill 1689
2 phebe born on the 10th of May 1690
3 perces born on the 10th of March 1692
4 Mehittabel born on ye 12th of January 1694
5 James born on ye 3th of March 1696
6 hannah born on ye 27th of May 1699
7 Elizabeth born on ye 5th of May 1701
8 pricila born on ye 18th of August 1702
9 Abigaiel born on ye 14th of August 1705

The Child of Joseph pratt & Martha pratt his Wife
1 pirses born on ye 12th of August 1704

The Children of Eliazar Jacson & hannah Jacson his Wife

1 John born on ye 19th of August 1692
2 Eliazar born on ye 18 of April 1694
3 Joannah born on ye 22^d of ffebruary 1696‡
4 Marcey born on ye 28 of November 1697
5 hannah born on ye 28th of April 1699
6 Mary born on ye 15th of April 1701
7 Abigall born on y^e (†) of october 1702

* It is evident that the clerk badly mixed the record of this family.
† Italics added by a modern hand.
‡ "first of november" was the original entry. The alteration has made the day illegible.

8 deborah born on ye 11th of March 170¾
9 Content born November 22^d 1705
10 Suzannah born 25 July 1706
11 Ransom born June 22^d 1708
12 Benjamin born on ye 2^d of August 1710   Deceased october 16 1713
13 Exsperiance born ye 18 of agust 1713
14 Ephraim born September 10th 1714

(To be continued.)

THE MAYFLOWER DESCENDANT

A Quarterly Magazine

OF

Pilgrim Genealogy and History

1902

VOLUME IV

BOSTON
PUBLISHED BY THE
MASSACHUSETTS SOCIETY OF MAYFLOWER DESCENDANTS
1902

PLYMOUTH, MASS., VITAL RECORDS.

(Continued from Vol. III, page 124.)

[Vol. I, p. 52] The Children of Elisha Holmes & sarah holmes his Wife

1 Marcy born June ye 26th 1696
2 Elisha born January 19th of 1698
3 Joseph born July 11th 1700
4 Elizabeth born March 13th 1702
5 Jabiz born January 28 1704
6 Elnathan born January 19 1705
7 John born March 27th 1707
8 Sarah born in March 1709

The Children of Elisha holme & Suanna his Wife

1 Rebecka born Agust 18th 1720
2 Nathaniel born Agust 18 1722

The Children of Micajah Dunham & Elizabeth Dunham his wife

1 Joshua born on ye 30th of June 1701
2 Joseph born on ye 12th of March 170¾
3 Abigaiel born on ye 19th of July. 1707

The Children of John Curtice

1 ffrances born on ye 20th of May 1696
2 hannah born on ye 20th of Aprill 1698
3 John born on ye 31 of March 1702
4 Elizabeth born on ye 20th of May 1704

The Children of Jacob Tinkcom & Lydia his Wife

1 Hannah Tinkcom Born Octr. 31. 1747.
2 Lydia Tinkcom Born Novr 15. 1749.
3 Mary Tinkcom Born. Novr 28. 1751
4 Jacob Tinkcom Born, Sep^t 10. 1754

[p. 53] The Children of helkiah Tincom & Ruth Tincom his Wife

1 helkiah born August 15th 1685
2 Mary born August 13th 1687
3 John born March 27th 1689
4 Jacob born June 15th 1691
5 Caleb born october 12th 1693
6 Sarah born on the 30th of January 1696 Deceased on ye 22^d of February 17½
7 Ebenazar born on y^e. 3^d of May 1698
8 Ruth born on ye 13th of ffebruary 1701
9 Peter Tinkcom born April 1st 1706.

The Children of Solomon Bartlett & Joanna his Wife

1 Solomon Bartlett Born July 18th. 1751.
2 James Bartlett Born Jan^{ry}. 2. 1754
3 Benjamin Bartlett Born, Novr. 14th 1755.
4 Abigail Bartlett Borne

The Children of Caleb Cook & Jane his Wife

1 John born on ye 5th of ffebruary 168¾
2 Marcy born on ye 21 of ffebruary 168¼ : Deseased ffebruary 11th 170½
3 Ann Cooke born on the 21 of August 1686
4 Jane born on ye 16th of March 168⅞
5 Elizabeth born on ye 30th of November 1691
6 Mary born on ye 20th: of August 1694
7 Caleb born on ye 17th of April 1697
8 James born on ye 19th of August 1700
9 Joseph born on ye 28 of November 1703

The Children of James howland & Mary his Wife

1 hannah born on ye 16th of october 1699
2 Abigaiel born ye 29th of october 1702
3 Elizabeth born on ye 2^d of december 1704
4 Thankfull born September 25th 1709
5 John Born March 14th 1711
6 James born August first 1713

[p. 54] The Children of Robert Cushman & Perses his Wife

1 Robert born on ye 2^d of July 1698
2 Ruth born on ye 25 of March 1700
3 Abigaiell born on ye 3^d of July 1701
4 Hannah born Desember 25th 1705
5 Thomas born ffebruary 14 1706
6 Joshua born october 14 1707
7 Jonathan born ye 28 July 1712

The Children of peter Tomson & Sarah Tomson his Wife

1 Sarah born october 30th 1699
2 Peter born on ye 30th of June 1701
3 James born on the second of ffebruary 170⅔
4 Joseph born on the 3 of June 1706

The Children: of Elish Cobb & Lidiah Cobb his Wife

1 Elisha born on the 11th of June 1704

2 Lemuel born on ye 10 of agust 1706
3 silvanos born on ye 18 of March 1709
4 Hust born June 20 1711 Deceased March 20th 17$\frac{12}{13}$
5 Lidiah born Apriel 17 1713
6 hanna born November 11th 1716
7 John born July 13 1719
8 Jabiz born on September: 6 1721
The Children of James Cobb & patience Cobb his Wife
1 Mallatiah born on the 22d of June 1706 Deseasd augst 20 1719
2 James born on ye 13 of June 1708
3 Girshom born August 1711 Deceased in agust 1714
4 Joanna born ye 9th of february 1715 Deceased february 16th 170$\frac{17}{18}$
5 Girshom born March 16th 170$\frac{16}{17}$
6 Martha born on ye 9th of ffebruary 170$\frac{18}{19}$

[p. 55] The Child of Jabiz Dunkin & Bethyah his Wife
1 Samuel born on the 22d of August 1705
The Children of: Benoney Lucos & of Repentance Lucos his Wife
1 Marey born on ye 4th of May 1684
2 Samuel born on ye 24 of July 1689
3 Joannah born on ye 9th of ffebruary 1691
4 Sarah born on ye 14 of Desember 1692
5 Elisha born on ye 7th of ffebruary 1699
6 Bethyah born on ye 29th of May 1704
The Children of John Barrows & Sarah his Wife
1 hannah born on ye 19th of ffebruary 1700
2 Samuel born on ye 11 of March 170$\frac{2}{3}$
3 Ruth born on ye 13th of June 1705
The Children of William Torrey & Mary his Wife
1 Mary Torrey Born, October 26th. 1749.
2. William Torrey Born, Octr. 30. 1751.
3. Anna Torrey. Born. Decr 6th. 1753
4. Joseph. Torrey. Born. Novr. 21st 1755 Deceased Ap: 25. 1757

[p. 56] The Children of Thomas howland & Joanna howland hi. wife
1 Consider born on ye 28th of august 1700
2 Joannah born on ye(*) June 1702 She Deceased June 5th 1715
3 Experiance born on ye last of November 1705
4 Thomas born November 23 1707
5 Elizabeth born May 23d 1710
6 hannah Born on ye: 19: Day of Desember 1712
7 Joanna born on ye 7th of May 1716 Deced 1810
8 Joseph born on ye 24 of July 1718
The Child of Thomas Dotey & Elizabeth his Wife
Thomas born on the 26 Day of January: 1704

* The day was omitted.

The Child of Edward Stephens Junr. & Phebe his Wife
Edward Stephens born Febry. 6th 1747/8.
The Children of Jobe Gibbs & Juduth Gibbs his Wife
Elizabeth born on the 15th of August 1706
The Child of Benjamin Bartlett Junr. & Jean his Wife
Benjamin Bartlett Born Augst. 18. 1752

[p. 57] The Children of John Faunce and of Abigaill Faunce His Wife
1: Nathaniell Born August ye. 27th 1706.
2: John Born May ye 2d 1709
3: Marsey Borne. octtober ye 31: 1711
4: Abigaill Borne May ye 22: 1715
5 Jane Borne. May ye 21: 1717:
6. Patience Born: July. ye. 13th: 1721
The Children of Beniamin Soule. and of. Sarah his Wife
1 Zachariah Born March ye 21 1694
2 Hanah Born March ye. 18: 1696
3 Sarah Born May ye. 9 1699
4 Deborah Born Aprill ye 23 1702
5. Beniamin Born June. ye 5th 1704.
The Child of Joseph Church & of Juduth Church his wife
1 Sarah born on ye 4th of August 1706
The Children of Nathl Warren & Sarah his Wife
1 Hannah Warren born Janry. 27th. 1735/6. Deceased March 28th 1736
2 (*) born Sept. 6. 1737. Deceased Sept 12. 1737
3 Nathaniel Warren born May 2. 1740. Deceased Sept. 4 1740
4 Sarah Warren born Janry. 8th 17†
5 Hannah Warren born, Mar: 14. 17†
6. Susannah Warren born, June 8. 1746
7 John Warren born, Novr. 18. 1748. Deceased. Augst. 30 1749
8. Abigail Warren born May 25. 1753
9 Ruth Warren born Augst: 30t. 1758

[p. 58] The Children of John Carver & Mary Carver his Wife
1 John born september: 7 1692
2 Robert born september 30th 1694
3 Mary born october 4th 1696
4 hannah born March 8·1700
The Children of James Drew, & Mary Drew his Wife
1 Hannah Drew born Novr. 25. 1751.
2 James Drew born April 16. 1754.
3 William Drew. Born Decr. 29. 1755. Deceasd. Octr. ye. 6th. 1757
4 Mary Drew. Born. Octr. 8th. 1757.
5 William Drew Born Sept. 29th. 1760
6 Sarah Drew Born Novr. 3. 1762

* Name omitted. † The years were not completed.

114

7 Priscilla Drew Born Aug^t: 11th. 1765 Carry^d. Down

The Children of John Andros
1 Sarah born March: 16: 169$\frac{4}{5}$
2 Joannah born December 26. 1697
3 John born october 22^d 1699
4 Mary born January 8th 1701
5 Ebenazar born May: 5: 1704

The Children of James Clark Junr. & Susannah his Wife
Abigail Clark Born Decr y^e. 22. 1752
John Clark Borne Jan^ry. 5. 1754

The Children of James Drew & Mary his wife
8 Lydia Drew born June 8th. 1767
9 Betsey Drew born Sep^t 12th. 1769 Deceas^d July 24th 1772

The Children of John Rickard Junior & sarah Rickard his Wife
1 James born November 15th 1706

The Children of Joell Ellice and Elizabeth Ellice his Wife
1 Joell born on y^e 21st of ffebruary 170:$\frac{8}{9}$
2 John born on y^e 18th of September 1714

The Chidren of Dennis Sturmey & Elizabeth his Wife
1 Rebeckah Sturmey Born Augst 25 1751. Deceas^d. Octr. 1751
2 Thomas Sturmey Born 13th of Jan^{ry}. 1753 New Stile

(To be continued)

PLYMOUTH, MASS., VITAL RECORDS.

(Continued from Vol. IV, p. 114.)

[p. 59] The Children of Jacob Willard & Sarah Willard his Wife
1 Sarah born ffebruary : 6th : 1704/5
2 Simon born on ye 19th of November 1706
The Children of Josiah Johnson, & Patience his Wife
1. Josiah Johnson Born Sept. 30th. 1748.
2. Patience Johnson Born March 10th. 1752.
3. Eleazer Johnson Born, Dec: 3. 1755.
The Children of Eliazar Dunham Junior & Meriam Dunham his Wife
1 Rebeckah born on ye 2d of ffebruary 1706
2 ffeare born March 13th 1708/9
3 Nathaniel January 4th 1710/11
4 Ezekell born July 14th 1713 Deceased June 28. 1714.
5 Ezekill born January 10th 1710/11
  Elizabeth born March 7th. 1723/4
  Jerusha born february : 2d : 1725/6
The Children of George Morton & Joanna Morton his Wife
1 Hannah born November 27th 1666
2 Manasseh born ffebruary 3d 1669
3 Ephraim born April 12th 1671
4 Joanna born June 27th 1673
5 Ruth born December 21 1676
6 George born July 16th 1679
7 Timothy born March 12th 1682
8 Rebeckah born July. 18th 1684
9 Elizabeth born November 20th 1686
10 Thomas born July 2d 1690

[p. 60] The Children of William Barnes & alse barnes his Wife
1 William born on the 5th of January 1706. Drowned Apr. 16. 1730*
2 lemuell born on ye 16th of ffebruary 1707 Deceased in 1751
3 Marcy born Desember 19th 1708
4 Benjamine born Desember 11 1711 Deceased
  Benjamin born Decr: 20th: 1717. Deceasd. April 12th. 1760
The Children of William Jerman, & Eleonar his Wife
1 William Jerman born May 22nd. 1747. Deceased Sept: 23rd. 1748

* "1" has been written over the "o."

54 Plymouth, Mass., Vital Records.

2. Mary Jerman born Sept. 23rd 1748.

The Children of John Harlow & Martha his wife
1. John born January 29 1706/7.
2. Elizabeth born September 1 1709 Deceas'd. July 4th 1710
3. Rebeckah born July 13th 1711 Deceas'd. Dec'r. 24. 1731. or 173(*)
4. Martha born July 7th 1715 Deceas'd. July 7. 1735.
5. Amaziah born Dec'r 18th. 1721
Mary Harlow born Dec'r. 5. 1717. Deceas'd. Dec'r. 19. 1717
Thankfull Harlow born, Feb'ry. 11. 1723/4. Deceas'd. Feb'ry. 22. 1723/4

The Children of William Cook & Tabitha Cook his Wife
1. hannah born the 8th of November 1707
2. Iidiah born ffebruary 4th 1710
3. Hulda born on ye 12 of Agust 1712
4. William born January 15th 1704/5
5. Elisha born March 10th 1706/7
6. Tabitha born July 8th 1719
7. Pricila born March : 13 : 1721/22

[p. 61] The Child of Nathaniel Morton & Mary Morton his wife.
Nathaniel born on ye 5th of Desember 1706

The Children of Bennijah Pratt & Mary Pratt his Wife
1 Mary born on ye 8th of April 1695
2 Sarah born on ye 15 of June 1697
3 Debora born october 18th 1698
4 Prisilla born November 21 1701
5 Abigail born July 6th 1703

The Children of Josiah Cotton & hannah Cotton his Wife
1 Hannah Cotton ye Daughter of Josiah Cotton & hannah his Wife was born Aprill 3d : 1709 Hannah deceased Octo'r 27. 1731
2 Mary born on the 14 of August 1710
3 John born on the 5th : of April 1712 Dec'd. Nov'r 1799 aged 77 years
4 Bethia born June 8th 1714
5 Theophilos born March 31st 1716
6 lucie born ffebruary 19th 1704/5
7 Josiah born January 19 1719/20 he Deceased : on : ye : first Day of agust 1720
8 A son born May 3d 1721 Deceased May 28 1721
9 Edward born June 20th 1722 Deceased July 6th 1722
10 Josiah born July 30 1723 Deceased october 23d 1723
11 Josiah Cotton born November 18th 1724
12 Edward Cotton born April 6th 1726. Deceased June 20th : 1726.
13 Rowland Cotton born July 27th. 1727. Deceased August 10th 1727
14 Margaret Cotton born January 23. 1729/30
15. Rowland Cotton born September 13. 1732. dead

The Children of Samuel Bates & Margeret bats his Wife

* The last figure is illegible.

Plymouth, Mass., Vital Records. 55

1 Thomas was born March 2d 1708/9
2 Samuel born : on ye 16 of April : 1713 :
3 John born November : 24 : 1716
4 Barnabas born January 15th 1707/8
5 Job born ye 14th of october 1721.

[p. 62] The Children of Samuel King Senior & Sarah King his Wife
1 Sarah born on ye 21 of ffebruary 1670
2 Joannah born on ye 16th Day of March 1672
3 Samuel born on ye 27 of March 1674
4 Mehitab born on ye 16 of June 1676
5 Bethyah born on the 21 of october 1678
6 Joseph born on ye 16 of ffebruary 1680
7 John born on ye 16 of March 1683
8 Eliazar born May 27 1685
9 Isaac born May : 6 : 1688
10 Martha born april 8th 1694

The Children of William Clarke Jun'er and Bethiah Clarke his wife
1 Nathaniel born october 30th 1709
2 Sarah born May 25 1712
3 Matthew born September 13th 1714

The Children of Elkanah Watson & Marsey Watson his Wife
John born the begining of october 1678 Died Sep'r. 9. 1731
Phebe born in June 1681
Mercy born in october 1683
Mary born in october 1688
Elizabeth*

The Child of William Green & Desire grene his Wife
Mary born March 8th 1710

The Children of Thomas Foster Jun'r, & Marcy his Wife
1. Hannah Foster Born, Sept'. 19th. 1748. Deceased April. 25. 1749
2. Lucey Foster Born Jan'r 13th. 1749/5. died of the Small pox in 1776
3. Thomas Foster Born Oct'r. 4. 1751.
4 Priscilla Foster born July 27. 1753. Deceas'd Aug'st 21st. 1775
5. George Foster Born Sep't 15th 1755.
6 Marcy Foster. Born Dec'r. 11th. 1758
Samuel Bartlett Son of Priscilla Foster Above named born April 28th 1775

[p. 63] "The Child of Joseph King Junior and Marsey King his Wife
Nathaniel born May 26 : 1707 : deseased february 7th : 1734/5

The Child of William Greene and Desire Greene his Wife
Mary born March ye 8 1710

The Children of Charles Church & Mary Church his Wife
1 Benjamin born on the first Day of November 1706
2 Deborah born January 12 1707

* This name is in a modern hand.

3 Charles born August 26 1710
4 Rebeckah born Aprill 15th 1713
5 Joseph born March 20th 1715
6 Sarah born ffebruary 26th 1701/2

The Children of John holmes & Sarah holmes his Wife
1 Patience born on ye 3d of November 1690
2 Nathaniel born on the 30th of August 1692
3 John born on ye 28 of May 1694
4 Cornelious born on ye 4th of January 1697/8
5 Sarah born october 28 1699

The Children of the sd John holmes and Exsperiance holmes his Wife
1 Samuel born November : 21 1704
2 Benjamin born october 9th 1706
3 Thomas born January 7th 1708/9
4 Suzanah born october. ye. 13 1711.

(To be continued)

PLYMOUTH, MASS., VITAL RECORDS.

(Continued from page 56.)

[p. 64] The Children of William Dunham and Annah Dunham his wife
1 William born on the fifth of Aprill 1710
2 Martha born on ye 8th of Desember 1713

The Children of John Wood* and Sarah wood his Wife
1 Sarah born on the 26 July 1709
2 Marey born on ye 8th of May 1711
3 John born ffebruary : 10 : 1701/2
4 Elydia born June : 6th : 1715 Deceasd being the wife of Jas Hovey Esqr Febry 23rd . 1771
5 Soloman born November 2d 1717
6 Isaac born March 18th 1719
7 Keziah born on ye 18 of Aprill 1721
8 Hannah born march 21 . 1722/3 . Deceased July 14 . 1723.
9 Experience born . Sepr . 12 1724.

The children of John Atwood & Experience his wife
Experience Atwood born April 4 . 1731
Elizabeth Atwood born April 23 . 1733
Experience Atwood born March 1 . 1734/5
George Atwood born Sepr . 19 . 1737.
George Atwood born february 26 . 1738/9

The Children of helkiah Tincom† & Elizabeth Tincom his wife
1 hannah born on the last Day of october 1710
2 Elizabeth born July 5 1713
3 Isaac born Desember 27th 1715
4 Sarah born Agust 5th 1718
5 Zedekiah born July : 11th 1721
John born September 29 1723 . deceased October 13th : 1723
Mary born September 14 . 1724
Martha born December 29 . 1726

* "alias Atwood Junr" written above in a different hand.

† "Junr" written above in a different hand.

THE MAYFLOWER DESCENDANT

An Illustrated Quarterly Magazine

OF

Pilgrim Genealogy, History and Biography

1905

VOLUME VII

BOSTON
PUBLISHED BY THE
MASSACHUSETTS SOCIETY OF MAYFLOWER DESCENDANTS
1905

Plymouth, Mass., Vital Records.

Ruth & Lydia born July 9 . 1729 . deceased Lydia 22 October 1732
Ebenezer born June . 26 . 1732
Lydia born March . 10 . 1734/5

[p. 65] The Children of John ffaunce Ju : and lidiah ffaunce his Wife

1 Juduth born January first 1707‡
2 lidiah born June 10th 1714
3 John born Aprill 13th 1716
4 Hannah born May 30th 1718
5 Mary born April 25th 1720
6 Mehitabell born Aprill : 11th : 172(*)
7 Rebeccah Faunce born September 15th 1724
   Mary born 1734. (See 166.) 2d w Ruth †

The Children of John Morton and Reliance Morton his Wife

1 John born November 15th 1706
2 Jonothan born ffebruary 10 1707 Deceased Desember 29 1708
3 Josiah born ffebruary 28 1709/10
4 A Daughter born Desember 11 1711 Deceased ye same Day
5 James born on ye 13th Day of May 1714
6 David born March 19th 1716

The Children of Joshua Bramhall and Sarah bramhal his Wife

:1: Cornelios born Agust 26 : 1708
:2: Silvanios born ye last Day of aprill 1712
:3: Joseph born Desember 20th 1717
4 Martha born March 21st 1718

The Children of Elisha Doty and Hanna ‡ Doty his Wife

1 Elisha born october 20th 1709
2 Samuel born June 16th 1712
3 hanna born october 10th 1714 Deceased
4 Edward born October 7th 1716
5 Hannah born September 5 . 1718
6 Paul born November 28 1721
7 Lois born August 26 . . 1724
8 Stephen born June 24 . 1726
9 James born August 27 . 1728

(To be continued.)

---

* "1721" or "1722," probably the latter.
† This line is in a modern hand.
‡ "Harlow" written above in a modern hand.

PLYMOUTH, MASS., VITAL RECORDS

(Continued from Vol. V, p. 100)

[p. 66] The Children of Job Cushman and Lidiah Cushman his Wife

1 Meriah Born february y̆e 16 17⅟₂
2 Job . Born february y̆e 20 . 171⅟₂
3 lidiah Born on y̆e last Day of october 1718

The Children of Jonathan Barnes & Sarah barnes his Wife

1 Sarah born on y̆e 9th of october 1709
2 Rebecah born March 14 1711
3 Lydia born January 30th 1714/5

The Children of Abraham Jackson, and Mary his Wife

1 . Mary Jackson Borne, Octᵇ 7 . 1742.
2 . Abraham Jackson borne, June, 2 . 1744 . Deceasᵈ July 1744.

The Children of Samuel : Wetherhead & Abigaill His Wife

1 : John Borne September yᵉ 20th 1708 :
2 . Rebekah Born September yᵉ 17th 1711

The Children of Abraham Jackson, and Bethiah his Wife.

1 . Isaac Jackson Borne July 28th 1745.
2 . Margaret Jackson Born, March 5th 1747/8.

[p. 67] The Children of Hunphry Turner and Mary Turner his Wife

1 Mary born June yᵉ 10th 1694
2 Ephraim born on yᵉ first of March 169⅞
3 Hunphray born october 19th 1699
4 Joseph born June 10th 1702
5 pricila born february 15th 169⅞ *
6 Bethiah born December 24 1709

The Children of Joseph Morton and Mary Morton his Wife

1 Joseph born on yᵉ 17th of January 1710 — Deceased January 5th 171⅟₂
2 Joseph born october 25 1711
3 hanna born June 29th 1713
4 Ezekel born Aprill 26 1718

The Children of James Swinnerton & Martha his Wife

1 William Swinnerton born March 28th 1745.
2 Martha Swinnerton born, Mar : 25 : 1747

The Children of Josiah Morton & Elizabeth Morton his Wife

1 Henery born on yᵉ 9th of November 1711 Deceased october 17th 1723
2 Josiah born on yᵉ 10th of Desember 1713
3 Elizabeth born yᵉ 14th of aprill 1716 She Deceased May 5th 1717
4 Ruth born on yᵉ 25 of March 1718
5 a Son born July 24 – 1720 . Deceased August 12th 1720
7 † a Daughter born April 29th 1722 . Deceased May 15th 1722
8 a Son born April 24th 1723 . Deceased May 17th 1723
9 a daughter born August 16th 1724 . Deceased September 4th 1724
10 Elizabeth born July 25th 1730.

[p. 68] The Children of Daved Bates and Abigaill bates his Wife

1 Remember born on yᵉ 10th of December 1711
2 David born agust 16th 1713
3 Joseph born on yᵉ 6th of September 1715
4 Mary born September 14th 1717
5 Abigail born on yᵉ 18th of agust 1719
6 Lydia born february 24th 1721/2
7 Ann born August 30th 1724

The Children of Ebenazar Dunham and ann Dunham his Wife

1 Seth born on yᵉ 10th of Desember 1708
2 Patience born february 5th 170⅞

The Children of Samuell Harlow, & Marcy his Wife.

1 Samˡˡ Harlow Born, Octʳ 22 . 1747.
2 Marcy Harlow Born Octʳ 20 . 1749. Deceased Septʳ 29 . 1750
3 Marcy Harlow Born April 10 . 1752

* Plainly an error for "170⅞."

† Between " 3 Elizabeth " and " 4 Ruth " was written " 4 John born June 18th 1716." which was crossed out. This doubtless caused the confusion in the numbering.

4 Jerusha Harlow, Feb^ry 13 . 1754
5 Josiah Harlow . Born Jan^ry 2nd 1756
6 James Harlow . Born Novr 23rd 1757 Deceas^d Jan^ry 10th 1758
7 George Harlow Born Jan^ry 18th 1759

The Children of Joseph Mitchel and Bathshua Mitchel his Wife

1 Sarah born on ye 16th of August 1711 Deceased about '10 months old
2 Hanna born ffebruary 14th 1713/4
3 Joseph born october 28 1714 Deceased July 16th 1715
4 John born June 18th 1716
5 Mary born ffebruary 2^d 1717/8
6 Sarah born october 14th 1719
7 Bathsheba born Agust 10 : 1721
8 Alce born July 21st 1723 . Deceased about 14 months old
   Joseph born January 4th 1724/5
   Benjamin 1728 *
   Martha 1731 *
   Ruth *

[p. 69] The Children of Robert Barrows and Bethyah Barrows his Wife

1 Jabiz born on ye 11th of october 1711
2 Lamuel born on ye 25th of March 1714
3 Thomas born September 13th 1716

The Children of Thomas Pitts & Mary his Wife

1 . A Daughter Not Named . Born July 23rd 1745 . Deceas^d Aug^st 7th 1745.
2 . Mary Pitts, Born Oct^b 16th 1748.

The Children of ffrances Curtice and Hannah Curtice his Wife

1 Janes born on ye 20th of January 1701
2 Elkana born Desember 1703
3 ffrances born Agust 10th 1705 Drown^d in Carolina in Decr 1739
4 Nathaniel born in March 1707
5 Silvanus born in february 170 9/10
6 Hannah born about ye Last July 1712
7 Lydia born about ye Midle of June 1718
8 Zacheus born about ye Midle of June 1720

The Children of Elisha Studson & Abigaiel Studson his Wife

1 Sarah born Agust 26th 1708
2 Eglah born october 7th 1710
3 Zeresh born November 29 1712
4 hopstill born May 21 1715

The Child of Lemuell Churchell, and Lydia his Wife

Nathaniel Churchell Born March 29th 1748.
Lydia Churchell the Wife of Lemuell Churchell above Deceas^d Sep^t ye 20th 1751

The Children, of Lemuell Churchell, & Abigail his Wife.

1 Lemuell Churchell Born June 9th 1754.
2 Abigail Churchell Born . Feb^ry 5th 1756
3 Ezra Churchell Born, Octr 11 . 1758.

(*To be continued*)

* These names are in a modern hand.

PLYMOUTH, MASS., VITAL RECORDS

(Continued from page 179)

[p. 70] The Children of Thomas Phillips & Rebeckah his Wife
1 John born September 20th 1707
2 lamuel born June 22d 1709
3 Bleaney born ffebruary 10th 1711/2
The Children of Stephen Doten, & Hannah his Wife
1 Mary Doten Born . July 16th 1746.
2 . Stephen Doten born Decr 4 . 1748.
3 . Sarah Doten born Jany 26 . 1750/1
4 . Marcy Doten born March 9 . 1753
5 . Hannah Doten born July . 8 . 1755.
The Children of Ebenazar Curtice and Mary Curtice his Wife
1 Jacob born october 11th 1710
2 Caleb born August : 15 : 1712 deceased November 19 . 1729
3 Mary born Desember 21st 1714
4 Sarah born August 19 1717
The Children of Ebenezer Curtis and Martha his wife
Eunis born June . 23 1723
Martha born July 3 . 1725
Seth born October 22 1727
Ebenezer born October 14 . 1731
The Children of John * Holmes and Sarah holme his Wife
1 Desire born on ye 13th of September 1712
2
3 Deborah born in January 1701/2
The Children of Joshua Newcomb, and Hannah his Wife
1 . Ruth Newcomb, Born Sept 21st 1741.
2 . Joseph Newcomb . Born May 31st 1745.
3 . Sarah Newcomb, Born, Octb 28th 1747.

* "King John " was written on the margin in the same hand and ink as the rest of the entry.

[p. 71] The Children of Capt Ephraim Morton & Suzanna Morton his Wife
1 Suzanna born May 14 1713
2 hannah born october : 16 : 1715
3 Sarah born May 6th 1718
4 Ephraim born June 10th 1722
5 Abigal born September 11th 1724
6 A Daughter born   Deceasd
7 Ichabod born, Jany 28 . 1729/30.
The Children of Thomas Harlow and Jedida harlo his Wif
1 Thomas born on ye 26 July 1712
2 Elizabeth born March 14th 1715 Deceased April 21st 1718
3 Jonathan born March 22d 1718
4 lidiah born June 4th 1721
5 Eleazer born Decr 13th 1723.
6 Jedidah born October . 3 . 1726
7 Nathaniel born July 22 . 1729.
The Children of thomas faunce* and Sarah faunce his wife
1 hannah born April ye 26 : 1713 She Deceased february 2 1701/2
2 Sarah Born february 23d 1701/2 Deceasd
The : Children of thomas faunce and lediah faunce his wife
1 Jeames : borne the 6 day of april 1719
2 thomas born the 10 of april 1721
3 Ruth born the the 24 of June 1723
4 Barnebe born June 10th 1726 . Deceased January 18th 1727/8.
5 Seth born July 30th 1729 Deceased August 4th 1729.
6 Peleg born November 20th 1730.
7 Lydia Faunce, born
8 Sarah Faunce, born   Deceasd

[p. 72] The Children of John Holmes and Marsey holmes his Wife
1 Mary born September 2d 1713
2 Peleg born September 28 1715
3 Josiah born on ye 15th Desember 1716
4 Jonathan born on ye 19th day of august 1719 . Deceased Decr 23 . 1726
Marcy born November 13th 1725.
John born June 22 . 1730
The Children of Richard holmes and hester holmes his Wife
1 Mary born ffebruary 5th 1701/2
2 Girshom bone october 13th 1714
3 Silvanos born Desember 27th 1716
The Children of Thomas Wethrell Junr, and Elizabeth his Wife
1 . Hannah Wethrell Borne, May 25th 1739 . Deceasd July 1740
2 . Lemuell Wethrell, Borne, May 1741 . Deceasd Mar : 1742
3 . Thomas Wethrell Born, Decr 4th 1742.
The Children of Charles little & Sarah little his Wife

* "Junr" has been written above in a different hand

The Wills of Georgᵉ³ and Deborah Soule

1 Sarah born Agust : 4 : 1713 she Deceased on yᵉ 2ᵈ of January 1714
2 Bethia born october 23ᵈ 1715
3 Charles born october 9ᵗʰ 1717 Deceased february 14ᵗʰ 1718
4 lucie born Aprill 30 : 1719
5 Sarah born Tusday at one AClock in yᵈ morning January 24ᵗʰ 17‡‡
6 . Charles born Novʳ 4 . 1723 . Deceased Novʳ 11ᵗʰ 1723

The Children of Josiah Morton Junʳ; & Melatiah Morton his Wife

1 . Benjamin Morton borne, Janʳʸ 18 . 1733/4 . Deceasᵈ Novᵇʳ 5 . 1735.
3 . Benjamin Morton borne Novᵇʳ 7 . 1737 . Deceasᵈ July 4 . 1739.
4 . Reliance Morton borne Febʳʸ 18 . 1739/4.
5 . Martha Morton borne March 29 . 1742
6 . John Morton borne Marᶜʰ : 21 . 1743/4 . Deceasᵈ Septᵗ 1 . 1745
2 . Seth Morton born Decʳ 8 . 1735
7 Mary Morton born April 5 . 1746.
8 John Morton born Augˢᵗ 30 . 1748
9 Josiah Morton born Septᵗ 11 1750 . Deceasᵈ Augˢᵗ 26ᵗʰ 1751
10 Josiah Morton, born Augˢᵗ 7ᵗʰ 1752
11 Sarah Morton b[orn] Augˢᵗ 11 1755

(*To be continued*)

PLYMOUTH, MASS., VITAL RECORDS

TRANSCRIBED BY THE EDITOR

(Continued from Vol. VII, p. 210)

[p. 73] The Children of Thomas Wetherel and Rebecah Wetherel his Wife

1 Rebecah Witherel born on ye first of Desember 1713 *deceased in 1761*
2 Thomas born ye last Day of July 1715 . *deceas^d May 9 . 1744 ✶*
3 William born March 6th 1718 *deceas^d in 1746 ✶*
4 James born the last Day of August 1720 . *deceas^d 1745 at Cape Breton ✶*

[Three given names, following the record of James, were crossed out and "A mistak of ye Nam" was written in the margin — Editor.]

Mary born on ye 5th of June 1722 *Married To Tho Mayhew July 8 1740 died Sep 3 . 1776.*
John Wethrell born May 13th 1725 *deceased at Surinam in 1763 ✶*
Marcy Wethrell born June 14 : 1727

Lemuel Wetherel born Sepr 2 . 1729 *Deceas^d Octr 1738 ✶*
Hannah Wetherel born August 5 . 1732 . *deceased June 10th 1736*

The Children of Samuel Kempton & Marsey Kempton his Wife
a Son born †
1 Marey ‡ born on the 12th of Desember 1707
2 Loes born on ye 12th of ffebruary 1710
3 Bathshua born on ye 17th of March 1712
4 Samuel Born April 7th 1714
5 John born ye 27th december 1716
6 Marcy born ye 12th of february 17 18/19
7 Sarah born ye 28 of february 1720/21 *deceased may ye 16*
8 Sarah born ye 16 June 1722 *deceased august 10*
Sarah born february 27 – 1723/4 *deceased July 19th 1724*
Sarah born June 11th 1725. *Deceased ✶*
Rebeccah born March 31 . 1731

The Children of John Mordo Junior and Ruth Mordo his Wife
1 Jennet born Desember 10th 1711
2 Robert born AGust 4th 1713

The Children of Samuell Morton & Ruth his Wife
1 Ruth Morton born Feby 8th 1748/9.
2 Rebeckah Morton born Aug^st 15 . 1751
3 Sarah Morton born Jan^ry 5 . 1755.
4 Priscilla Morton born April 28th 1759
5 Sam^ll Morton Born August 17th 1763

[p. 74] The Children of Nathan Ward & Elizabeth Ward his Wife
1 Thomas born october 18th 1705
2 Marcy born March 3th 1708
3 alse born october 4th 1710
4 Benjamin born october 27th 1713 *Dyed In Virginia ✶*
6 Ephraim born June 5 1720 *Deceased Decemb^r 15th 1748 ✶*
7 John born may 10th 1725 . about Sunsett.
5 Hannah born

The Children of Samuel Rider Junior and ann Rider his Wife
1 Cesiah born on the first Day of March 1704 ¾
2 Ezekiel Born on ye 22^d of May 1715.
3 Samuel born January 29th 17 17/18

The Children of Benjamin Morton & Hannah his Wife
1 Lydia Morton born March 1 . 1754.
2 . Hannah Morton born Aug^st 15 . 1755 . *Deceas^d Novr 1756.*
3 . Hannah Morton born January . 10th 1758
4 Barnaba Morton born Feby 4th 1759

* Words in italics are later additions to the record.

† This was interlined in a different hand.

‡ This name has been printed elsewhere as "Mercy", but the reading here given is verified by the Plymouth First Church records. In a list of baptisms in 1721 is found the following record: "Mary Lowis Bathua Sam^ll John Mercy. the 6 children of Samuell Kempton all baptized Sepr 24 Thomas Kempton being abt 17 . years old Covenanted upon his Account."

5. Benjamin Morton born Febry 28 . 1763.
6. Bartlett Morton born October, . 2 . 1766 . Thursday.

The Children of William harlow & Joanna harlow his Wife
1 Joanna born february 21st 170½
2 william born September 27th 1715
3 Mary born September 22d 1717
4 Hannah born November 20th 1721
5 Lydia born february 25th 1723/4
6 Isaac born April 21st 1726
7 Sarah born July. 21st 1728

The Children of David Goreham & Abigell his Wife
1 Mary Goreham Born Febry 20th 1751/2
2 Penelope Gorham Born July 10th 1757.

[p. 75] The Children of Thomas Clarke the son of Deacon Clarke and Mary Clarke his Wife
1 Marriah born Aprill 20th 1714
2 Sarah born September 16 . 1716
3 Thomas born on ye 18th of June 1718
4 Rebeck born June 28th 1720
5 Susanner born January ye 23d 17 22/23

The Children of Eliazer holmes and hannah his Wife
1 hannah born on the 27th Day of September 1712
2 Eleazer born on the 17 agust 1714
3 lidiah born July 31 1716
4 lemuel born 29th of october 1719
5 Elizabeth born 13th of October 1723
6 Ichabod born february 17 1725/6
7 Job born May 27th 1728
8 Jonathan born October 9th 1731
9 Joshua born August 5 . 1735

The Children of Ignatious Cushing & Marsey Cushing his Wife
1 hannah born January 1st 1710 & Deceased about 7 Dayes after
2 Ignatious Was born february 7th 1711 Deceased January 23d 170¾
3 Hannah born August 25 1714

The Children of Lemuel Barnes, & Sarah his Wife
1 Sarah Barnes, Born May 5 . 1751.
2 John Barnes, Born Decr 31 . 1752.
3 Lemuel Barnes . Born Janry 31 1754
4 Dorcas Barnes . Born Feby 5th 1756
5 Isaac Barnes Born Novr 6th 1757
6 Corban Barnes Born, July 23 . 1761

[p. 76] The Chldren of Elnathan Bartlet and hanna bartlet his Wife
1 Elnathan born february 12th 171¾
2 hannah born August 18th 1714

The Children of Ebenezer Dogget, & Elizabeth his Wife
1. Elizabeth Dogget Born Novr ye 9 . 1749.
2. Bathsheba Dogget Born Augst 4 . 1751 Deceased Octr 6th 1751.
3. Ebenezer Dogget Born Augst 25 . 1754.

Plymouth, Mass., Vital Records

The Children of Timothy Morton & Mary his wife
1 Charles born october 17th 1714
2 John born Desember 14th 1716 *Deceasd March 21 . 1739/40* *
3 Job born on ye first Day of aprill 1719 . *Deceased in Decemr 1761* *
4 Mary born February 8th 1721-22 *Dyed June 1[†] 1781 Deacn Foster's widow.* *
5 Silas born April 17 : 1727
Elizabeth born 19 of Dember 1732 deceased May 3 1734

The Children of Ebenezar Morton & hanah Morton his Wife
1 Mary born June 17th 1711
2 Edmond born November 16th 1713
3 Patience born on ye 16 June 1716 Deceased July 27th 1718
4 Zacheas born ye 20 of September 1718
Solomon Morton born May 16th 1727.

The Children of Zacheus Holmes & Ruth his Wife
1 . Content Holmes Born Janry 19 . 1755.
2 . Silvester Holmes Born Janry 12 . 1757
3 . Mary Holmes } Twins, Born June 25 . 1759.
4 . Sarah Holmes }

[p. 77] The Children of John Bradford Junio & Rebeckah his wife
1 Robert born october 18th 1706
2 Rebecah born Desember 14 1710

The Children of Nathaniel Bradford, & Sarah his Wife
1 . Nathl Bradford Borne July 26th 1748.
2 . Lemuel Bradford Born Febry 20th 1750/1.

The Children of Samuel Jackson & Elizabeth Jackson his Wife
1 Jeane born on ye 20th of July 1713
2 Elizabeth borne Aprill 10th 1716
3 Samuel borne June 28th 1718
Sarah born October 3 . 1722

The children of Stephen Churchil & Experianc Churchl his Wife
1 Ephraim born october 15 1709
2 My 2d Child born february 1710 Deceased the same Month 24 Day
3 Nathaniel born Desember 19th 1712
4 Mary born April 29 1716 Deceased Desember 13th 1716
5 Stephen Born AGust 24 1717
6 Zacaus born ye 30 day of october 1719 . *Deceased Novr 18th 1732* *
Benjamin born August 19th 1725

The Children of John Phillips and Elizabeth his Wife
1 Elizabeth Phillips Born March 14th 1752
2 John Phillips Born July. 10th 1755
3 Samll Phillips Born Augst 19th 1757.

(To be continued)

*Words in italics are later additions to the record.
†The second figure is doubtful,

PLYMOUTH, MASS., VITAL RECORDS

(Continued from page 13)

[p. 78] The Child of Judah Hall and Mehittabel hall his Wife
1 Judah born on the ffirst Day of June 1714
The Children of Ebenezer Bartlett, & Abigail his Wife
1 A Son Still Born, September the 3ᵈ 1750
2 Abigail Bartlett born August 21 . 1751 . Deceasᵈ Sepᵗ yᵉ 21 . 1751
3 Ebenezer Bartlett born at Barnstable . Janʳʸ 28 . 1754
4 Diman Bartlett Born at Barnstable, March 11ᵗʰ 1756 Deceasᵈ March 25ᵗʰ 1756
5 Thomas Bartlett . Born . at Plymᵒ April 16ᵗʰ 1757
6 Diman Bartlett Borne at Ditto Octʳ 9ᵗʰ 1759
7 Abigal Bartlett Born Novʳ 22 . 1762
The Children of Eleazar Churchill Junior and hanah Churchill his Wife
1 A son born May 16ᵗʰ 1712 Deceased July 21ˢᵗ 1712
2 Eliazar born ffebruary 26 1704⌿5 ‡
3 Josiah born July 20 1716
4 Jonathan born october 19 1720 *Decᵈ*

* Entries in italics are later additions to the record.

The Children of Daved Bradford and Elezabeth his Wife
1 Nathaniel born [*]ember 10ᵗʰ 1701*5 Deceased March 27ᵗʰ 1751* †
2 [*Josiah born yᵉ 20ᵗʰ of July 1716* ‡]
3 Jonathan born november 13ᵗʰ 1717
4 lidiah born Desember 23ᵈ 1719
5 Nathan born Aprill 3ᵈ 1722
The Children of Ichabod Holmes & Rebeckah his Wife
1 Remember Holmes Born July 19 . 1750   Mʳˢ Rebecca Holmes *above named Deceasᵈ July 22ⁿᵈ 1803* †
2 Rebecca Holmes Born July 5ᵗʰ 1753
3 Deborah Holmes Born June 19ᵗʰ 1755
4 Ichabod Holmes Born Augˢᵗ 23ᵗʰ 1757
5 Samuel Holmes Born   *Deceasᵈ* †
6 Samuel Holmes Born Augˢᵗ 29ᵗʰ 1761
7 Mary Holmes Born Sepʳ 25ᵗʰ 1763
8 a Son lived 2 Days only
9 Ellis Holmes Born March 27 . 1767
10 Ester Holmes Born March 13ᵗʰ 1769
11 Chandler Holmes Born March 5 . 1771
12 Elizabeth Holmes Born May 10ᵗʰ 1774 *She was Marryᵈ to Ichabod Shaw Junʳ. She Deceasᵈ Decʳ 26ᵗʰ 1795*
[p. 79] The Children of Manassh Kempton & Mehitabl Kempton his Wife
1 Manasseh born on yᵉ 13ᵗʰ of December 1715 Deceased July 26ᵗʰ 1717
2 Ruth born on yᵉ Seventh Day of March 1704⌿5
The Child of William Holmes and Ruth his Wife
1 . William Holmes Born Janʳʸ 12ᵗʰ 1743/4 . Deceased Janʳʸ 11ᵗʰ 1745/6
2 . Joannah Holmes Born Decʳ 30 . 1750.
3 . Luce Holmes . Born Octᵇ 16 . 1753
The Children of George Morton and Rebekah Morton his wife
1 Zeffaniah born on yᵉ last Day of Agust 1715
2 William born october 2ᵈ 1717 *Deceasᵈ Novʳ 15ᵗʰ 1750* †
3 George born ffebruary 6 1719/20
4 Rebecca born April 7 . 1724 . upon Tuesday. *Deceasᵈ Sepᵗ 23ʳᵈ 1759* †
The Child of William Morton Deceased, and Mary Morton, widdow of sᵈ William
William Morton Born, May 8ᵗʰ 1751.
The Children of heveland Torey & Elizabeth Tory his Wife
1 Heveland born May 10ᵗʰ 1716
2 John born october 13ᵗʰ 1717 *Deceased in December 1776* †

* "Des" appears to have been written over "nov"

† Entries in italics are later additions to the record.

‡ This record was crossed out, probably when the birth of Eleazer Churchill's son Josiah was entered a few lines above.

3 William born Desember 12 1719 Deceased April 25 1721
4 Nathaniel born october 12 1721
Thomas born October 5th 1723
William born August 21th 1725
Joseph born August 14th 1727.
Josiah born May 15th 1729

[p. 80] The Children of Joseph Holmes and Lidiah holmes his Wife
She was probably Lydia Griswold w of Jo Bartlett

1 ffeare born March 25th 1706
2 Josep born october 2d 1714 *Deceasd on a West India Voyage**
The Children of Job Holmes & Mehetable his wife
Lydia Holmes Born Febry 21 . 1753.
Jonathan Holmes Born, Jany 3 . 1755
The Chiltren of John May & ann May his Wife
1 Mary Born ffebruary 7th 1713
2 John Born Desember 8 1722 *Died in Sep 1769**
3 Sarah born the Last day of April 1724 . Deceased about June 5th 1724

The Children of Joseph Bartlet The Son of Samuel Bart[et] of Duxbery Deceased & lidiah Bartlet his Wife
1 Isaiah born March 25 1716
The Children of Daniel Diman & Elizabeth his Wife
1 Rebeckah Diman born May 29 . 1752.
2 . Daniel Diman, born Febry 22 . 1756.
3 . David Diman born Augt 27th 1758
4 . Elizabeth Diman born October . 31 . 1766 . Friday.
5 . Josiah Diman born August 30th 1760.
See Book 2nd page 53rd

[81] The Children of Barnabas Churchill & Lidiah Churchill his Wife
1 Barnabas born on ye 19th of october 1714
2 William born Desember 25 1716
3 Ichabod born on ye 12th of January 1711/8 *Deceasd Octr 1 . 1745.*
4 Joseph born May 19th 1721
5 lemuel born July 12th 1723
6 Isaac born May 31 . 1726
7 Thomas born Aprill 30 . 1730
8 Ebenezer born Novr 9th 1732
9 Lydia born March 24 . 1734/5
10 John Churchell born May 9 . 1739
The Children of William harlow Junior & Marsey his Wife
1 Sarah born November 5th 1715
2 Benjamin born November 20 1716
3 William born October 14th 1718
4 Hannah born January 14th 1719/20
5 . Marcy born february 14th 1721/2 . Deceasd January 1725/6
6 . Keziah born November 5th 1723 . Deceasd January 1725/6

7 . Samuel born September 7 . 1726
8 . Phebe born October 21 . 1728
9 . Rebecah born April 16 . 1732
10 . Seth born Sepr 10 . 1736.
The Children of William Bradford & Elizabeth his Wife
1 Elizabeth born Januer 10th 1714 Desed January 21st 1714
2 Charles born January 4th 170⅘
3 Sarah born Desember 15th 1718
4 Jerusha born Desember 20 1722
The Children of John Howard, and Enice his Wife
1 John. Howard Born, March 26th 1748 *Deceasd*
2 . James Howard Born, Novr 16th 1750 *Deceasd*
3 . Martha Howard Born Jany 27 . 1753 *Deceasd*
4 . Ebenezer Howard Born Jany 12 . 1755.
5 . Mary Howard . Born Augst 23 . 1757 . *Deceasd*
6 . Unice Howard . Born Novr 12 . 1759.
7 . Sarah Howard Born Jany 9th 1765

[p. 82] The Children of Nathaniel Jackson Juner & Abigail Jackson his Wife
1 Lemuel born September 12th 1713
2 Nathaniel born May 16th 1716
3 lydia born the last Day of october 1721
The Child of Samuel Totman & Deborah Totman his Wife
Simnion Born ye 21st of october 1716
The Children of Samuell Rogers, & Hannah his Wife
1 Priscilla Rogers Born July 6th 1751.
2 Samll Rogers Born Sept 16 . 1752 . old Stile : is Sept 5th N.S*
3 Hannah Rogers Born July . 18th 1754
4 Sarah Rogers Born Decr 18th 1756
The Chilldren of James Shurtleff and Faith Shurtleff his wife
1 Lydia Shurtleff born *Decd* wife of John Cornish
2 Elizebeth Shurtleff born February 15th 1736/7 *Deceasd* Febry 19th 1818
3 Hannah Shurtleff born *Deceasd*
4 Mary Shurtleff born
5 Faith Shurtleff born
The Children of Edward Stephens & Mary Stephens his Wife
1 Mary born June 21st 1710
2 hannah born April 11th 1712
3 Sarah born May 25th 1715
4 lemuel born Desember 5th 1716 Deceased June 20th 1718
Elizabeth born April 30th 1719
Edward born September 19th 1721
Eleazer born Decr 10 1723

(*To be continued*)

*Sic.

---

* Entries in italics are later additions to the record.

3 Samuel born June 20th 1714 . deceased the 5th July . 1724
4 Sarah born March 28th 1716

The Children of Samuel Nelson & Sarah Nelson his wife
5 Bathsheba Neson born July 15th 1719
6 Samuel Nicols Nelson born August 9th 1721
7 Ebenezer Nelson born Aug't 1 . 1723
8 Patience Nelson born Sep'r 1 . 1725

The Children of John Wotson & Sarah Wotson his Wife
1 John born Aprill 19 att 10 a Clock in y'e Morning Thirds Day 1716
2 George born fryday July 8th at : 8 a Clock in y'e morning 1718
The children of John Watson Esq'r & Priscilla his wife
William Watson born May 6th 1730 . on Wednessday at 10 a Clock morning

Elkanah Watson borne February 27th 1732 Sabath morning

The Children of Benjamin Bozworth and Joanna his Wife
1 Nathaniel born on y'e first of September 1709
2 Joanna born on y'e 19th of May 1714

The Children of John Rider, and Mary his Wife
1 . Micah Rider born Sep't 26 . 1736 . Deceased June 30th . 1737
2 . Hannah Rider born, Mar: 22 . 1738.
3 : Elizabeth Rider born, April 27 . 1740.
4 . Mary Rider born, July 25 . 1742
5 . Seth Rider born, Aug'st 11 . 1745.
6 . Nathaniel Rider born July 25 . 1747.
7 . William Rider born
8 . Micah Rider born Sep't 17 . 1752
9 . Phebe Rider . born Jan'ry 2 . 1755

[p. 84] The Children of John Rider and hannah Rider * his Wife
1 Sarah in Desember 1694 Sarah lived 4 yeares & 5 months
2 Marsy born November : 14 1696
3 Samuel born November 15th 1698
4 John born october 1700 he lived 3 years & 9 months
5 Ebenazar born November : 17 : 1702

The Children of John Rider and Mary Rider his Wife
1 hannah born March 20th 1707
2 John born March 26th 1709
3 Sarah born Desember 25 1712
4 Elizabeth born April 10th 1714
5 Mary born March 29th 1716
6 Charles born July : 26 1718

The Children of Hezekiah Bozworth & Bethyrah his Wife
1 hanna born November 17th 1703
2 hezekiah born May 27th 1716

The Children of John Howland, & Patience his Wife
1 . A Son Born Feb'ry 6th 1742/3 . Lived about Two Hours
2 . A Son Born July 20th 1744 . Lived about Two Hours
3 . Patience Howland Born Nov'r 11th 1746 . Deceas'd June 18th 1747

* See "John Rider's Wife Hannah Identified," page 256 of this issue.

PLYMOUTH, MASS., VITAL RECORDS

(Continued from page 87)

[p. 83] The Children of Samuel Nelson & Bathshaba Nelson his Wife
1 hannah born Desember 15th 1707
2 John born May 4th 1712

4. Patience Howland, Born Sept 23. 1749.

The Children of Benjamin Mory & Thankfull Mory his Wife
1 Mary born Desember 23d 1716
2 Meriah born ffebuary 22d 1740⅛
3 Marsy born aprel ye 1d 1721
4 Benjamin born April. 13 : 1727
5 John Born May 1729

The Children of Asa Hunt, & Sarah his wife
Ziba Hunt Born Janry 11th 1745/6
Buzi Hunt Born Janry 4. 1747/8 Deceasd Decembr 27 . 1753
Sarah Hunt Born May 8 . 1750.
A Son Still Born, Janry 4. 1747/8. was a Tin*
Asa Hunt Born at Duxboro, Janry 20th 1743/4 Dyed in Plymouth March ye 1st 1748/9

[p. 85] The Child of William Swift and lidiah Swift his Wife
1 Solomon born on ye 9th Day of June 1715
2 William born April 11th 1719

The Children of Jeremiah Holmes, & Phebe his Wife
1. Jeremiah Holmes born Decr 2 . 1750 . Deceasd
2. Jeremiah Holmes born Octor 31. 1752 old Stile
3 Peter Holmes born † Deceasd
4 Betsey Holmes born † Deceasd
5 Abigail Holmes born †
6 Phebe Holmes born †
7 Charles Holme born † . Deceasd
8 Charles Holmes born † . Deceasd
9 Andrew Holmes born Aug: 9th 1768
10 a Daughter Still born †
11 William Holmes born †

The Children of William Bradford Jun and of hanah his Wife
1 James Born ye 2d of July 1717
2 Zadock Born ye 30 day of July, 1719
3 Samuell Born April 4th 1721 Deceasd while a Minor
4 Eliphalet Born January 20th 1722/3

The Children of Peter Tinkcom & Mary his Wife
1 Jacob Tinkcom Born May 29 . 1738.
2 Arthur Tinkcom, Born June 7 . 1742.

The Children of Jabiz Shurtlif & Mary Shurtlif his Wife
1 Mary Born November 19th 1717 Deceased ffebruary 3d 1722/3
2 Jabiz Born on ye 5th of AGust 1719

The Children of Stephen Samson & Abigail his Wife
1 James Samson Born Novr 15th 1749 . Deceasd Sept 22nd 1751
2 . Stephen Samson Born July . 2 . 1751 . Deceasd July . . 1790
3 . James Samson Born, January. 11 . 1753.
4 . Abigail Samson . Born . Decr 7th 1754
5 William Samson . Born Febry 5th 1757 Deceasd Desmr 4th 1776
6 Enoch Samson Born March 18th 1759

*Sic.   † The date was not entered.

7 Penelope Samson Born June. 16th 1761
8 Rufus Samson Born March 21th 1764
9 Hennery Samson Born Sept 1st 1766

[p. 86] The Children of Simon Lazell & Margeret lazel his Wife
1 Joshua born May 5th 1717 Deceased July 9th 1718
2 Joshua born Sepr 30th 1719
3 Lydia born January 5th 1722/3

The Children of James Clark Junr. Son of James Clark Senr Deceasd & Hannah, his Wife
1 . Mariah Clark Born, Decr 13th 1748.
2 . Lothrop Clark Born, May 3 . 1751
3 . Mary Clark Born, Sept 10 . 1753 Deceased Janry 20th 1755
4 Mary Clark Born Janry 19th 1756 Deceasd April 1770
5 Hannah Clark Born March 9th 1758
6 Annah Clark Born July . 23 . 1760.
7 . James Clark, Born Sept 28 . 1762.
8 Sarah Clarke, Born Febry 13th 1765
9 Seth Clark . born May . 23rd 1767
10 John Clark . born Octr 22nd 1771

The Children of John Bratles & Martha Bratles his Wife
1 Jonathan born ye 28th of April 1718
2 Martha born ffebruary 15 1720
3 John born ffebruary 4th 1720/21
4 Edward born October 10th 1723
5 Mary born March 10 . 1725/6
6 Bathshuba born June 26 . 1728.
7 Timothy born August 15th 1730
8 Rebecca born July 19th 1732 . Deceased June 26 . 1733.
9 Samuell Born January 31st 1733/4

The Children of Joseph Churchel Junior & abiah his Wife
1 Abiah born october 9th 1717
2 Margoret born January 18 1740⅛
3 Joseph born July 14 1722
4 Samuel Churchell born June 24 – 1724
5 Joshua Churchell born July 4th 1726
Sarah Churchell born July 2 : 1728
Marcy Churchel born July 27 . 1733

The Children of Thomas Sears & Mehetabel his Wife
1 Mary Sears . Born [*] Deceased
2 . Marcy Sears Born May 3 . 1755.

[p. 87] The Children of Nicolos Drew and Abigail Drew his Wife
1 Joshua born october 21st 1709
2 Josiah born June 13th 1711
3 Nicolos born may 31st 1713
4 lemuel born About ye middle of march 1715
5 Joannah born June 18th 1717 by his Wife Reeckah † Drew

*The date was not entered.
†"Rebecca Morton" has been interlined, in a modern hand.

THE MAYFLOWER DESCENDANT

An Illustrated Quarterly Magazine

OF

Pilgrim Genealogy, History and Biography

1911

———

VOLUME XIII

———

BOSTON
PUBLISHED BY THE
MASSACHUSETTS SOCIETY OF MAYFLOWER DESCENDANTS
1911

226

Levy born January 11th 1718/19 deceased Sepr 1720.
James born April 27 , 1721 Deceased april 24th 1722
Abigail born [*]ber 14 . 1723 Deceased Augt 22d 1727
The Children of Nicholas Drew by his wife Lydia †
Rebeccah born May 3d 1731.
Lydia born ‡
The Child of Abraham Hicks & Bathsheba his Wife
John Hicks Born Febry 26th 1756
The Children of Lemuel Drew and hanah § Drew his Wife
1 Mary born october 19th 1716
2 Seth born May 4th 1718
3 Hannah born Augt 26th 1722
Lemuel Drew born . January 18th 1724/5
Sarah Drew born November 4th 1726
James Drew born Sepr 12 . 1728.
William Drew born february 14 . 1730/1
The Children of Thomas Clarke Se and Joanna Clark his wife
1 Willliam Born Aprill 14th 1718
2 Abigel Born august 5 day 1720
3 Lydia Born March 11th 1724/5 . deceased May 1727
The Child of Thomas Swift Junr & Rebecka his Wife
Jonathan Swift born, July 4th 1747

(To be continued)

PLYMOUTH, MASS., VITAL RECORDS

TRANSCRIBED BY THE EDITOR

(Continued from Vol. XII, p. 226)

[p. 88] The Children of Samuel Clarke & Mary Clarke his Wife
1 Sarah born January 23d 1717 . Deceasd June 5 . 1736
2 lucie born Aprill 30 1719
   Hannah born ye midle of October 1721
   Lurany born May 30 1726
   Samuel born March 1728/9

The Children of Ephraim Bradford & Elizabeth Bradford his Wife
1 Deborah born June 21st 1712
2 A son born June 1714 Deceased
3 Anna born July 25 1715
4 A Daughter born october 1716 Deceased
5 Elezebeth born November 3d 1717
6 Ephraim born January 1st 1718/9
7 Abigal born february 28th 1719/20
8 Lusanna born May 3 . 1721
9 Elijah born January 23 . 1722/3 Deceased
10 A Son born about March 28th 1723/4 Deceased

The Child of Ephraim Cole Junior & Sarah Cole his Wife
1 Ephraim born october 12th 1718
   Rebeckah Cole born June 1727.
   Sarah Cole born June 1730

The Children of Jonathan Eames Junr And Margaret his Wife
1 . Margaret Eames born Aprill 17 . 1744.
2 . Lydia Eames born Decr 26 . 1745.

[p. 89] The Children of Robert ffinney & Ann ffinney his Wife
1 lidiah born on ye 10th of March 1718
2 [Robert born on ye *] Josiah   Deceased on ye 30th of May 1720
3 Rebecca Finney born
4 Elizabeth Finney born July 14th 1724
5 . Jerusha born April. 19th 1728.

The Child of Samuel Mashall & Pricila Mashal his Wife
1 Elizabeth born January 2d 1701¼
   A son Deceased on ye 2d of may 1720
2 Samuel born March Ninth 1719
3 Mary born June 28 1722
   John born february 1725/6

* The words in italics were crossed out and the entry finished as printed. A space was left for the birth date.

The Children of Jacob Cooke Junor & Phebe Cooke his Wife
1 Jesse born on ye first Day of November 1717
2 Asa born on ye 12 day of June 1720
3 Phebe born Agust 5th 1722
4 Jacob born April. 19 : 1725

The Child of Jacob Cook Junr by his wife Mary
   Stephen born March 7th 1729/30

The Children of Isaac Morton, and Mariah his Wife.
1 . Hannah Morton Born Novr 3 . 1747 . Deceasd Janry ye 16 . 1748/9
2 . Hannah Morton born Sept 23 . 1749.
3 . Sarah Morton born Mar. 7 . 1752 old Stile
4   Isaac Morton . born Augst 6 . 1754 Deceasd
5   Abner Morton born July 15th 1758

[p. 90] The Children of John Tinckam & Ann Tinkam his Wife
1 Mary born June 25th 1718
2 Edward born February 2d 1710⁴⁄₆

The Children of Thomas* Spooner & Sarah Spooner his wife Said
   Thos Spooner Deceasd Decr 19th 1762 aged 68 years Said Sarah
   Spooner Aged 72 years Deceasd Janry 25 1767 1767
1 Ebenezar born october 26th 1718 Deceasd 1776.
2 Patience born october 17 1720 Deceasd July 23rd 1774
3 Joseph and Benjamin born ye 25th of March 1723 at one birth
4 Benjamin Deceased ye 19 of April 1723 & Joseph Deceased
   April 24 1723
5 Thomas born August 17th 1724 . Deceasd March 19th 1800
   Sarah born January 31 1726/7 Deceasd
   Jean born Augt 21 . 1729 Deceasd
   Ephraim born Decr : 28 . 1735 Decea'd March 22nd 1818

The Children of ffrances Billenton & Abigail Billenton his Wife
1 Sarah born on ye 11th of Desember 1702
2 Marcy† born on ye ffirst of January 1704
3 ffrances born february 16 1708
4 Jemima born June 12th 1710
5 Content born february 2d 1712
6 Abigaiel born october 21st 1716 Deceased Agust 14 : 171[‡]
7 Joseph born January 11th 1701¾

The Children of Ezekiel Morton, & Abigail his Wife.
1 Mary Morton born April 28th 1747.
2 . Ezekiel Morton born Febry 12 . 1748/9.

[p. 91] The Children of Thomas Swift and Thankfull Swift his wife
1 Lidiah Born ye 20 day of august 1718
2 Deborah born September first or Second 1720

* "Ebenezar" was first written, but was crossed out and "Thomas" interlined, in the same hand. On original page 138 is the following record: "Thomas Spooner Married to Sarah Nelson Desember 12 1717"

† "Marcy" has been written over "Sarah."

‡ The last figure has been altered and is now doubtful.

3 Elizabeth born the 28th of May 1723
4 Thomas Swift born January 11th 1724/5
5 Jerusha Swift born may 11th 1727.
6 Phineas Swift born february 25th 1731/2
7 Rhoda Swift born March 10th 1733/4
8 Thankful Swift born february 26 } 1737/8
9 Lemuel Swift born february 26 }
The abovenamed Thankfull Swift ye Daughter Deceas'd abo't May 26 . 1754

The Children of Josiah Dunham & Ruth Dunham his Wife
1 Amos born September 15th 1713
2 hannah born march 23 1719/20
3 : Charles born May 11th 1721 . Deceased About June 20th 1721
4 . Ruth born 25th June . 1722.
   Lydia born february 8th 1724/5
   Mary born July 30th 1727
   Josiah born March 27 . 1730

The Children of Nathaniel Chubuck & Mary Chubock his Wife
1 Benjamine born September 15th 1709
2 Ealles born April 5th 1715
3 Jonathan born february 5th 1716/17
4 Mary born AGust 14 : 1719
5 Susanna born October 11th 1726
these 3 children } Nathaniel born October 1st 1707
were born in   } Martha born December 18th 1708
Hingham   } Sarah born August 22th 1711

[p. 92] The Children of Joshua Gibbs & Marcey Gibbs his Wife
1 Temperence born october 5th 1712
2 Ruth born May Ninth 1715
3 Marcey born January Eleventh 1717
4 Bettey born AGust 27th 1720
5 Joshua Gibs born March ye 5th 1723/4
6 John Gibs born July 23th 1725
Phebe Gibs born November 28 . 1727

The Children of Soloman Silvester & Elezebeth Silvester his Wife
1 Ruben born February 3d 1719/20 Deceased Aprill 15th 1720
2 Nathaniell borne May 12 day 1721
3 Elizabeth borne June 3 . 1722
4 Abner borne Dec 25 . 1723.
5 Caleb borne may 1st 1725
6 Lydia borne November 4th 1726.
7 a Child born April 1st 1728 . deceased about 10 days old
8 Ruben born february 3d 1728/9 deceased about 3 months after
9 Ebenezer born June 26 . 1730
10 Joseph born february 28th 1731/2
11 Soloman born December 25 . 1733
12 Bartlet born Sep 8 . 1735
13 Hannah Borne Sept 1737.

The Child of Robert Dave and Debora Davey his Wife
1 Thomas Born November 19 1718

The Children of Jonathan Bishop, And Mary his Wife.
1 Jonathan Bishop Born Sep't 22nd 1745.
2 . Presbury Bishop (a Son) Born Jan'y 6 . 1746/7.
3 . Dorcas Bishop Born, AGust 23 . 1749.
4 . Ebenezer Bishop Born, AGust 12 . 1754
5 Mary Bishop Born Oct'r . 12 1757.

[p. 93] The Children of Eleazer Harlow and hannah Harlow his Wife
1 Elephas born on ye 5th Day of March 1716
2 lemuel born November 29th 1717*
3 Eleazar born on ye 17th of october 1719 Deceas'd Aug : 15th 1812

The Children of Elieazar harlow and Hannah Harlow his Wife
1 Elizabeth born April 21st 1721
2 Patience born on ye first Day of october 1722

The Children of Joseph Bartlet & Elizabeth Bartlet his Wife
1. William born on ye 27 Day of April 1718 Deceased,September 29 1718·
2 Silvanus born November 26th 1719
3 Jerusha born february 21st 1703/4†
4 lidiah born Desember 30th 1722
5 Zacheus born January 15th 1724/5 . Died March 6th 1780
6 Betty born January 3d 1726/7
7 Joseph born february 13 . 1728/9

The Children of Ebenazar holmes Jun and Patience Holmes his Wife
1 William on the 14th Day of August 1720
2 Ebnazar born April 4 1722
3 Patience Holmes born february 27th 1723/4 on thirdsday
4 Phebe Holmes born March 25th 1726
5 Jeremiah Holmes born January 5 . 1728/9
6 Peter Holmes born November 14th 1729 . Deceas'd Jan'y 10th 1746/7
7 John Holmes born January 7th 1731/2 . Deceased June 13 . 1733
8 John Holmes born November 27 . 1733·
9 Elizabeth Holmes born June 3d 1735
10 . Nath'll Holmes, born June 8 . 1737.
11 . Joseph Holmes, born May 16 . 1739.
12 . Abigail Holmes, born April 27 . 1742 . Deceas'd July 31 . 1742
13 . Gilbert Holmes, born March 13 1744/5.
14 . Esther Holmes born AGust 16 . 1747.

[p. 94] The Childen of George Conet & Mary his Wife
1 Charles born July 11th 1720
2 George born on ye 13th of January 1722/3
3 Elizabeth born June 3d 1726

The Children of Jonathan Eames and of Rebekah his Wife
1 Jonathan borne Decembr . 27 . 1715
2 . Isaac borne October 27 . 1717

*"8" was changed to "7."

3 . liidiah born ye last Day of october 1721
  Rebecah Ames born January 10th 1726/7
The Children of Josiah Stirtevant and Hannah Stirtevant his Wife
1 Josiah born September 4th 1720 died in Boston Augst 18 . 1775
2 Charles born January 14 1721-22
3 Zadok Sturtevant born April 19th 1724
4 William Sturtevant born April 12 . 1726
5 Hannah Sturtevant born Decr 7 . 1727.
6 Church Sturtevant born April 4th 1730.
7 Marcy Sturtevant born January 12 : 1732/3
8 John Sturtevant born July 3 . 1734

(To be continued)

PLYMOUTH, MASS., VITAL RECORDS

(Continued from page 36)

[p. 95] The Child of Quitton Crimble and Elizabeth Crimble his Wife
1 Holmes Born october 16th 1720 Decased March 20th 172¾
2 Charles Born November 13 : 1722
3 Elizabeth born August 23th 1725
4 Phebe Crymble born Decr 4th 1727 deceased april 14 . 1728
5 Murray Holmes Crymble born Sepr 27 . 1729
6 Phebe Crymble born february 20th 1731/2.
7 Abigal Crymble born June 29 . 1735
The Child of George holmes and lidiah holmes his Wife
1 George Born January 20th 1708/9
2 Richard Holmes born february 22th 1723/4
The Child of Benjamin Cartee & Elizabeth his Wife
Benjamin Cartee, borne Janry 22nd 1739/40
The Children of Gedian Ellece & ann his wife
1 Abigail Born November ye 19d : 1720
2 Gideon born . December 16 . 1722
3 Thomas born April . 25 . 1724 . Deceased 27 June 1724
4 Elener born July 6 . 1725
5 Elijah born Sepr 26 . 1727
6 Ebenezer born May 27th 1729
[p. 96] The Children of Josiah Clarke and Thankful his Wife
Elizabeth Born July 24 . 1719 Deceased Octor 19th 1719
Israiell Born on the 10th of September 1720
Elizabeth born January 31th 1724/5
a Child born January 31th 1724/5 Deceased the Same day
The Children of Lazarus Labaron & lidiah his Wife
1 lazaros Born May 7th 1721 Deceasd Novemby 15th 1784

Plymouth, Mass., Vital Records — 112

2 Joseph Born october yᵉ 7ᵗʰ 1722 . Deceased May 17 1761 ½ after 12 . A.M
3 Lydia born December 3 . 1724
Mary Lebaron born March 20 . 1731/2
Hannah Lebaron born April. 5 . 1734
Terress Lebaron born June 22 . 1736
Bartlett Le Baron born April 29 . 1739 Died July 24ᵗʰ 1806 see p. 186 . children by a 2ᵈ wife.

The Children of Ebenezer Donham and Abigail his wife
1 Abigal borne November 23 . 1720.
2 Samuel borne September 9ᵗʰ 1722.
3 Ebenezer borne September 21ˢᵗ 1724
4 John borne July 12ᵗʰ 1726.
5 Moses Donham borne, July 1728 . Deceased Febᵣᵧ yᵉ 11ᵗʰ 1744/5
6 Mary Donhan borne, June Deceased.
7 Barnabas Donham borne, Decʳ
8 William Donham borne, June

[p. 97] The Children of Elisha Bradford and Bathshua his Wife
1 Hannah Born on yᵉ 10ᵗʰ Day of Aprill 1720
2 Joseph Born Desember 7ᵗʰ 1721
3 Silvanus Born July. 6ᵗʰ 1723 . Deceased July 12ᵗʰ 1723
4 Nehemiah Born July 27ᵗʰ 1724
5 Luarama Born March 27 : 1726.

The Child James Rickard and Hanh his Wife
1 James Born on yᵉ 11ᵗʰ of June 1721

2 John Born July 22 1723
3 Benjamin Born June 7ᵗʰ 1726
Lothrop Born March 10ᵗʰ 1730/1.
William Born November 21ᵗʰ 1733
Hannah Born March 10 . 1736/7

The Child of Seth Cobb, and Sarah his Wife
Sarah Cobb Born May 17ᵗʰ 1739. See p. 179

The Children of Isaac King & Thankfull King his Wife
1 Isaac Born November 9ᵗʰ 1714
2 lidiah Born May 8ᵗʰ 1716
3 Marey Born october 26ᵗʰ 1717
4 Martha born July 25 1719
5 Jonathan born June 6 1721
6 Samuel born June 1ˢᵗ 1723 . Deceased Octoʳ 22 . 1724

The Children of Benjamin Bagnall, & Hannah his Wife,
Richard Bagnall born May 9 1752.

The Child of Jabez Mendall, & Meriah his Wife.
Benjamin Bagnall Born Janᵣᵧ 12 . 1755 . N. Stile

The Chilldren of Benjamin Bagnall & Sarah his wife
1 Hannah Bagnall born Augst 5ᵗʰ 1761
2 Benjamin Bagnall born Decʳ 20ᵗʰ 1762
3 Elizabeth Bagnall born Janᵣᵧ 10ᵗʰ 1766
4 Nicholas Spinks Bagnall born Octʳ 14ᵗʰ 1767

[p. 98] The Children of Judah West and Bethya West his wife
1 Charles born April 10ᵗʰ : 1719 & Deceased July 18ᵗʰ 1719

Plymouth, Mass., Vital Records — 113

2 Charles born Aprill 3ᵈ 1720 Deceasᵈ as Supposᵈ in yᵉ West : Indies in a Hurricane, abᵗ Augˢᵗ 8 . 1741
3 Juda born June 4ᵗʰ 1721
4 David born yᵉ 10ᵗʰ of Agust 1722 Deceasᵈ augᵗ 5 . 1745
5 Beththya born october 1723 Deceased May 24 . 1729.
6 Lydia born June 15 : 1725
7 William born May 31 . 1726 . Deceased August 2ᵈ 1726
8 Elizabeth born May 25ᵗʰ 1727 . Deceased August 2ᵈ 1727
9 Bethya born July 4ᵗʰ 1729 . Deceased August 9ᵈ 1729
10 William born June 16ᵗʰ 1730 . Deceased October 15ᵗʰ 1730
11 Samuel born 4ᵗʰ Augᵗ 1731
12 Joshua born 27 December 1732 . Deceasᵈ Sepᵗ 27 . 1733
13 Josiah born May 10 . 1734

The Child of Thomas Branch and Lidiah branch his Wf
1 Lidiah Born on The 26ᵗʰ of Agust 1721
2 Marcy born July 15ᵗʰ 1723
3 John born yᵉ 24ᵗʰ May 1725
4 Thankfull born June 5ᵗʰ 1727.
5 Thomas born November 24 . 1729
6 Experience born April 3ᵈ 1732

The Children of John Churchill Son to Serjant John Churchl and Beththya his Wife
1 Ebenazar Born November Sixth 1721
2 John Born october 24 1723 . Deceased Sepʳ 20ᵗʰ 1725
3 John Born April 15ᵗʰ 1727 . Deceasᵈ January 22ᵗʰ 1780

The Children of Joseph Shurtleff, & Sarah his Wife.
1 Mary Shurtleff Borne Augˢᵗ 4 . 1743.
2 Joseph Shurtleff Born Sept 29 . 1746
3 Bathshua Shurtleff, Born May 11 . 1752.

[P. 99] The Children of Elkanath Churchill & Suzannah his Wife
2 children at a birth on yᵉ 29ᵗʰ of November 1721 were born to them
2 Children
1 the name of their Son is Amaziah and their Daughter
2 Name is Meriah
Elkanah born April 10ᵗʰ 1726.

The Children of William Ellice & Joane his Wife
1 William born January 10ᵗʰ 1719
2 Experiance born July 15 1722
3 Eleazer Ellis born April 18ᵗʰ 1724
4 Thomas Ellis born June 20ᵗʰ 1726

The Child of Jabez Mendall, & Meriah his Wife.
Samuell Mendal Borne, Febᵣᵧ 16ᵗʰ 1746/7.

The Children of Elisha holmes Juno and Sarah holmes his Wife
1 Samuel born June 26ᵗʰ 1722
2. Sarah Holmes born August 28ᵗʰ 1724
3 . Susannah Holmes borne Novʳ 18ᵗʰ 1726.
4. Nathˡ Holmes borne, July 6 . 1730.
5. Elisha Holmes borne, Sepᵗ 4 . 1732.

Plymouth, Mass., Vital Records

6. Betty Holmes borne, Jan^ry 16 . 1734/5.
7. A daughter borne, not named, Deceased.
   a Son Borne, Between Susannah & Nath^ll and a Daughter
   borne after Betty Both Deceased, and not named — 9 in all

[p. 100] The Children of M^er John Mordoch and Mrs Phebe Mordoch his Wife

1 Joseph born Agust 21st 1720 Deceased September 6th 1720
2 Phebe born october 4th 1723

The Children of Mr Thomas Foster, & Mary his Wife

1 Mary Foster born Agust 4th 1745 . Deceased Sep^t 1 . 1746
2 Elizabeth Foster born Jan^ry 20 . 1746/7
3 Salome Foster born May 27 . 1749
4 Mary Foster born Jan^ry 29 . 1750/1
5 Seth Foster, born Feb^ry 6 . 1753 Deceas^d oct^br 18 . 1756
6 Job Foster, born May 3 . 1755
7 Eunice Foster born March 9 . 1757 . Deceas^d Mar: 16 . 1757
8 Seth Foster . born Feb^ry 26 . 1758.
9 Philemon Foster, born Mar: 7 . 1760
10 Susana Foster Born Janu^y 29 . 1762
11 Eunice Foster Born april . 15 . 1764

The Child of Mr Joseph Stacey and Mrs Patience Stace his Wife

hanna born January 21 1722/23

The Child John ffiney and Sarah ffiney his Wife

1 Sarah born November 19th 1722
   Phebe born february 8th 1724/5
   Josiah born february 5th 1726/7 . deceased Novr 16 : 1727
   Ruth born october 1st 1729 *
   John born October 18th 1730.

The Children of John Finney, & Susannah his Wife.

Josiah Finney Borne, Jan^ry 17th 1739/40.
Robert Finney Borne, Septemb^r 27th 1741.
Ezra Finney Borne, Novemb^r 26th 1743.
Silvanus Finney, Borne, Jan^ry 10th 1745/6.
Ephraim Finney Borne, Agu^st 1 . 1748.
William Finney Borne Novr 16 . 1750

[p. 101] The Children of Benjamin Norrice & Mary Norrice his Wife

1 Sarah born July 24 — 1718
2 Olliver born october first 1720
3 Mary born January 17th 1722/3
4 Abigal born October 31th 1725
5 Samuel born April . 25 . 1728
   Elizabeth born October 14 . 1731

The Child of James Barnes, & Sarah, his Wife.

James Barnes Born July 27 . 1755.

The Child of James Young and Rebeckah his Wife

Mary born on ye 10th of January 1722/23

* "9" has been written over "8."

The Children of Israiel fferren & Martha fferren his Wife

1 Israill born May 15th 1723
2 John Fearing born January 11th 1724/5
   Benjamin born September 21 . 1726.
   Ann Fearing born March 16th 1728/9.
   Noah fearing born febuary 10 . 1732
   David Fearing born October 21th 1733
   Elizabeth Fearing born Dec^r: 1 . 1736

[p. 102] The Children of Ebenezer * Bartlett and Mary Bartlet his Wife

1 Rebecka born July 7th 1719
2 lidiah born Agust 17th 1721 .
3 Nathaniel born January 31st 1722/23.

The Children of Thomas Ewer, & Lydia His Wife

Thomas Ewer Born Feb^ry 22nd 1749/5
Eleazer Ewer Born Aug^st 26th 1751.

The Children of Cornelis Holmes & lidia Holmes his Wife

1 patience Born on : ye 15th of Agust 1722
2 Cornelius born October 19 . 1723
3 Ebenezer born October . 4 . 1725 . deceased October 19th 1732.
4 Benjaman Born September 9 : 1731
   Ebenezer born January 17 : 1733/4
   Lydia born November 17 † 1735
   Priscilla Born Novr 6th 1738

The Children of Ebenezer Doggett & Elizabeth his wife

1 . Ebenezer . born July 5 . 1722 . Deceased . December 20th 1722.
2 . John borne february 6th 1723/4.
3 . Ebenezer born, July 17th 1726
4 . Samuel born January 20th 1728/9
5   a child born October 23 . 1730 . deceased November 1730

The Children of Joseph Bates, & Elizabeth his Wife.

1 . Elizabeth Bates borne March 8th 1741/2.
2 . Joannah Bates borne Novr 17 . 1743.
3 . David Bates, borne, Octr 5 . 1745.
4 . Samuel Bates born March 12th 1748/9.
5 . Lidya Bates born Novr 12th 1752.

[p. 103] The Children of Jacob Tinckham and Hanna Tinckham his Wife

1 Marcy born September 27 1722 : Deceased April . 20 . 1724
2 Jacob born february 28 — 1723/4

The Children of Robert Bartlett, and Rebeckah his Wife Continued
from page ye 184 . 8 Children there Recorded.
9 Josiah Bartlett Born Feb^ry 8th 1753.

* "Samuel" was first written, but was crossed out and "Ebenezer" interlined. The marriage of Ebenezer Bartlett and Mary Rider, on 3 July, 1718, is entered on page 139 of the same volume.

† The second figure appears to be a "7" written over a "2."

The Children of Nathaniell Cobb and Mary Cobb his wife
1 Mary born october 5th 1722
2 Nathaniel born September 19 — 1724
    Hannah born September 6th 1728
    Luce born June 24 . 1730
    Rowland born July 9th 1732
    Samuel Cob born January 18th 1735/6
The Children of Joseph Rider Junr* and Abigall his wif
1 William born october 11th 1723 Deceas{d} June 29th 1772
2 Abigall born April 18th 1726
3 Joseph born May 9th 1728 . Deceased July 4th 1728
4 Joseph born . June 15th 1729.
5 Hannah born October 27 : 1731 . Deceased Augst 3d 1732
6 Benjamin born September 8 . 1733
  Tilden born february 5 . 1735/6 Deceased June 30 1737
The Parents of the Above family Deceas{d} Vizt
Mr Joseph Ryder . July 18th 1737
Mrs Abigail Ryder Decr 5th 1766
[p. 104] The Children of Joseph Pearce and Elezabeth his wife.
1 hannah born March ye 10th 1723
2 Joseph born April ye 11th 1725
The Child of James Shurtleff, & Joanna Shurtleff, his Wife
James Shurtleff Born July 21 . 1745.
The Children of Thomas Morton Son of Decon morton and abigiel Morton his wife
1 Ruth born ye 11th of october 1723
2 Isaac Morton born May 8th 1725
3 Jonathan Morton born Nov{t} 28 . 1726
4 Thomas Morton born Augt 24 . 1728
5 Silvanus Morton born february 24th 1729/30
6 Abigal Morton born february 10 . 1731/2
7 Hannah Morton born December 31 . 1733
The Children of Ebenezer Cob Junr and Ruth his wife
1 Ebenezer born March 4th 1723/4
The Child of Ebenezer Cob Junr & Lydia his wife
  Ruth born November 6 . 1728
  Lydia born May 26 . 1730
The Children of Charles Rider, & Rebeckah his Wife
1 Luce Rider born Augst 14th 1742.
2 Jean Rider born July 22 . 1744.
3 . A Daughter not named, born Augst 24 . 1746 Deceas{d} Sept 13th 1746.
4 . Charles Rider born Feb{ry} 4th 1747/8 Deceas{d} at Phil{a}
5 Rebecca Rider born Jan{ry} 1st 1749/50
6 Elkanah Ryder born July 4th 1752

(To be continued)

* "Junr" was interlined in a different hand.

PLYMOUTH, MASS., VITAL RECORDS

(Continued from page 116)

[p. 105] The Children of Robert Harlow & Sussanna his wife
3 . & . 4 .   2 Borne, at Plimpton, R Harlow Says.
5 . Benjamin Borne the 12th day of September 1723
6 . Isaac borne August 3d 1725
7 . Robert borne January 30th 1727/8.
8 . Ruben borne April . 5th 1730
10 . James borne December . 7 . 1732
12 . Susanna . borne . April 13 . 1736 . Deceas{d} Feb{ry} 24th 1748/9

*The day was omitted.

1. A Son not named, borne, Aprill 1721 . (Deceased) Liv'd abo't 2 weeks
2. A Son, not named, borne June . 1722 . Deceas'd . Liv'd abo't 2 weeks
9. A Son Not named, born Dec'r 1731 . Deceas'd
11. A Son not named, borne Oct'br 1734 . Deceas'd
13. Mary Harlow Born May 5 . 1739.
A daughter born Nov'r 29 . 1729 . Deceased Dec'r 10th 1729
Mary born february 21 : 1730/1
Carry'd To Page 106.

The Children of John Bartlett and Sarah Bartlett his wife
1. Jerusha borne march . 21th 1723/4 . Deceased
2. Sarah borne January 20th 1725/6.
3. Hannah borne Dec'r : 13th 1727 Deceas'd April 1st 1778

The Children of John Bartlett and Sary his wife
1. Jerusha Bartlett born November 10th 1735
2. John Bartlett born february 26 . 1737/8
3. Genne Bartlett, borne, May 1740
4. Lewis Bartlett, borne, April 1 . 1743.
5. Abigail Bartlett born Nov'r 28 . 1745.
6. Mariah Bartlett, born April 8th 1748.

The Children of Seth Barnes & Sarah Barnes his wife
1. Elizabeth Barnes borne August 31th 1722
2. Sarah Branes* borne April . 27th 1724
3. Seth Barnes borne April . 25 . 1726
4. James Barnes borne May. 27 . 1728.
5. Mary Barnes born July 11th 1730
6. William Barnes born October 1st 1732
7. Joseph Barnes born february 8 . 1736/7
8. Benjamin born february 8 . 1736/7
9. Peter Wooden Barnes born, July 17th 1742.
10. Luce Barnes, born, Aprill . 9th 1745.
A Daughter Born, Between y'e birth of W'm & Joseph Lived about an hour.

[p. 106] The Children of Joshua Donham & Sarah Donham his wife
1 James Donham born y'e 16th of December 1723
2 Sarah Donham born January 26 : 1725/6.
3 Joshua Donham born November 27 . 1727
4 Marcy Donham born November 8 . 1729
5 Bathshua Donham January 7 . 1731/2.
6. Elizabeth Donham Borne June 10 . 1733.
7. Joshua Donham Borne Feb'ry 15 . 1735/6.
8 Luce Donham Borne Feb'ry 18 . 1737/8.
9. Levi Donham Borne June 1 . 1743.
10 Elisha Donham borne Nov'r 25th 1744

The Children of Benjamin Weeks & Mary Weeks his wife
1 Isaac Weeks born July . 21th 1722

* Plainly an error for "Barnes."

Elizabeth born february 14 . 1724/5
Jabesh born August 4th 1729
The Children of Robert Harlow, & Susannah his Wife Continued from page 105.
14th Elizabeth Harlow, born, Ap: 1 . 1743.
15 Submit Harlow, born. June 7 . 1745.
The Children of Robert Harlow, & Remember his Wife
1 Susannah Harlow, Born Nov'r 10 . 1750.
2 Lydia Harlow Born, July 10 . 1752.
The Children of Josiah Rider and Experience Rider his wife
1 Lemuel born November 24 1723 . Deceas'd . Mar: 4 . 1742/3
2 Experience born January 13th 1724/5
3 Sarah born May 7th 1726. Deceased July 20 . 1726.
4 Ruth born April . 20th 1727.
5 Mary born . March 22 . 1731/2
6 Isaac born July 5 . 1734
7 Lydia born february 5 . 1736/7
8 Mercy Borne April 8 . 1740
9 Josiah Borne Nov'r 25 . 1742 Deceas'd Aug'st 30 . 1743
10 Thomas Borne, Aug'st 28 . 1744.
17 *Caleb Rider Born Aug't 22 . 1746 . 1746
[p. 107] The Children of Seth Chipman & Priscilla his wife
2. Seth Chipman born October 31th 1724
The Child of Solomon Atwood, & Lydia his Wife
Lydia Atwood Born Sep't 11th 1749.
The Children of Joseph Warren and Alletheah his wife
1. Joseph Warren born June 21th 1724 . on a Saboth day
2. Elizabeth Warren born. Sep't 28th 1726.
3. Mary Warren born January 25th 1729/30
4. Priscilla Warren born April 19 . 1733 . Deceas'd Oct'r 2nd 1757
5. William Warren born June 18 . 1737
The Children of Caleb Stetson & Sarah his wife
1 Abishā born february 22th 1706
2 Elizabeth born October 14th 1709
3 Barzilla born December 17th 1711
4 Joshua born April 21th 1714
5 Jerusha born June 30th 1716
6 John born December 18th 1718
7 Jedidiah born Sep't 12th 1721
[p. 108] The Children of Nathaniel Morton & Rebecca his wife
1 Elizabeth born November y'e 12th 1720
2 Nathaniel born January 10th 1722/3
3 Eleazer born September 26 . 1724
4 Ichabod born December 28th 1726
The Children of Israel Bradford & Sarah his wife
1 Ruth born December y'e 11th 1702 . deceased about y'e beginning february 1702/3

*Sic.

2 Bathseba born November 8th 1703
3 Benjamin born . October 17th 1705
4 Abner born . December 25th 1707
5 Joshua born . June 23th 1710
6 Ichabod born . September 22th 1713
7 Elisha born . March 26th 1718

The Child of Wrastling Brewster & Hannah his wife
1 Wrastling Brewster born August 29th 1724

The Children of The Revd Mr Jacob Bacon, and Mary his Wife
1 Mary Bacon born Augst 18 . 1750.
2 Jacob Bacon born Augst 25 . 1751.
3 Thomas Bacon born Feb^{ry} 15 . 1753 . Deceased Augst 6 . 1753.
4 David Bacon, born Augst 24 . 1754.
5 Oliver Bacon, born, Oct^{br} 28th 1755.
6 Samuel Bacon born June . 3 . 1758.
7 Charles Bacon, born April, 8 . 1759 . Deceased Sep^t 16 . 1759

[p. 109] The Children of Robert Shattuck & Mary his wife
1 . Mary born March 9th 1719/20
2 Robert born June 3 . 1721
3 . Randel born April 27 . 1723 . Deceased

The Child of William Foster & Joanna his Wife
William Foster Born Novr ye 20th 1749.
S^d William Foster ye Father was Drowned, on his Passage, for Philadelphia 1749.

The Children of William Lucas & Mehetabel his wife
1 William Lucas born June 27th 1723 . Deceased May 29 1734.
2 Phebe Lucas born April 12 . 1725.
3 Priscilla Lucas born April . 19 . 1727.
4 Joseph Lucas born June 12th 1729.
5 Benjamin Lucas born June 21 . 1731
6 Isaac Lucas born June 1733 . Deceas^d Feb^{ry} 1743/4
7 William Lucas born July 29 1734 De
8 Mehetabell Lucas Born Feb: 24 . 1737/8.

The Children of Samuel Swift & Abigal Swift his wife
Elizabeth Swift born about ye 22th January 1717/8
James born March 1st 1720/1
Samuel born January 16th 1723/4

The Children of Zacheus Curtis, & Lydia his Wife.
1 . Zacheus Curtis born Octr 3 . 1743 . Deceased Sept^m ye 12th 1744
2 . Lydia Curtis, born Decem^{br} 31 . 1745.
3 . Hannah Curtis born April . 8th . 1748.
4 . Zacheus Curtis born Octr 19th 1753 .
5 . Nathaniel Curtis born Mar: 26th 1756
6 Mary Curtis born Feb^{ry} 24th 1764

[p. 110] The Children of Robert Johnson & Elizabeth Johnson his wife
1 Jane Johnson born August 15th 1716
2 Joseph Johnson born January 1st 1717/8

3 Sarah Johnson born february 9th 1719/20
4 Caleb Johnson born April 2^d 1722

The Children of Robert Carver & Mary Carver his wife
1 Elizabeth Carver born february 22th 1717/8
2 Mary Carver born September 14th 1721
3 Robert Carver born August 19th 1723

The Children of Nathaniel Morton Junr, And Rebeckah his Wife
1 Nathl Morton Born Novr 13 . 1754 . Dec^d
2 Meriah Morton . Born Jan^{ry} 19th 1758 . Dec^d
3 Rebecca Morton Born Decr 30 . 1761
4 Betty Morton born Sep^t 15th 1770 Dec^d 1790

The Children of Elisha Barrow & Thankfull Barrow his wife
1st Zacheus born february 13th 1719/20 Deceased July 3 . 1720
2 . a daughter born 1722 . Deceased
3 . Lydia born May, 8th 1723 Deceased September 6th 1723
4 . Elisha born November 13th 1724 . Deceased March . 5 . 1724/5
Patience born December 24 . 1729.

[p. 111] The Children of Seth Swift & Maria Swift his wife
1 . Mary Swift born . May 17th 1723
2 Seth Swift born . Decr 2^d 1724
Hannah Swift born . September 17th 1727

The Child of Edward Sparrow, & Jerusha his Wife
Edward Sparrow Born April 2 . 1745.

The Children of John Cooke & Elizabeth Cooke his wife
1 Silas Cooke born December 1st 1708
2 Paul Cooke born May 8th 1711
3 Robert Cooke born June 1714
4. Marcy Cooke born March 1718

The Children of Jonathan King, & Deborah his Wife
1 . Nathl King born Jan^{ry} 27th 1745/6
2 Lydia King born Novr 8th 1747.
3 Jonathan King born Decr 21 . 1749.
4 Luce King Born Augst 6 . 1752 . Deceas^d April 12th 1754
5 Abigail King born May 10th 1754
6 Mercy King born Feb^{ry} 14th 1756
7 Mary King born Aug: 22nd 1761

The Children of Benjamin Rider & Hannah Rider his wife
1 Amos Rider born September 14th 1720 . Deceased Sep^t 25 . 1744.
2 Lydia Rider born . february 4th 1721/2
3 Hannah born May 16 . 1723
4 Benjamin born . April 15th 1724
5 Abigal born february 6th 1725/6
6 Elizabeth born June 4th 1727.
7 Stevens born Decr 29 . 1728 . Deceas^d Decr 2 . 1745.
8 Jesse born february 1st 1730/1
9 William Rider borne May 25 . 1732.
10 Mary Rider borne Sep^t 14 . 1733.
11 Sarah Rider borne July 19th 1735.

Plymouth, Mass., Vital Records

[p. 112] The Children of Joseph Holmes & Mary his wife
1 Joseph Holmes born October 4th 1697
2 Ephraim Holmes born March 14th 1699
3 Mary Holmes born June 7th 1701
4 Sarah Holmes born April 12th 1703
5 Abigall Holmes born July 18th 1705
6 Jonathan Holmes born July 5th 1709
7 Micah Holmes born April 7th 1714
8 Keziah Holmes born March 23th 1719
The Children of Isaac Holmes & Mary his wife
1 Hannah Holmes born August 18th 1706
2 Mary Holmes born May 1st 1709
3 Zeruiah Holmes born October 29th 1714
4 Susannah Holmes born October 12th 1716
5 Isaac Holmes born April 7th 1722
The Child of Samuel Foster & Margett his wife
1 John Foster born August 23th 1724
Thomas Savery born Octor: 3d: 1681.
The Children of Thomas Savery & Esther his wife
1 Marcy Savery born June 21th 1706
2 Uriah Savery born April 30th 1708
3 Thomas Savery born April 26. 1710
4 Lydia Savery born July 25. 1712
5 Esther Savery born April 2. 1715
6 Samuel Savery born August 18. 1718
7 Mehetibell Savery born April. 15. 1721
[p. 113] The Children of Ebenezer Fuller and Joanna his wife
1 Josiah Fuller born May 15th 1722
2 Samuel Fuller born October 14th 1723. Deceased April 22th 1724
3 Rebeccah Fuller born April 23. 1725.
The Child of Lemuell Doten, & Jean his Wife
Jean Doten Born April. 23rd 1749.
The Children of James Howard & Sarah his wife
1 John Howard born January 12th 1723/4
2 Mary Howard born Febry 28th 1725/6
3 James Howard born Janry 18. 1727/8
4 Francis Howard borne Septr 12. 1731
5 Sarah Howard born Janry 1. 1733/4. 1733/4.
6 William Howard born June 10. 1742.
The Child of Thomas Sturmy and Rebecah his wife
1 Denniss Sturmy born february 15th 1724/5.
Thomas Sturmy born April. 8th 1730
The Children of Ebenezer Harlow, & Meriah his Wife
1 Thankfull Harlow borne August 13th 1740.
2 Meriah Harlow borne June 1. 1742.
3 Deborah Harlow borne June 18th 1744.
4 Ebenezer Harlow Born Septr 27 1746.
5 Andrew Harlow Born June 1749.

6. Philemon Harlow Born Febry 21. 1752.
[p. 114] The Children of Nathaniel Thomas Junr* and Hope his wife
1. Nathaniel Thomas born . January 5 . 1724/5 . deceased January 26th [worn]
2 Nathaniel Thomas born January 27th 1726/7 . deceased february 27 1727 [worn]
The child of Nathaniel Thomas and Hannah his wife
Hannah Thomas born June 20 . 1730.
The Child of Nathaniel Thomas Esqr & Elizabeth his wif[e]
Nathaniel Thomas borne October 17th 1742 . Deceasd June 16th 17 [worn]
John Thomas born, Sep. 27, 1745. Decd at Liverpool N. S. 1822
The Children of Robert Cooke and Abigal his wife
1 Charles Cooke born October 4th 1717
2 Nathaniel Cooke born December 19th 1719
3 Robert Cooke born March 12th 1721
4 Sarah Cooke born June 18th 1724.
The Children of Josiah Doty and Abigall his wife
1 Josiah Doty born April 18th 1715
2 Abigal Doty born December 3d 1716
3 Experience Doty born January 4th 1718/19
4 Patience Doty born february 10th 1720/21
5 Sarah Doty born June 2d 1723
The Children of Saml Barrows, & Desire his Wife
1 Luce Barrows, Born May 17th 1746
2 . Willis Barrows, Borne . Augst 6 . 1748
3 Isaac Barrows Borne July 1st 1750
4 Elizabeth Barrows Borne March 27th 1752
5 Lurany Barrows Borne January 16th 1754
6. Saml Barrows, Born March 21 . 1762.
[p. 115] The Children of John Crandon and Jean his wife
Jean Crandon born November 16th 1722
Grace Crandon born June 25th 1724.
John Crandon born January 30th 1725/6 . Deceased in ye West Indies September 4th 1745
James Crandon borne, March 21 . 1727/8.
Thomas Crandon borne, Decr 15 . 1729
The Children of Peleg Durfy & Mary his wife
1 Mary Durfy born March 21st 1724
2 Peleg Durfy born Sepr 5th 1724.
The Children of Asa Beale & Rheda his Wife.
1 . Susanna Beale Born july 2 . 1723 . Deceased Novr 19th 1729.

*"Junr" has been interlined in different hand and ink.

172 Plymouth, Mass., Vital Records

2. Margaret Beale Born Octr 25 . 1725 . Deceased Nov^{br} 13th 1729.
3. Rhoda Beale, Born May 15 . 1727.
4. Sarah Beale, Born Augst 23 . 1731.
5. Mary Beale, Born Dec^{br} 18 . 1733.
6. John Beale, Born Feb^{ry} 28 . 1735.
7. Elizabeth Beale, Born, March 21 . 1737.
8. Susanna Beale Born July 15 . 1729
9. Margaret Beale Born Augst 14 . 1740.

The Children of Benjamin Hanks & Mary his wife

1. Isaac Hanks born June 1st about one a clock in ye afternoon . 1725
2. Abigal Hanks born August 28th 1726 about 6 a Clock afternoon
3. William Hanks born October 23 . 1728 . about 5 a Clock in ye Morning
4. John Hanks born October, 5th 1730 . about 9 a Clock in ye forenoon
5. Richard White Hanks born November 8th 1734 at 11 a Clock in ye Morning
6. Uriah Hanks May 4 . 1736 . in the Morning
7. Benjamin Hanks born August 20th 1738.
8. Mary Borne June 7th 1741
9. Silas Hanks borne May 20th 1744.

[p. 116] The Child of Thomas Croad & Rachel his wife
Priscilla born . January 1st 1724/5 Deceased february 18th [worn]

The Children of James Clark Junr is James Clark ye 3^d, Son of John Clar[k]* and Meriba his wife
Rebeccah Clark born february 4th 1724/5
James Clark born April 30 . 1727

The Children of Jabez Cobb, and Sarah his Wife

1. John Cobb Born Jan^{ry} 29 . 1750/1.
2. Silvanus Cobb Born Ap: 2nd 1754.
3. Sarah Cobb, Born Decr 8 . 1757
4. Jabez Cobb Born Decr 20 . 1759.

The Children of James Clark Son of James Clark & Ann his w[ife]

1 James Clark born April 9th 1723 Deceas^d Feb^{ry} 6th 1815
2 Ann Clark born August 4th 1724
3 Abigal Clark born December 15th 1727

The Children of Richard Waite & Mary his wife

1 Mary Waite born february 27th 1722/3
2 Lydia Waite born January 25 . 1724/5
3 Martha Waite born April : 22 : 1727
4 Elizabeth Waite born July 27 . 1729 . Deceased September 16 . 1730
5 Abigal Waite born July 27 . 1731
6 Elizabeth Waite born April 15th 1734.
7 Sarah Waite born March 1st 1735/6
8 Thomas Waite borne april 3^d 1739 . Dec^d July 23 1740

*The words in italics were inserted when the record of James, born 1727, was entered. See also the second family following.

Plymouth, Mass., Vital Records 173

9 Thomas Waite born April 13th 1741 . Deceas^d Augst 25 17[worn]
10 . Hannah Waite Borne June 22 . 1743.
11 . Richard Waite born Octr 6 . 1745

[p. 117] The Children of James Cushman & Sarah his wife
1 Lydia Cushman born September 4th 1723
2 James Cushman born May 4th 1725.

The Children of Samuel Morton & Lydia his wife
1 Lydia Morton born March 24th 1724/5.
Samuel Morton born October 5th 1726
Benjamin Morton born October 10th 1728.
Ephraim Morton born April 23 . 1731.
Elisha Morton & Hannah Morton born April 1st 1734
Barneby Morton born Sepr 24 . 1735
Ephraim Morton borne Septr 12 . 1739
Sarah Morton borne March 15 . 1741.

The Children of Richard Bagnell & Elizabeth his wife
1 Benjamin Bagnell born December 19th 1724.
2 Hannah Bagnall Born   Deceased

The Children of Jonathan Darling, & Martha his Wife
1 Lydia Darling Born April 30 . 1750.
2 Benjamin Darling born Novr 1 . 1752 Old Stile is Novr 12 . 1752 . New Stile
3 Sarah Darling, Born, Oct^{br} ye 4 . 1754.
4 Mary Darling, Born, Augst ye 28 . 1756.
5 John Darling born Decr ye 23 . 1758

The Children of Josiah Carver & Dorothy his wife
Josiah Carver born June 29 1722 . Deceased July 6th 1722
a Daughter born April 29 . 1723 . deceased ye Same day
Josiah Carver born September 25 . 1724
Dorothy Carver born May 20th 1727 . deceased January 2^d 1730/1
James Carver born May 5th 1729 . deceased January 15 : 1730/1
a child born January 17th 1730/1 deceased the Same day.
Dorothy Carver born . Sepr 12 . 1736
Marcy Carver born August 1st 1738 Deceas^d July the 9th 1739.
Nathaniel Carver born September 24th 1740.
Marcy Carver born Augst 1 1743.
John Carver born, April 25th 1747.

[p. 118] The Children of Samuel Ellis & Marcy his wife
Mary Ellis born June 8th 1718
Hesther Ellis born April . 13 . 1721
Samuel Ellis born October 13 . 1722
Remember Ellis born . March 31st 1725
The Child of Joseph Jackson & Remembrance his wife
Joseph Jackson born March 31st 1725.
The Children of Nathaniel Bartlett & Abigall his wife
1 . Thomas Bartlett born December 7th 1725 . Deceased . 30th March 1 [worn]

2 . Susanna Bartlett born March 1st 1727/8.
3 . Mary Bartlett born april 30th 1730.
4 . Nathaniel Bartlett born September 20 . 1733
5 . John Bartlett, borne, Janry 3 . 1735/6
6 . Andrew Bartlett, borne, March : 16 . 1737/8 Deceasd Decr 9th 1808
7 . Abigail Bartlett borne, July . 3rd 1740 Deceasd Novr 15th 1766
8 . Hannah Bartlett, borne, Augst 11 . 1743.
The Child of John Sturtevant Junr & Sarah his wife John Born January 5th 1725/6.
[p. 119] The Children of Elkanah Morton and Elizabeth his wife
1 . Ephraim Morton born August 23th 1725 . Deceased at 20 mo & 8 days old
2 . Elisha Morton borne, Febry 13 . 1728 . Deceased, at about 13 mo. old
3 . A Son borne, Janry 21 . 1729/30 . Deceasd at 5 . days . old.
4 . Elkanah Morton, borne June 13 . 1731.
5 . Betty Morton, borne May . 9 . 1734.
6 . Phebe Morton, borne, July . 4 . 1739.
7 . Lazarus Morton, borne, April 5 . 1742 . Deceased May 12 . 1742.
The Children of Thomas Rogers & Priscilla his wife
1 . Ruth born April 30th 1722
2 . Priscilla born October 23 : 1723 . Deceased January 8 : 1723/4
3 . Desier born April 4th 1725.
4 . Willis born April 24th 1727 . Deceased Sepr 17 . 1730
5 . Samuel born November 7 . 1728
6 . Thomas born December 18 . 1730
7 . Hannah born August 10 . 1734
8 . Eleazer born March . 4 . 1735/6
9 . Priscilla born January 1 . 1739 . Deceasd Novr 20th 1747.
10 . John Rogers Borne Novr 24 . 1740.
The Child of Thomas Western & Mary his wife a Child Named Thomas born March 20th 1724/5 deceased June 23 . 1725
The Children of Consider Howland, & Ruth his Wife Continued from below
12th Experience Howland Born Janry 13 . 1747/8.
13 . John Howland Born Augst 2 . 1751 . Deceased Augst 30th 1751
14 . Joseph Howland Born Augst 2 . 1751.
15 . Hannah Howland Born June 11 . 1753.
The Children of Consider Howland and Ruth his wife
1 . Luce born January 27th 1725/6
2 . Elizabeth born february . 29th 1727/8
3 . Ruth born february 19 1729/30
4 . Mary born April 3 . 1732
5 . Thomas Southworth born March 31th 1734
6 . Consider born January 20th 1735/6 . Deceasd Febry 16 . 1742/3
7 . Joanna born Febry 20th 1737/8

8 . Martha Born December 22 . 1739
9 . Joseph Born Febry 20 . 1741/2 Deceasd May 12 . 1742.
10 . Bethiah Howland born Aprill 22 . 1743.
11 . Consider Howland born, Octr 1 . 1745.
Continued to ye accot Above

(To be continued)

PLYMOUTH, MASS., VITAL RECORDS

(Continued from page 175)

[p. 120] The Children of the Reverend mr Nathaniell Leonard & Priscilla his wif[e]

1. Anna Leonard born Novr 23 : 1725 . Deceased february 12th 1725/6
2. Sarah Leonard born Octor: 27th 1726
3. Anna Leonard born July 17th 1728.
4. Mary Leonard born July 8 : 1729 . deceased Sepr 26 . 1729
5. Nathaniel Leonard born Octor: 30 . 1730.
6. Priscilla Leonard born April . 18 : 1732
7. Daniel Leonard born January 9th 1733/4 deceased January 18 . 1733/4
8. Mary Leonard born April 2 . 1735 . deceased January 26, 1735/6
9. Elizabeth Leonard born July 3 . 1736
10. Ephraim Leonard born September 6 . 1737 deceased Novr 6 . 1737
11. Mary Leonard born September 11th 1738 . Deceasd Janry 1 . 1739.
12. Abiel Leonard borne November 5th 1740.

Carryd to page 124.

The Children of Benjamin Ellis and Hannah his wife.

1. Benjamin Elles born Aprill 11th 1724 . deceasd Aprill 26 . 1724
2. Hannah Ellis born April . 7th 1726.
3. A Child born, June 1st 1727 . Deceasd June 21st 1727
4. Sarah Elles, born, June 8 . 1728.
5. Benjamin Elles, born, Aprill 19th 1732.
6. Joseph Elles born, Sept 12 . 1734.
7. Susannah Elles, born, octbr 8 . 1736.
8. Freeman Elles born, Octbr 19 . 1738.
9. A Child born, Augst 25th 1740 . & Dyed ye Same day.
10. Nathll Elles born, octr 10th 1742 . deceased Octr 24th
11. Betty Elles borne Novr 28th 1746.

The Children of Samuell Bartlett Esqr & Elizabeth his wife

1. Lothrop Bartlett Borne Augt 16th 1723 . Deceased Sept 29 : 1723
2. A Daughter Still borne October 10th 1724
3. Elizabeth borne August 25th 1725 . Deceasd Sept 30th 1746
4. Margaret borne April 22 . 1728 . Deceased April 25 . 1729.
5. Hannah born August 15 . 1731 . Deceased April . 21 . 1732.
6. Margaret born April 15 . 1737 . Deceased Decr 31 . 1739

The Children of Sd Samll Bartlett Esqr & Elizabeth his Second Wife

1. Samuel Bartlett Born Septembr ye 3 . 1749 . Sabbath day about 3 Clock in ye afternoon . Deceased Monday July ye [*worn*] 1750 . at 7½ in ye forenoon

Plymouth, Mass., Vital Records — 200

2 Samuel Bartlett, Born, April ye 15 . 1751 Monday half after 1 Clock P.M.
3 Elizabeth Bartlett Born Aug^st 9 . 1753 Thirsday about 2 Clock in ye Morning.
Continued to page 1st 2nd Book.
The Children of Eleazer Morton Junr & Deborah his wife
1 Ambros Morton born July 12th 1725
2 Nathaniel Morton born April 16th 1727
The Children of Francis Le-Barron, & Sarah his Wife
1 Francis Le-Barron Borne Mar: 26 . 1722 . Deceas^d
2 Mary Le-Barron Borne oct^br 11 . 1723.
3 Isaac Le-Barron Borne Septr 7 . 1725 . Deceased July 22 . 1741 was Drowned at Ply
4 Sarah Le-Barron D^o oct^br 7th 1728.
5 a Daughter Borne   1727 Deceased
6 Francis Le-Barron D^o Aug^st 11 . 1731.
[p. 121] The Children of Robert Brown & Priscilla his wife
1 Priscilla born October 11th 1725
2 Mary Brown born March 15th 1727/8
3 Martha Brown born July 22th 1730
4 Rebecca
5 Robert
The Children of Edmond Tilsen & Elizabeth his wife
Hanah Tilsen born August 21th 1723
Peres Tilsen born July 16th 1725
The Children of Benjamin Bartlett & Abigail his Wife.
William Bartlett Borne Feb^ry 15 . 1741/2.
Priscilla Bartlett, borne Decr 3 . 1744.
Eliz^a Bartlett, born Oct^br 7 . 1746 . Deceas^d May 14th 1801 was the wife of Capt Nathaniel Ripley
The Children of Joseph Silvester Junr & Marcy his wife
Sarah Silvester born Oct^or 11 . 1721
Joseph Silvester born Oct^or 4 . 1723.
The Children of Samuel Bartlett & Hannah his wife
Samuel Bartlett borne June 10th 1726.
William Bartlett born february 14 . 1727/8
John Bartlett born September 6th 1729
Judah Barlet June 29 . 1732
[p. 122] The Children of Benjamin Bartlett and Lydia his wife
1 James Born July 12th 1725 : Deceased January 12th 1725/6.
2 Lydia born November 16 : 1726 . Deceas^d
3 Solomon Bartlett born October 2nd 1728.
4 Benjamin Bartlett born November 10 : 1730 . Deceased Feb: 1[*worn*]
5 Sarah Bartlett borne, Aprill 25 . 1733
6 Lydia Bartlett, borne, June 8 . 1735
7 Joseph Bartlett, borne Aug^st 1 . 1739.
The Children of Thomas Jackson & Hannah his wife
1 Hezekiah Jackson born September 2^d 1725 . Deceas^d

Plymouth, Mass., Vital Records — 201

2 Thomas Jackson born february 15 . 1728/9
3 Samuel Jackson born January 3 . 1730/1
4 Ruth Jackson Born Jany 8 . 1733
5 Hezekiah Jackson April 13 . 1738 . Deceas^d Feb^ry 10th 1768.
6 Nathaiel Jackson Born Feby ye 2 . 1742.
7 William Hall Jackson Born March . 9th 1744
8 Hannah Jackson Born July . 12 . 1747
9 Moley Jackson Born Nov^br 29 . 1749 Deceas^d
The Children of John Sparhawk and Hannah his wife
1 Sarah Sparhawk born September 27th 1726
2 Hannah Sparhawk born June 24th 1728 deceased June 15th 1729
3 John Sparhawk born May 7 . 1730 deceased June 20 . 1730
4 Hannah Sparhawk born August 14th 1732
5 John Sparhawk born January 19 . 1738/9 Deceas'd Novem^r 27 . 173[*worn*]
The Children of Ebenezer Swift & Mary his wife
1 Elizabeth Swift born Aug^st 22 . 1722 } both born at Yarmouth
2 Judah Swift born february 6 . 1723/4 }
3 Job Swift born July 17 . 1726.
Enoch & Micah Swift born July 25 . 1735
[p. 123] The Children of m^r James Warren & Penelope his wife
James born September 28th 1726 . died Novr 1808
Ann born July 5 . 1728.
Sarah born May 23 . 1730
Winslow born May 23 . 1733
Josiah born March 2^d 1735/6 . deceased April 22^d 1736
The Children of John Barnes Junr & Dorcas his wife
1 John Barnes born July 12th 1726 . on tuesday about 4 aclock in ye afternoon Deceas^d at Jamaica ye 20th or 22nd of Oct^br 1744
2 Lemuel Barnes born June 16 : 1729 . on Munday about 6 a Clock in ye morning
3 Corban Barnes born November 20th 1732 . on tuesday about 4 aclock in the Morning . Drowned off the Gurnet, & his Grandson, 1806 or 7
4 Mary Barnes borne July 17 . 1736 . on Saturday about Noon
5 Hannah Barnes, borne Aprill 8 . 1740 . Tuesday abo^t 1 Clock in ye Morn^g
6 Elkanah Barnes, born Novr 12 . 1742 . Fryday abo^t 7 Clock afternoon
The Childred of Joseph Holmes and Phebe his wife
1 Jonathan Holmes born Decr 14th 1726.
2 Pheba Holmes Born May 20th 1729
3 Desire Holmes Born May 6th 1731
4 Samuel Holmes Born March 14th 1733 Deceas^d at Novascotia in 1754
5 Hannah Holmes Born May 12th 1735 Deces^d June 25th 1751
6 Meriah Holmes Born May 18 . 1737 Deceas^d 9 weeks after
7 Jane Holmes Born Octr 14th 1738 Deceas^d Octr 13th 1740
8 Joseph Holmes Born March 14th 1741

9 Meriah Holmes Born June. 10th 1743 Deceasd July 25th 1751 Continued See Below
The Children of David Besse & Mary his wife
Samuel Besse born December 10th 1726
Thankfull Besse born Novr 10th 1727.
Nehemiah Besse born Augt 7 . 1729.
The Child of Joseph Swift, & Sarah his Wife
Mary Swift borne, August 1738 . Deceasd Decbr 1738
The Chilldren of Joseph Holmes & Phebe His wife Continued from Above
10 Elkanah Holmes Born March 27th 1745
11 Susannah Holmes Born Octr 8th 1747 Deceasd 12 weeks after
[worn] Holmes Born June 26th 1749
[p. 124.] The Child of Benjamin Besse & Martha his wife
Elizabeth Besse born December 4th 1726.
The Children of John Rickard, & Bathsheba his Wife
1 . Bathsheba Rickard born Febry 7 . 1749/5.*
2 . John Howland Rickard born July 2 . 1752.
3 Mary Rickard Born July 12th 1754
4 Benjamin Rickard Born July 12th 1756
5 Thomas Rickard Born June 29th 1758
The Children of Joseph Lewen and Hannah his wife
John Lewen born July 4th 1727
Moriah Lewen June 21 . 1730
The Children of Benjamin Cornish & Experience his wife
1 . Benjamin Cornish born July 17th 1727
2 . Susanna Cornish born September 16 . 1729.
3 . Marcy Cornish born March 20th 1731/2
4 John Cornish born June 6 . 1734
5 Experience Cornish born Decr 26 . 1740
6 Nathll Cornish borne Sept 28 . 1743. Deceasd
    a Son named Thos borne
The Children of Henry LittleJohn & Sarah his wife
Hannah born March 21th 1721/2
William born January 23th 1723/4
James born March 21 . 1727/8
The Children of ye Revd Mr Nathll Leonard & Priscilla his wife, Continued, from Page 120
13 . Margaret Leonard, Borne, Novr 21 . 1741.
14 . George Leonard, borne, Novr 28 . 1742.
15 Thomas Leonard, borne, Aprill 26 . 1744.
16 Phebe Leonard Borne Deceasd
[p. 125] The Children of Thomas Foster & Lois his wife
1 Thomas Foster born July 6th 1727.
2 Elisha Foster born May 12 . 1730. Deceased Novr 19 . 1730.
3 Gershom Foster, born Septembr 23 . 1733 . Deceased Novr 5 . 1739.

* Sic.

4 . Lois Foster, born June 9th 1735.
5 Deborah Foster born, March : 18 . 1736/7.
6 John Foster, born Jany 29 . 1738/9 . Deceased Augst 19 . 1739.
7 Gershom Foster, born, May. 16 . 1740 . Deceased Novr 5 . 1741.
8 . Hannah Foster, born March 1 . 1741/2 . Deceased July 4 . 1742.
The Children of Thomas Morton son of Thomas & Hannah his wife
Bathsheba born Sepr 18th 1727.
martha born february 24th 1729/30
The Children of Elkanah Totman and Sarah his wife.
Priscilla Totman born June 29 . 1728
Joshua Totman born May 22 . 1730
Elkanah Totman born April 18 : 1732 deceased August 4th 1732
The Children of Elkanah Totman and Elizabeth his wife
Elkanah Totman born May 23 . 1734
Sarah Totman born December 28 1735
Elizabeth Totman born . April 2 . 1738
Joseph Totman borne Janry 15 . 1741.
Dorothy Totman, borne, Febry 17 . 1743/4.
Abial Totman born March 1 . 1745/6
Caried the births to folio . 153.
[p. 126] Mer Wiliam Clark Was married unto hannah Griswell the 7th day of march 1677
Thomas ffaunce Was Married unto Jeann Nelson the 12th day of december 1672
Mer William Clark was Married unto Mrs Abiah Wilder on the 3d of August 1692
Baruch Jordan was Married unto Mary Wilder on ye 3d of August 1692
Thé Child of Francis Howard & Elizabeth His Wife
1 Francis Howard Born July 20th 1753
The Children of David Turner Junr, & Deborah his Wife
1 Ruth Turner Born July 31 . 1754. Wednesday about 4 Clock . P.M.
2 Deborah Turner Born March ye 11th 1756
3 Sarah Turner Born Novr 12th 1757.
[p. 127] 1 Elkanah Cushman Was married unto Elizabeth Cole the 10th of febuawary 1677 She deceased the 4th of Janawa[ry] 1681
2 Elkanath Cushman was married unto Martha Cooke March the 2 1683
3 John Mordo Was married unto lidia yong the 10th day of december 1686
4 Mer John ffuller Was Married unto hannah Morton the 24th day of March 1687
5 Nathn ffish Was Married to Deborah Barrows the 20th of december 1687
6 Henery Churchill Was Married unto Mary Doty widdow on the 8th of february 1688
Samuel Dunham Junior Was married unto mary harlow on the 30th of June 1680

204 Plymouth, Mass., Vital Records

John Cobb Junior was Married unto Rachill Soul on the 7th of September 1688

Edmon Weston was Married unto Rebeckah Soul on the 13th of December 1688

Heugh Cole Was Married unto Elizabeth Cook Widow the first day of January 1688

David Shepard Was Married unto Rebeckah Curtice on The 12th day of apriell 1699

[p. 128] 1 Giles Rickard Junor was married unto hannah Snow the 7th day of november 1683

2 William Churchill was married unto Liddiah Briant the 17th day of Jenaway 1683

3 George Bonam Junor was maried unto Elizabeth Jenney the 27th day of aprill 1681

4 Abraham Jacson Junior was maried unto Margarret hickst the 7th day of Janaway 1685

5 Samuell ffullour was maried unto mersey Eaton the 7th day of Janauary 1685

6 Josiah morton Was married unto Suzannah Wood thee 8th day of March 1686

7 John Gray Was married unto Joannah Morton the 9th day of december 1686

8 [*Samuell Lucas Was married unto patience Warren the 16th day of december 1686*]

9 Nathaniell Jacson Was married unto Ruth Jeny the 20th of december 1686

10 John Churchill Was married unto Rebekah Delleno the 28th day of december 1686

11 Edward Dote Was married unto Sarah Faunce the 25 of February 1662

12 John Morton Was married unto Mary Ring the 4th day of March 1687

13 Joshua Ransom Was married unto Mary Gifford the 21th day of February 1686

14 Jams Warren was Married unto Sarah doty the twenteth first day of June 1687

15 Frances Cook Was married unto Elizabeth Laythum on the second day of August 1687

16 Robert Bartlet was married unto Sarah the Daughter of Benjamen Bartlett Senior of Duxborrow the twenty eight day of december 1687;

[p. 129] 1 Jonathan Shaw Junior Was married unto Mehitabell Pratt the 29th day of december 1687

2 Ephraim Cole Was Married unto Rebekah Gray on the 3th of Janauary 1687

Eliazur Ring Was Married unto Mary Shaw the Eliventh day of January 1687

Plymouth, Mass., Vital Records 205

Eliazur Cushman was married unto Elizabeth Combs the 12th of January 1687

John Bradford was married unto Mersy Warren on the 6th of January 1674

Samuel Luces Was married unto Patience Warren on the 16th of December 1686

Josiah Finney Was Married unto Elizabeth Warren on the 19th of January 1687

Samuel Bradford was Married unto hannah Rogers on the 31 of July 1689

Robart Cuttlar was married unto Sarah Downham on the 31 of July 1689

Isaac King was married unto Mahitabel Bryant on the 13th of Agust 1689

John Carver was Married unto Mary Barns on the 24th of october 1689

Samuel Cornish was Married to Suzannah Clarke on the 27th day of october 1692

[p. 130] Benjamine Eaton was Married unto Mary Coombs the 18th of desember 1689

Samuel Rickard Was Married unto Rebekah Snow the 31st day of december 1689

Joseph King Was Married unto Elizabeth Bryant on the 15th day of January 1689 or 90

Jonathan Mory Was Married unto hannah Boorne on the 24th of January 1689

Thomas Clark Senior was Married unto Elizabeth Crow on the 12th of February 1689 or 90

Mer James Allen was Married unto mistris Elizabeth Cotton on the 2d of June 1690

Eliazar Jacson was Married unto hannah Ransom on the 29th day of January 1690*

Nathaniel harlow was Married unto Abigail Buck on the Seaventeenth day of March 1691

Nathaniel Dunham was Married unto Mary Tilson on the 21th day of January 1691*

Edmond Tilson was Marryed unto Elizabeth Waterman on the 28th of January 1691*

Robert Bartlet Was Married unto Sarah Cooke on the first day of April 1691

Joshua Ransom was Married unto Suzannah Garner on the 10th of March 1691*

Joseph Bartlet Junior was Married unto Lidia Grizwel on the 6th day of June 1692

John Sutton was Married unto Abigail Clarke June ye 6th 1692

[p. 131] Left Ephraim Morton Was Married unto the Widdow Mary Harlow on the 18th day of october 1692

* "1" was written over "2."

---

*This record has been crossed out. A duplicate record was entered on page 129 of the original.

Joseph Warren was Married unto Mehittabel Wilder on the 20th of desember 1692
Richard Cooper was Marryed unto hannah Wood on the first day of February 1692/3
John Doty Junior was Married unto Mahittable Nelson on the 2d of February 1692/3
John Buck of Sittuate was Married unto the widow Sarah Dotey on the 26th day of Aprill 1693
John Nelson Was Married unto Patience Morton on the 4th of May 1693
Ebenazar Cobb Was Married unto Mercy holmes on the first day of June 1693
Joseph Finney was Married unto Mercy Bryant on the 15th of June 1693
John Foster was Married unto hannah Studson November 16th 1692
Isaac Tincom was Married unto Sarah King November 17th 1692
John Barns was married unto Mary bartlet July 6th 1693
William Ring was Married unto hannah Shirmon on the 13th day of July 1693
Jeduthan Robbins was married unto hannah pratt on the 11th day of January 1693/4
Samuel dunham was Married unto the Widow Sarah Watson on the 15th day of January 1693/4
Georg Barrow was Married unto Patience Simmons on the 14th day of February 1694/5
Elisha Holmes was married unto Sarah Bartlet on the 2d day of September 1695
[p. 132] Ebenezar Holmes was Married unto phebe Blackmur on the 26th day of desember 1695
John Jacson was married unto Abigail Woodorth on the 25th day of desember 1695
Abiall Shurtleif was Married unto lidia Barnes on the 14th of January 1694/5
Frances lebaron was Married unto Mary Wilder on the Sixth day of September 1695
Caleb loring was married unto lidiah Grey on the Seaventh day of August 1696
Thomas Morton was Married unto Martha dotey on the 23d of desember 1696
Stephen Barnebe was Married unto Ruth Morton on the 10th of desember 1696
Thomas Holmes was married To Joanna Morton on the 6th day of January 1696/7
Nathaniel Houland was Married unto Martha Coole on the third Tusday of March : 1696/7
Benjamin Warren was Married unto Hannah Morton on the Twenty Second day of April 1697
Eleazar Prat and Hannah Kanedy was Married September 22d 1697

Nathaniel Holmes was Married unto Joana Clark on the 21 day of december 1698
David bozworth was Married To Marcy Stirtivant on The 18th day August 1698
Josiah Rickard Was Married unto Rebekah Eaton on The 21 of November 1699
Joseph Allen Was Married unto Mary doty december on the 21 1699
Joshua Mors Was Married unto Eliazebeth doty on the 12th day of December 1698
[p. 133] Mr Ephraime Little Was Married To Mrs Sarah Clarke on The 29th day of November 1698
Mr Thomas Lorein Was Married unto Mrs Deborah Cushin on the 19th day of April 1699
Thomas Tabor Was Married unto Rebekah Harlow July ye 4 1700
John Bryant Jun Was Married unto Mary West on The 11th of July 1700
William Bonney Was Married unto Mehetable King on The 11th day of July 1700
Frances Curtice Was Married unto hanah Bosworth on The 5 Day of November 1700
John Ellis Was Married unto Sarah holmes on The 7th of november 1700
John Churchell Was Married unto Desire holmes on The 19th of november 1700
Daniel Pratt Was Married unto Esther Wright on The 23d day of January 1700/1
Isaac Cushman was married unto Sarah Gibbs on the 28th of January 1700/1
Isaac lathrop was Married unto Elizabeth Barns on the 29th of december 1698
Micajah Dounham Was Married unto Eliazabeth Lazell on The 26 day of June 1701
Jacob Michell Was Married unto Rebekah Cushman on The 18 day of November 1701
[p. 134] Israell Bradford Was Married unto Sarah Bartlett November 27 ano 1701
John Bradford Was Maried unto Rebekah Bartlett November 27th ano 1701
Ebenazer Eaton Was Married unto Hanah Rickard November 2d ano 1701
Ephraime Kempton Was Married unto pattience Faunce June The 2d 1702
Joseph Stirtevant Was Married unto annah Jones December 5th 1693
Francis Billenton Was Married unto Abigaiel Churchill May 17 1702
Isaac Dotty Was Married unto Martha Faunce on ye 17 of March 1702/3
John Brigs of Rochester Was Married unto Ruth Barow of plimouth on ye 23d day of December 1701

THE MAYFLOWER DESCENDANT

An Illustrated Quarterly Magazine

OF

Pilgrim Genealogy, History and Biography

1912

———

VOLUME XIV

———

BOSTON
PUBLISHED BY THE
MASSACHUSETTS SOCIETY OF MAYFLOWER DESCENDANTS
1912

Robertt Waterman Was Married unto Mary Cushman on ye 19th of March 1702

Stephen Bryant Junior Was Married unto Bathsheba Brigs on ye 9th Day of September 1702

John pouldand Was Married unto Lidiah Tilson on ye 25th Day of october 1702

Josiah Washbond of Bridgwater Was Married unto Marsy Tilson on ye 11th Day of February 1702

Joseph Pratt Was Married unto Martha Lassell on ye 29th of March 170⅔

These Last Mentioned Six Couples Were Married by M^{er} Isaac Cushman Minester of ye Gospell at ye uper Sociaty in plimouth Township

(To be continued)

PLYMOUTH, MASS., VITAL RECORDS

Transcribed by the Editor

(Continued from Vol. XIII, p. 208)

[p. 135] Benjamin Curtice was Married unto Mary Bessee of Sandwidg on the 24th of desember 1700
John Eastland was Married unto Mary Finey octtober ye 29th 1702
James Reves was married unto deliverance Abrahams on ye 20 of November 1703
Experiance Bent Was Married unto Abaigaill Samson on ye 26th Day of Agust . 1703.
Nehemiah Stirtevant Was Married unto Ruth Samson December ye 9th 1703
William Churchell Was Married unto Ruth Bryant January ye 11th 1704
Abiall ffuller was Married unto Annis parker on the 19th of ffebruary 1704/5
John Faunce Was Married unto Abigaill Bryant on ye 20th day of November 1705
1 John Tilson was Married unto Lidiah Rickard March 27th 1706
2 Joseph Samson was Married unto Ann Tilson on ye 22 of April 1706
3 Joseph ffinney was Married unto Ester West September 19th 1706
4 Richard Wast was Married to Elizabeth Connaday october 21 1706
5 Danniel Pratt was Married unto Mary Washbon october first 1706
6 Edmond Tilson was Married unto hannah orket Desember 25th 1706
7 Samuel Stirtevant Junior was Married unto Mary Price January 20th 1706/7
William Stirtevant & Feare Cushman was married ffebruary 12th 1707
Joseph Rickard & Deborah Millar was Maried on the Nintenth of february 1707
William Clarke was married unto Bethyah Mayhew on the 4 of September 1707
Lieut Nathaniel Morton was Married unto Mary ffaunce on the 21 of february 1706

[p. 136] 1 Joseph Allen was Married unto Mary Dotey December 26th 1699
2 John Esland was Marreed unto Elizabeth Genney october 17 1700
3 Henerey Perrey was Married unto Mary pratt November 26th 1700
4 Job Simmons was Married unto hannah Bushop June 15th 1700
5 Jonathan Bryant Married unto Margret West february 27 1700
6 Nathaniel Holmes was Married unto Eleanar Bacor March 13th 1700
7 Ebenazar Eaton was Married unto hannah Rickard November 24 1701
8 Benjamin Bartlet was Married unto Sarah Barnes october 15th 1702
9 Jeremiah Jacson was Married unto hannah Rider october 27th 1702
10 John Esland was Married unto Mary ffinney october 29th 1702
11 Elisha Cobb was Married unto lidiah Rider february 4th 1702/3
12 Helkiah Bosworth was Married to Beththyah Boles ffebruary 20 1702/3
13 Elkana Cushman was Married unto Ester Barnes ffebruary 23d 1702/3
14 Thomas Doten was Married to Elizabeth Harlow ffebruary 24 1702/3
15 James Reves was Married to Deliverance Abrahams December 20 1703
16 Joseph Peterson was Married to Sarah Doten August 23d 1704
17 William Barns was Married to Alce Bradford November 20 1704
18 Samuel Nelson was Married to hannah ford December 13th 1704
19 Nicklos leechfeild was Married to Bathshabe Clarke January 3d 1704/5
20 James Cobb was Married to Patience holmes July 20 1705
21 Joseph Church was Married to Juduth Harlow November : 1 : 1705/6*
22 Joseph King was Married to Marsey Dunham November 17 1701
23 Joseph Holmes was Married to lidiah † Bartlet Janury 25th 1705
24 John Harlow was Married to Martha Dillino ffebruary 26 1705/6
25 Nathan Ward was Married to Elizabeth Pope March 7th 1705/6
26 John Harlow has married to Martha Dillino ffebry 26 1705/6
27 Samuel Nelson was married to Bathshebe Nicolds april : 1 : 1706
28 Samuel Kemton was Married to Marsey Dunham april 8 1706
29 Samuel Bates was married to Margeret Churchill November 20 1706

* Sic.

† Above, in a modern hand, has been written "Wid of Jo Bartlett Jr"

30 William Cook & Tabitha Hall were Joyned in Marriage on y^e 18th Day of March 170$\frac{4}{5}$ p^r John Thacher Justice of y^e peace
31 John Harlow was married to Martha Dilleno february 26 170$\frac{5}{6}$
32 Joseph Rider was married to Mary Southworth March 10 170$\frac{6}{7}$
33 Ebenazar Dunham was married to Annah ford May 2^d 1707
34 Joseph Bonney was Married to Margeret Phillips november 14 1707
35 Joshua Bamhall was Married to Sarah Rider November 20 1707
36 Retorne Weight to Mary labarron Desember 10 1707
37 Sam witherhead to abigaiell May January 2^d 170$\frac{7}{8}$
38 Mr Josiah Cotton to Mrs Hanah Sturtevant January 8th 170$\frac{7}{8}$
39 Eben Sponer to Mary Roos March 26 1708
40 Henery Rickard to Marsey Morton April 22^d 1708
41 Mr Edward Mitchell to M^{rs} allice bradford August 26 1708
42 Jonathan freman to Marsey bradford october 12 1708
43 William Dunham to Anna Norcutt Desemb: 9 1708
44 Edward Stevens to Mary Churchell December 23 1708
[p. 137] 1 Joseph Morton was Married unto Mary Chittenden May 30 1709
2 John holmes was Married unto Sarah Church october 7th 1709
3 Thomas Harlow was married to Jedidah Churchel December : 1 : 1709
4 Ebenazar Curtice was Married unto Mary Tinckam January 19 170$\frac{9}{10}$
5 William Greene was Married to Desire bacon on the 23 of march : 1709
6 Ephraim Bradford was Married to Elizabeth bartlet ffebry 13 170$\frac{9}{10}$
7 John ffaunce was Married to lydiah Cooke february 23^d 1709–10
8 Ignatious Cushing was married to Marcy Rickard April 4th 1710
9 Joel Ellis was Married to Elizabeth Churchill April 6 1710
10 Josiah Morton was Married to Elizabeth Clarke June : 1 : 1710
11 Stephen Barneb was Married to Judith Church July 11 1710
12 Joseph Mitchel was Married to Bathshaba lumbert october 12 1710
13 Robert Barrow was Married to bethiah ford April 25 1711
14 Mr Joseph Hall was Married to Mrs Mary Morton May 15 1711
15 Mr John Stirtevant was Married to Mrs Mary hascall July 12 1711
16 Thomas ffaunce was Married to Sarah Ford July 12 1711
17 Nathaniel Garner was Married to Sarah Turner Novembe 30 1711
18 Eliezor holmes was Married to hannah Silvester Desember : 6 : 1711
19 Elisha Studson was Married to Abigail bruster october 27th 1707
20 Timothy Morton was Married unto Mary Rickard January : 1 : 170$\frac{7}{8}$
21 John holmes was Married to Marsey Ford february 21 171$\frac{1}{2}$
22 Richard holmes was Married to Ester Wormwoll March 20 171$\frac{1}{2}$
23 John May was Married to Anne Warren April 8th 1712
24 Capt Ephraim Morton was Married to Suzannah Morton Aprill 10 : 1712

25 Elnathan Bartlet was Married to hannah Mansfeild Aprill 24 1712
[26 Middleton Church was Married to hannah Riord March 20 171$\frac{1}{2}$*]
26 Captain Thomas Barker was Married to Beththyah little May 22 1712
27 Charles little was Married to Sarah Warren october 9^h 1712
28 Ichabod Padduck was Married to Joannah ffaunce october 15 1712
29 Judah Hall was Married to Mehittabl Faunce october 21 1712
30 William Bradford Married to Elizabeth ffinney November 18 1712
31 Jabiz Shurtlif Married to Martha Weight ffebruary 19 1712/13
32 Eliazar Ring Married to Anna Wilder March : 23 : 17$\frac{12}{13}$
33 Barnabas Churchill was Married unto lidiah Harlow ffbruary : 4 : 1713
34 Samuel Rider Junior was Married to ann Eldred on The 17th of ffebruary 1713
35 William Harlow was Married to Joanna Jackson June 18th 1713
36 Jonathan Ames was Married to Rebecka Standford November 24 : 1713
37 George Morton was Married to Rebecca Churchill february 4th 170$\frac{3}{4}$
38 Manassieh Kempton to Mehittabl Holmes february 4 170$\frac{3}{4}$
39 Isaac King to Thankfull Barrows february 11th 170$\frac{3}{4}$
40 Joseph Hows to Hanah Rickard March 9th 170$\frac{3}{4}$
41 Hezekiah Bradford to Mary Chandler May 21st 1714
42 Sam Totman to Debrah Buck Jun 3^d 1714
43 John Barrow to bethyah King october 10th 1714
44 Samuel Steell to Sarah Cooper November 5 1714
45 Joseph Bartlet to Lidiah Nelson December 9 1714
46 William Bradford to hannah ffoster Desamber 9 1714
47 John Tinkham to Anna Gray Desember 30th 1714
48 Thomas hatch to Sarah Jackson Desember 30 1714
49 John Wotson to Sarah Roggers of Epswoge † January 26 1714
50 David Bradford to Elizabeth Finney february 23^d 170$\frac{4}{5}$
[p. 138] Serjant John Churchill Was Married unto The Widdo hanna Bartlet o^r the 4th Day of March 1715
Samuel Clarke Was Married unto Mary ffinney January 25th 170$\frac{4}{5}$
Josiah Dunham was Married unto Ruth Kempton ffebruary 2^d 170$\frac{4}{5}$
lemuel Drew To hannah Barnes December 22^d : 1715
Josiah Dunham To Ruth Kempton ffebruary 2^d 1715–16
Benjamin Samson was Married unto Rebeckah Cook March 19 1716
Simon Lazel To Margret Cooke Aprill 5th 1716
William harlow Junior Married To Marsey Rider february 24 1714–15
Nicolos Drew To Rebecaa Morton Aprill : 19 : 1716
Mordeca Ellis To Rebecca : Clarke octobe : 15 1715
Robert Jonson To Elizabeth Cooke october 27th 1715

*This entry has been crossed out in the original.
† "Ipswich" has been interlined, in a modern hand.

Plymouth, Mass., Vital Records — 38

Robert Davie To Deborah howes May 7th 1716
Peleg ford To Allice Warren May 10th 1716
Joseph Cobb To Hanna Clarke July 5th 1716
Girshom Bradford was Maried to pricila Weswall october 23d 1716
Jonathan Bryant Married to Mary little July 2d 1716
William Bartlet Married to Sarah ffoster July 5th 1716
Capt Benjamin Warren Married to Ester Cushman october 25th 1716
Robert Finney Married to Anne Morton November 15th 1716
Thomas Bartlet Married to Abigaiel Finney January 10th 1716/17
James Jonson Married to Anne Cooke february 6th 1716/17
Joseph Bartlett Married to Elezabeth Bartlet March 18th 1717
Robert Carver Married to Mary Cooke March 28 1717
Samuel Marshall Maried to priscila finney May 23d 1717
Thomas Clarke Married to Joanna Colman June 6 1717
Thomas Spooner Married to Sarah Nelson Desember 12 1717
Nathaniel Harlow Married to patience lucos Desembe 19 1717
Thomas Swift of Sanddwedg & Thankful Mory of plimouth was Married January 23d 1701/2 Josiah Cotton Justic
[Benjamin Bartlet Deceased March 10th 1717/8 *]
Thomas ffaunce Junior Was Married to Lidiah Barnebe May 29th 1718
William Perrey Was Marred to Ledia Barncbe august ye 5 1719
Joseph Vaughan narried to Elezabeth Shurtlif January 28th 1719/20
[p. 139] Judah West married to Bethiah Keen by mr Daniel Lewis Minister of Pembrook September 3d 1718

Persons Married By Mr Ephraim Little in the yeare 1718

1 Ebenaz Bartlet to mary Rider July 3d 1718
2 Samuel Nelson to Sarah Holmes September 12th 1718
3 Eben Curtice to Martha Doty october 7th 1718
4 Seth Jackson to Ester Dunham october 23d 1718
5 Solonon Silvester to Elezabeth Rider october 23d 1718
6 George Conett to Mary howland November 3d 1718
7 Josiah Carver to Dorithy Coole November 20th 1718
8 Henery Littlejohn To Sarah f Pratt Desember 4th 1718
9 George Holmes Maried to lidiah Wood febryary 5th 1718/19
10 Ignatious Cushing Married to Ruth Croad February 5th 1718
11 price Nicols Married to hanah Bartlet June 16th 1719
12 Nathan Thomas Married to Sarah Bartlet June 17 1719
13 Quintin Crimble Married to Elizabeth Holmes July 7th 1719
14 Robert Shattuck Married to Mary Pratt July 9th 1719
15 Elisha Bradford Married to Bathshua Brock September 7th 1719
16 Daved Turner Married to Ruth Jackson october 22d 1719
17 Joseph King Married to Mercy Spooner November 3d 1719
18 John Collens Married to Bathshua Dunham November 3d 1719
19 Elisha holmes Married to Suzannah Clarke November 4th 1719
20 Mr John Mordoch Married to Phebe Morton November 4 1719

* This entry has been crossed out, in the original.

† "Mary" was crossed out and "Sarah" interlined.

Plymouth, Mass., Vital Records — 39

21 John Jonson Married to Elizabeth Goole Janary 7th 1719/20
22 Ebenaz holmes Married to Patience ffinney Agust 20 1719
23 Gidian Ellis Married to Anna Clarke february 11th 1719/20

Mariages in ye year 1720 by Mr Little

1 Nathaniel Morton to Rebca Ellice Aprill 28 1720
2 John Bearse to Sarah Holmes May 12 1720
3 Lazaros Labaron to Lidiah Bartlet May 16 1720
4 Ebenazar Dogget to Elizabeth Rickard June 9 1720
5 Thomas Branch to Lidya Barow october 11 : 1720
6 James Rickard to hannah Howland June 29 1720
7 Nathaniel Cobb to Mary Waterman July 14 1720
8 Asa Beales to Rohoda Iathle Desember 8th 1720
9 Ebenazar Morton To Marcy ffoster february 2d 1720
10 Elkanah Churchill Suzanna Manchester febury 21 : 1720

Mariages in ye year 1721 by Mr Ephraim Little

Elisha Holmes To Sarah Bartlett March 7 1720/1
John Churchill to Bethiah Spooner february 1720/1
Peleg Eatlice to Mary Cooie June 19 1721
Anthony Decro to Elizabeth Bacon June 23d 1721
Joseph Silvester to Marcy holmes July 14 1721
Toby Crumwel to Bilka July 14 1720
[p. 140] Thomas Rogers Married To prissilla Churchill october 31st 1721

Mariages Solemnized

Mr Joseph Stacy To Mrs Patience Warren Aprell 11 : 1721
Ichabod Barlet To Susanah Sponer November 6. 1721
Jacob Tinkham To hannah Cobb November 16 1721
ffrances Lebaron To Sarah Bartlett November 23d 1721
Nathaniel Holmes To priscilla Pratt November 27th 1721
Samuel Bartlett to Elizabeth Lathrop December 22 1721
John ffinney To Sarah Bartlet * February 22d 1721
Before Mee Ephraim Little

Marriages Solemnized By Mr Little of Plimoth in the year 1722

1 John ffinney To Sarah Battict february 22d 1721/2
2 Joseph Langerell To Mary Thomas Aprill 5 1722
3 Seth Barns To Sarah Wooden Aprill 20 1722
4 Jams Clarke To Anna Rider June 8th 1722
5 Ednuond Tilson To Elizabeth Cooper June 12 1722
6 Nathaniel Thomas To hope Warren July 23d 1722
7 Joseph Warren To Alithea Chittenton Agust 22 : 1722
8 George Barrows To Desire Doty Agust 23 1722
9 James young To Rebecca Shepard october 12 1722
10 Ebenazar Cobb To Ruth Tinckham 8 1722 †
11 Joseph Rider To Abgaiel Warren November 4 1722

* Some one, in a modern hand, has interlined, above this name, the words "Rebecca Bryant," but "Sarah Bartlet" was not crossed out.

† The name of the month was omitted.

40

12 Samuel Rider To Mary Silvester Novembe 2ᵈ 1722
13 Richard Waite To Mary Barnes December 4 1722
14 Thomas Sterny To Rebeca Philips December 6 1722
15 Thomas Morton To Abigaill Pratt Desem 10 1722

James Cushman to Sarah Hatch December 24ᵗʰ 1722
Nathaniel Wood to Mary Adams January 14ᵗʰ 1722/3
John Sturtevant To Sarah Bartlett March 26 1723
John Bartlett to Sarah Cob April 4ᵗʰ 1723
Thomas Weston to Mary Howland April 19 : 1723
James Howard to Sarah Billington May 3 : 1723
Richard Bagnall to Elizabeth Poland May 6 : 1723
Israel Jackson to Mercy Donham June 28 : 1723
Joseph Lewing to Hannah Rogers Novʳ 4 : 1723
David Sturtevant to Sarah Holmes Novʳ 19 1723
Returned to yᵉ County Clerk

(To be continued)

PLYMOUTH, MASS., VITAL RECORDS

(Continued from page 40)

[p. 141] 1724 Mariages Solemnized by ye Reverend mr Nathaniel Leonard of Plimouth

Eleazer Faunce to Hannah Warren August 6th 1724
Caleb Tinkcom to Marcy Holmes October 20th 1724

Mariages Solemnized by Isaac Lothrop Esqr
Joseph Jackson to Remembrance Jackson february 20th 1723/4
Benjamin Ellis to Hannah Gibs March 25th 1724
Samuel Morton to Lydia Bartlett July 22th 1724
Benjamin Bartlett to Lydia Morton September 24th 1724
Elkanah Morton to Elizabeth Holmes October 1st 1724
Eleazer Morton Junr to Deborah Delano December 7th 1724
all above Returned to ye County Clerk

Marriages Solemnized by the Reverend mr Nathaniel Leonard of Plymouth

Francis Allen to Jane Kirk January 15th 1724/5
John Cooke to Hannah Morton January 21th 1724/5
Nathaniel Donham to Rebecca King January 26th 1724/5
Nathaniel Bartlett to Abigal Clarke April 8th 1725
Consider Howland to Ruth Bryant May 10th 1725
Ichabod Delano to Elizabeth Cushman May 20th 1725
Ephraim Washborn to Mary Polen the Marriage Solemnized by Isaac Lothrop Esqr January 13th 1725/6.
Nathaniel Howland and Abigail Billenton Married by Isaac Lothrop Esqr January 25th 1725/6.

Mariages Solemnized by the Reverend mr Nathaniel Leonard
John Peirce to Rebecca Donham July 19 : 1725
Stephen Barden Junr to Deborah Pratt Augt. 5 : 1725
Samuel Bartlett to Hannah Churchell Augt. 19 : 1725
Mr Tompson Phillips to mrs Hannah Cotton Sepr 30 : 1725
Allexander Mallise to Bathsheba Hill October 25 : 1725
Benjamin Cornish to Experience Gibs Novr. 11 . 1725
Jacob Tinkham to Judeth Hunt Novr. 18 : 1725
Phillip Lee to Elizabeth Jackson January 2 : 1725/6
Joseph Holmes to Phebe Churchell february 3 : 1725/6
John Moore to Mary Shattuck March 1 : 1725/6
William Foster to Hannah Rider March 17 : 1725/6
John Hayses & Bethiah Randall of Bridgwater were Married April 21th 1726 . by Josiah Cotton Justice of Peace
all above Returned to Josiah Cotton Esqr County Clerk.
[p. 142] Marriages Solemnized by the Reverend mr Nathaniel Leonard
Ebenezer Finney of Bristoll to Jane Faunce of Plymouth Augt: 18th : 1726'
Jonathan Barnes Junr: to Phebe Finney both of Plymouth Sepr 8th 1726
John Bacon Esqr of Barnstable & Madm Sarah Warren of Plymth Sepr 28 . 1726
Quominy & Dutchess Negros belonging to mr Phillips Married Octor 13th 1726
Peter Calee & Mary Marshall married Octor 21th 1726
John Tommas to Abigall Donham both of Plymth Novr 1st 1726
Lazerus Samson to Jemina Holmes . both of Plymr Novr 3 . 1726
Isaac Little to Sarah Church both of Plymouth December 1st 1726

Marriages Solemnized by Isaac Lothrop Esqr
Ebenezer Rider to Thankfull Silvester March 16th 1725/6
Thomas Morton Junr to Hannah Nelson March 29th 1726
Nathan Delano to Bathsheba Holmes June 29th 1726

Marriages Solemnized by the Reverend mr Nathaniel Leonard
The Revd mr Rohart Ward of Wenham Married to mrs Margaret Rogers of Plymth February 16 . 1726/7

Barnabas Shurtleff of Plympton & Jemima Adams Married . March 16 1726/7
Joseph Bartlett & Sarah Morton both of Plymouth Married April . 4 . 1727
Samuel Totman & Experience Rogers both of Plym^th Married April 17 . 1727
Ebenezer Cobb Junr & Lydia Stephens both of Plym^th Married Decr 14 . 1727
Benjamin Lothrop Junr of Barnstable & Experiance Howard of Plymouth Married Decr 22 . 1727.
Ebenezer Cobb of Plymouth and Mary Thomas of Middleberough married February 8 . 1727/8

marriages Solemnized by Isaac Lothrop Esqr
Samuel Doty and Marcy Cob married April 10th 1727
Joshua Finney and Hannah Curtis married September 28 . 1727

Marriages Solemnized by ye Reverend m^r Nathaniel Leonard
Nehemiah Riply and Sarah Atwood married June 6th 1728
Thomas Scarret and Alse Ward married August 6 : 1728
Jo a Negro man belonging to m^r Nathaniel Thomas & Phebe a Negro Woman belonging to m^r Haviland Torry married October 28. 1728
Elkanah Delano and Mary Sanders married Octo^r 31 . 1728.
Ephraim Samson of Duxberough & Ruth Shepherd of Plymouth Married November 14th 1728.
Samuel Cole and Marcy Barnes married November 14th 1728
Timothy Burbank of Boston Now residing in Plymouth & Mary Kempton of Plymouth married December 12th 1728.
Jonathan Freeman of Plimton & Sarah Rider of Plymouth Married December 19th 1728.
Thorton Gray & Katherine White married Decr 20th 1728
James Holmes & Content Silvester married January 30th 1728/9
Mathew Lemote and Marcy Billington Married February 18th 1728/9
[p. 143] 1729 Marriages Solemnized by the Reverend m^r Nathaniel Leonard
Edward Stevens and Marcy Silvester both of Plymouth Maried April. 3 . 1729
Redolphus Hatch of Provincetown & Esther Holmes of Plymouth married april 3^d 1729
Thomas Doane of Chatham & Sarah Barnes of Plymouth married may 20 . 1729
Thomas Totman & Lucretia Rose both of Plymouth Married May 30: 1729
Jack and Mariah Negroes belonging to m^r Jonathan Bryant June 30 . 1729
Jacob Lewis and Bathsheba Mallis both of Plymouth Married July 8 . 1729

John Watson Esqr & m^rs Priscilla Thomas both of Plymouth Married July 8 . 1729
Jacob Tayler of Barnstable and Mary Atwood of Plymouth married July 24th 1729
Seth Doggett & Elizabeth Delano both of Plymouth Married Sep^tem^r 9 . 1729
Isaac King & Hannah Harlow both of Plymouth Married October 28 . 1729
John Cushing Esqr of Scituate and m^rs Mary Cotton of Plymouth married November 20 . 1729.
John Hambleton and Elizabeth Jones both of Plymouth Married Feb^ry 10 . 1729/30

Marriages Solemnized by the Reverend m^r Nathaniel Leonard
Thomas Ward and Joanna Donham both of Plymouth were married march 4th 1729/30.
Ephraim Churchel & Priscilla Manchester both of Plymouth were married March 27 . 1730.
Thomas Westron & Prudence Conant both of Plymouth were married May 4th 1730
m^r William Dyre of Boston & m^rs Hannah Phillips of Plymouth were married May 18th 1730
Deacon John Atwood & m^rs Experience Peirce both of Plymouth were married June 8th 1730
Nicholas Drew & Lydia Doggett both of Plymouth were married August 10th 1730
Ebenezer Finney of Barnstable and Rebecca Barnes of Plymouth were married September 22 . 1730
John Studly and Elizabeth Doten both of Plymouth were married September 24 . 1730
Jabez Holmes and Rebecca Harlow both of Plymouth were married September 30 . 1730.
[p. 144] Marriages Solemnized by ye Reverend m^r Nathaniel Leonard
Samuel Cornish & Meribah Clark both of Plymouth were Married March 30 1731
Jacob Curtis & Fear Donham both of Plymouth were married May 7 . 1731.
Cato a Negro man belonging to m^r Thomas Foster and Jenne a Negro woman belonging to m^r John Foster were married May 21 . 1731
Jonathan Bartlett & Thankfull Barnes both of Plymouth were married July 15 1731
William Kempton & Mary Brewster both of Plymouth were married July 29 . 1731
John Waterman & Hannah Cushman were married August 17 : 1731
Lemuel Fish of Rochester & Deborah Barden of Plymouth were married Sepr 14 . 1731.
Thomas Kempton & Mary Holmes both of Plymouth were married Sepr 28 . 1731

John Harlow Junr & Mary Ryder both of Plymouth were married Oct^{or} 4 . 1731

Elnathan Holmes & Rebecca Churchell both of Plymouth were married Oct^o 7 1731

Francis Curtis Junr & Elizabeth Barnes both of Plymth were married Novr 23 . 1731

Dolphin a Negro man belonging to m^r Nathaniel Thomas Junr & Flora a Negro woman belonging to m^{rs} Priscilla Watson were married Novr 29 . 1731

Cornelius Clark of Rochester & Susanah Donham of Plymth were married Decr 2 1731

m^r Josiah Carver & m^{rs} Bethiah Churchell both of Plymth were married Jan: 11 . 1731/2

Dick & Pebe Negroes belonging to Decon Torry of Plymth were married Feb: 8 . 1731/2

John Blackmore of Rochester & Sarah Holmes of Plymth married March 15 1731/2

Samuel Lucas & Abigail Shaw both of Plimton were married by Josiah Cotton Justice of Peace February 29 . . 1731/2.

Marriages Solemnized by ye Rev^{ed} Mr Nath^{ll} Lenoard

Giles Gnash & Remembrance Jackson Both of Plym^o ware married Ap^{ll} 3 . 1732

Nicolis Spink of north kingston in Narragansit and Mary Jackson of Plym^o ware married Septem^r 29th 1732

Caleb Stetson & deborah Morton Both of Plym^o ware Married Novr 8 : 1732

Benjaⁿ Roggers & Phebe hardin Both of Plym^o ware Married october 13 : 1732

Peter English & alse Randell Both of Plym^o ware Maried July 26 1732

John Wetherhead & Remember Bates Both of Plym^o ware Married Novr 30 : 1732

John Case Resident and Rebeckah Peirce of Plym^o ware Married december 13 : 1732

Barnabas holmes and abigall Shepard Both of Plym^o ware Married decem 21 1732

Cornelius Warren of Middleborough & Mercy Ward of Plym^o war Married Jenauary 18 1732/3

Isaac Lothrop Junr & Priscilla Watson Both of Plym^o Ware Maried Jany 28 1732/3

Abiall Pulsifur & Bethiah Cotton Both of Plym^o Ware Married March 1 : 1732/3

Samuell Doten and Joanah Bosworth Both of Plym^o ware Married April 3 : 1733

[p. 145] Mr Thomas Gardner of Newport on Rhode Island & Mrs Margaret Bryant of Plymouth were married at Plymouth June 27 . 1734 Coram me : Nathaniel Leonard Eccleas

Marriages Solemnized by the Reverend m^r Nathaniel Leonard*
Marriages Solemnized by the Reverend m^r Nathaniel Leonard*

Ichabod Samson Junr of Duxberough & Marcy Savery of Plymouth were married at Plymouth April 2^d 1734

Samuel Hubbard & Hannah Polden both of Plymouth were married at Plymouth April 8 . 1734

Paul Cooke of Kingston & Joanah Holmes of Plymouth were married at Plymouth April 29 . 1734

Thomas Sears and Elizabeth Bartlett both of Plymouth were married at Plymouth May 16 . 1734

William Davis and Elizabeth Bagnald both of Plymouth were married at Plymouth May 21 . 1734

Nathaniel Warren and Sarah Morton both of Plymouth were married at Plymouth May 23 . 1734

Cuffe a Negro man belonging to m^r Isaac Lothrop Junr and Nanne a Negro woman belonging to m^r Samuel Bartlett Junr were married at Plymouth June 5 1734

[p. 146] James a Negro man belonging to Deacon John Atwood and Nanne a Negro woman belonging to m^r Robert Brown were married were married at Plymouth June 13 . 1734

Joshua Donham Resident in Plymouth and Ann Revis of Plymouth were married June 25 . 1734

Capt John Dyer & m^{rs} Hannah Morton both of Plymouth were married at Plymouth June 27 . 1734

Elkanah Hamblen of Barnstable & margaret Bates of Plymouth were married at Plymouth August 16 . 1734

Noah Samson and Jemima Rider both of Plymouth were married August 22 . 1734

Francis Merifield and Content Billenton both of Plymouth were married at Plymouth October 18 . 1734

Silvanus Cob and Elizabeth Kider both of Plymouth were married at Plymouth October 22 . 1734

Jeremiah Howes of Yarmouth & Mariah Morton of Plymouth were married at Plymouth October 24 . 1734

m^r William Dyre and m^{rs} Hannah Howland both of Plymouth were married at Plymouth October 29 . 1734

Isaac Doten and Mary Lannan both of Plymouth were married at Plymouth November 5 . 1734

Jabez Holmes and Sarah Clarke both of Plymouth were married at Plymouth November 12 . 1734

Jack a Negro man belonging to m^r Samuel Kempton & Bess a Negro woman belonging to m^r Thomas Wethrel were married at Plymouth November 13 . 1734

Abner Corpe of Plymouth and Hannah Ransom of Halifax were married at Plymouth November 25 . 1734

Nathaniel Thomas Esqr & m^{rs} Mary Allen both of Plymouth were married at Plymouth November 28 . 1734

* Between these two entries is a blank half page.

John Ryder Junr and Mary Drew both of Plymouth were married at Plymouth December 5 . 1734
Joseph Whitemore & Abigal Hatch both of Plymouth were married at Plymouth January 2ᵈ 1734/5
Samuel King & Mary Rose both of Plymouth were married at Plymouth January 16 . 1734/5
Jonathan Darleng & Lydia Cob both of Plymouth were married at Plymouth February 20ᵗʰ 1734/5.

(To be continued)

PLYMOUTH, MASS., VITAL RECORDS

(Continued from page 76)

[p. 147] Marriages Solemnized by the Reverend mr Nathaniel Leonard

James Hovey and Lydia Atwood both of Plymouth were married march 20 . 1734/5

Lemuel Barnes and Lydia Barnes both of Plymouth were married May 21 . 1735.

Nathaniel Bosworth and Lydia Sampson both of Plymouth were married May 28 . 1735.

Lemuel Jackson and Ester Savary both of Plymouth were married June 5 . 1735.

John Atwood Junr and Joannah Drew both of Plymouth were married October 9 . 1735

Capt Josiah Carver and mrs Mercy Faunce both of Plymouth were married October 23 . 1735.

John Goddard and Lydia Polden both of Plymouth were married November 10 . 1735.

mr Anselm Lothrop and mrs Mary Thomas both of Plymouth were married January 8 . 1735/6

Nicholas Drew and Bathshebath Kempton both of Plymouth were married January 29 . 1735/6.

Marrage Solemnized by Samll Bartlet Esqr
James Wood & Deborah Fish were married January 21 . 1735/6

Marriage Solemnized by Josiah Cotton Esqr
viz: Joshua Rafe & nab Shanks, were married Decr 1 . 1736
John Deerskins & Kate Shanks were maried Novr 9th 1737

Marriages Solemnized by the Reverend mr Nathaniel Leonard
mr Charles Dyre and mrs Luce Cotton both of Plymouth were Married at Plymouth March 25 . 1736

Thomas Holmes Junr and Elizabeth Cobb both of Plymouth were married at Plymouth April 13 : 1736

mr Seth Cobb and mrs Sarah Nelson both of Plymouth were married at Plymouth April 20th : 1736

The Reverend mr Andrew Crosswell and mrs Rebekah Holmes both of Plymouth were married at Plymouth May 6 . 1736.

Jabez Hammond of Rochester and Abigail Faunce of Plymouth were married at Plymouth May 12 : 1736

Benjamin Cartee resident and Elizabeth Marshall of Plymouth were married at Plymouth May 27 . 1736

James Cornish and Abiah Churchell both of Plymouth were married at Plymouth Sepr 2, 1736

Jonathan Diman of Rehoboth and Hannah Morton daughter of Joseph Morton of Plymouth were married at Plymouth October 14 . 1736

Gershom Holmes and Lydia King both of Plymouth were married at Plymouth October 21 . 1736

Ebenezar Tinkham and Jane Pratt both of Plymouth were married at Plymouth Novr 9 : 1736.

[p. 148] William Gammon of Boston and Hannah Hubbard of Plymouth were married at Plymouth December 16 : 1736

Joseph Swift and Sarah Lebaron both of Plymouth were married at Plymouth January 21 . 1736/7

James a Negro man belonging to John Murdoch Esqr and Kate a Negro woman belonging to Colln Lothrop were married Febry 3 . 1736/7

Samuel Kempton Junr of Plymouth & Mabel Soul of Duxborough were married at Plymouth Febry 9 : 1736/7

Ezekiel Rider and Margeret Churchell both of Plymouth were married at Plymouth February 10th 1736/7

a marrige Solemnized by Josiah Cotton Esqr
Mathew Unquit & Sarah Acquit Indians both of Plymouth were Married February 10th 1737/8

mr Uriah Savory & mrs Deborah Bump of Rochester were married*

mr Josiah Swift of Sandwich & mrs Mary Mory of Plymouth were maried by A: Bourn Justice of the Peace at Large May 26 . 1738

Marriages Solemnized by the Reverend Nathaniel Leonard at Plymout[h]
Thomas Bates & Lydia Savory both of Plymouth were married March 9 1736/7.

mr Francis Adams & mrs Keziah Atwood both of Plymouth were married april . 4 . 1737.

Benjamin Bartlett & Hannah Stephens both of Plymouth were married april 8 . 1737.

James Cushman & Hannah Cobb both of Plymouth were married april 11 . 1737

Charles Morton & Mary Shattuck both of Plymouth were married april 28 . 1737.

mr Caleb Shareman of marshfield & mrs Deborah Ring of Plymouth were married May 12 . 1737.

mr Thomas Murdoch & mrs Elizabeth Doggett both of Plymouth were married may 16 . 1737.

*No date entered.

mr Abner Holmes & mrs Bathshebeth Nelson both of Plymouth were married October 20 . 1737

Lemuel Robins of Plinton & Ester Dunham of Plymouth were married November 15 . 1737.

mr John Cooper & mrs Hannah Rider both of Plymouth were married December 8 . 1737

Timothy Hely & Elce Chubbuck both of Plymouth were married December 22 . 1737.

mr Job Bourn of Sandwich & mrs Lydia Swift of Plymouth were married January 19 . 1737/8.

[p. 149] mr Return Wait & mrs Martha Tupper both of Plymouth were married february 7th 1737/8

John Staff & Rebekah Sterny both of Plymouth were married february 21 . 1737/8.

Joseph Smith & Lydia Barnes both of Plymouth were married at Plymouth May 2d 1738.

Stephen Churchell junr & Hannah Barnes both of Plymouth were married at Plymouth July 4 . 1738

Benjamin Harlow & Elizabeth Stephens both of Plymouth were married at Plymouth . July 25 . 1738

Nathaniel Freeman & Martha Donham both of Plymouth were married at Plymouth September 4 . 1738.

Thomas Wright & Abijah Rogers both of Plymouth were married at Plymouth September 14 . 1738.

Joseph Holmes & Hannah Donham both of Plymouth were married at Plymouth October 2d, 1738

Eleazer Churchell junr & Sarah Harlow both of Plymouth were married at Plymouth October 19 . 1738

Lemuel Cob & Fear Holmes both of Plymouth were married at Plymouth November 30 . 1738

Benjamin Warren junr & Rebekah Doty both of Plymouth were married at Plymouth December 14 . 1738.

Nathaniel Shurtleff & Lydia Branch both of Plymouth were married at Plymouth January 1st 1738/9.

Zepheniah Holmes & Sarah Bradford both of Plymouth were married at Plymouth January 23 . 1738/9

Alexander Dow and Sarah Duncan both of Plymouth were married June 18 . 1739

Mr William Bowdoin of Boston and mrs Phebe Murdoch of Plymouth were maried July 12 . 1739.

Ebenezer Sampson & Hanah Harlow both of Plymouth were married September 14 . 1739.

Seth Luce of Wareham and Hannah Morton of Plymouth were maried February 14 . 1739/40

Moses Nummuck and Sarah Deerskins were maried October 15 . 1739 . Pr Josiah Cotton Esqr

Abiel Shurtleff & Lucy Clark both of Plymouth were Maried at Plymouth March 24 . 1739/40.

Elkanah Cushman & Lydia Bradford both of Plymouth were Maried at Plymouth March 31 . 1740

[p. 150] The following Mariages were Solemnized by Revd Mr Nathaniel Leonard.

Mr Thomas Mayhew & Mrs Mary Wethrel both of Plymouth were maryed at Plymouth July 8th 1740

Isaac Atwood & Lydia Waite both of Plymouth were Maried at Plymouth August 26th 1740.

Noah Peniss & Abigail Chummuck (Indians) both of Plymouth were maried at Plymouth Augt 27 . 1740.

Lemuel Harlow of Plymouth & Joanna Paddock of Middleboro . were maried at Plymouth Septr 1 . 1740.

David Sepitt & Joanna Scoke (Indians) both of Plymouth were maried at Plymo Octo 1 1740.

Levi Stephens of Boston & Mary Marshall of Plymo were maried at Plymo Octo 29th 1740.

Asa Hatch & Mary Waite both of Plymo were Maried at Plymoth Nov 6 . 1740

Joseph Abbott & Mercy Kempton both of Plymouth were maried at Plymouth Janry 15 . 1740.

Edward Winslow & Hannah Dyre were Maried at Plymouth April 10th 1741 . pr Isaac Lothrop Esqr

The following mariages were Solemnized by the Revd Mr Nathll Leonard.

Amos Dunham and Abigail Hill both of Plymouth were maried at Plymoth April 1 . 1741.

Silvanus Holmes & Mercy Harlow were maried at Plymouth April 6th 1741.

John Torrey & Deborah Reed both of Plymouth were maried at Plymouth April 16 . 1741.

George Holmes junr & Lydia West were maried at Plymouth April 21 . 1741.

Benjamin Bartlet & Abigail Morton both of Plymo were maried at Plymouth May 4 . 1741.

Thomas Brace & Eliza Barnes both of Plymo were maried at Plymo June 3 . 1741.

William Holmes and Ruth Morton both of Plymouth were maried at Plymo July 23 . 1741

[p. 151] Gideon Bradford of Plymton and Jane Paddock of Plymouth were maried at Plymouth Octo 8 . 1741.

Josiah Churchell & Patience Harlow both of Plymoth were maried at Plymouth Decr 1 . 1741

William Harlow junr & Hannah Littlejohn both of Plymo were maried at Plymo April 5 . 1742.

John Howland & Patience Spooner both of Plymouth were maried at Plymouth May 27th 1742.

Benjamin Barnes, & Experience Rider, both of Plymo, Marryed at Plymouth, June 14 . 1742.

Plymouth, Mass., Vital Records

160

The Revᵈ Mʳ Samuell Veazie of Duxboro & Mʳˢ Deborah Samson of Kingston, Marryᵈ at Kingston, Augˢᵗ 6 . 1742
Barzillia Stetson, & Ruth Kempton, both of Plymᵒ, Marryd at Plymᵒ; Septʳ 6 . 1742.
Robert Shattuck, & Ruhama Cook, both of Plymouth, Marryed at Plymouth, September yᵉ 9ᵗʰ 1742.
Theophilus Cotton, and Martha Saunders, both of Plymouth, Marryed at Plymᵒ Octʳ 29 . 1742.
Lemuell Bartlett, & Mary Doty, both of Plymᵒ Marryed at Plymouth, November 25ᵗʰ 1742.
Henry Saunders Junʳ, of Wareham, & Mary Hambleton, of Plymouth, Marryed at Plymᵒ Decembʳ 13 . 1742.
Joseph Shurtleff, & Sarah Cobb, both of Plymouth, Marryed at Plymouth, Decʳ 9 . 1742.
Joseph Ruggles of Hardwick, & Hannah Cushman of Plymouth, Marryed at Plymᵒ Janʳʸ 13 . 1742/3
Thomas Faunce yᵉ 4ᵗʰ & Sarah Bartlett both of Plymᵒ Marryed at Plymouth, January 20ᵗʰ 1742/3.
Job Hammond (Negro) and Hannah Quoy (Indian) Marryᵈ at Plymouth, Febʳʸ 17 . 1742/3.
Noah Bradford, & Hannah Clarke, both of Plymouth, Marryed at Plymᵒ March 10 . 1742/3
William Keen, & Ruth Sarjant, both of Plymᵒ Marryed at Plymouth, March 17 . 1742/3.
Doctʳ Lazarus Le Barron, & mʳˢ Lydia Cushman, Both of Plymᵒ Marryed at Plymᵒ May 2ⁿᵈ 1743
[p. 152] The following Marriages, Were Solemnized, by yᵉ Revᵈ Mʳ Nathaniell Leonard of Plymᵒ Viz.
Josiah Whittemore of CharlesTown, & Mary Hatch of Plymᵒ, Marryed at Plymᵒ May 26 . 1743.
Francis Penias, & Mary Thomas Indians, Marryed at Plymouth, May 30ᵗʰ 1743.
David Curtis of Scituate, & Hannah Ward of Plymouth, Marryed at Plymᵒ, September yᵉ 22 . 1743.
John Bradford of Plimpton, & Elizabeth Holmes of Plymouth, Marryed at Plymᵒ Novʳ 10 . 1743.
Mʳ John Greenleaf of Boston, & Mʳˢ Priscilla Brown of Plymouth, Marryed at Plymᵒ December 8ᵗʰ 1743.
Peter Daniel, & Sarah Waterman (Indians) Marryed at Plymouth, December yᵉ 18ᵗʰ 1743.
Amos Donham, & Ann Mackelroy, both of Plymouth, Marryed at Plymouth, Febʳʸ 13ᵗʰ 1743/4.
Ephraim Ward, & Sarah Donham, both of Plymouth Marryed at Plymouth, Febʳʸ 14 1743/4
Gideon White of Marshfield, & Joannah Howland, of Plymouth, Marryed at Plymouth, Febʳʸ 23 . 1743/4
Phillip Vinceat of Yarmouth, & Phillippe Rider of Plymouth; Marryed at Plymouth, March 9ᵗʰ 1743/4

161

Ezekiel Donham, & Patience Holmes both of Plymouth, Marryed at Plymᵒ, March 14ᵗʰ 1743/4
James Shurtleff, & Joannah Tupper, both of Plymouth, Marryed, at Plymouth, May 17 . 1744.
James Swinnerton, & Martha Battles, both of Plymᵒ Marryed at Plymouth, July 17 . 1744.
Barnabas Churchell Junʳ, & Lydia Holmes both of Plymᵒ, Marryᵈ at Plymᵒ Novʳ yᵉ 13ᵗʰ 1744
Mʳ Thomas Foster, & mʳˢ Mary Morton, both of Plymᵒ, Marryed at Plymᵒ, Novʳ yᵉ 13ᵗʰ 1744.
Thomas Pitts, & Mary Howard, both of Plymᵒ, Marryᵈ at Plymouth, Novʳ 15ᵗʰ 1744.
Moses Sachamus, & Kate Deerskins (Indians) both of Plymᵒ, Marryᵈ at Plymᵒ Janʳʸ 2 . 1744/5
Joseph Fulgham, & Rebeckah Young, both of Plymᵒ Marryᵈ at Plymouth March 1 . 1744/5
Gave in a List of 32 Marriages To yᵉ Clerk of yᵉ Sessions May 23ʳᵈ 1745

(To be continued)

Plymouth, Mass., Vital Records

PLYMOUTH, MASS., VITAL RECORDS

(Continued from page 161)

[p. 153] The Child of mr Tomson Phillips and Hannah his wife
Hannah Phillips born July 20th 1728
The Children of Mr John Watson, & Elizabeth his Wife
1. Elizabeth Watson born Decr 4th 1745.
2. John Watson born Augst 26 . 1747.   *Died Feb. 1826**
3. Daniel Watson born Septr ye 6 . 1749 . Deceasd June 19 . 1756.
The Children of Mr George Watson, & Abigail † His Wife.
1. George Watson born Augst 30th 1749 . Deceasd Sept 26th 1749.
2. A Son Still born March 11th 1750/1.
The Children of Zephaniah Swift & Lydia his wife
Lydia born Sepr 13th 1728.
Alce born April 25th 1731
The Chilldren of Jabez Harlow & Experience his Wife
1. Jabez Harlow Born Febry ye 9th 1754
2. Experience Harlow Born April 29 . 1756.
3. Nathaniel Harlow Born Janry 27 . 1758
4. Rebeckah Harlow . Born Janry 6th 1760 . Deceasd April 10th 1766
5. John Harlow Born April ye 14 . 1762
The Children of Isaac Little & Sarah his wife
Joseph Little born January 16th 1727/8.
George Little born June 19 . 1730
Sarah Little born November 8 . 1732.
The children of Francis Allen & Jane his wife.
Francis Allen born January 31 . 1727/8
Jenny Allen born January 1st 1732/3
[p. 154] The Child of John Clarke & Rebecca his wife
John Clarke born October 9th 1728.
Rebeckah Clarkke born October 4th 1734.
The Children of Jonathan Barnes junr & Phebe his wife
1 . Mary Barnes born April 24 . 1728 . Deceased June 29th 1729.

* The words in italics are in pencil, in a modern hand.
† "Saltonstall of Haveril" and "in 1748" have been added in a modern hand.

Plymouth, Mass., Vital Records

2 . Margaret Barnes born June 14 . 1732.
3 . Jonathan Barnes born May 21 . 1735.
4 . Nath[ll] Barnes born June 18 . 1740.
5 . Zacheus Barnes born April . 8 . 1743.
The children of Nehemiah Riply and Sarah his wife
Peter Riply born April 20th 1729 . Deceased July 27th 1729
Nehemiah Riply born 25 * . 1730 Deceased
Nath[ll] Ripley born March . 1 . 1732/3
Nath[ll] Ripley Born March 4 . 1742/3
Experience Ripley Born Feb[ry] 5 . 1746/7
[†] Scarret borne June 18th 1729
The Child of Thomas Scarret and Alse his wife
The Child of James Donham & Elizabeth his Wife
Sarah Donham born June 4 . 1750
[p. 155] The Children of Samuel Cole and Marcy his wife
James Cole born September 12th 1729 . deceased Dec[r] 10th 1729
Ephraim Cole born November 14th 1730 . Deceased January 25th 1730/31
Samuel Cole born November 14 : 1731 . Died March 18 . 1811
The Children of Joseph Le Barron, & Sarah his Wife.
1 . Joseph Le Barron Born, Jan[ry] 22 . 1747/8 . on Fryday at 5 Clock, In y[e] afternoon . Deceas[d] Oct[r] 1 . 1748.
2 Sarah Le Barron born Feb[ry] 22 . 1748/9
The Children of Samuel Doty and Marcy his wife
Samuel Doty born August 15th 1729
one born february 9 . 1731/2 deceased in the beging of March following
Marcy Doty born January 14th 1732/3
Hannah Doty born March 8th 1734/5
Sarah Doty born August 5 . 1736
The child of Isaac Howland & Elizabeth his wife
William born May 2[d] 1725.
The Children of Timothy Burbanks and Mary his wife
1 . Mary Burbanks born July 24th 1730
2 . Timothy Burbank born february 9th 1731/2
3 . Isaac Burbank born December 22 . 1733
4 . Rebeckah Burbank born february 19 . 1735/6
5 . Hannah Burbank born October 21 . 1740.
6 . Ezra Burbank, Borne Feb[ry] 20th 1737/8
7 . Joseph Burbank borne, May 22 . 1743.
8 . Lucey Burbank born May 4 . 1745
9 . Marcy Burbank, born March 17 . 1747/8.
10 . David Burbank . born . April . 1 . 1750
[p. 156] The Children of Jacob Tayler and Mary his wife
1 . Jacob Tayler born January . 18th 1729/30
2 . Sarah Tayler born September 10th 1733

* The month was not entered.

† A blank was left for the first name.

3 . Rebeckah Tayler born October 6th 1735
4 . Leavitt Tayler born July 14th 1738 . 1738.
5 . Mary Taylor born, Feb[ry] 17 . 1740/1.
6 . Edward Taylor, born, June 20th 1743 . Deceased July 4th 1749
7 . Hannah Taylor, born, Jan[ry] 31 . 1744/5 . Deceased July 11th 1745
8 . Hannah Taylor Born Dec[r] 18th 1746 . Deceas[d] July 14th 1747.
9 . Hannah Taylor born June 15 1748 . Deceased June 22 . 1748.
10 . Lydia Taylor Born . July . 15 . 1749
11 . Hannah Taylor Born Feb[ry] 2 . 1753 . (old Stile) at Barnstable.
Continued Below
The Children of Mathew Lemote and Marcy his wife
1 Mathew Lemote born August 18th 1730 . Deceased July 15 . 1733
2 Joseph Lemote born November . 30 . 1732 Deceased July 22 . 1733
3 Abigal Lemote born June 6 . 1733 * Deceased . October 25 . 1734
4 Marcy Lemote born October 29 . 1734.
5 Susannah . Lemote June 30 . 1736
6 Mathew Lemote June 25 . 1738 . Deceased . Sept[r] . 1739.
7 Mary Lemote borne, Feb[ry] 17th 1739
8 George Lemote, borne Dec[r] 24 . 1741
9 Abigail Lemote borne Feb[ry] 2 . 1743/4
The Children of Nathan † Delano & Bathsheba his wife
Ruth Delano born April 5th 1726
Sarah Delano born March 5th 1728/9
Bathshebah Delano born May 16 : 1731
Joannah Delano born June 10 . 1733
Hannah Delano born May 1st 1735.
Nathan Delano borne Octob[r] 26 . 1737
Amassa Delano borne Octob[r] 22 . 1739
Ichabod Dellano born July . 7th 1742
The Children of Thomas Kempton & Mary his wife
1 margret Kempton Born december 7 1732
2 mary Kempton born June 15th 1736 . Deceas[d] 1736
3 Richard Kempton born October 28 . 1739.
4 Mary Kempton borne
The Children of Tayler & Mary his Wife Continued from above
12 . Priscilla Tayler Born, at Yarmouth, July 25th 1754.
[p. 157] The Child of Isaac Lothrop Jun[r] & Hannah his wife
Freeman Lothrop born Dec[r] 7 : 1730 . Deceased January 9th 1730/1
The Children of Isaac Lothrop Jun[r] & Priscilla his wife
Isaac Lothrop born December 11th 1735 . Died 1808
Nathaniel Lothrop born Nov[r] 26 . 1737.
Thomas Lothrop born February 10 . 1739/40 Deceas[d] Jan[ry] 23 . 1794
Caleb Lothrop born Thursday Nov[r] 25 . 1742 Deceas[d] at Martinneco May 28th 1766
Priscilla Lothrop born, Aug[st] y[e] 1st 1747 . Died 1810

* The last figure appears to have been altered from "4" in the same ink.

† "Capt" has been interlined in a different hand and ink.

242 Plymouth, Mass., Vital Records

The Children of John Washburn and Abigal his wife
John Borne May 8th 1730.
Abigal Borne february 17th 1731/2
Mary borne November 21 . 1734.
Marcy born July 31 . 1736 . deceased March 4th 1737/8
Seth born April 17th 1738 . *Died April 27 1826* *
Phillip born Septr 5 . 1739.
Thankfull Washburne born Aug^st 14 . 1742
The child of Thorton Gray & Katherine his wife
Thorton Gray born . October 22th 1729.
The Child of m^r William Dyre † & Hannah ‡ his wife
William Dyre born february 8th 1730/1
(2^d wife Hannah D of Thomas Howland in 1734) §
Hannah Dyre born May 21 . 1736 . Deceasd June 21 . 1737.
Hannah Dyre born : Septr 15 . 1737
The Children of Josiah Churchell & Patience, his Wife.
1st Josiah Churchell borne, Octr 23 . 1742 . Deceas^d Octr 25 . 1742
2 . Josiah Churchell borne Novr 28 . 1743 . Deceas^d
3 . Thaddeus Churchell . born Novr 29 . 1745.
4 . Patience Churchell born Novr 23 . 1747.
5 Samuel Churchill born July 10th 1754
6 Enos Churchill Born March 10 1759
7 Silvanus Churchill Born Janu^y 23rd 1765
[p. 158] The Child of John Winslow and Mary his wife
Josiah born September 5th 1730 . deceased . March 1st 1730/1
The Children of Thomas Ward and Joanna his wife
  . Ebenezer Wa^rd born July 4th 1731 . Deceas^d Septr 3rd 1746 . In Jamaica
  . Elizabeth Ward Born, Octr 19 . 1733.
3 . Jonathan Ward Born, Novr 16 . 1735.
4 . Joanna Ward, Born Septr 15 . 1737.
5 Mary Ward, Born, Jany 4 . 1739/4 . Deceas^d March 16th 1796
6 . Hannah Ward, Born, Jany 21 . 1743/4.
7 . Thomas Ward Born, July 5 . 1745.
8 . Ebenezer Ward Born, Jany 13 . 1747/8.
The Children of Lazerus Samson & Jemima his wife
1 Jemima Samson born June 2^d 1731.
The Children of Lazarus Samson and Abigall his wife
1 Susannah Samson born January 22 . 1734/5
2 Ephraim Samson born . Decr 30 . 1736 . Deceas^d Aug^st 12 . 1744.
3 Lazerus Samson born January 19 . 1737/8 Deceas^d July 26 . 1744.
4 Mary Samson, born Jany 27 . 1740/1.
5 William Samson Borne March 7th 1742/3 . Deceas^d July 21 . 1744

* The words in italics are in pencil, in a modern hand.
† "of Boston" has been interlined in a modern hand.
‡ "Phillips in 1730" has been interlined in a modern hand.
§ This entry, in parentheses in the original, is in a modern hand.

243

6 . Lazarus Samson, Born, Aug^st 20 . 1746.
The Children of Thomas Totman & Lucretia his wife
Ebenezer Totman born January 6th 1730/31
John Totman born January 29th 1732/3
Mary Totman born June 11th 1734
[p. 159] The Children of Ebenezer Rider & Thankfull his wife
Lydia Rider born October 16 . 1729
Ebenezer Rider born Sepr 3 . 1731
John Rider born October 12 . 1733
Thankfull Rider born Octr 28 . 1735.
The Children of James Holmes and Content his wife
1 Zacheus Holmes born April 10 . 1729
2 . Solomon Holmes born June 2 : 1731
3 . Janes Holmes born August 29 . 1733
a Daughter borne   Deceas^d
4 . Seth Holmes born Novr 3 . 1735.
A Daughter born   Deceased
5 . Nathaniel Holmes born Jan^ry 25 . 1738.
6 . Lathrop Holmes borne Jan^ry 26th 1740.
7 Barnabas Holmes borne, Aug^st 6 . 1743
8 Caleb Holmes Born Octr 11th 1745
9 Ezra Holmes Born, March, 15th 1747/8.
The Children of John Elles & Rose his wife
Jabesh. Ellis born february 26 . 1731/2.
Mary Ellis born September 27 . 1733
John Ellis born August 25 . 1735
The Children of Ephraim Ward & Sarah his Wife
Benjamin Ward born Octr 18th 1744.
Sarah Ward born   Deceas^d July 18th 1748.
The Children of Benjamin Churchill, & Ruth his Wife
1 Wilson Churchill Born, April 28th 1746
2 Benjamin Churchell born Novr 17 . 1748
3 . Abner Churchell, born April . 8 . 1750.

(*To be continued*)

THE MAYFLOWER DESCENDANT

An Illustrated Quarterly Magazine

OF

Pilgrim Genealogy, History and Biography

1913

———

VOLUME XV

———

BOSTON
PUBLISHED BY THE
MASSACHUSETTS SOCIETY OF MAYFLOWER DESCENDANTS
1913

PLYMOUTH, MASS., VITAL RECORDS

Transcribed by George Ernest Bowman

(Continued from Vol. XIV, p. 243)

[p. 160] The Children of Benjamin Lothrop & Experience his wife
1 Hannah Lothrop born July 6th 1729 . Deceasd May 25th 1736
2 John Lothrop born June 7 : 1731 Deceasd . June ye 30th 1761
3 Benja Lothrop born Octo 10th 1733
4 Thomas Lothrop borne Octo 11, 1735 Decd June 1736
5 Thomas Lothrop borne april 29th 1737 Decd Sept 18 . 1737
6 Nathll Lothrop borne Decr 24th 1738 Deceasd Janry 22 . 1739
7 Joseph Lothrop borne Febry 2nd 1741.
8 Thomas Howland, Lothrop, Borne Febry 6th 1743 —

The Children of Samuel Cornish and Meribah his wife
1 Samuel Cornish born february 26 . 1731/2
2 Hannaniah Cornish born Octr 15 . 1734.
3 A Daughtr borne, Decr 30 . 1736 . Deceasd Janry 10 . 1736/7
4 Abigail Cornish borne, Ap: 18 . 1741 . Deceasd

The children of Samuel Rider & Mary [Silvester*] his wife
1 Moriah Rider born Decr 2d 1724
2 Hannah Rider born Novr 26 . 1726
3 Mary Rider born Octor 2 . 1728
4 Sarah Rider born Augt 6 . 1730
5 Lois Rider born Septemr 15 . 1732
6 Saml Rider borne, May 25th 1735.
7 Martha Rider borne, Janry 30 . 1737.
8 Deborah Rider borne . Augst 18 . 1741.
1 Child Dead Borne viz the first Child, & Was before Moriah

[p. 161] The Children of John Harlow Junr & Mary his wife
1 Jabez Harlow born November 19th 1732
2 John Harlow borne March 10th 1733/4.
3 Ebenezer Harlow . borne Novr 5 . 1735.
4 Silvanus Harlow, borne, June 7 . 1738.
5 Jesse Harlow, borne, Janry 31 . 1739/4 †

* "Silvester" was written in the same hand and ink as the rest of the entry, but was crossed out and "his wife" added in a different ink.
† Sic.

6 Ezra Harlow, borne, August 28 . 1741.
7 Martha Harlow borne Janry 8 . 1743/4
8 Mary Harlow Borne, Octr 21st 1747 . Deceasd July 8th 1748.
9 Lydia Harlow Born June 9th 1748.
10 Zacheus Harlow Born May 27 . 1753
11 Mary Harlow Born March 18th 1750
12 Lazarus Harlow . August 11th 1755.

The Children of Ephraim Cob & Margaret his wife
1 Susannah Cob born february 1st 1730/31 . Deceasd Decr 30th 1766
2 Abigail Cob born May 4th 1732   Deceased,
3 Rebeckah Cob, born   Deceased,
4 A Son not Named born   Deceased,
5 A Daughter not Namd born   Deceased,
6 John Cobb, borne
7 Rebeckah Cobb, born
8 Lazarus Cobb born

The Children of Frances Curtis Junr & Elezebeth his wife
Lydia Curtis Born Aprill 17 : 1732.
James Curtis born Decr. 20 . 1735 Dec. Janry 15th 1767

The Child of Jacob Johnson & Sarah his Wife
Sarah Born Aprill 18 : 1732
Jacob Johnson born february 21 . 1733/4
Thomas Johnson January 7th 1735/6
Josiah Johnson born Sepr: 16 1738

[p. 162] The children of Samuel Burge & Jedidah his wife
Jabez Burge born April 25th: 1733
Nathaniel Burge born January 22 : 1734/5

The Children of Ebenezer Bartlett & Rebeckah his wife
1 James Bartlett born Novr: 5th 1733
2 Chloe Bartlett born August 26 . 1735, deceased Sepr: 19 . 1736
3 Thomas Bartlett born April . 11 . 1737 . deceased August 14th 1737
4 Rebecah Bartlett born June 28 . 1738 . Deceased Sept . 1738.
5 Phebe Bartlett born October 9th 1740.
6 Chloe Bartlett Borne May 24 . 1743 Deceased May 13th 1744
7 Rebeckah Bartlett borne May 29 . 1745.
8 A Daughter Still Born, May . 7 . 1749.

The Children of Abner Perry & Joaanah his wife
Joseph & Benjamin Perry born October 13th 1733

The Children of Timothy Heeley, & Alice his Wife
1 Benja Heeley born Decr 14th 1738.
2 Timothy Heeley born March 25 . 1741 . Deceased, July 21 . 1745.
3 Alice Heeley born April 24 . 1743.

The Child of Mica Gibs & Sarah his wife
Thankfull born March 6th 1732/3.

[p. 163] The Children of John Blackmer & Sarah his wife
1 Branch Blackmer born January 27 . 1732/3
2 John Blackmer born September 17–1734 . deceased December 13 . 1734.

3. Sarah Blackmer born January 20, 1735/6
4. John Blackmer born March 1st 1737/8
5. Susanna Blackmer borne March 13th 1739/40
6. Marcy Blackmer, Borne, Oct 24. 1742.
7. Jerusha Blackmer, Borne, Jan'y 20. 1744/5.
8. Bettey Blackmer Borne. Nov. 4. 1746.
9. Experience Blackmer Born. May 18th 1750.

The Child of Abiel Pulcifer . & Bethiah his wife
Joseph Pulcifer born December 8th 1733 . on Saturday about 8 a clock in morning

The Children of Elisha Holmes Jun', and Mary his Wife.
1. Jerusha Holmes Borne, June 26th 1740.
2. Mary Holmes Borne, Augst 3 . 1741 . Deceas^d Decr 9th . 174[il-legible]
3. Mary Holmes Borne Augst 13 . 1742
4. Bartlett Holmes borne Aprill 2 . 1744.

The children of Elnethan Holmes & Rebeckah his wife
Sarah Holmes born December 14 : 1732 thirdy about 10 aclock in ye Morning
Rebeckah Holmes born July 4 . 1734 . thirsday about 11 aclock before noon
Elnathan Holmes born December 7, 1735

The Children of Thomas Polden, & Deborah his Wife
1. Thomas Polden Borne augst 1 . 1735 . Deceased aprill 28 . 1736
2. William Polden Borne Sep^t 18 . 1738
3. Rebeckah Polden Borne June 1 . 1740
4. James Polden Borne June 28 . 1742.
5. Jonathan Polden borne, Decr 5th 1744.
6. Lydia Polden born, Novr 5 . 1747.
7. Elizabeth Polden born June 11th 1750.
8. Hannah Polden born Decr 24 . 1752

[p. 164] The Children of Thomas Faunce ye 3^d & Hannah his wife
Bathsheba Faunce born January 25th 1733/4.
Hannah Faunce born february 27 1735/6
Daniel Faunce born October 11 . 1738
Sarah Faunce, borne

The Children of Silas West & Mary his wife
1. Sarah West born, Jan^{ry} 31 . 1732/3 . Deceas^d March 1732/3
2. Jean West born June 6 . 1734
3. Mary West born April 18 . 1736
4. Silas West born february 3 . 1737/8
5. John West born November 18th 1739.
6. Charles West born Octr 20th . 1742.
7. Bethiah West born } Twins . July 20 . 1745.
8. William West born }

The Children of William Wethrell & Rebeckah his Wife
1 Hannah Wethrell Born Oct 3 * . 1740

*This date was written over another and is nearly illegible. Above, in the same hand and ink, is written "is oct^r 3rd".

2 Rebeckah Wethrell Born May 15 . 1744 . Deceased April 13th 1748.

The Above is Entered page 171.

The Children of Jonathan Mory & Elizabeth his wife
Jonathan Mory born May 25 . 1730
Thomas Mory born May 19 . 1732
Elizabeth Mory born April 23 . 1734

The Children of William Churchell, & Susannah, his Wife
1. Rebacah Churchell Born, Octr 31 . 1747
2. Mordica Churchell Born, April . 24th . 1749.
3. William Churchell Born, Jan^{ry} 24 . 1750/1 *
4. Susanna Churchell Born, April 23 . 1756 *

[p. 165] The Children of John Waterman and Hannah his wife
1. Elkanah Waterman born March 20th 1732/3.
2. John Waterman born July 27 . 1735 . Deceas^d March 9th 1735/6
3. Elizabeth Waterman borne Augst 15th 1737.
4. John Waterman borne, Octr 17th 1739. Deceased Augst 17th 1741.
5. Hannah Waterman borne, March : 10th 1741/2.
6. John Waterman borne, March 27th 1744 . Deceas^d July 27th 1744.
7. James Waterman borne, May 11th 1745.

The Children of Walter Rich and Rebeckah his wife
1. Elizabeth Rich born April 28 . 1734
2. Nathaniel Rich born August 27 . 1735
3. Eleazer Rich borne July 21 . 1737
4. Rebecca Rich was borne July 9th 1739
5. Ebenezer Rich was born April 6, 1741 . Deceas^d Augst 4 . 1742
6. Ann Rich born August 12th 1745.

The Children of Jonathan Bartlett and Thankfull his wife
1. James Bartlett borne, Feb^{ry} 28th 1731/2.
2. Sarah Bartlett born August 8th 1734
3. Thankfull Bartlett born December 21 . 1738 . Deceas^d Sept 14th 1739
4. Jonathan Bartlett, borne May 18 . 1742.
5. Luce Bartlett borne Decr 17 . 1744.
6. William Bartlett born Octr 25th 1747.
7. Thankful Bartlett born Jan^{ry} 18th 1749/5.†

[p. 166] The Children of Barnabas Hedge & Marcy his wife
1. Marcy Hedge, born November 27 : 1734 . Died Sep^t 1779 (Mrs. Davis ‡)
2. Lemuel Hedge, born, Sep^t 20 . 1736 . Deceased Octr 3 . 1736
3. Abigail Hedge, born, Decr 2 . 1737.
4. Barnabas Hedge, born, May . 3 . 1740 . Died Feby 1814 ‡
5. Lemuell Hedge born, June 25 . 1742 . Deceas^d July 7th 1742
6. Lothrop Hedge, born, Novr 5 . 1744 . Deceased, Jan^{ry} 20 . 1744/5
7. Sarah Hedge, born, June . 5th 1746.

* A space was left between these two entries.
† Sic.
‡ The words in italics are in a modern hand.

The Child of Nathaniel Swift & Abia his wife
Rufus Swift born November 24th 1734
The child of John Faunce Jun' & Ruth his wife
Mary Faunce born October 24th 1734 (See . 65 . page)
The children of Samuel Doty Jun' & Johannah his wife
Hannah Doty born february 15th 1733/4
Johannah Doty born June 15th 1736
The Child of Nathaniel Morton, & Mary his Wife
Mary Morton born, Augst 8th 1734.
[p. 167] The child of Nathan Cob and Joannah his wife
William Cob born february 8th 1734/5.
Elizabeth Cob born December 28 . 1736.
The Child of Joshua Drew and Joannah his wife
Levi Drew born May 21 . 1734.
Isaac Drew born June 4 . 1736
Josiah Drew born March 25th 1738.
Joshua Drew borne 24th of May . 1740.
William Drew borne Febr^y 23^d 1741
Ephraim Drew, borne . April 23rd 1743.
Patience Drew, borne, Jan^{ry} 25th . 1745/6
The children of John Holmes and Lois his wife
1 . Lois Holmes born January 3^d 1734/5 . Deceased . Sep^t 11 . 1736
2 . Marcy Holmes Borne Augst 9 . 1736.
3 . John Holmes Borne July 16 . 1738
4 . Nehemiah Holmes Borne July 12 . 1740 as stands Entred, in this book page, 182.
5 . Lois Holmes borne Octr 18 . 1744.
6 . Margaret Holmes borne Feb^{ry} 3rd 1746/7.
7 . Ruth Holmes Born Jan^{ry} 15 . 1748/9.
The Child of John Dyer and Hannah Dyer his wife
John Dyer born May 11th 1735 on Saboath day morning between three & four a Clock
[p. 168] The Children of Benjamin Rogers and Phebe his wife.
John Rogers born January 28 . 1733/4
Hannah Rogers born April 5 . 1735.
The Children of Icabod Samson and Marcy his wife
Thomas Samson born January 15th 1734/5
Marcy Samson born October 8th 1736
See page 195.
The Child of James Crandon & Sarah his Wife
John Crandon Born Decr 24th 1751
The Children of Jacob Curtis and Fear his wife
1 . Elizabeth Curtis born May 24th 1732.
2 . Sarah Curtis born July 14 . 1734.
3 . Caleb Curtis born July . 13 . 1737 . Deceas^d July 29th 1740.
4 . Fear Curtiss born May 12 . 1740
5 . Jacob Curtiss borne Augst 10 , 1742
6 . Mary Curtis borne March 19 . 1744/5.
7 . Hannah Curtis borne April . 24 . 1747.

The Children of Thomas Savery & Priscilla his wife
1 . Bethiah Savery born 19th february 1733/4
2 . Thomas Savery born July 1 . 1736 *
3 . Priscilla Savery born May 8 . 1739
4 . William Savery borne Augst 12 . 1744
5 . Esther Savory born Jan^{ry} 7 . 1746/7
6 . Ruth Savory born June 8th 1749 . Deceas^d Sep^t 14th 1754
7 . James Savory born Decemb^r 3 . 1752.
8 . Ruth Savory born March 27 . 1755.
9 . Lemuel Savory born July 7 . 1757.
The Child of Bridget Mecabe
Rebeccah Fling born february 28th 1734/5.
[p. 169] The Children of John Nelson & Mary his wife
1 . Mary Nelson born April 12 . 1733
2 . Lydia Nelson born October 21 . 1734 . deceased Decr 12 1737
3 . Hannah Nelson born April 15 . 1737
4 . Samuel Nelson borne July 13 . 1739 . Deceas^d April 19th 1749 . was Killed, by a Mill.
5 . Thomas Nelson borne August 27th 1741 . Deceased Decr 16 . 1748.
6 . John Nelson Borne June 26 . 1745 . Deceased Feb^{ry} 17th 1746/7
7 . John Nelson Borne Feb^{ry} 14th 1747/8
The Children of William Kempton & Mary his wife
William Kempton borne february 7 . 1731/2
Ephraim Kempton born May 17 . 1734
The Children of Samuel King jun^r & Mary his wife
1 Seth King born January 26 . 1735/6
Twins { Marcy King Born April 16th 1739.
        { Mary King Born April 16 . 1739.
4 Elizabeth King born April 21 . 1742.
5 Susannah King born May 8 . 1744.
[p. 170] The Children of Nathaniel Donham Junr and Ann his wife
1 . Elijah Donham born february 7 . 1735/6
2 . Hannah Donham born January 27 1738/9
3 . Susannah Donham born Novr 14 . 1741.
4 . Rebeckah Donham, borne, Novr 13 . 1743.
5 . Abner Donham, born, Octr 12 . 1746.
The Children of John Case and Rebecah his wife
John Case born february 3^d 1735/6 deceased
John Case born July 14th : 1737
The Children of Jeremiah Hows and Meriah his wife
1 . Silvanus Hows born September 8th 1735
2 . Rebecca Howes born June 6 . 1738.
3 . Eben^r Howes borne November 19 . 1740.
4 . Meriah Howes born April 3 . 1743
5 . Jerusha Howes, born Octr 29 . 1746.
6 . Sarah Howes, born June . 10 . 1751
The Children of Lemuel Jackson and Esther his wife
1 . Jacob Jackson born April 25 . 1736 Deceas^d Augst 12 . 1737.

* "Died March 12 . 1822" has been added in pencil.

Plymouth, Mass., Vital Records

3 . David Jackson born February 12 . 1740 . Deceas^d Sep^t 4 . 1742.
2 . Lemuell Jackson born July 17th 1738 . Deceas^d Decr 16 . 1739
4 . Lemuel Jackson born April 17 . 1752.
[p. 171] The Child of Lemuel Barnes*
The child of Sarah Faunce daughter of Thomas Faunce Junr
Jabez Faunce born October 31 . 1735 †
The Children of Joseph Bramhall & Sarah his Wife
1 . Edmond Bramhall Born, Fryday June 23^d 1749.
2 . Joseph Bramhall Born Jan^{ry} 4 . 1750/1
3 . William Bramhall, Born June 21 . 1752.
The child of Elisha Cob jun^r & Priscilla his wife
Lemuel Cob born january 9th 1735/6
The children of Joshua Shareman & Deborah his wife
1 . Joshua Shareman born Sep^t: 17 : 1736 . Deceas^d
2 . Nathl Shareman borne   Deceased
3 . Deborah Shareman, borne
The Children of Wm Wethrell, & Rebeckah his Wife
1   Hannah Wethrell Born Octr 3 . 1740.
2   Rebeckah Wethrell Born May 15 . 1744 Deceased April 13 . 1748
See page 164.
[p. 172] The Children of Nathaniel Foster & Marcy his wife
1 . Mary Foster . born May 28 . 1736
2 . Marcy Foster Born, Decr 2 . 1737.
3 . Nathl Foster Born, Augst 9 . 1739 . Deceas^d Decr 11 . 1739.
4 . John Foster Born, Novr 13 . 1740.
5 . Hannah Foster Born, March 21 . 1742/3 . Deceas^d Novr 11 . 1743
6 . Peter Foster Born, Novr 29 . 1745.
See his Chilldren by his 2nd wife Lib^r 2nd page 13th
(He m Abigail Billings of Little Compton 1748) ‡
The Children of Noah Samson and Jemima his wife
Southworth Samson born September . 19 . 1735
Deiser § Samson born March 19th 1737/8
Elizabeth Samson Born March 5 . 1739/4 . ‖
The Child of Nathaniel Churchell and Mary his wife
Experience Churchell born August 27th 1735
The Child of Silvanus Cobb & Elizabeth his wife
Elizabeth Cobb born May 1st 1736

(To be continued)

* This entry was left unfinished.
† 5 has been written over 6.
‡ This line is in a modern hand.
§ Probably an error for Desire.
‖ Sic.

PLYMOUTH, MASS., VITAL RECORDS

(Continued from page 44)

[p. 173] The children of Joseph Bartlett Junr Son of Benjamin Bartlett and Jean his wife

1. Benjamin Bartlett born July 22^d 1736
2. Marcy Bartlett born Aug^st 7 1738
3. Jean Bartlett born Jan^ry 10 1740/1 Deceas'd April . 7 . 1741.
4. Joanna Bartlett born Octr 17 . 1742
5. Joseph Bartlett born Decr 8 . 1745
6. Elkanah Bartlett born Jan^ry 1 . 1746/7
7. David Bartlett } Twins . Born Jan^ry 31 . 1753
8. Jonathan Bartlett }

The Children of Michael Burn & Elizabeth his wife
1. Margeret Burn born January 8th 1736/7
2. Elizabeth Burn born November 28 . 1738
3. Samuel Burn born October . 8 . 1740, Deceas'd May 8th 1741.
4. Timasin Borne Feb^ry 13 . 1741.
5. Michael Burne, Borne, Sep^t 21 . 1744.
6. George Burn Borne Novr 1 . 1746.

The Child of Josiah Morton jun^r & Maletiah his wife
Seth Morton Born, December 8 . 1735
Transcribed to page 72

The Children of James Landman and Joannah his wife
William Landman born January 1st 1725/6
Thomas Landman born June 11 . 1728
Joannah Landman born february 3 . 1730/31
Edward Landman born October 5th 1733

[p. 174] The Children of Isaac Doty & Mary his wife
1. Isaac Doten born July 11th 1735
2. James Doten born January 22 . 1736/7
3. Hope Doten born, Feb^ry 19 . 1738/9
4. Mary Doten born Feb^ry 12 . 1740/1 . Deceas^d April 24th 1741
5. Jeane Doten born Feb^ry 12 . 1740/1 . Deceas^d May . 5 . 1741
6. Ichabod Doten born, Sep^t 15 . 1742 . Deceas^d Sep^t 28 . 1747
7. Thomas Doten born Decr 24 . 1744
8. Mary Doten born Feb^ry 4 . 1746/7
9. Jean Doten born April 16th . 1749 . Deceas^d Aug^st 10th 1750
10. William Doten born July . 21st 1751
11. Rebeckah Doten born April 20th 1754 Deceas^d Sep^t 5th 1754
Continued to page 176th

The Child of Thomas Bates & Lydia his wife
Sarah Bates born Dec^r : 16 . 1737

The Children of John Valler & Mary his Wife
1. Sarah Valler borne Octr 29 . 1734.
2. Ann Valler borne Octr 24th 1736 . Deceased Aug^st 1 . 1738.
3. John Valler borne . Aug^st 1 . 1739.
4. Silvanus Valler borne Novr 21 . 1742.
5. Silas Valler, borne June 1744
6. Anne Valler, borne, Septr 9th 1746
7. Simeon Valler born Decr 13th 1748.
8. Lois Valler born Novr 15 . 1752 O. S.

The children of Ezekiel Rider & Margeret his wife
1. Kesia Rider born Decr 12th 1737.
2. Joseph Rider born March 22^d 1738/9
3. Deborah Rider borne July 20th 1740.
4. Samuel Rider borne Oct^o 18th 1741
5. Lemuell Rider, borne, July 24 . 1743 . Deceased Aug^st 4th 1743
6. Patience Rider, borne, July 7 . 1744.
7. Lemuell Rider, borne July 7 . 1745.
10. Margaret Rider, born March 15th 1748/9.
8. Ezekiel Rider Born Decr 31 . 1746 . Deceased Jan^ry ye 19th 1746/7
9. A Child Still Born . March ye 15 . 1747/8 was a Son.
11. Ezekiel Rider born Jan^ry 14 . 1750/1
12. Sarah Rider Born Novr 14 . 1752.
Ezekiel Riders Chilldren Continu^d To Page 175th

The Children of Joseph Mory and Mary his wife
1 Abigal Mory born December 15 . 1733
2 A Daughter Still Borne
3 Joseph Mory born May 9th : 1737.
4 Mary Morey Borne August 27 . 1739
Elisha Morey Borne May 14 . 1741.
Philemon Morey borne May 15th 1743.
Hannah Morey, Borne June 5 . 1745.

[p. 175] The Child of Anslem Lothrop & Mary his wife
Joseph Lothrop born 20 f July . 1737
Transcribed See page 180

The Children of Jabez Gorham, & Mary his Wife
1. James Gorham Born July 23 . 1751 Deceas^d 1751

Plymouth, Mass., Vital Records — 112

2. Jabez Gorham Born Sept 13 . 1753

The Children, of Gershom Holmes & Lydia his wife
1 Gershom Holmes Born february 4 . 1738/9
  Gershom Holmes Born   Deceas{d}
2. Lydia Holmes Born Augst 1741 . Deceas{d} June 1742
3. Richard Holmes born Octr 20 . 1743
4. Isaac Holmes born Octr 9 . 1745
5. Lydia Holmes born Octr 7 . 1747
6. Thankfull Holmes borne Sept 20 . 1749
7. Joseph Holmes born July 7 . 1751
8. The Child of Lemuel Jackson & Esther his wife*

Lemuel Jackson born July 17th 1738*

The Children of Benjamin Deleno, & Lydia His Wife
Benjamin Deleno Borne Novr 29 1746 . Deceased Decr 10th 1746.
Lydia Deleno Borne Novr 29 1746.
Being Twins

The Chilldren of Ezekiel Rider . And Margarett his Wife
Continued from folio . Page 174th
13 Joshua Rider Born June 22nd 1755
14 Ezra Rider Born March 6th 1757 . Deceas{d} Novr 12th 1760
See his Chilldren by his Other Wife the Other book of the Town page
73rd

[p. 176] The Children of Nicholas Drew and Bathsheba his wife
1 Abigal Drew born July 10th 1737 deceased August 5 : 1738
2. Abigal Drew born January . 3 . 1738/9.
3. Lois Drew, borne Feb{ry} 22 . 1740/1 . deceas{d} Augst 7th 1742.
4 Nicolas Drew borne May. 19 . 1743.
5. Josiah Drew born Augst 6 . 1745.
6. Abbet Drew born Novr 25 . 1747.
7. Samuel Drew born Decr 3 . 1749.
8. David Drew, born, Feb{ry} 17 . 1752.
9. Stephen Drew, born July 23 . 1754
The Child of Benjamin Bartlett junr & Hannah his wife
Stevens Bartlett born May 7 . 1739.
The Children of Isaac Doten & Mary his wife Contn{d} from p. 174th
12. Jabez Doten Born Decr 27th 1755
13 Jno Palmer Doten Born June 19th 1758 . Deceased . Sept 21 . 1760.
14. Rebeckah Doten Born . April 2 . 1762.
The Children of Nathaniel Shirtleff & Lydia his wife
1 Nathaniel Shurtleff born Novr 24th 1739 . Deceas{d} Octr 8 . 1748.
2 Lydia Shurtleff, borne Octr ye 1 . 1741
3. Thomas Branch Shurtleff borne Augst 9 . 1743 . deceas{d} Augst 19 . 1744.
4. Sarah Shurtleff, borne May 14 . 1745 . Deceas{d} Sept 26th 1748
5. Marcy Shurtleff born Feb{ry} 18th 1746/7 . Deceas{d} May 1 . 1748
6 Thankfull Shurtleff born Feb{ry} 4th 1748/9
7 Nathaniel Shurtleff born June 27 . 1751.

* This entry is crossed out. See original page 170.

Plymouth, Mass., Vital Records — 113

8 William Shurtleff born Decr 15 . 1753
9. Sarah Shurtleff born Novr 18 . 1755 . Deceas{d}
10 Mary Shurtleff born Sept 27 . 1749*
11 Paticience Shurtleff born Jan{ry} ye 12 . 1762.

[p. 177] The Children of Jabez Holmes & Sarah his wife
1. Rebecah Holmes born October 25 . 1736.
2. Jabez Holmes born . July 1st 1738 Deceased, April 29 . 1739.
3. Mary Holmes born May 12 . 1740
4. Sary Holmes born July 10 . 1742
5. Stephen Holmes borne, Octr 13 . 1744 . Deceas{d} Aprill 13 . 1745.
6. Mariah Holmes born, Feb{ry} 20 . 1745/6
7. David

The Children of Ebenezer Tinkcom & Mary his wife
1. Sarah Tinckcom born Novr 22 . 1733
2. Ebenezer Tinckcom born february 20 . 1735/6
The Children of sd Ebenezer Tinkcom & Jean his wife
1. Mary Tinckcom born October 7 . 1737 . Deceas{d} April, 18th 1739
2. Mary Tinkcom Borne, April 9th 1739 . Deceas{d}
3. Ebenezer Tinkcom Born, April 14th 1741.
4. James Tinkcom Born Jan{ry} 19th 1743/4
5 Phebe Tinkcom Born, July . 12th 1746.
6. Susannah Tinkcom, Born . Sept 15th 1748.
7. Priscilla Tinkcom Born July 26th 1755
The Child of Thomas Gardner & Hannah his wife
Mary Gardner born October 27 . 1738 . desesed
The Child of Seth Nicholson & Margaret his wife.
Seth Nicholson borne Feb{ry} 25 . 1745/6
The Children of Lemuell Cobb, & fear his Wife
Lydia Cobb Borne July 22 . 1741.
Lemuell Cobb Borne Augst 14 . 1743.

[p. 178] The Children of Joseph Smith & Lydia his wife
Sarah Smith born february 9th 1738/9
Lydia Smith born May 23rd 1744.
The Children of Joseph Bartlett junr & Sarah his wife
Sarah: Bartlett born January 23 . 1736/7.
Joseph Bartlett born october 12th 1738
Thomas Bartlett borne May 31st 1742.
Josiah Bartlett, borne, Decr 1 . 1744 . Deceas{d} June 26 . 1746
Martha Bartlett born, Feb{ry} ye 4 . 1746/7
Hannah Bartlett born, Novr 30th 1749.
The child of Abner Holmes & Bathsheba his wife
Abner Holmes born January 6 . 1738/9 (see page 184)
[p. 179] The Child of Seth Cobb & Sarah his wife
Sarah Cobb born may 14th 1739 on Thursday
see p. 97
The Children of Caleb Tinckham and Mercy his wife
1. Mercy borne May 8th 1726

* Sic.

Plymouth, Mass., Vital Records — 114

2. Patience borne July 16th 1729
3. Fear born November 5th 1731
4. Sarah born December 28th 1733
5. Nathaniel born August 12th 1736
6. Caleb born March 20th 1738

The Children of Capt Charles Dyre & Lucy his wife:

Charles Dyre borne August 13 . 1738
2. Lucy Borne March 31 . 1741

The Children of Doct^r William Thomas & Mary* his wife

William Born February 16 . 1739
2. Ann Thomas Born July 14th 1741
4. Elizabeth Thomas Born Jan^{ry} 17th 1747 Deceas^d Feb^{ry} 1749
   [*Mary Thomas Born   Deceased Apr 13^t 1749 †*]
3. Peter Thomas Born Decr 15th 1744

[p. 180] The Children of Joseph Morton Junr & Anna his wife

1. Peres borne February 3 . 1739

The Child of Benjamin Warren Junr and Rebecca his Wife

1 Benjamin Borne March 13 . 1739/40

The Children of Barnabas Hedge & Mercy his wife

1 Abigail Borne December 2 . 1737 } Transferred to page . 166
Barnabas Borne May 3 . 1740.

The Children of Ansell Lothrop & Mary his wife

1 Joseph Lothrop Born July 20th 1737 . Deceased October 6 . 1738
2. Mary Lothrop born October 1st 1739
3. Betty Lothrop born Augst 14 . 1741
4. Ansell Lothrop born. March 16 . 1742/3.
5. Joseph Lothrop born Sept 20th 1745 . Deceas^d Novr 18th 1746.
6. William Lothrop born April 15 . 1748.
7. Lydia Lothrop. Born . July . 12 . 1750 . *Murthred & Willm Beadle her Husband with four Children at Weathersfield in the State of Connecticutt* ‡

[p. 181] The Child of Abiel Shurtleff & Lucy his wife

1 Abiel Shurtleff borne, January 20th 1740/1

The Children of Capt Francis Adams and Keziah his Wife

1 Francis Adams Borne May 21 . 1738 Deceas^d July 23 . 1738
2 Samuel Adams Borne November 10th 1740 Deceas^d June 18 . 1741
3. Saml Adams Borne, June 26 . 1742.
4 Lydia Adams Borne Feb^{ry} 28 . 1743/4 . *Died in Middleboro Lydia Crane 1824* §
5. Keziah Adams Borne March 4th 1745/6
6. Francis Adams, Born Novr 26th 1750.

The Children of John Witherhead, & Remem^{ber} his wife

1. Rebeckah Wetherhead borne Sep^t 28 1733 Deceased Octr 8th 1733

115

2 Mary Witherhead borne Sept 12th 1735.
3. Rebecca Witherhead borne November 21 . 1737.
4. Remember Witherhead borne Jan^{ry} 23 . 1739
5. Marcy Witherhead born Octr 3 . 1742
6. { Saml Wetherhead born Augst 6 . 1745 . Deceas^d Sept 10th 1745
7. { John Wetherhead born Augst 6 . 1745.
   was Twins

The Child of Thomas Harlow jun^r & Patience his wife

1. Elizabeth Harlow born Jan^{ry} 13th 1738.
2 Patience Harlow, borne July 23 . 1741.
3. Elijah Harlow, borne Decr 16 . 1743.
4. Mary Harlow, born, Novr 13 . 1746.
5 Thomas Harlow, born, Oct^r . 6 . 1751 . Deceas^d Octr 14 . 1751
6 Abigail Harlow Born, April 9 . 1753 . N. Stile

[p. 182] The Child of Nath^{ll} Morton & Rebecca his wife

Nathaniel Morton borne November . 9 . 1741.

The Child of Nath^{ll} Morton, & Mariah his Wife

Nath^{ll} Morton borne Novr ye 27th 1731.

The Child of Richard Webber & Priscilla his wife.

Priscilla Borne April 12th 1741.

The Children of John Holnes & Lois his wife.

1 Nehemiah Born July 12 . 1740.   See page 167.

The Children of Edward Winslow Esqr & Hannah his wife.

1 John Winslow Borne Thursday May th 14 . 1741 . at seven Clock in the morning . Obiit July 17th 1742 . on Saturday Night . at half an hour after Twelve
2. Penelope Winslow, Borne, Aprill 19th 1743.
3 Sarah Winslow borne Feb^{ry} 24 — 1744/5 being Sabbath day.
4. Edward Winslow Born, Feb^{ry} 20 . 1746
5. A Son born March 11th 1748 . Deceas^d within a few hours after

(*To be continued*)

---

* "Papillon" has been written above in a modern hand.
† This entry has been crossed out.
‡ Words in italics were entered in a modern hand.
§ Words in italics are in pencil, in a modern hand.

PLYMOUTH, MASS., VITAL RECORDS

(Continued from page 115)

[p. 183] The Children of Elkanah Cushman & Lydia his wife
1 Elkanah Cushman borne Nov'r 13th 1741 . being Fryd[ay]
The Children of Mary Crowley Single Woman
Thomas Farmar } Twins . Born April 11th 1745
John Farmer
The Children of Thomas Holmes jun'r & Elizabeth his wife
1 Thomas Holmes borne July 18th 1739.
2. & 3'd Jemima & Elizabeth Twins borne Sept'r 28 . 1741
4. Sarah Holmes Nov'r 12 . 1744.
5. Marcy Holmes, Feb'ry 3 . 1745/6.
The Children of Ephraim Churchell & Priscilla his wife viz't
1 Mary Churchell borne August 14th 1730.
2   borne Decem'r 19th 1731 . Dec'd 30th 1731
3 Charles Churchell borne April 25 . 1733
4 Zacheus Churchell borne Feb'ry 20, 1734
5 Ephraim Churchell borne July 27th 1738
6 Priscilla borne Jan'ry 8 . 1739.
7 Ellis Churchell borne Nov'r 25th 1742
8. Ansell Churchell borne March 29 . 1745.
9. John Churchell . Born, July 16th 1748.
The Children of Ebenezer Sampson & Hannah his wife
1 Ebenezer Sampson borne March 3'd 1740.
2 Elizabeth borne July 24th 1741

Plymouth, Mass., Vital Records

3. Hannah Samson borne, Oct² 2 . 1744
4. John Samson borne, Oct' 21 . 1746.
5. George Samson, Borne, Augst 22 . 1748
6. Sarah Samson Born, May 25 . 1751.
7. Lydia Samson Born, July 16 . 1753 . Old Stile
8. Mary Samson Born June 4th 1755.
9. Benjamin Samson, Novr 28th 1757 Born . Deceas^d June 21 . 1759
10. Benjamin Samson Born May 25th 1760 . Deceased Sep^tr 4 . 1761
Continued to 2nd Book 40th

[p. 184.] The Children of Benjamin Harlow & Elizabeth his wife vizt
1. Keziah Borne July 20 . 1740.
2. Stephen Harlow Borne, Augst 19 . 1742.
3. Eliz^a Harlow . Borne, Sep^t 5 . 1744 . Deceas^d Sep^t 6th 1745
4. Elizabeth Harlow, Born, Augst 21 . 1747.
The Child of Abner Holmes & Bathsheba his wife.
Bathsheba Borne November 17 . 1741. (*See page 178*) *Ent^d* *
The Children of John Cobb & Sarah his wife
1. John Borne January 3 . 1735/6 Deceas^d Augst 7th 1762.
2. Josiah Borne Feb^{ry} 22 . 1738/9 Deceas^d Sep^t 10th 1744.
3. Mary borne October 19 . 1741 Deceas^d Augst 6th 1799
4. Sarah Cobb born . Decr 11 . 1745.
a Daughter Borne not named, Born between, Mary & Sarah, was born aprill 13th 1744 . & Lived 11 Days.
Robert Bartlett Continued to page 103
The Children of Robert Bartlett & Rebecca his wife
1. Robert Bartlet Borne August 15th 1735
2. Ephraim Bartlet borne Sept^t 8th 1737
3. Rebecca Borne May 20th 1739
4. Isaac Borne Septr 14th 1742.
5. Lazarus Bartlett, born, Octr 25 . 1744.
6. Joshua Bartlett born Ap. 1 . 1747
7. James Bartlett . Born Augst 16 . 1749 Deceased Decr 8 . 1749
8. Susannah Bartlett Born Jan^{ry} 16 . 1750/1
See page 103

[p. 185.] The Children of Eliakim Tupper, & Mary his Wife.
1. Ruth Tupper Borne July 28th 1741.
2. Mary Tupper, Borne, May 15 . 1743.
3. [†]
4. [†]
Charles Tupper Born Augst 19th 1748
The Children of Barzilla Stetson & Ruth his Wife
1. Barzilla Stetson borne Decr ye 21 . 1742.
2. Jedediah Stetson, born July 17th 1745.
3. Sarah Stetson . Born . June ye 26th 1749
4. Mehittable . Stetson . Born . Sep^t ye 30th 1751

The Children of Jonathan Harlow, & Sarah his Wife
1. Ansell Harlow, Borne, April 25 . 1743.
2. Jonathan Harlow, borne Decr 30 . 1746.
3. Sarah Harlow born Augst 13th 1751.
4. Jedediah Harlow, born June 18th 1755.
5. Lucy Harlow . . Born March 9th 1758
6. Maray Harlow . Born October ye 28 . 1761.
7. Clarrissa Harlow . Born . Oct^r . 16th 1765.
The Children of James Faunce, & Sarah his Wife
1. Nathaniel Faunce borne Augst 16th 1743.
2. James Faunce Borne Feb^{ry} 18 . 1744/5
3. John Faunce Borne, July 7th 1747.
4. Seth Faunce Born, Octr 2 . 1749.
[p. 186] The Child . of William Wood . & Elizabeth his Wife
Elizabeth Wood, Borne Augst 17 . 1743 . Deceas^d March 3rd 1750/1
The Child of Ebenezer Holmes the 3rd and Susannah his wife.
Ebenezer Holmes born, Octr 1 . 1745.
The Children of Doct^r Lazarus . Le:Barron, and Lydia his Second Wife See p 96 — children by a former wife
1. Isaac Le:Barron Borne, Jan^{ry} 25th 1743/4 on Wednesday, at one Clock P.M.
2. Elizabeth Le:Barron Born Decr 21 . 1745 . on Saturday, about 5 Clock in ye Morning.
3. Lemuel Le:Barron, Born, Sep^t ye 1st 1747 . on Tuesday Morning, at 7 of ye Clock.
4. Francis Le:Barron, Born, Sep^t ye 3rd 1749 . deceas^d September 1773 S. Carolina
5. William Le:Barron Born, Augst ye 8th 1751 on Thirsday at 6 Clock in the morning
7. Margaret Le:Barron Born, July ye 5th 1755 . on Saturday, at 9 Clock in ye Evening . Deceas^d Novr 20 . 1756
6. Priscilla Le:Barron Born, Augst ye 3 . 1753 on Fryday morning half an hour after . 6 Clock see p. 96. chil. by former wife
The Children of George Holmes Junr & Lydia his wife
1. Lydia Holmes born Deceased
2. George Holmes born, Augst 8 . 1742
3. Lydia Holmes born, Deceased
4. Richard Holmes born, June 1 . 1745.
[p. 187] The Children, of Benjamin Barnes, & Experience, his Wife.
1. Elce Barnes, Born April 2 . 1743.
2. Marcy Barnes . born July . 8th 1745.
3. Bradford Barnes Born August 1st 1747.
4. Benjamin Barnes Born . Jan^{ry} 14 . 1749/50.
5. Josiah Barnes born Jan^{ry} 15th 1752 old Stile
6. Isaac . Barnes born June 16th 1754
7. Experience Barnes born May 11th 1756
8. Sarah Barnes born June 13th 1760

* Words in italics are in a different hand.

† No names were entered in these spaces.

The Children of Lemuell Barnes, & Lydia his Wife
1. Hannah Barnes borne Augst 6 . 1735.
2. Lydia Barnes borne Sep^t 9 . 1737.
3. William Barnes, borne Mar: 4 . 1740/1.
4. Lemuell Barnes borne Mar: 30 . 1743 . Deceas^d July 29 . 1743
5. Alice Barnes borne, June 30th 1744.
6. Lemuell Barnes borne Augst 11th 1746
7. John Barnes . borne Sep^t 11 . 1748.
8. Isaac Barnes born May 2 . 1750 . Deceased Octr 1750
The Children of Eleazer Holmes Junr, & Esther his wife
1. Hannah Holmes born, Aprill 18th 1744 . Deceas^d.
2. Jane Holmes borne July 15th 1747.
3. Eleazer Holmes Born, May 27 . 1749 . Deceas^d in 1751
4. Bettey Holmes . Born . Augst 27th 1754
5. Marcy Holmes, Born Octr 17 . 1756
6. Eleazer Holmes, Born, May 18th 1759
2 Twins Born Between ye Births of Eleazer, & Betty, Deceased Soon after they were Born, & not named

[p. 188] The Children, of William Harlow Junr, & Hannah his wife
1. Sarah Harlow, borne . Jan^{ry} 4th 1742/3.
2. William Harlow, borne July . 11th 1744.
3. Isaac Harlow born June 20th 1746
4. Zephaniah Harlow . born, May . 7 . 1748.
5. Hannah . Harlow . Born . March 25th 1751 . Old
6. Simeon Harlow Born Jan^{ry} 1st 1754 . New Stile
7. Marcy Harlow Born May . 7th 1756.
8. James . Harlow . Born July 28 . 1760
The Children of Amos Rider, & Ruth his Wife.
1. A Son not Named borne June 4 . 1742 . Dyed on or about June the 8th 1742.
2. Thomas Rider, borne May 14 . 1744.
Since s^d Amos's Death s^d Thomas's name is altered and is now Amos Rider.
The Children of Jonathan Sanders, & Elizabeth his Wife
1. Mary Sanders borne March 22 . 1741/2
2. Elizabeth borne Augst 12 . 1744.
3. Jonathan Sanders, borne, Feb^{ry} 5 . 1746/7 . Deceas^d Octr 1 . 1747.
The Children of Sam^{ll} Lanman & Elizabeth his Wife
1. Samuell Lanman Born Novr 28 . 1752.
2. Elizabeth Lanman, Born Novr 2 . 1755.
3. Rebeckah Lanman, Born Octr 31 . 1757
4. Peter Lanman, Born Sep^t 21 . 1759.
5. Thomas Lanman . Born Novr 20 . 1763
[p. 189] The Children of Zephaniah Holmes & Sarah his Wife
1. Bradford Holmes, Borne Octr 9 . 1739 . Deceas^d May 14 . 1740
2. Zephaniah Holmes, borne July 30th 1741
3. Sarah Holmes born . Decr 23 . 1743

* "21" appears to have been altered to "1".

4. Luce Holmes, born, June 13th 1747.
5. Deborah Holmes born . April 8th 1750
The Children of Lemuell Bartlett, & Mary his Wife
1. Lemuell Bartlett borne Jan^{ry} 29th 1743/4.
2. William Bartlett borne, Octr 20 . 1746.
3. Mary Bartlett, born Decemb^r 4 . 1749.
4. Jean Bartlett born April . 28 . 1752 Deceased Sep^t 15 . 1753
5. Jean Bartlett born June . 28 . 1754
6. Stephen Bartlett . Born . Nov^r . 5th 1756
7. Rebeckah Bartlett Born April 14th 1760,
8. Rufus Bartlett Born August . 21st 1762
The Children of Edward Doten, & Phebe his wife
1. Elisha Doten borne . Novr 21 . 1743.
2. Edward Doten born . Octr 13 . 1745
3. Thomas Doten born . March 6 . 1747/8
4. John Doten . born Augst 9 . 1750
5. Lemuell Doten Born Augst 7 . 1753
6. James Doten Born, Novr 18 . 1757.
[p. 190] The Children of Thomas Wright & Abijah his wife
1. Elizabeth Wright borne Jan^{ry} 24 . 1738/9 Deceased Novr 18 . 1739
2. Elizabeth Wright borne, Decr 19 . 1740
3. William Wright borne June 5 . 1743.
The Children of Ephraim Holmes & Sarah His Wife
1. Elizabeth Holmes borne June 20th 1743.
2. Ephraim Holmes borne, Sep^t 16 . 1745.
3. Joanna . Holmes born, Augst 19th 1748.
4. Nathaniel Holmes born, April 14 1751 old Stile
5. Sarah Holmes . born . May 3 . 1756.
6. Bathsheba Holmes . born Septr 19 . 1758.
A Son Born, Augst 1754 . not Named, Lived about 6 Hours . was in Course ye 5th Child.
7. Bathsheba Holmes born Nov. 28th 1763
The Children of Nathl Donham, & Rebeckah his wife
1. A Daughter, not named, Borne Deceas^d
2. Nath^{ll} Donham borne
3. Silas Donham borne
4. Rebeckah Donham, borne,
5. Hannah Donham borne,
6. Elizabeth Donham, borne,
7. Martha Donham, borne,
[p. 191] The Children of David Curtis & Hannah his Wife
1. Elizabeth Curtis borne, Augst 23 . 1744.
2. David Curtis borne June . 10 . 1746.
The Children of William Clarke, & Experience his Wife
1. Nathl Clarke borne, Decr 24th 1738 . Deceas^d July 27th 1744.
2. William Clarke, borne, March 19 . 1740/1.
3. Josiah Clarke, borne, June 19th 1743 . Deceased July 26 . 1744.
4. Lydia Clarke borne June 23rd 1744

5. Nath¹¹ Clarke born Jan^ry 13th 1747
6. Josiah Clarke born Decr 15th 1750
7. Thomas Clarke born March 15 : 1753
8. Experience Clarke born August 3rd 1755
9. Abigail Clarke born May 7th 1758

The Children of John Kempton, & Elizabeth his Wife
1. Jerusha Kempton borne, Aug^st 29th 1738.
2. John Kempton borne . July 22nd 1740.
3. Elizabeth Kempton, borne, June 21st 1742.
4. Nath¹¹ Kempton borne July . 23rd 1744 . Deceased . August . 19 . 1756
S^d Kempton had 2 Children, born at one birth, In May . 1737 . one borne dead, ye other Deceased.
5. Hannah Kempton Borne Novr 22 . 1747
6. Mary Kempton Borne Sepr 15 . 1749
7. Deborah Kempton Borne July 7th 1751
8. Samuel Kempton Borne Feb^ry 14 . 1753
9. Zacheus Kempton Borne December ye 4 . 1754.
10. Sarah Kempton Borne May . ye 18 . 1756
11. Joannah Kempton Borne March ye 14 . 1758
12. Nath¹¹ Kempton Borne June 6 . 1762

[p. 192] The Child of Amos Donham, & Abigail his Wife
Amos Donham borne Novr 8 . 1741 . Deceas^d Feb^ry 1 . 1741/2
The Children of Amos Donham, & Ann his Wife
1. Robert Donham borne, Sep^t 3 . 1744.
2. Mary Donham Born, Octr 13 . 1746 Deceased June 19 . 1747
3. Anne Donham Born July 10th 1748.
4. Amos Donham Born Jan^ry 3 . 1750/1.
5. Ruth Donham Born, Feb^ry 11 . 1753.
6. Mary Donham Born, March 18th 1755.
7. Josiah Donham Born, Feb^ry 8th 1757
8. Catharine Donham Born August 30th 1759 . Deceas^d Augt 30 . 1760
9. Abigal . Donham Born Feb^ry 3 . 1763

The Children of Samuell Doty Junr & Joannah his Wife
1. Hannah Doty borne, Decr 10th 1733.
2. Joannah Doty borne, June . 1737.
3. Sam¹ Doty borne, April 1739.
4. Nath¹ Doty, borne, Octr 10 . 1740.
5. Elizabeth Doty, borne June 6 1744.

The Children of Sam¹ Kempton Junr, & Mabell his Wife
1. A Child Still borne Viza   July 5 . 1737.
2. Sam¹ Kempton borne, Novr 5 . 1738 . At 6 Clock in ye Morn
3. Mabell Kempton borne blind, Octr 28 . 1740 D
4. Lydia Kempton borne, May 31st 1742.
5. Oliver Kempton borne, Septr 16th 1743.

(To be continued)

PLYMOUTH, MASS., VITAL RECORDS

(Continued from page 164)

[p. 193] The Children of Eleazer Churchell, Junr & Sarah his Wife
1. Hannah Churchell borne, July 14th 1739 . Deceas^d Aug^st 13th 1739.
2. Hannah Churchell, borne June 15th 1740.
3. Sarah Churchell borne Decr 27 . 1741 . & Lived about 14 Months
4. Marcy Churchell borne April¹ . 27th 1743.
5. Eleazer Churchell, borne, Octr 31 . 1744.
6. James Churchill, born, Jan^ry . 9 . 1746/7.
7. Asa Churchill, born Decr 20 . 1748 . Deceas^d Octr 5 . 1749
8. Silvanus Churchill born, July 6 . 1750 Jan^ry 29 . 1754 . Deceas^d
9. A Daughter Still Born
10. Sarah Churchell Born, March 29th 1755.
11. Joseph Churchell Born July 3rd 1757
12. Phebe Churchell Born June 9 . 1759.

The Children of Israell Clark, & Deborah his wife
1. Josiah Clarke borne, Jan^ry 18 . 1743/4
2. Jerusha Clark, born Octr 28 . 1745.
3. Thomas Clark born, Novr ye 17th . 1747.
4. Thankfull Clark . born Jan^ry 23 . 1749/5.*
5. Lurania Clark born March 23 . 1751/2 old Stile.
6. Bettey Clark born Jan^ry 16 . 1754.
7. Abigail Clark . born May 13 . 1756
8. Olive Clark born Jan^ry 1st 1759
9. Grace Clark born June 22nd 1761
10. Seth Clark born April 10th 1766

The Children of Thomas Faunce, Son of Thomas Faunce Junr and Sarah his Wife
1. John Faunce Born, Octr 26th 1743.
2. Thomas Faunce Born, Octr 22 . 1745.
3. Thaddeus Faunce Born
4. Lydia Faunce Born
5. Sarah Faunce Born
6. Ansell Faunce Born
7. Priscilla Faunce Born April 1st 1758
8. Stephen Faunce Born Novr 5th 1760
9. Jerusha Faunce Born Ap¹ 21st 1763
10. George Faunce Born Octob^r 1st 1765

[p. 194] The Children of Elkanah Delano, & Mary his Wife
1. A Son not Named Borne 1729 . Lived about three weeks, and Dyed with ye Small pox.

*Sic.

2. Elkanah Delano, borne Nov² 2 . 1730.
3. Hannah Delano, borne, Dec² 19 . 1732.
4. Mary Delano, borne, May . 7 . 1735.
5. Barzilla Delano, borne, Sep² 10 . 1737.
6. Eunis Delano, borne, Aug⁵ᵗ 1 . 1741.
7. Deborah Delano, borne, May 22 . 1743.
8. Sarah Delano born, Dec² 6 . 1746.

The Children of Stephen Churchell Jun² & Hannah his Wife

1 Sarah Churchell borne · July 18ᵗʰ 1739 Deceas⁴ Aug⁵ᵗ 13 . 1740.
2 Marcy Churchell borne July 18 . 1739 Deceas⁴ July 13 . 1740 Twins
3 Stephen Churchell borne July 17ᵗʰ 1741 . Deceas⁴ Sept 14ᵗʰ 1742
4 Stephen Churchell borne June 7 . 1743.
5 Hannah Churchell borne Feb² 14 . 1744/5.
6 Zadock Churchell borne July . 16 . 1747.
7 Peleg Churchell, borne July 9 . 1749. Deceased Oct² 5 . 1750.

The Children of Joshua Swift & Jane his Wife

1 Abigail Swift, borne, March 8 . 1739.
2 Joseph Swift, borne, Feb² 5 1742.
3 Jean Swift, borne, June 6 . 1744.
4 John Swift born, Sep² 15 . 1746
5 Lusanna Swift, Feb² 9 . 1748/9
6 [*]
7 [*]

[p. 195] The Children of Eleazer Faunce, & Hannah his Wife

1. Hannah Faunce Borne, Nov² 2 . 1725.
2. Elizabeth Faunce borne, Sep² 14 . 1727 . Deceas⁴ Feb² 13 . 1727/8
3. Patience Faunce borne, Jan² 22 . 1729/30.
4. Mary Faunce borne June 2 . 1731.
5. Abigail Faunce borne, Feb² 22 . 1734/5.
6. Priscilla Faunce borne Jan² 25 1738/9 . Deceas⁴ Mar: 3ʳᵈ 1740/1

The Children of Ichabod Samson, & Marcy his Wife

1 Esther Samson, borne Aug⁵ᵗ 24 . 1738.
2 Elnathan Samson, borne, July 28 . 1740.
3 Ichabod Samson, borne, Aprill, 12 . 1742.
4 Sam¹. Samson borne . April 2 . 1745.
(See page 168.)

The Children of Nath¹¹ Croade, & Elizabeth his Wife

Elizabeth Croade Borne, May 31 . 1743 . Deceas⁴ Sep² 17ᵗʰ 1744
Nathaniel Croade Borne Sep² 5ᵗʰ 1745

The Children of John Thomas, & Abigail† his Wife

1. John Thomas Born July 16 . 1727.
2. James Thomas borne, Dec² 16 . 1729.
3. A Son Still born Dec² 4 . 1731.

* No names were entered for these numbers.
† "Dunham in 1726" has been interlined in a modern hand.

4. Jonathan Tho⁵ born, July 14 . 1733 . Deceased May 14 . 1734
5. Nath¹ Thomas borne, Aprill 20 . 1735.
6. Mary Thomas, born May 11 . 1738.
7. Susannah Thos. born Feb² 17 . 1741.
8. Abigail Thos born July 14 . 1743 . Deceas⁴ July 20 . 1743
9. William Tho⁵, born, Aug⁵ᵗ 5 . 1744.
10. Ichabod Thomas, born June 28 . 1748.
11. Ephraim Thomas, born July 4 . 1752.

[p. 196] The Children of Josiah Whittemore, & Mary his wife

1. Mehitable Whittemore born April 15 . 1744.
2. Thomas Hatch Whittemore, born Aug⁵ᵗ 14ᵗʰ 1747
3. Josiah Whittemore, born Sept² 8ᵗʰ 1749.
4. Joannah Whittemore, born March 21 . 1752.

The Childⁿ of Theophilus Cotton, & Martha his Wife

1. Theophilus Cotton borne July 11ᵗʰ 1744.
2. John Cotton borne, Jan² 10 . 1745/6.
3. Rowland Cotton Borne, April 30 . 1748 . Was Drowned . Aug⁵ᵗ 15 . 1759
4. Bethiah Cotton Born Feb² 11ᵗʰ 1749/50.
5. Wᵐ Crowe Cotton Born, Dec² 14 . 1751.
6. Josiah Cotton borne Nov² 7 . 1753
7. Edward Cotton Borne . April 17 . 1759   Ent⁴

The Child of Alexander Dow, & Sarah his Wife

Alexander Dow, borne May, 31 . 1741

The Child of Joseph Jackson, & Mary his Wife

Remembrance Jackson borne Jan² 6ᵗʰ 1742/3.

The Children of Will:ᵐ Keen, & Ruth his wife

1 Elizabeth Keen Borne, Jan² 1⁵ᵗ 1743/4
2 Ruth Keen borne June 25ᵗʰ 1746.
3 Grace Keen born Sep² 26ᵗʰ 1748.

Sarah Weston Daughter of Prudence Weston born January 12 . 1746/7.

[p. 197] The Children of the Rev⁴ Mʳ. Jonathan Elles, and Patience his Wife.

1. Deborah Elles Born Aprill 8 . 1740 . Deceas⁴ July 12ᵗʰ 1740
2. Luce Elles Borne April 14 . 1742.
3. Mary Elles, Borne April 27 . 1744.   Deceas⁴ May 1 . 1756

The Children of Silvanus Bartlett, & Martha his wife

1. Waite Bartlett, Borne April 7ᵗʰ 1744 . Deceas⁴ June 13ᵗʰ 1744.
2. Joseph Bartlett, Borne, May, 22 . 1745 . Deceas⁴ May 1 . 1756
3. Elizabeth Bartlett Born March 28 . 1749 . Deceas⁴
3 Silvanus Bartlett Born   Deceas⁴ May 1 . 1756
5. Silvanus Bartlett Born Jan² 18 . 1750/1.
6. Mary Bartlett Born Feb² 21 . 1753.
7. Abner Bartlett Born March 2 . 1755.
8. Martha . Bartlett Born June 27 . 1757.
9. Jerusha Bartlett Borne October 16 . 1759   Decsed october 25 . 1759

Plymouth, Mass., Vital Records

10 Joseph Bartlett Borne Dec^r . 16 — 1761
11 Jerusha Bartlett Born ye 24 May 1764
12 Francis Bartlett Born
13 Sophia Bartlett born
14 Jesse Bartlett born . Octr 28th . 1772
Sylvanus Bartlett the Father died Novr 16th 1811 . born Decr 1 1719 . Aged 92
Martha Bartlett the Mother died Decr 30 . 1809 . born Ap^l 6 1726 . Aged 83.

The Children of John Goddard, & Lydia his Wife
1. John Goddard borne Augst 8 . 1736
2. Sarah Goddard born May . 14 1738
3. Lemuell Goddard, born Septr 21 . 1739.
4. Benj^a Goddard, born Sept 21 . 1745.

The Children of Thom^s Davee & Hannah Davee his 2nd Wife.
1 Johnson Davee Born July . 16th 1762
2 George Davee Born March 10st 1764

[p. 198] M^{er} Thomas prince Esquir . deceased on the 29 of March 1673 : Who for Sixteen years past was govener of plimouth Colony and god Made him a great blesing to his people therein
M^{er} Thomas Southworth desceased on the 8th of desember 1669
Maior William Bradford Deceased february ye 20th 170¾ Being Neare 80 years of age.
The Widow Mrs Mary Bradford Deceased January 6th 170⅘
Mrs Joseph Bradford Deceased July 10th 1715 being Neere 84 years of age.

The Children of Jonathan Churchell & Hannah His Wife
1 Jonathan Churchell Borne ye 18th March 1744/5.
2. Jesse Churchell Born Octr ye 30th 1746.
3. Samuel Churchell Born, Jan^{ry} ye 15 . 1749/5 * : Deceas^t May 20th 1753
5 Hannah Churchill Born Jan^{ry} ye 3 1760 . Deceas^t June 1st 1760
4 Not Named Born October ye 30 1752   Lived abo^t 8 Days
6 Francis Churchill Born June ye 1st 1761
7 Hannah Churchill Born March 28 : 1763
8 Ruben Churchill Born Augst 1st 1765

The Children of Thomas Davee, and Sarah his Wife
1. Robert Davee, borne, Sep^t 13 . 1741
2. Thomas Davee, born, oct^r 20 . 1743
3. William Davee born April 20 . 1746
4. Deborah Davee born May 28 . 1749 . Deceas^d may 4^t 1759
5. Betty . Davee born Jan^{ry} 29 . 1752 old Stile . 1751/2.
6. Joseph Davee born Augst 29^t 1756
7 Solomon Davee born July 12^t 1759
8 John Davee born Sepr 12th 1761
{ 9 Johnson Davee born July: 16 : 1762 } Entred over y^e
{ 10 George Davee born March 10th 1764 } Other Side †

* Sic.
† See original page 197.

[p. 199] Rebeckah Morton Borne Widdow of the Late, George Morton Deceased, Dyed February ye 3rd 1758.
Esther Holmes, Wife of Eleazer Holmes, Deceased August ye 26th 1759
Mistris Alse Bradford deceased the 27th of March 1670
Mistres Mary Carpenter deceased the 20th day of march 1687 being Entered into the 91 year of her age
Mistris Pricila Cooper desceased on the 28th of desember 1689 being Entered in to 92^d yeare of her age
Nathl Thomas Esqr Deceased, Feb^{ry} 24th 1738.
John Thomas Esqr Deceased, Augst 7 . 1737.
Jemina Samson, wife of Lazarus Samson Deceased, July 28– 1731.
Lydia Bartlett, Wife, of Benjamin Bartlett Deceased Octr 21st 1739.
Mary Donham (widdow of ye Late Saml Donham Deceas^d) Deceased, January 8th 1743 . In ye 84th year, of her age
William Donham Deceased November ye 12th 1745   In ye 62 year of his age
Deacon Thomas Harlow, Deceased, Novr 12th 1746
William Morton Deceased, Novr 15th 1750
Hannah Ring (Widdow of William Ring Deceased) . Deceased July 8th 1745 In the 77th Year of her Age
Hannah Doten (widdow of John Doten of Plimton Deceased) Deceas^d at . Plymouth April ye 15th 1754 In . the 67th Year of her Age
Stephen Churchell Deceased, Octr 6th 1750
Eleazer Churchell Deceased, Septr 21 . 1754.
Eleazer Holmes Deceased . Augst 27th 1754
Lydia Le Barron, Wife of Doct^r Lazarus Le Barron Deceased.
Mrs Flizabeth Lothrop, Widdow (of The Honourable Isaac Lothrop Esqr Deceased) Deceased October the 19th 1757, about 10 Clock A.M.   Was Daughter of Mr Jonathan Barnes, & Elizabeth his Wife, and Born Augst ye 16th A.D. 1677 1677.
Hannah Churchill Widdow, of ye Late Eleazer Churchell Deceased; Dyed, September ye 19th 1757
Joseph Holmes . Deceas^d Feb^{ry} 20th 1749
[p. 200] M^{er} nathaniel morton Secretary of plymouth Colony and a pilar in the Church here deceased June 28 * 1685 Being Entred into the Seventy third yeare of his age.
Roas The wife of Thomas morton Deceased the 31th day of november 1685
William Greene deceased the 7th day of october 1685
Phebe the Wife of John Morton desceased the 11th day of June 1686
Elizabeth the Wife of Elkanah Cushman deceased the 4th day of Januaway 1681
The Widow Lettes deceased the 2th day of July 1687.
William Bradford Junor deceased the 5th day of July : 1687
Deacon finney Deceased the 7th day of Januawary 1687 Being Nere four Score years of age

* "29" was interlined, apparently in the same hand.

THE MAYFLOWER DESCENDANT

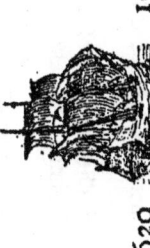

1620   1920

A QUARTERLY MAGAZINE OF
PILGRIM GENEALOGY AND HISTORY

VOLUME XVI

1914

PUBLISHED BY THE
MASSACHUSETTS SOCIETY OF
MAYFLOWER DESCENDANTS

BOSTON

Samuel Dunham Sun of John Dunham was burned to death in his house on the 24th of . January 1687 88 :
Hannah The Wife of Mr William Clarke Deceased on the 21th of February 1687 88 being : Entered into the 29th yeare of her age
Sarah the Wife of Robert Bartlet Deceased on the 20th of february 1687 88
Rebkah the Wife of Thomas Clarke deceased on the 3d of Aprill 1688
John Moyses deceased on the 22d of Aprill 1688
An the Wife Samuel King : se deceasd on the 4th of May 1688 :
Esthur Jordan Deceased on the 26th of may 1688
Georg Watson deceased on the 31 day of January 168 [*worn*] Being Entered into the 87th yeare of his age

(*To be continued*)

PLYMOUTH, MASS., VITAL RECORDS

Transcribed by the Editor

(Continued from Vol. XV, p. 214)

[p. 201] Joseph Warren Senior deceased May the 4th 1689
hannah harlow deceased June the 27th 1689
Samuel Garner deceased on the 3d of September 1689
Samuel harlows Sone Samuel deceased on the 2d of Septem: 1689 his daughter pricilah deceased on the 6th of September 1689
BenJamine howland Sone to Joseph howland and Elizabeth howland his Wife deceased September the 7th 1689
Joseph deceased September the 8th 9 1689
Mary the wife of Joshua : Ransom deceased on the 25th of october 1689
Josiah Clarke deceased on the 7th of october 1689
Thomas Morton Senior deceased on the 4th of November 1689
Elkanath Watson Edward doty Senior and his Son John doty Were all drowned on the 8th of february 1689or90
Martha dunham the Wife of Samuel dunham Senior of plymouth desceased on the 26 of April 1690
Desire the Wife of Nathaniel Southworth of plimouth descseased desember 4th 1690
Benijah pratt the Sone of John pratt descseased desember 4th 1690
The Widow hannah Rickard deceased on the 22d of december 1690
Lettis the Wife of Andrew Ring descseased the 22d of february 1690/1
Patience Doty deceased on the 26th of february 1690/1
John Jorden deceased on the 14th of March 1691
Richard Write deceased on the 9th of June 1691
Mris hart deceased on the 9th of June 1691
Edward May deceased Agust 10th 1691

[p. 202] My deere Mother Whitteney deceased Agust the 16th 1691 Being Entered into the 77 yeare of her age, *Recorded by Elder Faunce**
My ant Sarah Bonam deceased Agust 25th 1691 being Entered into the yeare of her age — *Recorded by Elder Faunce**
Serjant William Harlow deceased Agust 25th 1691 being entered into the 67 yeare of his Age
My ant ann Morton the Wife of my uncle Ephraim Morton deceased on the 6th day of September 1691.   *P Elder Faunce**
Lidiah Nelson the Wife of John nelson deceased on the Eleventh day September 1691
on the 10th day of december 1691 That precious and Eminant Servant of god deceased The Elder Thomas Cushman being Entered into the 84 yeare of his age

*The words in italics are in a modern hand.

John Barrows deceased february the 14th 1691or92
John Dunham Senior deceased Aprill 6th 1692 being Entered in to the 79th yeare of his age
Elizabeth Doty the Wife of John doty Senior desceased on the 21th of November 1692
Mary the Wife of Jonathan Mory Senior deceased on the 26th day of September 1692
Left Ephraim Morton deceased october 5th 1693
Andrew Ring deceased on the 22 of february 1693/4
Josiah Morton deceased on the 29th day of May 1694
Abigail the Wife of Stephen Bryant Senior deceased on the 24 of october 1694
William Hoskins Senior deceased on the 7th day of September 1695
my Sister Sarah the Wif of John Buck of Sittuat deceased on the 27th day of June 1695

[p. 203] Elizabeth the Wife of deacon Thomas Clerke deceased on the 13th day of November 1695
An Rider the mother of Samuel Rider deceased the forteenth of december 1695
Mary Holmes the daughter of Mer John Holmes of duxbery deceased on the Eight day of March 1695/6
Joseph Warren deceased desember 28th 1696
Richard Warren deceased January 23d 1696/7
Mer Thomas Clarke deceased on the 24th of March 1697 being Entered into the 98th yeare of his Age
William Hannur deceased March 31 1697
John Nelson deceased on the 29th of Aprill 1697 . being Entered into the 54th yeare of His age
Abigail Bradford deceased on the 4th of May 1697
John Holmes Senior deceased on the last of July 1697
Mary the wife of Samuel waterman deceased August : 3d : 1697
Joshua praat deceased february 16th 1697/8
Marsy Wood deceased on the 4th of March 1697/8
The Widdow Mary dounham deceased on the 20th of March 1698
William Blackmur deceased october 7th 1698
The Aged Widow Mary Cushman deceassed November The 28th day of 1699.
Barak Jourdaine deceassed The first day of december 1699
Sarah The Wife of John Holmes Deceasd On The 27 day of october 1700
Mrs Sarah Warren Deceassed Novembr 24th 1700
Jabiz Warren deceased Aprill 19th 1701 drowned : at : sea
John doty Senior deceased May 8th 1701

[p. 204] Elizabeth Holmes deceased on the 2d of August 1701
The Widow Esther Jordan deseased March 12th 1702
Elizabeth Esland deseased Aprill 18th 1702 being Entered into the 26 yer
hannah Rider the Wife of John Rider Deceased January : 17th 1703

Plymouth, Mass., Vital Records

Sergant Joseph Bartlett Deceassed Aprill ye 9th 1703

George Bonan Senior deseaced April 27th 1704 being upward of 85 yer of Age

Mersey Rickard the Daughter of the Widow hannah Rickard Deceased on the 21 of June 1706 being 26 years of aged

The Widow pricila Warren Deceased on ye 15 of May 1707 being Near 74 yeares of age

Remember the Wife of Abraham Jacson Senior deceased on the 24th Day of July 1707

Joseph Church Deceased on the 19th Day of october 1707 betwen 9 & 10 at Evening

M^{er} Nathaniel Warren Deceased october 29th 1707

M^{rs} hannah Stirtevant the Wife of John Stirtevan Deceased on march first 170$\frac{8}{9}$ Aged

The Widow hannah Rickard Deceased on the first of Aprill 1709 Aged

Rebeckah the Wife of John Churchel Deceased April 7th 1709

Leftenant Nathaniel Morton Deceased July: 7th: 1709 after about 17 weks Confinement & Indured aboundance of paine with wonderfull patience Lived Desired and Dyed Lamented

Ruth Barnebe The Wife of Stephen barnebe Deceased December 21 1709 being 33 years of agee

James Warren y^e Son of Richard warren Deceased Deceased on the 25th of Desember 1709 being in the 30th year of his age

Giles Rickard Deceased on the 29 of January 170$\frac{9}{10}$

The Widow Abigaiel Coole Deceased on the 20th of ffebruary 170$\frac{9}{10}$

The Aged Wido febe ffinney Deceased on the 9th of Desember 1710 in the Evening being as was Judged in her 92 yeare of agee

Left Jonathan Mory Deceased May 19th 1708 being Entered into the 75 yer of his age

M^{rs} hannah Bartlet the Wife of Mr Joseph Bartlet Deceaced March 12 170[zworn] being Entered into the 72^d yeare of her life

John Clarke Deceased January 17th 170$\frac{1}{2}$

Samuel Dunham Senor Deceased January 20th 170$\frac{1}{2}$ being in his 89 years of age

William Harlow Deceased January 28th 170$\frac{1}{2}$

Mr Joseph Bartlett Deceased February 18 170$\frac{1}{2}$ being nere

M^{er} John Rickard Deceased on y^e 25th Day of Aprill 1712

Mrs Mary Rickard Deceased on y^e 28th of august 1712

Docter Thomas Little Deceased Desember 22^d 1712 in y^e 38 yea of his age

on the 29th of November 1712 Was Capt Tewe and all his Ship Comp Drowned Going of from their Ship in their boat where She Rid in Grea[t] Disstres in a dreadfull Storme and In ye Evening of that Day Come on Shore on the beach & there staved

(To be continued)

PLYMOUTH, MASS., VITAL RECORDS

(Continued from page 64)

[p. 205] on y^e 26th Day of June 1713 Nicolos May Esther Rickard and Daved Shepards Child Deceased

Abigail The Wife of Thomas Snell Deceased on y^e 27h of May 1713

Marsey Cooke Deceased on y^e 11th of ffebruary 170$\frac{3}{4}$

Nathaniel Churchel Deceased on y^e 24th Day of March 1714

Rebecka Cole Deceased on y^e 2d of July 1714 Ephraim Cols Daughter

William barns y^e Son of John barns was Drowned July 23 : 1714

Sarah holmes The Wife of Elisha Holmes Dyed in Travil July 24 1714

Mr Jonathan Barns Deceased on the 20th of August 1714 being Entered into y^e 71st yeare of his life

Abraham Jacson Senior Deceased october 4th 1714

Elkath Cushman Juner Deceased on y^e 9th of January 170$\frac{4}{5}$

Charles Littles Daughter Sarah Deceased January 2 170$\frac{4}{5}$

Elnathan Bartlet Deceased ffebruary 7th 170$\frac{4}{5}$

John Cobb Deceased ffebruary 21st 17$\frac{4}{5}$ being neare being in y^e 83d yeare of his life

Sarah Tinckom Deceased ffebruary 22d 1714

Jonathan Perry Deceased March 6th 170$\frac{4}{5}$

Mrs Hanna Little The Wife of mr william little Deceased Aprill : 12 : 1715

Abigail The Wife of Nicolos Drew Deceased Aprell 22d 1715

The Widow Patience Nelson Deceased May 3d 1715

Capt James Warren Esquire Deceased May 30th 1715 in y^e 50 yer of his age

Caleb Carver Deceased May 31st 1715

Hanna Ring The Daughter of William Ring & hanah his Wife Decesed on ye first Day of June 1715 in ye 18th yeare of her age

Joanna howland The Daughter of Thomas howland Deceased June ye 5th 1715

Mer Joseph Bradford Deceased July 10th 1715 aged : 84 :

Samuel Rider Deceased July 18th 1715

hanna Warren The Wife of Benjamin Warren Deseased November 3d 1715

Mary Morey The Daughter of Jonathan Mory Deceased November : 23d 1715

Mary Churchill The Wife of Eliazar Churchill Deceased Desember 11th 1715

Mary harlow Deceased January 3d 170$\frac{5}{6}$

Samuel Lucos Deceased January 17th 170$\frac{5}{6}$ aged : 54

Sarah The Wife of Thomas ffaunce Junior Deceased March 3d 1716

Eleazar Churchill Deceased March 5th 1716

Jabiz Dunkin ffell overbord from a Sloop Coming from Bostorn on y^e 6th Day March 1716 : and Was lost

Desre the Wife of John Woshbon Deceased September 23d 1716 being Delevered then of a child both Deceased

Elizabeth Cole ye Daughter of Ephraim Cole Deceased Desember 17th 1716

[p. 210*] Sarah King deceased on the 23d day of April 1738 in the Eighty & Eight year of her Age

Debro Shareman Deceased on the 29th of August 1738 the wife of Caleb Shareman

the child of Caleb Shareman deceased the 5th day of September being 3 weeks & one day of old 1738.

Seth Cobb

The Honourable Isaac Lothrop Esqr Deceased, Septr 7 . 1743

Mr Thomas Howland Deceased December ye 2 . 1739.

Sarah Bartlett, wife of John Bartlett, Deceased,

Mary Kempton, Wife of Thos Kempton Deceasd

Thomas Clarke Deceased, Augst 25th 1744

Abigail Donham, Wife of Amos Donham . Deceasd Decr 15 . 174[*worn*]

Rebeckah Holmes, Wife of Jabez Holmes, Deceasd Decr 24 . 1730

Mrs Sarah Bartlett. (Relict Widdow, of Robert Bartlett, Deceased) Deceased Febry . 8th 1744/5.

Mary wife to Abraham Jackson, Deceasd Febry 1740/1

Mary 2nd wife to sd Jackson Deceasd . July 2 . 1744

* Pages 206–209, both inclusive, were omitted in numbering.

Lemuell Cobb . Deceased — October yͤ 22ⁿᵈ . 1743
Sarah Holmes, Wife of Elisha Holmes Junʳ Deceased July 4 . 1738.
Rebeckah Holmes, Wife of Jabez Holmes Deceasᵈ Decʳ 24 . 1730 and
   Jabez, Son to sᵈ Jabez & Rebeckah Lived about 7 months
John Morton Deceased Febʳʸ 4 . 1738/9
Reliance Morton Wife to sᵈ John, deceased, Decʳ 4 . 1735.
Mrs Elizabeth Bartlett Wife of Samˡ Bartlett Esqʳ (Daughter of
   Isaac Lothrop Esqʳ Deceased) Deceased November yᵉ 1 . 1745 .
   10 Clock A M
Samuell Harlow Deceased
Hannah Harlow Deceased (his wife)
Mary Morton, wife of Timothy Morton, Deceased March 22ⁿᵈ 1734/5.
Bethiah West, Wife of Judah West Deceasᵈ Decʳ 16 . 1745.
Ann Finney, wife to Robert Finney, Deceased
Captˡ Ephraim Morton Dyed·of yᵉ Small pox Decʳ 30ᵗʰ 1729.
Abigail Withered, (wife of Samˡ Wetherhead Deceasᵈ) deceasᵈ Augˢᵗ
   20ᵗʰ ADom : 1743·
Elkanah Totman, dyed at Luisburgh, Oct 5ᵗʰ 1745
Thomas Clarke Deceased.
[p. 211] Lois Foster, Wife of Thomas Foster, Deceasᵈ September yᵉ
   21. 1743·
Nathˡ Thomas Esqʳ, Deceasᵈ at LewisBurgh Septʳ 23 . 1745·
Deacon John Foster, Deceased Decʳ . 24 . 1741
Marcy King yᵉ Wife of Joseph King, Deceased, Janʳʸ . 15ᵗʰ 1744/5 .
   aged 76 years wanting about one month
Rodolphus Hatch, Deceased, Janʳʸ yᵉ 1 . 1743/4
Joshua Drew Deceased, March 27ᵗʰ 1748.
John Barnes Deceased, September yᵉ 11ᵗʰ 1745·
Patience Donham, the Wife of Ezekiel Donham Deceased, Febʳ .
   10ᵗʰ . 1748.
Ephraim Churchell Deceasᵈ Decʳ 13ᵗʰ 1748.
Priscilla Churchell his Wife Deceasᵈ Decʳ . 15ᵗʰ 1748.
Rebeckah Bartlett, Wife, of Ebenezer Bartlett Deceasᵈ May yᵉ 11ᵗʰ
   1749.
Sarah Sanson, Wife of Jonathan Samson, Deceasᵈ Augˢᵗ 22 . 1748
Jean Doten Wife of Lemuell Doten, Deceased, June 3 . 1749.
Susannah Harlow, Wife of Robert Harlow, Deceased, Febʳʸ 17
   1748/9
Sarah yᵉ Wife of James Howard, Deceased, Decʳ 27ᵗʰ 1748
James Howard yᵉ Son of James Howard, Deceased May yᵉ 9 . 1749.
   Dyed of the Small Pox at Jamaica
Thomas Wethrell Junʳ Dyed with a fever, at Jamaica In May yᵉ 9ᵗʰ
   or 10ᵗʰ day ADom 1744.
Captˡ Benjamin Warren, Deceased, May 30ᵗʰ*
William Wethrell, Dyed of yᵉ Small Pox, in London 1746
James Wethrell Dyed, at Lewisburge, Cape Breton In Anno Domini
   1745

*The year was not entered.

Mʳ Thomas Wethrell Dyed Aprill 21ˢᵗ 1743.
Martha Harlow, the Wife of John Harlow, Deceased. April yᵉ 2ⁿᵈ
   1749.
Nathˡ Bradford Deceased March yᵉ 27ᵗʰ 1751.
Annah King, Wife of Eleazer King of Plymouth, Dyed at Plimton
   February yᵉ 8ᵗʰ in yᵉ Evening ADom : 1750/1. In yᵉ 85ᵗʰ year
   of her Age
John Holmes yᵉ Son of Elisha Holmes, Deceasᵈ March 19ᵗʰ . 1750/1
Captˡ Seth Cobb Deceased, Septʳ yᵉ 17ᵗʰ 1739.
[p. 212] Mrs Lydia Holmes, Wife of Mʳ Joseph Holmes, (In 1703 Was
   widdow of Mʳ Joseph Bartlett Junʳ Deceased) Departed this
   Life, On Monday yᵉ 6ᵗʰ of January 1752 Aged Eighty Years, In
   September Last.
Asa Hunt Deceased Janʳʸ . 29 . 1752. Was Drowned Near Clarks
   Island. Aged 41 years yᵉ 8ᵗʰ day of May 1751
Mʳ John Sturtevant Senʳ Deceased Febʳʸ yᵉ 4 . 1752 N. S. Aged
   Ninety Three years, & five Months
Mʳ Return Waite Deceased, October yᵉ 3 . 1751 In the 73 year of
   his age
James Clark yᵉ 3ʳᵈ Deceased . August . yᵉ . 8ᵗʰ 1727
Ruth Turner (Wife of David Turner) Deceased March 28ᵗʰ 1755 .
   on Fryday about 8 Clock in the forenoon She was Born Novem-
   ber 1700.
Patience Harlow, Wife of Thomas Harlow, Deceased January yᵉ 6ᵗʰ
   1755.
Hannah Bagnall, Wife of Benjamin Bagnall, Deceased May the 5ᵗʰ
   1755
Thomas Sears, Deceased . 1755.
Bathsheba Hicks, wife of Abraham Hicks Deceasᵈ June 22ᵈ 1756
John Rider Deceased, March 11ᵗʰ 1756
Lydia Le-Barron yᵉ 2ⁿᵈ wife of Doctor Lazarus Le-Barron, Deceased
   October yᵉ 28ᵗʰ 1756
Lydia Bartlett Wife of Benjamin Bartlett Deceased In November
   Anno Domini 1739.
Captˡ Benjamin Bartlett, dyed of yᵉ Small Pox In Jamaica, February .
   1755.
Priscilla Drew Wife of Lemuel Drew Deceasᵈ Octobʳ 2ⁿᵈ 1757
Mrs Sarah Watson, wife of John Watson Esqʳ Deceased, July 2 . 1725 .
   Æ. 31.
John Watson Esqʳ Deceasᵈ Septˡ 9ᵗʰ 1731 Æ. 53.
Mrs Elizabeth Watson, Wife of John Watson Esqʳ Deceased Septʳ 14 .
   1750 Æ. 28.
John Watson Esqʳ Deceased, Janʳʸ . 3 . 1753. Æ. 37.
Mrs Abigail Watson Wife of George Watson Esqʳ Deceasᵈ March 15ᵗʰ
   1750/1 . Æ. 22.
[p. 213] The Children of Samuell Kent, And Desire his Wife Born
   at Marshfield
1. Samuel Kent Born July 2 . 1729.

Plymouth, Mass., Vital Records

2. Nathl Kent, Born Febry 25 . 1732.
3. Desire Barker Kent Born June 25th 1735
4. Hannah Kent Born Augst 4 . 1737.
5. John Kent Born Octr 13 . 1739.
6. Sarah Kent Born Augst 6 . 1741.
7. Hulda Kent, Born Decr 2 . 1743.
8. Ichabod Kent, Born Decr 13 . 1744
The Above Born at Marshfield . Entd Octr ye 4th 1756
[p. 214] The Children of Saml Nichols Nelson, & & Elizabeth his Wife.
1. Alathea Nelson born, Novr 20 . 1745 . Deceasd
2. Saml Nelson born Augst 7 . 1747.
3. Patiance Nellson born May 17 . 1749
4. Sarah Nellson born Aug. 2nd 1754
5. Alathea Nellson born Janry 27th 1758
6. Joseph Warren Nellson born Novr 9th 1761
7. Priscilla Nellson born July . 31st . 1765
8. Betty Nellson born Janry 11th 1768
The Child of The Revd Mr Thomas Frink and Isabella his Wife . Viz
Peter Frink Born Janry 2 . 1745/6.
The Children of Barnabas Churchell Junr, and Lydia his Wife
1. Elizabeth Churchell born, Janry 16 . 1745/6.
2. Barnabas Churchell Born Novr 25th 1747.
3. Job Churchell Born Janry 15 . 1750/1 Deceasd 14th 1753.
4. Saml Churchell Born Janry 9 . 1753 Deceasd 31 . 1753.
5. Seth Churchell Born Octr 1 . 1754
6. Job Churchell Born August. 17th 1756
7. Lydia Churchell Born Decr 16th 1758.
[p. 215] The Children of Josiah Morton the third, and Experience, his wife
1. Simeon Morton born, June 16th . 1743 . Deceased June 9th 1753
2. Sarah Morton born, July 22 1746 Decesd Octobr 3rd 1747
3. Thomas Morton Born Decembr 15th 1748
4. Elizabeth Morton Born January 10th 1752 Dcasd
5. Josiah Morton Born May 31st 1756
6. Anasa Morton Born Septemr 9th 1758 Deceasd
7. William Morton Born January 27th 1761
8. Ruth Morton Born October 19th 1763
The Children of Abial Shurtleff, & Luce his Wife
1. Abial Shurtleff, born Janry 20th 1740/1 . Deceased July 23rd . 1742.
2. Abial Shurtleff, born Septr 15 . 1742.
3. Clark Shurtleff born Janry 7 . 1744/5.
4. Noah Shurtleff born, June 12 . 1747.
5. Lucy Shurtleff born May . 21st . 1750
6. Levi Shurtleff born May 14th 1754
7. Samuel Shurtleff born May 15th 1759
The Children of Isaac Tinkcom & Kezia His Wife
1. Briggs Tinkcom Born June 21th 1740.

Plymouth, Mass., Vital Records

2. Elizabeth Tinkcom Born April 26th 1743.
3. Isaac Tinkcom Borne Octr 22nd 1745.
The Children of James Nicholson, & Hannah his Wife
Elizabeth Nicholson born Febry 19 . 1745/6.
Thomas Nicolson born, Aprill . 10th 1748.
[p. 216] The Children of Joseph Churchell, & Meriah his Wife.
1. Ichabod Churchell Borne, Augst 9th 1746.
2. Joseph Churchell Born July . 14 . 1748.
3. Lucey Churchell, Born . Augst 22 . 1750
The Children of Isaac Thomas, and Mary his Wife
1 Isaac Thomas Born Febry 4th 1749/5
2. Joshua Thomas Born Febry 4th 1749/5 . Deceasd Febry 20th 1749/5. Were Born at one Birth.
The Child of John Churchell, and Sarah his Wife.
Sarah Churchell born June 11th 1750 . Deceased Oct. 29th 1796
[p. 217] The Children of John Jones, & Sarah his Wife
1. John Jones born July 9th 1742.
2 Thomas Jones born Sept 20 . 1744.
3. Sarah Jones born March 25 . 1747.
4. James Jones born Decembr 9 . 1749
The Children of John Atwood Junr & Joanna * his Wife
1 Rebeckah Atwood born June 22 . 1737.
2. John Atwood born Augst 11 . 1739
3. George Atwood born Sept . 2 . 1741
4 Elijah Atwood born July 20 . 1743 . Deceasd Sept 19th 1743.
5. Abigail Atwood born April . 18 . 1745.
6. Micah Atwood born April 14 . 1747.
7. William Atwood born Febry 19 . 1749
8. Sarah Atwood born April . 6 . 1751.
9 Mary Atwood . born
The Children of John Thomas Junr, & Abigail his Wife
1. Abigail Thomas Born June 12 . 1748.
2 A Daughter Born Novr 5 . 1750 . Deceased Novr 7 . 1750
3. Sarah Thomas Born Janry 18th 1752.
4. Jonathan Thomas Born Janry 14th 1759
[p. 218] The Children of Thomas Jackson Junr & Sarah his Wife
1. Sarah Jackson Born April 22 . 1752 Deceased Octr . 3 . 1752
2. Sarah Jackson Born . Augst 6 . 1753
3. Hannah Jackson Born, July 12 1755
4. Thomas Jackson Born, July 7 . 1757
5. Lucy. Jackson Borne July 10th . 1759
6. Daniel Jackson Borne Augst 24th 1761
7 William Jackson Born July . 14th 1763
8 Priscilla Jackson Born Ap: 13th 1765
9 Hannah Jackson Born Janry 16th 1767 Deceasd June 12th 1767
10 Lydia Jackson Born Ap: 8th 1768
11 Charles Jackson Born Mar. 1st . 1770

*"Drew 1735" has been interlined in a modern hand.

90

12 Rebecca Jackson Born Feby 19th 1772
13 Woodworth Jackson Born Feby 20th 1774
The Children of Benjamin Rider Junr & Bettey his Wife
1 Stephen Rider Born April 16th . 1750
2. Bettey Rider Born April 15 . 1752.
3. Mary Rider Born March 25 . 1754
4 Priscilla Rider Born Feb^y . 7 . 1756
5 Jesse Rider Born June . 8th 1758
The Children of Joseph Treeble, & Sarah his Wife
1 Joseph Treeble Born Novr 4th 1751 1751
2. Sarah . Treeble Born Octr 29th 1754
3 Lydia Treeble Born Sept 27th 1762
4 Anna Treeble Born Augst 10th 1765
5 Betsey Treeble Born July 26th 1770

(To be continued)

PLYMOUTH, MASS., VITAL RECORDS

(Continued from page 90)

[p. 219] 1752
Augst 18 A Purpose of Marriage, Between Thos Hinkley Junr of Barnstable, & Phebe Holmes of Plymouth
22 A purpose of Marriage, Between Robert Brown Esqr and Mrs Elizabeth Murdoch, Both of Plymouth
29 A purpose of Marriage, between Saml Totman of Plymouth, & Sarah Reding of Berkley
Sept. 16. A purpose of Marriage, between Silvanus Morton & Mary Stephens both of Plymouth
Octr 28 . A purpose of Marriage, Between Nathl Donham & Hannah King both of Plymouth
28 . A purpose of Marriage, Between M^r. Joseph Fulgham, & Mrs Lurania Clark, both of Plym^o
Novr 4 A Purpose of Marriage Between Lemuell Churchell & Abigail Rider both of Plymouth
A Purpose of Marriage, Between Saml Elles of Plym^o & Lydia Lobdell of Plymton
11 A Purpose of Marriage, Between Thomas Cornish & Elizabeth Burton, both of Plymouth
Decr 2 . A purpose of Marriage, between Joseph Lucas of Plym^o & Mary Rickard of Kingston.

1753
Jan^{ry} 27 . A purpose of Marriage Between William Bundick Pearson & Phebe Holmes, both of Plym^o
Feby. 10 A purpose of Marriage, Between Zacheus Bartlett & Margaret Barnes both of Plymouth
March 9 A purpose of Marriage, Between Ebenezer Ransom of Plimton, & Rebeckah Harlow of Plymouth
10 A Purpose of Marriage, Between Alpheus Witon of Plimton, & Ruth Grafton of Plymouth
10 . A purpose of Marriage, Between James Doten & Bathsheba Delano, both of Plymouth
April 7 A purpose of Marriage, Between M^r. Thomas Davis, & M^{rs}. Marcy Hedge both of Plym^o
14 A Purpose of Marrage Between Samuel Doten & Mary Cook Both of Plymouth
28 A purpose of Marriage, Between Cornelius Holmes Junr, & Lydia Drew both of Plymouth Spoke for p^r Geo: Holmes
28 A Purpose of [Marria]ge Between Ichabod Bartlett Junr & Hannah Rogers

[p. 220] 1753
May 5 A purpose of Marriage, Between M^r. David Tuner* Junr & Mrs Deborah Lothrop, both of Plymouth
5 A purpose of Marriage, Between Abner Sylvester, & Abigail Washburn, both of Plymouth
12 A purpose of Marriage, Between M^r. George Watson of Plym^o, & Mrs Elizabeth Oliver of Middleborough
June 23 . A. purpose of Marriage, Between Nathan Simmons of Kingston, and Lydia Holmes of Plymouth Spoke for by Joseph Delano
July 21 . A purpose of Marriage, Between Archippus Fuller of Plimton, & Mariah Churchell of Plymouth
21 . A purpose of Marriage, Between Robert Roberts, & Margaret Decort—both of Plymouth
28 . A purpose of Marriage, Between Zedekiah Tinkcom, & Marcy Tinkcom ye 2nd, Both of Plymouth
Augst. 4 . A purpose of Marriage Between Nathl Morton Junr. and Rebeckah Jackson, both of Plymouth
11 . A purpose of Marriage between Saml West & Elizabeth Rich, both of Plymouth.
25 . A purpose of Marriage, Between Benj^a Morton & Hannah Faunce ye 2nd, Both of Plymouth
Sep^t 1 . A Purpose of Marriage, Between Saml Ransom of Plimton, & Content Merryfield of Plymouth.
8 . A purpose of Marriage, Between Thomas Southworth of Freetown, (Resident in Plymouth) and Sarah Ward of Plymouth (Goddard promises pay)
Oct^b. 2 . A Purpose of Marriage, Between William Coomer of Duxborough, & Mabell Kempton of Plymouth Spoke for & paid, by Isaac Delano
Novr. 3 A purpose of Marriage Between William Weston of Plimton & Mary Westron of Plym^o. (Spoke for p^r Ruben Harlow)
3 A purpose of Marriage, between Isaac Little of Plym^o & Hannah Soule of Plimton
3 A Purpose of Marriage, Between Mr Saml Jackson & Mrs Experience Atwood, both of Plymouth
Novr 24 . A^i purpose of Marriage, Between Zacheus Holmes of Plymouth & Ruth Briant of Bridgwater

1753
Jan^{ry} 5 A purpose of Marriage, Between Robert Perrigo, & Susannah Holmes, both of Plym^o. (Spoke for by Ebenezer Churchell Junr)
12 A purpose of Marriage Between Benj^a Holmes of Dartmouth & Thankfull King of Plym^o

[p. 221] 1749
Oct 7 A Purpose of Marriage, Between John Harlow and Lydia Holmes, Both of Plymouth

*Sic. See original page 126 [Ante, 13 : 203] for children of David Turner, Jr., and Deborah.

Plymouth, Mass., Vital Records

7th A Purpose of Marriage, Between, William Serjeant and Mary Rider, Both of Plymouth

14 A Purpose of Marriage, Between Paul Doten, and Ruth Rider. both of Plymouth

14 A purpose of Marriage, Between, Benjamin Smith, and Sarah Tinkcom (Daughter of Mrs Marcy Tinkcom) Both of Plymouth

Novr 4 A Purpose of Marriage, Between James Doten, & Ruth Finney both of Plymouth.

Dec. 2 A purpose of Marriage Between Isaac Harlow, & Jerusha Finney both of Plymouth

9 A purpose of Marriage between Denis Sturmey, of Plymo. and Elizabeth Cook Late of Boston, Now Resident, in sd Plymo

16 A purpose of Marriage, between Reuben Bisbe of Plinton and Lydia Faunce of Plymouth

23 A purpose of Marriage, between Ebenezer Bartlett . and Abigail Finney, Both of Plymouth.

30th . A Purpose of Marriage, Between Solomon Bartlett, and Joanna Holmes, Both of Plymouth.

1749/5 A Purpose of Marriage, Between Simon Moses, & Sarah Adams, Indians, both of Plymouth.

1749/5
Febry 24 . A purpose of Marriage, Between, Mr William Thomas of Plymo., And Mrs Marcy Logan of Boston

March 3 . A purpose of Marriage, Between Robert Harlow Junr and Jean West . Both of Plymo

10 A purpose of Marriage between Seth Swift Junr and Desire Holmes, both of Plymouth

24 A purpose of Marriage, between Thomas Silvester, & Martha Tinkcom of Plymouth Both

31 A purpose of Marriage, between Wm Morton, & Mary Warren (Daughter of Joseph Warren) Both of Plymouth

April 21 A Purpose of Marriage, between Thomas Warren & Lydia Barnaby, both of Plymo

26 A Purpose of Marriage, between Ebenezer Doten of Plymton, and Marcy Whitten of Plymo

28 A Purpose of Marriage, between James Barnes, and Sarah Nash, both of Plymouth

May . 5 A purpose of Marriage, Between Samll Rogers, and Hannah Bartlett both of Plymo

5 A purpose of Marriage, Between Abraham Hicks a[nd] Bath[sheba] Donham, both of Plymouth

[p. 222] 1750
May 12 . A Purpose of Marriage, Between James Thomas of Plymouth, and Abigail Waterman of Plimpton

19 A purpose of Marriage, Between Richard Durfey [*] of Freetown, & Mrs Rebeckah Cole of Plymouth

*"Junr" has been crossed out here.

19 A purpose of Marriage, Between Mr Wm Davis, & Mrs Rebeckah Easdell, Both of Plymouth

June 9 . A purpose of Marriage, Between Mr Robert Davee of North Yarmouth, & Mrs Marcy Morton of Plymo

9 A purpose of Marriage, between Jacob Albertson, and Margaret Nicholson, both of Plymouth.

July 14 A purpose of Marriage, Between Jabez Cob, & Sarah Bartlett both of Plymouth.

14 A Purpose of Marriage, Between Jabez Goreham of Barnstable, and Mary Burbank of Plymouth

Augst 4 A Purpose of Marriage Between, Benjamin Cornish Junr, & Rhoda Swift Both of Plymouth.

Sepr 1 . A purpose of Marriage, between James Clark Junr of Plymouth and Susanna Hascoll of Rochester.

22 . A purpose of Marriage, between Samuell Shareman, and Experience Branch, both of Plymouth

29 A purpose of Marriage, between Benjamin King of Plymouth, and Betty Lovell of Kingston

Octr 13 A Purpose of Marriage, between Benjamin Bagnall, and Hannah Jackson, both of Plymouth

13th A Purpose of Marriage, between William Sutton, and Lydia Rider, both of Plymouth wch Wm Morton, Spoke for, & promises to pay

27 A purpose of Marriage . between Joseph Treble, and Sarah Howard, both of Plymouth

Decr 22 . A Purpose of Marriage, Between Mr Wm Bradford, of Warren, In ye Collony of Rhode Island : & Mrs Mary Le:Barron of Plymouth

Decr . A Purpose of Marriage, Between Mr Edward Curtis of Stoughton, & Mrs Sarah Freeman of Plymouth

1750/1
Febry 2 . A . Purpose of Marriage, between William Davis, and Sarah Dogget, both of Plymo

23 . A Purpose of Marriage, between John King Junr of Plimpton, and Hannah Pearce of Plymo

23 . A Purpose of Marriage, between Josiah Torrey & Marcy Atwood Both of Plymouth

Mar: 2 A purpose of Marriage, between Benja Bartlett Junr & Jean Elles, Both of Plymouth

[p. 221½] [A Purpose of Marrage Between Boston Negro Man Slave To Mr William Barnes & Hannah Hammond Indian Woman Both of Plymo April 4th 1747*]

1750/1
March 2 . A Purpose of Marriage Between James Drew, and Mary Churchell, both of Plymouth

9 A purpose of Marriage, Between John Lewen and Sarah Holmes both of Plymouth

*This entry has been crossed out. See original page 234.

168

April. 3 . A Purpose of Marriage Between Lemuell Barnes, & Sarah Le:Barron both of Plymouth
6 . A purpose of Marriage, between Thomas Jackson Junr and Sarah Tayler, both of Plymouth
6 . A purpose of Marriage, between David Gorham and Abigail Jackson, both of Plymouth
13 . A Purpose of Marriage, between Thomas Crandon & Ruth Howland, both of Plymouth, as John Lothrop Says Crandon of Plymo who Come for ye Publishment Recd 2 half pistereens.
May . 4 . A Purpose of Marriage, between Thomas Rogers Junr & Elizabeth Ward . Both of Plymouth
18 . A Purpose of Marriage, between Daniel Diman, and Elizabeth Morton, Both of Plymouth
June 1 . A Purpose of Marriage, between David Leach of Bridgwater, and Hannah Newcomb of Plymouth (ye Publishment Spoke for ₱ Isaac Little)
June 19th Sent Leach ye Cirtificate ₱ Joseph Harvey.
22 A purpose of Marriage, Between Saml Swift Junr of Plymo, and Thankfull Ashley of Rochester.
29 A purpose of Marriage, between Eliphalet Bradford of Plymouth, and Hannah Prince of Duxborough
29 A purpose of Marriage Between Francis Howard, & Elizabeth Curtis The Second, Both of Plymouth
July . 27 A purpose of Marriage, Between, Seth Barnes Junr, and Hannah Williams, Both of Plymouth
Sept. 7 A purpose of Marriage, Between Cornelius Morrey & Sarah Johnson, both of Plymouth
7 A Purpose of Marriage, Between Mr John Torrey of Plymouth, and Mrs Mary Tilley of Boston
21 A purpose of Marriage, between John Morrey & Jerusha Swift, Both of Plymouth
21 A Purpose of Marriage, Between Mr Lemuel Drew, and Mrs Priscilla Warren (Daughter of Mr Joseph Warren) Both of Plymouth
[p. 222½] 1751
Sept. 28 . A purpose of Marriage, Between Walter Rich & Experience Totman, both of Plymouth
Octr 12 A Purpose of Marriage, between Saml Lanman of Plymouth, & Elizabeth Elles of Middleborough
26 A purpose of Marriage Between, Moses Sachamus & Sarah Nummock, both of Plymouth Indians.
Decr 7th A Purpose of Marriage, Between Mr Nathl Crosman of Taunton & Mrs Esther Hatch of Plymouth
7th A purpose of marriage, Between David Davis of Plymo, & Sarah Cousins, of Edgertown, Martha's Vineyard
13th A purpose of Marriage, Between Phinelas Swift of Plymouth, and Rebeckah Phillips of Sandwich.

169

1752
Janry A Purpose of Marriage Between Jonathan Holmes of Plymouth
A Purpose of Marriage, Between William Gammons & fear Curtis, both of Plymouth
Mar. 7 . A purpose of Marriage, Between Job Holmes of Plymo and Mehetabell Stewart of Sandwich
14 . A purpose of Marriage, Between Josiah Gibbs of Sandwich and Marcy Cornish of Plymouth
14 . A purpose of Marriage, Between James Howard of Plymouth, And Marcy Warren of Middleborough
21 A purpose of Marriage, Between Thomas Sears of Plymouth, and Mehetabel Fish of Sandwich
April 11 . A Purpose of Marriage, between Isaac Tinkcom & Re-member Cooper, both of Plymouth
May 23 . A purpose of Marriage, Between Joshua Totman and Joanna Scarret, both of Plymouth
30 . A purpose of Marriage, between William Bartlett & Mary Bartlett, both of Plymo
June 13 A purpose of marriage, Between Jabez Harlow & Experience Churchell Both of Plymo
18 A purpose of Marriage, Between Joseph Rider of Province Town, and Thankfull Polden of Plymouth
23 . A purpose of Marriage, Between Nathl Williams & Mary Vincent, both of Plymouth
24 A purpose of Marriage, Between Abijah Fisher of Norton, and Mary Washburn of Plymouth
July 25 A purpose of Marriage, Between John Swift of Sandwich, and Desire Swift of Plymouth
Augst 1 A purpose of Marriage, Between John Phillips, and Lydia Morton ye Second, Both of Plymouth
[p. 223] Marriages Solemnized By ye Revd Mr Jacob Bacon of Plymouth

1749
May 29 . James Crandon, & Sarah Delano, both of Plymouth
July 4 . Reuben Chandler of Duxboro, & Hannah Tilson of Plymo.
Octr. 26 . William Serjeant, & Mary Rider, both of Plymo.
Novr. 2 . Paul Doten, & Ruth Rider, both of Plymo.
13 . Benjamin Smith, & Sarah Tinkcom, both of Plymo.
1749/5
Janry. 4 . Isaac Harlow & Jerusha Finney, both of Plymo.
Febry. 8 . Jabez Gibbs of Sandwich & Susanna Cornish, of Plymo.
March 27 . Robert Harlow Junr, & Jean West both of Plymo.
29 . Seth Swift Junr & Desire Holmes, both of Plymo.
April 23 . Thomas Silvester & Martha Tinkcom, both of Plymo.
24 . James Doten, & Ruth Finney, both of Plymo.
26 . Reuben Bisbe & Lydia Faunce, both of Plymo
26 . Solomon Bartlett & Joanna Holmes, both of Plymo.
Recd ye Certificates . May 28th 1752. All Marryed in Plymo

June 11 . James Barnes & Sarah Nash, both of Plym° Marryed at Plym°
28 . Dennis Sturmey, & Elizabeth Cook both of Plym° Marry'd at D°
Sep.r 25 . Thomas Warren, & Lydia Barnaby, both of Plym° Marry'd at D°
Gave a List to y.e Clerk of y.e Sessions June 27 . 1757
Rec'd June 15 . 1752 . M.r Bacons List as below

1751
June 20 . Thomas Crandon & Ruth Howland, both of Plym°, Marry'd at Ply°
27 Benj.a Bartlett Jun.r & Jean Elles, both of Plym°, Marry'd at Plym°
Oct.r 21 . Daniel Diman, & Eliz.a Morton, both of Plym° Marry'd at Plym°

1750/1
Feb.ry 20 . William Davis, & Sarah Dogget, both of P[l]ym° Marryed at Plym°

is feb.ry 20 . 1750/1
1752 . Rec'd June 6 . 1753 . M.r Bacons List, as below
April 3 . Nath.l Crosman of Taunton, & Esther Hatch of Plym°.
16 . Josiah Gibbs of Sandwich, & Marcy Cornish of . Plym°.
May 4 . Isaac Tinkcom, & Remembrance Cooper, both of Plym°.
July 28 . W.m Bartlett, & Mary Bartlett, both of Plym°
Nov.r 23 . Lemuel Churchill, & Abigail Rider, both of Plym°
Dec.r 7 . Thomas Cornish, & Elizabeth Burton, both of Plym°.

1753
April 26 . James Doten, & Bathsheba Delano, both of Plym°.
Gave in a List To y.e Clerk of the Sessions, July y.e 8th 1757 All Marryed at Plym°.

[p. 224] Marriages Solemnized, by the Rev.d M.r Nath.l Leonard

1749/5
Feb.ry . 15th Simon Moses, & Sarah Adams Indians, both of Plym° Marry'd at Plym°

May 10 . William Morton, & Mary Warren Daughter of Joseph Warren both of Plym°. Ditto
June 12 . Ebenezer Doten of Plimpton, and Marcy Whitten of Plymouth, Marryed at Plymouth.
July 19 . Jacob Albertson, & Margaret Nicholson, both of Plym°.
Aug.t 30 . Richard Durfey of Freetown, & Rebeckah Cole of Plymouth, Marryed at Plymouth
Oct.r 16 . Benjamin King of Plymouth, & Betty Lovell of Kingston Marryed at Plymouth.
25 . Sam.l Rogers, & Hannah Bartlett, both of Plym° Marry'd at Plym°.
Nov.r 8 . Sam.l Shareman, & Experience Branch, both of Plym° Marry'd at Plymouth
15 . Jabez Goreham of Barnstable, & Mary Burbank of Plymouth, Marryed at Plymouth
16 . Jabez Cobb, & Sarah Bartlett . both of Plym° Marry'd at Plym°

1750/1
Jan.ry 31 . Edward Curtis of Stoughton, & Sarah Freeman of Plymouth, Marryed at Plym°
Rec'd M.r Leonards List of Marryages Feb.ry 29 . 1752 Viz

March 22 . William Bradford of Warren, In Rhode Island Colony & Mary Le:Barron of Plym°, Marry'd at Plymouth
April . 4 . James Drew & Mary Churchell, both of Plym°, Marry'd at Plym°.
4 Joseph Trible & Sarah Howard, both of Plym°, Marry'd at Plym°.
11 William Sutton & Lydia Rider Both of Plym° . Marry'd at Plym°
17 Lemuel Barnes & Sarah Le:Barron Both of Plym° . Marry'd at Plym°
25 John King Jun.r of Plimton & Hannah Peirce of Plymouth Marryed at Plymouth
29 Benjamin Bagnall & Hannah Jackson Both of Plym° Marry'd at Plym°
May . 20 . Thomas Jackson Jun.r & Sarah Taylor Both of Plym° Marry'd at Plym°
July . 1 David Gorham & Abigail Jackson Both of Plym° Marry'd at Plym°
July .11 Abraham Hicks & Barshabah Donham Both of Plym° Marry'd at Plym°
Octob.r 25 John Lewen & Sarah Holmes Both of Plym° Marry'd at Plym°
31 Thomas Rogers Jun.r & Elizabeth Ward Both of Plym° Marry'd at Plym°
Nov.r 4 Lemuel Drew & Prisilla Warren Both of Plym° Marry'd at Plym°
19 Walter Rich & Experance Totman Both of Plym° Marry'd at Plym°
28 Moses Sachamus & Sarah Nummock Indiens Both of Plym° Marryed at Plymouth
Oct.r 17 Francis Howard & Elizabeth Curtis, both of Plymouth, Maryed at Plymouth

[p. 225] Marriages Solemnized by y.e Reverend M.r Thomas Frink of Plymouth.

1744
Dec.r 6 . Sam.l Nicholls Nelson, & Elizabeth Warren both of Plym°. Marryed at Plymouth.
Gave List to Clerk of y.e Sessions May 23 . 1745.
1745
Oct.r 3 Daniel Robin & Sarah Sanders Indians of Plymouth Were marryed at Plym° Oct.r 3rd 1745
Oct.r 4 'Thomas Ling and Elizabeth Mackfun Both of Plym° marryed at Plym° Oct.r 4th 1745
Oct.r 31 Amariah Churchell and Elizabeth Sylvester Both of Plym° marryed at Plym° Oct.r 31th 1745

172

1745/6
Febry 25. Thomas Burge, and Patience Doty, both of Plymo, Marryed at Plymo, Febry 25. 1745/6.
Gave List to ye Clerk of ye Sessions. Mar: 12 1745/6
May 5th Nathll Hatch & Ruth Rider, both of Plymouth, Marryed at Plymouth, May 5th 1746.
30 Amaziah Harlow & Lois Doten both of Plymo. Marryed at Plymouth May 30th 1746
July 24. Ezekiel Morton, & Abigail Morton, both of Plymo, Marryed at Plymouth, July 24th 1746
℣ List Recd. Febry 5 Viz
Octr. 21. Thomas Swift Junr, & Rebeckah Clark, both of Plymo Marryed at Plymo Octr 21. 1746
Novr. 3 Benjamin Churchell, & Ruth Delano, both of Plymo. Marryed at Plymo, Novr. 3. 1746.
20. Peres Tilson, & Elizabeth Doty, both of Plymo. Matryd at Plymo. Novr. 20th 1746

1746/7
Janry. 8 Doughty Randall, of Scittuate, & Elizabeth Tilson of Plymo, Marryed at Plymo. Janry 8th 1746.
Febry. 5. Jacob Tinkcom, & Lydia Donham, both of Plymo. Marryed at Plymo, Febry 5th 1746
Gave List To ye Clerk of ye Sessions, Aprill 11th 1747.

(To be continued)

PLYMOUTH, MASS., VITAL RECORDS

(Continued from page 172)

[p. 226] Marriages, Solemnized, By yᵉ Revᵈ Mʳ Thos Frink Continued,

1747 June 3 . Mʳ William Greenleaf of Boston, & Mʳˢ Mary Brown of Plymᵒ, Marryᵈ at Plymᵒ

Oct. 13 . Lemuell Churchell, And Lydia Silvester Both of Plymᵈ, Marryed at Plymouth

Novʳ 26 Joseph Bramhall & Sarah Tillson Both of Plymᵒ Marryᵈ at Plymouth

1747/8 March 8 Elkanah Churchell Junʳ & Susannah Bartlett Both of Plymᵒ Marryᵈ att Plymᵒ

Gave List to yᵉ Clerk of yᵉ Sessions . Marː 17ᵗʰ 1747/8

March 24ᵗʰ 1747/8 . Lemuell Doten, and Jane Fish, Both of Plymᵒ Marryed at Plymouth

Marː 31 . Thomas Hinkley, & Elizabeth Decoster, Both of Plymouth, Marryed at Plymouth

Gave in a List to yᵉ Clerk of yᵉ Sessions July yᵉ 8ᵗʰ 1757

Marriages Solemnized by Edward Winslow Esqʳ of Plymᵒ Justice of the Peace

1751 Oct 17ᵗʰ Viz John Morrey, and Jerusha Swift, both of Plymouth Marryᵈ at Plymouth Octʳ . 17ᵗʰ 1751.

Oct. 17ᵗʰ Cornelius Morrey, and Sarah Johnson, both of Plymouth Marryed at Plymᵒ Octʳ 17ᵗʰ 1751

1757 July yᵉ 8ᵗʰ Gave A List In, to the Clerk of the Sessions

[p. 227] Marriages Consummated By Samˡ Bartlett Esqʳ Justice of The peace . For yᵉ County of Plymᵒ

1735 . Janʳʸ 21 or 22 James Wood of Plymouth . & Deborah Fish of Plymᵒ at Plymouth.

1738 June 13 Simeon Totman of Plymᵒ; & Sarah Littlejohn of Plymᵒ at Plymouth

29 Willᵐ Clark, of Plymᵒ; & Experience Doty of Plymᵒ at Plymouth

Augˢᵗ 3 Edward Doten of Plymᵒ; & Phebe Phinney, of Plymᵒ at Plymouth

Sepᵗ 5 William Harlow of Plymᵒ or Bridgwater & Hannah Bartlett of Plymᵒ was Marryed at Plymᵒ

1738/9 Marː 21 or 22 Joshua Swift of Sandwich . & Jane Faunce of Plymᵒ. Was Marryed at Plymᵒ.

May 8 David Morton of Plymᵒ. & Rebeckah Finney of Plymᵒ. at Plymouth

1740 Augˢᵗ 18 John Jones of Plymᵒ & Sarah Barnes of Dᵒ at Plymouth

1741 April 16 . Edwᵈ Sparrow, of Plymᵒ. & Jerusha Bradford of Dᵒ at Plymouth

June 30 . Mʳ Ezra Whitmarsh of Plymᵒ, & Mʳˢ Dorothy Gardner, of Dᵒ at Plymᵒ

July 3 Jonathan Sanders of Wareham . & Elizᵃ Tinkcom of Plymᵒ was Marryed at Plymᵒ.

1742 May 13 William Wood of Plymᵒ. & Elizᵃ Finney of Dᵒ at Plymouth

19 Epᵐ Holmes, of Plymᵒ. & Sarah Finney of Dᵒ at Plymᵒ.

1742/3 . Marː 3 Peter West of Kingston . & Lydia Keen of Kingston Was Marryed at Plymᵒ.

14 Gideon Gifford of Rochester, & Lois Jackson of Plymᵒ. Maryed at Plymᵒ

July 7 Silvanus Bartlett of Plymᵒ & Martha Waite of Plymᵒ at Plymᵒ

1744 May 7 Seth Nicholson of Harwich, & Margaret Moore of Plymo Marryᵈ at Plymᵒ.

29 Thomas Williams & Hannah Bagnall, both of Plymᵒ Marryed at Plymouth.

Gave List to Clerk of yᵉ Sessions these 18 Marriages

1745 Septʳ 26 Jacob Decoster, & Elizabeth Cole both of Plymᵒ. Marryed at Plymouth . Gave List To yᵉ Clerk of Sessions marː 12ᵗʰ

1746 April 7 Joshua Bemon, & Sarah Shurtleff, both of Middleboro Marryed at Middleboro

Gave List To yᵉ Clerk of yᵉ Sessions, Apː 11 . 1747.

[p. 228] Marriages Consummated by Samˡ Bartlett Esqʳ Continued.

1748 July 13ᵗʰ . Daniel Peak Resident in Plymᵒ. & Rhoda Beal, of Plymᵒ. Marryᵈ at Plymᵒ. Gave List to yᵉ Clerk of yᵉ Sessions July yᵉ 8ᵗʰ 1757

1752 Septʳ 21 . John Swift of Sandwich, & Desire Swift of Plymᵒ Marryed in Plymouth.

Octʳ 18 . John Phillips, and Lydia Morton yᵉ Second, both of Plymouth, Marryᵈ at Plymouth

1753 March 30 William Bundick Pearson, and Phebe Holmes, both of Plymouth, Marryed at Plymouth

Octʳ 2 . Samuell Ransom of Plimton, & Content Merryfield of Plymouth, Marryed at Plymouth

Novʳ 5 . Alpheus Witon of Plimton, & Ruth Grafton, of Plymouth, Marryed at Plymouth

1755 May 28 . Samˡ Crow of Providence In the Collony of Rhode Island, & Hannah Rider of Plymᵒ Marryᵈ at Plymouth

1756 . Sepᵗ 2 . Quosh, Negro Man, Servant, To Doctor Lazarus Leꞏ Barron, & Phillis Negro Woman, Servant to Capᵗ Theophilus Cotton, Both of Plymᵒ. Marryed at Plymouth

1757 July yᵉ 8ᵗʰ Gave A List In, to the Clerk of the Sessions . 7 Marriages

1758 April 20ᵗʰ Silvanus Howes, & Thankfull Rider, Both of Plymᵒ Marryed at Plymouth.

1759 April 29 . John Totman & Elizabeth Harlow, Both of Plymouth Marryed —— at Plymouth.

Dᵈᵈ List to yᵉ Clerk of yᵉ Sessions . May 17ᵗʰ 1759 . 2 Marriages

(To be continued)

THE MAYFLOWER DESCENDANT

A QUARTERLY MAGAZINE OF PILGRIM GENEALOGY AND HISTORY

VOLUME XVII

1915

PUBLISHED BY THE
MASSACHUSETTS SOCIETY OF MAYFLOWER DESCENDANTS
BOSTON

PLYMOUTH, MASS., VITAL RECORDS

TRANSCRIBED BY THE EDITOR

(Continued from Vol. XVI, p. 255)

[p. 229] Marriages Consummated, by Josiah Cotton Esqr Justice of ye peace, for ye County of Plym^o

1743 . June 7 . Cornelius Holmes of Plym^o, To Marcy Doten of Plym^o. Marryed at Plym^o.

Gave List to Clerk of ye Sessions

1749 Sept 14 Thomas Sawyer, and Margaret Cotton both of Plymouth Marry^d at Plymouth

Gave in a List, To ye Clerk of ye Sessions . July ye 8th 1757.

Marriages Solemnized by Thomas Foster Esqr of Plym^o., One of his Maj^{tys} Justices of Peace, for ye County of Plym^o

1748/9 Feb^{ry} 9 James Weston of Middleborough, and Abigail Donham of Plymouth

Gave in a List of ye Same, To ye Clerk of ye Sessions July ye 8th 1757

1757 Novr 4 . Benjamin Smith & Sarah Doten . Both . of . Plymouth Marry^d at . Plymouth

Nov^{br} . 17th Benjamin Goodwin of Boston, & Hannah Le:Barron of Plymouth, Marryed at Plymouth,

Nov^{br} 21 . Capt. Josiah Sturtevant Junr of Hallifax, & Mrs Lois Foster of Plym^o. Marryed at Plymouth

D^{dd} List to ye Clerk of ye Sessions, wth ye Entrys in ye 2nd Books May 17th 1759

1754 . Marriages Solemnized by the Revd Mr Elijah Packard Pastor of ye 2nd Precinct, in ye Town Plymouth,

April . 3 . Simon Mahomman, & Phebe Robbens, Indians both of Plym^o

April 11 . Zacheus Holmes, of Plymouth, And Ruth Bryant, Resident In Plymouth

June 11 . Seth Barnes Junr & Elizabeth Rider, both of Plymo
Septr 1 . Job Brewster of Duxboro, & Elizabeth Elles of Plymo all ye above, Marryed In Plymouth
1756 May 20 . Thomas Cornish & Ann . Bates Both . of . Plymo Marryd at Plymouth
Gave in List, To ye Clerk of ye Sessions July ye 8th 1757
[p. 230] Marriages Consummated By the Revd Mr Jonathan Elles of Plymouth.
1740 August 24th Ebenezer Harlow & Meriah Morey Both of Plymo marryed at Plymouth
Novr 13 Nathaniel Morton & mary Elles Both of Plymo marryed at Plymo
Febry 19 Jonathan Tobey of Sandwich & Deborah Swift of Plymo marryed at Plymo.
1742 march 18 Thomas Clark & Ruth Morton Both of Plymo marryed at Do
April 22 Jonathan Harlow & Sarah Holmes Both of Plymo marryed at Do
1743 Augst 11 Josiah Morton the Third & Experience Elles Both of Plymo marryd at Do
Septr 29 Edwd Tinkcom of Kingston & Lydia Rider of Plymo marryd at Plymo
1744 March 11 Joseph Croswell of Groton & Jerusha Bartlett of Plymo Marryd at Do
1743 Decr 14 Eleazer Holmes Junr & Esther Elles Both of Plymo Marryd at Do
1744 Novr 29 Joslin Cepet & Joannah Cepet Indians Both of Plymo marryd at Do
1745 April 11 Ebenezer Holmes ye 3rd & Susannah Holmes Both of Plymo marryd at Do
1744 Augst. 5 William Fish & marcy Morrey Both of Plymo marryd at Do
Gave List to ye Clerk of ye Sessions . Mar: 12 . 1745/6
1746 Novr. 11 . John Thomas Junr & Abigail Clark, Both of Plymo. Marryd at Plymo.
13 Willm Churchell, & Susannah Clark, Both of Plymo. Marryd at Do
1747 Augst 6 . James Clerk, Junr & Hannah Swift, Both of Plymo Marryd @ Do
1748 April 12 . Saml Churchell of Plymton, & Marcy Elles of Plymo Marryd at Plymouth.
July 5 . Mr Jonathan Parker Pastor of a Church at Plimpton, & & Mrs Lydia Bartlett of Plymo. Marryd at Plymouth
Novr 2 . Jeremiah Squib, Mollato of Plymo, & Mary Scoke Indian Woman of Plymo. Marryed at Plymo.
10 . Abner Silvester & Jedidah Harlow, both of Plymo Marryed at Plymouth.
1749 March 30 . Thomas Ewer of Barnestable & Lydia Harlow of Plymo Marryd at Plymo

May . 6 Benjamin Rider Junr & Betsey Bartlett Both of Plymo Marryd at Plymo
Sept 15 . Robert Harlow & Remembrance . Wetherhead . Both of Plymo. Marryd at Plymouth
Octr. 26 Zacheus Mendall of . Sandwich & Mary Swift . of Plymo. Marryd at Plymouth
Gave in List, To ye Clerk of ye Sessions . July ye 8th 1757
[p. 231] Marriages Consummated, By the Revd Mr Nathaniel Leonard of Plymo
1745 April 11 Elkanah Shaw of Middleborough & Johannah King of Plymo marryed at Plymo.
25 Ebenezer Donham of Plympton & Phebe Luces of . Plymo mard at Plymo
July 28 Jirah Fish of Sandwich & Hannah Finney of Plymo Marryd at Do
August 15 Caleb Sharmon & Rebeckah Ryder Both of Plymo marryd at Do
Septr 10 Azariah Whitten of Plympt & Rebeckah Holmes of Plymo marryd at Do
23 Joseph Churchell & mariah Ryder Both of Plymo marryd at Do
1745/6 Febry 10 Stephen Doten & Hannah Bartlett Both of Plymo marryd at Do
March 6 Benja Deleno of Doxboro & Lydia Jackson of Plymo marryd at Do
Gave List to ye Clerk, of ye Sessions, March 12 . 1745/6.
1746 April 28 Lemuell Holmes & Abigail Rider Both of Plymo marryed at Plymo
June 19 John Howard & Eunice Curtis Both of Plymo marryd at Do
July 3 Jabez Mendal of Plympton & maria Churchell of Plymo marryd at Do
29 James Watkins & Jerusha Rider Both of Plymo marryd at Do
August 28 William Jerman & Eleoner Thomas Both of Plymo marryd at Do
Octr 28 Benja Eaton of Kingston & Mary Tinkcom of Plymo Marryd at Do
Novr 6 Josiah Bradford & Hannah Rider Both of Plymo marryd at Do
24 Nathaniel Bradford & Sarah Spooner Both of Plymo Marryd at Ditto
Decr 11 James Howard Junr & Thankfull Branch Both of Plymo Marryd at Do
15 Samuell Harlow & Marcy Bradford Both of Plymo Marryd at Do
25 Nathaniel Goodwin & Lydia LeBarron Both of Plymo marryd at Do
1746/7 Janry 1 Thomas Patison & Susannah Beale . Both of . Plymo Marryd at Do
22 Josiah Carver Junr & Jerusha Sparrow Both of Plymo Marryd at Do
27 Edward Wright & Elizabeth Decoster Both of Plymo Marryd at Do

Plymouth, Mass., Vital Records — 6

March 19 Isaac Morton & Meriah Lewen Both of Plym⁰ Marry⁴ at D⁰

Gave List To y⁴ Clerk of y⁴ Sessions, Aprill 11th 1747.

1747 April 23rd Joseph LeBarron & m⁹ Sarah Leonard Both of Plym⁰ marry⁴ at Plym⁰

May 14 M⁸ Nath⁺ll Torrey & m⁸ Anne Leonard Both of Plym⁰ Marry⁴ at Plym⁰

July 16 Edward Stephens Jun⁸ & Phebe Harlow Both of Plym⁰ marry⁴ at Plym⁰

Sept 24 Jonathan Samson & Sarah Drew Both of Plym⁰ marry⁴ at Plym⁰

Oct⁸ 29 Eleazer Stephens & Sarah Silvester Both of Plym⁰ marry⁴ at Plym⁰

Nov⁸ 5 m⁸ Th⁸ Foster Jun⁸ & m⁸ Marcy Wetherell Both of Plym⁰ marry⁴ at D⁰

14 Job Morton & mary Barnes Both of Plym⁰ Marry⁴ at Plym⁰

16 Samuell Morton & Ruth Rogers Both of Plym⁰ Marry⁴ at Plym⁰

[p. 232] Marriages Consumated By the Rev⁴ M⁸ Nathaniel Leonard of Plym⁰ Continued

1747 Nov⁸ 16 Josiah Johnson & Patience Faunce Both of Plym⁰ marry⁴ at Plym⁰

Nov⁸ 23 Ebenezer Churchill & marcy Branch Both of Plym⁰ marry⁴ at Plym⁰

Dec⁸ 10th Guiney & Hagar (Negros) Ware marry⁴ at Plym⁰ Dec⁸ 10th 1747.

Gave List To the Clerk of y⁴ Sessions, March 16th 1747/8.*

Gave List to y⁴ Clerk, of y⁴ Sessions, March 17th 1747/8.*

1748 April 19th Zephaniah Morton, & Jerusha Donham, Both of Plym⁰ Marry⁴ at Plym⁰

21st M⁸ David Stockbridge of Hanover, & m⁸ Jean Reed of Plym⁰ Marryed at Plymouth.

May 5th M⁸ Benjamin Lothrop of Kingston, and m⁸ Deborah Thomas of Plym⁰ Marryed at Plymouth.

12th M⁸ Isaac Thomas, & M⁸ Mary Hatch, Both of Plym⁰, Marry⁴ at Plym⁰

June 30th Joseph Pearce & Rebeckah Eames, Both of Plym⁰, Marry⁴ at Plym⁰

July 11th Timothy Fales Esq⁸ of Bristoll, & M⁸ Elizabeth Thomas, of Plymouth, Marryed at Plymouth.

14th John Rickard, & Bathshua Morton, Both of Plym⁰, Marry⁴ at Plym⁰

Oct⁸ 10th Sam⁺ll Marshall Jun⁸ and Sussannah Bartlett, both of Plym⁰. Marryed at Plymouth.

25th Ichabod Holmes, & Rebeckah Elles, Both of Plym⁰, Marry⁴ at Plym⁰

Oct⁸ 13 Solomon Atwood, & Lydia Cushman, Both of Plym⁰ Marry⁴ at Plym⁰

*Sic.

Plymouth, Mass., Vital Records — 7

31st James Donham, & Elizabeth Wood, Both of Plym⁰, Marry⁴ at Plym⁰.

Nov⁸ 3. Silas Morton, & Martha Morton, both of Plym⁰. Marry⁴ at Plym⁰.

24th Samuell Bartlett Esq⁸ & M⁸ Elizabeth Wethrell Both of Plym⁰ Marryed at Plymouth.

Dec⁸ 29 Moses Barrows Jun⁸ of Plimpton, To Deborah Totman, of Plym⁰, Marryed at Plymouth.

1748/9 Jan⁸⁸ 5. Ebenezer Doggett, & Elizabeth Brace, both of Plym⁰. Marry⁴ at Plym⁰.

19 Stephen Samson & Abigail Morton, both of Plym⁰, Marry⁴ at Plym⁰.

Mar. 15. William Foster, & Joannah Lanman, both of Plym⁰, Marry⁴ at Plym⁰.

20th Martin Wright, & Sarah Beale, both of Plym⁰ Marryed at Plym⁰.

21st Jonathan Darling, & Martha Bramhall, both of Plym⁰ Marry⁴ at Plym⁰.

Sep⁸ 14. John Churchill, & Sarah Cole both of Plym⁰ Marry⁴ at Plym⁰.

Oct⁸ 5 Jonathan Morton, & Rebeckah Wethrell, both of Plym⁰ Marry⁴ at Plym⁰.

12th Jeremiah Holmes, & Phebe Crymble, both of Plym⁰ Marry⁴ at Plym⁰.

13th Scipio Negro man belonging to Deacon Torrey, & Hager negro Woman, belongs to Doct⁸ Lazarus Le:Barron. Marry⁴ at Plym⁰.

26th John Harlow & Lydia Holmes both of Plym⁰ marryed at Plym⁰.

1749/5 Ebenez⁸ Bartlett & Abigail Finney Both of Plym⁰, Marryed at Plymouth January 11th 1749/50*]

[p. 233] 1748. Nov⁸ 12th A Purpose of Marriage, Between Martin Wright, and Sarah Beale Both of Plymouth.

Dec⁸ 10th A Purpose of Marriage, Between Ebenezer Dogget, and Elizabeth Brace. Both of Plym⁰

24th A Purpose of Marriage, Between, Stephen Samson and Abigail Morton, Both of Plym⁰

1748/9 Jan⁸⁸ 21 A Purpose of Marriage, Between Thomas Ewer of Barnstable, & Lydia Harlow of Plym⁰.

21st A Purpose of Marriage, Between James Weston of Middleboro and Abigail Donham of Plymouth.

Feb⁸⁸ 18. A Purpose of Marriage, Between William Foster & Joannah Lanman, Both of Plymouth.

25 A Purpose of Marriage, Between, Jonathan Darling, & Martha Bramhall, Both of Plymouth.

Mar. 4 A purpose of Marriage, between Joseph Ashley Jun⁸ of Rochester, and Elizabeth Swift of Plym⁰

11. A purpose of Marriage, between M⁸ Levi Potter, of Bristoll, and M⁸ Hannah Bradford of Plym⁰

*See Mayflower Descendant, Volume XVI, p. 166.

18 A Purpose of Marriage Between Jonathan Morton, & Rebeckah Wethrell Junr, Both of Plym^o

Ap: 22 James Crandon, & Sarah Delano, both of Plymouth, Published at Plymouth.

29th . A Purpose of Marriage, Between Jeremiah Holmes, & Phebe Crymble both of Plymouth

May 13th . A Purpose of Marriage, Between, Mr Benjamin Rider Junr & Mrs Elizabeth Bartlett Both of Plym^o.

13th . A purpose of Marriage, Between Zacheus Mendall of Sandwich and Mary Swift of Plymouth

15th A Purpose of Marriage, Between The Revd Mr Jacob Bacon of Plym^o, & Mrs Mary Wood of Boxford.

June 10th A Purpose of Marriage, Between, Reuben Chandler, of Duxborough, And Hannah Tilson of Plymouth

Aug^st 5 A Purpose of Marriage, Between, Mr John Churchill, & Mrs Sarah Cole Both of Plym^o

12 . A purpose of Marriage between, Robert Harlow, & Remember Wethred Both of Plym^o

Sep^t 23rd Scipio Negro Servant to Deacon Haviland. Torrey and Hagar negro Servt to Doctr. Laz^s Le:Barron Both of Plymouth, published at Plymouth.

30th A purpose of Marriage, Between John May of Plymouth & Anna King of Plimton.

Octr. 6 A Purpose of Marriage Between Jabez Gibbs of Sandwich, & Susannah Cornish of Plym^o

[p. 234] 1746/7 Feb^ry 21 A purpose of Marriage, Between Isaac Morton and Mariah Lewen, both of Plymouth

April 4 . A purpose of Marriage, between Boston Negro Slave to Mr Wm Barnes, and Hannah Hammond Indian woman . Both of Plym^o.

8 A Purpose of Marriage, between Eleazer Robbens of Plimpton, & Rebeckah Jackson of Plym^o

11th A Purpose of Marriage, between Edwd Stephens Junr, & Phebe Harlow, both of Plym^o.

11th A purpose of Marriage, between Nathl Torrey, & Anne Leonard, both of Plym^o

May 2 A purpose of Marriage, Between Jonathan Samson, & Sarah Drew, Both of Plymouth

2 A Purpose of Marriage, Between, Mr Will Greenleaf of Boston, & Mrs Mary Brown of Plymouth

9th . A Purpose of Marriage, Between Thomas Hinkley Junr of Harwich, & Jane Fish of Plymouth

June 27 . A Purpose of Marriage, Between Lemuell Churchill, & Lydia Silvester, Both of Plym^o

July 18 . A Purpose of Marriage, Between Josiah Johnson, & Patience Faunce, both of Plym^o.

Aug^st 15. Thomas Bumpas of Plym^o, and Marcy Stewart of Barnstable, This day Published ; in order for Marriage

15th A Purpose of Marriage, Between Rueben Carver of Marshfield, & Phebe Holmes of Plymouth

Sep^t 12th A Purpose, of Marriage, Between Wm Thoma[s] Junr of Plymouth ; & Susannah Howland of Marshfield.

19th A Purpose of Marriage, Between Joseph Bramhall & Sarah Tilson, Both of Plymouth

26th A Purpose of Marriage, Between Mr Thomas Foster Junr, & m^rs Marcy Wethrell, Both of Plymouth

Octr 3 . A purpose of Marriage, Between Job Morton, & Mary Barnes Both of Plym^o

17 A purpose of Marriage, Between Ebenezer Churchell & Marcy Branch, both of Plym^o

[p. 235] Octr 31 1747 A Purpose of Marriage Between Mr Thomas Torrey of Plymouth, and Mrs Abigail Thomas of Pembrook

Novr 7 . A Purpose of Marriage, Between Saml Bartlett of Plymouth Esqr And Mrs Abigail Magoun, of Pembrook *made Void by Mutuall Consent**

7 . A Purpose of Marriage, Between Seth Barnes Junr of Plym^o. and Hannah Delano of Rochester.

Novr 14 A Purpose of Marriage Between Ginney Negro . Belonging To Joshua Drew and Hager Negro Belonging To ye Revd Mr Nathaniel Leonard . Both of Plym^o

A Purpose of Marriage In October, Between Sam^ll Morton, & Ruth Rogers, Both of Plymouth.

21 A Purpose of Marriage Between Elk^a Churchell Junr, & Susannah Bartlett Both of Plym^o.

28 . Stephen Ca[l]ey of Plym^o, & Catherine Flanega of Chatham, Published

Decr 26 . A purpose of Marriage, Between Amos Howes of Plym^o, & Sarah Ripley of Duxborough.

1747/8 Jan^ry 3 . A Purpose of Marriage Between Mr Sam^ll Churchell of Plimpton, & Mrs Mary Elles of Plymouth.

5th A purpose of Marriage, between Joseph Pearce & Rebeckah Eames, Both of Plymouth

Feb^ry 6th A Purpose of Marriage, Between Zephaniah Morton, & Jerusha Donham, both of Plym^o

27 a Purpose of Marriage Between Thomas Hinkley & Elizbeth Decoster Both of Plym^o

27th A Purpose of Marriage, Between, Lemuell Doten and Jean Fish, Both of Plymouth.

Mar^r 12 : A Purpose of Marriage, Between Mr David Stockbridge of Hanrover, And Mrs Jean Reed of Plymouth

Apr 8 A Purpose of Marrige Between Mr Isaac Thomas, & Mrs Mary Hatch, Both of Plym^o

(*To be continued*)

* The words in italics are on the margin of the page.

PLYMOUTH, MASS., VITAL RECORDS

(Continued from page 9)

[p. 236] 1748 April 16th A Purpose of Marriage, Between Mr Benjamin Lothrop of Kingston, And Mrs Deborah Thomas of Plymouth

May 13 A Purpose of Marriage, Between ye Revd Mr Jonathan Parker of Plimpton, & Mrs Lydia Bartlett of Plymo

28 A Purpose of Marriage, Between, John Rickard, and Bathshua Morton, Both of Plymo.

June 4th A purpose of Marriage, Between Mr George Watson of Plymouth, & Mrs Abigail Saltonstall of Haverhill.

18th A purpose of Marriage, Between Timothy Fales Esqr of Bristoll, and Mrs Elizabeth Thomas of Plymouth.

25 A Purpose of marriage, Between Mr Nath¹ Foster of Plym° and mrs Abigail Billings, of Little Compton

29 A Purpose of Marriage, Between Daniell Peak now Resident In Plymouth and Rhoda Beal of Plymouth.

Sep¹ 3 . A purpose of Marriage, Between Sam¹ Marshall Jun¹, & Susannah Bartlett, both of Plym°

3 . A Purpose of Marriage, Between Mr Abraham Hammatt of Boston, & Mrs Luce Howland of Plym°.

10th Mr William Torrey of Plym° and Mrs Mary Turner of Pembrook. This day published at Plymouth.

17th A Purpose of Marriage, Between Jeremiah Squibb Indian or Molatto Man ; & Mary Scoke, Indian Woman . Both of Plym°

17th A Purpose of Marriage, Between, Solomon Atwood, and Lydia Cushman, Both of Plymouth.

17th A Purpose of Marriage, Between Silas Morton, and Martha Morton, Both of Plymouth

17th A Purpose of Marriage, Between, Abner Silvester, And Jedidah Harlow Both of Plymouth.

Oct¹ 1st A Purpose of Marriage, Between Ichabod Holmes and Rebeckah Elles, Both of Plymouth.

1st A purpose of Marriage, Between John Carver and Grace Crandon, Both of Plym°

15 A purpose of Marriage, Between James Donham and Elizabeth Wood, Both of Plymouth

Nov¹ 5 A Purpose of Marriage, Between Mr Thos Sawyer and Mrs Margaret Cotton, Both of Plym°

5 A Purpose of Marriage, Between, Sam¹ Bartlett Esqr & Mrs Elizabeth Wethrell, Both of Plymouth.

5 A Purpose of Marriage, Between Moses Barrows Junr of Plimton & Deborah Totman of Plymouth

(To be continued)

PLYMOUTH, MASS., VITAL RECORDS

(Continued from page 124)

[p. 237] Sam¹ Bartlett . Town Clerk

1742/3 Mar: 12 . A Purpose of Marriage Between William Elles Junr, of Plym°, & Patience Gibbs of Sandwich.

19 A Purpose of Marriage, Between Jona Eames Junr of Plymouth, & Margaret Barter of Boston.

April 16 . A Purpose of Marriage, between Doct¹ Lazarus LeBarron, of Plymouth, and Lydia Cushman Widdow (of Elka Cushman Deceasd) of Plymouth

23 . A Purpose of Marriage, Between Job Cobb & Patience Holmes, Both of Plym°.

23 A Purpose of Marriage, between Josiah Whittemore of Charles Town, & Mary Hatch of Plym°.

May 14 A purpose of Marriage, between Francis Benias Indian of Plym°, and Mary Thomas Indian Woman, of Plimpton.

21 . A purpose of Marryage, between Cornelius Holmes and Marcy Doten widdow, both of Plymouth

June 4 A Purpose of Marriage, Between Silvanus Bartlett, & Martha Waite, both of Plym°

Augst 9 . A purpose of Marriage, Between John Bradford of Plymton and, Elizabeth Holmes of Plym°.

12 . A Purpose of Marriage, between Sam¹ Vaughan, & Lydia Morton, both of Plymouth.

13 A Purpose of Marriage, between Eleazer Rickard of Plymton, And Martha King of Plymouth.

17 John Cooper of Plym°, or Late Resident in Plym°, And Remembrance Walker of Plym°, This day published.

27 A Purpose of Marriage, between Jona Churchell of Plym°, and Hannah Worster of Sandwich

29 . A Purpose of Marriage, between David Curtis of Scituate, and Hannah Ward of Plymouth.

Septb 3 . A Purpose of Marriage, Between Ebenez¹ Spooner, of Plymouth ; and Mary Morton of Middleborough.

Octb 24 A Purpose of Marriage, Between mr John Greenleaf of Boston, & mrs Priscilla Brown of Plymouth

29 A Purpose of Marriage, Between, Eleazer Donham, of Plymouth, & Eliza Conner widw of Hannover.

29 . A Purpose of Marriage, Between Seth Nicholson, of Harwich, & Margaret Moore of Plymouth

[p. 238] 1743
Nov⟨r⟩ 5 . A Purpose of Marriage, Between Ephraim Ward and Sarah Donham both of Plym⟨o⟩.

5 . A Purpose of Marriage, Between Peter Daniell, & Sarah Waterman, both of Plym⟨o⟩ Indians.

Jan⟨y⟩ 26 . 1743/4 A Purpose of Marriage, Between Phillip Vincent Jun⟨r⟩ of Yarmouth, & Phillippe Rider of Plymouth.

28 . A purpose of Marriage, between Gideon White of Marshfield, and Joannah Howland of Plym⟨o⟩.

28 . A Purpose of Marriage, Between Amos Donham, & Ann Mackelroy, Both of Plymouth

28 A purpose of Marriage, Between Ezekiel Donham, & Patience Holmes, both of Plymouth

Feb⟨y⟩ 4 . A Purpose of Marriage, Between Jon⟨a⟩ Hammond of Rochester, & Sarah Jones of Plymouth

18 . A purpose of Marriage, Between Sam⟨l⟩ Nicholls Nelson, & Elizabeth Warren (Daughter To Joseph Warren), both of Plymouth

March 17 . A purpose of Marriage, between Joseph Crosswell, of Groton, in Connecticutt, & Jerusha Bartlett, of Plymouth.

24 . A Purpose of Marriage, between, M⟨r⟩ John Watson of Plymouth, & M⟨rs⟩ Elizabeth Reynolds of Bristoll

April 28 . A Purpose of Marriage, between James Shurtleff, & Joannah Tupper, both of Plymouth.

May 16 . A purpose of Marriage, between Thomas Williams & Hannah Bagnall, both of Plymouth

June 30 . A Purpose of Marriage, between James Swinnerto⟨n⟩ & Martha Battles, Both of Plymouth

July 25⟨th⟩ A purpose of Marriage, between William Fish of Sandwich, & Marcy Morrey of Plym⟨o⟩.

Aug⟨st⟩ 25 . A purpose of Marriage, between Barnabas Churchell Jun⟨r⟩ & Lydia Holmes, Both of Plymouth.

Sept 1 . A purpose of Marriage, between Abraham Jackson of Plym⟨o⟩, & Bethiah Witon of Plympton.

3 A purpose of Marriage, Between Daniel Robin Ind⟨n⟩ man & Abigail Ralph Indian Woman, both of Plymouth

22 . A purpose of Marriage, between Jonathan Bishop of Plym⟨o⟩, And Mary Woolston of Sandwich

[p. 239] 1744 Sept⟨r⟩ 29⟨th⟩ A Purpose of Marriage Between Jonathan King of Plymouth, And Deborah Carver of Marshfield.

Oct⟨r⟩ 20 . A Purpose of Marriage, Between, Thomas Pitts, & Mary Howard, both of Plym⟨o⟩.

27 A Purpose of Marriage, Between, M⟨r⟩ Thomas Foster and M⟨rs⟩ Mary Morton, both of Plym⟨o⟩uth.

Nov⟨r⟩ 3 . Sam⟨l⟩ Barrows Jun⟨r⟩ of Plimpton ; & Desire Rogers of Plymouth Published

3 Josselyn Sepit Indian, & Joannah Sepit Indian woman, both of Plymouth, Published

10⟨th⟩ . Moses Sachamus, and Kate Deerskins, both of Plymouth, Published

24 Ebenezer Donham of Plympton and Phebe Lucas of Plymouth Published.

1744/5 Jan⟨ry⟩ 26 . A Purpose of Marriage, between Elkanah Shaw of Plimpton, & Joannah King of Plym⟨o⟩.

26⟨th⟩ A Purpose of Marriage, between Thomas Burge, and Patience Doty both of Plymouth.

Feb⟨y⟩ 2 . A Purpose of Marriage between Joseph Fulgham, & Rebeckah Young, both of Plym⟨o⟩.

16 A Purpose of Marriage, between Ebenez⟨r⟩ Holmes y⟨e⟩ Third, and Susannah Holmes, both of Plymouth

26 . A purpose of Marriage, between Jacob Decoster, & Elizabeth Cole, both of Plymouth.

March 2 . A Purpose of Marriage, between Eleaz⟨r⟩ Harlow of Duxboro, and Abigail Clark of Plym⟨o⟩. Cirtifict Aug⟨st⟩ 23 . 1745

2 . A Purpose of Marriage, between Thomas Ling & Elizabeth Mackfun, both of Plymouth

30⟨th⟩ A purpose of Marriage, between Ezra Allen and Mary Durfey, both of Plymouth

Ap: 6 . A Purpose of Marriage between John Doten of Plimpton, and Hannah Shareman of Plymouth

20 A purpose of Marriage, between Jirah Fish of Sandwich, and Hannah Finney (Wid⟨w⟩) of Plymouth.

May 18 A purpose of Marriage between Joseph Churchell & Meriah Rider, both of Plymouth.

June 22 A Purpose of Marriage, Between Azariah Witon of Plimpton and Rebeckah Holmes of Plymouth

[p. 240] 1745 . June 22 A Purpose of Marriage, Between, Caleb Shareman, and Rebeckah Rider, Both of Plymouth.

Aug⟨st⟩ 10 . A Purpose of Marriage, between John May Jun⟨r⟩, of Plym⟨o⟩, & Bathshua Blackwell of Sandwich

30 . A Purpose of Marriage, between Sam⟨l⟩ Smith, & Grace Crandon, both of Plym⟨o⟩.

24⟨th⟩ Amaziah Churchell, and Elizabeth Silvester, both of Plymouth, this day, Published.

Sept 7 . A Purpose of Marriage, Between, Daniel Robbin and Sarah Sanders both of Plym⟨o⟩th, Indians.

Nov⟨r⟩ 22 . Nath⟨ll⟩ Morton * of Plym⟨o⟩. and Martha Tupper, of Sandwich Published.

Dec⟨r⟩ 21 . A purpose of Marriage, Between Eleazer Elles of Plym⟨o⟩, and Deborah Gibbs of Sandwich.

1745/6 Jan⟨ry⟩ 25 . A purpose of Marriage, between Christopher Dewet and Susannah Beale, both of Plymouth

25 . A purpose of Marriage, between, Benjamin Delano of Duxboro, and Lydia Jackson of Plymouth.

* "Jun⟨r⟩" was interlined in the same hand, but crossed out.

134 Plymouth, Mass., Vital Records

25 A purpose of Marriage, between Stephen Doten, & Hannah Bartlett, both of Plymouth.

Mar. 29 A Purpose of Marriage, between James Swift of Plym°., and Elizabeth Loreing of Barnstable.

April 5. A Purpose of Marriage, between Ezekiel Morton, & Abigail Morton, both of Plymouth

12th. Jabez Mendall of Plimpton, and Mariah Churchell of Plymouth Published.

12th. John Howard, and Eunice Curtis, both of Plym°. Published.

12th Lemuell Holmes, and Abigail Rider, both of Plymouth — Published.

19th. Nathl. Hatch and Ruth Rider, both of Plymouth, Published.

26th James Watkins, & Jerusha Rider, both of Plym°. Published.

May 3. Josiah Bradford & Hannah Rider, both of Plym°. Published.

31 James Howard Junr., & Thankfull Branch, both of Plym° Published.

June 14 : Thomas Swift Junr And Rebeckah Clark, both of Plymouth Published.

July 12. John Thomas Junr, and Abigail Clark, both of Plym°. Published.

[p. 241] A purpose of marrage betwen Wiliam Swift of Sandwich & Kezia Rider of Plymouth March 30. 1733

A Purpose of Marriage Between Moses Cole of Dorchester Indian, and Patuence DearSkin of Plymouth April 7 1733

A purpose of Marriage Betwen Mr Nathll Morton of Plym° & mr Mary Shaw of Plymton April 21 1733

A Purpose of Marriage Betwen Joseph Mory and Mary Swift Both of Plymouth April 25 . 1733

A purpose of Marriage Betwen Joseph Wanpum and Paticience DearSkin Indians Both of Plymouth April 27 1733

A purpose of marriage between Thomas Sears and Elezebeth Bartlett Both of Plymouth April 28 . 1733

A purpose of marriage Between Joshua Drew and Juana Kempton Both of Plymouth April 28 : 1733

A purpose of marriage, Between John holmes and Lois Kempton Both of Plymouth April 28 1733

A purpose of Marriage Betwen Isaac Tomson and Sarrah Penis Both of Plymouth April 28 1733

A purpose of Marriage between William Griffing and Sarah Curtis both of Plymouth Decr. 29th : 1733.

A Purpose of Marriage between Nathaniel Churchell & Mary Curtis both of Plymouth January 2d 1733

A Purpose of Marriage between Noah Samson and Jemima Rider both of Plymouth february 23 . 1733/4

A Purpose of Marriage, between mr Jeremiah Howes of Yarmouth and mrs Meriah Morton of Plymouth March 7th 1733/4

A Purpose of Marriage between Nathan Cob of Plymouth and Joannah Bennet of Middleberough March 9th 1733/4.

A Purpose of Marriage between Mordecai Ellis & Mol Samons both Indians of Plymouth March 9th 1733/4

Plymouth, Mass., Vital Records 135

A Purpose of Marriage between Nathaniel Warren and Sarah Morton both of Plymouth March 23d 1733/4

A Purpose of Marriage between William Davis & Elizabeth Bagnald both of Plymouth April 10th 1734.

A Purpose of Marriage between Joshua Donhum now resideing in Plymouth and Ann Revis of Plymouth April 13. 1734

A Purpose of Marriage between Cuffe a Negro Man Servant to mr Isaac Lothrop Junr and Nanne a Negro woman Servant to mr Samuel Bartlett both of Plymouth May 18th 1734.

[p. 242] A Purpose of Marriage between John Dyer and Hannah Morton both of Plymouth May 25th 1734

A Purpose of Marriage between John Norris and Mary Tupper both of Agawam within the Township of Plymouth May 25 . 1734

A Purpose of Marriage between Jabez Holmes and Sarah Clarke both of Plymouth May 25 . 1734.

A Purpose of Marriage between James a Negro man Servant belonging to Decon John Atwood and Nanne a Negro Woman Servant belonging to mr Robert Brown both of Plymouth May 25 . 1734

A Purpose of Marriage between Elkanah Hamlen of Barnstable and Marget Bates of Agawam in the Township of Plymouth Plymouth June 7th 1734.

A Purpose of Marriage between mr Thomas Gardner of Newport in Rhoad Island and mrs Margaret Bryant of Plymouth June 13th : 1734.

A Purpose of Marriage between Abner Corpe of Plymouth & Hannah Ransom of Plimton July 8th 1734

A Purpose of Marriage between mr James Shurtleff of Plimton and mrs Faith Jackson of Plymouth July 27th 1734

A Purpose of Marriage between Silvanus* Curtis of Plymouth and Dorothy Delano of Duxberough . August 2d : 1734.

A Purpose of Marriage between mr Silvanus Cob and mrs Elizebeth Rider both of Plymouth August : 17th 1734.

A Purpose of Marriage between Bradford Freeman & Sarah Church both of Plymouth August 17th : 1734

A Purpose of Marriage between Mr John Bartlett of Plymouth and Mrs Sarah Gray of Falmouth August 24th 1734.

A Purpose of Marriage between Francis Merifeild and Content Billington both of Plymouth August 30th 1734

A Purpose of Marriage between Daniel Robins & Mary Whood Indian[s] both of Plymouth September 7th 1734

A Purpose of Marriage between John Rider and Mary Drew both of Plymouth September 21th 1734

A Purpose of Marriage between mr Isaac Doty and mrs Mary Lanman both of Plymouth October 5th 1734.

A Purpose of Marriage between mr William Dyre and mrs Hannah Howland both of Plymouth October 14th : 1734

* "Silvanus" has been written over "Nathaniel".

A Purpose of Marriage between Jedediah Wing of Rochester and Elizabeth Gifford of Plymouth October 15th 1734

A Purpose of Marriage between Nathaniel Thomas Esqr and Madam Mary Allen both of Plymouth Octor 26 : 1734

[p. 243] A Purpose of Marriage between Samuel Quacom and Kate Shanks Indians both of Plymouth November 2 . 1734

A Purpose of Marriage between Accalabe Jeffry a Mallatto man and Betty Simons and Indian Woman both of Plymouth November 5th 1734

A Purpose of Marriage between Samuel King and Mary Rose both of Plymouth . November 9th 1734

A Purpose of Marriage between Nathaniel Bosworth and Lydia Samsen both of Plymouth November 23d 1734

A Purpose of Marriage between mr Nathaniel Foster of Plymouth and mrs Marcy Thatcher of Midleberough Novr 23 . 1734

A Purpose of Marriage between Joseph Whitenore and Abigal Hatch both of Plymouth November 30th 1734.

A Purpose of Marriage between Thomas Haublen of Rochester and Ruth Gibs of Agawam in the Township of Plymouth Decb 10 . 1734 to be set up next Saturday come Sennet.

A Purpose of Marriage between Jonathan Darling and Lydia Cob both of Plymouth January 11th 1734/5

A Purpose of Marriage between Nathaniel Dunham of Plymouth and Anna Peterson of Duxberough february 1st 1734/5

A Purpose of Marriage between mr James Hovey & mrs Lydia Atwood both of Plymouth february 19 . 1734/5.

A Purpose of Marriage between mr Elisha Cob junr of Plymouth and mrs Prissilla Merrick of Harwich . March. 8th : 1734/5

A Purpose of Marriage between Lemuel Jackson of Plimton and Esther Savery of Plymouth March 25th 1735.

A Purpose of Marriage between Zacheus Burge of Sandwich and Temperance Gibbs of Plymouth . April 12 : 1735.

A Purpose of Marriage between mr John Atwood junr and mrs Joannah Drew both of Plymouth April 26 . 1735

A Purpose of Marriage Between Cornelius Morton of Plymouth and Jean Johnson of North yarmouth May 3d 1735

A Purpose of Marriage between mr Lemuel Barnes and mrs Lydia Barnes both of Plymouth May 3 . 1735

A Purpose of Marriage between mr Silvanus Bramhall of Plymouth and mrs Mary Bennet of Midleberough . May 6th 1735.

A Purpose of Marriage between mr John Cobb and mrs Sarah Bartlett of Plymouth May 13th 1735

A Purpose of Marriage between mr Joshua Shareman and mrs Deborah Croade both of Plymouth . July 12th 1735

A Purpose of Marriage between Joseph Bartlett of Plymouth and Jean Swift of Sandwich August 2d 1735

A Purpose of Marriage between mr Josiah Carver and mrs Marcy Faunce both of Plymouth Septr 13th 1735

[p. 244] A Purpose of Marriage between Mordecai Ellis and Hannah Jonas Indians both of Plymouth Sepr. 16 : 1735

A Purpose of Marriage between Phillip Sachemus and Esther Peck Indians both of Plymouth October 4th 1735.

A Purpose of Marriage between mr Abiah Keith of Bridgwater and mrs Jean Faunce of Plymouth October 9th 1735

A Purpose of Marriage between John Goddard and Lydia Polden both of Plymouth October 11th 1735.

A Purpose of Marriage between mr Thomas Holmes Junr and mrs Elizabeth Cob both of Plymouth November 8th 1735

A Purpose of Marriage between John Ring now Resideing in Plymouth and Rebeckah Stermy of Plymouth Novr 21 . 1735

A Purpose of Marriage between mr Anselm Lothrop and mrs Mary Thomas both of Plymouth December 27th . 1735.

A Purpose of Marriage between mr Nicholas Drew and Mrs Bathshebah Kempton both of Plymouth Decr 27 . 1735

A Purpose of Marriage between James Wood and Deborah Fish both of Plymouth January 3d : 1735/6

A Purpose of Marriage between Benjamin Cartee now Residing in Plymouth and Elizabeth Marshal of Plymouth January 7th 1735/6.

A Purpose of Marriage between mr Seth Cobb and mrs Sarah Nelson both of Plymouth January 13th : 1735/6 Sett up January 24th 1735/6

January 15th 1735/6. George Holmes came and forbid the banes betwixt James Wood and Deborah Fish by reason he Suposed her former husband Fish was yet liveing in the Law

A Purpose of Marriage between mr Jonathan Dinan of Rehoboth in the County of Bristol and mrs Hannah Morton daughter of mr Joseph Morton of Plymouth . february 14th : 1735/6

A Purpose of Marriage between John Kempton of Plymouth and Elizabeth Randel of Plimton february 28th 1735/6

A Purpose of Marriage between mr Charles Dyre & mrs Lucie Cotton both of Plymouth March 10th 1735/6

A Purpose of Marriage between James Morton of Plymouth and Mehitebel Churchel of Plimton March 20th 1735/6

A Purpose of Marriage between mr Jabez Hamond of Rochester and mrs Abigal Faunce of Plymouth March 27th 1736.

A Purpose of Marriage between mr Abiel Pulcefer of Plymouth and mrs Sarah Noyse of Boston, April 18th : 1736

A Purpose of marriage between mr Andrew Croswel and mrs Rebeckah Holmes both of Plymouth April 21th 1736

A Purpose of Marriage between James Cornish and Abiah Churchell both of Plymouth June 5th 1736

A Purpose of Marriage between Gershom Holmes and Lydia King both of Plymouth August 1736

[p. 245] A Purpose of Marriage between John Patee and Hannah Morton both of Plymouth . Sepr 4th 1736

THE MAYFLOWER DESCENDANT

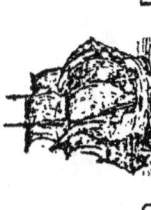

1620 1920

A QUARTERLY MAGAZINE OF PILGRIM GENEALOGY AND HISTORY

VOLUME XVIII

1916

PUBLISHED BY THE
MASSACHUSETTS SOCIETY OF
MAYFLOWER DESCENDANTS
BOSTON

Plymouth, Mass., Vital Records

A Purpose of Marriage between Thomas Harlow Jun' of Plymouth and Patience Tilson of Plimton Sep' : 4th 1736

A Purpose of Marriage between Ezekiel Rider & Marget Churchell both of Plymouth Sep'. 16th : 1736

A Purpose of Marriage between Cipio a Negro man belonging to mr John Rickard of Plymouth and Hannah a Negro Woman belonging to mr Samuel Smith of Sandwich October 2d . 1736

A Purpose of Marriage between Ebenezer Tinkcom and Jeane Pratt both of Plymouth. October 23 . 1736.

A Purpose of Marriage between Joshua Shachemus and Betty Poaquenett

A Purpose of Marriage between Joshua Rafe and Nab Shanks Indians both of Plymouth November 4th . 1736.

A Purpose of Marriage between John Walker and Remembrance Nash both of Plymouth Nov' 5 . 1736

A Purpose of marriage between Jeremiah Atequeen and Moll Simons Indians both of Plymouth Nov' 13 . 1736

A Purpose of Marriage between William Gammons of Boston and Hannah Hubbard of Plymouth Nov'. 27 1736.

A Purpose of Marriage Between Samuel Kempton Jun' of Plymouth and Mabel Sole of Duxborough Nov'. 27 . 1736

A Purpose of marriage between Benjamin Bartlett Jun' and Hannah Stevens both of Plymouth Dec' 14th 1736.

A Purpose of Marriage between Antipas Hammond of Rochester and Abigal Swift of Plymouth . Dec' 21 . 1736

A Purpose of Marriage between Peter Tinkcom and Mary Wood both of Plymouth December 23d 1736.

A Purpose of Marriage between mr Joseph Swift and mrs Sarah Lebaron both of Plymouth January 8th 1736/7

A Purpose of Marriage between Lemuel Robins of Plimton and Esther Donham of Plymouth february 3d 1736/7

A Purpose of Marriage between between Thomas Bates and Lydia Savory both of Plymouth february 3d 1736/7

A Purpose of Marriage between mr Caleb Shareman of Marshfeild and mrs Deborah Ring of Plymouth february 5th 1736/7.

A Purpose of Marriage between Lemuel Drew Jun' and Hannah Donham both of Plymouth february 12 . 1736/7

A Purpose of Marriage between mr John Cooper & mrs Hannah Rider both of Plymouth March 19th . 1736/7

A Purpose of Marriage between mr Charles Morton & mrs Mary Shattuck both of Plymouth March 19th : 1736/7

(To be continued)

PLYMOUTH, MASS., VITAL RECORDS

Transcribed by the Editor

(Continued from Vol. XVII, p. 198)

[p. 246] A Purpose of Marriage between m^r Thomas Murdoch & m^{rs} Elizabeth Doggett both of Plymouth March 19th 1736/7

A Purpose of marriage between m^r Thomas Gardner of Plymouth and m^{rs} Hannah Baker of Boston March 19th 1736/7

A Purpose of Marriage between m^r Francis Adams & Keziah Atwood both of Plymouth March 19th 1736/7

A Purpose of Marriage between m^r James Cushman & m^{rs} Hannah Cobb both of Plymouth March 19th 1736/7.

A Purpose of Marriage between m^r Josiah Connet & Mima B[*]ant Indians both of Plymouth March 19th 1736/7.

A Purpose of Marriage between m^r Abner Holmes & m^{rs} Bathsheba Nelson both of Plymouth April 16th 1737.

A Purpose of Marriage between m^r Benejah Pratt & m^{rs} Elizabeth Winslow both of Plymouth April 22th 1737.

A Purpose of Marriage between Jo Titus Ned and Esther Lawrance Ned Indians both of Plymouth April 30th 1737

A Purpose of Marriage between Jabez Twiney and Mary Sinons Indians both of Plymouth Sepr 10th 1737.

A Purpose of Marriage between m^r Joseph Holmes son of Nathaniel Holmes of Plymouth deceased and m^{rs} Lydia Bradford of Brantry September 24th 1737.

A Purpose of Marriage between m^r Joseph Smith and m^{rs} Lydia Barnes both of Plymouth October 15th 1737.

A Purpose of Marriage between Joseph Gifford of Agawam in the Township of Plymouth and Content Irish of Little copton October 22th 1737

* A hole in the paper has destroyed about two letters here.

A Purpose of Marriage between John Deerskins and Kate Shanks Indians both of Plymouth October 22th 1737

A Purpose of Marriage between m^r Lemuel Cobb and m^{rs} Fear Holmes both of Plymouth November 5th 1737.

A Purpose of Marriage between m^r Timothy Morton and m^{rs} Marcy Wilson both of Plymouth November 12th 1737

A Purpose of Marriage between m^r Ebenezer Brigs of Rochester and m^{rs} Betty Gibs of Agawam in the Township of Plymouth Novr 22th 1737

A Purpose of Marriage between m^r Timothy Heley and m^{rs} Alce Chubbuck of Agawam both in the Township of Plymouth Novr 26. 1737

A Purpose of Marriage between Mathew Unquit and Sarah Acquit Indians both of Plymouth December 10th 1737

A Purpose of Marriage between m^r Benjamin Harlow and m^{rs} Elizabeth Stevens both of Plymouth December 24: 1737.

A Purpose of Marriage between m^r Job Bourn of Sandwich & m^{rs} Lydia Swift of Plymouth December 27th 1737 to send ye certificate to John Blackwell

A Purpose of Marriage between m^r Return Waite & m^{rs} Martha Tupper both of Plymouth January 14th 1737/8

A Purpose of Marriage between m^r Josiah Swift of Sandwich & m^{rs} Mary Mory of Plymouth January 17th 1737/8 not paid

[p. 247] A Purpose of Marriage between Richard Tommas and Marcy Cunnet Indians both of Plymouth January 21th 1737/8 not paid

A Purpose of Marriage between m^r Simeon Totman and m^{rs} Sarah Littlejohn both of Plymouth January 21th 1737/8.

A Purpose of Marriage between m^r John Staff and m^{rs} Rebecah Sterny both of Plymouth february. 4th 1737/8

A Purpose of Marriage between m^r Josiah Cunnet of Midleberough and m^{rs} Sarah Norris of Agawam in the Township of Plymouth february 14th 1737/8

A Purpose of Marriage between m^r Isaac Hamblen of Rochester and m^{rs} Marcy Gibs of Agawam in the Township of Plymouth february 20th 1737/8.

A Purpose of Marriage between m^r Thomas Wethrell jun^r of Plymouth and m^{rs} Elizabeth Lothrop of Barnstable. May 13th 1738.

A Purpose of Marriage between William Harlow and Hannah Bartlett both of Plymouth May 26 . 1738 . not paid

A Purpose of Marriage between m^r Nathaniel Freeman and m^{rs} Martha Donham both of Plymouth May 27th 1738

A Purpose of Marriage between Ebenezer Besse and Deborah Sanders both of Agawam in the Township of Plymouth June 3^d 1738.

A Purpose of Marriage between m^r William Clarke & m^{rs} Experience Doty both of Plymouth June 10th 1738

A Purpose of Marriage between m^r Stephen Churchell jun^r and m^{rs} Hannah Barnes both of Plymouth June 10th 1738

A Purpose of Marriage between m^r Benjamin Warren jun^r and m^rs Rebecah Doty both of Plymouth June 18th 1738

A Purpose of Marriage between m^r Edward Doty and m^rs Phebe Finney both of Plymouth July 8th 1738

A Purpose of Marriage between m^r Uriah Savory of Plymouth and m^rs Deborah Bump of Rochester. August 5th 1738. p^d

A Purpose of Marriage between m^r Joseph Holmes and m^rs Hannah Donham both of Plymouth august 26th 1738

A Purpose of Marrage between Mr Thomas Wright and Abijah Roger both of Plymouth August 1st 1738

A Purpose of Marriage between Mr Joseph Morton Junr and m^rs Annah Bulluck of Rehoboth August 2^d . 1738

A Purpose of Marriage between m^r Miles Standish jun^r of Duxberough and m^rs Mehetibel Robins of Plymouth Sepr 20 1738

A purpose of marriage between m^r Eleazer Churchell jun^r and m^rs Sarah * Harlow both of Plymouth

[p. 248] A Purpose of Marriage between m^r Joseph Rider Junr of Plymouth and m^rs Elizabeth Crosman of Taunton Novr 11th 1738.

A Purpose of Marriage between m^r Nathaniel Shurtleff and m^rs Lydia Branch both of Plymouth November 22th 1738

A Purpose of Marriage between the Reverend Jonathan Ellis of Plymouth and m^rs Patience Blackwell of Sandwich Novr 29 . 1738.

A Purpose of Marriage between m^r Isaac Tinckcom of Plymouth and m^rs Keziah Wornall of Duxberough Decr 15th 1738. p^d

A Purpose of Marriage between m^r Zephaniah Holmes and m^rs Sarah Bradford both of Plymouth Decr 15 : 1738

A Purpose of Marriage between m^r Joshua Swift of Sandwich and m^rs Jean Faunce of Plymouth January 13th 1738/9.

A Purpose of Marriage between m^r John Barnes Senr of Plymouth and m^rs Ann Bonum of Plimton February 9th 1738/9.

A Purpose of Marriage between Jack a Negro man belonging to m^r Thomas Holmes of Plymouth and Patience a Molatto woman belonging to m^r Barnabas Churchell of s^d Plymouth March 17th 1738/9.

A Purpose of Marriage between m^r John Finny of Plymouth and m^rs Susanna Prat of Plimton March 31 . 1739.

A Purpose of marriage between in^r David Morton and m^rs Rebecah Finny both of Plymouth March 31 . 1739

Plymouth April 2^d 1739. Joannah Tupper came to my House and forbid the Banes of John Finnys marrying with Susanna Prat in as much as the s^d Finny had promised her marryage & that no thing but death should part & that he had asked her father & mothers consent.

A Purpose of Marriage between Ebenezer Burge jun^r of Plymouth and m^rs Zerviah Ney of Sandwich May 14th 1739

* "Hannah" was first written, but was crossed out and "Sarah" interlined, in the same hand and ink.

A Purpose of Marriage between m^r Charles Samson of Plymouth & m^rs Mary Church of Scituate May 26 . 1739

A Purpose of Marriage between m^r William Bowdoin of Boston and m^rs Phebe Murdoch of Plymouth June 2^d 1739.

A purpose of Marriage between m^r Ebenezer Harlow and Mrs Moriah Mory both of Plymouth . June 9 . 1739

A purpose of marriage between m^r Elisha Holmes Junr of Plymouth and m^rs Mary Ellis of Sandwich July 7th 1739.

A Purpose of Marriage between m^r Ebenezer * Samson & m^rs Hannah Harlow both of Plymouth July 14th 1739.

A Purpose of Marriage between m^r Seth Luce of Wareham & m^rs Hannah Morton of Plymouth August 11 . 1739

[p. 249] A Purpose of Marriage between m^r Joseph Abbet & m^rs Marcy Kempton both of Plymouth Sepr 1 . 1739

A Purpose of Marriage between m^r Nathaniel Morton and m^rs Mary Ellis both of Plymouth Sepr 29 . 1739

A Purpose of Marriage between Moses Nummuck and Sarah Deerskins Indians both of Plymouth Octob^r 11 . 1739

A purpose of Marriage between m^r Thomas Davie and m^rs Marcy Bartlett both of Plymouth Novr 11th 1739

A Purpose of Marriage between m^r Robert Toxe and m^rs Hannah Clarke both of Plymouth Novr 17 . 1739.

A Purpose of Marriage between m^r Thomas Shurtleff and m^rs Marcy Warren both of Plymouth Decr 8th 1739

A Purpose of Marriage between m^r Jonathan Tobe of Sandwich and m^rs Deborah Swift of Plymouth Decr 27 . 1739.

A Purpose of marriage between m^r Thomas Mayhew & m^rs Mary Wethrell both of Plymouth february 8th 1739/40

A purpose of marriage between William Cunnet Junr of Plymouth & Moll Wicket of Sandwich both Indians in the County of Plymouth & Sandwich february 23 1739/40

A Purpose of Marriage between m^r Abiel Shurtleff & m^rs Luce Clarke both of Plymouth february 23 . 1739/40

The Intention of Marriage between m^r Elkanah Cushman & m^rs Lydia Bradford both of Plymouth March 8 . 1739/40

A Purpose of Marriage between m^r Lemuel Harlow of Plymoth and Joanna Paddock of Middleborough April 26 . 1740.

A Pŭrpose of Marige between m^r James Celler & Jane Crandon both of Plymouth May 10 . 1740.

A purpose of Marriage between Noah Peniss & Abigail Chumuck both of this Town Indians. July 19 . 1740.

A purpose of Marriage betwen m^r John Jones and Sarah Barnes both of Plymouth July 26 . 1740.

A Purpose of Marriage between m^r David Sepitt & Joanna Scoke Indians both of Plymoth Septr 21 . 1740

* "Benjamin" was first written, but was crossed out and, "Ebenezer" interlined, in the same hand and ink.

A Purpose of Mariage between Isaac Wood & Lydiah Wait both of Plymouth August 7 . 1740:

[250] A Purpose of Mariage between Levi Stephens of Boston & Mary Marshall of Plymoth Sept'r 27 . 1740.

A purpose of Marriage between Joshua Newcomb of Truro & Widdow Hannah Holmes of Plymoth Sept'r 27 . 1740

A purpose of Mariage between Asa Hatch and Mary Waite both of Plymouth Oct'o 18 . 1740.

A purpose of Mariage between Joseph Abbot & Mercy Kempton both of Plymouth November 22 . 1740

A purpose of mariage between Edward Sparrow and Jerusha Bradford both of Plymouth November 29 . 1740.

A purpose of Mariage between Thomas Tobey of Sandwich and Elizabeth Swift of Plymouth Dec'r [*illegible*] 1740.

A purpose of mariage between John Torrey & Deborah Reed both of Plymoth Jan'ry 17 . 1740

A purpose of Mariage between Silv'a Holmes, & Mary Harlow Jan'ry 17 . 1740 . both of Plymouth

A purpose of Mariage between Amos Ryder & Ruth Faunce, both of Plymouth March . 14 . 1740.

A purpose of Mariage between Charles Rider of Plym'o & Rebecca Bartlet of Duxborough March 14 . 1740.

A purpose of mariage between Amos Dunham of Plym'o & Abigal Hill of Plymouth March 14 . 1740.

A purpose of Mariage between Edward Winslow & Hannah Dyre both of Plymouth . March 21 . 1740.

A purpose of Mariage between William Holmes & Ruth Morton both of Plymouth March 21 . 1740.

N. B. The publication between William Holmes & Ruth Morton was taken down y'e Same Week it was Set up, (by whom I do not know.)

A purpose of Mariage between George Holmes jun'r & Lydia West both of Plymouth March 28 . 1741.

A purpose of mariage between William Holmes & Ruth Morton both of Plymouth April 4 . 1741

A purpose of Mariage between Benj'a Bartlett & Abigail Morton both of Plymouth April 17 . 1741

A purpose of mariage between Joseph Bates of Plym'o and Betty Gibbs of Sandwitch — May 16 1741

(*To be continued*)

PLYMOUTH, MASS., VITAL RECORDS

(*Continued from p. 32*)

[p. 251] A purpose of mariage between Thomas Brace and Elisabeth Barnes both of Plymouth May 16 . 1741.

A purpose of mariage between Gideon Bradford of Plympton & Jane Paddock of Plymouth May 16 . 1741

A Purpose of Mariage between Joseph Sachemus of Plym'o & Lydia Peacken Sandwich June 6th 1741. Indians.

A purpose of mariage between Abraham Jackson of Plymouth & Mary Whiteing of Plymton Oct'o 12 . 1741.

A purpose of Mariage between Sam'll Sepitt & Sarah Ryder both of Plym'o Oct'o 18 1741.

A purpose of mariage between William Wood & Eliz'a Finney both of Plym'o Oct'o 25 . 1741.

A purpose of mariage between Tho's Clarke & Ruth Morton : both of Plym'o Oct'o 31 . 1741

A purpose of Mariage between Israel Clarke of Plym'o & Deborah Pope of Sandwich Oct'o 31 . 1741.

A purpose of Mariage between Josiah Churchell & Patience Harlow both of this Town Oct'o 31 . 1741

A purpose of mariage between William Harlow jun'r & Hannah Littlejohn both of Plym'o Mar. 19 . 1741.

A purpose of mariage between Ephr'm Holmes & Sarah Finney both of Plym'o April 10 . 1742.

A purpose of mariage between Josiah Morton y'e 3'd & Experience Ellis both of this Town April 10 . 1742

A purpose of mariage between Seth Finney of Boston & Lydia Eames of Plym'o April 16th 1742.

A purpose of mariage between m'r Jn'o Howland & m'rs Patience Spooner both of Plym'o april 16 . 1742

A purpose of mariage between Barzilla Stetson & Ruth Stutson * both of Plym'o April 24 . 1742

---

* On original page 151, the marriage record reads "Barzillia Stetson, & Ruth Kempton, both of Plym, Marryed at Plym'o, Sept'r 6 . 1742." See *Mayflower Descendant*, 14 : 160.

A purpose of mariage between Eleazr Holmes junr & Ester Ellis both of Plymo May 8th 1742

A purpose of Mariage between Benja Barnes and Experience Rider both of Plymo May 15. 1742

a purpose of Mariage between Edward Tinkam of Plymo & Sarah Ryder* of Plymo & Lydia Ryder* of Kingston July 17th 1742

[p. 252] A purpose of mariage between Robt Shattuck & Ruhami Cook both of Plymoth Augt 14th 1742

a purpose of mariage between Zacheus Curtiss of Plymo and Lydia Thomas of Dartmouth Augt 28th 1742

a purpose of mariage Ephrm Paddock of Plymo & Sarah Bradford of Plymton Septr 3d 1742

A purpose of mariage between Ephraim Quoy & Mercy Peniss both of Plymo Indians Septr 3 . 1742

a purpose of mariage between Theophilus Cotton & Martha Sanders both of this Town Octo 16 . 1742.

a purpose of Mariage between Josiah Cunnett & Hannah Quoy both of Plymo Indians Octo 23 . 1742

a purpose of mariage between Joseph Shurtleff & Sarah Cobb both of Plymo Octo 31 . 1742

a Purpose of mariage between Henry Sanders of Warham & Mary Hambleten of Plymo Novr 21 . 1742

a Purpose of Mariage between Thomas Faunce 4th & Sarah Bartlett both of Plymouth Novr 27 . 1742

a Purpose of mariage between mr Joseph Ruggles of Lambstown [Hardwick†] & mrs Hannah Cushman of Plymo Decr 4 . 1742

a Purpose of Mariage between Nathll Croade & Eliza Carte both of Plymo December 11th 1742

a purpose of mariage between Peter Daniell & Hanah Ryder Indians both of Plymo Janry 8 . 1742

a purpose of mariage between Job Hammond (Negro) & Hanah Quoy (indian) both of Plymo Janry 30 . 1742.

A purpose of mariage between Noah Bradford and Hannah Clarke both of Plymo Febry 13 . 1742

A purpose of Mariage between Archelaus Lane now resideing in Plymo & Remembrance Walker of sd Plymo Febry 19 . 1742 spoke for pr Isaac Little of Plymo Febry 23 . 1742 sd Lane came to my House & Declared sd Publishment was. Spoke for Contrary to his knowlege & Consent

A Purpose of Mariage Between William Keen and Ruth Serjeant both of Plymo Febry 19 . 1742

A purpose of mariage between Gideon Gifford of Rochester and Lois Jackson of Plymouth Febry 27th 1742.

* The Kingston records show the intentions of Edward Tinkham of Kingston and Lydia Ryder of Plymouth, on 17 July, 1742, and the Plymouth town records [Mayflower Descendant, 17 : 4] show the marriage of Edward Tinkham of Kingston and Lydia Ryder of Plymouth, on 29 September, 1743.

† The word "Hardwick" has been interlined, in a different hand and ink.

[p. 253] 1746 Augst 2 . A purpose of Marriage, Between Willm Jerman and Eleonar Thomas, both of Plymouth

30th A purpose of Marriage, Between Benja Eaton of Kingston, & Mary Tinkcom of Plymo

Sept 17th A Purpose of Marriage, Between David Wood of Plympton and Rebeckah Pratt of Plymouth

Sept 13th A Purpose of Marriage, Between Benja Churchell & Ruth Delano, Both of Plymouth.

27 . A Purpose of Marriage, between Mr Peres Tilson & mrs Eliza Doty . both of Plymo

Octr 11 . A Purpose of Marriage, between Willm Churchell and Susannah Clark . both of Plymouth

11th A Purpose of Marriage, between Nathl Bradford & Sarah Spooner, both of Plymouth.

18th A Purpose of Marriage, between [*] Dowty Randall of Scituate & [*] Eliza Tilson of Plymo

25 . A Purpose of Marriage, between Nathl Goodwin & Lydia Le-Barron, both of Plymo

Novr 22 A Purpose of Marriage, Between Eleazer Stephens, & Sarah Silvester, both of Plymo

29 A Purpose of Marriage, Between Joshua Finney, of Plymo, & Elisabeth Pope of Sandwich

29 A Purpose of Marriage, Between Saml Harlow, and Marcy Bradford, Both of Plymouth

Decr 13 . A Purpose of Marriage, Between, Thomas Pattison & Susannah Beale, Both of Plymouth

27 . A Purpose of Marriage, Between Josiah Carver Junr, & Jerusha Sparrow . Both of Plymouth

Janry 3 A Purpose of Marriage, Between Mr Joseph Le-Barron & mrs Sarah Leonard, both of Plymo

10 A Purpose of Marriage, between Edward Wright, & Elisabeth Decoster, both of Plymo

17 . A Purpose of Marriage, Between Jacob Tinkcom, & Lydia Donham, Both of Plymouth

24th A Purpose of Marriage, Between Thos Spooner Junr of Plymo, and Deborah Bourn of Marshfield

Febry 14 . A Purpose of Marriage, Between James Clark Junr and Hannah Swift, Both of Plymo

[p. 254] a purpose of marrage Between Elkanah Totman and Elisebeth Donham Both of plymouth July ye 7 1733

A Purpose of Marrage between Archibold Fisher and Elizabeth Decost both of Plymouth August 4th 1733

A Purpose of Marrage between Joslen Cepit & Desire Whood Indians both of Plymouth August 4th 1733

A Purpose of Marrage between mr Ebenezer Dogget & mrs Desire Rickard both of Plymouth August 11th 1733

* "Mr", before "Dowty", and "Mrs", before "Eliza", were crossed out, apparently in the same ink as the rest of the record.

A Purpose of Marriage between Ichabod Samson Junr of Duxberough and Marcy Savory of Plymouth August 17th 1733

A Purpose of Marriage between John Faunce Junr of Plymouth and Ruth Samson of Plinton September 15th 1733

A Purpose of Marriage between Ebenezer Sanders and Sarah Peters Indians both of Plymouth September 19th 1733.

A Purpose of Marriage between John Palmer of Scituate & Jean Doty of Plymouth Sepr 21th 1733.

A Purpose of Marriage Between John Valler and Mary May both of Plymouth September 22. 1733

A Purpose of Marriage between m^r Lazerus Samson and m^{rs} Abigal Shurtleff both of Plymouth October 6th 1733.

A Purpose of Marriage between Thomas Polden of Plymouth and Deborah Spooner of Dartmouth October 13. 1733

A Purpose of Marriage between Nathaniel Thomas Junr Esqr of Plymouth and m^{rs} Elizabeth Gardner of Marshfeild. October 27th 1733.

A purpose of Marriage between Paul Cooke of Kingston and Joannah Holmes of Plymouth Novr 21th 1733.

A Purpose of Marriage between Robert Bartlett and Rebeckah Wood both of Plymouth Novr 21th 1733

A Purpose of Marriage between m^r Nathaniel Howland of Plymouth and Yetmercy Palmer of Bristol Novr 24. 1733

A Purpose of Marriage between Samuel Hubberd and Hannah Polden both of Plymouth November 24th 1733

A Purpose of Marriage between m^r Barnebas Hedge of Yarmouth and m^{rs} Marcy Cole of Plymouth Decr 21. 1733.

A Purpose of Marriage between Solomon Sepit and Sarah Farrow Indians both of Plymouth Decr 22 1733

[p. 255] A Purpose of Marriage Between Mr Jacob Tayler of Barnstable and m^{rs} Mary Atwood of Plymouth June 30th 1729.

A Purpose of Marriage Between Mr Nathaniel Thomas Junr of Plymouth & m^{rs} Hannah Robinson of Duxberough. Augt 16. 1729

A Purpose of Marriage Between m^r Seth Doggett and m^{rs} Elizabeth Delano, both of Plymouth Augt 23. 1729

A Purpose of Marriage Between m^r Isaac King & Hannah Harlow both of Plymouth September 6th 1729

A Purpose of Marriage Between John Hambleton and Elizabeth Jones both of Plymouth October 24th 1729

A Purpose of Marriage between John Cushing Junr Esqr of Scituate & m^{rs} Mary Cotton of Plymouth Novr 1st 1729.

A Purpose of Marriage between Thomas Ward & Joanna Donham both of Plymouth. Novr 1st 1729.

A Purpose of Marriage Between m^r Isaac Lothrop Junr of Plymouth and m^{rs} Hannah Freeman of Harwich. Novr 8th 1729.

A Purpose of Marriage between Joseph Treeble Residing in Plymouth and Ann Jones of s^d Plymouth Decr 6th 1729.

A Purpose of Marriage between Ebenezer Bryant of Plinton and Elizabeth King of Plymouth Decr 6th 1729

A Purpose of Marriage between Cornelius Brigs of Rochester and Thankfull Burges of Plymouth December 27th 1729.

A Purpose of Marriage between Ephraim Churchell and Priscilla Manchester both of Plymouth March. 14th 1729/30

A Purpose of Marriage between John Studly and Elizabeth Doty both of Plymouth March 28th 1730.

A Purpose of Marriage between Thomas Western and Prudence Conant Both of Plymouth April. 18th 1730.

A Purpose of Marriage between m^r William Dyre of Boston and Mrs Hannah Phillips of Plymouth May 4th 1730

A Purpose of Marriage between m^r John Atwood and m^{rs} Experience Peirce both of Plymouth May 19th 1730

A Purpose of Marriage between m^r Nathaniel Morton & m^{rs} Meriah Clarke both of Plymouth June 17th 1730.

A Purpose of Marriage Between m^r Thomas Kempton of Plymouth and m^{rs} Esther Throop of Bristol. June 19th 1730.

A Purpose of Marriage between m^r Nicholas Drew & m^{rs} Lydia Doggett both of Plymouth. July 18th 1730.

A Purpose of Marriage between m^r Ebenezer Finney of Barnsta[ble] and m^{rs} Rebeccah Barnes of Plymouth August 1st 1730.

A Purpose of Marriage Between Nathaniel Thomas Esqr of Plymouth and Madam Anna Leonard of Norton August 8th 1730.

[p. 256] A Purpose of Marriage between Jabez Holmes and Rebecca Harlow both of Plymouth August 29th 1730

A Purpose of Marriage between Silas West & Mary Cob both of Plymouth Sep 26th 1730

A Purpose of Marriage between Tobe and Dutch, negroes both of them Servants to Joseph Warren of Plymouth October 28. 1730

A Purpose of Marriage between m^r Jonathan Bartlet & Mrs Thankfull Barnes both of Plymouth December 5th 1730.

A Purpose of Marriage Between Samuel Cornish Junr and Meribah Clarke both of Plymouth January 16th 1730/31

A Purpose of Marriage between John Waterman and Hannah Cushman both of Plymouth. february 4th 1730/1

A Purpose of Marriage between Jacob Curtice and Fear Donham both of Plymouth March 6th 1730/1

A Purpose of Marriage between Joseph Donham of Plymouth and Jean Randel of Scituate March 13th 1730/1

we the Subcribers Select men of the Town of Plymouth declare that the above named Joseph Donham is not an Inhabitant in s^d Town according to Law dated at Plymouth March 16. 1730/1

    Isaac Lothrop
    Benj^a Warren
    John Foster

A Purpose of Marriage between Jacob Johnson & Sarah Clarke both of Plymouth April 17th 1731

A Purpose of Marriage between Samuel Holmes of Plymouth and Mary Lewis of Falmouth April 24th 1731.

A Purpose of Marriage between Cato Negro Servant to mr Thomas Foster and Jenne Negro Servant to Decon John Foster both of Plymouth May 6th 1731.

A Purpose of Marriage between Lemuel Fish of Rochester and Deborah Barden residing in Plymouth May 22th 1731

A Purpose of Marriage between Capt John Gould of Plymouth and mrs Sarah Clark of Chilmark in Dukes County : May 29th 1731.

A Purpose of Marriage between William Kempton and Mary Brewster both of Plymouth July 3d 1731

A Purpose of Marriage between Thomas Kempton Junr and Mary Holmes both of Plymouth July 24th 1731.

A Purpose of Marriage between Elnathan Holmes and Rebeccah Churchell both of Plymouth August 7th 1731.

A Purpose of Marriage between mr Josiah Morton Junr of Plymouth and mrs Maletiah Finney of Barnstable August 14th 1731

A Purpose of Marriage between Joseph Peach and Lydia Jeffry Indians both of Plymouth August 14th 1731

[p. 257] A Purpose of Marriage between John Harlow Junr and Mary Rider both of Plymouth Augt 28th 1731

A Purpose of Marriage between Benjamin Gifford of Plymouth and Mary Lawton of Portsmouth in Rhoad Island October 29th 1731.

A Purpose of Marriage between mr Cornelius Clark of Rochester and Susanna Donhaun of Plymouth . October 30th 1731.

A Purpose of Marriage between Dolphin a Negro man Servant belonging to Nathaniel Thomas Junr and Flora a negro woman Servant belonging to mrs Priscilla Watson both of Plymouth November 6th 1731

A Purpose of Marriage between mr Francis Curtis Junr & mrs Elizabath Barnes both of Plymouth . November 10th 1731.

A Purpose of Marriage between Dick a negro man Servant belonging to mr Nathaniel Thomas Junr and Phebe a Negro Woman Servant belonging to Mr Haviland Torry both of Plymouth Dcember 4th 1731

A Purpose of Marriage between mr Josiah Carver and mrs Bethiah Churchell both of Plymouth Novr 20th 1731

A Purpose of Marriage between Ebenezer Bartlett of Plymouth and Rebekah Dimond of Rehoboth Plymouth february 5th 1731/2

A Purpose of Marriage between Samuel Burge of Plymouth and Jedidah Gibs of Sandwich february 16th 1731/2

A Purpose of Marriage between John Blackmore Junr of Rochester and Sarah Holmes of Plymouth february 18th 1731/2

A Purpose of Marriage between Gyles Nash and Remembrance Jackson both of Plymouth february 19th 1731/2.

A Purpose of Marriage between Thomas Faunce the third of Plymouth and Hannah Damond of Scituate Plymth March 25 . 1732

A Purpose of Marriage Between Micah Gibs & Sarah Sanders both of Agawam within the Township of Plymouth April 7th 1732.

A Purpose of Marriage between Mordecai Ellis and Desire Whood Indians both Residing in Plymouth April 14th 1732.

A Purpose of Marriage between Ebenezer Tinkcom of Plymouth and Mary Bonney of Plimpton Plymouth April 19th 1732.

A Purpose of Marriage between John Case Resident in Plymouth and Rebecah Peirce of Plymouth. May 6th 1732*

A Purpose of Marriage between Quomeny a Negro Man Servant belonging to Josiah Cotton Esqr and Kate a Negro Woman Servant belonging to mr John Murdoch both of Plymouth May 27: 1732.

A Purpose of Marriage between mr Walter Rich of Boston and Rebeccah Morton of Plymouth June 16 1732

[p. 258] A Purpose of Marriage between Peter English and Alce Randel both of Plymouth June 24th 1732.

A Purpose of Marriage between Nicolas Spink of North Kingston in Naraganset and Mary Jackson of Plymouth . June . 30th 1732

A Purpose of Marriage between Barnabas Holmes & Abigal Shepherd both of Plymouth August 5th 1732

A Purpose of Marriage between Nathaniel Chubbuck Junr and Tabitha Besse of Agawam within the Township of Plymouth Augt 12th 1732

A Purpose of Marriage between Samuel Doty Junr and Joannah Bosworth Junr both of Plymouth September 9th 1732

A Purpose of Marriage between Joseph Lewen of Plymouth and Rejoyce Walker of Eastham Sepr 9th 1732

A Purpose of Marriage between John Wetherhead & Remember Bates both of Plymouth September 17th 1732

A Purpose of Marriage between Benjamin Rogers and Phebe Harden both of Plymouth September 17th 1732.

a purpose of Marriage between Quomeny a Negro Servant belonging to Josiah Cotton Esqr and Mary Hamshere Indian woman both of Plymouth Sepr 30th 1732

A Purpose of Marriage between Caleb Stetson and Deborah Morton both of Plymouth October 21 . 1732.

A Purpose of Marriage between Benjamin Wanno Indian of Plymouth and Leah Tompom Indian of Barnstable Novr 4 . 1732

A Purpose of Marriage between Benjamin Cole of Plimpton and Rebekah Harlow of Plymouth Novr 9th 1732

A Purpose of Marriage between James Winslow of Plymouth & Susannah Conant of middleberough November 14 . 1732.

A Purpose of Marriage between John Barker now residing in Plymouth and Meriah Cushman of Plymouth Novr 16 : 1732

A Purpose of Marriage between John Nelson & Mary Morton both of Plymouth November 25th 1732

A Purpose of Marriage between Cornelius Warren of Middleberough and Marcy Ward of Plymouth Decr 15 1732

A Purpose of Marriage between mr Isaac Lothrop Junr and Madam Priscilla Watson both of Plymouth Decr 23 1732.

A Purpose of Marriage between mr Abiel Pulcifer and mrs Bethiah Cotton both of Plymouth January 20th 1732/3

---

* In the margin, opposite this entry, is written "June 10"

Plymouth, Mass., Vital Records

A purpose of marriage between Thomas Savery of Plimouth and Priscilla paddock of midleabourough march 10 1732/3

A purpose of Marrgie Between Samuell Bumpus of Barn[stable] and Sarrah Roggers now Residing in Plymouth March 2 [*]

[p. 259] A Purpose of Mariage between Elisha Perry of Sandwich & Anna Sanders of Agawam within the Township of Plymouth Sepr 4th 1725

A Purpose of Marriage Between m^r Tomson Phillips of Jemaco In the West Indies & m^{rs} Hannah Cotton of Plymouth Sepr 9th 1725

A Purpose of Marriage Between Joseph Holmes & Phebe Churchell both of Plymouth October 9th 1725.

A Purpose of Marriage Between Allexander Malli[se]† and Bathsheba Hill both Residing in Plymouth Octr 9th 1725

A Purpose of Marriage Between Nathan Delano & Bathsheba Holmes both of Plymouth October 14th 1725.

A Purpose of Marriage Between Thomas Foster of Plymouth and Lois Fuller of Barnstable October 16th 1725.

A Purpose of Marriage Between Joseph Cornish of Plymouth and Patience Pratt of Scituate . October 30th 1725

A Purpose of Marriage Between m^r John Sparhawk of Plymouth and m^{rs} Hannah Jacob . of Scituate Octr 30th 1725.

A Purpose of Marriage Between Jacob Tinkcom and Judeth Hunt both of Plymouth Novr 2^d 1725.

A Purpose of Marriage between m^r Thomas Morton Junr & m^{rs} Hannah Nelson both of Plymouth . Decr 4th 1725.

A Purpose of Marriage between John Moore Resideing in Plymouth & Mary Shattuck of Plymouth . Decr 4th 1725

A Purpose of Marriage between Phillip Lee & Elizabeth Jackson Decr 11th 1725

A Purpose of Marriage between Nath^{ll} Howland & Abigal Billington both of Plymth December 18th 1725.

A Purpose of Marriage between Silvanus Hall of Plymouth & Elizabeth Dogget of Marshfield . December 25th 1725.

A Purpose of Marriage between m^r John Winslow of Plymouth and m^{rs} Mary Little of Marshfield . January 21th 1725/6.

A Purpose of Marriage between William Foster of Sandwich and Hannah Rider of Plymouth January 21th 1725/6.

A Purpose of Marriage between Ebenezer Rider and Thankfull Silvester both of Plymouth february 12th 1725/6.

A Purpose of Marriage between Benjamin Besse and Martha Chubbuck both of Agawam within the Township of Plymouth March 20th 1725/6

Jonathan Barnes & Phebe Finny Published May 1726

A Purpose of Marriage between m^r Ebenezer Finney of Bristoll and m^{rs} Jean Faunce of Plymouth June 4th 1726.

A Purpose of Marriage between Peter Cole & Mary Marshall both of Plymouth July 16th 1726. m^r Robert Brown forbid the bans July 18th 1726 by Reason the s^d Mary Marshall is his Servant Octo^r 20th m^r Brown Consented

Lef^t Josiah Finney Published to Mrs Marcy Thomas of Marshfeild Augt 6 . 1726

m^r Isaac Little & m^{rs} Sarah Church Published . Sepr 3 : 1726.

(To be continued)

* Illegible.

† See marriage on original page 141. [Mayflower Descendant, 14 71]

PLYMOUTH, MASS., VITAL RECORDS

(Continued from page 125)

[p. 260] John Bacon Esqr of Barnstable Publisht to mrs Sarah Warren of Plymouth Sepr 10th 1726.

A Purpose of Marriage Between John White & Ruth Shepherd both of Plymouth September 17th 1726

A Purpose of Marriage between Joshua Larance of Rochester and Elizabeth Sprague of Plymouth : October 6th 1726.

A Purpose of Marriage between Lazerus Samson & Jemima Holmes both of Plymouth October 7th 1726.

A Purpose of Marriage between John Tommas & Abigal Donham both residing in Plymouth . October 15th 1726.

A Purpose of Marriage between Jonathan Bryant of Kingstone and Mary Eastland of Plymouth . November 12th 1726.

A Purpose of Marriage between Jedediah Hatch of Scituate and Sarah Churchell of Plymouth Novr 30th 1726 sd Hatch ordered it to be taken down again ye Same day at night about 10 a clock A Purpose of Marriage Between the Reverend mr Robert Ward of Wenham and mrs Margaret Rogers of Plymouth . December 16th 1726

A Purpose of Marriage between James Bumpass of Rochester and Marjery Norris of Agawam in the Township of Plymouth January 12th 1726/7.

A Purpose of Marriage between Joseph Bartlett and Sarah Morton both of Plymouth . January 21th 1726/7

A Purpose of Marriage Between Barnabas Shurtleff of Plimpton and Jemima Adams of Plymouth . febry 10th 1726/7.

A Purpose of Marriage Between John Clarke of Plymouth and Rebecca Hathaway of Dighton in the County of Bristol . March 18th 1726/7

A Purpose of Marriage Between mr Samuel Doty and mrs Marcy Cob both of Plymouth . March 25th 1727.

A Purpose of Marriage Between Samuel Totman And Experience Rogers both of Plymouth March 25th 1727.

A Purpose of Marriage between Joshua Finney & Hannah Curtise July 29th 1727

A Purpose of Marriage between Elkanah Totman and Sarah Churchell both of Plymouth . August 26th 1727

A Purpose of Marriage between Nathan Whood Junr & Rachel Jeffry Indians both of Plymouth Sepr 23d 1727.

A Purpose of Marriage between mr Nehemiah Riply & mrs Sarah Wood both of Plymouth November 8th 1727

A Purpose of Marriage Between Ebenezer Cob Junr & Lydia Stevens both of Plymouth . November 25th 1727

A Purpose of Marriage Between mr Benjamin Lothrop Junr of Barnstable and mrs Experience Howland of Plymouth December 1st 1727.

A Purpose of Marriage Between mr Ebenezer Cob of Plymouth and mrs Mary Thomas of Middleberough December 14th 1727.

A Purpose Marriage between John Smale of Provinceton & Hannah Barnebe of Plymouth february 24th 1727/8.

[p. 261] A Purpose of Marriage between mr Joshua Freeman of Plymouth and mrs Patience Rogers of Ipswich April 9th 1728.

A Purpose of Marriage between Thomas Scarrot and Alse Ward both of Plymouth. July 19th 1728.

A Purpose of Marriage between John Price and Esther Prat both of Plymouth August 9th 1728 . Daniel Prat forbid ye banes

A Purpose of Marriage between Thomas Ward Junr Residing in the Town of Plymouth And Marcy Ward of Plymouth August 26th 1728.

A Purpose of Marriage between Samuel Cole and Marcy Barnes both of Plymouth Sepr 7th 1728.

A Purpose of Marriage between Jonathan Freeman of Plimton and Sarah Rider of Plymouth Sepr 7th 1728.

A Purpose of Marriage between Jonathan Mory Junr of Plymouth and Elizabeth Swift of Sandwich Sepr 14th 1728.

A Purpose of Marriage between Elkanah Delano & Mary Sanders both of Plymouth October 12th 1728.

A Purpose of Marriage between Ephraim Samson of Duxberough & Ruth Shepherd of Plymouth October 18th 1728.

A Purpose of Marriage between Timothy Burbanks of Boston now residing in Plymouth and Mary Kempton of Plymouth Novr 2 . 1728

A Purpose of Marriage between Mathew Lemote & Marcy Billington both of Plymouth Novr 16th 1728.

A Purpose of Marriage between Thorton Gray & Katherine White both of Plymouth. Novr 20th 1728.

A Purpose of Marriage between James Holmes and Content Silvester both of Plymouth Decr 28th 1728.

A Purpose of marriage between Joseph Cole of Plimton & Mary Stevens of Plymouth January 28th 1728/9.

A Purpose of Marriage between Thomas Doan of Chatham in the County of Barnstable and Sarah Barnes of Plymouth february 15th 1728/9

A Purpose of Marriage between Elisha Doty Junr of Plymouth & Deborah Tubs of Duxberogh february 22th 1728/9

A Purpose of Marriage between Redolphus Hatch late of Province Town in the County of Barnstable now residing in Plymouth and Esther Holmes of Plymouth . March 1st 1728/9.

A Purpose of Marriage between Edward Stephens And Marcy Silvester both of Plymouth March 15th 1728/9

A Purpose of Marriage between Thomas Totman & Lucrecy Rose both of Plymouth May 10th 1729.

A Purpose of Marriage Between John Watson Esqr & mrs Priscilla Thomas both of Plymouth June 14th 1729.

A Purpose of Marriage Between Jacob Lewis & Bathsheba Mallis June 21th 1729.

[p. 262] Marriges Solemnized By ye Revd Mr Nathl Leonard.

1752 April 15 . James Howard of Plymouth, & Marcy Warren of Middleboro Marryed at Plymouth

June 13 . William Gammons & Fear Curtis, Both of Plymo Marryd at Do

July 14 . Joshua Totman & Johanna Scarret, Both of Plymo Maryd at Ditto

23 . Abijah Fisher of Norton, & Mary Washburn of Plymouth Marryed at Plymouth

Octr 18 . Silvanus Morton & Mary Stephens, both of Plymo Marryed at Ditto

19 . Jabez Harlow & Experience Churchill, both of Plymo Marryd at Do Joseph Rider of Province Town, & Thankfull Polden of Plymouth Marryed at Plymo July 13 . 1752

Novr 9 . Thomas Hinckley Junr of Barnstable, & Phebè Holmes of Plymouth Maryed at Plymouth

Recd ye List March 2 . 1753 . & Entered

1753 Aprill 12 Zacheus Bartlett & Margaret Barnes Both of Plymo Marryd at Plymo

May . 24 Thomas Davis & Mercy Hedge Both of Plymo Marryd at Ditto

24 Eben: Ransom of Plimton, & Rebeckah Barlow of Plymo Marryd at Ditto.

Augst 13 Mr Joseph Fulgham, & Mrs Luranah Clark, Both of Plymo marryd at Ditto

Sepr 20 Benjamin Morton & hannah Faunce, Both of Plymo marryd at Ditto.

26 . Archipus Fuller of Plimton, & Mariah Churchell of Plymo marryd at Ditto

Novr 13 Nathaniel Morton Junr & Rebeckah Jackson ; Both of Plymo marryd at Ditto

15 Ichabod Bartlett Junr & hannah Rogers, Both of Plymo marryd at Ditto

22 William Weston of Plimton, & Mary Westron of Plymo Marryd at Ditto

1754 Janry 3 . Samuell Jackson and Experiance Atwood Both of Plymo marryd at Ditto

March 14 John Bacon of Barnestable & Joanna Foster of Plymo marryd at Ditto

May . 30 The Revd Mr Elijah Packard, & Mrs Mary Rider Both of Plymo marryd at Ditto

June 20 Arthur Shepherd Resident in Plymo & Mary Morton of Plymo marryd at Ditto

July . 18 Samuel Torrey of Boston, & Deborah Torrey of Plymo marryd at Ditto

Sept 16 Zacheus Churchell & Mary Trask Both of Plymo marryd at Ditto

Oct 16 Elkanah Waterman & Mary West, Both of Plymo marryd at Ditto

Novr 28 Ephraim Dexter of Rochester, & Martha Wait of Plymo marryd at Ditto

Decr 5 Nathaniel Holmes & Lydia Churchill, Both of Plymo marryd at Ditto

12 Ebenezer Nelison, & Ruth Jackson, Both of Plymo marryd at Ditto

19 George Peckham, of Providence, & Jerusha Bartlett of Plymo marryd at Plymouth.

Continued to Book ye 2nd page 252

To the Honerable Isaac Lothrop Esqr

Whereas the Province Law makes provision that all births & deaths shall be registred by the Town Clerk in the Several Towns within said Province These are to Informe your Honner that Josiah Sturtevant of Plymouth in ye County of Plymouth in New England had a child born in or about the month of April Last past and the sd Sturtevant neglecteth to give Notice thereof as according to the direction of the Law. I do therefore pray your Honner to give forth a Warrant for sd Sturtevant to appear before your Honner that he may be dealt withall as according to ye direction of the Law

Plymouth Decr 30th 1724

John Dyer
Town Clerk

[p. 263] Ebenezar Holmes publeshed to patiene ffiney on ye first of agust 1719

Elisha Holmes published To Suzanna Clark August 7 1719

John Johnson Publeshed To Elisabeth Goold august. 21 1719

Elish Bradford publeshed to Bathsheba Brock agust 22 : 1719

Job Prince of plimouth published to abigail Cimbol of plimptown September ye 5 — 1719

Joseph King publisht To ye Widow Marcy Spooner october 3 1719

David Turner publisht To Ruth Jacson october. 5 : 1719

Josiah Sturdefunt publisht to Hannah Church of Sittuate october 9th 1719

Gidion Ellice & Anna Clarke published octobe 10th 1719

Mr John Mordow to phebe Morton october 24th 1719

Ichabod Standish publisht to phebe ring october ye 30 — 1719

Joseph Pearce was Publisht to Elezebeth Ring on ye 20 of november 1719

Ebenazar Dunham was published to Abigaiel Smith Desem 12 1719

Joseph vahan & Elizabeth Shurtlif Janewary 14 1719/20

John Barse to Sarah Holmes published January 23d 1719/20

Benjamn Rider to hannah Stephens of marshfeild published february 29 1719/20

John Goole published to Mary Coombs March 28 1720

Nathaniel Morton published to Recka Ellece Aprill 2d 1720

Nathaniel Jackson Jun published to Reeckah Powin April 8th 1720

lazaros labaron published to lidia Bartlet Aprill 16 1720

Nathaniel Cobb published to Mary Waterman Aprill 23d 1720

Thomas Branch published to lidiah Barrow April 23 1720

Ebenazar Doged published to Elizabeth Rickard on ye 14 Day of May 1720

James Rickard published to hanna howland May 14th 1720

Tobe and Billa published May 20th 1720

Eleazar Harlow published to Hannah pratt of plimton on ye 21st Day of May 1720

Richard Church & anna stirtvent published June 18 : 1720

Rasteling Bruster of plim & Hannah Thomas of Duxbero Agust 17 1720

[p. 264] Ase Beale was publisht to Rhoda Lathle ye 1 day of october 1720

Peter Hopkins was publisht to priscilla prat Ye 3 day of october 1720

Ebenazar Morton of Middlebery published to Marsy Foster 24 december 1720 ye 24

Elkana Churchill pubeshed to suzanah Manchester January 28 1720

John Churchill published to Bethya Sponer January 28 1720

Elish holmes Jun: published to Sarah Bartlett February 16 : 1720/21

Thomas Woshbon Published to Elizabeth Howland february 18th 1720/21

Eben fuller published to Joanna Gray March : 17th 1721

Thomas peters & Rebecka Shepard March 18 1721

Mr Joseph Stace to Mrs patien Warren March 25 : 1721

John finney of plimton To Rebekah Bryant May 13 1721

peleg Durfey publisht to Mary Cole May ye 27 1721

Anthoney Coast Marrener and Elisabeth bacon both now residing In plymouth publisht June ye 10 1721

Joseph Silvester publisht to mercy holmes July ye 7 day 1721

Seth Chitman* publisht to priscilla bradford august ye 7 day 1721

Thomas Rogers published to picila Churchill october 12 1721

Jacob Tinckham published To hanna Cobb october 14th 1721

Ichabod Bartlet published to Suzanna Sponer octobe 23 1721

Nath: Holmes published to pricilla prat November 9 : 1721

ffrances Labaron publ: to Sarah Bartlet November 9th 1721

Samuel Bartlet Published to Elizabeth Latherop ; on the first Day of December 1721

John finey published on ye first Day of Decembe to Sarah Bartlet 1721

Joseph Sangerele Published To Mary Thomas of Duxberouh february 17 1721

George Barrows Ju: published To Desir Doty March 10th 1721/22

Seth Swift published To Meriah Morey March 17 : 1721/22

Seth Barns to Sarah Wooden March 24 1722

Edmond tilson publisht to Elisabeth Coper : aprel ye 17 1722

James Clark published to Anna Rider Aprill 21 1722

* An error of the town clerk. The name should have been "Chipman", as shown by the marriage, on the Kingston Church records, and by the will of Priscilla's father, Maj. John³ Bradford (William²).

John pratt publish to pricila Bryant April 21 1722
Joseph Warren to allatheah Chi[tten]ton * April 18 1722
[p. 265] Isral Ferren published to Martha Gibbs May 2ᵈ 1722
Willian Lucust publisht to meheible doty may: yᵉ 4 : 1722
Nathaniel Thomas published to hope Warren July 7ᵗʰ 1722
July 21ˢᵗ 1722 Richard Weight published to marey Barnes of plimouth
Ebenazar Cobb published to Ruth Tinckham July 28ᵗʰ 1722
Jesiah Feney publisht to abigaiel briant august yᵉ 11 1722
Robert Jones published to Mary Stuard Agust 18 1722
Johnathan barns : publisht to yᵉ widow Mercy Doty august 25 1722
James Clarke Junio published to Meriba Tuper of Sandwich September first 1722
Joseph Rider published to abigaiel Warren September first 1722
James young & rebecker Shepard was publisht yᵉ 6 September 1722
Samuel Rider published to Marey Silvester September 15ᵗʰ 1722
Josiah Rider published to Experiance Jenney or Jennes october : 4 : 1722
Thomas Philips Published to abigaiel Rider october 20ᵗʰ 1722
Thomas Morton published to Abigaiel pratt November 3ᵈ 1722
Jams Cushmon published to Sarah Hatch November 3ᵈ 1722
Nath Wood published to Mary Adams November 17ᵗʰ 1722
Thomas Stoormy published to Rebeckah philips November 23 1722
Thomas Western published to Mary Howland Desembe 18 1722
James Howard A Stranger published to Sarah Billenten Desember 22ᵈ 1722
Edward Crowly published to Jane Rich Desembe 27ᵗʰ 1722
Samuel Foster published To Margeret Tilden Desember 29 : 1722
John Bartlett published To Sarah Cobb January 5ᵗʰ 1722/23
Addam Jones of plymouth publisht to Mary Cran of diten January yᵉ 30ᵗʰ 1723
John Sturtavant publisht to yᵉ widow Sarah barlit fabuary yᵉ 9ᵗʰ 1723
John Stirtevant published to the Widow Sarah Bartlet ffebruary 9ᵗʰ 172¾
Joshua Dunham Published To Sarah Pratt ffebruary 16ᵗʰ 1722/3
Samuel Norrice published to Marcy Jones March 8ᵗʰ 1722/3
Caleb Cooke published To Abigaill Howland April 11ᵗʰ 1723
Richard Bagelet published to Elizabeth polon April 27ᵗʰ 1723
Israel Jackson published to Marcy Dunham on yᵉ [†]1 of may 1723
Joseph lewing published to hanna Rogers July 3ᵈ 1723
Jacob lewes publisht to Sarah Reavis September : 25ᵗʰ 1723
beniamin Elis publisht to hannah gibs october yᵉ 29 1723
David Stirtevant publisht To Sarah holmes november first 1723
James Warren publisht to penelepe winslow december yᵉ 27ᵗʰ 1723
Samuell baker publisht to Susaner mitchel yᵉ 5ᵗʰ of January 1723/24
Joseph Jackson to Rembrance [Jackson ‡] february first [1]723/24

* See marriage record, in Mayflower Descendant, 14:39.
† The first figure is doubtful — probably "1".
‡ "Jackson" has been interlined in a modern hand. See marriage, in Mayflower Descendant, 14:70.

[p. 266] The Children of Richard & mingo his Wife both servants to Mr Joseph[h *worn*]
1 Margeret born on yᵉ 9ᵗʰ of January 1701 She was baptized 1708
2 Mary born on yᵉ 22 of June 1708 } these 2 Children was both baptized the 27 of Jun. 1708
3 Marth born June 22 1708
George Jonson the son of hanna Jonson was born at plimouth on the 16 Day of february 170⅘
Eleazer Faunce & Hannah Warren * Published March 30ᵗʰ 1724
Elkanah Morton & Elizabeth Holmes Published March 30ᵗʰ 1724
Samuel Morton & Lydia Bartlett Published may 16 — 1724.
Caleb Tinkcom & Marcy Holmes Published Augˢᵗ 8ᵗʰ 1724
Benjamin Bartlett Published to Lydia Morton [†] 1724
mʳ Robert Brown Published to Priscilla Johnson of Boston Sepʳ 12. 1724
Thomas Jackson Published to Hannah Woodward of Little Compton Sepʳ 22 : 1724.
Isaac Jackson Published to Sarah Bridgett of Scituate October 17 — 1724.
The Reverend mʳ Nathaniel Leonard Published to mʳˢ Priscilla Rogers of Ipswich Nov: 7. 172[4]
Eleazer Martin Junʳ & Deborah Delano Published. November 21ᵗʰ 1724.
Nathaniel Donham & Rebeccah King Published Decʳ 18ᵗʰ 1724
mʳ John Cooke Published to mʳˢ Hannah Morton Decʳ 19ᵗʰ 1724
Ichabod Delano & Elizabeth Cushmans Publishment Sot up. Decʳ 26ᵗʰ 1724
Francis Allen & Jane Kirk Publishment Sot up January 2ᵈ 1724/5
Consider Howland & Ruth Bryant Publishment Set up March 13. 1724
Nathaniel Bartlett & Abigal Clarke Published March. 13ᵗʰ 1724/5
Ichabod Washborn & Bethiah Phillips Published March. 13ᵗʰ 1724/5
Robert Cushman Junʳ & Marcy Washborn Published April 17ᵗʰ 1725
mʳ John Barnes Junʳ and mʳˢ Dorcas Corben of Haverill April. 28ᵗʰ 1725
John Peirce & Rebecca Donham Published May 22ᵗʰ 1725
A Purpose of Marriage between Barnabas Seabury of Bridgwater and Abigal Cooke of Plymouth. May 29ᵗʰ 1725
A Purpose of Mariage between Stephen Barden Junʳ of Midleboro & Deborah Prat of Plymouth June 26ᵗʰ 1725. Quinten Crimble forbid the banes by reason he had an Indenture on sᵈ Barden Since agreed
A Purpose of Marriage between Samuel Bartlett & Hannah Churchel both of Plymouth June 26ᵗʰ 1725.
A Purpose of Marriage between Samuel Dexter of Falmouth and Elizabeth Burg of Agawam within yᵉ Township of Plymouth July 31ˢᵗ 1725.

* "Morton" was first written, but was crossed out and "Warren" interlined in the same hand and ink. See marriage, in Mayflower Descendant, 14 : 70.
† The month and day were omitted.

A Purpose of Marriage between Benjamin Cornish & Experience Gibs both of Plymouth August 19th 1725

A Purpose of Mariage between Elkanah Shaw of Plimpton & Hanna[h] Cushman of Plymouth . August 28th 1725

[p. 267] 1754 Jan'y 19 . A Purpose of Marriage, Between John Robinson of Plymouth. And Elizabeth Studley of Hannover Daughter of M'r Eliab Studley.

Feb'y 2. A Purpose of Marriage, Between The Rev'd M'r Elijah Packard, & M'rs Mary Rider, Both of Plymouth

9 A purpose of Marriage, Between, M'r John Bacon of Barnstable, & M'rs Joanna Foster of Plymouth

March 16 A purpose of Marriage, Between Joshua Pocknot Indian Man, & Sarah Adams Indian Woman both of Plym

16 A purpose of Marriage Between Simon Mahomon, & Phebe Robbin Indians, both of Plym°

30 A Purpose . of . Marrage . Between . Edward . Lanman . of . Plymouth And Joan Tobey . of Sandwich

Ap: 27. A purpose of Marriage, Between M'r Seth Barnes Jun & M'rs Elizabeth Rider, both of Plymouth

May . 4 . A purpose of Marriage, Between M'r Job Brewster of Duxboro, & M'rs Elizabeth Elles of Plymouth

18th A . Purpose . of . Marriage Between Elkanah Waterman And Mary . West . Both of . Plymouth

25 A purpose of Marriage Between M'r Arthur Shepherd Resident in Plymouth & M'rs Mary Morton of Plymouth

June 1 . A purpose of Marriage, Between Nath'l Holmes and Lydia Churchell both of Plymouth

June 1 . A purpose of Marriage, Between Thomas Morton & Mary Morton Daughter of M'r Nath'l Morton Both of Plymouth

8 A purpose of Marriage, Between M'r Joseph Watson Resident in Plym° & M'rs Marcy Wadsworth of Duxboro

15 A purpose of Marriage, Between M'r Sam'l Torrey of Boston, and M'rs Deborah Torrey of Plymouth

20 A purpose of Marriage, Between Elisha Witon Jun of Plimton, and Betty Holmes of Plym°

De'd the Certificate To Edward Doten Nov'r 9th

Aug'st 2 . A purpose of Marriage, Between Noah Penes & Patien[ce] Wampom both of Plymouth Indians

3 . A purpose of Marriage, Between M'r Ebenezer Nel[son*] and m'rs Ruth Jackson

10 A Purpose of Marriage, Between Lemuel Fish, Joanna Doten, both of Plymouth

Aug'st 17th A purpose of Marriage, Between Zacheus Churchell and Mary Trask Both of Plymouth

[On fly-leaf, at back of book.] Abigal Cornish . deceased y'e Last day of May . 1724

[END OF VOLUME I OF ORIGINAL RECORDS. — *Editor.*]

* See marriage, on original page 262.

PLYMOUTH, MASS., VITAL RECORDS

(*Continued from page 146*)

[Vol. 2, p. 1] The Children of Samuell Bartlett Esq'r, and Elizabeth his wife. Continued from page 120. First Book.

4th Lothrop Bartlett Born, Aug'st 7 . 1755. Thirsday, half an hour After 7 Clock A M Deceased June 13th 1756

5th Hannah Bartlett, Born . April y'e 11th 1757 Monday, about 1 Clock A M

6 . Isaac Bartlett, Born Oct'r 5th 1759, on Fryday, about half after 2 aClock P.M

The Child of Joseph Silvester, and Susannah his Wife

Joseph Silvester, Born July 15 . 1755.

The Children of Thomas Davis and Mercy his Wife

1 Sarah Davis, born June 29th 1754. Dec'd Nov'r 10 . 1821 in Plym°

2 Thomas Davis born June 26 . 1756 Deceas'd, at Boston, January 21st 1805

3 William Davis born July 13th 1758 Dec'd January 6 . 1826 . in Plym°

4 John Davis born Jan'ry 25th 1761

5 Samuel Davis born Mar: 5th 1765

6 a Daughter born Aug'st 7th & deceas'd y'e 14th Aug'st 1766

7 Isaac Davis . born . Octob: 7th 1771

8 Wendell Davis born Feb'ry 13 1776.

The Children of William Bartlett, & Mary his Wife

1. Hannah Bartlett, Born Nov'r 8th 1752.

2. William Bartlett, Born, Aug'st 9 . 1754.

3 a Daughter not named. Born July . Deceased July

4 Samuell . Bartlett . Born July . 24th 1757

5 Judah Bartlett . Born December 14 . 1759 . deceased May 27 : 1791

6. Amasa Bartlett . Born June . 23 . 1763.

7 Mary Bartlett . Born Novemb'r 16th 1765

8 Sarah Bartlett . Born July . 30th 1768

9 Thomas Bartlett . Born Jan'ry 9th 1770

Plymouth, Mass., Vital Records

10 Nathaniel Bartlett . Born June . 28th 1772
Mrs Mary Bartlett above named the mother of the Above family Deceasd July 16th 1785
[p. 2] The Child of the Revd Mr Elijah Packard . and Mary . his Wife

1. Abigail . Packard Born Aprill 5th 18th 1755

The Children of Joshua Totman, & Joanna, his wife
1. Joshua Totman Born, June 3 . 1753
2. Betty Totman, Born Jany 9 . 1756.
3. Elkanah Totman Born Augst 18 . 1758.
4. Thomas Totman Born Decr 24th 1760.

The Child of Mary Ward.
1 James Beeten Born Janury 8th 1761

The Chilldren of Samuel Sherman . & Experiance his Wife
1 Samuel Sherman Born Decr 1st 1751. Died Novr 9th 1818.
2 Elijah Sherman Born Octr 29th 1753
3 Lydia Sherman . Born . Octr 16th 1755

[p. 3] The Children of Ebenezer Churchill Junr & Jean his Wife
1. Ebenezer Churchell Born, Oct 5 . 1755.
2. Timothy Churchell Born Jany 21 . 1757
3. John Churchell . Born Febry 4th 1759 . Deceasd August 23rd 1760
4. Jean Churchell . Born Jany 6 . 1761.
5. John Churchill, Born June 24 . 1763.
6. Martha Churchill born January . 10 . 1767 . Saturday.

The Chilld . of . Nathaniell Holmes . And Lydia His Wife
1. Nathaniell Holmes Born Decr 16th 1755.

The Children of Mr Elkanah Watson & Patience his Wife
1. Marston Watson Born May 28th 1756.
2. Elkanah Watson Born Jany 22 . 1758 . at 12 aClock, Sabbath Day.
3. Priscilla Watson Born Sepr 30 . 1760
4 Patty Watson Born October yr 16 . 1762
5 Lucia Watson Born Novemr yr 11 . 1765

[p. 4] The Children . of Ebenezer Silvester, & Mary his Wife
1 Ebenezer Silvester, Born June 18th 1756 . Deceasd April 24th 1760
2 Lemuel Silvester Born May 24th 1758
3 Caleb Silvester Borne June 17th 1760
4 Joseph Silvester Born Augst 15th 1763
5 Solomon Silvester Born Octobr 17 : 1764

The Child of Ebenezer Churchell Junr & Jean his wife
Timothy Churchell Born Jany 21 . 1757. Entd page . 3rd

The Child of John Wall, & Ruth Wall, his Wife
Ruth Wall . Born June 25th 1756.

[p. 5] The Children of Thomas Silvester, & Martha, his Wife
1. Thomas Silvester, Born, Febry 11th 1750/1
2. Sarah Silvester Born June 5 . 1753.
3. Hannah Silvester Born March 4 . 1756.

The Children of Samuell Elles, & Lydia his Wife
1. Sarah Elles . Born March 10 . 1755.

2. Nathaniel Elles, Born Jany 30 . 1757.

The Chilldren of James Shurtleff . & Faith his wife
1 Lydia Shurtleff born June 16th 1735 Deceasd Augst 19th 1764
2 Elizabeth Shurtleff born Febry 15th 1736/7
3 Hannah Shurtleff born Jany 11th 1739/40
4 Molley Shurtleff born April 1741 Deceasd May 1742
5 Faith Shurtleff born March 25th 1745

[p. 6] The Child of Seth Barnes Junr, & Elizabeth, his Wife
Elizabeth Barnes, Born Decr 25th 1754.

The Children of Edward Burt & Elizabeth his wife
1. Tamson Clark . born Decr 28 . 1817.
2. Silas Hathaway   Febr 21 . 1820
3. Benjamin Thomas   Mar: 5 . 1822
4. John E. Burt   Decr 27 . 1823
5. Charity S. Burt   Febry 17 . 1826
6. Charlotte H   Mar: 29 . 1828.
7. Elizabeth C   Sept: 25 . 1830
8. William B   June : 6 . 1832
9. Almira Burt   Augt 31 . 1833 . deceased Sept 20 . 1833
10. Eunice D. Burt*   Decr 8 . 1837.
11. Adoniram Burt*   July. 29 . 1836 . died June 7 . 1837
12. Thomas B. Burt.   Feby . 15 . 1839.

The Children . of . Jacob Tayler & Jemimah his Wife
1 Jemimah Tayler Born Aprill 11th 1757.
2. Mary Tayler Born May 19th 1759.
3 Joannah Tayler Born August ye 11 . 1761
4. Jacob Tayler, Born, May 15th 1763.
5. Edward Tayler Born Septr 5t 1765
6 Sarah
7 Elizabeth
8 Lucy

The Children . of . John . Washburn Junr & Lydia his Wife
1 John Washburn . Born . Decr 28th 1755
2. Abial . Washburn . Born Novr 21st 1757.
3 Benjamin Washbn Born Augt. 14th 1761
4 Prince Washburn Born Sept 9th 1763
5 Lydia Washburn Born Oct 1st 1765
6 Thomas Washburn born Decr 16th 1767

[p. 7] The Children of Silvanus Morton & Mary his Wife
1 Abigail Morton Born June 10 . 1753.
2. James Morton Born Sept 3 . 1755.

Henry W. Green & Elizabeth his wife, their Children.
1. Henry T. Green born 1833, 19th April.
2 Harriet Elizabeth 1838 . 31st . Dec.

The Children of . Alezander Roberson & Abigail his Wife
1 Alexander Roberson Born May 29th 1752
2 Micah Roberson Born April 8th 1755

*Before these two entries is written "vice versa"

Children of Richard Green & Mary T. Green his wife

1. Rachel T. Green born 1828 . December 16
2. Mary Jane Green   1832 March . 12
3. Richard F Green   Dec. 10 . 1833*
4. Charles G. Green   Dec. 14 . 1834†
5. George Franklin   1836 . Ap¹. 8.
6. Edward Everett   1837 . Nov. 16.

[p. 8] The Chilldren of Benjamin Cornish Jun. & Rhoda his Wife

1. Deborah Cornish Born June 25ᵗʰ 1753
2. Susannah Cornish Born March 4ᵗʰ 1755
3. William Cornish Born March 3ʳᵈ 1757
4. Rhoda . Cornish . Born Jan^ry 16ᵗʰ 1759.
5. Stephen Cornish Born Decem^r 25ᵗʰ 1760
6. Nancey Cornish Born Decem^r 22ⁿᵈ 1762
7. Benjamin Cornish Born Jan^ry 25ᵗʰ 1765
8. Sarah Cornish Born
9. George Cornish born 1 Novr 1767
10. Lenuel Cornish born [‡] Deceas^d

The Children of Jonathan Morton, & Rebeckah his Wife

1. Cary Harris Morton Born July 18ᵗʰ 1750.
2. Jonathan Morton Born, Feb^ry 25ᵗʰ 1753 Deceased April 17 . 1753
3. George Morton Born Aug^st 15 . 1757.

The Children of Samuel Chandler & Jerusha, his Wife

1. Samuel Bartlett Chandler bor, 1832 . July 14.
2. David Lothrop Chandler   1834 . May . 16.
3. Everline Coleman "   1835 . Novr 2
4. John Brown Chandler   1837 . Octr 7.

[p. 9] The Children . of . William Barnes & Mercy his Wife

1. Abigail . Barnes Born August . ye 7ᵗʰ 1755.
2. Marcy . Barnes Born Dec^r . 15ᵗʰ 1757
3. William Barnes, Born Jan^ry 2 . 1760

The Chilldren of Richard Holmes & Mercy his wife

1. Elizabeth Holmes born Octr 15ᵗʰ 1764 Deceas^d Feb^ry 5ᵗʰ 1782
2. Richard Holmes born July 5ᵗʰ 1766
3. William Holmes born March 26ᵗʰ 1768
4. Lydia Holmes born Jan^ry 8ᵗʰ 1770
5. Polley Holmes born May 18ᵗʰ 1779

The Chilldren of Jesse Rider . & Bethiah§ his Wife

1. Bethiah Rider Born Feb^ry 21ˢᵗ 1755
2. James Rider Born Decemb^r 8ᵗʰ 1756

The Children of Leavitt T. Robbins & Lydia his wife

1. Lydia Johson   born 1833 . December 21

---

* "1834 Decr 14" was first written, but it was crossed out with pencil, and "Dec. 10 . 1833" written, in a different hand and ink.
† "1833 . Decr 10 " was first written, but it was crossed out with pencil, and "Dec. 14 . 1834" written, in a different hand and ink.
‡ Space was left for the date.
§ "Thomas " has been interlined above, in a modern hand.

---

2. Elizabeth Fuller   1834 . November 25
3. Leavitt Taylor   1837 . Septr 2
4. Lemuel Fuller   1839 . Jan^ry 22.

[p. 10] The Children . of Thomas Morton . & Mary his Wife

1. Nathaniel Morton . Born Decr 7ᵗʰ 1754
2. Thomas . Morton . Born Jan^ry 15ᵗʰ 1757
3. William Morton Born Octob^r 13ᵗʰ 1759
4. Jesse Morton Born August . 8ᵗ 1761
5. Mary Morton Born Septr 23ʳᵈ 1763
6. Andrew Morton Born Septr 23ʳᵈ 1765
7. Martha Morton Born Decr 21 1767

Twins 8 } Tabor Morton Born Jan^ry 8ᵗʰ 1770
      9 } Andrew Morton Born Jan^ry 8ᵗʰ 1770

The Children of William C. Green & Marcia his Wife

1. William Henry born 1830 Sept. 13ᵗʰ
2. Nathaniel Holmes born 1832 . April 6
3. Marcia Ann   1833 . July 20 deceased
4. Marcia Ann   1835 . July 14 deceased

The . Chilldren . of . Lemuel . Fish & Joannah his Wife

1. Jane Fish . Borne Decr 1ˢᵗ 1754
2. Lemuel Fish . Borne Octr 17ᵗʰ 1756
3. Deborah Fish Borne
4. Johannah Fish Borne Sep^t 29ᵗʰ 1760.
5. Samuel Fish Born July . 17 . 1762
6. Lucy Fish born [*] Deceas^d
7. Caleb Fish born
8. Lucy Fish born
9. Eliz^a Fish born
10. Mary Fish born
11 Lemuel Fish born May 12ᵗʰ 1779.

[p. 11] The Child of Robert Roberts, & Margaret, his Wife
John Roberts, Born July 28ᵗʰ 1757.

The Children of Nathan Bacon Robbins & Lucia his Wife

1. Lucia Rider Robbins . born . 1824 . Ap^l 11ᵗʰ
2. Mary Bacon Robbins,   1826 . Jan^ry 13.

The Children of Nathan Bacon Robbins & Lucia his 2^d Wife

1. Hannah Tilden Robbins born 1831 . Sept 23^d.
2. Nathan Bacon Robbins   1834 . July . 31.

The Children of Ichabod Shaw, & Priscilla his Wife

1. Priscilla Shaw Born Jan^ry 11 . 1758.
2. Mary Shaw Born Aug^st 2 . 1760.
3. Experience Shaw, Born, July . 1 . 1762.
4. Desire Shaw Born June 7 1765
5. Lydia Shaw born Aug^st 15ᵗʰ 1767
6. Ichabod Shaw born Novr 21ˢᵗ 1769
7. Southworth Shaw born Feb^ry 3rd 1772 Deceas^d
8. Lucy Shaw born June 2nd 1773
9. Southworth Shaw born July 28ᵗʰ 1775

---

* Space was left for the date.

216   *Plymouth, Mass., Vital Records*

10 Sarah Shaw born May 4th 1778.
11 Nansey Shaw born Jany 4th 1781 Deceased
12 John Atwood Shaw born April 18th 1783
13 Samuel Shaw . born . Septemb: 22 1785 Deceased
[p. 12] The Children of Caleb Stetson & Abigail his Wife
1. Caleb Stetson Born August 12 . 1755.
2. Bradford Stetson Born May 20 . 1757.
Children of Orrin Bosworth & Jane his wife, viz
1. Jane Taylor, born, 1831 . May 5.
2. Orrin Waterman, 1835 . Decr 8
The Child of Orrin Bosworth & Betsey his 2d wife
3. Hannah Elizabeth born 1838 Augt 4th
The Children of Zacheus Churchell, & Mary his Wife
1. Elezabeth Churchell Born Jany 24 . 1755
2. Zacheus Churchell Born Decr 1 . 1757
3. Mary Churchell Born Novr 24 . 1758
4. Ephraim Churchell Born Sepr
The Children of Bourn Spooner & Hannah his wife.
1. Nathaniel Bourn Spooner, born 1818 . Feby 2d *Should be 1815.**
2. William Thomas Spooner, born 1817 April 25
3. Charles Walter Spooner born 1824 . Apl 27.
4. John Adams Spooner . born 1826 . Augt 27
5. Edward Amasa Spooner born . 1830 Jany 7.
Marnion Born at New Orleans Aug. 13 . 1819.
[p. 13] The Children of George Watson Esqr and Elizabeth his Wife.
1. Mary Watson Born April 15 1754
2. George Watson, Born July 24 1757 . Deceased Augst 10th 1757
3. Sarah Watson, Born March 23 1759
4. Elizabeth Watson Born August 29 1764 Deceased September 14 1764
5. Elizabeth Watson Born Febry 19th 1767
Mrs Eliza Watson Mother of the Above Family Deceasd Febry 19th 1767
The Child of Lemuel D Holmes & Polly his wife viz
Mary Antoinette Holmes, born January 6th . 1837.
The Chilldren of Nathaniel Foster, & Abigail His Wife,
1. Hannah Foster . Born June 15th 1749 Deceasd Sept 18th 1750
2. Sarah Foster Born Sept 10th 1750
3. Nathaniel Foster Born Sept 28th 1751
4. Abigail Foster Born Mar: 9th 1753
5. Gershom Foster Born July 6th 1754
6. Hannah Foster Born Octr 1st 1755
7. Betty Foster Born Aprill 1st 1757.
See his Children by his first wife Libr 1st page 172.
The Children of Amasa Bartlett & Esther his wife.
1. Amasa S. Bartlett, born 1834 . August 5th
2. Mary Ann Bartlett   1838 . Feby 9th

(*To be continued*)

---

* The words in italics are in a different hand and ink.

THE MAYFLOWER DESCENDANT

1620　1920

A QUARTERLY MAGAZINE OF
PILGRIM GENEALOGY AND HISTORY

VOLUME XIX

1917

PUBLISHED BY THE
MASSACHUSETTS SOCIETY OF
MAYFLOWER DESCENDANTS
BOSTON

PLYMOUTH, MASS., VITAL RECORDS

TRANSCRIBED BY THE EDITOR

(*Continued from Vol. XVIII, p. 216*)

[p. 14] The Child . of . William Huston & Elizabeth his Wife
William Huston . Born July . 22nd 1755.
The Children of Thomas Cornish, & Anne his Wife
1 Elizabeth Cornish Born March 2 . 1757.
2 Thomas Cornish, Born Sept 22 . 1758.
3. Josiah Cornish, Born Oct 15th 1760.
4. Anna Cornish . Born Feb 24th 1763.
5 Abigal Cornish Born Nov 24th 1764
6 Samuel Cornish Born Jan 10th 1767.
The Children of . Branch Blackmer & Sarah his Wife
1 Mary . Blackmer . Born Feb 21st 1758 . Deceasd
2. Sarah Blackmer, Born July 2 . 1759 . Deceasd
3 William Blackmer born Oct 27 . 1760
4 John Blackmer born Jan 8 . 1763
5 Sarah Blackmer born Nov 28th 1764
Twins { Mary Blakmer born July 10th 1767
       { Mercy Blackmer born July 10th 1767
8 Betty Blackmer born Nov 3rd 1769
9 Richard Blackmr born Nov 1st 1772
Twins { 10 Branch Blackmer born April 10th 1775
       { 11 Ivorey Blackmer born April 10th 1775
[p. 15] The Chilldern . of William Serjant . & Mary his Wife
1 Experience Serjant . Born May 1st 1750
2 Ruth . Serjant . Born Decemb 27th 1751

Plymouth, Mass., Vital Records

3. Mary Serjant Born July 22 . 1754
4. Elizabeth Serjant Born March 22nd 1756 Deceased March 28th 1758
5. Lydia Serjant Born Jany 1st 1758
6. Elizabeth Serjant Born June 10th 1760
7. Sarah Serjant Born April 4th 1762
8. Hannah Serjant Born July . 10th 1764

The Children of Benjamin Lucas, & Lydia his Wife
1. Bela Lucas, Born Febry 3 . 1757.
2. Isaac Lucas Born Jany 6 . 1759
3. Abigail Lucas Born March 8 . 1761.
4. Ezra Lucas Born . May 19 . 1763.
5. Lucey Lucas Born March 24th 1765
6. Lydia Lucas Born July 24th 1767
7. Naomi Lucas born June 2nd 1770

The Children of George [Henry*] Griffin & Marcia his wife
1. George Henry Griffin, born, 1833 . July 29th
2. Hannah Elizabeth, born, 1835 . June 6th.
3. Sarah Williams, born, 1837 . June 13th.

[p. 16] The Childd of Ebenezer Fuller . & Lowis His Wife
1. Ebenezer Fuller. Born Febry 4th 1758

The Children of John Gardner & Ann his wife.
1. William Gardner born in Roxbury
2. Susan Gear Gardner born 1824 August 24
3. Ann Maria Gardner born 1830 July 20
4. John Gardner born 1832. Novr 9.
5. Andrew Gear Gardner . 1834. Decr 2.
6. Mary Clark Gardner 1837 . May 9.

The Child of Benja Allen, & Beza his Wife
Benjamin Allen, Born, Octr 11 . 1755.

The Children of Nathan Simmons & Lydia his wife.
1. Nathan born July . 29 . 1754 . deceased august . 11 . following.
2. Nathan born august . 1st. 1755.
3. Bennet born august . 17 . 1757.

Said Nathan Simmons dyed November . 3 . 1758 . Aged . 27 . years & . 6 . months.

Children of Chandler Carver & Catharine his Wife
1. Lucy Carver born March 28 . 1837.
2. James M Carver March 5 . 1839.

[p. 17] The Children of Mr William Watson, & Elizabeth his Wife.
1. William Watson Born Augst 18 . 1757.
2. Elizabeth Watson Born Febry 17th 1759
3. Benjamin Watson Born Febry 8th 1761
4. Ellen Watson Born April 12th 1764

The Children of John Stephenson, & Elizabeth his Wife
1. John Stephenson Born Octr ye 13th 1757.
2. Elizabeth Stephenson Born in Bostson may 15th 1760
3. Jasper hall Stephenson Born Jany 18th 1766
4th Child see above
4. Willm Stephenson born Apl 27th 1767

The Children of Joshua Holmes & Hannah Holmes his Wife
1. Elizabeth Holmes Born Augst 8 . 1756.
2. Joshua Holmes Born, March 28 . 1759.

Children of Charles Westgate & Lydia his wife.
1. Charles Howard Westgate, born 1832, May 29
2. Nancy Polden Westgate born 1835, Febry 19
3. Susan Polden Westgate born 1838 April, 28.

[p. 18] The Children of Joseph Rider ye 3rd & Thankfull his wife.
1. Samuel . Rider . Born Novr 28th 1752 Deceasd Decr ye 19th 1752
2. Samuel . Rider . Born . June 25th 1754
3 a Daughter . not named . born July . 18th 1757 . Deceasd the same day
4. Hannah Rider Born Augst 17 . 1760.
[5 Joanna Ryder born Aug. 19th 1781*]

The Children of Thadeus Faunce & Mary Anna his wife.
1. Elizabeth Davis born 1834 . Novr 22d
2. Mary Ann born 1836 . Augt 10th.
3. Thadeus born 1839 . Apl 4th

The Children of John Cobb & Hannah his Wife
1. Hannah . Cobb Born in Kingston June 17th 1756
2. Patience . Cobb Born in Plymo April 29th 1758
3. Joannah Cobb Born Decr 4 . 1759.
4. Lydia Cobb Born Novr 3 . 1761.
5. Sarah Cobb . Born . Novr 5 1762.
6 Abigail Cobb Born Novr 30th 1765

The Children of John Cobb & Pearces his 2nd wife
1 William Cobb born June 24th 1767
2 Elizabeth Cobb born Novr 14th 1769
3 Eleonar Cobb born Novr 26th 1770
4 John Cobb born April 22nd 1773
5 Ruth Cobb born Octr 13th 1775
6 Perces Cobb Born Decr 31 1777 Deceasd Jany 2nd 1782
7 Josiah Cobb born Novr 3rd 1780
8 Perces Cobb . born June 16th 1783

[p. 19] The Child of Willm Gammons & Fear his Wife
Rebeckah Gammons, Born March 1753.

Samuel Alexander Jrt & Charlotte his wife
1. Catharine Elizabeth born January 21 . 1830
2. Samuel Thomas " July 24 . 1833
3. John Knowls " March. 2 . 1837

The Child of John Dyre & Mary his Wife
John Dyre Born May 25th 1758

*This entry evidently was an error, and it was partially erased. The record will be found on original page 78, among the children of Joseph Rider, Jr, and Abigail his wife.

† "Jr" was added in a different hand

*"Henry" has a line through it, with an "x" above, referring to "x Washington" at the bottom of the page, written in a different hand

The Child of James Timberleck & Lydia his wife
Sarah Timberleck born June 27th 1775
Children of Oliver Holmes & Pamela his Wife
1. Amelia Anne born, 1831, May 31
2. Maria Thomas born 1833, June 28
3. Fanny Winsor born 1835, Mar. 24
4. Mehetable Pain " 1839 Feby 3.
[p. 20] The Chilldren of. William Weston & Mary His Wife
1 Lewis Weston . Born . August 22nd 1754
2 William Weston Born July . 17th 1757
3 Comer Weston born
The Chilldren of Samuel Doten & Mary Doten his Wife
1 Rebeckah Doten . Born . Novr 30th 1753 Deceasd Decr 14th 1753
2 Samuel . Doten . Born July 15th 1758
Mary Doten Born, Sept 18, 1762
[p. 21] The Children of John Cornish & Lydia his Wife.
2. Hannah Cornish Born, April 3 . 1758.
1 A Son Borne, June 1757 . & Dyed a few Minutes after its Birth.
3. A Daughter Born Decr 3 . 1759 . and Lived about one Week.
4. Mary Cornish Born March 1761 is March ye 1st
5. Lydia Cornish Born April 19th 1763
The Children of John Cornish & Sarah his 2nd wife
John Cornish born Janry 5th 1771 Deceasd
2. John Cornish born Novr 22nd 1772
2. Freeman Cornish born Augst 27th 1774 Deceasd
3. Sarah . Cornish born Novr 22nd 1776
4 Spooner Cornish born Janry 10 . 1779
The Children of Nathl Washburn, & Mary his Wife
1 Mary Washburn Born July 27 . 1758 . Deceased Decr 15th 1759.
2 Nathaniel Washburn Born August ye 1 . 1760
3 Mary Washburn . Born . Febry ye 17 1764.
The Chilldren of John Cornish & Elizabeth his wife
Freeman Cornish & } Twins borne Octo 24th 1782
Clark . Cornish
Phebe Cornish born April 20th 1785
[p. 22] The Chilldern of Zacheus Bartlett & Margarett his Wife
1 Phebe Bartlett Born March 16th 1754
2 Elizabeth Bartlett Born Octr 21st 1758
Children of James Diman & Rebecca his wife
1 Rebecca Harlow, born May 17 . 1834
2 Mary Boylston " Mar: 29 . 1837
The Chilldren of William Carver & Margarett his Wife
1 Thomas Carver born Octr 4th 1755
2 William Carver born Augst 2nd 1757
3 Branch Carver borne Octr 17th 1759
The Child of Joseph Fulgham & Rebackah Fulgham his Wife
Charles Fulgham Born June 13th 1749

Children of Joseph Wright and Sally his wife
1 Sarah Robbins born January 1st . 1832
2 Joseph Wright born April 21th . 1834
[p. 23] The Chilldren of Elkanah Waterman of Mary His Wife
1 Mary Waterman Born March 23rd 1755
2 Mercy Waterman Born July 30th 1757
The Children of Patrick Morris, & Mary Morris his Wife
1. John Morris Born, October ye 24th 1758.
2. James Morris, Born, Sept ye 9th 1761.
The Children of John Jones, & Lydia Jones his Wife
1 John Jones Born, March 2 . 1759 . Deceasd Oct 22nd 1761
2 John Jones Born Janry 14th 1763
3 Benjamin Jones Born May 20th 1767
4 Ebenezr Jones born at Kingston 14th Septemr 1769 Deceasd
5 Lydia Jones born Novembr 13th 1771
6 Ebenezr Jones Born Sept 12th 1774
The Children of Thomas Diman & Polly his Wife.
1. Sophia Sampson born in 1832 . May 14th
2. Abby Philips born in 1833 . Sept 26th
4 Mary Harlow born in 1837 . Feby 24th } born in Boston
3. Polly born in 1835 . July 31st   deceased
[p. 24] The Children of George Glover, & Mary his Wife
1. Mary Glover Born July 16 . 1758
2. George Glover Born Febry 23 . 1761
3. Margaret Glover, Born, April . 10 . 1763
4. Samll Glover Born August 1st 1764
The Children of John Wiswell & his Wife
1. Priscilla Thomas born October 29, 1828.
2. John Bradford born June 1, 1837.
The Chilldren of Nathaniel Torrey & Anna His Wife
1 Elizabeth Torrey . born Febry 5th 1747/8
2 Nathaniel Torrey born Octr 8th 1750
3 Priscilla Torrey born Octr 2nd 1754
4 Annah Torrey . born July 11th 1756
5 Sarah Torrey born Augt 7th 1758 Deceasd April 4th 1759
Daniel Torrey born   decd in U. S. army*
John Torrey born*
Children of Nathaniel Barnes & Hannah his wife.
1. Betsey Goddard Barnes born 1821 . May 6
2. John Ellis Barnes born 1826 July 25
3. Nathaniel Barnes born 1829 . Feby 23.
The Child of Sally Burgess
named Horatio Spooner, born March 6 . 1825.
Child of Nathan Hall & Sally his wife
Nathan Thomas Hall, born October 11th . 1828.

(To be continued)

*These two entries are in a different hand.

PLYMOUTH, MASS., VITAL RECORDS

(Continued from page 9)

[p. 25] The Children of Thomas Mayhew, & Mary Mayhew his Wife

Mary Mayhew, Born April 22nd 1742. Deceas'd Feb'y 9th 1812
Thomas Mayhew, Born Sept 9. 1744.
Anna Mayhew, Born Dec'r 11. 1746. Died at L Island N'York 1826
Elizabeth Mayhew Born Feb'y 13. 1748. Deceas'd Dec'r 4. 1756.
William Mayhew Born Nov'r 28. 1751. Deceas'd April. 2. 1752
Sarah Mayhew, Born Jan'y 18. 1753. Deceas'd 1789
William Mayhew Born Aug'st 1. 1755.
Betty Mayhew. Born March 5. 1757.
Lucy Mayhew Born July 30. 1760. deceased July 6. 1766
The Children of Solomon Silvester, and Hannah Silvester his Wife

1 Hannah Silvester Born, April 13th 1759.
2. Elizabeth Silvester Born, Feb'y 8. 1762.
3 Solomon Silvester Born July y'e 5th 1764
4 George Silvester Born. June 25th 1766
5 Lucy Silvester Born Sept 4th 1768
The Children of Francis Polden & Catharine B. his Wife
1. Harriet Thomas born May 9th 1837.
The Children of George F. Lanman & Abby his Wife.
1 George Francis, born February 1835.
2. Samuel Ellis, born January. 1837.
[p. 26] The Children of John Russell, & Marcy Russell his Wife
1. John Russell Born July 8th 1758.
2. James Russell Born Jan'y y'e 3d 1760 Deceas'd Sept 28th 1792
3. Thomas Russell Born Oct'r 3. 1761. Dec'd September 24th 1802
4. Mercy Russell Born June 18 1763. Dec'd September Deceas'd
5 Abigail Russell Born May 4th 1766 Deceas'd
6 Nancey Russell Born May 24th 1767
Jane Russell
Nathaniel Russell
George Russell
The Children of John Russell & Mary his wife
1 John Russell born Aug: 13th 1786
2 Thomas Russell born July 19th 1788

3 Charles Russell born Aug: 24th 1790 Dec'd Nov: 2nd 1791
4 Mary Russell born Oct'r 5th 1792
5. Nancey Russell born July 2nd 1795 Deceas'd Aug: 10th 1797
6. Charles Russell born Dec'r 11th 1798
7. James Russell born
The Child of Edward Lanman & Abiah his Wife
William Lanman Born April y'e 8th 1759
The Children of James Prince & Eunice his wife
1 Polley Prince . born April 11th 1784
2 Thomas Prince born Jan'y 17th 1786
3 Lydia Prince born Aug: 14th 1788
Child of Jesse Cunningham & Sarah his wife
Sarah Elizabeth born, February 21. 1834
[p. 27] The Child of Samuel Dogget & Deborah his Wife
Deborah Dogget Born Aug'st 8th 1758
Children of America Rogers & Eliza his wife
1. William Rogers, born 1836. February 14th
2. Lydia Holmes Rogers born December 21. 1837.
The Children of Levi Drew, & Mary Drew, his Wife
1. Mary Drew Born, Nov'r 9. 1756.
2. Joanna Drew Born June 11. 1759. Deceased, Nov'r 9. 1760.
3. Levi Drew Born, July 29. 1761. Deceased September* 9. 1762.
4. Lydia Drew Born August 3rd 1764
5 Levi Drew . born Dec'r 10th 1766
6 John Milk Drew Born March 21st 1769
Children of Winslow Drew and Abby his wife
1. Augusta Winslow born July 12. 1833
2. Edward Winslow born July 7. 1835
[p. 28] The Children of Joseph Trask, & Jerusha Trask, his Wife
1 Joseph Trask Born, Sept 27 1758.
2 Thomas Trask Born Feb'y 11. 1760
3 Priscilla Trask Born October 27th 1761
4 William Trask Born Aug'st 2 : 1763
Children of David Cobb Holmes & Louisa his wife.
1. David Winsor, born Ap'l 11. 1832
2. Andrew ⎱ Twins, born March 19. 1833.
3. Albert   ⎰
4. Louisa born January 10. 1835
5. Mary Smith, born Nov 3. 1836
The Children of James Harlow & Jerusha his Wife
1. Nathaniel Harlow born Jan'y 12th 1759

*"December" was first written, but was crossed out and "September" written above it, in the same hand and ink.

2. Susanna Harlow* Born July 12th 1761
3. James Harlow, Born August. 5th . 1763.
4 Reubin Harlow born Augst 12th 1766
Children of Thomas Allen & Betsey his wife. viz
1. Thomas Jefferson Allen, born March 23d . 1839
[p. 29] The Children of Ebenezer Donham Junr, and Hannah Donham his Wife
1. Abigail Donham Born, August 10th 1757.
2. Ebenezer Donham Born, Janry 12 . 1759.
Children of Asa Thomas & [†] his wife viz:
Fanny Thomas was born March 26, 1819
Asa Thomas Jr. was born August . 25, 1820
Alanson Thomas was born Sept 21, 1822
Gamaliel Thomas was born . Augt 10, 1824
Eleazer Thomas was born July 5, 1827
Ezra Thomas was born August . 5, 1829.
The Child of Thomas . Churchell & Mary his Wife
Gamaliel Churchell Borne Augst 30th 1759
Children of George Augustus Drew & Ruby his wife
1. Georgianna Drew, born, May 17 . 1836
2. Charles Lee Drew, born, March 5 . 1839
Children of George Washburn & Priscilla his 2d Wife
1. George born Feby 28 . 1828
2. Priscilla D. Washburn born . Jany 28 . 1830
[p. 30] The Children of Peleg Faunce & Mary his Wife
1 Eleazer Faunce Born Decr 16th 1757
2 Peleg Faunce Born Decr 2nd 1759
3 Joseph Faunce Born April 4th 1763
4 Benjamin Faunce Born Augst 18th 1765
Children of George P. Fowler & Margarett his wife
1. Margarett Elizabeth . born November 11th . 1832
2. Harriet Frankson born October 19th . 1834
3. Sophia Hersey born Apl 26th. 1836 deceased March 26 . 1837.
4. Thomas Bartlett born Jany 11th . 1839.
The Children of Joshua Battles & Experience his Wife
1 Martha Battles borne May 15th 1758
2 Experience Battles borne Aug: 18th 1760
3. Joshua Battles, born July . 19th 1762.
4. Timothy Battles, Born Augst 6th 1764.

* "Holmes" was first written, but was crossed out and "Harlow" interlined, in the same hand and ink.
† A blank space was left for the name of the wife.

Children of Daniel J. Lewis & Sarah his wife.
1. James Augustus, born May 20th . 1833
2. Albert born May 19th . 1835
3. William born Mar: 6th . 1839

(To be continued)

PLYMOUTH, MASS., VITAL RECORDS

(Continued from page 93)

[p. 31] The Child of James Carver, & Hope Carver his Wife
James Carver Born Sept 28 . 1757.
Children of Elisha Nelson & Abigail his wife
1. George William born June 3d . 1823.
2. Hannah Thomas born Augt 15th . 1828
The Child of John Cobb, & Hannah Cobb his Wife
Joannah Cobb, Born Decr 4 . 1759. is Entred page 18th*
Children of Charles Nelson & Lucy his wife.
1. Lucy born July, 29 . 1830
2. Charles born June, 7, 1833
3. Harriet born May, 16, 1836.
[p. 32] The Child of John Totman, & Elizabeth Totman his Wife
1 John Totman Born, Decr 26 . 1759
Reubin Totman Born June 23rd 1766
Asaph Totman born May 4th 1769
Children of Lemuel Bradford & Bathsheba his wife
1. Lemuel, born May 22d . 1813
2. Charles, born Jany 28th . 1821
3. Winslow, born Novr 4th . 1826
4 Lydia Nelson Mar: 29th . 1830
5 Hannah Everson, Mar: 26 . 1833
6 Ebenezer Nelson, Octr 31 . 1836.
The Children of Cornelius Holmes Junr & Lydia Holmes his Wife
1. Cornelius Holmes Born Decr 3 . 1754.
2. Benjamin Holmes Born, Decr 16 . 1759.
The Children of Daniel Prat, & Lydia Prat, his Wife
1. Lydia Prat Born Augst 27 . 1760.
2. Hopefull Prat Born Sept 25 . 1761.
3 William Cobb Pratt born Febry 21st 1764
4 Daniel Pratt . born Decr 12th 1765
5 Ruth . Pratt . born April 30th 1768
6 Joshua Pratt . born June 20th 1770

*This family was recorded in full on original page 18.

[p. 33] The Child of Samuell Calderwood, & Priscilla Calderwood his Wife.

Sam.ll Calderwood, Born, Sept 1. 1761

The Children of.William LeBaron & Sarah his Wife

1 William born November 9th 1775 deceased the 17th
2 Sarah born December 16th 1776 mondy morn eight OClock A.M.

Twins { 3 Mary born August 27th 1778 } Thursday ten OClock
      { 4 Lucy born August 27th 1778 } A.M
5 Priscilla born March 7th 1781 Wednesday four OClock A.M.
6 Eliza. born May 1785

The Children of Solomon Holmes, & Abigail Holmes his Wife
1. Nathaniel Holmes, Born, Nov.r 19th 1760.
2. Abigail Holmes, Born . July. 4 . 1762.
3. Solomon Holmes . Born Jan.ry 1 1764
4. Thomas Holmes Born

The Above named Abigail Holmes Deceas.d Nov.r 15th 1766
Children of W.m Hall & Susan his wife,
1. Susan Williams, born, 1834 . December 23d
2. John Frederick, born, 1837. April. 22d
3. William Curtis, born, 1839. January 12th

Children of Andrew Mackie & Hitty his wife.
1. Andrew born February 21 . 1823
2. John Howel Mackie, born Aug.t 24 . 1826.

[p. 34] The Children of Samuel Donham Jun.r & Susannah his Wfe
1 Samuel Donham borne. Oct.r 9th 1758
2. Elizabeth Donham born Jan.ry 31 . 1761
3 Susannah Donham born May 20th 1763
4. Deborah Donham born Sept 24th 1765
5 Ichabod Donham born Jan.ry 8th 1768
6 Elijah Donham . born Feb.ry 3rd 1770 Deceas.d Sept 30th 1773
7 Nath.ll Thomas Donham born March 18th 1772 Deceas.d Octob.r 28th 1773
8 Nansey Donham born Nov.r 11th 1774
9 Ephraim Donham born Jan.ry 6th 1777 Deceas.d Jan.ry 5th 1786
10 Andrew . Donham born June 23rd 1779
11 Lewis . Donham born Aug : 28th 1785

1761. The Children of John Donham, & Mary Donham, his Wife
1. Moses Donham Born Jan.ry 23rd 1757.
2. Mary Donham, Born, Dec.r 16th 1758.
3 Salome Donham Born Ap.r 12 : 1762
4 John Donham Born Nov.r 16th 1764

Children of James Hall and Mary his Wife
1. Isaac Thomas, born June 29th. 1834

Children of John Thomas & Hannah his Wife
Eunice Burr Thomas born Ap.l 7 . 1824

[p. 35] The Children of James Warren Esq.r, & M.rs Marcy Warren his Wife
1. James Warren Born Oct.r y.e 18th 1757. [*Died 1821**]
2. Winslow Warren Born March 24th 1759. Deceas.d Nov.r 4th 1791
3. Charles Warren, Born, April. 14. 1762. Deceas.d at S.t Lucar in Spain Nov.r 30th 1784
4. Henry Warren Born March 21 . 1764. [*Died 1828**]
5 George Warren born Sept 20 . 1766 Deceas.d at Augusta District of Main Feb.ry 1800

James Warren Esq.r the father of the above famely Deceas.d Nov.r 28th 1808

The Children of Henry Warren Esq.r & Mary his wife
1 Marcia Otis Warren Sept 26th 1792 [*Died 1858**]
2 Winslow Warren Jan.ry 14 1795
3. Pelham Winslow Warren Jan.ry 14th 1797 [*Died 1848**]
4 Charles Henry Warren Sept 29th 1798
5 James Warren March 6th . 1801 deceas.d Feb.ry 12th 1814
6 Mary Ann Warren Sept 2nd 1803 [*Died 1834**]
7 Richard Warren June 5th 1805
8. George. Warren April 10th 1807 [*Died 1855**]
9 Edward. Warrin Sept 8th 1809

The Children of William Bradford & Alice his wife
1. Mary Ann born January 15 . 1822.
2. Alice S born October 26 . 1823.
3. Nancy born Nov.r 24 . 1827
4. William born Aug.t 11 . 1829
5. Eudora born June 9 . 1831

[p. 36] The Children of Nathaniel Morton & Mary his wife
1 Nathaniel Morton Borne April 13th 1747 Deceas.d Aug.st 8th 1758
2. Nathaniel Morton Borne July . 3rd 1749 Deceas.d July 17th 1753
3 Lemuel Morton Borne July 9th 1757 new Stile Dec.d 1827

The Children of Peleg Faunce & Olive his Wife
1. Daniel Wooster†, born Jan.ry 3d . 1829
2. Caroline Augusta, born May 23d . 1833.

*The entries printed in italics are additions in pencil, and all in one hand, therefore made in 1858, or later

† "Wooster" has been crossed out with pencil, and "Worcester" interlined in a different hand and ink.

THE MAYFLOWER DESCENDANT

1620   1920

A QUARTERLY MAGAZINE OF PILGRIM GENEALOGY AND HISTORY

VOLUME XX

1918

PUBLISHED BY THE
MASSACHUSETTS SOCIETY OF
MAYFLOWER DESCENDANTS
BOSTON

The Chilldren of Joseph Pearse & Rebeckah his Wife
1 Joseph Pearse borne Octr 11th 1749
2 Elizabeth Pearse borne Aug: 28th 1751
3 Rebeckah Pearse borne Novr 11 . 1753
Robert King and Eliza his Wife, their children
1. Eliza Ann, born May 15th . 1834
2. Robert Williams born March 12 1837.
3. Hannah Lewis born March. 29 . 1839.

(*To be continued*)

PLYMOUTH, MASS., VITAL RECORDS

Transcribed by the Editor

(Continued from Vol. XIX, p. 152)

[p. 37] The Chilldren of Isaac Atwood . & Lydia his wife

3 Thomas Atwood . borne Decr 22nd 1744
4 Isaac Atwood . borne July . 17th 1747
5 Waite . Atwood . borne Decr 17th 1749
6 Zacheus Atwood . borne Jan^{ry} 10th 1752 Old Stile
7 Lydia Atwood borne Jan^{ry} 11th 1754
8 Hannah Atwood . borne Sep^t 9th 1756

Two Chilldren belong^s to the Above family not Ent^d in their places in Course

Viz 1 Isaac Atwood borne . July 1741 Deceas^d Augst 1741
2 Lydia Atwood borne June 1743. Deceas^d July 1743

The Children of John Patee, and Margaret Patee his Wife

1. Ann Patee Born . April 3 . 1758.
2 John Patee . Born July 21 . 1759.
3 Levi Patee . Born July 27th 1761
4 Ephraim Patee Born [April 2^d 1763*]
5 Silvenus Patee Born Augst 4th 1765
6 Hannah Paty . Born
7. Margaret Paty . Born
8. Thomas Paty . Born

The Child of William Rider Junr, & Betty Rider his Wife.
Hallet Rider Born, Augst 17 . 1760.

Child of Joshua Pratt & Mary Ann his Wife, viz
Mary Ann Goodwin Pratt. born August 26 . 1838.

[p. 38] The Childdren of Jobb Cobb, And Patience Cobb, his Wife
1. Lydia Cobb. Born, June 30th 1744. Deceased, Augst 26th 1745.
3. Cornelius Cobb, Born June 30 . 1747.
2. Jobb Cobb, Born Octr 17 . 1745.
4. Rowland Cobb . Born Augst 20 . 1748. Deceased Augst 28th 1748.
5. Lydia Cobb Born . Novr 22 . 1750. Deceased August 20 . 1753.
6. Nehemiah Cobb Born August 23 . 1752. Deceased Sept 8th : 1753
7. Neheemiah Cobb, Born July 28 . 1754.
8. David Cobb. Born Augst 1 . 1756.

* An attempt has been made to erase this date.

9 Patience Cobb, Born June 19th 1759.

The Children of Mr Nath^{ll} Goodwin, & Lydia Goodwin his Wife

1. Nath^{ll} Goodwin, Born May 21 . 1748 . O. S. 5 Clock P.M. Saturday . died Mar : 8 . 1819.
2. Lydia Goodwin Born, May 10 . 1750 . O S. 9 Clock . A.M. Thursday
3. John Goodwin Born, Octr 18 . 1751 . O. S. 10 Clock P.M. Fryday.
4. Lazarus Goodwin, Born March 22 . 1753 New Stile, 9 Clock P.M. Thursday Deceased June 27th 1795 . 10, oClock P.M.
5. William Goodwin Born, Jan^{ry} 10 . 1756 N. S. 8 Clock P.M. Saturday
6. Thomas Goodwin, Born, Augst 31 . 1757 N. S. 4 Clock, AM. Wednesday
7. Mercy Goodwin, Born, March 22 . 1759 . 4 Clock . A.M. Thursday
8. Roby Goodwin Born, July 21 . 1761 10 Clock A.M. Tuesday Deceas^d Decr 5th 1761 Saturday 1 Clock PM
9 Francis Lebaron Goodwin Born Sept 29th 1762 N S. Wednesday 3 Clock PM
10 Anna Goodwin Born August 11th 1765 N S. Sunday 9 Clock PM Deceas^d July 14th 1766
11 George Goodwin born Jan^{ry} 13th 1767

The Children of William Straffin & Sophia his wife

1. William Turner, born Novr 1824*
2. Sophia Bartlett, born Sep^{tr} 1st . 1826.*

[p. 39] The Child of John Mackeel & Susanah Mackeel his wiffe
1 Abigail Mackeel Born August ye 28th 1757.

The Children of Sam^{ll} Bryant, & Eleonar Bryant, his Wife
1. Sarah Bryant Born, Decr 23rd 1758.
2. Samuel Bryant Born, April 14th†
3. Lydia . Bryant . Born

Children of Wm M. Jackson & Sylvina his Wife
1. Sylvina Augusta Jackson, born December 8 . 1828
2. William Spenser Jackson, born, January 15 . 1830. dec^d Sep^t 27 . 1833.
3. Morton Spenser Jackson, born March‡ 25th 1836. deceased Octr 29 . 1836

*These children have been crossed out. They were entered again on original page 242.

†The year was not recorded.

‡ "April" was first written, but was crossed out, and "March" written below the line.

Plymouth, Mass., Vital Records

The Child of Jeremiah Howes, & Hannah Howes, his Wife

Meriah Howes Born Jan'y 30th 1762.

The Child of Benjamin C. Finney & Elizabeth his Wife

1. Elizabeth Atwood, born May 2 . 1835.

[p. 40] The Children of James Polden, & Elizabeth Polden, his Wife

1 William Polden Born Dec'r 18 . 1761.
2 James Polden Born Aug'st 20th 1764.
3 Elizabeth Polden Born Aug'st 4th 1766
4 Hannah Polden Born Jan'y 17th 1770.

The Children of Cap't John Burgess & Susan his wife

1. Susan Burgess, born, Nov'r 28, 1808
2 Anna born. Sep't 30, 1810.
3. Catharine born Dec'r 11, 1815
4. Mary Ann born Aug't 23, 1817.
5. John born Dec'r 10, 1819;

And of Sophia his Wife.

1. Albert Thomas, born Sep't 3d 1825
2. Sophia, born July 1st . 1828.

The Children of Ebenezer Samson, And Hannah Samson His Wife

10 Continued from the first Book Page 183.*
11 Caleb Samson Born May . 3rd 1762
12. Ebenezer Samson Born April 1 . 1764

The Children of Asa Kendrick & Charlotte his wife

1. Reuben born March 12 . 1838.

The Children of James Burgess & Betsey Otis, his Wife.

1. Elizabeth James, born April 23d . 1838.

[p. 41] The Children . of Jacob Johnson Jun'r & Hannah Johnson his Wife

1. Joseph Johnson Born Oct'r 21 . 1760.
2. Thomas Johnson, Born . Sep't 9 . 1762
3 Abigail Johnson Born Mar : 22nd 1764
4 Mason Johnson Born Feb'ry 11th 1766
5 Jacob Johnson Born Jan'ry 8th 1768

The Children of Isaac Barnes Jr . & Betsey Thomas his Wife

1. Isaac, born, May 19, 1820
2. Thomas Davie, Feb'y 27, 1822.
3. Samuel Davis, July 8, 1829.

The Children of Isaac Barnes Jr & Lucy C. his Wife.

1. George Winslow, born Sep't 19 . 1832.

2 James Franklin, born Oct'r . 18, 1834.
3. Betsey Davie, born Feb'y 8, 1836.
4. Mary Frances, born Mar : 3, 1839.

The Children of Cornelius Morrey . & Sarah Morey His Wife

1 Mercy Morrey Born June 10th 1754
2 Sarah Morrey Born May . 25 . 1756
3 Elijah Morrey Born June . 1 . 1759
4 Cornelius Morrey Born May . 25 . 1761
5 Josiah Morrey . Born May . 23 . 1763
6 Silvanus Morrey . Born July 27 . 1767

The Children of Isaac M. Sherman & Hope his Wife

1. Betsey D. Sherman, born August 27 . 1814.
2. Isaac M. born July 25, 1816.
3. Winslow P. born Dec'r 31, 1818.
4. Mary D born June 25, 1821.
5. Hannah born Oct'r 9, 1823
6. Abby L. born Jan'y 12 . 1826.
7. Leander Lovell born Nov'r 12 . 1829.

The Child of Isaac M. Sherman & Sally his Wife.

George Sherman, born March 13, 1834.

(To be continued)

---

* See Mayflower Descendant, Vol. XV, pages 159, 160, for the first ten children.

THE MAYFLOWER DESCENDANT

1620 — 1920

A QUARTERLY MAGAZINE OF
PILGRIM GENEALOGY AND HISTORY

VOLUME XXI

1919

PUBLISHED BY THE
MASSACHUSETTS SOCIETY OF
MAYFLOWER DESCENDANTS
BOSTON

PLYMOUTH, MASS., VITAL RECORDS

TRANSCRIBED BY THE EDITOR

(Continued from Vol. XX, p. 73)

[p. 42] The Children of the Rev⁴ M' Chandler Robbins, & M'ˢ Jane Robbins, his Wife.*

1 Chandler Robbins Born, Thirsday yᵉ yᵉ 19th of August 1762. Half hour after 12 aClock, at noon.
2 Jenney Robbins Born Feby yᵉ 5 . 1764. Deceased July, 1801
3 Hannah Robbins Born Sepᵗ 24th . 1765 Deceasᵈ July 17th 1766
4 George Robbins Born March 8th . 1767 Deceasᵈ Mar: 13th 1767
5 Hannah Robbins born Sept 29th 1768 on thursday at ½ past 12 a Clock P.M
6 Isaac Robbins born June 19th 1770 a tuesday at ¼ past 11 aClock P.M
7. Philemon Robbins born March 23 . 1777 Decᵈ 1827†
8 Samuel Prince Robbins born April 20, 1778.
9. Peter Gilman Robbins born December 10, 178t

The Children of Ichabod Simmons & Marcia his Wife.
1. Marcia Ann Bates, born . April 11th . 1830.
2. Ichabod—born, Decʳ 24th . 1831.
3. Joann Adelaide, born. Novʳ 24th . 1834.
4. Victorine Annette born, Septʳ 9th . 1837.

The Children of Josiah Waterman, & Fear Waterman his Wife.
1. Joshua Waterman, Born, Decʳ 1 . 1757.
2. Josiah Waterman, Born Janʸ 19 . 1760.
3. Jerusha Waterman Born June 19 . 1763.

The Children of Lewis Harlow & Betsey his Wife
1. Elizabeth Frances, born August 1st 1822.
2. Lewis Otis born October 9th . 1824.
3. Lucy James born Septʳ 5th . 1827.
4. Charles Goodwin born October 19th . 1830.

[p. 43] The Children of Mʳ John Cotton & Hannah Cotton his Wife born at Plymouth.
1. Rosseter Born March . 23 . 1758 wednesday about . 1 . or 2 . AM.
2. Joanna Born October . 7 . 1761 . Tuesday . near midnight

---

* A note on the margin, in another hand and ink, is as follows: "He was published to Thankfull Hubbard of Guilford 1759. See page 120 — 1760". The year 1760 is given in the intention of marriage, recorded on page 120. — Editor.

† Apparently, "6" was first written, and "7" written over it.

Plymouth, Mass., Vital Records

3. Sarah Born March 28 . 1763 . 3 . a clock AM. Monday.
4. Elizabeth born June . 30 . 1765 . 10 . AM. Sabbath.
5. Lucy Cotton born Feb'y 12th 1768. 2 . A.M. Friday.
6. Ward Cotton born March 24th 1770. 7 . A.M. Saturday.

His Children born at Hallifax.

1. Josiah born august . 14 . 1747 . [or 25 . N.S.] . 3 . aclock AM. Friday.
2. Hannah—December . 1 . 1748 . [12 . NS.] . 3 . aclock AM. Thursday.
3. Mary—November . 15 . 1750 . [26 . NS.] 2 . or . 3 . aclock PM. Thursday.
4. John—March . 27 . 1753 . NS. 8 aclock AM Tuesday.
5. Sophia—July . 14 . 1755 . NS. 2 . aclock AM Monday.

The Children of Richard Durpha & Sarah Durpha his Wife

1. Sarah Durpha Born March ye 23rd 1763 Deceas^d
2. Thomas Durpha Born September ye 4 . 1764
3. Hannah Durfey Born April ye 5th 1767 Deceas^d
4. Mary Durfey Born Sepr ye 13th 1769 Deceas^d

The Child of Richard Durfey Above named & Elizabeth his 2nd wife

Richard Durfey . born Octr ye 8th 1771

The Children of Jeams Coad & Hannah Coad his Wife

1. Sarah Coad Born Jan^ry 20th 1764
2. Mary Coad Born Novr 6th 1765

The Children of Levi Robbins & Harriett his Wife

1. Harriet Newell, born April 1st . 1832.
2. Maria—born May 11th . 1838

[p. 44] The Children of Thomas Crandon and Ruth Crandon his Wife

1. Jean Crandon Born Octr 21 . 1753 Betwixt 7 . & 8 Clock Sunday Morning
2. James Crandon Born Augt 1 . 1755 Betwixt 7 . & 8 Clock Tuesday Evening
3. Thomas Crandon Born Augt 20 . 1757 . at Two Clock Friday morning
4. Ruth Crandon Born Ap^r 22 1760—20 moments after one in the after noon of a Tuesday
5. John Crandon Born Ap^r 14 . 1763 Betwixt 10 . & 11 Clock Thrisday morning
6. Benj^a Crandon Born Octob^r 24th 1764*

The Children of John Douglas and Mercy Douglas his Wife

1. John Douglas Born Octr 26 . 1761

* "4" has been written over a "5".

2. Jean Douglas Born May 30 . 1763

The Children of James Thomas, & Hannah Thomas his Wife.

1. Hannah Thomas Born, Aug^st 31 . 1761.
2. James Thomas Born, July 10 . 1763. Deceas^d Decr 28th 1763
3. Waterman Thomas born July 13th 1766
4. Isaac Thomas born May 29th 1768

The Chilldren of Barnabas Hedge the 3rd & Tryphena His Wife

1. James Goreham Hedge born October 13th 1812
2. Sarah Thomas Hedge born Aug^st 11th 1814
3. William Hedge born Novr 9th 1815

[p. 45] The Children of James Holmes Junr and Remember Holmes his Wife

1. James Holmes Born Novr 21 . 1763
2. a Son Not Named Born Sepr 11th 1765 Deceas^d Sepr 12th 1765
3. Zepheniah Holmes born Decr 24th 1766
4. Rufus Holmes born July 19th 1769
5. Remember Holmes born May 23rd 1772 } are twins
6. Robert Holmes born May 24th 1772

The Children of Barnabas Hedge & Hannah Hedge His Wife

1. a Daughter Born October ye 14 . 1763 . & Lived Ab^ot an Hour
2. Barnabas Hedge Born Septemb^r 15th 1764

The Children of Barnabas Hedge Junr Esqr & Eunice Dennie Hedge his wife

1. Barnabus Hedge ye 3rd born Novr 13th 1791
2. Hannah Hedge born Jan^ry 19th 1793 Deceas^d Feb^ry 2nd 1796
3. Eunice Dennie Hedge born Aug^st 17th 1794 Deceas^d Septr 29th 1794
4. Eunice Dennie Hedge born Septemb^r 1st 1795 Deceas^d Octob^r 18th 1795
5. Isaac Lothrop Hedge born March 8th 1797 Deceas^d Septr 22nd 1797
6. Isaac Lothrop Hedge born Decr 7th 1798
7. Thomas Hedge born Octr 22nd 1800
8. Abigail Hedge born Novr 22nd 1802
9. Hannah Hedge born Aug^st: 1st 1804
10. Eunice Dennie Hedge born June 28th 1806
11. Ellen Hobert Hedge born July . 5 . 1808
12. John Sloss Hobert Hedge born March 8th 1810 Deceas^d Octob. 17th 1810
13. Priscilla Lothrop Hedge born May . 5th 1811 Deceas^d Octr 31st 1814
14. Elizabeth Hedge born Novr 28th 1813
15. Priscilla Lothrop Hedge born July 11th 1816

Plymouth, Mass., Vital Records

[p. 46] The Children of William Bartlett Junr & Rebecca Bartlett His Wife

1. William Bartlett Born November 14th 1761
2. Zacheus Bartlett Born November 29th 1763
3. Thomas Bartlett . Born August 16th 1766
4. Jabez Bartlett Born Octr 15th 1768

The Children of James Bradford & Eleanor his wife.

1. Eleanor born 1821 . February 17th
2. James born 1823 . February 10th
3. Nathaniel 1832 . October 10th.

The Child of Josiah Finney jun^r & Alice Finney His Wife

1. Olley Finney, Born Feb^ry 2 . 1764

Children of Thomas Hedge & Lydia G. Hedge, his wife.

1. Mary Ellen Hedge, born 12th, May 1825
2. Abby Burr Hedge, born 17th, Sept. 1826
3. Edward Goodwin, born 11th . Octr 1828
4. Albert Goodwin, born 19th . May . 1832
5. Lydia Goodwin, born 24th Jan'y 1834
6. Thomas B. Hedge, born 6th . July 1838.
7. Wm Hedge born

[p. 47] The Children of Richard Coopper & Hannah Coopper His Wife

1. Hannah Coopper Born July 1st 1761
2. Richard Coopper Born Jan^ry 30th 1763
3. Elizabeth Coopper Born July 25th 1764

The Children of William S. Burbank & Abigail his Wife.

1. Abigail William, born, 1824 . August 13th
2. Ezra Lewis, born, 1828 . February . 12th.
3. Priscilla Ann, born, 1830 . March, 23d
4. William Sherman, born, 1832 . July 3d.
5. Calvin Perkins, born, 1834 . November 12th.
6. Elijah Walker, born 1837 . February 3d.

The Children of Benjamin Bartlett & Jemima Bartlett His Wife

1. Jane Bartlett Born July 21st 1762. Deceased
2. Mary Bartlett Born August 1st 1763. Deceased
3. Jemima Bartlett Born } Twins Decr 8th 1764.
4. Mercy Bartlett Born
5. Benjamin Bartlett Born Octr 20th 1766
6. Elizabeth Bartlett born July 6th 1769

The Children of Joshua Hathaway & Rebeca his wife.

1. George A. Hathaway, born, 1814 May 24.
2. Charles F. Hathaway, born, 1816 . July 1.
3. Betsey W: Hathaway . born, 1819 . July 5

4. Joshua T. Hathaway, born 1821 . May 11.
5. Frederick C. Hathaway, born, 1823 . Mar^h 30
6. John A. Hathaway, born, 1825 . Feb^ry 25.
7. Sarah Carver, born, 1827 . Augt 18.
8. Samuel G, born, 1829 . Octr 6.
9. Sarah Ann, born, 1832 . Feby 5.
10. Edward Emerson born, 1835 Decr 17

[p. 48] . The Children of Silvanus Harlow & Desire Harlow His Wife

1 Jesse Harlow Born July 21th 1761
2 Silvanus Harlow Born March 3rd 1764
3 Desire Harlow born Aug^st 2nd 1767
4 Ephraim Harlow born Feb^ry 22nd 1770

The Children of Stephen Thomas & Sarah his Wife

1. Nancy Everson, born August 22d . 1827.
2. Justus August 16th. 1829
3. Charles Novem^r 29th . 1833.
4. Sarah Ann March 10th . 1836.
5. Susan Frances October 6th . 1838.

The Child of Elijah Morrey & Rebecca Morrey his Wife

1 Silas Morrey Born June 1st 1764

The Children of Seth Benson & Bathsheba his Wife

1. Seth Benson, born 1824 . August 25.
2. Bathsheba Thomas, born Novr 26, 1825
3. George born June 23, 1828
4. Lydia West born Decr 26, 1829.
5. Elias Thomas born Feby 24, 1832
6. Ellis born May 22, 1833.
7. Lucinda Thomas, born Sept^t 14, 1837.

Children of Timothy Berry & Maria his Wife.

1. Maria E. born June 18 . 1826
2. Antoinette L. July 21 . 1829.
3. William T. April 6, 1833.
4. Mary T. Decr 4 . 1836.
5. Timothy Decr 4 . 1836
6. Harriet S. Oct. 11 . 1843

(To be continued)

PLYMOUTH, MASS., VITAL RECORDS

(Continued from page 23)

[p. 49] The Child of Ezra Burbank & Prisscilla Burbank His Wife

1 Ezra Burbank Born June 30th 1764

The Children of John Atwood Jr & Hannah his Wife.
1. Nancy Churchill born February 12th . 1829.
2. John Murray born June 4th . 1835
3. Adoniram March 27th . 1837
4. Hannah Tuffs March 27th . 1839.

The Children of William Crumbie & Zerviah Crumbie his Wife both Deceas{d} before Calvin

1 William Crumbie Born May 24th 1764 Deceas{d}
2 Kimbull Crumbie born July . 17th 1767 Deceas{d}
3 Anne Crombie born [*] Deceas{d}
4 Anna Crombie born Sept 12th 1771 . Deceas{d}
5 Calvin Crombie born Augst 29th 1773 Deceas{d} Feb{ry} 26th 1815 [Polly†]

The Children of Albert Finney & Lucinda his Wife.
1. Albert Thomas, born July 20 . 1834
2. Charles Harlow, born October 28, 1835
3. Costellow Sept 20, 1837.
4. Thomas Weston born, Octobr 7 . 1838

[p. 50] The Child of Samuel Eddy & Anna Eddy His Wife
1 Samuel Eddy Born June 21st 1764

The Children of Richard Pope & Eunice his Wife.
1. Richard Pope, born, December 11th . 1823
2. Richard Thomas born, May 25th . 182[‡]
3. William Wallace June 29th . 1826
4. Lydia Covington June 2d . 1829
5.th Eunice born Feb{ry} 25th . 1832
6. Lucy Ann born Feby 3d . 1835
7. Rufus [H.§] born June 20th . 1838.

* The date was not entered.
† "Polly" was added, later, in pencil.
‡ The last figure of the year was not entered.
§ "H" was interlined in a different hand and ink.

The Children of Isaac Jackson & Lydia Jackson His Wife
1 Robert Jackson Born March 20th 1765 Deceas{d} at Sea March 26th 1793
2 Abraham Jackson Born Decr 30th 1766
3 Isaac Jackson born April 27th 1769 . Deceas{d} July 5th 1770
4 Hosea Jackson born May 29th 1771.
5 Hannah Jackson born July 10th 1773.
6 Ransom Jackson born July 10th 1775
7 Isaac Jackson born Augst 6th 1777 . Deceas{d} Sept 11th 1796
8 Lydia Jackson born Octobr 4th 1779
9 Oliv{e} . Jackson born Feb{ry} 24th 1782
10 Nancy Jackson born July 28th 1784
11 Salley Jackson born Sept 22nd 1787

The Children of Thomas McLaughlin & Lovisa, his Wife
1. Thomas, born Feby 8 . 1808
2. Freeman Thomas Sept 20, 1809
3. Seth Mar : 3 . 1812
4. Lovisa Thomas Feby 14, 1815
5. Mercy Warren July 19, 1817,

The Children of Fred{c} Cotton & Elizabeth his wife.
1. Elizabeth, born October 26 . 1822
2. Sarah O, born March . 4 . 1826

[p. 51] The Children of Bartlett Lebaron & Mary Lebaron His Wife
1 Mary Lebaron Born May 18th 1762
2 Hannah Lebaron Born Jan{ry} 16th 1764

The Child of Josiah Drew & Sarah W. his wife
1. Sarah D. Drew born October 24th . 1838.

The Children of Seth Harlow & Sarah Harlow His Wife
1 Benjamin Harlow Born July 28th 1764
2 Seth Harlow . Born July . 14th 1766

The Children of Benjamin Bramhall & Mary his wife.
1. Robert Eldridge, born Sept 4 . 1834.
2. Albert Nelson, born Ap{l} 14 . 1839.

The Children of Samuel Dixon & Ruby, his wife
1. Samuel Russell, born, Ap{l} 24, 1834.
2. Calvin Luther, born, Novr 15, 1835
3. Jacob Washburn, born Ap{l} 20, 1839.

(To be continued)

PLYMOUTH, MASS., VITAL RECORDS

(Continued from page 95)

[p. 52] The Children of Capt Joseph Fulgham & Lurania Fulgham His 2nd Wife

Joseph Fulgham Born October 1st 1756 Deceasd
Mercy Fulgham Born Decembr 11th 1760 Deceasd
Hannah Fulgham Born Januy 4th 1764 Deceasd
The Child of Joseph Fulgham & Rebeckah his wife Viz his first wife
1 Charles Fulgham Born June 13th 17[*]
The Children of Benjamin Barnes & Elizabeth Barnes His Wife
1 Elizabeth Barnes Born August 22nd 1762, Deceasd Apr 1764
2 Benjamin Barnes Born April 14th 1764
The Children of Seth Luce Holmes & Saloma his Wife
1. Sarah Elizabeth, born March 8 . 1827
2. Rebecca W. Holmes, born June 20, 1830
3. Saloma N, born Feby 3, 1834
4. Seth Luce born July 30, 1838
5. Lydia Morton born July 30, 1838.
The Child of James Doten junr & Elizabeth Doten his Wife
1 Hope Doten Born June 15th 1765
Children of Joseph Gifford & Elizabeth his Wife
1. Elizabeth, born June 20th 1839.†
[p. 53] The Children of Benjamin Warren & Jane his wife.
1. Benjamin born may . 12 . 1766.
2 Rebeckah Warren Born Febry 28th 1768
3. Salley Warren Born Augst 30th 1769
The Child of Hezekiah B. Reed & Mary his Wife
1. Mary Freeman, born July 19th . 1831.
The Child of Daniel Diman & Susannah his 2nd wife
Susannah Diman born March 7th 1770
The Children of Henry Seymour & Nancy his Wife
1. Nancy Seely, born, 1827 . May 2d
2. Margarett Augusta, 1831 . Jany 22d.
The Children of Elijah Walker & Hannah his Wife
1. Antoinette A, born, October 7th . 1832
2. Elizabeth B. born, Feby 14th, 1837.
3. Paulina Ross, born July 2d, 1839
[p. 54] The Children of Mr Samll Pearce & Elizabeth Pearce His Wife
1 Experience Pearce Born May 2nd 1764
2 Elizabeth Pearce Born Decr 22nd 1765

* The last two figures of the year were not entered.
† See also original page 60.

3. Sarah Pearce Born
4 Samuel Pearce Born March 19th 1769
Children of Samuel Lamman & Content* his wife
1. Ellis Thomas, born, July 25th . 1812
2. George Francis, born Augt 9th . 1814.
3. Sarah Holmes, born Apl 18th . 1817.
4. Samuel Ellis, born Sept 11th . 1819
5. Elizabeth, born Octr 7th . 1821
6. Ellis Thomas, born June 3d . 1824
The Gilldren of Ephraim Spooner & Eliza his Wife
1 A Son Born April 1st 1764 livd About 20 Hours
2 Elizabeth Spooner Born Sept 5th 1765 Deceasd April 17th 1767
3 Ephraim Spooner Born May 3rd 1767 Deceasd Decr 2nd 1769
4 A Daughter Sillt Born April . 12th 1769
5 Ephraim Spooner . born April 4 . 1771 Deceasd Aug: 1775
6 Sarah Spooner . born August 13th 1772
7 Thomas Spooner born Feby 11th 1775
8 James Spooner born Feby 5th 1777
9 Ebenezr Spooner . born Jany 20th 1779
The Children of Ichabod Bearce Jr & Sally his Wife,
1. Sarah Ann, born May 27th . 1833
2. Lucy James, born May 17th . 1836
[p. 55] The Children of John Bartlett junr & Sarah Bartlett His Wife
1 Sarah Bartlett Born January 29th 1758 Deceasd April 9th 1758
2 Sarah Bartlett Born August : 14th 1759
3 Eunice Bartlett Born Novembr 21st 1761
4 John Bartlett Born Novembr 17th 1763
5 Deborah Bartlett Born July : 8th 1765
The Children of John Cambell & Sarah Holmes his Wife.†
1. Sarah born April 18th . April 18th . 1837.
2. William Wallace born July 17th . 1839
The Child of Ezra Corban & Hannah Corban His Wife
1 Dorcas Corban Born augst 22nd 1765
Children of Nathan Haskins & Keziah his Wife§
1. Sarah Royal born Jany 7th 1826
2. Nathan Thomas July 15th 1828
3. George Henry Augt 24th, 1831
4. Keziah Davis born Jany 22d, 1834
Children of Robert Swinborn & Keziah his wife§
1. Jane Johnson born August 6 . 1838.

* "Temperance" was first written, but it was crossed out and "Content" interlined, in a different hand and ink. See also original page 61.

† Still-born.

‡ See also original page 61.

§ See also original page 58.

164 Plymouth, Mass., Vital Records

[p. 56] The Children of Joseph Mitchell & Mary Mitchell His Wife
1 Joseph Mitchell Born November 14th 1760
2 James Mitchell Born March 23rd 1763
3 Ebenezer Mitchell Born August 23rd 1765
4 Mary Mitchell born Feby 3 . 1768
Children of Prince Doten & Susan or Sukey his Wife
1st Susan born December 16 . 1809.
2d. Phebe born December 31 . 1811
3d. Hannah born April 18 . 1814
4th. Prince born October 3 . 1816
5th. Sarah Ann born Decr 7 . 1818.
6th Naomi born Jany 14 . 1821
7th. George Henry born July 7 . 1830
The Children of Joseph Lucas & Mary Lucas his Wife
1 Benjamin Lucas Born Febry March 15th 1755
2 Phebe Lucas Born Febry 24th 1757
3 Lovisa Lucas Born July 8th 1759
4 Elnathan Lucas Born March 1th 1762
5 Ansell Lucas Born April 15th 1764
6. Molle Lucas born April . 18 . 1766.
Children of Nathaniel C. Covington and Catharine his Wife
1. Catharine was born Augt 26 . 1836
Twins { 2 Nathaniel born May . 20 1839
        { 3 William born May 20 1839
[p. 57] The Children of Seth Morton & Mercy Morton His Wife
1 Mercy Morton Born July 28th 1762
2 Elizabeth Morton Born August 26th 1765
Children of Capt Winslow Holmes & Lydia his wife
1st. Betsey born August 1st . 1825
2d. Winslow S. born Feby 29 . 1827.
3d. Lydia born Apl 22 . 1828
4th. Lydia Mason born July 5 . 1829.
5th. Henry B born Decr 18 . 1831
6th Bathsheba J. born Oct 14 . 1833.
7th. Emeline Frances born Sept 3 . 1836.
Capt Winslow Holmes, the father, was born Novr 2d . 1801 He was lost at sea; sailed from Boston 3d . Octr 1836, and was never heard from Afterwards.
Lydia his wife was born May 29th . 1804
The Children of William Dunham, & Abigail Dunham his Wife
1 William Dunham Born, August . 15th 1765
2 Joseph Donham born Novemr 24th 1770
The Children of John Torry & Meriah Torry his Wife
1 John Torry born 31st of May 1778 decd Octr 12 . 1779
2 Meriah Morton Torry born 31st of March 1780.
The Children of John Torry & Elizabeth Torry his Wife
1 John Torry Born ye 17 . of October 1784 decd 19th

Plymouth, Mass., Vital Records 165

2 Elizabeth Harlow Torry born ye 22 Feby 1786.
3 John Torry Born Jany ye 4th 1790.
4 Jesse Harlow Torry Born ye 9 of May 1793.
5 George Washington Torry Born ye 8 of Feby 1800.
The Children of John Carver & Sarah his wife
1. John was born, Feby 13 . 1824
2. Sarah Jane June . 26 . 1827.
3. Nathaniel Jany . 16 . 1835
John Carver the father was born Jany 12th . 1800
Sarah the Mother was born December 31st 1802
[p. 58] The Children of Ichabod Morton & Zilph Morton His Wife
1 Ephraim Morton Born Feby 13th 1759 Deceasd January 23rd 1761
2 Ichabod Morton Born Jany 2nd 1761
3 Hannah Morton Born Novenr 22nd 1762
The Children of Abraham Jackson & Harriet his W
1 Abraham Jackson born Jany 30th 1821
2 John G. March 8th 1823
3 Thomas O. June 30th 1825
4 Horace April 6th 1828
5 George H. Jany 17th 1830
6 Isaac C. Feby 2d 1832
7 Isaac W. Feby 4th 1834
8 Edward H. July 9th 1835
9 Harriet O. Sepr 21st 1837
The Children of Silvanus Holmes, & Mercy Holmes his Wife,
1 Mary Holmes Born, Janury 1st 1743 Old stile
2 Silvanus Holmes Born, Novemr 11th 1744 Old stile
3 Rebecca Holmes Born, Janury 13th 1747 old stile
4 Ansel Holmes Born Novemr 20th 1749 old stile
Children of Nathan Haskins & Keziah his Wife*
1. Sarah Royal, born January 7 . 1826.*
2. Nathan Thomas, born. July 15 . 1828.*
3. George Henry born . Augt 24 . 1831*
4. Keziah Davis born Jany 22 . 1834*
Child of Robert Swinborn & Keziah his Wife*
1. Jane Johnson . born August 6 . 1838.*
[p. 59] The Children of Ebenezer Harlow junr & Rebecca Harlow His Wife
1 Rebecca Harlow Born June 29th 1759
2 Mary Harlow Born Novr 18th 1761
3 Ebenezer Harlow Born Jany 7th 1765
The Chilldren of Samuel Bartlett Junr & Eliza his wife
1 Samuel Bartlett born June 19th 1767
2 Nathl Bartlett born Jany 22nd 1769
3 Cornelus Bartlett born Jany 19th 1771

*These entries have been crossed out, and "Duplicate entry" written on the margin. See original page 55.

Plymouth, Mass, Vital Records

The Children of Samuel Bartlett Junr & Betty Bartlett His Wife
1 Mercy . Bartlett Born October 19th 1755
2 Betty Bartlett Born Decr 13th 1757
3 William Bartlett Born march 16th 1759
4 John Bartlett Born Decemb^r 14th 1760
5 Joseph Bartlett Born June 16 : 1762
All Born at North Carolina See Above
The Children of Samuel Battles & Alise Battles His Wife
1 Elizabeth Battles Born Sepr 17th 1763
2 Polley Battles Born Decr 2nd 1765
[p. 60] The Children of Isaac Mackee, & Sarah Mackee his Wife
1 Isaac Mackee Born August 4th 1764.
2 William Mackey born Jany 29th 1765
3 Mary . Mackey born June 30th 1767 Deceas^d Octob^r 27th 1768
4 Martha Mackey born Decr 17th 1768
5 Hannah Mackey born Octr 12th 1770 Deceas^d Decr 27th 1770
The Children of William Drew & Sarah his wife . viz
1. William born Feby 14 . 1805
2. Lucy born Feby 28 . 1807.
3. Gamaliel born Novr 15 . 1808
4. Elizabeth born Augt 13 . 1810
5. Stephen born Sept 27 . 1812
6. Sarah Woodward, born Aug 24 . 1814
7. Joann March 31 . 1817.
8. Reuben born Feby 14 . 1819
9. Charles born Jany 11 . 1821 died 1821 . Decr 2d
10. Sophronia born Augt 27 . 1822
11. Charles born Sept 30 . 1824 died . 1825 . Feby 20
12. James born Ap^l 23 . 1826
The Children of Ephraim Bartlett & Marcy Bartlett his Wife
1 James C Bartlett Born August 7th 1760
2 Silvanus Bartlett Born Septem^r 16 1762
3 Susannah Bartlett Born Septem^r 20th 1764
The Children of Job Rider & Sally his wife viz
1. Sally born Novr 8th . 1809
2. Lydia William born . March 24, 1811
3. Joseph . born April 12th . 1813
4. Job . born Sept. 5th 1815
5. Betsey . born . Novr 13th 1817.
6. Thomas born . Decr 19th 1821
7. Henry Cassady, born Ap^l 24th . 1825.
The Child of Joseph Gifford & Elizabeth his wife.*
1. Elizabeth Gifford, born 1839 . June 26th.*

(To be continued)

See also original page 52.

THE
MAYFLOWER DESCENDANT

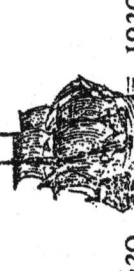

1620　1920

A QUARTERLY MAGAZINE OF
PILGRIM GENEALOGY AND HISTORY

VOLUME XXII

1920

PUBLISHED BY THE
MASSACHUSETTS SOCIETY OF
MAYFLOWER DESCENDANTS
BOSTON

PLYMOUTH, MASS., VITAL RECORDS

Transcribed by the Editor

(*Continued from Vol. XXI, p. 166*)

[p. 61] The Child of John Rogers & Mary Rogers His Wife
1 John Rogers Born October 19th 1762
The Children of Seth Morton & Mercy his wife
1 Seth born December 8th . 1797
2. Mercy . S. born Febr 14th . 1800
3. William Morton born Febr 20 . 1802
4. James born June 4 . 1806.
5. Betsey born Augt 4 . 1808
6. Harriet born Augt 15 . 1811.
7. Henry born May 25 . 1815

8. Caroline born Apl 15. 1818.

The Children of Samuel Sherman & Betty Sherman His Wife

1 Thomas Sherman Born April 18th 1762.
2 William Sherman Born Novem 23 1764.
3. Andrew Sherman born January. 24. 1767. Saturday.

The Children of Samuel Lanman & Content* his Wife

1. Ellis Thomas, born 1812, July, 25th.
2. George Francis, born, 1814. Augt 9th
3. Sarah Holmes, born, 1817. Apl 18th
4. Samuel Ellis, born, 1819. Sept 11th
5. Elizabeth . born, 1821 . Oct 7th.
6. Ellis Thomas, born., 1824 . June 3d

Children of John Campbell & Sarah H. his Wife†

1. Sarah born, 1837. Apl 18
2. William Wallace, born. 1839. July . 17th.

[p. 62] **The Children of Thomas Burgess & Patience Burges his Wife**

1 Elizabeth Burges Born Sepr 28th 1745.
2 Thomas Burges Born Augt ye 10 . 1748

The Children of John Kempton Junr and

1 Nanny Robbertson Born August ye 2 . 1760
2 Sarah Robertson Born September . 29. 1762

The Children of Nathaniel Hatch & Ruth his Wife

1 Mary Hatch Born Augt ye 16 . 1746.
2 Ruth Hatch Born Augt 1749

The Children of William Thomas junr & Rebeccah Thomas His Wife

1 Dorothy Born August 31st 1762
2 William Thomas Born October 2nd 1765

The Children of Southworth Barnes & Lucy his Wife

1. Georgianna Barnes, born January 17, 1834.

[p. 63] **The Children of Docter William Thomas & Mercy Thomas His Wife**

1 Joshua Thomas Born January 19th 1751
2 a female Child Born March . 5th 1752 Deceasd Soon After
3 Margeret Thomas Born March . 8th 1753
4 Joseph Thomas Born Janry 8th 1755
5 Nathl Thomas Born Novr 23rd 1756
6 John Thomas Born April 1st 1758
7 Mercy Thomas Born Novr 28th 1759

The Child of John Kempton junr & Mary Kempton His Wife,

1 Nathl Hatch Kempton Born August 16th 1765
2 Charles Kempton born Febry 20th 1768
3 Seth Kempton . born Sept 15th 1773

* "Temperance" was first written, but it was crossed out, and "Content" written above, in a different hand. See also original page 54.

† See also original page 55.

‡ Entry unfinished. See original page 63.

4 Zacheus Kempton . born Sept 14th 1775
5 Lemuel Kempton . born July 28th 1778
6 Mary Kempton . born July 1st 1781
7 Samuel Kempton . born Sept 15th 1783
8 Joseph Kempton . born Sept 2nd 1785.
9 Stephen Kempton born June 30th 1787

The Child of Territ Lester & Sarah Lester His Wife

1 Sarah Lester Born October 1st 1760

The Children of William Bartlett & Susan his wife.

1. Susan Louisa born January 1 . 1815.
2. Betsey Thacher born March 30 . 1818
3. John born June 14 . 1820
4 Eliza Ann born June 26 . 1825

[p. 64] **The Children of Elisha Morton, & Elizabeth Morton His Wife**

1 Elisha Morton Born May 23rd 1761 Deceasd Sepr 30th 1763
2 Elizabeth Morton Born July 4th 1764

The Children of Ellis Churchell & Patience Churchell his Wife

1 Ellis Churchell Born June . 24 . 1765.
1. Marcia Ellen, born, 1820 . September 21.
2. Jacob William, born, 1822 April 25th.

The Children of Charles Boult . & Lydia Boult His Wife

1 Lydia Boult Born May 13th 1757.
2 Elizabeth Boult Born July 9th 1759

The Children of John Taylor and Nancy his Wife.

1. John Taylor, born 1821. November 4.th
2. Nancy Catharine, 1827, October, 8th.

The Children of William G. Dunham & Nancy his Wife.

1. Sally born March 17 . 1836
2. Robert born March 10 . 1837.
3. William born . Sept 10 . 1838.

[p. 65] **The Children of Deacon John Torrey & Mary Torrey His Wife**

1 Haviland Torrey Born July 20th 1752 Deceasd October 13th 1756.
2 John Torrey Born Sepr 20th 1754
3 Elizabeth Torrey Born June 22nd 1756 Deceasd November 19th 1756
4 Mary Torrey Born Febry 10th 1759
5 Elizabeth Torrey Born Decr 20th 1762 Deceasd July 6th 1763
6 George Torrey Born Novr 20th 1765

The Children of Isaac Symms & Hannah Symms His Wife

1 Hannah Symmes Born Janry 30th 1766
2 Isaac Symms Born June 5th 1767.

The Child of Phineas Pierce & Dorcas M his Wife.

1. Phineas born 1834 . February 8th.

The Children of Seth Holmes & mary his wife.

1. Deborah Holmes born August . 6 . 1763.
2. Mary Holmes born June . 24. 1765.
3. Rebekah Holmes born January . 8 . 1767.

4. Seth Holmes born May 19th 176[*]
5. Silvina Holmes born May 25th 1770
6. Stephen Holmes born Decr 19th 1771
7. Jerusha Holmes born Octr 15th 1773 Deceasd Febry 15th 1782
8. Amasa Holmes born June 2nd 1775
9. Caleb Holmes born April 4th 1777
10. Nathan Holmes born Febry 15th 1779
11. Jesse Holmes born May 9th 1781
12. Jerusha Holmes born June 2nd 1783

[p. 66] The Child of John Holmes & Abigail his wife
1. Abigail Holmes born Decr 26th 1766

The Children of William Davie & Marcia his Wife.
1. George Davie born August 1 . 1832
2. Marcia Torrey born August 26, 1834.

The Children of Corbin Barnes & Mary his Wife†
1. Mary Barnes born Octr 14th 1766†
2. Elizabeth Barnes born Jany 26th 1771†

The Children of Hosea Churchill & Eunice his Wife.
1. Hosea born 1813 . July . 24th.
2. Betsey W. born . 1815 . Decr 18th.
3. Silas M. born . 1817 . Decr 10th.
4. Bartlett } born 1822 . June, 5th.
5. Henry }
6. John Clark . born 1827 October 1st.

The Child of Joseph Warren & Mercy his Wife
1. Joseph Warren born Augst 18th 1765. *Died in Charleston S. C. an Episcopal minister*‡

The Children of George Harlow & Lydia his Wife.
1. Nathaniel Ellis, born 1813 . Dec 6th.
2. Lydia Ellis, born 1816, June 2d.
3. George Henry born 1817, Decr 3d
4. Lydia born 1819, May . 17th
5. Esther born 1821 . July 22d
6. George Henry 2d . born 1823, October 15th.

[p. 67] The Children of Samuel Bartlett Esqr & Elizabeth Bartlett His First Wife
1. Lothrop Bartlett Born August 16th 1723 Deceasd Sepr 29th 1723
2. A Daughter Still Born October 10th 1724
3. Elizabeth Bartlett Born August 25th 1725 Deceasd Sept 30th 1746
4. Margerett Bartlett Born April 22nd 1728 Deceasd April 25th 1729
5. Hannah Bartlett Born August 15th 1731 Deceasd April 21st 1732
6. Margerett Bartlett Born April 15th 1737 Deceasd Decr 31st 1739

* "9" was first written, but an attempt appears to have been made to change it to "8".
† These entries have been crossed out. Nine children are recorded on original *page 95*.
‡ The entry in italics is in a later hand.

Transcribed From the First Book Page 120
The Children of Samuel Bartlett Esqr & Elizabeth Bartlett His Second Wife
1 Samuel Bartlett Born Sepr 3rd 1749 Sabbath Day About 3 Clock in ye Afternoon Deceasd Monday July 2nd 1750 at 7½ Clock in ye Forenoon
2 Samuel Bartlett Born Apr 15th 1751 Monday half after 1 Clock P M
3 Elizabeth Bartlett Born Augst 9th 1753 Thursday about 2 Clock in ye Morning
4 Lothrop Bartlett Born August 7th 1755 Thursday half an hour After 7 Clock A M Deceasd June 13th 1756
5 Hannah Bartlett Born Apr 11th 1757 Monday About 1 Clock A M
6 Isaac Bartlett Born Octobr 5th 1759 Fryday Abot half After 2 Clock P M

The Children of Charles Marcy & Abigail his Wife
1. Susan Packard born 1818 . October 18th (misplaced & a mistake)*

The Children of Thomas Torrey & Lydia his Wife
1. Lydia Ann, born March 8th . 1822
2. Elizabeth Thomas, bprn August 7 . 1824
3. Lucy Haviland, born Apl 15th . 1828

[p. 68] The Chilldren of Lemuel Goddard & Nancey his Wife
1 Sarah Goddard born Novr 15th 1762
2 Lemuel Goddard born Novr 21st 1764

The Children of George Simmons Jr & Fanny Fox, his Wife
1. George Augustus Simmons born 1829 . December 15th.
2 Lorenzo Frederick 1831 . May 10th
3. Fanny Wilkins 1833 . Novr 28th
4. Isabella 1836 . Jany 24th
5th. Moses 1838 . Apl 13th.

The Children of George Lemont & Catherine his Wife
1 Francis Lemont born Sept 12th 1766.
2 Mercy Lemont born Octr 16 . 1768

The Children of Robert Hutchinson & Deborah his Wife.
1. Susan A. Hutchinson, born July 22d 1812
2. Deborah . B. born Feby 8 . 1814
3. Robert Hutchinson born Sept 15 . 1816
4. Lydia D. born Octr 10 . 1818.

The Children of Robert Hutchinson & Deborah his second Wife
1 Betsey E. Hutchinson, born Sept 22 . 1822
2 Joshua B born Augst 29 . 1824
3 Emeline born Augt 30 . 1832
4. Adeline born Jany 31 . 1839.

The Children of Jonathan Polden & Mary his Wife
1 Mary Polden . Born Aug: 27th 1766.
2 Jonathan Polden Born Jany 8th 1770

*Printed as recorded. See original page 88.

PLYMOUTH, MASS., VITAL RECORDS

Transcribed by Miss Ethel A. Richardson

(Continued from p. 36)

[p. 69] The Chilldren of Joseph Rider Jun[r] *the Son of Joseph Rider*[*] & Elizabeth his Wife

1 Hannah Rider born Feb[ry] 14th 1739/40
2 Mary Rider . born Nov[r] 8th 1741
3 Nath[l] Rider . born June 13th 1744
4 Job Rider . born June 9th 1746
5 Elizabeth Rider born Sep[t] 16th 1748
6 Bathsheba Rider born Nov[r] 7th 1750
7 Sarah Rider . born April 15th 1753
8 Desiah . Rider . born March 10th 1755
9 Pheba Rider . born March 7th 1757
10 Huldah Rider . born May 1st 1760 Deceas[d] Sept 1760

The Chilldren of Benjamin Drew & Elizabeth his Wife

1 Elizabeth Drew born Dec[r] 2nd 1765
2 Benjamin Drew born Feb[ry] 7th 1767
3 Bathsheba Drew born March 17th 1768 Deceas[d] March 29th 1768
4 Ebene[zr] Drew born Dec 21st 1769 Deceas[d] Aug : 27th 1771
5 Margaret Drew born July 30th 1771
6 Ebenezer . Drew born May 1st 1773
7 Mallechi Drew born Nov[r] 10th 1774
8 Desire . Drew born Sep[t] 21st 1776
9 Simeon . Drew born May 24th 1780

The Chilldren of Nathan Bacon & Mary his Wife

1 Nathan Bacon Born Aug[st] 5th 1767
2 Molley Bacon Born Jan[ry] 15th 1771
3 George Bacon Born Aug[st] 23rd 1773

Children of Prince Doten and Susan his wife.[†]

1. Susan Doten, born Dec[r] 16. 1809[†]
2. Phebe Doten, born Dec[r] 31. 1811[†]
3. Hannah Doten, born Ap[l] 18. 1814[†]
4. Prince Doten, born Oct[r] 3. 1816[†]
5. Sarah Ann born, Dec[r] 7. 1818[†]
6. Naomi Doten . born Jan[y] 14. 1821[†]
7. George Henry, born July 7. 1830[†]

[*] The words in italics were interlined in the same hand, but in different ink.
[†] These records were crossed off, and "Entered before" written in the margin. See original page 56.

36
3 Thomas Polden Born Nov[r] 1st 1774
4 George Polden Born July 6 . 1776

The Children of Henry Erland & Sally C. his Wife

1. Henry Thomas Erland, born August 28 . 1828.
2. Edwin Francis Erland, born Feb[y] 19 . 1833.

(To be continued)

Plymouth, Mass., Vital Records

[p. 70] The Chilldren of Nathaniel Carver & Sarah his Wife
Nathaniel Carver born Jan⁷ 18ᵗʰ 1766
Children of Thomas Bassett & Abby his wife
1. Angeline Stephens, born Apˡ 10. 1836
2. Jesse Thomas born Sepᵗ 24. 1838.
The Child of Ebenezʳ Ward & Lydia his Wife
Thomas Ward Born Decʳ 26ᵗʰ 1765
Children of Newell Raymond and Celia his Wife
1. Cordelia Ann, born August 27, 1835
2. Joseph Newell born February 20, 1838.
The Child of William Barnes & Mary his Wife
William Barnes born May 21ˢᵗ 1767
Children of Joseph Taylor and Sarah his Wife
1. Frances Elizabeth, born January 27. 1830.
2. George Washington, born Novemʳ 16. 1832.
3. Joseph born August, 8. 1834.
4. Sarah Jane born Janu⁷, 10. 1839.
[p. 71] The Chilldren of John Finney Junʳ & Rebeckah his Wife
1 Ruth Finney . born Feb⁷ 11ᵗʰ 1757
2 Sarah Finney . born Feb⁷ 19ᵗʰ 1758
3 Elizabeth Finney . born Feb⁷ 22ⁿᵈ 1761
4 James . Finney . born Augˢᵗ 15ᵗʰ 1764
5. John . Finney. born Sepᵗ 3ʳᵈ 1766
Children of Atipas Brigham & Mercy his Wife
1. Antipas Brigham, born Augˢᵗ, 10. 1828.*
2. Mercy Ann born Feb⁷ 16. 1830.
The Children of John Otis & Hannah his Wife
1 Temporance Otis born June 18ᵗʰ 1766
2 Hannah . Otis born June 1768†
The Children of Amaziah Harlow & Ruth his Wife
1 Ruth T. Harlow, born May 19. 1830
2. Martha Dandridge Washington, born, July 16, 1835
3. James William, born December 14. 1837.
The Chilldren of William Warren & Rebeckah his Wife
Rebeckah Warren born Sepᵗ 1ˢᵗ 1765
Alatheah Warren born Apː 1ˢᵗ 1767
The Children of Heman Robbins & Mary Ann his Wife.
1. Mary Elizabeth, born March 31, 1833
2. Almira F. born May 22, 1834
3 Jesse L born Jan⁷ 17, 1836.
4. Caroline A. born July 8, 1837.
5. Charles Henry born May 24, 1839.

* "1828" has been added in pencil, on the margin. The marriage of Antipas Brigham and Mercy S. Morton, on 12 May, 1825, was recorded on original page 217.
† The day of the month was not entered.

[p. 72] The Chilldren of Zacheus Barnes & Hannah his Wife
1 Pheba Barnes Born March 14ᵗʰ 1766
2 Hannah Barnes Born Jan⁷ 10ᵗʰ 1768
3 Lydia Barnes Born March. 12ᵗʰ 1771
4 Jonathan Barnes Born*
5 Jerusha Barnes born*
The Child of Wᵐ Savary & Ruth Ann his Wife
1. Augusta S. born February 22ᵈ 1838
The Child of Robert Decoster & Johanna his Wife
Elizabeth Decoster Born at Boston June 23ʳᵈ 1757
The Children of Seth McHurin & Nancy his Wife
1. Nancy McHurin, born August 12, 1836.
2. Susan Maria born August 22. 1838.
The Chilldren of Joseph Totman & Elizʰ his Wife
1 Sarah Totman . Born July 4ᵗʰ 1765
2 Hannah Totman Born Novemʳ Sepᵗ 13ᵗʰ 1767
3 Joseph Totman Born Apː 5ᵗʰ 1770
Children of John Darnley & Joann B. his Wife
1. Betsey Ann born February 6th. 1837.
2. William Henry born Feb⁷ 26. 1838
[p. 73] The Child of Josiah Clark & Hannah his Wife
Joseph Clark Born Nov⁷ 9ᵗʰ 1767
Children of Stephen Turner & Sally his Wife.
1. Stephen Turner jr born September 11th 1822.
2. Sally Turner born . August 28th, 1824
3. Mary Ann born August 19th. 1826.
4. Lydia D. born July 4th. 1828
5. Benjamin Franklin, born March 6th. 1832.
6. Martha Thomas born . Decemʳ 17th. 1833.
7. Emeline Frances born Feb⁷ 19th. 1836.
The Chilldren of Thomas Spooner Junʳ & Deborah his Wife
1 Nathaniel Spooner born March 8ᵗʰ 1748 Deceasᵈ Decʳ 29ᵗʰ 1748
2 Anna Spooner . born March 8ᵗʰ 1748 Deceasᵈ May 24ᵗʰ 1757
3 Sarah Spooner . born April 5ᵗʰ 1754 Deceasᵈ Feb⁷ 21ˢᵗ 1757
4 Thomas Spooner . born June 28ᵗʰ 1756 Deceasᵈ was Drownᵈ
5 Nathˡ Spooner . born Octʳ 24ᵗʰ 1758
6 John Spooner. born July 12ᵗʰ 1762.   Deceasᵈ March 29ᵗʰ 1764
The Chilldren of Ezekiel Rider & Lydia his Wife
1 Ezra Rider born June 11ᵗʰ 1764 Deceasᵈ Aug: 21ˢᵗ 1764
2 Seth Rider born July 4ᵗʰ 1765
3. Ezra Rider. born . Sepᵗ 9ᵗʰ 1766
See his children by a former wife, Towns first book of Records of births &c, page 175ᵗʰ†

* The date of birth was not entered
† Mayflower Descendant, 15 : 112.

108   Plymouth, Mass., Vital Records

Child of John Spinney & Sophia his Wife
1. Daniel Jackson Spinney born Dec' 2. 1838.
[p. 74] The Child of William Harlow Jun' & Sarah his Wife
1 Sarah Harlow Nov' 3rd 1765
2 Deborah born June 22d 1768 dec'd 21st Dec'm 1775
3 William Jan'y 16th 1771
4 Deborah Sep't 14th 1778
5 Southworth Jan'y 26th 1781
The Children of George Bramhall & Zilpah his wife
1 Zilpah Bramhall born Jan'y 25th 1768
2 Mary Bramhall born Sept 26. 1769
The Children of Charles Churchell & Sarah his Wife
1 Charles Churchell born Oct' 3th 1767
2 Joseph Churchell . born Nov' 15th 1769
3 Rufus Churchell born April 12th 1772
4 Samuel Churchell born Sept 23 1774
5 Elkanah Churchell born Mar: 10th 1777
6 Sarah Churchell born Nov' 12th 1779
7 Ephraim Churchel born May 16th 1782
[p. 75] The Children of Ebenez' Harlow y'e 3rd & Lydia his wife
1 Zebulon Harlow born Aug'st 11th 1763 Deceas'd April 28th 1771
2 Andrew Harlow born Octob. 11th 1770
3 Ebenezer Harlow born Nov' 14th 1772 } Twins
4 Zebulon Harlow born Nov' 14th 1772 }
5 Philemon Harlow born Dec' 30th 1774
6 George Harlow born Feb'y 4th 1778
7 James Harlow born Aug'st 24th 1781
8 Asa Harlow . born at S't Georges : Riv' Eastw'd Feb'y 26th 1784
9 Hose Harlow . born*
The Children of Robert Donham & Ruth his Wife
1 Anna Donham born Oct' 17th 1768
2 Ruth Donham born Aug'st 23rd 1770
3. Sarah Donham born June 17th 1775
4 Robert Donham born Nov' 26th 1778
5 Josiah Donham born May 15th 1781 Dec' 30th 1782 Deceas'd
6 Betsey Donham born July 10th 1785
7 Elener Donham born May 13th 1789
8 Lydia Donham born Sep't 4th 1791
The Chilldren of Moses Reding . & . Sarah his wife
1 Sarah Reding born June 27th 1767
2 a Daughter Allso born at the Same time not named Deceas'd June 29th 1767
3 Bruse Reding . born Sep't 4th 1769
4 Bennet . Reding born Jan'y 18th 1771

(To be continued)

*The date of birth was not entered.

PLYMOUTH, MASS., VITAL RECORDS

TRANSCRIBED BY MISS ETHEL A. RICHARDSON

(Continued from page 108)

[p. 76] The Chilld of Zedekiah Tinkcom & Mercy his Wife
1 Sarah Tinkcom born May 8th 1768
Children of Zepheniah Bradford & Sally his Wife
1 Charles Coban, born October 6. 1824.
2. Priscilla Morton born Ap¹ 22. 1826.
3. Zephaniah born May 29. 1827.
4. Elizabeth Richardson born April, 16, 1829
5. Rebecca Holmes " March, 18. 1835.
6. Sarah James " March. 6. 1839.
7 Adeline Augusta " March 25, 1844
The Chilldren of Eleazʳ Rogers & Bethiah his Wife
1 Bethiah Rogers born July 15th 1758
2 Thomas Rogers born Octobʳ 5th 1765
3 Samuel Rogers born Augst 21st 1767
4 Priscilla Rogers born June 25th 1769

Plymouth, Mass., Vital Records

The Children of Bartlett Faunce & Lydia his Wife.
1. Bartlett born 1811. June 17th
2. Charles L, 1814. March 27th.
3. George Henry, born July 18th, 1817.
The Children of Jonathan Churchell Junʳ & Lydia his Wife
1 Olive Churchell born Octʳ 26th 1768
2 Mary Churchell born July 22nd 1770
[The Children of William Collingwood & Ellen . his Wife*
1. Mary Collingwood, born November 28. 1825*
2. Eleanor " born October 14. 1827*
3. James " born March 14. 1830*
4. Thomas " born Decʳ 2. 1831*
5. Jane " born March 2. 1834*
6. Robert " born Septʳ 28. 1836*]
[p. 77] The Child of Mʳ John Barrows & Sarah his Wife
1 John Barrows born Novembʳ 15th 1768
2 William Barrows born June 7th 1770
3 Thomas Barrows born June 18th 1772.
The Children of John Foster & Elizabeth his Wife
1 John Foster born July 18th 1768
2 Elizabeth Foster born March 8th 1770
3 William Foster born †
4 Peter Thatcher Foster born †
The Children of John Chase & Abigail his Wife.‡
The Children of Stevens Mason & Lydia his Wife
1 Stevens Mason born yᵉ 20th March 1769
2 Susanna Mason born January 10th 1771
3 Lydia Mason born March. 20th 1772
4 Polly Mason born Sept 11th 1773
The Children of Nathˡ Brown Faunce & Rebecca his Wife
1. Rebecca Jane, born, March 31. 1835
2. Martha Ellen, born. Decʳ 17. 1836
3. Nathaniel Brown. Decʳ 13. 1838.
Mʳ Nathaniel Brown the Father deceased Decʳ 13. 1838.
[p. 78] The Children of Joseph Rider Junʳ yᵉ Son of Ezekiel Rider & Abigail his Wife
1 Joseph Rider born Augst 14th 1768
2 William Ryder born May 22nd 1772 Deceasd
3 Michael Ryder born April 15th 1775
4 Margaret Ryder born June 22nd 1777
5 Abigail Ryder born Sept 15th 1779
6 Joanna Ryder born Aug: 19th 1781
7 William Ryder born in Salem Febʳʸ 15th 1784 Deceasd Decʳ 1785 in Salem

*The record of this family was crossed out. See original Volume III, page 34.
† No date was entered.
‡ Space was left, but no children were entered.

180 Plymouth, Mass., Vital Records

The Children of William Savory & Lydia his Wife
1 a Daughter born [*] Lived about 2 Days
2 William Savory born Sept 2nd 1769

The Children of Joseph Davis & Mary, his Wife.
1. Sarah Elizabeth Davis, born, May 3d. 1829.
2. Nancy Rogers Davis, born, Dec' 3d. 1830
3. Hannah Ackus Davis, born, Aug' 27th. 1834
4. Francis Edward Davis, born, July. 31st. 1836.
5. Susan Nichols Davis, born, Sep' 16th. 1838.

The Child of Eleaz' Stephens & Susannah his wife
Susannah Stephens born Octob' 27th 1766
said Susannah the Mother Deceas'd Dec' 30th 1766
The Child of Eleaz' Stephens & Elizabeth his wife
Sarah Stephens born Dec' 23rd 1772

[p. 79] The Child of James Lawrance & Abigail his wife
Joseph Lawrance born Oct' 29th 1769

The Children of John F. Dunham & Lydia his Wife.
1. Hannah Nickerson Dunham, born, March 11th. 1823.
2. Saloma Nickerson Dunham, born, Sep' 20th. 1827.
3. George Foster Dunham, born, Oct' 31st 1831.
4. Betsey Foster Dunham, born, Aug' 23d. 1833.
5. Lydia Ann Dunham, born, July 14th. 1837.

The Children of Abraham Tisdall & Experience his wife
1 Samuel Tisdall born†
2 Abraham Tisdall   } are twins bon September 21st 1768
3 Isaac Tisdall

The Children of Isaac Austin & Bethiah his Wife.
1. Isaac L. born, 1824. May 15th
2. Alva C. born, 1826. June 15th
3. Elizabeth Owen, born 1829. Nov' 26
4. Selden born 1833. July. 30
5. Henry Carter born 1836. Jan'y 5th.

The Children of Hennery Highton & Eliz' his wife
1 Hennery Highton born July 15th 1769
2 Margaret Highton. born July 5th 1771

The Children of Isaac Robbins & Eliza his wife.
1. Isaac Marshal, born August 9th. 1826.
2. James Hewit, born, October 1st. 1830.
3. Curtis Holmes, born June 26th. 1832.
4. Sarah Elizabeth, born March 13th. 1826.‡

[p. 80] The Chilldren of Ephraim Morton & Sarah his wife
1 Ephraim Morton born Dec' 28th 1747 Deceas'd Dec' 14th 1756
2 a Sonn born Dec' 12th 1749 Deceas'd Same Day
3 Osborn Morton born Feb'y 7th 1750/1

*Space was left for the date, but it was not filled in.
† No date was entered.
‡ So entered. Probably an error for "1836."

Plymouth, Mass., Vital Records 181

4 Edward Morton born Sep' 3rd 1753
5 Ichabod Morton born March 18th 1756 Deceas'd Nov' 27th 1756
6 a Son Still born Oct' 2nd 1757
Ephraim morton d Ap' 27. 1758*

The Child of Phillip Leonard & Hannah his Wife
Nathaniel Warrin Leonard born Feb'y 7th 1768

The Children of William Barnes & Phebe his Wife
1. William M. Barnes, born, Ap'l 16. 1822.
2. Winslow C. Barnes, born, June, 23. 1829.
3. Ellis D. Barnes, born. June 29. 1831.
4. Caroline F. Barnes, born Sep't 8. 1834.
5. Charles C. Barnes, born May 18. 1838.

The Child of Bartlett Holmes & Lucy his Wife
Bartlett Holmes born Dec' 19th 1768

Children of Lewis Weston 2d and Martha his wife
1. Sylvanus Bartlett Weston, born, March, 10, 1821
2. Edward L. Weston, born March, 8, 1828.
3. Horace Weston, born May, 4. 1825.
4. Sophia Weston, born March, 14. 1831.
[p. 81] The Child of Barnabas Holmes & Mercy his Wife
Barnabas Holmes born Nov' 29th 1769

The Children of Job Churchill & Hannah T. his wife.
1. Barnabas Churchill, born Sep' 30th. 1810.
2. Job Churchill born, Jan'y 17th. 1812.
3. Sylvanus Harlow Churchill, Feb'y 23d. 1815.
4. Hannah T. Churchill, born, Jan'y 1st. 1817.
5. Sally Churchill, born, Dec' 27th. 1819.
6. Sally Churchill, born, Nov' 23d 1821.
7. Cornelius Bradford, born, Mar'h 26. 1824.

The Children of John Bartlett y' 3rd & Dorothy. his wife
1 Lewis Bartlett born March 20th 1770 Deceas'd Jan'ry 9th 1772
2 Dolley Bartlett born Nov' 30th 1771
3 John Lewis Bartlett born March 4th 1774 Deceas'd Ap: 1st 1776
4 John Bartlett born Feb'y 4th 1776
5 Henry Bartlett born Jan'y 25th 1778

The Children of Thomas Farmer & Susannah his wife
1 Thomas Farmer born June 8th 1770
2 Mary Farmer born Jan'y 15th 1776

The Children of David Harlow & [ ] his Wife†
1. David L. Harlow, born, Feb'y 25. 1825.
2. Isaac N. Harlow, born, Jan'y 26. 1828.
3. Ezra Harlow born, July 19. 1829.
4. Ezra Harlow born, Dec' 18. 1830.
5. Henry M. Harlow born, Aug't 19. 1833
6. Ann Eliza Harlow born, Mar'h 9. 1836
7. Hannah Harlow born, Aug't 12. 1838

* This entry is in a different hand and ink.
† The wife's name was not entered.

Plymouth, Mass., Vital Records

[p. 82] The Children of Thomas Wethrell & Anne his Wife
1 William Wethrell born Sept 4th 1769 Dec'd Sep'r y'e 6 . 1770
2 Anne May Wethrell born Januar'y y'e 31st 1771
3 Thomas Wethrell born Feb'y y'e 12. 1773
4 Elizabeth Wethrell born March y'e 10th 1775
The Chilldren of Thomas Wethrell & Sarah his wife
1 William Wethrell born, January y'e 29 1781
2 Isaac Wethrell born December y'e 3'rd 1783
3 Sarah Wethrell born April y'e 19 1787
4 Lucia Wethrell born July y'e 1789 dec'ed
5 Hariot Wethrell born March 1792
The Children of Lemuel Drew & Eliz'a his wife
1 Lemuel Drew born April 12th 1769
2 Seth Drew born June 12th 1771 . deceased Feb'y 4 1838
3 Elizabeth Drew born June 22nd 1773
4 Margaret James Drew born July 21st 1775
5 George Drew born Aug'st 20th 1777
6 William was born, September 21 1779
7. Sarah was born August 27. 1781 deceased March 20. 1829
8. Joseph was born November 15. 1783. deceased March 4. 1786
9. Thomas was born December 9. 1785.
10. Joseph was born December 30. 1787 deceased April 11. 1821
11. Isaac was born August 14. 1790
     Carried to the foot of the page
The Children of Robert Roberts & Sarah his wife
1 Mary Roberts born Octob'r 4th 1769
2 Robert Roberts born Sept 23rd 1771   Dec'd in Boston 1826
3 Sarah Roberts . born Aug'st 17th 1773
Deac: Lemuel Drew the father of the above named family was born November the 14th day old style in the year 1744, and was married February 25th, in the year 1768, to Elizabeth Rider
Mrs Elizabeth Drew, the mother was born Sept 16, in the year 1748.
Deac. Lemuel Drew deceased, May 24. 1825.
Mrs. Elizabeth Drew deceased Nov'r 3. 1815.
[p. 83] The Children . of William Curtis & Hannah his wife
1 William Curtis born August 10th 1769
2 Hannah Curtis born Sep't 3rd 1771
3 James Curtis born Nov'r 25th 1773
The Children of Lemuel Simmons jr & Priscilla his Wife.
1. Priscilla C. Simmons born Nov'r 1st 1819
2. Mary S. Simmons born Ap'l 23d 1821.
3. Lemuel born Jan'y 23d 1823.
4. Eunice T. Simmons born Mar: 30. 1824
5. Lemuel   "   Feb'y 26. 1826.
The Children of Robert Gamble & Rebeckah his wife
1 George Gamble born Septemb'r 30th 1759
2. Mary Gamble born Sep't 27th 1762.

Plymouth, Mass., Vital Records

Children of Robert Cowin & Ann, his Wife.
1. Mary Ann Cowin, born 1836. May 20th.
2. Sarah Frances born, 1838. June. 7th.
The Child of Daniel Whitman & Mary his wife
John Whitman born may 28th 1769. *Mary,* *Daniel,* *The Father d 1777 æ 33**
The Children of Jacob Covington & Patty his wife.
1. Elam born July 1st. 1817.
2. Mary Holbrook born Feb'y 13. 1820
3. Martha Ann born Oct'r 10. 1822
4. Edwin born July 24. 1825
5. Harriet born Mar 6. 1827
6. Hellen born, June 3. 1830
7. Jacob born Mar: 1. 1832
8. Leonard born Mar: 1. 1834.
[p. 84] Amasa the Son of Abigail Wate Born April 22nd 1764
The Children of Sam'l Doten Holmes & Betsey his wife
1. Elizabeth Mason born November 11th. 1812
2. Harriet . born January 11th. 1815
3. Rebekah born February. 21st. 1819.
4. Mercy Johnson, born November 26th. 1822. died Oct'r 2. 1826.
5. Emeline Frances, born, January 27th. 1825.
6. Samuel Doten, born Ap'l 26th 1827.
7. Joseph Johnson, born Ap'l 25th Sep't 1829.†
The chilldren of Phillip Washburn & Silence his wife
1 Sarah Washburn born Jan'ry 13th 1766
2 Phillip Washburn born Aug'st 9th 1767
Twins { 3. Israel Washburn born Feb'ry 20th 1770
       { 4 Levi Washburn born Feb'ry 20th 1770 Deceas'd March 4th 1770
Child of Thomas May & Cordelia his Wife.
1. Cordelia Frances born February 26. 1835.
The Children of Peleg Stephens & Sarah his wife
1 Asa Stephens born Oct'r 27th 1761
2 William Stephens born Dec 11th 1770
The Children of John Macomber & Eleanor. his Wife.
1. Eleanor born December 21. 1825.
2. Betsey Ann, born. January. 21. 1827.
3. Augusta Jane   "   July 3d 1830.
4. Emeline   "   Aug't 20th 1832.
5. John Alfred   "   June 3d 1835.
[p. 85] The Child of Mary Beal:
Simeon Rathmel born June 5th 1761
The Children of William D. Simmons & Harriet. his Wife.
1. William D. born July 7th. 1833.

*These entries in italics are in a different hand and ink.
†This record is printed just as recorded.— Editor.

THE MAYFLOWER DESCENDANT

1620   2020

A QUARTERLY MAGAZINE OF
PILGRIM GENEALOGY AND HISTORY

VOLUME XXIII

1921

PUBLISHED BY THE
MASSACHUSETTS SOCIETY OF
MAYFLOWER DESCENDANTS
BOSTON

---

184 *Plymouth, Mass., Vital Records*

2. Ferdinand Augustus, born, April 1st 1837.
3. Harriet Louisa born, June 24. 1839.
The Child of Ezra Finney & Hannah his wife
Hannah Finney born October 8th 1769
The Children of James M Bradford . & Betsey M. his Wife.
1. Elizabeth M. born June 3d. 1833.
2. James M. born Jany 7th. 1835
3. Branch Johnson " Novr 10th 1838.
The Child of Seth Nicholson & Lydia his wife
Seth Nicholson born Jan^{ry} 15th 1769
The Children of Benjamin Bagnell & Lucy his Wife
1. Lucy Emily born September 13th. 1822.
2. Betsey Crocker born February 7th. 1825
3. [*] born March 13th. 1837
[p. 86] The Children of Ansell Harlow & Hannah his wife
1 Rebeckah Harlow born Decr 10th 1770
2 Sarah Harlow born May 28th 1773
3 Hannah Harlow born May 8th 1775
4 Jedidah Harlow . born, May 19th 1778
5. Ansell Harlow born . Augst 20th 1780
6 Stephen Harlow born Novr 27th 1783 Deceas^d
7. Mary Harlow born July 26th 1785
The Child of William King & Susannah his wife
Sussannah King born Sep^t 25th 1771.
The Children of David Drew 2^d & Ann his Wife
1. David Lewis, born August 2d. 1834
2. Harrison Warren, born Decr 2d. 1836
3. Sally Ann, born Novr 4th. 1838.
The Children of Jonathan Harlow Junr & Betty his wife
1 Mercy Harlow born Augst 31st 1770
2 Lewis Harlow born Augst 18th 1772
3 Elea^r Harlow born July 27th 1774
4 Jonathan Harlow born Novr 18th 1776
5 John Harlow born Sep^t 16th 1778
6 Lemuel Harlow born Novr 6th 1780
7 Ivorey Harlow born Mar. 12th 1783

(*To be continued*)

* The name was not entered.

PLYMOUTH, MASS., VITAL RECORDS

TRANSCRIBED BY MISS ETHEL A. RICHARDSON

(Continued from Vol. XXII, p. 184)

[p. 87] The Children of Joshua Shaw & Margaret his wife
1 Hannah Shaw born Novr 18th 1765
2 Elizabeth Shaw born Sept 22nd 1767
3 Joshua Shaw . born Sep^t 4th 1769 Deceas^d Sep^t 10th 1771
4 Joshua Shaw born Jan^{ry} 26th 1772

The Children of Ebenez^r Robbins & Eunice his wife
1 Levi Robbins born Jan^{ry} 21st 1761
2 Ebenez^r Robbins . born Augst 4th 1762
3 Thaddeus Robbins . born Augst 25th 1764
4 Consider Robbins . born May. 25th 1766 Deceas^d June 20th 1766
5 James . Robbins born Octr 29th 1767
6 Ansell . Robbins born Sep^t 29th 1769
7 Levi Robbins born Augst 29th 1771 Deceas^d May 11th 1772

The Child of Thomas Lewis & Sarah Lewis his wife
Thomas Lewis born April 4th 1771

The Children of Maj. Benjamin Ryder & Patience his wife
1 Patience Ryder born Feb^{ry} 16th 1777
2 Abigail Ryder born June 2nd 1779

Child of William Gooding & Mary Ann, his Wife
1. William Putnam born August 13th.*

[p. 88] The Childdren of Nathaniel Leonard & Bethiah his wife
1 Nathaniel Leonard born July 18th 1765
2 William Leonard born Octr 11th 1767
3 Thomas Leonard born Sep^t 27th 1770

The Childdren of John Bartlett 3^d & Me
1 Abigail Bartlett born Octr 20th 1763
2 John Bartlett born Sep^t 21st 1766
3 Ellis Bartlett born May 21st 1770
4 Ivory Bartlett born July 28th 1772

The Child of Hezekiah Jackson & Elisa|
Elisabeth Jackson born Feb^{ry} 10th 1768

The Child of Charles Marcy & Abigail l
1. Susan Packard bornǂ

The Children of Charles Marcy & Char
1. James Warren born June 10th. 1818.
2 Mary Ann born Sepr 25th. 1820.

*The year was not entered.
ǂ The date was not entered.

[p. 89] The Children of Isaac Harlow Junr & Martha his wife
1 Isaac Harlow born February 8th 1771 lost at sea June 1790
2 Stephen Harlow born May. 15th 1775.
3 Joseph Harlow born Oct^r . 11th 1776
4 Bradford Harlow born Decr 13th 1778 deceased Sep^t 7th 1782
5 Sylvanus Harlow born Octr. 26th 1780
6. Lewis Harlow born May 11th 1783
7. Timothy Harlow born July 27th 1786
8 Bradford Harlow born July 24. 1788

The Children of Andrew Bartlett & Lydia his wife
1 Andrew Bartlett . born Jan^{ry} 21st 1765.
2 Caleb Bartlett . born March 3rd 1767
3 Henery Bartlett born . Novr 1st 1768
4 Stephen Bartlett born . Sept 1st 1770
5 Hosea Bartlett born . March 24th 1772.

The Child of Ephraim Luce & Ruth his wife
Hannah Luce born Novemb^r 2nd 1772.

The Children of Capt Simeon Sampson & Deborah his wif[e]
1 Lydia Sampson born March 8th 1760 Deceas^d 1762
2 Lydia Cushing Samson born Octr 21st 1762
3 Simeon Sampson . born Decr 8th 1765 Deceas^d March 10th 1766
4 Simeon Sampson . borne Decr 8th 1766 Deceas^d Decr 10th 1766
5 Deborah Sampson . born April 25th 1768
6 a Son born Octr 16th Deas^d a few Days after
7 Isaac Sampson . born Octr 16th 1771 Deceas^d Novr 29th 1782
8 Mary Sampson . born June 3rd 1775 Deceas^d
9 Mercy Samson born June 12th 1777
10 Marah Sampson born [*] Decea^d Octr 1st 1777
11 Martha Washington Samson born Sep^t 9th 1779 Decea^d Sept 25th 1780
12 George Washington Sampson born Decr 27. 1781
13 Meriah Sampson born Jan^{ry} 4th : 1784

[p. 90] The Child of Susannah Lee
Deborah Farling born Jan^{ry} 6th 1761

The Children of Richard Durfy & Grace his Wife
1. Susan T. Durfey born 1822. October 30th
2. Abby H. Durfey born . 1824. Novr 8th
3. Richard T. Durfey born 1826. October 9th.
4. Benjamin B. Durfey . 1828. August 19th.

The Children of Thomas Doten & Jerusha his wife
1 Jerusha Doten born Feb^{ry} 18th 1770
2 Meriah Doten born Jan^{ry} 18th 1773

The Children of Zephaniah B Lucas & Eliza his Wife.
1. Emely H. Lucas, born January 29th. 1820
2. Ivory B. Lucas, born July 30th. 1822

*The date of birth was not entered.

Plymouth, Mass., Vital Records

The Child of Ichabod Tinkcom & Mary his wife
Mary Tinkcom born Jan'y 2nd 1773
The Children of Ebenezer Davie & Mercy his Wife.
1. Curtis Davie, born, 1827.
2. Mercy Ann Davie " 1829. September, 12th.
3. Sarah W. Davie " 1833. September, 6th.
4. Emeline Davie " 1835. September, 29th.
   September, 6th.
[p. 91] The Children of David Lothrop & Bathsheba his wife
1 a Daughter Still born Dec'r 1771
2 Bathshebah May Lothrop born Aug: 6th 1773.
The Child of Judah Bartlett & Jerusha his wife
1. Eliza Ann, born April 20. 1826
The Children of Judah Bartlett & Eliza his Wife
1. Jerusha H.   born 1832. November 25th
2. John Franklin " 1835. June 19th.
3. Martha Washington " 1837. Nov'r 9th
The Chilldren of Thomas Nicolson & Sarah his wife
1 Sarah Nicolson born Oct'r 7th 1771
2 Hannah Nicolson Born July 21st 1773
3 Polley Nicolson Born Sep't 25th 1775 Deceas'd
4 Eliza Nicolson born July 11th 1777
5. Lucy Nicolson Born July 28th 1778
6 Nancey Nicolson Born Feb'y 22. 1780 Deceas'd
7. Thomas Nicolson Born Aug: 5th 1782 Deceas'd
8. James Nicolson Born May 10th 1784 Hannah his wife
The Children of Thomas Nicolson & Hannah his wife
1 Samuel Nicolson born Dec'r 22nd 1791
2 Hannah Otis Nicolson born Nov'r 18th 1793
3. Daniel Nicolson born March 11th 1796 is March 11th 1796 Deceas'd
March 5th 1815
4 Carroline Nicolson born July 15th 1798
The Child of James Barnes & Sarah his wife
James Barnes born July 20th 1755
The Children of Clement Bates & Irene his Wife.
1. Ruby, born, 1814, December 12th
2. Ozen, born, 1816. December 27th
3. Ira, born, 1819. June 15th
[p. 92] The Chilldren of Pelham Winslow Esq'r & Joanna his wife
1 Mary Winslow born July 28th 1771
2 Joanna Winslow born June 30th 1773
The Chilldren of Thomas Ellis & Jerusha his wife
1 Betty Ellis born April 2nd 1770
2 William Ellis born Dec'r 22. 1771

Plymouth, Mass., Vital Records

The Children of Lemuel Fish Reed & Eunice his Wife.
1. Lucy Ann,   born January 12. 1822.
2. Cordelia Green, "   July 4 1834
3. Henry Holmes   "   Dec'r 8. 1836
4. Richard Williams—May 11. 1839.
The Children of Zepheniab Harlow & Patience his wife
1 Zepheniah Harlow born April 24th 1773
2 Patience Harlow born Mar: 5th 1775
3 Freeman Harlow born Dec'r 24 1776
4 Josiah Harlow born Sep't 4. 1780
5 Betsey Harlow born Oct'r 27 1782
6 Elen Harlow born Aug't 12. 1787
[p. 93] The Child of Isaac Atwood & Hannah his wife
Isaac Atwood born June 11th 1772.
The Children of Barnabas Otis & Mary his wife
1 Henry Otis Born in Scituate Sep't 1782 Deceas'd
2 Barnabas Otis Born March 12th 1785
3 Henry. Otis Born Feb'y 6th 1787. Deceas'd
4. Mary. Otis. Born Octob'r 17th 1790
Child Eunice born Sep't 2nd 1768
6 Child Phillip born June 27th 1774
These two Chilldren were made free by their master Edward Winslow
Esq'r
7 Easter born May 28th 1775 which s'd Ceasor says Edw'd Winslow
Esq his wifes master Gave the Child to him & his wife
The Chilldren of John Goddard & Mary his wife
1 Mercy Goddard*
2 Lydia Goddard*
3 Mary Goddard*
4 John Goddard. born May 28th 1769
[p. 94] The Chilldren of Robert Barrows & Rebeckah his wife
1 Robert Barrows born May 20th 1765
2 Ebenezr Barrows born March 18th 1767
The Child of John Wetherhead & Submit his wife
Mary Wetherhead born March 2nd 1777
The Children of John Chase Jr & Lydia his Wife
1. Zenas Ripley, born August 10th. 1833.
2. Lydia Allen, born Septem'r 14th. 1836.
The Children of John Allen & Esther his wife
1 Esther Allen born July 13th 1769
2. Eliz'a Allen . born Feb'y 7th 1772
3. John Allen . born August 2nd 1774
4 William Allen born Feb'y 18th 1779
[p. 95] The Child of James Savory & Mercy his wife
Mercy Savory born March 31st 1796

*The date was not entered.

The Children of Corben Barnes & Mary his wife
1 Mary Barnes born Octobr 14th 1766
2 Rebeckah Barnes born Augst 30th 1768.
3 Betsey Barnes born Jan'y 26th 1771.
4 Charlotte Barnes born Febry 11th 1774
5 Corbin Barnes born May 5th 1776. Deceasd July 20th 1777
6 Corbin. Barnes born July 4th 1778
7 Pattey. Barnes born July 5th 1781
8 Deborah. Barnes Born April 3rd 1785.
9 Abigail Barnes. Born Febry 27th 1789 is 1789
The Child of Bennoni Shaw & Ruth his wife
Ruth Shaw Born July 3rd 1774
The Children of Frederick Robbins & Jane his Wife.
1. Mary Jane, born March 11. 1828.
2. Charles Frederick, born Novr 13. 1830.
3. Isabella Grayham, born June 28. 1834
[p. 96] The Childran of Richard Nutting & Mehitable his wife
Richard Nuting Born Janry 8th 1768
Joseph Nutting born June 1st 1773
Benjamin Nutting born June 1st 1773 Deceasd Octr 1st 1773
Mehitable Nutting born March 17th 1775
John Nutting born May 4th 1777
The Child of Jesse Harlow & Elizabeth his wife
Elizabeth Harlow born Sept 18th 1762.
The Child of Henry Gibbs & Eliza Ann his Wife,
Martha Bourne, born May 8th. 1830
The Children of George Prise & Abigail his wife
1 Jenna Prise Born Decr 10th 1773
2 Sarah Prise Born Sept 4th 1775 Deceasd Febry 7th 1776
3 George Prise Born Decr 3rd 1777 Deceasd March 21st 1778
The Children of Benjamin Peirce & Mary his wife
1. Judith   born December 1802
2. Melzar   born December, 1804
3. Lucy   born December. 1807.
4. Benjamin   "   February. 1812.
5. Mendall   "   June 1815.

(To be continued)

PLYMOUTH, MASS., VITAL RECORDS

Transcribed by Miss Ethel A. Richardson

(Continued from page 12)

[p. 97] The Children of David Bacon & Abigail his wife
1 Lucy Bacon born Jany 24th 1778
2 David Bacon . born Octr. 15th 1779
3. Abigail Bacon born March 15th 1782
4. Elizabeth Bacon. born Octr 18th 1784
5. Henry Samson Bacon born Jany 8th 1787 Deceas^d Jan^ry 21st 1787
6. Jacob Bacon. born March 4th 1788
7 Rufus Bacon born Feb^ry 13th 1792
8 Mary Bacon born Sep^t 16th 1794
9 Charles Henry Bacon born Aug: 25th 1797 Deceas^d Sept 26th 1802
The Children of James Newbury & Susannah his wife
1 James Newbury born June 12th 1773
2 Lemuel Newbury born Decem^br 9th 1775
The Child of Perez Pool and Lydia his wife, viz:
David Vining, born April 26, 1823.
The Chilldren of Andrew Campbell & Bathshua his wife
1 Susannah Campbell born Aug: 24th 1775
2 Mary Campbell born Jan^ry 23rd 1777
3 Andrew Campbell . born Jan^ry 12th 1779
The Children of Nathan Holmes & Polly his Wife
1. Mary, born April 18. 1827
2. Elizabeth " Decr 5. 1828.
3. Nathan " Ap^l 15. 1831
4. Frederick " Ap^l 9. 1835.
[p. 98] The Chilldren of Enoch Randal & Phebe his wife
Enoch Randal born July 26th 1767
Phebe Randal born Aug: 9th 1769
Lucy Randal born Sep^t 1st 1771
William Randal born Aug: 7th 1773
Mercy Randal born April 2nd 1777
The Chilldren of Sam: Drew & Elizabeth his wife
1 Abbit Drew . born Jan^ry 7th 1773
2 Rebeckah Drew born July 5th 1775 Deceas^d
3 Nicholas Drew born Decr 27th 1776
4 Elizabeth Drew born April 27th 1784
5. Samuel Drew . born Aug : 11th 1787
6. Rebecca Ames Drew born Novr 12th 1790
Joseph Perce Drew born Octr 10th 1795

The Children of Nathaniel Bradford* & Rebecca his wife
1 Nathaniel Bradford born Novr 26th 1775
2 Joseph Bradford born March 12th 1778 *Died Ap^l 15 1853*†
3 John Howland Bradford born July 14th 1780
4 Sarah Bradford. Jany 8th 1783
5 Ephraim Bradford June 28th 1785
6 Rebecca Bradford Feb^ry 15th 1788
7. Benjamin Willis Bradford Jan^ry 15th 1791
The Children of Joseph Bradford & Nancy Barnes‡ his Wife.
1. Nathaniel Barnes Bradford born May 16 . 1803 . lost at sea —1818
2. Joseph Bradford born Augt 10 . 1805 . died at sea .1839
3. Edward Winslow Bradford, born Augt 4 . 1807
4. James Madison Bradford. born Feby 18 . 181b
[p. 99] The Children of John Thomas & Anna his wife
Mary–Anna born Jany 14 . 1774
John born Octob^r 5 . 1775
Nathl Gardner, born Sep^t 28 1777
Frederick born Decem^r 1779 Decem^r 20
The Child of Josiah Bemis & Joanna his wife
Joanna Bemis born Jany 26th 1782
Child of George A Hathaway & Patience§ his Wife
1. Abby Seaver, born Feby 18. 1838.
The Children of Isaac Churchell & Sarah his wife
1 Isaac Churchell born Jan^ry 11th 1781
2 Salley Churchell born Feb^ry 10th 1783
The Children of Francis‖ Goddard & Caroline his Wife
1. Caroline Frances born Novr 25th . 1833.
2. Mary James. born Jany 19th .1837.
3. Sarah Elizabeth born July. 20th . 1839
[p. 100] The Children of Samuel Churchel & Eliz^a his wife
1 Samuel Churchell born May 3rd 1779
2 Caleb Churchell born March 25th 1782
3 Mendal Churchell born April 13th 1786
4 Lucy Churchell born June 24th 1788
5 Henry Churchell born July 29th 1790
The Chilldren of Jesse Churchell & Abigail his wife
1 Jesse Churchell born Novr 10th 1772 Deceas^d Novr 12th 1772
2 Jesse Churchell born Novr 20th 1773
3 Lemuel Churchell born Decr 5th 1775

* A note in the margin, in a later hand, reads as follows: "His father was Nathaniel & his mother was Sarah Spooner: she afterwards m Judge Benjn Willis."
† The entry in italics is in a different hand and ink.
‡ The name "Barnes" is interlined, in a different hand.
§ "Davie" has been interlined, in pencil.
‖ "J" has been interlined, in pencil.

THE MAYFLOWER DESCENDANT

1620   2020

A QUARTERLY MAGAZINE OF
PILGRIM GENEALOGY AND HISTORY

VOLUME XXIV

1922

PUBLISHED BY THE
MASSACHUSETTS SOCIETY OF
MAYFLOWER DESCENDANTS
BOSTON

---

4 Abigail Worchester Churchell born June 25th 1778 Deceasd Sept 6th 1778
5 Joseph Churchell born Octr 10th 1779
6 Abigail Churchell born Mar: 23rd 1782 Deceasd July 24th 1783.
7 David Churchell born July 30th 1784 Deceasd Janry 11th 1788.
8 Simeon Churchell born June 25th 1786
9 Hannah Churchell borne Mar: 24th 1789
10. David Churchell borne July 16th 1795
The Child of William Drew & Eunice his wife
Betse Lewis Drew born Decr 25th 1780
Sd William Drew was lost at Sea as Supposd in Comeing in a Cartell Ship from Hallifax, to Boston in Decr 1781

(To be continued)

PLYMOUTH, MASS., VITAL RECORDS

Transcribed by Miss Ethel A. Richardson

(Continued from Vol. XXIII, p. 188)

[p. 101] The Children of William Goodwin & Lydia Cushing his Wife
1 Simeon Samson Goodwin born July 23d 1782.
2 William Goodwin born November 22d 1783.
3 a Son born April 1st 1785 lived ab^t 4 Hours.
4th Isaac Goodwin born June 28th 1786.
The Children of Joseph Faunce & Mercy his wife
1 Eleaz^r Faunce born Jany 11th 1786
2 Joseph Faunce born Sep^t 15th 1787
The Children of Lemuel Morton, Azubah Cushman Morton his wife
1 Nathaniel Morton born May 27th 1789
2 Lemuel Morton born April 9th 1792
3 Elizabeth Cushman Morton born Novr 8th 1796
4 Mary Ellis Morton. born Sep^t 5th 1799
5 Nancy Morton born Feby 5th 1801
[p. 102] The Chilldren of Bartlett Marshell & Ruth his wife
1 Ruth Marshell born Aug: 8th 1778
2 Bartlett Marshell born Aug: 11th 1780
3 Samuel Marshell born May 2nd 1783
The Children of William Davis & Rebecca his wife
William Davis born April 20th 1783 Dec^d March 28th 1824
Nathaniel Morton Davis born March 3 1785
Thomas Davis born*
Elizabeth Davis born*

*The dates were not entered.

The Children of Jonathan Farnam & Dorcas his wife
Sarah Barnes born March 4th 1785
Dorcas Farnum born Decr 18th 1786
The Children of Wendal Hall & Mary Ann, his Wife
1. Mary Wendal, born January 25th. 1830
Of Betsey his wife previous.
1. John Atwood born Sep^t 22d. 1828
[p. 103] The Chilldren of Joseph Robbins & Eliz^a his wife
1 Joseph Robbins born at Plimton Novr 4th 1779
2 Mercy Robbins born Augst 1st 1781
3 Lemuel Stephens Robbins born Jan^{ry} 25th 1783 Decease^d April 1st 1786
4 Betsey Robbins born Octr 21st 1785
Joseph Robbins the Father Aboves^d born in Kingston Decr 12th 1757
The Children of Rosseter Cotton & Priscilla his wife
1 Thomas Jackson Cotton born Jan^{ry} 17th 1785
2 Charles Cotton born Octob^r 7th 1788
3 Polley Cotton born May 20th 1790 Dec^d Augst 26th 1791
4 Polley Cotton born March 9th 1792 Dec^d Sept 24th 1793
5 Rosseter Cotton born Jan^{ry} 27th 1794 Dec^d Jan: 30th 1796
6 Sophia Cotton born May 18th 1796
7. Rosseter Mather Cotton born July 11th 1798
8 John Winslow Cotton born March 29th 1800
9 Rowland Edwin Cotton born Jan^{ry} 4th 1802
10. William Cushing Cotton born April 17. 1804 Dec^d Augst 23 1805
The Child of Corbin Barnes Junr & Phebe his wife
Lemuel Barnes born Jan^{ry} 12th 1785
The Children of Edward Doten & Esther, his Wife
1. Edward was born October 1st 1800
2. Samuel " June 22d 1803
3. Esther " Octr 17th. 1806
4. Lewis " Feby 27th. 1813
5. Lemuel " Mar 26th 1816.*
6. Phebe " Novr 18th 1815.*
7. Hannah " October 15th 1819
8. John " Feby 27th 1823.
[p. 104] The Children of Joseph Bartlett ye 3rd or fourth & Lucy his wife
1 Joseph Bartlett born Novr 15th 1770
2 Zepheniah Holmes Bartlett born Feb^{ry} 17th 1772
3 Lucy Bartlett born March 25th 1775
4 Bradford Bartlett born Decr 15th 1776
The Children of Thomas Burges Junr & Lydia his wife
1 William Burges born Feb^{ry} 2nd 1782
2 Polley Burges } Twins born Aug: 19th 1784
3 Lydia Burges }

*Sic.

Plymouth, Mass., Vital Records — 16

The Children of Charles Faunce & Jerusha his Wife
1. Abigail Thomas, born . March 11th . 1839.
The Child of Sylvanus Donham Mary his wife
   Sylvanus Donham, born Aug: 5th 1780
Children of Richard Bagnell 2d & Lydia his wife, viz
1. Susan Sampson, born October 7th . 1819.
2. Richard William born Decr 2d . 1822.

[p. 105] The Children . of Richard Bagnal & Bethiah his wife
1 Samuel West Bagnal born Augst 19th 1785 Deceasd Febry 14th 1786
2 Samuel West Bagnal born Sept 9th 1787.
3 Hannah Jackson Bagnal born May 11th 1790
4 Benjamin Bagnal born Sept 17 . 1792
5 Joseph . Bagnal born Mar: 5th 1795
6. Nancey Ellis Bagnal born Sep. 18th 1797 Deceasd
7. Nancey Ellis Bagnal . born Febry 11th 1799
8 Richard . Bagnal . born Janry 12th 1802

The Chilldren of Elkanah Bartlett & Sarah his wife
1 Elkanah Bartlett born Decr 29th 1769
2. David Bartlett born July 24th 1775
3 John Bartlett born July 30th 1777
4 Jonathan Bartlett born June 17th 1779 . Deceasd Sept 1780
5 Jonathan Bartlett born Aug: 9th 1782
6 Salley Bartlett born Janry 10th 1786
7 Jenne . Bartlett born } may 27th 1792
8 Joanna Bartlett born }

The Children of Zacheus Bartlett Junr & Hannah his wife
1 James Bartlett born Janry 28th 1785
2 William Bartlett born Febry 4th 1787
3 Hannah Bartlett borne Aug: 6th 1795

The Children of John S. Payne & Deborah his Wife
1. Reuben Church'll, born April 5th . 1815
   Of Susan his wife.
1. Stephen Payne, born Sept 16 . 183[*]
2. Hannah Sherman " Augt 28 . 1836
3. John Sampson " Mar: 7 . 1838.

[p. 106] The Child of Eleazer Holmes Junr & Polley his wife
1 Esther Holmes born Febry 9th 1786.
2 Eleazer Holmes Born
3 Mary Holmes Born
4 James Avery Holmes Born—by Elizabeth his wife

The Children of Jacob Albertson & Lydia his wife
1 A Son Still born June 25th 1778
2 Martha Albertson born Aug: 30th 1779
3 Joseph Ryder Albertson born Decr 4th 1781 Deceasd Sept 9th 1782
4. Lydia Gardner Albertson born Octr 19th 1783
5 Margaret Albertson . born July 28th 1785 Deceasd Octr 27th 1785

*The last figure was omitted.

Plymouth, Mass., Vital Records — 17

The Children of Asa Peirce & Eliza his Wife
1. Amanda Stephens, born August 1st . 1839.
The Children of Daniel Jackson & Rebecca his wife
1 Daniel Jackson born April 19th 1787
2 Rebecca Jackson born . Sept 22nd 1789
3 Abraham Jackson born Novr 29th 1791
4 Jacob Jackson born Janry 9th 1794
5 William Morton Jackson born Feb: 4th 1796
6 Thomas Taylor* Jackson born Sept 11th 1798
7 Isaac Carver Jackson born Decr 22d 1799
8 William Morton Jackson born may 30th 1802

[p. 107] The Chilldren of Jacob Albertson & Margaret his wife
1 Jacob Albertson born Janry 30th 1752
2 William Albertson born
3 Elizabeth Albertson born
4. Rufus Albertson born

The sd Jacob Albertson the Father of the family abovesd born in North Carrolina in the County of Pasquetank and was Drownd on a fishg Voyg from Plimo in the year
Said Margaret his wife Deceasd at Plimo

The Chilldren of Cornelus Cobb & Gase† his wife
1 Cornelus Cobb born Febry 10th 1775
2 Betse . Cobb . born May 6th 1777
3 Grace Cobb born May 31st 1781
4 Isaac E Cobb born Janry 19th 1789 deceased Janry 14 . 1821

The Chilldren of Joseph Holmes & Rebecca his wife
1 Joseph Holmes born Sept 8th 1770
2 Rebecca Holmes born Sept 28th 1772
3 Cornelus Holmes born June 15th‡ 1774
4 Ansell Holmes born Ap: 23rd 1777
5 Barter Holmes born Oct 19th 1779

[p. 108] The Children of James Clark Jun: & Lucy his wife
1 Jonathan Clark born March 19th 1785 Deceasd April 21st 1785
2 Bartlett Clark born Janry 29th 1786 Deceasd April 26th 1786
3 James Clark born March 15th 1787 Deceasd Augst 2nd 1804
4 Lucy Clark born Aug. 11 . 1788
5 Thankfull Clark born June 9th 1791
6 Sarah Clark born April 10th 1794
7 Rebecca Clark born June 24th 1796
8 Ezra Clark . born March 20th 1798
9 David Clark . born May 2nd 1800
10 Lewis Clark . born . June . 11th 1802

*"Taylor" is interlined, in a different hand and ink.
†Cornelius Cobb and Grace Eames, both of Plymouth, were married 15 May, 1774. See page 266 of this original volume of records.
‡"5" was written over "4".

Plymouth, Mass., Vital Records

The Child of James Harlow Jun.r & Sarah his wife
James Harlow born Aug: 27th 1785
The Children of William Atwood & Harriet his wife.
1. Edward Winslow, born . December 22d . 1835.
2. Harriet Elizabeth, born, Feb.y 22 . 1839.
The Chilldren of Cornelius Morrey & Jerusha his wife
1 Elijah Morrey born Aug.st 27th 1784
2 Sarah Morrey born July 22nd 1786
3 Cornelus Morrey born March 14th 1789
4 William Morrey born Sep.t 11th 1791
5 Jerusha Morrey born July 22nd 1794
6 Josiah Morrey born June 22 . 1797
The Children of W.m Drew 3d and Ann his Wife
1. William Warren, born 1831 . January
2. Frederick Augustus, born 1833 . November, 16
3. Augusta Ann born 1837. August . 10.
[p. 109] The Child of Joshua Thomas Esq: & Isabella his wife
1 John Boies Thomas born July 28th 1787
See this family in page 110
The Children of James Reed & Lucy his wife
1 Betsey Reed born June 1st 1789
2 James Reed born Nov.r 24th 1791
3 Polley Reed born April 28th 1794
4 Ruth Reed born Oct.r 26th 1796
5 Lemuel Fish Reed born May 4th 1800
2 Daughters of the above family there names were Ruth Reed both of them were born between Polley & Ruth above named one liv.d about 2 years the other about ten Days
8 Samuel Reed was born April 24th 1803
9 Hezekiah Bryant Reed born June 10th 1805
10 Henry Reed born March 1808
11 Salley Reed born June 7th 1811
The Children of Judah Dellano & Penelope his wife
1 Salome Dellano born   Deceas.d
2 Penelope Dellano born   Deceas.d
3 a Daughter born not named   Deceas.d
4 Elizabeth Dellano born April 4th 1786 tuesday half past 8 aClock A. M
5 Henry . Dellano born July 6th 1788 Sunday 53 minutes past 9 aClock A. M
6 Judah Dellano born Feb.y 26th 1792
7 Priscilla Dellano born Dec.r 11th 1793
The Chilldren of Seth Ryder & Hannah his wife
1 Seth Ryder born Sep.t 7th 1788
2. Hannah Ryder born Sep.t 7th 1788 Deceas.d were Twins
3. Hannah Ryder born Oct.r 23 1789
4. Mary Ryder born Sep.t 4th 1792
5. Esther Ryder born Sep.t 6th 1794
6 John Ryder born Oct.r 18th 1797
7. Nathaniel Ryder born April 30th 1801
[p. 110] The Children of Joshua Thomas Esq.r & Isabela his wife
1 John Boyse Thomas born July 28th 1787
2 William Thomas born March 15th 1788
3 Joshua
The Chilldren of William Straffin & Susannah his wife
1 William Straffin born Jan.ry 10th 1770
2 George Straffin born March 9th 1771
3 Lucy Straffin born Jan.ry 11th 1773 Deceas.d Jan.ry 31st 1773
The Chilldren of Robert Finney & Lydia his wife
1 Lydia Finney born
2 Robert Finney born June 17th 1768
3. Clark Finney born
4 George Finney born March 2nd *
5. Josiah Finney born
6 Elkanah Finney born
7 Experiance Finney born April 6th *

(To be continued)

---

* The year was not recorded.

THE
MAYFLOWER DESCENDANT

A QUARTERLY MAGAZINE OF
PILGRIM GENEALOGY AND HISTORY

VOLUME XXV

1923

PUBLISHED BY THE
MASSACHUSETTS SOCIETY OF
MAYFLOWER DESCENDANTS
BOSTON

PLYMOUTH, MASS., VITAL RECORDS

TRANSCRIBED BY MISS ETHEL A. RICHARDSON

(*Continued from Vol. XXIV, p. 19*)

[p. 111] 1754. In order for Marriages.
Augst 31 A Purpose of Marriage, Between Mr James Warren Junr of Plymouth; And Mrs Marcy Otis of Barnstable
31 A Purpose of Marriage, Between James Wade of Bridgwater, and Anna Clark of Plymouth. James Clark Junr Spoke for ye Publishment.
Sep^t 7 A Purpose of Marriage, Between Caleb Stetson of Plym^o and Abigail Bradford of Plimton
21 A Purpose of Marriage, Between Jesse Rider, and Bethiah Thomas, Both of Plymouth

Oct 5 A purpose of Marriage, Between Mr George Peckham, of Providence, In the Collony of Rhode Island, And Mrs Jerusha Bartlett of Plymouth

12 A purpose of Marriage, Between Mr Ephraim Dexter, of Rochester, & mrs Martha Waite of Plymouth

19 A purpose of Marriage, Between Mr Elkanah Watson of Plymouth, And Mrs Patience Marston of Manchester

Novr 1 A purpose of Marriage, Between Samll Crow of Providence In the Collony of Rhode Island, & Hannah Rider of Plymouth Spoke for by, and Ddd To Joshua Finney

1 A Purpose of Marriage Between Corban Barnes, & Rebeckah Atwood—Both of Plymouth

23 A purpose of Marriage, Between William Carver, (ye third) of Marshfield, & Margaret Kempton of Plymouth

26 A purpose of Marriage, between Mr John Wall of Greenwich In ye Collony of Rhode Island &c. and mrs Ruth Lucas of Plymouth
A Purpose of Marriage Between Joseph Silvester, & Susannah Cobb Both of Plymouth

Decr 7 A Purpose of Marriage Between Thomas Bayley Resident in Plymouth, and Sarah Langlee of Plymouth

14 A Purpose of Marriage Between John Washburn Junr and Lydia Prince, Both of Plymouth

Janry 4 A Purpose Of Marriage, Between James Lakey of Plymouth; And Margaret Beard, now Resident In Plymouth Chargd to A Donham

Feb: 22 A Purpose of Marriage, Between Mr Nathaniell Little of Tiverton, and Mrs Keziah Adams of Plymouth

22 A purpose of Marriage, Between Alexander Anderson Resident In Plymo, and Jean Seller of Plymouth

Mar: 1 A purpose of Marriage, Between William Huston, and Elizabeth Waite, Both of Plymouth

15 A purpose of Marriage Between Benjamin Lucas of Plymo and Lydia Crocker of Plimton

29 A purpose of Marriage, Between Benjamin Allen of Plymouth, and Beza Delano of Kingston wms Spoke for by Williams

[p. 113]* In Order for Marriages

1755 April . 5 A Purpose of Marriage Between John Brown of Truro & Sarah Little of Plymouth

5 A Purpose of Marriage Between Mr Jacob Tayler and Mrs Jeminah Samson Both of Plymouth

26 A purpose of Marriage, Between William Barnes, and Marcy Lemote both of Plymouth

May 3 A Purpose of Marriage Between Ebenezer Churchell Junr and Jean Fisher Both of Plymouth Chargd R Roberts

June 28 A Purpose of Marriage Betwen Mr Andrew Thomson And Mrs Elizabeth Murdoch Both of Plymouth

July 5 A Purpose of Marriage, Between George Stephens of Providence, In ye Collony of Rhode Island &c. And Elizabeth Donham of Plymouth

19 A purpose of Marriage, Between John Marshall, & Jerusha Watkins, Both of Plymouth

Augst 16. A purpose of Marriage, Between, Between Mr William Sever of Kingston, And Mrs Sarah Warren of Plymouth

16 A Purpose of Marriage, Between, George Little of Plymouth; And Abigail Soul of Plimton Spoke for ℅ W. Rich

Octr 10 A Purpose of Marriage, Between James Cole of Plimton, and Deborah Davenport of Plymouth

17 A. purpose of Marriage, Between John Donham; And Mary Thomas, Spoke for Ebenr Donham Junr

25 A purpose of Marriage, Between Charles Boult, and Lydia Curtis, both of Plymouth

Novr 1 A purpose of Marriage between Thomas Roberson, and Elizabeth Collons, Both of Plymouth

1 A purpose of Marriage, Between, Benjamin Robbens of Plymouth, & Abigail Cushman of Kingston

1 A Purpose of Marriage, Between Josiah West of Plymouth, and Elizabeth Griffen of Plimton

8th A Purpose of Marriage, Between Samll Donham Junr And Susannah Thomas, both of Plymouth

15 A Purpose of Marriage, Between Mr Samuell Dogget, And Mrs Deborah Foster, Both of Plymouth

A Purpose of Marriage Between Joshua Holmes, and Hannah Doten, Both of Plymouth Spoke ℅ Thomas Mitchel

22 A Purpose of Marriage, Between Capt Nathan Delano and Mrs Sarah Cobb, Both of Plymouth

A Purpose of Marriage Between William Keen and Margret Drew Both of Plymouth Spoke for ℅ Nicolas Drew

29 A Purpose of Marriage, Between John Bartlett Junr, and Sarah Bartlett, Both of Plymouth

Decr 3 A Purpose of Marriage Between Thomas Mitchell and Elizabeth Totman Both of Plymouth

[p. 114] 1755. In Order For Marriage

Decr 6. A Purpose of Marriage, Between, Mr Benjamin Lincoln of Taunton; And Mrs Marcy Carver of Plymo

1756 Febry 3 A Purpose of Marriage, Between Joshua Prat of Plimton, and Eunice Jackson of Plymouth Spoke for ℅ Seth Fuller Abiels Son, wth Certificate

21 A Purpose of Marriage Between John Cornish & Lydia Shurtleff Both of Plymouth

28 A Purpose of Marriage Between James Carver and Hope Doten Both of Plymouth

A Purpose of Marriage Between Ebenezer Donham Junr and Hannah Morton (Daughter of Lydia Morton) Both of Plymouth

* Page 112 was omitted, in numbering.

PLYMOUTH, MASS., VITAL RECORDS

(Continued from page 54)

[p. 115] 1756 In order for Marriages.

July 17 A Purpose of Marriage Between Thomas Robinson, and Ruth Hatch Both of Plymouth

31 A Purpose of Marriage Between Snow Keen of Pembrook And Rebeckah Burbanks of Plymouth Spoke for ⅌ Joseph Trask

Augst 13 A Purpose of Marriage Between Peleg Faunce, & Mary Faunce Both of Plymouth, Spoke for ⅌ Nathll Holmes

14 A Purpose of Marriage, Between Mr Lazarus Le-Barron Junr; and m{rs} Mary Lothrop, both of Plymouth

21 A Purpose of Marriage, Between Samuel Soule of Duxboro, & Mehetabel White of Plymouth

28 A Purpose of Marriage, Between, Mr William Watson of Plymouth; & m{rs} Elizabeth Maston of Salem

Octr 2 A Purpose of Marriage Between Josiah Waterman And Fear Tinkcom Both of Plymouth

2 A Purpose of Marriage Between Mr John Wethrell, and Mrs Sarah Crandon Both of Plymouth,

2 A Purpose of Marriage, Between Isaac Churchell of Boston, and Sarah Cobb of Plymouth

Novr 6 A Purpose of Marriage Between Ebenezer Fuller of Plymouth And Lowis Rider of Middleborough

6 A Purpose of Marriage Between John Mackeel, And Susannah Samson, Both of Plymouth

11 A Purpose of Marriage Between Lemuell Swift of Plymouth, and Rebecca Whitfield of Rochester

27 A Purpose of Marriage Between, Eleazer Rogers, and Bethiah Savery, Both of Plymouth

A Purpose of Marriage, Between Branch Blackmer, And Sarah Waite Both of Plymouth

A Purpose of Marriage, Between Ebenezer Rider, And Sarah Rider Both of Plymouth

A Purpose of Marriage Between, Obediah Osbern, of Rhode Island, And Jerusha Kempton of Plymouth

Decr 11 A Purpose of Marriage Between Levi Drew of Plym{o} And Mary Milk of Boston

18 A Purpose of Marriage Between John French of Hampton, In the Government of Newhampshear, and Rhoda Peck of Plymouth

1757 Jan{ry} 11 A Purpose of Marriage Between John Humphrys (Late of Boston) Negro man now of Plymouth & Beck Wicket of Plym{o}

15 A purpose of Marriage, Between Ezra Stetson of Rochester, & Sarah Rider of Plymouth Spoke for by Ebenez{r} Cobb Junr

March 13, A Purpose of Marriage, Between Micah Sepit, & Mary Sepit, Both of Plymouth, Indians

17 A Purpose of Marriage, Between, Thomas Cornish, and Ann Bates, both of Plymouth

20 A Purpose of Marriage Between Benjamin Holmes, and Rebeckah Drew Both of Plymouth

April 10 A Purpose of Marriage Between Territ Lester Now of Plymouth and Sarah Little of Plymouth

17 A Purpose of Marriage Between Mr David Turner and Mrs Rebeckah Warren Both of Plymouth

24 A Purpose of Marriage Between Nathaniel Washburn and Mary Rider Both of Plymouth

May 15 A Purpose of Marriage Between Nathaniel Bartlett Junr & Lydia Barnes (Daughter of Lemuel Barnes Deceas{d}) Both of Plymouth

22 A Purpose of Marriage; Between James Bunker of Sherburn in the County of Nantuckit, & Hannah Shurtleff of Plymouth

27 A Purpose of Marriage Between John Jones & Lydia Tinkcom Both of Plymouth

June 5 A Purpose of Marriage, Between Mr William Chambers and m{rs} Susannah Lemote; Both of Plymouth

12 A Purpose of Marriage Between Quosh, (Negro Man Servant To Doctr Lazarus LeBarron) and Phillis (Negro Woman, Servant To Capt{t} Theophilus Cotton,) Both of Plymouth

23 A Purpose of Marriage, Between Pero Molatta Man; & Hannah Malatta Woman; Both Slaves to Mr John Murdoch of Plymouth   Charg{d} Murdoch

July 3 A Purpose of Marriage Between Ebenezer Holmes Junr & Hannah Nellson Both of Plymouth

July 9 A Purpose of Marriage, Between Joshua Totman & Elizabeth Rogers, Both of Plym{o} Spoke for ⅌ John Churchell Junr

July 9 A Purpose of Marriage, Between, Barnabas Fountain of Plymouth And Elizabeth Joyce of Marshfield, Spoke for ⅌ T. Burbank Junr

(To be continued)

[p. 116] 1757 In order for Marriage
Febry 5 A Purpose of Marriage, Between Mr Ichabod Shaw & mrs Priscilla Atwood, both of Plymouth
19 A Purpose of Marriage Between John Patee & Margaret Finney Both of Plymouth Spoke for ℔ Seth Morton
26 A Purpose of Marriage Between John Finney Junr & Rebeckah Holmes, Both of Plymouth,
Mar: 25 A Purpose of Marriage, Between Nathaniel Thomas & Margaret Newcom, Both of Plymouth
April 2 A Purpose of Marriage Between James Harlow, & Jerusha Holmes Both of Plymouth
9 A Purpose of Marriage, Between, Mr Thomas Foster Junr of Marshfield; and Mrs Mary Foster of Plymouth.
9 A Purpose of Marriage Between Elisha Holmes Junr of Plymo, & Sarah Ewer, of Barnstable
May 21 A Purpose of Marriage, Between, Isaac Rider of Middleboro, and Bridget Nash of Plymouth
July 9 A Purpose of Marriage, Between, Mr John Russell, & Mrs Marcy Foster, Both of Plymouth
16 A Purpose of Marriage, between Mr John Dyer & mrs Mary Barnes, both of Plymouth
23 A Purpose of Marriage, Between Between Benjamin Smith, & Sarah Doten (Daughter of Samuel Doten Deceasd) Both of Plymouth
August 6 A Purpose of Marriage, Between Solomon Silvester, & Hannah Churchel Both of Plymouth
20 A Purpose of Marriage, Between John Goddard, & Mary Polden, Both of Plymouth.
27 A Purpose of Marriage Between, Mr Benjamin Goodwin, of Boston, & Mrs Hannah Le-Barron, of Plymo
Sept 10 A Purpose of Marriage, Between Joshua Battles, & Experience Cornish, Both of Plymouth,
Octb 1 A Purpose of Marriage, Between Thomas Mitchell of Bridgwater; And Keziah Swift of Plymouth
1 A purpose of Marriage, Between, George Codding of Taunton, And Mary Faunce of Plymouth
22nd A purpose of Marriage, Between James Reynolds, of Northkingston, In ye Collony of Road Island &c: and Elizabeth Donham of Plymouth
[p. 117] In order for Marriage
1757 Novb 5 A purpose of Marriage, Between, Capt Josiah Sturtevant, Junr of Hallifax & Mrs Lois Foster of Plymouth
5 A Purpose of Marriage, Between Ichabod Waterman of Plymouth, And Hannah Rogers of Kingston
26 A Purpose of Marriage, Between Eseck (Negroman Servant To George Watson Esqr) & Rose (Negro Woman Servant To Wm Clark) Both of Plymouth
26 A Purpose of Marriage Between Benjamin Bagnall & Sarah Totman Both of Plymouth
26 A Purpose of Marriage, Between George Glover, & Mary Fisher Both, of Plymouth,
Decr 3 A Purpose of Marriage Between John Rider & Priscillah Churchill Both of Plymouth
10 A Purpose of Marriage Between Robert Hosee & Mary Churchell Both of Plymouth
24 A Purpose of Marriage Between Joseph Trask; & Jerusha Kempton Both of Plymouth
1758 Janry 10 A Purpose, of Marriage, Between Edward Lanman of Plymo & Abiah Briant of Plimton.
14 A Purpose of Marriage, Between Samuell Briant and Eleoner Tinkcom, Both of Plymouth
21 A Purpose of Marriage, Between William Ozment. Late of Boston Now Resident in Plymouth & Elizabeth Donham of Plymouth

(To be continued)

PLYMOUTH, MASS., VITAL RECORDS

(Continued from page 141)

Febry 4* A purpose of Marriage Between Ebenezer Harlow, Junr & Rebeckah Bartlett Both of Plymouth

4 A purpose of Marriage Between Theodotious Ford, & Hannah Burbanks Both of Plymouth

10 A Purpose of Marriage, Between John Dillingham of Sandwich, & Sarah Blackmer of Plymouth

11 A Purpose of Marriage Between Ichabod Morton & Zilpah Thare Both of Plymouth

April 1 A Purpose of Marriage Between Jacob Doten of Plymouth & Sarah Cobb of Kingston

5 A Purpose of Marriage Between, Silvanus Howes, and Thankfull Rider, Both of Plymouth.

15 A purpose of Marriage, Between Gideon Hersey of Abbington, and Elizabeth Atwood of Plymouth

[p. 118] 1758. In Order for Marriage

May 5 A purpose of Marriage, Between Thomas Churchill, of Plymouth, & Mary Ewer of Barnstable

6 A Purpose of Marriage, Between ye Revd Mr Noah Hobart of Fairfield In Connecticut; And Mrs Priscilla Lothrop of Plymouth

20 A Purpose of Marriage Between Thomas Matthews of Plymo & Desire Gifford of Rochester

27 A Purpose of Marriage, Between Silvanus Harlow, & Desire Samson, Both of Plymouth

July 15 A Purpose of Marriage, Between mr Paul Leonard of Raynham, Mrs Mary Rider of Plymouth

Augst 12 A Purpose of Marriage Between Mr Billings Throop of Bristol, & Mrs Hannah Morton of Plymouth

25 A purpose of Marriage, Between, Richard Durfey Junr of No Kingston, In ye Collony of Rhoad Island, & Providence And Sarah Bayley of Plymouth.

Sept 9 A Purpose of Marriage, Between Joseph Bent, & Elizabeth Waterman, Both of Plymouth,

Octr 21 A Purpose of Marriage, Between Ephraim Bartlett, & Marcy Churchell, Both of Plymouth,

Novr 17 A purpose of Marriage, Between, Robert Bartlett Junr of Plymouth, And Lucey Woodworth, of Norwich, in ye Collony of Connecticut. Spoke for by Seth Harlow

18 A Purpose of Marriage Between Thomas Crosbey, & Elizabeth Beale, Both of Plymouth.

*Of the year 1758.

Decr 2 A Purpose of Marriage Between Joseph Mitchell & Mary Tinkcom Both of Plymouth

15 A purpose of Marriage, Between Silas West, And Rebeckah Withered, Both of Plymouth

1759 Jan^{ry} 27 A Purpose of Marriage Between Mr Jeremiah Howes & Mrs Hannah Churchill Both of Plymouth

Feb^{ry} 3 A Purpose of Marriage Between Micah Swift of Wareham & Abigail Swift of Plymouth

[p. 119] In Order for Marriages

1759 Feb^{ry} 10 A purpose of Marriage Between John Totman & Elizabeth Harlow both of Plymouth

[24 A Purpose of Marriage, Between Peleg Stevens & Sarah Beale, Both of Plymouth*]

24 A Purpose of Marriage Between Peleg Stevens Resident, In Plymouth, and Sarah Wright of Plymouth *This Purpose Ent^d anew Ap: 9th as below by Desire of said Peleg Stevens so this Entry Void*†

24 A Purpose of Marriage, Between Thomas Doty Esqr of Plym^o & Mrs Abigail Leonard of Boston,

27 A Purpose of Marriage, between Robert, Gamble Resident in Plym^o & Rebeckah Polden of Plymouth,

March 10 A Purpose of Marriage Between John Pool now Resident in Plymouth, & Jean Allen ye 2nd of Plymouth,

23 A Purpose of Marriage Between Moses Sachamus, & Susannah Harrey Indians, both of Plymouth,

31 A Purpose of Marriage Between Daniel Pappoon now Resident in Plym^o & Mary Lemont of Plymouth

Ap: 7 A Purpose of Marriage, Between John Williams, Resident in Plymouth, & Lydia Goddard of Plymouth.

9 A Purpose of Marriage, Between Peleg Stevens‡ now Resident in Plymouth, & Sarah Wright of Plymouth,

21 A Purpose of Marriage Between Mathew Claghorn of Chilmark & Jean Bartlett of Plymouth

27 A purpose of Marriage, Between Mr Nathl Bartlett of Plym^o, & Mrs Rebeckah Elles of Sandwich. Spoke for by Jacob Johnson

June 21 A purpose of Marriage Between Daniel Prat of Plimton & Lydia Cobb of Plymouth

July 7 A purpose of Marriage Between Mr Joseph Kempton of Dartmouth, & Mrs Mary Lothrop of Plymouth,

August 4 A purpose of Marriage, Between John Humpry Negro Man, & Mary Paul Indian Woman, Both of Plymouth,

Sept 22 A. Purpose of Marriage, Between Willm Rider Junr of Plym^o; and Betty Mitchell of Dartmouth.

*This entry has been crossed out.
†The words in italics are in the same hand and ink as the seventh entry following.
‡ See seventh entry preceding.

[p. 120] In Order for Marriages

1759 Novr 17th A Purpose of Marriage Between Solomon Holmes, & Abigail Bartlett, Both of Plymouth,

24 A Purpose of Marriage, Between Benjamin Bartlett Junr & Jemimah Holmes, Both of Plymouth.

Decr 1 A Purpose of Marriage Between Mr Thomas Finney of Bristol & Mrs Elizabeth Clark of Plymouth.

15 A Purpose of Marriage, Between, Jacob Johnson Junr of Plymouth, & Hannah Mason of Sandwich

22 A Purpose of Marriage, Between Jabez Dogget of Middleborough, & Rebeckah Rich of Plymouth

1760 Jan^{ry} 19 A Purpose of Marriage Between Benjamin Bagnall of Plymouth & Sarah Shurtleff of Plimton

19 A Purpose of Marriage, Between Joseph Barnes, & Hannah Rider, Both of Plymouth

Feb^{ry} 2 A Purpose of Marriage Between Nicholas Spinks, & Sarah Goddard, both of Plymouth

15 A Purpose of Marriage, Between, Francis Crapoo Junr of Rochester; & Margaret Beale of Plymouth.

22 A purpose of Marriage, Between Nathaniel Holmes & Cloe Sears Both of Plymouth

22 A purpose of Marriage, Between Thomas Savory Junr of Plymouth, & Zilpa Barrows of Plimpton

(To be continued)

THE MAYFLOWER DESCENDANT

1620   2020

A QUARTERLY MAGAZINE OF
PILGRIM GENEALOGY AND HISTORY

VOLUME XXVI

1924

PUBLISHED BY THE
MASSACHUSETTS SOCIETY OF
MAYFLOWER DESCENDANTS
BOSTON

PLYMOUTH, MASS., VITAL RECORDS

TRANSCRIBED BY MISS ETHEL A. RICHARDSON

(Continued from Vol. XXV, p. 189)

March 1* A purpose of Marriage Between Daniel Finn, now Resident in Plymouth, & Mary Samson of Plymouth.

22 A purpose of Marriage, Between John Rider Jun' of Plymouth, & Susannah Briant of Plimton.

29 A Purpose of Marriage, Between William Cunnet, & Mary Squib, Indians, Both of Plymouth.

April 12 A Purpose of Marriage, Between, the Rev'd M' Chandler Robbins of Plymouth, And M'rs Thankfull Hubbard of Guilford, In y'e Collony of Connecticut.

12 A Purpose of Marriage, Between James Thomas of Plinton & Hannah Barnes of Plymouth,

May 31 A Purpose of Marriage, Between James, Negro man (Servant to M' Tho' Jackson) & Rose Negro woman (Servant To M' William Clark) both of Plymouth

[p. 121] In order for Marriages

1760 July 19th A Purpose of Marriage, Between Elisha Morton, & Elizabeth Mitchell, Both of Plymouth.

25 A Purpose of Marriage Between Hasadiah Job & Betty Pepit Indians Both of Plymouth

Sep't 19 A Purpose of Marriage, Between Seth Jackson of Plymouth, And Ann May of Hallifax.

Oct' 29 A Purpose of Marriage Between Nathaniel Tupper & Susannah Blackmer both of Plymouth

Nov' 1 A Purpose of Marriage Between M' William Crumbie of Plymouth & M'rs Zerviah Kimball of Andover

22 A Purpose of Marriage Between Samuel Calderwood now Resident in Plymouth & Priscilla Bartlett of Plym°

Dec' 6 A Purpose of Marriage Between John Dugless now Resident in Plymouth & Mary Holmes of Plymouth

13 A Purpose of Marriage Between Joshua Bramhall Jun' & Rebeckah Sears both of Plymouth

A Purpose of Marriage Between Jn° Harlow y'e 3rd & Rebeckah Howes Both of Plymouth

A Purpose of Marriage Between Patrick Morris now Resident in Plymouth & Mary Vincent of Plymouth

A Purpose of Marriage, Between William Case of Boston, & Joanna Ward of Plymouth

*Of 1760.

27 A Purpose of Marriage Between Mr Robert Slocumb of Liverpool in Nova Scotia & Faith Shurtleff of Plymo

1761 Janry 3 A Purpose of Marriage Between Richard Cooper and Hannah Samson, Both of Plymouth

17 A Purpose of Marriage, Between, Thomas Holmes Junr and Marcy Bartlett, Both of Plymouth.

Febry 7 A Purpose of Marriage Between Thomas Trask, & Hannah Waterman, Both of Plymouth.

7 A Purpose of Marriage, Between, Mr John Churchell of Plymouth & Mrs Hephzibah Pemberton of Boston

14 A Purpose of Marriage, Between Samuell Sherman, and Betty Sears, Both of Plymouth

Mar: 7 A Purpose of Marriage, Between Faunce Hammond of Rochester, And Mary Holmes of Plymouth

[p. 122] 1761. In order for Marriage

Mar: 21. A Purpose of Marriage, Between Einathan Holmes, & Bathsheba Holmes, Both of Plymouth

April 11. A purpose of Marriage, Between Saml Gray of Kingston & Eunice Delano of Plymouth

11. A purpose of Marriage, Between Nathaniel Leonard, & Bethiah Rider, Both of Plymouth

18th A purpose of Marriage Between Ebenezer Samson Junr of Plymouth and Priscilla Pratt. of Middleborough

May 2 A purpose of Marriage, Between Mr John Holmes of Plymouth, & Mrs Abigail Finney of Bristoll.

30th A Purpose of Marriage, Between Mr Barnabas Hedge Junr of Plymouth, And Mrs Hannah Hedge of Yarmouth

June 6 A Purpose of Marriage Between Seth Morton & Marcy Sampson, Both of Plymouth

July 25. A purpose of Marriage, Between Samuel Kempton Junr & Elizabeth Sampson, Both of Plymouth.

Augst 1 A Purpose of Marriage, Between, William Bartlett Junr & Rebeckah Trask. Both of Plymouth.

August 15 A Purpose of Marriage Between Ebenezar Fuller & Hannah Rider Both of Plymouth

22. A Purpose of Marriage: Between ye Revd Mr Chandler Robbin of Plymouth; And Mrs Jane Prince of Boston

25. A Purpose of Marriage. Between Joseph Lovell of Barnstable, & Elizabeth Harlow of Plymouth.

29. A Purpose of Marriage, Between James Polden, and Elizabeth Beale, Both of Plymouth.

Octr 3. A Purpose of Marriage, Between, Adam Allen, Negro Man, & Susannah Sachamus, Indian Woman, Both of Plymouth

10 A Purpose of Marriage Between Isaac Cole & Martha Harlow Both of Plymouth

A Purpose of Marriage Between Cesar Negro Man Slave To Mr Elkanah Watson: And Esther Woman Slave To Edward Winslow Esqr Both of Plymouth

[p. 123] In order, for Marriages. Continued:

1761 Octr 16. A purpose of Marriage, Between John Hall Resident, in Plymouth, & Marcy Leach, of Plymouth

Novr ye 14 A purpose of Marriage. Between Mr Benjamin Willis Junr of Bridgwater: And Mrs Sarah Bradford of Plymouth

Decr 2 A Purpose of Marriage, Between Mr Saml Peirce of Bristoll, In the Collony of Rhode Island &c: & mrs Elizabeth Hersey of Plymouth

Decr 2. A Purpose of Marriage, Between Mr Silvanus Bramhall and mrs Marcy Warren, Both of Plymouth

5. A Purpose of Marriage, Between Thomas Davee and Hannah Rogers, Both of Plymouth

12. A purpose of Marriage, Between Thomas Harlow, of Plymouth, & Anna Fuller of Plimpton

26. A Purpose of Marriage, Between, The Revd Mr Ammi-Ruhamah Robbins, of Norfolk, in ye Collony of Connecticut, And Mrs Elizabeth Lebarron of Plymouth

26. A Purpose of Marriage, Between, Brittan Hammond Negro manslave, to John Winslow Esqr of Marshfield; And Hannah, Negro Woman Slave, to James Hovey Esqr of Plymouth

1762 Janry 16 . A purpose of Marriage, Between Joseph Bartlett the Third, & Lydia Cobb, Both of Plymouth.

16th A Purpose of Marriage, Between John Rogers, and Mary Holmes, Both of Plymouth.

23 A Purpose of Marriage Between Richard Kimbell Resident in Plymouth & Susanna Donham of Plymo

23 A Purpose of Marriage Between William Polden and Susannah Lee Both of Plymouth

Febry 13th A purpose of Marriage, Between Benjamin Barnes, And Elizabeth Holmes both of Plymouth.

[p. 124] 1762 In Order for Marriage Continued

Febry 13 A Purpose of Marriage Between Ezra Burbank And Priscilla Savory Both of Plymouth

A purpose of Marriage Between Gershom Holmes of Taunton & Deborah Dellano of Plymouth

20th A purpose of Marriage, Between Mr Saml Battles, & Mrs Alice Barnes, Both of Plymo

27 A Purpose of Marriage, Between Jacob Wompus, of Plymton & Jean Atkins, of Plymouth Indians

March 6. A purpose of Marriage, Between Thomas Smith Resident in Plymouth; And Marcy Leach of Plymouth.

27. A purpose of Marryage, Between Jesse Harlow, and Elizabeth Sampson, Both of Plymouth

April 3. A purpose of Marriage, Between, Lemuell Goddard, & Nancy Kingston, Both of Plymouth.

April 10. A purpose of Marryage, Between Mr Bartlett LeBarron & mis Mary Esdell Both of Plymouth

June 12. A Purpose of Marriage, Between, Isaac Mackey & Sarah Harlow, Both of Plymouth.

July 10th A purpose of Marriage, Between, James Coade and Hannah Ward, Both of Plymouth.

10 A Purpose of Marriage Between Mr William Rickard And Miss Martha Tilley Both of Plymouth

31st A Purpose of Marriage, Between Seth Holmes, and Mary Holmes, Both of of Plymouth.

Augst 14. A Purpose of Marriage, Between Seth Ewer, of Barnstable; & Lydia Holmes, of Plymouth.

Octr 23. A Purpose of Marriage, Between Mr Ezekiel Rider, And Mrs Lydia Atwood, Both of Plymouth.

Novr 6 A Purpose of Marriage Between Stephen Smith of Sandwich And Deborah Elles of Plymouth

12 A Purpose of Marriage Between Mr John Bartlett Third And Mis Mercy Elles Both of Plymouth.

[p. 125] In Order for Marriages Continued

1762 Novr[r]d A Purpose of Marriage Between George Atwood And Joanna Bartlett Both of Plymouth

Decr 18 A Purpose of Marriage Between James Holmes Jur And Remember Wetherhead Both of Plymouth

20 A Purpose of Marriage Between John Phillips Negro Man & Patience Robbins Indian Woman Both of Plymouth

1763 Jany 1 A Purpose of Marriage Between Mr Benjamin Warren of Plymouth & miss Jane Sturtevant of Kingston

A Purpose of Marriage, Between mr David Stoops of Taunton, and miss Margaret Marrifield of Plymth

8th A purpose of Marriage, Between, Coll: Stephen Miller of Milton, And miss Hannah Dyre, of Plymouth

Febry 5. A purpose of Marriage, Between, Elijah Morrey, and Rebecca Wast Both of Plymouth.

Febry 12 A Purpose of Marriage Between Samll Eddy of Middlebor And Anna Morton of Plymouth Entred Below

Febry 12 A Purpose of Marriage, Between, Samuell Eddy of Middleboro, And Anna Morton of Plymouth

12. A Purpose of Marriage Between Seth Harlow and Sarah Warren Both of Plymouth

Apr 2 A Purpose of Marriage Between Josiah Finney Junr and Alice Barnes Both of Plymouth

9th A Purpose of Marriage, Between Mr Andrew Croswell Junr of Boston; & Mss Mary Clark, of Plymouth.

23rd A purpose of Marriage, Between Mr Joseph Warren, and Mrs Mercy Torrey, Both of Plymouth.

May 7 A Purpose of Marriage, Between Zephaniah Holmes Junr & Mercy Withered, Both of Plymouth

June . 11. A purpose of Marriage, Between Joseph Holmes, & Phebe Bartlett, Both of Plymouth

18 A Purpose of Marriage Between Mr Rufus Ripley of Kingston, and Miss Mary Shurtleff of Plymouth

[p. 126] 1763 In Order For Marriages Continued

Sepr 12 A Purpose of Marriage Between John Kempton Junr And Mary Hatch Both of Plymouth

24. A Purpose of Marriage . Between Mr Samuell Harlow, And Mrs Mary Morton, Both of Plymouth.

Oct 8 A: Purpose of Marriage, Between Isaac Jackson of Plymouth; & Lydia Barrows of Plimpton.

8 A Purpose of Marriage, Between, Amos Jefery of Plimpton & Phebe Sepit of Plymouth, Indians.

29th A Purpose of Marriage, Between Judah Bartlett, & Love Sprague . Both of Plymouth.

A purpose of Marriage Between Mr James Bartlett And Elizabeth Bates Both of Plymouth

Novr 26 A purpose of Marriage Between, William, Harlow Junr and Sarah Holmes Both of Plymouth

Decbr 10th A Purpose of Marriage. Between Mr Ephraim Spooner And Miss Elizabeth Shurtleff Both of Plymouth

1764 Febr 22 A purpose of Marriage Between Joseph Totman And Elizabeth Curtis Both of Plymo

March ye 31 A purpose of Marriage, Between Richard Holmes And Mercy Barnes, both of Plymouth

April 14th A purpose of Marriage, Between George Le Mot[e] and Catherine Nicolson Both of Plymouth,

April 27th A purpose of Marriage, Between Mr Perez Tilsson, & Mrs Sarah Wethrell, Both of Plymouth,

May 18th A purpose of Marriage, Between . Mr Daniel Hill. of Black Point, In Casco Bay; & Mrs Elizabeth Holmes of Plymouth.

July 14 A purpose of Marriage, Between Ebed Negro Man Servant to mrs mary Thacher of Middleboro And Betty Cunnit of Plymouth Indian Woman

July 21 A Purpose of Marriage Between William Donham And Abigail Thomas; Both of Plymouth

[p. 127] In Order for Marriages Continued

1764 August 18 A Purpose of Marriage Between Mr William Warren & Miss Rebecca Easdell Both of Plymouth

yr 18th A Purpose of Marriage Between Mr James Doten & Miss Elizabeth Kempton Both of Plymouth

yr 18th A Purpose of Marriage Between Mr Silas Donham & Mrs Bethiah Bartlett Both of Plymouth.

25 A Purpose of Marriage Between Mr Ellis Churchill & Miss Patience Churchill Both of Plymouth.

Septmbr 8 A Purpose of Marriage Between Mr Eleazer Churchill . junr & Mrs Jane Rider, Both of Plimouth.

A Purpose of Marriage Between John King & Thankfull Homes Both of Plimouth.

* Blotted — probably "22d" — Editor.

44

15 A Purpose of Marriage Between Mr Benjamin Drew of Plimouth & Mis^s Elizabeth Doggett Of Plimton

22 A Purpose of Marriage Between Mr Jacob Johnson of Plymouth & M^{iss} Eunice Cushman of Plimton

October 13 A Purpose of Marriage Between Mr Nathaniel Carver, & Mis^s Sarah Churchill Both of Plimouth.

27 A Purpose of Marriage, Between Mr William Barne[s] & Miss Mary Rider the Second; Both of Plimouth

Nov^{br} 3 A Purpose of Marriage Between Mr Jonathan Bartlett ju^r & Mis^s Mary Doty Both of Plimouth

Novr 10 A Purpose of Marriage Between John Bates of Hanover & Hannah Silvester of Plimouth

10 A Purpose of Marrige Between Josiah Doten & Deborah Rider Both of Plimouth

A Purpose of Marriage Between Mr George Holmes & Anne Rich, Both of Plimouth

Nov^{br} 17 A Purpose of Marriage Between George Toto of Kingston & Zilpa Buckley of Plimouth

(To be continued)

PLYMOUTH, MASS., VITAL RECORDS

(Continued from page 44)

[p. 128] In Order For Marriages Continued

1764 Novr 17 A Purpose of Marriage Between Mr Ebenezer Gorham jun^r of Barnstable, & Mrs Hope Carver of Plimouth.

Novr 29th A Purpose of Marriage Between Mr Andrew Bartlett & Mis^s Lydia Churchill Both of Plymouth

A Purpose of Marriage Between Mr Isaac Burbanks of Plymouth & Mis^s Mary Marble of Swansy

1765 Jan^{ry} 19 A Purpose of Marriage Betwen Jonathan Polden & Mary Ward, Both of Plymouth.

Feb^{ry} 16 A Purpose of Marriage, Between Mr Isaac Symms of Plimouth . & Mis^s Hannah Davis . of Charlestown.

23 A Purpose of Marriage, Between Mr Hezekiah Jackson of Plimouth, & Mis^s Elizabeth Thacher of Barnstable.

Ap^r 6 A Purpose of Marriage Between Mr Ezra Corban of Killingley, & Mrs Hannah Barnes of Plimouth

A Purpose of Marriage Between Mr James Seller and Rebeca Cobb Both of Plymouth

20 A Purpose of Marriage Between Nath^{ll} Doten & Mercy Rider Both of Plymouth

*Isaac Addington was clerk of the court at Boston.

May 11 A Purpose of Marriage Between Mr John Otis And Mis^s Hannah Churchill Both of Plymouth

11 A Purpose of Marriage Between John Atwood, & Lydia Holmes, Both of Plimouth.

June 2 A Purpose of Marriage Between Ebenezer Ward & Lydia Polden Both of Plimouth

July 13 A Purpose of Marriage Between Elkanah Barnes & Hannah Bartlett, Both of Plymouth

27 a Purpose of Marriage Between Ansell Churchill and Bethiah Holmes Both of Plimouth

August 31 a Purpose of Marriage Between Nath^{ll} Barnes, & Lydia Curtis Both of Plimouth

Octob^r 3 A Purpose of Marriage Between Joshua Shaw, & Margerett Atwood Both of Plimouth

[p. 129] In Order For Marriages

1765 Octob^r 10 A Purpose of Marriage Between Bartlett Holmes, & Lucey Bartlett Both of Plimouth

12 A Purpose of Marriage Between Mr Charles Churchill & Mrs Sarah Churchill Both of Plimouth

14 A Purpose of Marriage Between [*] Seth Washburn of Plimouth & Fear Howard of Kingston

17 A Purpose of Marriage Between Phillips Washburn of Plimouth & Silence Davis of Kingston

19 a Purpose of Marriage Between Thomas Bartlett & Betty † Bartlett Both of Plimouth

A Purpose of Marriage Between [*] Nathanel Ripley & Elizabeth Bartlett Both of Plimouth

A Purpose of marriage Between Mosses Reading & Sarah Jones ye 2nd Both of Plimouth

A Purpose of Marriage Between Abraham Tisdell of Taunton & Experience Totman of Plimouth

Novr 23 A Purpose of Marriage Between Mr Corban Barns & Mis^s Mary Phinney. Both of Plimouth

27 A Purpose of Marriage Between Robert Finney & Lydia Clark Both of Plimouth

Decr 15 a Purpose of Marriage Between Ebenezer Harlow jun^r & Lydia Doten Both of Plimouth

1766 Jan^{ry} 25 A Purpose of Marriage Between, Philip Leonard & Hannah Warren Both of Plimouth

A Purpose of Marriage Between Mr Eleazer Stevens & Mrs Susannah Silvester Both of Plimouth

Feb^{ry} 22 A Purpose of Marriage Between . James Bartlett of Plimouth & Zerviah Knowlton of Middleboro

* "M^r" was written here, but apparently an attempt was made to erase it.

† "Elizabeth" was first written, but was crossed out, and "Betty" interlined, in the same hand and ink.

[p. 130] In Order For Marriage

1766 March 1st A Purpose of Marriage Between Elkanah Lucas, of Plimton & Mehitable Lucas, of Plimouth
15 A Purpose of Marriage Between Jonathan Watkins Resident in Plimouth & Lucy Donham of Plimouth.
Publishments. 1766.
March. 22. Gamaliel Arnold of Duxborough to Hannah waite of Plymouth
22. Isaac Morton to Ruth Tinkham both of Plymouth.
April. 12. Robert Davie to Elizabeth Churchell both of Plymouth.
19. Enoch Randall to Phebe Tinkcom both of Plymouth.
19. Stephen Churchill to Lucy Burbank both of Plymouth.
May. 3 Mr Prince Wadsworth of Duxborough to Mrs Zilpah Ellis of Plymouth.
17 Nathanael Barnes to Jerusha Blackmer both of Plymouth.
April. 26. Barnabas Donham to Lydia Cole both of Plymouth.
June. 21. Isaac Bartlett to Lois Harlow both of Plymouth.
July. 5. Thomas Sylvester to Elisabeth Donham both of Plymouth.
19. Samuel Bartlett junr to Elisabeth Jackson both of Plymouth.
Aug: 9. John Whitehorn of Newport in Rhode-Island to Thankful Holmes of Plymouth.
23. James Cobb junr of Kingston & Melatiah Holmes of Plymouth.
30. John Cobb & Persis Lucas both of Plymouth.
30. Andrew Hill resident in Plymo to Elizabeth Burgis of Plymo
Sept. 6. Josiah Clark of Plymouth to Hannah Harlow of Middleborough.
6. Lemuel Leach to Sarah Holmes both of Plymouth.
Oct. 11 Benjamin Goddard to Mary Morton both of Plymouth.
25. Isaac Morse of Middleboro to Jemima Pratt of Plymouth.
25. Oliver Kempton of Duxborough to Experience Ripley of Plymouth
[p. 131]
Publishments. 1766.
1766 novembr 1. Alexander Dow & Lydia Eames both of Plymouth.
1. Elijah Harlow to Patience Drew both of Plymouth.
22. William Savery to Lydia Holmes both of Plymouth.
Decemr 27. Mr John Churchill junr of Plymo to Mrs Sarah Prat of Bridgwater.
1767 February . 21 . Joseph Burbank to Joanna Holmes both of Plymouth.
28. Peter Shurtleff of Plimpton to Rebekah Holmes of Plymouth.
March 21 Ezra Harlow To Susannah Warren both of Plymouth
George Bramhall To Zilpah Richmond both of Plymouth
28 William Clark Junr To Sarah Howard both of Plymouth
Joseph Rider Junr To Abigail Atwood both of Plymouth
July 11 Thomas Ellis To Jerusha Clark both of Plymouth
19 William Duey To Rebeckah Cole Junr both of Plymouth
Zacheus Morton To Sylvester Aken both of Plymouth

Augst 29 Jonathan Olever Resident in Plymouth To Mehitable Stetson of Plymo
Sept 5 John Bishop Resident in Plymouth, To Abigail Holmes of Plymo
12 Mr Jonathan Churchell Junr of Plymouth To Mrs Lydia Gilbert of Hingham
12 Mr Stevens Mason To Mrs Lydia Simmons both of Plymouth.
19 Mr Reubin Washburn & Mrs Meriah Holmes both . of Plymouth
25 Mr William Loring of Plimton To Mrs Lucy Rider of Plymouth
Mr Robert Donham. To Mrs Ruth Hatch both of Plymouth
Octor 3 Mr John Barrows of Plymouth To Mrs Sarah Manning of Cambridge
10 Mr Jonas Clark of Boston To Mrs Martha Rickard of Plymouth
Mr Samuel Rider To Mrs Jane Swift . both of Plymouth
Mr Josiah Johnson of Plymo To Mrs Batisheba Barrows of Plimton
Mr John Foster To Mrs Elizabeth Rider both of Plymouth
24 Thomas Faunce Junr To Mary Curtis both of Plymouth
31 Mr Lemuel Drew To Mrs Elizabeth Rider ye 2nd both of Plymo
Seth Nicholson To Lydia Holmes. Both of Plymo
Decr 2 Mr John Fuller of Plimouth To Mr Rebeckah Robbins of Plymton
19 Thomas Howard To Ruth Holmes Both of Plymouth
Lemuel Harlow of Plimton To Johanna Holmes of Plymouth
26 The Revd Mr Samuel West of Dartmouth To Mrs Experience Howland of Plymouth
[p. 132] Publishments In ordr for Marriage
1767 Decr 25 Mr Consider Drew of Duxboro To Mrs Jean Ellis of Plymouth
Mr Nathaniel Corrish of Plymo & Mrs Abigail Swift of Ditto
1768 January 2 Mr John Samson To Mrs Hannah Shareman both of Plymouth
9 Mr Samuel Harlow To Mrs Remember Holmes both of Plymouth
30 Mr Peter Thomas of Plymo To Mrs Mary Cushing of Duxboro
Mr William Curtis Junr of Pembrook To Mr Hannah Tinkcom of Plymo
March 5 Cuff Negro Man Servant To George Watson Esqr & Nanne Negro woman Servant to Samuel Bartlett Esqr both of Plimouth
19 Mr Daniel Gifford of Sandwich To Mrs Sarah Vallur of Plimouth
19 Mr Thomas Davie Junr & Mrs Jenne Holmes both of Plimo

(To be continued)

PLYMOUTH, MASS, VITAL RECORDS

(Continued from page 87)

April 4* William Campble Resident in Plimouth & Rebeckah Gamble of Plimouth
9 Zadock Howard of Plim° & Experience Bearce of Bridgwater
16 Isaac Holmes of Plimouth & Ruth Ransom of Plimton
23 M' Seth Pain of Eastham & M'ˢ Sarah Sears of Plimouth
30 Silvanus Finney & Mary Morton both of Plimouth
   Joseph Bramhall of Plim° & Keziah Thomas of Kingston
May 14 Thomas Farmer & Susanna Tinkcom both of Plimouth
21 William Boult & Johanna Ward yᵉ 2ⁿᵈ both of Plimouth
June 11 James Murfee & Mary Mcfarling now Residents in Plim°
18 Hennery Highton now Resident in Plim° & Eliz° Polden of Plim°
July 2 William Dave & Lydia Harlow both of Plimouth
9 M' Ezra Harlow of Midd° & M'ˢ Betty Ellis of Plimouth
16 Ichabod Bearce of Pembrook & Esther Holmes of Plimouth
   Ephraim Darling now Residing in Plimouth & Rebeckah Bartlett of Plim°
   M' Daniel Hose & M'ˢ Hannah Bartlett both of Plimouth
23 M' Ephraim Holmes Jun' & M'ˢ Lucy Barnes both of Plimouth
30 M' John Bartlett yᵉ 3ʳᵈ & M'ˢ Dorothy Carver both of Plim°
Aug 6 M' Thomas Doten & M'ˢ Jerusha Howes both of Plimouth
   William Bassett Now Resident in Plimouth & Abigail Lee of Plimouth
20 M' Thomas Wethrell, & M'ˢ Anna May, Both of Plimouth
Septem' 10 M' John Allen & M'ˢ Esther Savory both of Plimouth
17 M' Caleb Rider & M'ˢ Hannah Mackfarling both of Plimouth
[p. 133] 1768 Publishments in order for Marriage
October 1 Solomon Holmes, & Mary Dellano, Both of Plimouth
   Elisha Doten, & Mercy Harlow yᵉ 2ⁿᵈ Both of Plimouth
   Elkanah Bartlett, & Sarah Atwood, both of Plimouth
   Samuel Hollis now resident in Plim° & Abigail Drew of Plim°
8 Gilbert Holmes & Mercy Holmes both of Plimouth
15 M' Nathaniel Jackson & M'ˢ Elizabeth Foster both of Plimouth
   M' Thomas Usman of Bristol in the Colony of Rhode Island & M'ˢ Salome Foster of Plimouth
29 M' Ellis Holmes & M'ˢ Content Howland both of Plimouth
   John Randall Now Resident in Plim° & Lurany Bearce of Plim°

* p. 68 Under "Publishments In order for Marriage"

*"On original page 258 is the marriage on 18 November, 1768, of 'Elis Holmes & Content Howland both of Plimouth'"

5 Isaac Tinkcom of Plimo & Lydia Rider of Middleborough
19 Silvanus Holmes Junr & Rebeckah Churchell, both of Plimouth
19 John Rickard Junr of Plimton, & Lydia King of Plimouth
26 Barnabas Holmes To Mercy Holmes Both of Plimouth
26 James Lawrance of Plimo & Abigail Ewer of Sandwich
26 Thomas Watson now Resident in Plimouth & Sarah Lester of Plimo
30 Isaac Howland & Sarah Doten Both of Plimouth
Decr 2 John Cooper & Sarah Samson . Both of Plimo
10 Ezra Finney . & Hannah Luce Both . of Plimouth
17 John Cornish & Sarah Bartlett . both . of Plimouth
1769 Janry 7 Mr Nathaniel Goodwin Junr & Mrs Molley Jackson both of Plimo
21 Ephraim Luce & Ruth Morton . Both . of Plimouth
April 8 Mr Daniel Diman of Plimo & Mrs Susannah Southworth of Middo
15 Mr John Watson & Mrs Luca Marston both of Plimouth
Seth Luce . & Sarah Blackwell both . of Plimouth
May 20 Mr Amos Donham & Mrs Abigail Faunce both of Plimouth
June 24 Joseph Holmes, & Rebeckah Eames, both of Plimouth,
July 8 Benja Boyston Resident in Plimo & Mercy Bartlett of Plimo
Richard Bab & Meriah Bartlett Both of Plimouth
Wait Atwood & Susannah Marshell ye 2nd both of Plimouth
Augst 12 Robert Robards now Resident in Plimo & Sarah Westron* of Plimouth
Sept 9 Nathan Cobb & Jerusha Harlow both of Plimouth
[p. 134] 1769 Publeshments in order for Marriage
Sept 9 William Straffen now Resident in Plimo & Susannah Kember of Plimouth
23 Mr Joseph Sylvester & Mrs Susannah Tupper, both of Plimo
23 Silas Vallar & Mercy Morrey both Plimouth,
23 Mr Nicholas Drew Junr, & Mrs Mercy Holmes, both of Plimo
30 Nathaniel Shearman & Meriah Clark both of Plimouth
Octobr 7 William Smith now Resident in Plimo & Sarah Stetson of Plimouth
14 Lothrop Holmes & Mary Bartlett ye 2nd both of Plimouth
21 David Curtis of Plimo & Mary Wing of Sandwich
21 Jonah Bisbey Junr of Pembrook & Ruth Sherman of Plimouth
Mr Edward Clark of Boston & Mrs Elizabeth Watson of Plimouth
Novr 18 Joseph Bartlett ye 4th & Lucy Holmes Both of Plimouth
Decr 8 Ansell Harlow, & Hannah Barnes, both of Plimouth
23 William Donham of Plimo & Mercy Raymond of Middleboro
1770 Janry 6 James Waterman & Johanna Wood both of Plimouth
13 Mr Robert Bartlett & Mrs Jenna Spooner both of Plimouth
20 John Swift of Plimo & Elizabeth Gibbs of Sandwich

20 Jonathan Harlow Junr & Elizabeth Blackmer both of Plimouth
Febry 3 Mr Samuel Shareman & Mrs Jerusha Morton both of Plimouth
March 3 Mr John Bartlett of Plimouth & Mrs Sarah Seaberry of Duxboro
3 Nicholas Smith & Susannah Churchell both of Plimouth
3 Isaac Harlow & Martha Swinnerton both of Plimouth
3 Silvanus Morton & Hulda Holmes both of Plimouth
10 Barnabas Ellis of Plimouth & Ruth Mendall of Rochester
24 John Faunce of Plimouth & Jenne Paddock of Middleboro

(To be continued)

* On original page 264 is the marriage, on 27 August, 1769, of " Robert Roberts Now resident in Plimo & Sarah Weston of Ditto ".

PLYMOUTH, MASS., VITAL RECORDS

(Continued from page 141)

[PUBLISHMENTS IN ORDER FOR MARRIAGE]

April 21* Lemuel Cobb, & Hannah Kempton, both of Plimouth,
21 Isaac Atwood, of Plimouth & Hannah Chubbuck of Abington
28 Mr Thomas Spooner & Mrs Mary Bartlett both of Plimouth
May 5 Thomas Sears & Rebeckah Rider both of Plimouth
June 9 David Lothrop, & Bathsheba May, both of Plimouth
[p. 135] Publishments in ord^r for Marriage
1770 June 16 Pelham Winslow Esqr & Mrs Joanna White ye 2nd both of Plimouth
30 James Harlow & Hannah Dellano both of Plimouth
July 14 Miles Long, & Thankfull Clark both of Plimouth
28 Jacob Decoster & Priscilla Rogers both of Plimouth
Sep^t 1 Mallicha Dellano of Duxboro & Patience Burges the 2nd of Plimouth
1 Richard Durfey & Elizabeth West both of Plimouth
22 Mr Joseph Bartlett Junr & Mrs Mary Bartlett both of Plimouth
29 William King, & Susannah Harlow, both of Plimouth
Octob^r 13 William Williams & Thankfull Thrasher both of Plim^o
27 Nathl Churchell Junr & Bettey Rider both of Plimouth
Novr 3 John Howard Junr of Plim^o & Eleanor Cobb of Kingston
3 Ichabod Thomas & Hannah Morton both of Plimouth
3 Benjamin Eaton & Hannah Holmes both of Plim^o
17 Thomas Hatch Whittemore & Thankfull Holmes both of Ditto
Decr 1 Jesse Churchell & Abigail Worcester both of Plimouth
8 James Wollins & Ruth Donham (Daughter of Mr Cornelius Donham) both of Plimouth

*April 21, 1770.

THE MAYFLOWER DESCENDANT

1620 2020

A QUARTERLY MAGAZINE OF
PILGRIM GENEALOGY AND HISTORY

VOLUME XXVII

1925

PUBLISHED BY THE
MASSACHUSETTS SOCIETY OF
MAYFLOWER DESCENDANTS
BOSTON

Plymouth, Mass., Vital Records

14 William Ephraims & Elizabeth Nero both of Plimouth
22 Thomas Edward Burrows now Resident in Plim° & Eliz° Rogers in Plimton
29 Samuel Morton & Joanna Totman both of Plimouth
29 John Atwood Jun' & Deborah Doten both of Plimouth
1771 Jan'y 5 George Donham now resident in Plim°, & Anna Donh^m of Plim°
Feb'y 9 M' Benjamin Rider Jun' & M's Sarah Jones, both of Plimouth
16 M' William Breck of Boston, & M's Margaret Thomas of Plimouth,
M' Thomas Southworth Howland, & M's Abial Hovey both of Plimouth,
March 9 M' John Churchell Jun' of Plim° & M's Mary Bradford of Plimton
9 M' Thomas Lanman & M's Rebakah Kempton both of Plimouth
9 Job Tack Negroman & Mehittable Cuff Indian woman both of Plim°
John Edwards & Lydia Samson both of Plimouth
[p. 136] Publishments in order for marriage
1771 March 16 David Bates of Plim° & Sarah Fish of Sandwich
16 Thomas Covington & Sarah Treeble y° 2nd both of Plimouth
30 John Barnes & Margaret Rider, both of Plimouth,
April 6 M' William Thomas, & M's Mary Howland, both of Plimouth,
May 3 Aaron Sekins & Tabitha Raymond both Residents in Plimouth
3 Nathaniel Raymond Resident in Plimouth & Thankfull Baker of Barnestable
4 Nehemiah Holmes of Plimouth, & Fear Reding of Midd°
4 Richard Holmes Jun' & Abigail Dammon both of Plim°
4 Ansel Holmes & Martha Howard both of Plimouth
20 James Hovey Esq' & M's Mary Harlow both of Plimouth
25 Seth Lawrance of Plimouth & Mary Peck now resident In Plimouth*
June 22 Cornelius Bramhall of Falmouth in Casco bay & Mercy Torrey of Plimouth
29 Joseph Bramhall & Rememb' Robbins both of Plimouth
July 6 Thomas Hackman & Lydia Sutton both of Plimouth
20 Micah Thomas of Kingston & Lydia Holmes of Plimouth
27 Cornelus Morrey & Ruth Holmes both of Plimouth
27 The Rev^d M' Joseph Pennimon of Bedford & M's Hannah Jackson of Plimouth
Septemb: 8 M' Thomas Nicholson, & M's Sarah Mayhew, both of Plimouth
28 John Churchell y° 3rd & Elizabeth Ames both of Plimouth

(*To be continued*)

---

* A marginal note shows that the fee was returned.

PLYMOUTH, MASS., VITAL RECORDS

Transcribed by Miss Ethel A. Richardson

(Continued from Vol. XXVI, p. 190)

[PUBLISHMENTS IN ORDER FOR MARRIAGE]

Novr 2* Thaddeus Faunce & Elizabeth Sylvester ye 2nd both of Plimouth
9 Zepheniah Harlow & Patience Johnson both of Plimouth
16 Ebenezer Cobb & Martha Cole both of Plimouth
20 George Samson & Mary Kempton both of Plimouth
20 James Howard & Margaret Holmes both of Plimouth
30 Josiah Whittemore, & Experience Serjant, both of Plimouth
7 Ichabod Tinkcom & Mary Goreham, both of Plimouth
[p. 137] Publishments in order for Marriages
1771 Decr 21 John Cornish of Plimouth & Phebe Pope of Dartmouth
28 Job Rider & Rebeckah Diman . both . of Plimouth
1772 . January 4 Silas Negro man (Servant to Mr Daniel Diman) & Venis Negro woman (Servant to Mrs Elizabeth Stephenson) both of Plimouth
11 Samuel Norris Junr of Wareham & Jedidah Swift of Plimouth
Feby 1 Josiah Johnson Junr & Bethiah Rider both of Plimouth
8 Mr Eleazer Stephens & Mrs Elizabeth Jackson both of Plimouth
8 Joseph Treeble Junr & Sarah Donham . Both of Plimouth
22 Thomas Cooper & Experience Holmes . both . of Plimouth
22 Timothy Swinerton & Hannah Curtis both of Plimouth
March 21 Samuel Drew & Elizabeth Pearce both of Plimouth
April 18 William Coye & Ruth Savory both of Plimouth
25 Jonathan Belchar, now resident in Plimouth, & Mary Beals of Plimouth
May 9 Mr Peleg Wadsworth Junr of Duxboro, & Mrs Elisabeth Bartlett ye 2nd of Plim^o
9 Michael Poor, now resident in Plim^o, & Mary Glover of Plimouth
June 13 Thomas Holmes, & Sarah Tinkcom, both . of Plimouth
13 Nathaniel Rider of Plimouth & Priscilla Bradford of Plimouth
20 David Holmes & Rebeckah Morton ye 3rd both of Plimouth
20 Elisha Corbin of Dudley & Experience Barnes . of Plimouth
27 Willard Sears of Plimouth & Sarah Robbins of Plimton
July 11 Benoni Shaw now resident in Plimouth & Ruth Serjant of Plimouth
18 Mr Jonathan Tufts & Mrs Elizabeth Nicholson both of Plimouth
Mr John Thomas Junr & Mrs Anna Mayhew both of Plimouth
Augst 8 Mr John Lothrop & Miss Lydia Goodwin both of Plimouth
15 Lemuel Taber, now Resident in Plim^o, & Hannah Atwood of Plimouth
22 Joshua Bartlett, & Mary Harlow, both of Plimouth
Mr Nathaniel Lewis, & Mrs Hannah Drew, both of Ditto
Ezra Holmes, & Lydia Curtis, ye 2nd both of Ditto
Sep^t 5 Nathaniel Cobb now resident in Plimouth & Sarah Holmes of Ditto
12 James Newberry & Susannah Perry both of Ditto
19 Mr Ebenezer Churchill ye 3rd & Miss Jane Bartlett both of Ditto
[p. 138] Publishments in order for Marriage
1772 Sep^t 26 David Morton of Plimouth & Deborah Blackwell of Sandwich
Mr Robert Bartlett of Plimouth & Mrs Hopestill Seaberry of Duxboro
Oc^{tr} 12 Silvanus Bartlett Junr of Plimouth & Sarah Loring of Plimton
17 Lothrop Clarke . & Mary Rider . both of Plimouth
24 Stephen Doten . Junr & Elizabeth Holmes . both of Plimouth
Novr 21 Ezekiel Rider Junr of Plim^o & Elizabeth Jenna of Dartmouth
28 Zadock Churchill & Bathsheba Rider both of Plimouth
Decr 5 Dunking Campbell now Resident in Plimouth & Susannah McKeel of Plimouth
12 Willson Churchill & Lydia Darling both of Plimouth
Josiah Drew & Sarah Shareman both of Plimouth
26 Benjamin Gammons of Plimton & Deborah Cornish of Plim^o
1773 Jan^{ry} 2 Mr Charles Dyre & Miss Bethiah Cotton both of Plim^o
13 Jeremiah Connel resident in Plim^o & Jane Sulliven of Kingston
Feb^{ry} 6 Lucas Donham Resident in Plim^o & Rebeckah Wood of Plimton
George Price resident in Plim^o & Abigail Thomas ye 2nd of Plim^o
27 James Holmes of Plimouth & Anna Fish of Sandwich
Zepheniah Morton . & Rebeckah Pearce . both of Plimouth
March 20 Charles Rider of Plim^o Lurania Peterson of Duxboro

*2 November, 1771.

46

April 3 Eliab Richmond & Hannah Holmes both of Plimouth
May 1 James Shurtleff & Priscilla Torrey . both of Plimouth
June 12 William Mclathly of Kingston & Eliza Luce of Plimouth
　　See Octr 4th 1773
26 Samuel Gibbs Junr of Sandwich & Abiah Swift of Plimouth
July 3 Solomon Bartlett Junr of* Abigail Torrey both of Plimo
17 Thomas Gibbs of Sandwich & Abigail Ellis of Plimouth
24 Willm Bradford & Ruth Donham both of Plimouth
31 Samuel Bates of Plimouth & Joannah Fish of Sandwich
11† William Finney . & Elizabeth Sherman both of Plimouth
[p. 139]　　In Order For Marriage
1773 Sept 25 Elkanah Corbin now resident in Plimouth & Hannah Harlow of Plimouth
25 Benjamin Thomas now resident in Plimouth & Lydia Faunce of Plimouth
Octr 4 William McLathley now resident in Plimouth & Elizabeth Luce of Plimouth .　sd Mclathley was published & misscall'd June 12th last See page 138th
23 Solomon Thomas of Middo‡ & Sarah Harlow of Plimouth
30 Jobb Cobb of Plimouth, & Ruth Cobb of Kingston
Solomon Atwood Junr & Hannah Rogers both of Plimouth
Cornelius Donham & Lydia Atwood both of Plimouth

(To be continued)

PLYMOUTH, MASS., VITAL RECORDS
(Continued from page 46)

[PUBLISHMENTS IN ORDER FOR MARRIAGE]

Novr 20* Joseph Holmes Junr & Lydia Serjant both of Plimouth
27 Joseph Bramhall Junr & Experience Blakmer both of Plimo
Ansel Gibbs of Sandwich & Elizabeth Morton of Plimouth
Decr 11 William Warren, & Elizabeth King; both of Plimouth
18 William Holland now resident in Plimo & Joanna Atwood of Plimouth
18 Mr Nathaniel Brett of Bridgwater & Mrs Mary Dyre of Plymo
25 Thomas Clarke & Lydia Ellis both of Plimouth
1774 Janry 1 John Goodwin & Hannah Jackson both of Plimouth
Febry 26 Cornelus Cobb & Grace Eames both of Plimouth
March 5 Elijah Sturtevant of Kingston & Mary Bartlett of Plimouth
19 David Drew . & .Elizabeth Atwood both . of Plimouth
John Wootten & Elizabeth Sherman both of Plimouth

* November, 1773.

---

* Sic.
† There is nothing to show whether this is in July, August or September. They were married 21 October, 1773. [See original page 266 of the same book.]
‡ Middleborough, Mass.

26 Ephraim Bartlett & Elizabeth Kempton both of Plimouth
Samuel Rider of Plimouth & Peggy Keen of Pembrook
April 2 John Totman of Plimouth & Mary Sylvester of Scituate
9 James Churchell & Lydia Nickolson both of Plimouth
June 18 James Savory & Mercy Burbank both of Plimouth
18 Levi Harlow & Mercy Barnes both of Plimouth
[p. 140]   I* order For Marriage
1774 July 23 Jonathan Dellano of Plim° & Ruth Dellano of Duxboro
Samuel Cooper & Mary Smith both of Plimouth
Aug: 13 Ralph Merrey & Lucy Cobb both of Plimouth
Sept 24 James Hovey Esqr of Plim° & Mrs Margarett Connell of Boston
Oct [†] The Revd Mr Jacob Bacon of Plim° & Mrs Mary Whitney of Dorchester
29 Amos Wood of Midd‡ & Rebeckah Barrows of Plimouth
Benjamin Barnes Junr & Deborah Holmes both of Plim°
Novr 5 Paul Doten Junr & Elizabeth Churchell both of Plim°
12 Mr Isaac Le Baron Junr & Mrs Martha Howland . both of Plim°
12 Mr William Le Baron & Mrs Sarah Churchell both of Plim°
19 Mr Isaac Symms & Mrs Hannah Cobb both of Plim°
26 John Black now resident in Plimouth, & Sarah Morton of Plimouth
26 Mr Abraham Hammet & Mrs Priscilla Lebaron both of Plimouth
Decr 3 Thadeus Churchell & Assenath Dellano both of Plim°
10 Mr Nathaniel Morton Junr & Mrs Joanna Delano both of Plimouth
10 James Timberlake now resident in Plim°, & Lydia Boult ye 2nd of Plimouth
12 Abner Bartlett & Anna Hovey both of Plimouth
31 Nicolas Davis Junr of Kingston & Martha Morton ye 3rd of Plim°
31 Simeon Harlow & Susannah Churchell ye 2nd both of Plimouth
1775 Janry 14 Thomas Jackson ye 5th Now resident in Plimouth & Sarah Holmes of Plimouth   The above Publishment was not sett up by reason the woman Vizt Sarah Holmes Desired it might not be
14 Christopher Gunderson now resident in Plimouth & Sarah Wright of Plimouth
28 Ebenezr Churchell & Patience Faunce both of Plimouth
28 Andrew Campbell Junr Now resident in Plimouth & Bathshebah Rickard ye 2nd of Plimouth
[p. 141]   In order For Marriage
1775 Febry 11 Lemuel Bradford & Mary Samson both of Plimouth
18 Jeremiah Connell & Elizabeth Engles both of Plimouth
25 Crosbe Luce & Elizabeth Totman both of Plimouth
March 4 Mr Caleb Churchell & Mrs Patience Nellson both of Plimouth
John Holmes Junr & Priscilla Marshell . both of Plimouth
6 Zoeth Hammond of Dartmouth & Lowis Valler of Plimouth

* Sic.
† The day is either 8 or 5—probably intended for 8.
‡ Middleborough, Mass.

11 Mr Isaiah Doane Now resident in Plimouth & Mrs Hannah Bartlett of Plimouth
25 Rufus Sherman of Plimton & Phebe Rider of Plimouth
May 6 Stephen Marten of Dartmouth & Abigail Mcfarling of Plim°
Nathaniel Bradford & Rebeckah Holmes both of Plimouth
27 Josiah Bartlett, & Martha Holmes, both of Plimouth
June 24 Joshua Eldredge of Truro & Elizabeth Dammon of Plimouth
July 8 Jabez Harlow . & Content Holmes . both of Plimouth
15 John King & Elizabeth Harlow both of Plimouth
15 James Collings of Truro & Lois Robbins of Plimouth
22 George Bartlett & Sarah Churchell both of Plimouth
Aug: 5 Mr Benjamin Rider Junr & Miss Patience Howland both of Plim°
Mr Thomas Morton Junr & Mrs Ruth Warren both of Plim°
Septem 2 James Chummuck & Bethiah Cook . both of Plimouth
23 Benjamin Hoye resident in Plimouth & Elizabeth Sturmey of Plim°
Jacob Allbertson & Lydia Rider both of Plim° ye 2nd Instant
Mr David Thurston of Rowley & Mrs Mary Bacon of Plim° ye 2nd Instant
30 John Wetherhead of Plimouth & Submitt Harlow of Hallifax
Mr Andrew Croswell of Plim° & Mrs Sarah Palmer of Falmouth
Octr 28 Francis Howard & Mary Donham both of Plimouth
Decr 2 Eleazer Morton & Jemima Taylor both of Plimouth
9 George Lemont & Thankfull Whittemore both of Plimouth
William Cuffs now Resident in Plim° & Hannah Donham of Plimouth
[p. 142]   In order for Marriage
1775 Dec: 30 John Landers of Sandwich & Patience Bates of Plimouth
Eleazer Churchell Junr & Abigail Bartlett both of Plimouth
James Samson & Sarah Smith both of Ditto
1776 Janry 13 Samuel Rogers & Abigail Churchell . both of Ditto
20 Amos Rider & Mehetable Olever both of Ditto
Febry 17 Samuel Robbins & Sarah Holmes both of Ditto
March 16 Amaziah Churchell Junr & Elizabeth Bartlett both of Ditto
Joshua Totman & Elizabeth Sutton both of Ditto
Ephraim Finney & Mary Bartlett both of Ditto
Thomas Mayfield of the Colony of Connecticut & Millson Barrows now Resident in Plimouth
Amos Peter Indian man of Plimton & Mercy Penes Indian woman of Plimouth
23 Ezekiel Morton Junr & Faith Churchell both of Plimouth
May 10 Mr Seth Parker of Falmouth & Mrs Sophia Cotton of Plimouth
June 28 Mr Jonathan Gibbs of Wareham & Hannah Clarke of Plimouth
29 Mr Timothy Goodwin & Miss Lucy Shurtlef Both of Plimouth

THE MAYFLOWER DESCENDANT

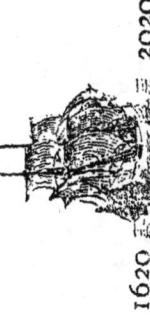

1620 2020

A QUARTERLY MAGAZINE OF
PILGRIM GENEALOGY AND HISTORY

VOLUME XXVIII

1930

PUBLISHED BY THE
MASSACHUSETTS SOCIETY OF
MAYFLOWER DESCENDANTS
BOSTON

Plymouth, Mass., Vital Records

July 5 Mr John Churchill Junr & Mrs Olive Cobb both of Plimouth
12 Mr Ebenezr Nye of Falmouth & Mrs Hannah Cotton of Plim
Aug: 9 Ebenezr Besse of Wareham & Betsey Doten of Plimouth
23 Mr Nathaniel Atwood of Plimton & Mrs Lydia Boult of Plimo
Sept 7 Mr Nathaniel Jackson & Mrs Martha Bartlett both of Plimouth
Josiah Clark Junr & Elizabeth Cornish both of Plimouth
28 Moses Reding & Priscilla Rider . both of Plimouth
Octr 19 Azariah Thrasher of Plimouth & Pheba Standish of Hallifax
Novr 9 Joseph Bates of Plimouth & Mehittable Wright of Ditto .
30 William Doten & . Abigail Sylvester both of Plimouth
Decem : 14 Samuel Churchell & Elizabeth Churchell both of Plimouth
21 Ebenez: Howard, & Bethiah Rogers . both . of Plimouth
Mr Robert Brown; & . Mrs Mary Bramhall both of Plimouth
[p. 143]   In order for Marriages
1777 Jany 4 George Deverson Resident in Plimouth & Elizabeth Stephenson of Plimouth
18 William Bartlett ye 3rd & Mercy* Holmes boath of Plimouth
Zacheus Curtis & Deborah Turner Both of Plimouth
March 15 Richard Bagnal & Bethiah West Both of Plimouth
April . 5 Samuel Dutch now Resident in Plimo & Susannah Straffen of Plimouth
5 Stephen Drew of Plimouth & Jerusha Bryant . of Middo
19 Bartlett Marshell & Ruth Doten both of Plimouth
31 John Nellson & Sarah Holmes both of Plimouth
May 17 Mr John Torrey & Mrs Meriah Morton both of Plimouth
24 Azariah Thrasher & Mary Wetherhead both of Plimouth
31 Jonathan Bartlett & Lydia Ellis both of Plimouth
Augt 16 John Faunce of Plimouth & Susannah Clark . of Rochester
16 Ebenezr Luce & Lydia Harlow . both of Plimouth
23 Thomas Clark Junr of Plimouth & Deborah Fuller of Plimpton
Sept 6 Jacob Howland & Sarah Holmes both . of Plimouth
20 Benjamin King of Plimouth . & Lydia Donham of Plymton
27 Mr David Bacon & Mrs Abigail Samson both of Plimouth
Samuel Horton Resident in Plimo & Hannah Doten of Plimouth
John Mack Catto Resident in Plimouth & Mary Samson of Plimouth
Octobr 4 John Phillips & Rebeckah King both of Plimouth
18 John Washburn Junr of Plimo & Experience Totman Plimton
Novr 8 Peter Holmes & Mary Brooks both of Plimouth
Willm Anderson now resident in Plimo & Priscilla Tinkcom of Plimo
James Emery now Resident in Plimo & Joanna Fish of Plimouth
15 Abner Baker of Rochester & Hannah Morton of Plimouth

* "Deborah" was first written, but was crossed out and "Mercy" interlined, in the same hand and ink.
† So recorded.

PLYMOUTH, MASS., VITAL RECORDS

(Continued from Vol. XXVII, p. 178)

Transcribed by George Ernest Bowman

[Vol. 2, p. 144]   In Order for Marriages

1777 Novr 15 Mr John Goodwin of Plimouth & Mrs Fear Thatcher of Barnestable
29 Caleb Bartlett & Elizabeth Holmes both of Plimouth
Decr 10 Obediah Wickit, & Bathsheba Hammat Indians both of Plimouth
17 John Butterworth & Elizabeth Bott both of Plimouth
23 John Hutchenson now Resident in Plimouth & Jane Kirk of Plimouth
Edward Morton & Sarah Morton both of Plimouth
1778
Jan^ry 24 Jacob Guardna Resident In Plim° & Rachel Finley of Plim° William Cornish & Mary Swift both of Plimouth
April 4 Ebenez^r Dogget & Lydia Holmes both of Plimouth
May 4 Lemuel Barnes Junr & Jedidah Harlow both of Plimouth
4 Lemuel Tucker of New Glasgo & Sarah Black of Plimouth
16 William Milligen, Resident in Plimouth, & Eunice Howard ye 2nd of Plimouth
30 John May & Mercy Foster ye 2nd both of Plimouth
June 3 Ezekiel Raymond Junr & Sarah Perkins both of Plimouth
6 Sylvanus Donham & Mary Treebles both of Plimouth
17 Thomas Bartlett Junr & Sarah Rider both of Plimouth
20 Perez Wright of Plimouth & Sarah Rickard of Plimton
July 11 John Blaqch Resident in Plimouth, & Rebeckah Morton ye 2nd of Plimouth
George Donham of Plimton & Pheba Lucas of Plimouth
18 William Atwood & Lydia Savery both of Plimouth
25 William Weston Junr & Mary Churchill both of Plimouth
Aug. 8 John Chase Resident in Plim° & Rebeckah Donham of Plimouth
8 William Hewston & Mary Churchell both of Plimouth
29 Lemuel Doten & Phebe Persons both of Plimouth
Thomas Winslow of Duxboro & Hannah Torrey of Plimouth
[p. 145] 1778   In Order For Marriages
Sept 12 Barnabas Holmes & Priscilla Holmes both of Plimouth
Mr William Hall Jackson of Plim° & Mrs Sarah Goreham Barnestable
19 Mr Daniel Bell of Boston & Mrs Sarah Ryder of Plymouth
Richard Pearce Resident in Plimouth & Abigail Barnes of Plim°
Ent^d Octr 25th 1778

26 Daniel Thrasher of Plimouth & Lydia Wright of Plimton*
Charles Renoff of Rehoboth & Marcy Doten of Plimouth*
28 Branch Churchell & Mary Churchell both of Plimouth
28 James Field of Taunton & Mary Drew of Plimouth
1779 Feb^ry 12 Zacheus Harlow & Hannah Barnes both of Plimouth
12 Lazarus Harlow & Sarah Darling both of Plimouth
Robert Wharton & Mary Burr both of Plimouth Published Decr 5th 1778
John Fish ye 3rd of Sandwich & Lydia Bates of Plimouth Published Decr 12th 1778
March 8 Mr Martin Brimmer of Boston & Miss Salley Watson of Plim° Posted up ye 13th Currant
April 3 Thomas Goodwin & Desire Ryder both of Plimouth
17 Elisha Nye of Sandwich & Sarah Morrey of Plimouth
Nathaniel Brown Resident in Plimouth & Rebeckah Doten of Plimouth Ent^d March 27th
May 1 M^r Le Baron Bradford of Bristol & Miss Sarah Davis of Plim°
1 Peter Gilbert now Resident in Plimouth & Mary Gamble of Plim°
22 Ansell Faunce of Plimouth & Hope Besse of Middleboro
June 5 Capt Thomas Doten & Mrs Lowis Bartlett Both of Plimouth
June 26 Deac^n Jonathan Diman & Mrs Rebeckah Brown both of Plim°
Octob^r 16 James Carver & Mary Harlow both of Plim°
23 Barnabas Raymond of Middleboro & Bethiah Jackson of Plim°
30 Ebenez^r Luce & Sarah Holmes both of Plimouth
Nov^br 6 Jabez Churchell of Middleb° & Lovise Lucas of Plimouth
Joshua Swift, & Nance Cornish both of Plimouth
Decr 18 Peter Kimber & Ruth Turner Both of Plimouth
1780 Jan^ry 1 William Harlow ye 3rd & Susanna Harlow Both of Plimouth
1 Mr Thomas Wethrell & Miss Sarah Jackson both of Plimouth
15 Lemuel Robbins & Mary Atwood both of Plimouth
Feb^ry 5 Joshua Wright & Susannah Parsons both of Plimouth
[p. 146] 1780   In order For Marriage
Feb^ry 12 William Coomer of Duxboro, & Priscilla Anderson of Plim°
26 Joseph Jennings & Mary Cotton Both of Plimouth
March 11 Noah Waterman of Hallifax & Esther Ellis of Plimouth
25 Mr Jonathan Farnam of Duxboro & Miss Dorcas Barnes of Plim°
25 Jabez Doten & Hannah Sylvester both of Plim°
31 James Cushman of Kingston & Mercy Morton of Plim°
April 22 Phineas Swift Junr of Plim° & Sarah Ellis of Sandwich
22 Isaac Churchell & Sarah Morton ye 2nd both of Plim°
May 3 Josiah Morton ye 3rd of Plim° & Mary Whiting of Plimton

(To be continued)

* "Octr 25th" is interlined between "Plimton" and "Plimouth". It is doubtful to which it belongs.

PLYMOUTH, MASS., VITAL RECORDS

(Continued from page 35)

[In Order For Marriage]

June 3* Sylvanus Shaw & Rebeckah Donham both of Plimouth
  Cornelus Holmes Junr & Eliza Lanman both of Plimo
24 George Samson of Plimton & Hannah Cooper of Ditto
24 Andrew Deburroughs Negro Man Resident in Plimo & Sarah Bow Negro woman of Plimouth
29 Mr John Cotton Junr of Plimo & Mrs Lucy Little of Kingst[on]
Sept 9 Mr John Reed Junr of Boston & Miss Mercy Goodwin of Plimo
16 Samuel Lanman Junr & Sarah Cobb both of Plimo
  William Drew & Eunice Howard ye 2nd both of Ditto
30 Barnabas Churchell & Sarah Faunce both of Ditto
Octr 7 William Ryder Junr & Lydia Churchell both of Ditto
Novr 10 Ezra Holmes & Thankfull Long both of Ditto
18 Isaac Barnes & Lucy Harlow both of Ditto
26 John Cotton ye 3rd & Experience Jackson both of Ditto
Decr 9 James Harlow Junr & Hannah Bagnal both of Ditto
30 Osborn Morton & Patience Cobb ye 2nd both of Ditto
9 † Bela Lucas of Plimouth & Hannah Lucas of Plimton
1781 Janry 6 William Barnes & Jane Fish both of Plimo
13 William Donham of Plimouth & Deborah Hooper of Bridgw[ater]
20 Josiah Bemis Junr of Waltham & Joanna Fish of Plimouth
[p. 147] 1781 Publishments in Order for Marriage
Janry 20 Judah Delano Junr of Duxboro & Penelope Samson of Plimouth
27 Josiah Soul Indien man & Ame Nummuck Indien woman Both of Plimouth
27 James Prince of Kingston & Eunice Foster of Plimouth
Febry 17 Abner Samson of Duxboro & Ruth Burges of Plimo
24 Mr Stephen Samson & Mrs Deborah Turner both of Plimouth
March 3 Mr Samuel Jackson Junr & Mrs Hannah Southworth both of Plimo
3 Bartlett Sylvester & Thankfull Washburn both of Plimo
17 Thomas Burges Junr & Lydia Treeble both of Plimo
April 13 Samuel Donham Junr of Plimo & Eliza Morton of Plimton
23 Noah Curtis of Pembrook & Deborah Luce of Plimouth
30 Lemuel Holmes Junr & Rebeckah Bartlett both of Plimo
  Paul Mcferson & Hannah Thomas ye 2nd both of Plimo
May 5 Samuel Doten & Eunice Robbins both of Plimo
June 9 Thomas Morton ye 3rd & Sarah Bartlett both of Plimo
July 28 Simeon Valler & Ruth Holmes both of Plimo

* Of 1780.
† Sic.

Sept 1 Mr Barnabas Otis of Boston & Mrs Mary Rickard of Plimo
8 Mr William Davis & Mrs Rebeckah Morton both of Plimo
  Mr Nathaniel Thomas & Mrs Priscilla Shaw both of Plimo
  Ebenezr Robbins & Mercy Doten both of Plimo
15 Mr William Goodwin Junr & Mrs Lydia Cushing Samson both of Ditto
29 Peleg Faunce Junr & Hannah Churchell both of Ditto
Octr 25 George Watson Esqr of Plimo & Mrs Phebe Scot of Newport in the State of Rhode Island
Decr 1 John Cornish & Elizabeth Clark both of Plimo
15 Joshua Besse Junr of Wareham & Mercy Morton of Plimo
22 Benjamin Churchell Junr & Phebe Randal both of Plimo
1782
Janry 5 Jeremiah Holmes Junr & Anna Robinson both of Plimo
  Nathaniel Goodwin Esqr of Plimo & Mrs Ruth Shaw of Bridgwat[er]

(To be continued)

THE MAYFLOWER DESCENDANT

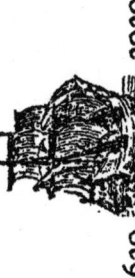

1620　2020

A QUARTERLY MAGAZINE OF
PILGRIM GENEALOGY AND HISTORY

VOLUME XXIX

1931

PUBLISHED BY THE
MASSACHUSETTS SOCIETY OF
MAYFLOWER DESCENDANTS
BOSTON

PLYMOUTH, MASS., VITAL RECORDS

Transcribed by George Ernest Bowman

(Continued from Vol. XXVIII, p. 71)

[Vol. 2, p. 148] 1782 Publishments in order for Marriage
March 16 Zacheus Kempton & Sarah Robinson both of Plimouth
13 Josiah Badger now Resident in Plimouth & Mary Raymond Plim° Nimphas Marston, & Eliz^a Cooper both of Plim°
20 Thomas Bates of Midd° & Susannah Cornish of Ditto*
July 1 Caleb Raymond, & Deborah Harlow, both of Ditto
Sep^t 21 Robert Bearse of Kingston & Abigail Lucas of Ditto
Joshua Holmes Junr & Abigail McKeel both of Ditto Ent^d Aug 31st 1782
29 James Perrey of Rochester & Mary Cornish of Ditto
Octr 26 Mr Lewis Weston, & Miss Lucy Churchell both of Ditto
Novr 2 Cornelus Morrey & Mercy Bates both of Ditto
2 Nathaniel Harlow & Mary Shaw both of Ditto
9 Mr Thomas Jackson . Junr Of Plim° & Miss Lucy Sampson of Kingston
16 Samuel Bartlett Junr & Joanna Taylor both of Plimouth
1783 January 4 Mr Seth Briggs of Rochister & Mrs Lucy Bartlett of Plimoui[th]
18 Samuel Wright Junr Plimton & Sarah Richmond of Ditto
William Burges of Plim° & Mary Samson of Ditto
23 John Chubbuck, & Lowis Bumpas both of Plim°
Joseph Bates Jur. & Rebeckah Harlow both of Ditto
Feb^{ry} 15 Jasper Hall a Negro & Vilot Otis an Indien Call^d Residents in Plim°
29† Rowland Cobb now resident in Plimouth & Jerusha Bartlett of Plimouth
29† James Bartlett Junr & Mary Taylor both of Plimouth
May 1 Stephen Swift & Phebe Mendal beth of Plimouth
17 Corbin Barnes Junr & Phebe Holmes both of Plimouth
24 Seth Churchell & Elizabith Sylvester both of Ditto
31 William Robbins of Plim° & Lewis Doten of Kings^n
June 25 Josiah Thomas Indien man of Abington, & Mary Webquist Indien Woman of Plim°
28 Heman Sturtevant of Wareham & Betsey Bartlett of Plimouth
June 28 Isaac Holmes & Margaret Eames both of Plimouth

(To be continued)

* "Ditto" in these intentions always means Plymouth.—Editor.
† So recorded. 1783 was not a leap year.

PLYMOUTH, MASS., VITAL RECORDS

(Continued from page 90)

[p. 149] 1783 In Order for Marriage
June 25 Mr Rosseter Cotton, & Mrs Priscilla Jackson, both of Plimouth
Mr Stephen Marcy of Bradford County of Middlesex & Mrs Lucy Jackson of Plimouth
Augst 30 William Holmes Jun. & Margaret Morton Both of Plimouth
[1784 Jan^{ry} 31 Mrs Margaret Morton Desires me not to Give a Certificate to Mr Holmes*]
Octr 18 Mr John Torrey & Mrs Eliz^a Harlow both of Plim°
Novr 8 Peter Lanman & Mary Holmes both of Plim°
William Bartlett ye 3rd & Deborah Holmes both of Plimouth
Cornelus Morrey & Jerusha Harlow both of Plimouth
10 Fortune Howland Melattow man & Ama Numuck Indien Woman both of Plimouth
Decemb^r 20 Thomas Doty of Plimton & Joanna Waterman of Plimouth
1784 January 3 Levi Whitting resident in Plimouth & Ruth Finney of Plimouth
10 Bennet Simmons now Resident in Plim° & Sarah Cooper of Plim°
10 Lemuel Morton & Sarah Drew both of Plimouth
14 Nathaniel Bartlett Junr & Elizabeth Marshel both of Plimouth
17 James Clark Junr & Lucy Bartlett both of Plimouth
31 John Mendal of Plim° & Thankfull Burges of Wareham
31 William Persons & Abiah Thrasher both of Plimouth
Feb^{ry} 14 Coomer Weston & Patty Cole both of Plimouth
Ezra Thomas of Plimouth & Lucy Sturtevant of Plimton
James Collings of Plimouth & Polley Avery of Truro
21 Lothrop Turner & Elizabeth Morton both of Plimouth
March 13 Zacheus Bartlett Junr & Hannah Thomas ye 2nd both of Plimouth
John Burges & Anna Treeble both of Plimouth
[p. 150] 1784 In order for Marriage
March 27 James Bumpas & Margaret Chubbuck both of Plim°
27 Samuel Churchell Junr & Sarah Thomas both of Plim°
27 Allden Fuller of Sandwich & Mary Ellis of Plim°
April 3 Mr Stephen Doten & Mrs Jane Donham both of Plim°
3 James Polden & Bethiah Donham ye 2nd both of Plim°
10 Jonathan Hill now resident in Plimouth & Mary Serjant of Plimouth
May 1 Nathl Ellis & Jane Bartlett both of Plimouth

* This entry was interlined here, in the same hand.

28 George Thrasher & Rachel Holmes both of Plimouth
29 Samuel Holmes & Mary Finney both of Plimouth
June 5 Ichabod Holmes Junr & Rebecca Harlow ye 4th both of Plim-outh
July 10 Daniel Jackson & Rebecca Morton both of Plimouth
10 Barnabas Holmes Junr & Mercy Bates both of Plimouth
24 John Bartin of Duxboro & Abigail Simmons Plim^o
24 Nathaniel Spooner & Mary Holmes both of Plimouth
August 1 Solomon Churchill & Betsy Bartlett both of Plimouth
14 Pera Smith Mulattow Man & Betty Thomson Mulattow Woman both now Resident in Plim^o
18 Daniel Lawrance & Lydia Bartlett both of Plimouth
21 William Cassaday & Lydia Finney 2nd both of Plimouth
28 Jesse Harlow Junr & Hannah Turner both of Plimouth
Sep^t 5 Elnathan Holmes Junr of Plim^o & Deb^o Brewster of Kingston
12 Samuel Hermon Cole* of Kings^n & Lydia Sylvester of Plimouth
William Doten & Jane Churchell both of Plimouth
Mr Isaac Symms & Mrs Joanna Holland both of Plimouth
Lemuel Joseph of Wareham & Sarah Sepit of Plim^o both Indiens
William Stephens & Esther Allen both of Plimouth
Joseph Bartlett ye 4th & Rebecca Churchell both of Plimouth
[p. 151] 1784   In order for Marriage
September 18 John Washburn, & Mary Churchell, both of Plimouth
25 James Harlow Junr & Sarah Blackmer Junr both of Plim^o
Octob^r 2 Joseph Bartlett ye 3rd & Anna Clark both of Plim^o
2 Jonathan Russell of Barnestable & Rebecca Turner of Plim^o
9 James Brand Indien Man of Pembrook & Betty Sepit Indien Woman of Plymouth
16 Daniel Perry Sandwich & Phebe Bartlett of Plim^o
16 Zacheus Holmes of Plimouth & Merriam Churchell Plimton
18 Israel Hoyt, & Susannah Perkins both of Plimouth
23 Moses Donham of Plimton & Margaret Morton of Plimouth
30 Jacob Swift & Rememb^r Ellis both of Plimouth
30 William Keen & Lydia Holmes both of Plimouth
November 6 Jonathan Thrasher & Nanse Swift both of Plimouth
10 Jasper Hall Negro man & Ruth Sachemas Indien Woman both now residents in Plimouth
13 Benjamin Washburn & Bathsheba Churchell both of Plimouth
27 Stephen Raymond of Wareham & Eliz^a Holmes Plim^o
Decr 11 Caleb Howland of Plimouth & Mary Sylvest^r of Hanover
11 Joseph Faunce & Mercy Bartlett both of Plimouth
18 Eleazer Holmes Junr & Polley Barnes both of Plimouth
1785 Jany 15 Levi Pate & Elizabeth Finney both of Plimouth
March 5 Elijah Sherman & Hannah Thomas both of Plimouth
12 Doct^r James Thacher of Plimouth & Mrs Susannah Hayward Bridg'w

*In the margin is: "Abial Washb^n to pay"

April 12 Charles Bartlett & Abigail Churchel both of Plimouth
Ellis Harlow & Sarah Harlow both of Plimouth
23 Nath^ll Swift of Sandwich & Betse Ellis of Plimouth
Prince Negro man & Barberry Negro woman both of Plimouth
[p. 152] 1785   In Order for Marriage
April 23 Mr Jesse Dunbar of Scituate & Mrs Sarah Wethrell of Plimouth
30 Abial Washburn & Olive Finney both of Plimouth
May 15 Samuel Bradford & Lucy Churchell both of Plimouth
June 4 Nathaniel Clark Junr of Hanover & Abigail Donham of Plimouth
4 Sylvester Holmes & Grace Clark both of Plimouth
18 Elnathan Lucas & Lydia Cornish both of Plimouth
Enoch Tupper now resident in Plim^o & Martha Battles of Plim^o
Rufus Robbins Junr & Temperance Otis both of Plimouth
2* Lemuel Savery & Elizabeth Deverson both of Ditto
Octr 15 Capt James Russell & Miss Experience Shaw both of Ditto
Octr 22 Job Brewster & Elizabeth Polden both of Ditto
29 Samuel Conklin now resident in Plimouth & Deborah Barrows of Plimouth
Novr 5 Lemuel Bartlett Junr & Mary Holmes both of Plimouth
5 Josiah Bradford & Elizabeth Holmes both of Plimout[h]
12 Silas Morrey & Eunice Donham both of Plimout[h]
12 George Churchell & Elizabeth Harlow both of Plimou[th]
Decr 2 Sylvanus Pate & Hannah Barnes both of Plimouth
9 William Morton Junr & Eunice Bartlett both of Plimou[th]
Thomas Torrey Junr & Elizabeth Holmes both of Plimou[th]
17 John Dugless & Elizabeth Goddard both of Plimouth
24 Waite Atwood & Rebecca Bartlett both of Plimouth
1786 Jan^ry 6 Ransom Thomas of Midd^o & Deborah Donham of Plimouth
29 Caleb Morton & Rebecca Warren both of Plimouth
Feb^ry 25 Capt Thomas Sturges of Barnestable & Mrs Eliz^a Jackson of Plim^o
Thomas Clark & Abigail Morton both of Plimouth
March 4 Issacher Howland & Mary Mitchel both of Plimou[th]
[p. 153]   Publishments In order For Marriage
1786 March 18 Elias Nye of Plimton & Elizabeth Bartlett of Plim^o
April 1 Ebenez^r Samson Junr & Susannah Finney both of Plimouth
1 Benjamin Morton Junr of Wareham & Rebecca Swift of Plim^o
15 Prince Washburn & Ruth Stetson ye 2nd both of Plimouth
18 Benjamin Samson of Kingston & Priscilla Churchell of Plimouth[h]
22 Isaac Cobb of Plimton, & Eunice Donham of Plimouth
Mr Francis Cushing of Scituate & Miss Lucy Dyre of Plimouth
Mr John Davis & Miss Ellen Watson both of Plimouth
6 Mr John Russell & Miss Polley Jackson both of Plimouth
6 Solomon Davee & Jedidah Sylvester both of Plimouth

* So entered.

May 20 Joseph King now resident in Plim° & Asenath Pratt of Plimouth
June 3 Amaziah Harlow & Lucy Torrey both of Plimouth
23 Samuel Rickard Junr of Plimton & Priscilla Holmes ye 2nd of Plimouth
July 7 Abraham Bumpas & Elizabeth Besse both of Plimouth
  Dolphin Mando negro man now resident in Plimouth & Cate Quonda negro woman of Plimouth
27 Thomas Kitridge Negro man now resident in Plimouth & Patience Robbins Indien woman of Plimouth
Sep^t 2 Samuel Nellson & Lucy Ellis both of Plimouth
  Bartlett LeBaron & Lydia Dogget both of Plimouth
16 George Prise now resident in Plim° & Susanna Farmer of Plim°
16 Prince Hall Negro man of Bridgwater & Alise Crook Indien woman of Plim°
16 Josiah Cornish & Abigail Clark both of Plimouth
16 Joshua Thomas Esqr of Plimouth & Miss Isabella Stevenson of Boston
23 Elisha Perrey of Sandwich & Lurany Clark of Plimouth
23 Samuel Morton Junr & Mary Washburn both of Plimouth
Octr 7 Eben: Nellson Junr & Lydia Robbins both of Plimouth
7 Samuel Brooks & Eliz^a Jackson both of Plimouth
7 Benjamin Bramhall & Priscilla Burbank both of Plimouth
[p. 154] 1786 Publishments in order for Marriage
Octr 14 Mr Franc^s LeBaron Goodwin, & Miss Jane Robbins both of Plim°
Octr 28 Sylvanus Sturtev^t now resident in Plimouth & Hannah Ryder of Plimouth
Novr 4 Noah Bumpas of Wareham & Mercy Bumpas of Plimouth
Decr 2 David Thrasher of Plim° & Elizabeth Donham of Plimton
Decemb^r 16 Stephen Paine & Hannah Samson ye 2nd both of Plimouth
1787 Jan^ry 6 John Barrit now resident in Plim° & Hannah Holmes of Plimouth
6 William Holmes Junr & Hannah Doten, both of Plimouth
20 Thaddeus Ripley & Mary Shurtleff both of Plimouth
March 10 Noah Gale, now resident in Plim° & Rebecca Chase of Plimouth
10 Amasa Morton & Hannah Morton both of Plimouth
24 Seth Ryder & Hannah Bartlett both of Plimouth
May 5 Nathaniel Bartlett ye 3rd & Hannah Faunce both of Plimouth
19 Joseph Swift & Lucy Holmes both of Plimouth
26 George Davie of Plimouth & Sussanna Farn of Boston
2* Mr Daniel Diman of Plim° & Mrs Mary Smith of Bristol
2* Andrew Anderson now resident in Plimouth & Eliz^a Raymond of Plim°
9 Ichabod Shurtleff now Resident in Plim° & Betty Petingell of Bridgwater

* So recorded.

16 John Ripley now resideing in Plimouth & Lucy Doten of Plimouth
23 William Morton Junr & Pamelia Howland both of Plimouth
July 18 Benjamin Sepit Indien man of Plim° & Rosanna Mingo Mulatto Woman of Sandwich
Aug^s: 4 John Taylor now Resideing in Plimouth & Mercy Bryant of Plimouth
4 Richard Holmes Junr & Sarah Howard both of Plimouth
11 Reubin Churchell & Hannah Samson ye 2nd both of Plimouth
11 Benjamin Gibbs of Sandwich & Deborah Pope of Plimouth
11 Joseph Barnes Junr & Elizabeth Treeble both of Plimouth
  William Rogers & Elizabeth Bartlett both of Plimouth
[p. 155] 1787 Publishments in order for Marriage
Sep^t 1 Gershom Holmes of Taunton & Mercy King of Plimouth
8 Rufus Bartlett & Mercy Churchell both of Plimouth
11 John Hoskins now resident in Plim° & Eliz^a Bagnal of Plim°
15 John Rich now resident in Plim° & Eloner Holmes of Plim°
Octob^r 6 Eleaz^r Nicols now resident in Plimouth & Eliz^a Holmes of Plim°
13 Ichabod Morton Junr & Sarah Churchell both of Plimouth
27 Barnabas Holmes of Plim° & Anna Dammon of Pembrook
28 The Honourb^l Nathaniel Niles Esqr Fairlee in the State of Vermont & Miss Elizabeth Watson of Plimouth
3* Thomas Jackson ye 3rd & Sarah May both of Plimouth
  Enoch Randal & Ruth Donham both of Plimouth
Novr 9 Mordica Ellis, & Lydia Swift both of Plimouth
Decemb 1 Abraham Jackson & Lydia Eltnes both of Plimouth
22 Judah Bartlett & Mercy Sylvester both of Plimouth
29 Gideon Holbrook & Sarah Clark both of Plimouth
1788 Jan^ry 5 Nathaniel Cooper & Margaret Glover both of Plimouth
19 Amasa Bartlett & Sarah Taylor both of Plimouth
Feb^ry 16 Hezekiah Nellson of Plim° & Mrs Abigail Holmes of Kingston
16 Lemuel Harlow of Plim° & Phebe Lovil of Barnestable
March 4 Lemuel Thomas of Midd° & Eliz^a Donham of Plimouth
15 John Stephens, & Eliz^a Battles both of Plimouth
April 5 Mr William Jackson of Plimouth & Miss Nancy Barnes of Scituate
  Samuel Samson of Midd° & Lydia Holmes of Plimouth
June 28 Daniel Garlu Negro Man of Plimouth and Anstus Allen Mulatto woman of Nantuckit
July 4 Charles Bradford & Priscilla-Morton both of Plimouth

(To be continued)

* So recorded.

THE MAYFLOWER DESCENDANT

1620　2020

A QUARTERLY MAGAZINE OF
PILGRIM GENEALOGY AND HISTORY

VOLUME XXX

1932

PUBLISHED BY THE
MASSACHUSETTS SOCIETY OF
MAYFLOWER DESCENDANTS
BOSTON

PLYMOUTH, MASS., VITAL RECORDS

TRANSCRIBED BY THE EDITOR

(*Continued from Vol. XXIX, p. 129*)

[Vol. 2, p. 156] 1788 Publishments in order for Marriage
July 10 Thomas Torrance of Plim° & Betsey Harris of Boston
Melatiah Morse of Rochest'ʳ & Joanna Swift of Plimouth
12 Samuel Stephens & Desire Harlow both of Plimouth
William Donham & Elizabeth Foster both of Plimouth
Aug'ˢᵗ 9 Caleb Fish & Sarah Paine both of Plimouth
16 Joseph Sinson Negroman of Boston, & Candis Gardner Negro woman of Plimouth
23 James Reed, now resident in Plimouth, & Lucy Fish, of Plimouth
30 John Bacon & Priscilla Holmes yᵉ 2ⁿᵈ both of Plimouth
Oct'ʳ 11 Thomas Russell Esq'ʳ of Boston & Miss Elizᵃ Watson of Plimouth
Nov'ʳ 1 Pompe Negroman & Barbery Negro Woman Both of Plimouth
8 Joseph Holmes & Polley Finney both of Plimouth
8 Sylvanus Harlow Jun'ʳ & Katharine Manter both of Plimouth
15 Joseph Johnson & Betsey Blackmer both of Plimouth
Decemb 26 Daniel Mayo Jun'ʳ of Wellfleet & Mary Bartlett of Plimouth
1789 Jan'ʳʸ 2 Richard Austin now resident in Plim° & Rebecca Atwood of Plim°
8 Cap'ᵗ Thomas Nicolson & Miss Hannah Otis both of Plim°

10 Kimbell Cronbie & Deborah Davie both of Plimouth
Lemuel Morton & Azubah Cushman Rickard both of Plimouth
19 Charles Holmes & Sarah Raymond both of Plimouth
Graften Manter now resident in Plimouth & Lydia Leach of Ditto
Solomon Bartlett Jun: of Plim° & Lydia Wood of Plimton
23 Lamson Hathaway resident in Plym° & Rebecca Battles of Plimouth
Feb'y 7 Thomas Holmes & Phebe Holmes both of Plimouth
Samuel Sherman Jun: & Lydia Doten both of Plimouth
14 Job Morton of Plimouth & Patience Crooker of Plimton
Benjamin Robbins & Esther Allen both of Plimouth
March 7 Isaac Holmes & Mary Poor both of Plimouth
[p. 157]   In order for Marriage
1789 March 14 Ansell Bartlett & Elizabeth Churchell both of Plimouth
21 Andrew Bartlett Jun'r & Sarah Holhrook both of Plimouth
28 M'r Jonathan Tuffts & Miss Priscilla Drew both of Plimouth
May 30 George Cornish of Plimouth & Joanna Reed of Freetown
July 8 Edward Megounds now resident in Plimouth, & Mary Covel of Plimouth
Aug'st 1 Nathaniel Carver Jun'r & Joanna Churchell both of Plim°
8 Joseph Whiting & Sarah Morton y'e 2'nd both of Plim°
15 Cap't George Donham & M'rs Patience Churchell both of Plim°
29 Spinks Bagnal & Nancy Crooker both of Plim°
James Doten y'e 3'rd & Patty Torrey both of Plim°
Jasper Hall Stephenson & Rebecca Harlow both of Plim°
Septemb: 5 Seth Clark Plim° & Eunice Ellis of Sandwich
8 Benjamin Warren Jun'r of Plimouth & Sarah Lewis of Wellflt
19 William Barnes Jun'r & Mercy Carver y'e 2'nd both of Plimouth
Lewis Holmes & Betsey Sherman both of Plimouth
Benjamin Cornish Jun'r & & Experience Cornish both of Plimouth
Asa Barrows & Deborah Dewe* both of Plimouth
26 M'r Perez Briggs of Wareham & Miss Mary Foster of Plimouth
3† Francis Bartlett & Auya Cornish both of Plimouth
10 Benjamin Whiting & Martha Harlow both of Plimouth
17 Edward Taylor & Mary Sylvester both of Plimouth
24 Seth Clark & Mary Tupper both of Plimouth
Josiah Cotton Esq'r of Plimouth & Miss Rachel Barnes of Scituate
31 John Blackmer Jun'r of Plimouth & Sarah Hovey of Rochest'r
Nov'r 7 Freeman Cobb of Wellfleet & Rachel Holbrook of Plimouth
12 Nathaniel Holmes Jun'r & Jerusha Bartlett both of Plimouth
12 M'r Benjamin Ives Gilman of Marietta Western Territory & Miss Hannah Robbins of Plimouth
19 Reubin Harlow & Hannah Johnson both of Plimouth
[p. 158]   In order for Marriage
1790 Jan'ry 9 Benjamin Crandon & Susanna Bishop both of Plimouth
19 Branch Dillingham of Sandwich & Abigail Bartlett of Plimouth

* The marriage record, 25 October, 1789, on original page 273, gives this name as "Dewey".
† Apparently "Oct'r" was omitted, before the "3".

30 William Clark Jun'r & Zilpah Bramhall 2'nd both of Plimouth
February 27 Samuel Smith, & Hope Doten, both of Ditto
April* Warren Lucas & Abigail Bartlett both of Plimouth
17 M'r John Sever of Kingston & Miss Nancy Russel of Plimouth
M'r George Goodwin of Vasselborough & Mis~ Lucy Cotton of Plimouth
May 1 Eleazer Ellis Jun'r of Plim° & Deborah Ellis of Sandwich
8 Seth Ryder & Salley Bartlett both of Plimouth
May 29 John Alden Jun'r of Midd° & Susannah Donham y'e 2'nd of Plim°
June 5 Perez Peterson of Duxboro & Betsey Nellson of Plimouth
July 10 Thomas Sherman & Priscilla Calderwood both of Plimouth
22 Thomas Nellson & Abigail Holmes y'e 2'nd both of Plimouth
24 William Coye & Mary Carver both of Plimouth
31 Diman Bartlett & Lydia Barrows both of Plimouth
Aug'st 26 Josiah Finney Jun'r & Rebecca Warrin both of Plimouth
Septemb'r 1 From this day I Endeavour'd to take pay for recording the names as well as for the Publishment, & Certificate, at the Request of The Rev'd Chandler Robbins, and the Advise of James Sullivin & Joshua Thomas Esq'rs (at least for those persons marry'd in Plimouth)
4 Benjamin Swift of Wareham & Hannah Cornish of Plimouth
4 Richard Francis Johnson of Kingston & Mary Turner of Plimouth
18 Henry Bartlett & Clarrassa Harlow both of Plimouth
Thomas Farmer & Margaret Pate both of Plimouth
25 John Tilson of Hallifax & Desire Shaw of Plimouth
Oct'r 1 Lothrop Turner & Susanna Stephens both of Plimouth
1 Samuel Rogers Jun'r & Joanna Samson both of Plimouth
15 Caleb Jenkins of Scituate & Elizabeth Tillson of Plimouth
Nov'r 6 Thomas Johnson & Susannah Sylvester both of Plimouth
13 Kimbel Crombie & Deborah Jackson both of Plimouth
[p. 159]   Publishments in order for Marriage
1790 Dec. 18 Seth Nicolson & Meriah Harlow both of Plimouth
1791 January 14 William Leonard & Rebecca Bartlett both of Plimouth
Feb'y 12 William Holmes & Lucy Harlow both of Plimouth
12 Ansel Robbins & Hannah Cobb both of Plimouth
14 Francis Liberty Negro man, & Sarah Newport Indien Woman both res in Plimouth
March 19 Ellis Brewster & Nancy Holmes both of Plimouth
April 4 Lemuel Doten of Duxboro & Patty Mackey of Plimouth
May 7 Ellis Holmes & Grace Symms both of Plimouth
10 Asa Raymond of Sandwich & Mercy Norris of Plimouth
14 Peleg Churchel & Hannah Hose both of Plimouth
John Virgen & Priscilla Cooper both of Plimouth
28 Avery Dellano of Duxboro & Betsey Faunce of Plim°
Benjamin Clark & Lydia Atwood both of Plimouth
Joseph Cooper & Lucy Taylor both of Plimouth

* The day of the month was not entered.

June 4 Stephen Churchill Junr of Plym^o & Elizabeth Gray of Kingston
18 Owin Harris & Mercy Holmes both of Plimouth
July 9 Consider Robbins of Carver & Abigail Bartlett of Plimouth
23 Thomas Savery of Plimouth & Abigail Everson of Plimouth
30 Lemuel Bradford, & Lydia Holmes, both of Plimouth
Augt 13 Mr Eleazer Ellis of Plim^o & Mrs Jerusha Gibbs of Sandwich
George Ryder & Deborah Chandler both of Plimouth.
27 Mr Nathaniel Lewis & Miss Lucy Shaw both of Plimouth
Caleb Bartlett & Rebeca Holmes both of Plimouth
Sep^t 3 Joseph Warren Nelson & Alethear Warren both of Ditto*
14 Cornelius Holmes of Carver & Rhoda Richmond of Ditto*
17 Benjamin Ransom Junr of Carver & Rebecca Finney ye 2nd of Plimouth
Andrew Bartlett Jun & Sarah Holbrook both of Plimouth published March [illegible] 1791 omitted in its place
[p. 160] 1791   Publishments in order for Marriage
Sep^t 17 William Sturtevant & Salle Warren both of Plimouth
24 Henry Warren Esqr & Miss Mary Winslow both of Plimouth
Silas Donham Junr & Lydia Polden both of Plimouth
28 Enos Covil & Mary Bessee both of Plimouth
Octr 8 Seth Dogget & Jemima Harlow both of Plimouth
22 John Clark & Betsey Long both of Plimouth
25 Ebenez^r Skiff of Chilmark on Marthas Vineyard & Deb^o Ellis Plym^o
Ellis Mendal of Plym^o & Hannah Hammond of Carver
27 Michel Bowland now in Plymouth a native of Ireland late from Newfound Land & Mercy Lemoat of Plym^o
Nov: 5 Elisha Morton Junr & Salley Ellis both of Plym^o
12 George Manter & Nancey Richmond both of Plymouth
19 John Calderwood & Patience Churchel ye 3^d both of Plymouth
Ansel Harlow & Thankfull Bartlett both of Plymouth
Ezra Burbank Junr of Plym^o & Lydia Drew of Eastown
Decr 10 Bartlett Marshal & Bathsheba Doten ye 2^d both of Plym^o
Benjamin Goddard & Hannah Luce both of Plym^o
17 Josiah Diman of Plym & Sukey Gray of Barnestable
1792 Jan^{ry} 4 Prince Brown & Martha Harrey, People of Colour, both now resident in Plymouth
21 Seth Luce & Jedidah Barnes both of Plymouth
March 3 Enos Churchell & Mary Pain both of Plymouth
10 Ansel Lucas & Susannah Donham both of Plymouth
24 Benjamin Reed of Midd^o & Anna Chubbuck of Plymouth
Lewis Churchell & Nancey Mitchel both of Plymouth
William Nellson & Bathsheba May Lothrop both of Plymouth
29 Samuel Battles Junr & Deb^o: Atwood both of Plymouth
April 14 Hezekiah Jackson & Sarah Nicolson both of Plymouth
21 Benjamin Washburn & Abigail Bartlett both of Plymouth
[p. 161] 1792   Publishments in order for Marriage
May 19 George Ellis & Experience Clark both of Plymouth.

* "Ditto" in these Intentions always means Plymouth.

June 10 Ebenezer Barrows & Clarrissa Bartlett both of Plymouth
23 John Charles Martin resident in Plymouth & Sarah Holmes ye 2nd of Plymouth
30 Stephen Raymond of Plymouth & Ruth Chubbuck of Plym^o
Ephraim Chubbuck of Plym^o & Abigail Nye of Wareham
John Doten & Sarah Morton ye 2nd both of Plymouth
Aug: 18 John Taylor & Mercy Burges both of Plymouth
25 Joseph Samson & Sarah Manter both of Plymouth
Sylvanus Morrey & Lydia Ellis both of Plymouth
Lemuel Leach Junr & Susanna Harlow both of D^o
Sep^t 1 Richard Durfey Junr & Mary Holmes both of Plym^o
8 Daniel Diman & Patience Holmes . both . of Plymouth
26 Mr Lot Haskel of Rochester & Mrs Elizabeth Cotton of Plym^o
Octob^r 20 John Mitchel of Duxboro & Joanna Ransom of Plym^o
27 Nathaniel Bartlett ye 4th & Mary Bartlett both of Plym^o
Pebody Bartlett & Lucy Turner both of Plym^o
Novr 3 Zachere Soul of Kingston & Nanse Donham of Plym^o
17 Lemuel Drew Junr & Salle Bartlett both of Plymouth
24 Zenas Sturtevant of Hallifax & Eliza Serjant of Plymouth
Decr 5 Isaac Morse Jun of Midd^o & Hannah Bessee of Plym^o
11 William Ellis Junr of Plym^o & Hiphzibah Blackwell of Sandwich
15 Barnabe Faunce Junr & Sarah Carver both of Plymouth
Spinks Bagnal of Plym^o & Mehitable Finney of Plimton
Thomas Pope of Bridgwater now Resident in Plymouth & Mary Howland ye 2nd of Plym^o
1793 Jan: 5 George Bartlett Junr & Silvinay Holmes both of Plymouth
Branch Dillingham of Sandwich & Ruth Holbrook of Plym^o
Joseph Balston & Polley Doten both of Plymouth
7 Rufus Holmes & Patience Clark both of Plymouth
[p. 162] 1793   Publishments in order for Marriage
Jan^{ry} 9 David Turner & Lydia Washburn both of Plymouth
26 William Blackmer & Mary Bly both of Plymouth
Feb^{ry} 2 Wrastling Brewster Junr of Kingston & Martha Symms of Plymouth
6 Robert Bessee of Plym^o & Mary Conant of Wareham
March 2 Robert Finney & Sarah Leach both of Plymouth
2 Thomas Washburn & Hannah Smith both of Plymouth
8 Bazaliel Lucas of Carver & Sarah Sears of Plymouth
23 Nathan Reed & Lydia Bartlett both of Plymouth
29 Ebenez^r Pumroye now resident in Plymouth & Elizabeth Mitchell of Plymouth
April 8 William Davee Junr & Experience Stetson ye 2nd both Plymouth
18 Isaiah Cobb & Lydia Chubuck both of Plymouth
May 11 Ignatious Cushman of Plimton & Ruth Washb^n Plymouth
26 Abraham Howland & Elizabeth Finney both of Plym^o
June 1 Thomas Leonard & Sarah Babb both of Plym^o
8 Andrew Holmes of Plym^o & Sarah Conant of Wareham
July 20 Isaac Thomas & Hannah Barnes both of Plym^o

Aug: 15 Mr Chandler Robbins of Hollowell in yᵉ County of Lincoln*
& Miss Harriot Lothrop of Plymouth
24 Abraham Thomas of Middlebᵒ & Nancey Donham of Plymᵒ
Jacob Johnson Junʳ & Betsey Bates both of Ditto
David Cornish & Mercy Holmes both of Ditto
31 Lewis Churchell Junʳ of Plymᵒ & Desire Barker Brewster of Duxboro
Septʳ 11 Nathan Burges of Plymᵒ & Deborah Hunt of Duxboro
Octʳ 5 Timothey Perkins resident in Plymᵒ & Rebecca Donham of Plymᵒ
Ephraim Harlow & Jerusha Doten both of Plymouth
John Burbank & Lydia Mason both of Plymouth
[p. 163] 1793   Publishments in order for Marriage
Octʳ 31 Thomas Caswell of Carver & Susannah Wing of Plymouth
Novʳ 16 Nathaniel Holmes Junʳ & Sarah Bagnal yᵉ 2ⁿᵈ both of Plymouth
William Barnes yᵉ 3ʳᵈ & Sarah Treeble Junʳ both of Plymouth
23 Levi Lucas of Carver & Mʳˢ Hannah Jackson of Plymouth
Samuel Ryder Junʳ & Nancy Donham both of Plymouth
29 Mr Naaman Holbrook & Mʳˢ Hannah Finney both of Plymᵒ
Thomas Davee & Betsey Barnes both of Plymᵒ
Sylvanus Rogers & Salley Finney both of Plymᵒ
Decʳ 7 Lewis Bartlett now resident in Plymᵒ & Hannah Paty of Plymᵒ
Barnabas Donham Junʳ & Phebe Froberry both of Plymᵒ
14 Nehemiah Savery & Sarah Cornish both of Plymᵒ
Charles Robbins of Plymᵒ & Mary Bacon of Barnesta[ble]
Mʳ John Morong of Salem & Miss Hannah Nicolson of Plymouth
23 Mʳ John Watson Junʳ of Plymouth & Mʳˢ Permela Howard of Duxboro
1794 January 4 Joseph Treeble yᵉ 3ʳᵈ & Polley Holmes both of Plymouth
11 Jube Hedge & Judah Tuner people of Colour both of Ditto
Daniel Goddard & Bulah Simmons both of Plymᵒ
Ichabod Besse of Pembrook & Jerusha Doten yᵉ 2ⁿᵈ of Plymᵒ
Febʳʸ 1 Charles Jackson & Lucy Cotton both of Plymᵒ
8 Thomas Bryant & Eunice Lobdel people of Colour both now resident in Plymouth
10 John Clark of Plymᵒ & Eloner Shurtieff of Carver
15 William Morton yᵉ 3ʳᵈ of Plymouth & Permelia Rose of Sandwich
22 Mʳ William Crombie Junʳ & Miss Deborah Jackson both of Plymouth
Mʳ John Danforth Dunber of Charlton County of Worchester & Miss Nancy Crombie of Plymouth
John Swift Junʳ & Penelope Richmond both of Plymouth
March 1 William Straffin & Prudence Turner both of Plymouth
8 Samuel Sturtevant of Hallifax & Eloner Holmes of Plymouth
Joseph Code of Plymouth now resident in Bridgwater and Salley Atwood of Bridgwater

(To be continued)

* Now in Maine.

PLYMOUTH, MASS., VITAL RECORDS

(Continued from page 78)

[p. 164] 1794   Publishments for Marriage
April 5 Thomas Rogers & Elizabeth Barnes yᵉ 2ⁿᵈ both of Plymᵒ
12 Seth Harlow Junʳ & Priscilla Nellson both of Plymᵒ
16 Benjamin Cooper & Susanna King both of Plymouth
25 Thomas Bartlett yᵉ 3ʳᵈ & Margaret James Drew both of Plymouth
Nathaniel Sylvester & Alice Finney both of Plymouth
May 10 Isaac Covington & Mary Samson both of Plymouth
20 Thomas Clark of Plymᵒ & Ruth Hovey of Rochester
24 Charles Churchell of Plymᵒ & Jedidah Haws of Newbeadfᵈ
Joseph Doten & Elizabeth Allen both of Plymᵒ
6* Ephraim Besse of Wareham & Rebecca Manter of Plymᵒ
July 5 Ichabod Shaw Junʳ & Betsey Holmes both of Plymᵒ
Augˢᵗ 23 Salathiel Perrey of Wareham & Mercy Doten of Plymᵒ
Zepheniah Bartlett & Elizabeth Samson both of Plymᵒ
Septʳ 4 Caleb Wright of Plymᵒ & Egerthy Shaw of Carver
13 Elkanah Bartlett Junʳ & Rebecca Holmes yᵉ 2ⁿᵈ both of Plymᵒ
Octʳ 4 Caleb Bryant & Betsey Barnes both of Plymouth
8 Mr Lemuel Holmes of Kingston & Miss Patience Harlow of Plymᵒ
Mʳ Mathew Cushing & Miss Lydia Drew both of Plimᵒ
18 James Bartlett yᵉ 3ʳᵈ of Plymᵒ & Silvina Bates of Sandwich
Ephraim Everson & Sarah Atwood both of Plymᵒ
Mʳ Gardner Coffin of Sherburn on Nantuckit and Miss Mary Jackson Goodwin of Plymouth
Uriah Ripley & Sarah King both of Plymᵒ
25 Heman Churchell & Jane Churchell both of Plymᵒ
Novʳ 1 Samuel Bartlett & Zilpah Morton both of Plymᵒ
William Sherman & Elizabeth Drew both of Plymᵒ
15 John Bartlett Junʳ & Mary Morton both of Plymᵒ
22 America Brewster & Sarah Cobb yᵉ 2ⁿᵈ both of Plymᵒ
Thomas Paty & Jerusha Barnes both of Plymᵒ
[p. 165]   Publishments in order for Marriage
1794 Decʳ 6 James Caswell & Dorcas Brooks, people of Colour, both of Plymouth.
25 Ebenezʳ Donham Junʳ of Carver & Priscilla Morton of Plymᵒ
Ezra Morton of Carver & Polley Allen of Plymᵒ

* So recorded.

1795 January 3 Daniel Finney & Sarah Cooper both of Plymouth
10 Edward Winslow Junr of Duxboro & Rebecca Harlow of Ditto*
17 Ichabod Donham of Plym^o & Betty Wood of Midd^o
Feby 14 John Turner of Scituate & Pearce† Washburn of Plymouth
March 14 Seth Drew of Plymouth & Temperance Pigslee‡ a resid^nt in Plym^o
21 Thomas Long & Bathsheba Churchell both of Plymouth
21 John Edwards & Sarah Covington both of Plym^o
June 6 Nathan Whiteing & Rebecca Doten both of Ditto
13 Joseph Jennings & Sarah Holbrook both of Ditto
20 Charles Thomson now resident in Plym^o & Sarah Boyse of Ditto
William Goddard & Salley Barnes both of Ditto
25 Anseln Rickard & Margaret Drew both of Ditto
Aug: 1 Joseph Shurtleff & Silvina Battles both of Ditto
Mr William Jackson & Miss Mercy Russell both of Ditto
Sep^t 5 Henry Richmond & Submit Wetherhead both of Ditto
12 John Anderson, now a Resident in Plym^o, & Elizabeth Anderson of Plymouth
Mr Joseph Bartlett of Woburn & Miss Anna May Wethrell of Plymouth
Octr 1 Billey Saunders a resident in Plymouth & Phebe Holmes of Plymouth
3 Ephraim Whiteing & Elizabeth Bartlett both of Plymouth
10 Seth Robbins & Betsey Holmes both of Plymouth
17 William Brewster, & Elizabeth Taylor, both of Plymouth
24 Rowland Holmes of Plym^o & Phebe Dugless of Plymouth
31 Joshua Prat of Plymouth & Rebecca Mitchel of Kingston
Nath. Warrin Leonard of Midd^o & Mary Warren of Plymouth
[p. 166] Publishments in order for Marriage
1795§ Seth Holmes Junr & Jerusha Blackmer both of Plymouth
Novr 28 Ebenez^r Ellis Junr of Plym^o & Susannah Hacket of Midd^o
William Serjant Junr & Abigail Faunce both of Plymouth
Decr 5 Jacob Josselyn & Abigail Ryder both of Plymouth
19 John Clark & Grace Holmes both of Plymouth
Josiah Cotton Junr & Temporance Robbins both of Plymouth
1796 Jan: 3 Daniel Harow now a resident in Plymouth & Jane Barnes of Plymouth
9 Prince Manter & Lucy Bessey both of Plymouth
16 Ellis Bartlett & Anna Bartlett both of Plymouth
Nathaniel Thomas & Jane Jackson both of Plymouth
30 Eleaz^r Ellis Junr of Plym^o & Mercy Nye of Sandwich

* "Ditto" means Plymouth in each case.
† The marriage of "John Turner Junr of Scituate & Perces Washburn of Plym^o" on 17 August, 1795, is recorded on original page 279.
‡ The marriage of "Seth Drew & Temporence Pixly both of " Plymouth, is recorded on original page 276.
§ The month and day were not recorded.

Feby Capt James Seaver of Kingston & Miss Jane Russell of Plymouth
13 Nathan Reed & Rebecca Morton both of Plymouth
27 George Samson & Patience Ryder both of Plymouth
27 Benjamin Wright & Deborah Samson both of Plymouth
27 David Bartlett & Polley Carver both of Plymouth
6* Amaziah Harlow Junr & Martha Albertson both of Plymouth
Mar: 12 Isaac Sturtevant of Plym^o & Eliz^a Darling of Midd^o
19 Zepheniah Holmes & Bethiah Churchell both of Plymouth
Lewis Harlow & Hannah Churchell both of Plymouth
Mr John Watson & Mrs Eunice Goodwin both of Plymouth
26 Oliver Keeys & Lydia Bagnal both of Plymouth
David Warren & Sally Donham both of Plym^o
April 16 John Clark of Hanover & Polly Roberts of Plymouth
23 John Allen & Meriah Smith both of Plymouth
Doct^r Zacheus Bartlett, & Miss Hannah Jackson, both of Plym^o
[p. 167] 1796 Publishments for Marriage
May 21 Samuel Holmes Junr & Mary Thomas both of Plym^o
Thomas Pope & Priscilla Mitchell both of Plym^o
Seth Morton & Mercy Savery both of Plym^o
28 Mr John Goddard of Carver & Miss Grace Haynan Otis of Plym^o
George Burges & Deborah McLathley both of Plymouth
June 19 Mosis Sepit & Deborah Jeffery Indiens both of Plym^o
Thomas Goodwin Junr & Abigail Croswell both of Plym^o
Aug: 13 Reubin Ellis of Plymouth & Patience Blackwell of Sandwich
Stephen Harlow & Charlotte Barnes both of Plymouth
20 Clark Finney & Polley Wetherhead both of Plymouth
Sep^t 3 Jeremiah Hoskins & Lucy Cowit both now residents in Plym
Hoskins came from Freetown & Cowit from Barnestabl
Joseph Holmes Junr & Mary Battles both of Plymouth
10 John Doten of Plymouth & Polly Wright of Plimton
John Michael Merop a resident in Plymouth & Sarah Gould of Plymouth Merop came from [†] or the Western Territory with Doct^r Hayward Say 2 year ago
17 Zepheniah Harlow Junr of Plym^o & Salley Thomas of Kingston
24 Elias Shaw of Carver & Lydia Faunce of Plymouth
Octob^r 8 Robert Davee & Jerusha Trask both of Plymouth
George Straffin & Mary Simmons both of Plymouth
15 Calvin Crombie & Naoma Jackson both of Ditto
29 James Wright Junr of Plymouth & Mercy Shaw of Carver
Nathaniel Holmes ye 6th & Elizabeth Drew both of Plymouth
Novr 5 William Bradford & Nanse Balston both of Ditto
12 Abraham Whiteing of Kingston & Sally Robbins of Plymouth
19 Nathaniel Harlow & Sally Holmes both of Ditto
Joseph Ryder of Plym^o & Rebecca Fuller of Kingston
26 George Finney & Abigail Finney both of Plymouth
Rufus Churchell & Eunice Covington both of Plymouth

* So recorded.
† A blank was left, but no place was entered.

[p. 168] 1796   Publishments for Marriage
Nov'r 26 Chandler Holmes & Phebe Atwood both of Plymouth
Jonathan Polden of Plym° & Esther Hollis of Kingston
Dec'r 2 Nathaniel Besse of Rochester & Tabethy Chubbuck of Plymouth
Nathaniel Clark y'e 3'rd & Lydia Samson both of Ditto
Arunah Bartlett now resident in Plym° & Rememberance Holmes of Plymouth
Jeremiah Holmes Jun'r of Plym° & Mary Lucas of Carver
Edward Lanman Jun'r of Plym° & Matha Newcomb of Welfleet
Dec'r 24 John Collings now resident in Plym°, a native of London & Martha Harris of Plymouth
31 William Harlow Jun'r of Plym° & Elizabeth Jackson of Norton
1797 Jan'r'y 13 Jesse Muxsom of Wareham & Mercy Wadsworth of Plym°
14 Nicolas Drew & Azuba Wood both Plymouth
27 Abner Rickard of Croydon in the State of Newhampshire & Lydia King of Plym
29 Lazarus Lucas & Nanse Code both of Plymouth
Thomas Covington, & Elizabeth Hewston both of Plymouth
Feb'r'y 4 Clark Raymond Resident in Plymouth & Sarah Hall of Plymouth
25 Jonathan Shaw a resident in Plymouth & Sally Bartlett of Plym° (M'r Shaw Came from Middlbo)
March 11 Ezra Harlow Jun'r & Lydia Davee both of Plymouth
Josiah Carver & Elizabeth Davee both of Plymouth
18 John Bartlett & Ruth Shaw both of Plymouth
Andrew Bartlett Jun'r of Plym° & Elizabeth Hammond of Rochester
25 Charles Howard of Bridgw'r & Eloner Howard of Plym°
April 6 Benjamin Keys & Polley Norris both of Plymouth
22 John Sylvester & Lydia Edwards both of Plymouth
Benjamin Holmes & Meriah Thomas both of Plymouth
30 William Ellis & Mary Ellis both of Plymouth
May 1 Jabez Pryor of Duxboro and Sally Holmes of Plymouth
[p. 169] 1797   Publishments in order for Marriage
May 13 William Cobb Esq'r of Falmouth Casco bay & Elizabeth Ripley Jun'r of Plymouth
20 Daniel Churchill & Salle Collings both of Plymouth
Samuel Burbank & Salla Coye both of Ditto
27 Thomas Polden of Plymouth, & Tryphona Westgate now a Resident in Plymouth
Thomas Atwood of Plym° & Mehitable Shaw of Abing't'n
June 3 George Polden & Jedidah Mclathley, both of Plymouth
24 John Wanfor a resident in Plymouth (he came from the County of Norfolk in the Kingdom of Great Brittain as a Drummer in the late warr with America,) and Lydia Raymond of Plymouth
27 George Briggs of Middleboro & Patience Holmes of Plym°
July 1 Barneby Morton & Eliz'a Doten both of Ditto
22 Abial Washburn Plym° & Abigail Briggs of Midd°

Aug: 12 Caleb Battles & Jane Ryder both of Plymouth
Ichabod Davee & Joanna Bartlett both of Plymouth
12 or 18* Joseph Holmes y'e 3'd & Martha Dyre both of Plymouth
19 Isaac Josselyn of Pembrook & Mary Balstom of Plymouth
Isaac Symms & Mary Whitman both of Plymouth
Ebenezer Holmes & Margaret Howard both of Plymouth
Sep'r 16 Cap't Benjamin Warren & M'rs Lewis Doten both of Plymouth
23 Joseph Holmes Jun'r & Lydia Lucas both of Plymouth
Octo'r: 7 Ezra Finney & Lydia Bartlett both of Plymouth
Thomas Faunce & Lucy Holmes both of Plymouth
14 Solomon Finney & Patience Churchell both of Plymouth
21 Thomas Sears & Susannah Morton both of Plymouth
21 John Michael Merop now resident in Plymouth and Elone'r Holmes of Plymouth Merop Came to this Town with Doct'r Hayward About 3 years ago
21 Ephraim Morton & Sarah Howland Jun'r both of Plymouth
Nov'r 4 Freeman Bartlett & Salley Stephens both of Plymouth
[p. 170] 1797   Publishments in order for Marriage
Nov'r 11 David Holmes Jun'r & Polley Holmes both of Plymouth
Jesse Bartlett & Betsy Lewis Drew both of Plymouth
18 Barnabas Holmes y'e 3'rd & Thankful Gammons both of Ditto
25 John Carver & Betsey Holmes both of Ditto
Ebenezer Mitchell & Joanna Rogers both of Ditto
1798 January 13 George Rogers & Sally Harlow both of Ditto
Ebenezer Davee & Lydia Curtis both of Ditto
27 Samuel Rand a resident in Plym° & Susanna Atwood of Ditto
February 3 Cap't Robert Roberts & Miss Elizabeth Harlow both of Ditto
10 Sylvanus Shurtleff resident in Plym° & Polley Clark of Ditto
14 Thomas Cornish & Jerusha Holmes both of Plymouth
24 Hezekiah Jackson of Plym° & Elizabeth Fails Dinnan of Bristol in the State of Rhode Island
March 3 Thomas Donham of Carver & Silvina Shurtleff of Plymouth
Nathaniel Churchell & Susanna Harlow y'e 2'nd both of Plym
17 William Manter & Mehitable Ellis both of Plym
Henry Jackson & Huldah Holbrook both of Ditto
24 Cap't Eleazer Holmes & Betsey Avery both of Ditto
April [†] Isaac Banks & Abigail Babb both of Ditto
Bartlett Sears & Bathsheba Drew both of Ditto
14 Hose Bartlett & Mercy Bartlett both of Ditto
Samuel Churchell y'e 3'rd & Bathsheba Collings both of Ditto
Southworth Shaw & Meriah Churchell both of Ditto
14 Truman Bartlett & Experience Finney both of Ditto
21 Samuel Rogers & Betsey Babb both of Ditto
Joseph Sampson & Zurviah Burge both of Plym°
May 5 M'r Thomas Wethrell Jun'r & Miss Nancy Shaw both of Plym°
Josiah Swift Jun'r of Wareham, & Polley Ellis of Plymouth

(To be continued)

*So recorded.
†The date is doubtful—possibly 1 was intended.

PLYMOUTH, MASS., VITAL RECORDS

(Continued from page 119)

[p. 171] 1798   In order for Marriage*
May 12‡ William Cunnit & Nabbe Amos Indiens both of Plym°
25 Joshua Ryder & Hannah Howland both of Plym°
   Jacob Howland Ju' & Jane Hovey both of Ditto‡
26 William Sever Esq' of Kingston & Mrs Mercy Russell of Ditto
   Noah Perkins & Lowis Huckins both now residents in Plym°
   James Robbins & Olive King both of Plymouth
June 9 Elkanah Finney & Lucy Morton both of Plymouth
   William Allen & Betsey Holmes both of Plym°
   Thaddeus Churchill Ju: of Plym° & Mercy Fuller of Kingston
16 George Bacon & Betsey Ryder both of Plym°
22 Stephen Holmes & Rebecca Bartlett both of Plym°
July 21 Joshua Torrey & Sarah Doten y° 2nd both of Plym°
28 Zabdial Weston of Duxboro & Sarah Boise both of Plymouth
Aug': 5. Cary Harris Morton & Bethiah Johnson of Plym°
12 James Trent of Boston & Bethiah Johnson of Plym°
13 John Green a Native of Ireland now resident in Plymouth Lucy Ripley of Plymouth§
18 Ezekiel Seakins now a resident in Plymouth who Came from the State of Vermont & Ama Raymond of Plymouth
   David Moses & Sarah Cowit Indiens of Plymouth

*This means "Intentions of Marriage".— Editor.
† Above the date is written "Charg'd Dea: Bartlett".
‡ "Ditto" means Plymouth, in each case.
§ A note in the margin, beside this entry, reads "Isaac Howland to pay".

23 Timothey Phillips Negro man of Boston & Vilot Hedge of Plymouth
25 Stephen Doten Jun' & Abigail Clark both of Plymouth
25 Jonathan Harvey & Hannah Bates both of Plymouth
25 Clark Bartlett & Mercy Bartlett both of Plymouth
Sep': 2 Jonathan Polden & Sarah Rogers both of Plymouth
   This Sarah Rogers came from [*] to Plymouth
8 Samuel Churchill Jun. Elizabeth Totman both of Plym°
   James Cushing Jun' & Joanna Barnes both of Plymouth
22 Sylvanus Churchill & Lydia Churchell both of Plym°
[p. 172] 1798   In order for Marriage
Oct' 12 Thomas Bartlett y° 3rd & Ruth Rogers both of Plymouth
20 George Bartlett & Rebecca Lanman y° 2nd both of Plymouth
   Levi Reed of Pembrook & Lucy Doten of Plymouth
   Lewis Weston & Betsey Lanman both of Plymouth
27 Seth Finney & Sarah Churchell y° 2nd both of Plymouth
   Nathaniel Jackson & Deborah Harlow both of Plymouth
Nov' 3 Samuel Cornish & Lucy Holmes both of Ditto
   Rufus Bartlett Jun' & Rocksiade Bartlett both of Ditto
   Lemuel Nellson of Plym° & Scintha Cobb of Kingston
   Sylvanus Rogers & Polley Mason both of Plym°
   John Mevas & Sarah Rhodes Alies Phillis Quacum people of Colour both of Plym°
10th Ephraim Bartlett Jun' & Abigail Holmes y° 2nd both of Ditto
   Amasa Holmes & Elizabeth Bartlett both of Ditto
17 John Fitzgerald a native of Ireland now resident in Plymouth & Anna Raymond now Resident in Plymouth said Raymond Came from Middleboro or Freetown about two years ago
Dec' 1 Nathaniel Bradford Jun' & Deborah Wright both of Plym°
   Joshua Bartlett of Plym° & Lucy Tillson Donham of Carver
   Stephen Pain & Suke Bates both of Plym°
   Bradford Barnes & Jenna Holmes both of Plymou[th]
8 Josiah Mehurin a resident in Plym° & Patience Burges Perce of Plym° Mr Mehuerin came from Bridgwater
15 Nathan Holmes & Ruthey Cobb both of Plym°
1799 Jan'y 2 Jesse Pearce & Susanna King both of Plym°
19 Joseph Obrian a Resident it‡ Plym° & Deborah Gault of Wareha[m] Mr Obrian Came from Newfoundland to Plym° in 1797
26 Robert Holmes of Plym° & Desire Perce of Plymouth
   Amaziah Churchill Jun' & Martha Doten both of Plymouth
   Daniel Doten & Sarah Edwards both of Plymouth
[p. 173]   Publishments in order for Marriage
1799 February 2 Olever Kempton & Sarah Harlow Jun' both of Plymouth
9 William Coye & Rebecca Brown both of Plymouth
   John Bumpas of Carver & Betsey Chubbuck in Plymouth

* Space was left, but the place was not entered.
† Sic.

THE MAYFLOWER DESCENDANT

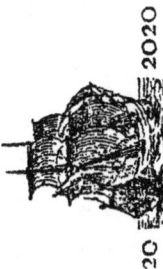

A QUARTERLY MAGAZINE OF PILGRIM GENEALOGY AND HISTORY

VOLUME XXXI

1933

PUBLISHED BY THE
MASSACHUSETTS SOCIETY OF MAYFLOWER DESCENDANTS
BOSTON

Plymouth Mass., Vital Records

March 9 Francis Ellis & Joanna Briggs both of Plymouth
Ebenez: Holmes ye 3rd of Plymouth & Sarah Sturtevant of Kingston
Ebenez Drew & Deborah Ransom both of Plymouth
23 John Bartlett Junr & Rebecca Ryder both of Plymouth
31 Stephen Bartlett of Plymouth & Polley Nye of Sandwich
April 20 Mr John Locke of Ashby & Miss Hannah Goodwin of Plym-
  outh
May 24 Mr Josiah Diman of Plym^o & Mrs Sophia Samson of Plimton
25 Mr John Taylor of Barnestable & Miss Lucia Watson of Plymouth
27 Benjamin Ellis & Elizabeth Pigslee both now residents in Plymouth
  Ellis came from Chatham is the son of Eben: Ellis and Pigsle is
  the Daughter of Benjamin Pigslee he came from Freetown
June 6 Dominnicus Hovey now of Plym^o & Eliz^a Clark of Plymouth
Sep^t 7 Abner Holmes & Polley Bradford both of Plymouth
? Sylvanus Bramhall & Ruth Marshell both of Plymouth
21 John Atwood & Nancy Churchell both of Plymouth
21 John Battles & Elizabeth Cobb both of Ditto
29 John Meleck & Polley Tuckerman Indiens both of Plymouth
Octob: 5 Caleb Finney & Lydia Comington* both of Plymouth
12 Belcher Manter Junr & Sarah Wright ye 2nd both of Ditto
The Revd Ward Cotton of Boylston & Miss Rebeckah Jackson Plym-
  outh
19 Ezra Howard of Duxboro & Rebecca Holmes of Plymouth
Mr John Bishop Junr & Miss Elizabeth Holbrook both of Plym^o
William Holland of Plymouth, & Eliz^a Roberts, of Boston,
Ransom Jackson of Plymouth & Sarah Faunce of Carve[r]
[p. 174] 1799 Publishments in order for Marriage
Novr 3 Ansel Holmes & Salley Bartlett both of Plymouth
23 Nathaniel Robbins Plym^o & Ruth Robbins of Carver
Decr 3 Darbey Barnes late from Newfound Land now a resident in
  Plymouth & Mary Cowit resident in Plymouth (She is Daughter
  of Jesse Cowit a man of Colour who Came into this Town lately
  from Barnestable)
14 Woodworth Jackson & Meriah Morton Torrey both of Plymouth
14 Simon Richmond & Lydia Anderson Simmons both of Plymouth
Finney Leach & Mercy Bartlett both of Plymout[h]
21 Capt Anselm Gibbs of Wareham & Miss Lucy LeBaron of Plymouth
27 Caleb Morton & Hannah Leonard both of Plymouth
Ichabod Shaw Junr & Esther Holmes both of Plymouth

(To be continued)

---

* On page 280 is recorded the marriage, on 10 November, 1799, of "Caleb Finney & Lydia Covington both of Plym^o marryd at Plym^o".

PLYMOUTH, MASS., VITAL RECORDS

TRANSCRIBED BY THE EDITOR

(Continued from Vol. XXX, p. 190)

[Vol. 2, p. 174]
1800 Febry 1 Doctr Nathaniel Bradstreet & Miss Mary Crombie both of Plymouth
15 Capt Nathaniel Russell & Miss Martha LeBaron Both of Plymouth
22 Stephen Doten ye 3rd of Plymo & Hannah Wright of Plimton
March 8 Thomas Doten & Polley Donham both of Plymouth
Ephraim Holmes & Polley Bradford both of Plymouth
Samuel Robbins Junr of Plymouth, & Pamelia Donham now resident in Plymouth
April 4 Benjamin Battles & Zilpah Wadsworth both of Plymouth
Anthoney Dike Junr & Polley Curtis both of Plymouth
12 Jonathan Hill of Plymouth formerly of Bridgwr & Mary Hines resident in Plymouth
Thomas Bradford & Polley Holmes both of Plymouth
19 Zadock Packard of Bridgwater & Rebecca Phillips of Plymo
Lazarus Morton & Sally McCarter both of Plymo
26 George Perkins & Experience Battles both of Plymouth
[p. 175] 1800 Publishments in order for Marriage
May 30 The Revd James Kendall of Plymo & Miss Sarah Poor of Andover
June 21st Haywood Gardner A resident in Plymo & Mehitable Pain of Plymo
July 19 James Howard & Hannah Churchell both of Plymouth
Aug. 2nd Sylvanus Bisbey of Rochester & Lydia Jackson ye 2nd of Plymouth
Sept 6 Levi Thomas of Plymouth & Lydia Thomas of Bridgwater
6 Benjamin Barnes Junr of Plymo & Rebecca Shurtleff of Carver
Oct 4 Sylvanus Sampson & Ruth Burges both of Plymouth
11 Rufus Goddard & Elizabeth Bartlett both of Plymouth
25 William Southwick resident in Plymouth & Hannah Churchell of Plymouth
15 Benjamin Perce of Duxboro & Polley Sampson of Plymouth
Joseph Bradford & Nancy Barnes both of Plymouth
22 Thomas Marsh of Boston & Mercy Bramhall of Plymouth
29 Jacob Johnson & Abigail Bates both of Plymouth
Decr 3 Ebenezer Covil of Plymouth & Mary Carter of Kingston
19 Ephraim Dugles of Plymouth & Deborah Hoskins of Freetown
20 Caleb Faunce & Rebecca Brown both of Plymouth
27 Mr Salsberry Jackson, & Miss Salley Goodwin, both of Plymouth
10 Mr John Allen of Salem & Mrs Polley Nicolson of Plymouth
10 John Cooper & Jerusha Cobb both of Plymouth
1801 23* Joseph Swift of Plymouth & Rosanna Cornish of Middleboro
Febry 21 Richard Blackmer & Nancy Ellis both of Plymouth
Wait Atwood & Polley Treeble both of Plymouth
28 Isaac Drake is Resident In Plym & Elizabeth Morton of Plymouth
28 Robert Donham Junr & Sarah Goddard both of Plymouth
March 14 Israel Clark & Phebe Cornish both of Plymouth
21 Gideon Hovey & Betsey Clark both of Plymouth
28 Beza Hayward Esqr of Bridgwr & Mrs Experience Russell of Plymo
James Woodward of Duxboro & Polley Burges of Plymouth
[p. 176] 1801 Publishments in order for Marriage
April 11 George Morton of Plymo & Betse Bartlett Falmouth Casco Bay
Ansel Holmes & Pattey Barnes both of Plymouth
18 Isaac Bartlett & Fear Cobb both of Plymouth
25 William Randal Plymo & Hannah Thomas of Kingston
June 6 Samuel Bartlett Junr & Olive Bartlett both of Plymouth
6 Ansell Bartlett Junr & Polley Lanman both of Plymouth
6 John Churchill & Nancy Jackson both of Plymouth
27 James Spooner & Margaret Symms both of Plymouth
Thomas Whitmarsh & Chloe Simmons both of Plymouth
July 31 Lothrop Clark Junr & Polley Bartlett both of Plymouth
Augst 10 Christopher Wadsworth of Plymouth & Elizabeth Gibbs Sandwich
16 George Bramhall & Lucy Morton both of Plymouth
Sept 1 John Porter of Abington & Eloner Doten of Plymouth
Sept 5 Nehemiah Burbank of Plymouth & Hannah Torrey of Waymouth
5 Elkanah Churchell & Eunice Finney both of Plymouth
George Dellano of Duxboro & Lydia Burges of Plymouth
Samuel Virgen & Esther Cooper both of Plymouth
16 William Holmes Junr & Ruth Morton 2nd both of Plymouth
19 William Weston ye 3rd & Polley Samson Holmes both of Plymo
26 Ebenezer Robbins & Mercy Bartlett both of Plymo

*The month was not entered.

Sept 28 Levi Tinkcom resident in Kingston & Eliza Cowit of Plymouth
Octr 10 Edmond Churchill & Mary Hewston both of Plymo
  Peter Holmes & Salley Harlow both of Plymouth
24 William Whitmarsh & Fanney Hatheway both of Ditto
31 Edward Doten of Plymo & Esther Hollis resident in Plymouth
  Jesse Robbins & Sarah Turner Curtis both of Ditto
Novr 14 Joseph Bumpas & Lydia Wingford both of Ditto
21 Hunnewell Haskel of Rochester & Lucy Ellis of Ditto
[p. 177]   Publishments in order for Marriage
1801 Novr 21 Samuel Churchell Junr & Nancy Comington both of Plymouth
  Caleb Churchell & Lydia Grennolds both of Plymouth
Decr 5 George Ellis Junr & Mercy Harlow both of Plymo
19 Jesse Holmes & Mary Bartlett both of Ditto
1802 Janry 1 Thomas Ellis of Plymouth & Rebecca Burges of Sandwich
9 John King & Polley Briggs both of Plymouth
February 27 Doctr Nathaniel Lothrop & Miss Lucy Hammet both of Plymouth
27 Atwood Drew & Lydia Ryder ye 2nd both of Plymouth
March 6 John Pate Junr & Assenah Churchell both of Plymouth
  Samuel Barnes & Lucy Stetson both of Plymouth
11 Thomas Morton 4th & Nancy Paty both of Plymouth
13 Zacheus Holmes & Charlotte Wing both of Plymouth
20 Beza Perkins & Lucy Besse both of Plymouth
27 Clark Johnson of Plymouth & Silva Gibbs of Sandwich
  Lemuel Cobb Junr of Plymouth & Clarrissa Samson of Duxboro
9 David Covill & Susanna Mirick both of Plymouth
10 Pelham Bradford of Plymo & Joanna Downs resident in Plymo
17 Edward Stephens of Carver & Lucy Nellson of Plymouth
24 Nathaniel Doten & Mary Farmer both of Plymouth
May 1 Samuel Holmes ye 3rd & Salley Luce both of Plymouth
22 William King & Huldah Battles both of Plymouth
June 5 William Ellis Jur & Betsey Harlow both of Ditto
July 31 Elisha Macumber & Mary Gullifer both now residents in Plymouth
Aug: 7 Levi Lucas & Betsey Davee both of Plymouth
  John Holmes & Polley Fearing both of Plymouth
14 John Chase & Abigail Rogers both of Plymouth
28 Jacob Tinkcom a Resident in Plymo & Rebecca Morton of Ditto
Septr 25 Lazarus Symms & Mary Weston Junr both of Ditto

(To be continued)

PLYMOUTH, MASS., VITAL RECORDS

(Continued from page 4)

[p. 178] 1802 Publishments in order for Marriage
Novr 6 Diman Bartlett & Hannah Harlow both of Plymouth
  Josiah Morton Junr of Plymouth & Abigail Windsor of Duxboro
13 Stephen Gammons of Plymouth & Dorothy Tenter a Resident in Plymo
20 Prince Goodwin of Plymo & Lettis Barker of Scituate both Negros
  Samuel Holmes Junr of Plymouth & Polley Sturtevant of Kingston
  Calvin Donham & Hannah Harlow ye 2nd both of Plymouth
24 Elkanah Bartlett Junr & Sarah Code both of Ditto
27 William Drew of Plymouth & Priscilla Washburn of Kingston
3* Ichabod Harlow of Plymouth & Patience Holmes of Kingston
11 Rufus Robbins & Margaret Howard both of Plymouth
  Boston Parsons & Patty Hall Indiens both of Plymouth
18 William Hewston Junr & Ruthe Finney Junr both of Plymouth
25 Malletiah Bartlett & Martha Bartlett ye 3rd both of Plymouth
25 Olever Porter of Midd°† & Susannah Raymond of Plymouth
  Consider Clark & Sarah Sampson Both of Plym
1803 Janry 1 Job Cobb Junr & Nancey Doten Both of Ditto
8 Mr George Jackson of Plymouth & Miss Susan Willard of Boxber[worn]
15 David Drew Junr & Salley Churchell both of Plymouth
  Joseph Whiteing & Polley Morton both of Plymouth
29 Josiah Bradford & Polley Robbins both of Plymouth
Febry 12 Seth Eddy Resident in Plymo & Sophia Holmes of Plymo
March 2 Stephen Hill Tucker a: Resident in Plymouth & Rebecca Stephenson of Plymouth
9 Perkins Raymond & Elizabeth Drew both of Plymo
11 Zacheus Harlow Junr & Nancey Gammons both of Plymo
  Heman Cobb & Betsey Whitmarsh both of Plymo

* This apparently was in December. — *Editor.*
† Middleborough, Mass.

19 Mr Benjamin Warren & Mrs Patience Diman both of Plymo
April 16 Ephraim Morton & Dorcas Brown both of Plymo
23 Jabez Churchell & Mercy Bartlett both of Plymo
30 Stephen Faunce Junr & Betsey Shurtleff both of Plymo
[p. 179] 1803   Publishments for Marriage
May 13 Samuel Cole Junr a resident in Plymo & Salley Norton of Plymo
14 Joseph Davee & Hannah Faunce both of Plymouth
June 3 Moses Hoyet & Joanna Luce both of Plymouth
18 Doctr Benjamin Shurtleff of Boston & Miss Salley Shaw of Ditto*
25 Lucas Shaw & Mehitable Manter both of Plymouth
July 16 Joseph Hoyet resident in Plymouth & Susanna Hoyet of Ditto*
    Malletiah Holmes† & Lydia Luce both of Ditto
Aug: 8 Caleb Raymond Junr & Lydia King both of Ditto
15 Ephraim Finney & Phebe Wright both of Plymo
20 Ezekiel Ryder & Polley Holmes both of Plymo
27 Capt Gideon S Allden of New Bedford & Miss Priscilla LeBaron of Plymouth
    John Swift Junr of Plymo & Joanna Cornish of Middleboro
    Job Hoskins & Susanna Ellis both now residents in Plymouth Hoskins I think is an inhabitant of Rochester, Ellis's name was Hackit of Middleboro ‡
Septr 3 John Cornish Junr & Polley Nicols both of Plymouth
    Levi Vaughan of Carver & Phebe Donham of Plymouth
Octobr 1 Elijah Morrey & Grace Cornish both of Plymouth
1 Samuel Dickson & Polley Churchell both of Plymouth
8 James Chummuck Junr & Hannah Sept Indiens both of Plymouth
    Simeon Volentine & Bathsheba Wicket Junr Indiens both of Ditto
22 Paul Doten of Plymouth & Elizabeth Cobb of Carver
22 George Simmons & Mercy Bates both of Plymouth
29 Deacn Lot Harlow & Miss Polley Boylstone both of Plymouth
    Joseph Lock Esqr of Billereica & Miss Lydia Goodwin of Plymouth
Novr 5 Simeon Dike of Plymouth & Mary Gibbs of Wareham
19 David Covill of Plymouth & Cinthea Basset of Harwich
    Barnabas Churchell & Lydia Cole both of Plymouth
26 Ichabod Howland of Plymo & Deborah Crocker of Carver
    Amos Whiteing & Priscilla Holmes the 2d both of Plymouth
[p. 180] 1803   Publishments for Marriage
Novr 30 Samuel Alexander of Kingston & Deborah Paty of Plymo
    Ephraim Paty of Plymouth & Betsey Fuller of Kingston
    William Atwood & Temperance Churchell both of Plymouth
17 Hosea Vaughan & Jedidah Harlow both of Plymouth

* "Ditto" means Plymouth, in each case.
† The marriage record (original page 372) on 25 July, 1803, reads "Melatiah Howard & Lydia Luce both of Plymouth,"; and the original church records read "Melatiah Howard & Lydia Luce both of Plymouth". — Editor.
‡ This is all in one hand and entered at one time. — Editor.

31 John Holmes of Duxboro & Polley Holmes of Plymouth
    Thomas Spear & Clarrisse Harlow both of Plymouth
    Lemuel Rickard of Crydon* & Abigail Shurtleff of Plymouth were publishd Decr 24th
1804 Janry 19 John Treeble & Bathsheba Holmes both of Plymouth
    James Treeble & Susanna Holmes both of Plymouth
21 Lot Covill & Mehittable Weeks both of Plymouth
    Lilleston Banks & Sarah Johnson both of Ditto
    Vaspasian Wing & Hulda Bates both of Ditto
28 Jesse Robbins & Betsey Churchell both of Ditto
Febry 4 Lewis Finney & Elizabeth Weston both of Ditto
    William Morton of Plymouth & Catherine Gibbs of Sandwich
    John Aderson resident in Plymouth & Sarah Fish of Ditto
    Micah Bompo resident in Plymouth & Nabbe Stephens of Ditto both people of Colour
11 Thomas Jarvis of Boston & Judath Hedge of Plymouth both People of Colour
21 Ichabod Peterson of Duxboro & Sintha Holmes of Plymouth
24 Ephraim Leonard of Middleboro & Elizabeth Churchell of Plym
March 2 John Bates & Margaret Besse both of Plymouth
    Benjamin Lawrance of Sandwich & Abigail Packard of Plymouth
    David Ripley Junr of Plimton & Hannah Wadsworth Cuffs of Plymouth
    Ephraim Churchell & Salley Finney both of Plymouth
16 Joseph Harrington of Dugless & Salley Raymond of Plymouth
23 Robert King & Salley Wing both of Plymouth
[p. 181] 1804   Publishments for Marriage
May 12 Edward Freeman of Sandwich & Lucy Churchell of Plymouth
    Caleb Battles & Lucy Ryder both of Plymouth
19 Allden Lucas & Deborah Barnes both of Plymouth
    Lewis Goodwin & Anna Lucas both of Plymouth
    Samuel Briggs & Salley Morrey both of Plymouth
16 Ichabod Hall & Priscilla Cowit people of Colour both Resident in Plymouth
July 7 Samuel Nute of Bridgewater & Mary Weston Junr of Plymo
14 Josiah Morton ye 3rd & Lucy Burges both of Plymouth
    George Raymond of Plymouth & Priscilla Shaw of Middleboro
21 Mr Daniel Roberts Elliot of Waynsborough State of Georgia and Miss Betsey Hayward Thacher of Plymouth
28 Nathan Churchell & Elizabeth Sylvester both of Plymouth
    Joseph Churchell & Mercy Goodwin both of Plymouth
Aug: 4 Benjamin Dillard & Mary Covington both of Plymouth
11 James Allen of Boston & Priscilla Brown of Plymouth
Sept 2 Barnabas Faunce of Plymouth & Abigail Sturtevant of Carver
    Cooner Weston & Hannah Doten both of Plymouth

*Croydon, N. H. See marriage record, 9 January, 1804, on original page 280. — Editor.

8 John Rogers & Mercy Wright both of Plymouth
15 William Jackson Esq[r] of Plym[o] & Mrs Esther Parsons of Scituate
Abiather Smith resident in Plym[o] & Mehitable Gardner of Plymouth
George Armor resident in Plym[o] & Catherine Hubbard of Plymouth both people of Colour
Noah Morse of Middleboro & Patience Bryant of Plymouth
28 Doct[r] Abraham Haskell of Luningb* & Mrs Experience Cotton of Plym[o]
29 Doct[r] Isaac Barrows of Plymouth & Miss Rebecca Hammond of Wareham
Octob[r] 6 William Drew Jun[r] & Salley Holmes both of Plymouth
27 Thomas Williams Resident in Plym[o] & Polley McCarter of Plym
Nov[r] 3 Levi Ripley of Kingston & Mary Covington of Plymouth
4 George Savery & Mary Lanman both of Plymouth
[p. 182] 1804 Publishments for Marriage
Nov[r] 10 John Burges Jun[r] & Susanna Samson both of Plymouth
Thomas Burges 3rd & Lucy Lanman both of Plymouth
17 John Harlow Jun[r] & Betsey Harlow Torrey both of Ditto
28 Thomas Holmes Jun[r] & Eunice Morton both of Ditto
Dec[r] 9 Willson Churchell of Plym[o] & Ruth Hinkley of Barnestable
15 Ebenezer Howard & Thankfull Le Moat both of Plymouth
1805 Jan[ry] 5 John Bartlett y[e] 3rd & Jerusha Davee both of Plymouth
19 William Dunber of Hallifax & Jerusha Holmes of Plym[o]
26 Thomas Holmes & Mercy Snow both of Plymouth
Lathley Haskins & Susanna Hoyet both Residents in Plymouth
Feb[ry] 9 John Gray Jun[r] of Kingston & Sarah Battles of Plymouth
16 Cap[t] George Drew & Miss Fanney Glover both of Plymouth
March 9 John Gooding & Deborah Barnes both of Plymouth
Daniel Clark & Martha Bramhall both of Plymouth
April 2 Ignatious Perce & Betsey Bessey both of Plymouth
6 Joshua Bartlett & Elizabeth Goodwin both of Plymouth
M[r] Thomas Jackson & Miss Sarah Lebaron both of Plymouth
13 Melzer Whiteing of Plymouth & Welthey Dellano of Kingston
20 Caleb Alexander Spooner resident in Plym[o] *he Came from New bedford*† & Nancey Simmons of Plymouth
May 18 William Nye & Lucy Sylvester both of Plymouth
William Putnam Ripley of Plym[o] & Mary Briggs of Dighton
June 1 Eleazer Sears & Polley Morton both of Plymouth
8 Cap[t] Jesse Harlow & Miss Salley Cotton both of Plymouth
10 Cannadey Reed resident in Plym[o] & Sarah Moses of Plymouth
July 2 Josiah Sturtevant & Lucy Clark both of Plymouth
6 John Mitchell Tessier Resident in Plymouth & Waite Shurtleff of Carver

*The marriage record, on original page 373, calls the groom "of Rochester", but the church records, under the year 1804, read: "Oct. 22 Doct[r] Abraham Haskell of Lunenburg to Mrs. Experience Cotton of Plymouth." — *Editor.*
†The words in italics have been interlined, in the same hand and ink.

20 Edward Morse Jun[r] of Rochester & Anna Holmes of Plymouth
Aug[st] 10 Jacob Curtes Sarah Churchell both of Plymouth
John Perce & Betsey Warren Doten both of Plymouth
[p. 183] 1805 Publishments for Marriage
August 31 Edmond Sears & Lucy Holmes both of Plymouth
Sept[r] 28 John Faunce & Hannah Samson both of Plym[o]
Oct[r] 12 John Hall & Mary Pigslee both residents in Plymouth
19 Joab Thomas Resident in Plymouth & Lois Doten of Plymouth
Thomas Fish Jun[r] of Pembrook & Cintha Doten of Plymouth
Nov[r] 16 William Leonard & Susanna Bartlett both of Plymouth
Joseph Wright & Lucy Burges both of Plymouth
Dec[r] 7 Nathan Holmes & Euphamy Bartlett both of Plymouth
Freeman Cornish & Jenna Ellis both of Plymouth made Void by mutual Consent
Chandler Burges & Jane Morton both of Plymouth
13 John Burges of Plymouth & Ruth Sprague of Duxboro
28 Alpheus Richmond & Abigail Simmons both of Plymouth
1806 January 25 Lyman Adams of Albeny State of New York & Elizabeth Goddard of Plymouth
Feb[ry] 1 William Finney & Patty Harlow both of Plymouth
3 Benjamin Norris & Mehitable Cahoon both of Ditto
4 Uriah Savery of Rochester & Jenna Ellis of Plymouth
8 James Polden of Plym[o] & Lucy Holmes of Kingston
March 1 Freeman Cornish of Plymouth & Sarah Reed of Middleboro
1 David Burbank & Polley Bryant both of Plymouth
Josiah Donham & Betsey Donham both of Plymouth
15 Benjamin Lucas Jun[r] of Plymouth & Perces Lucas of Carver
Josiah Robbins & Experience Morton both of Plymouth
Ephraim Bradford & Hannah Morton both of Plymouth
22 Richard Holmes y[e] 3rd and Polley Ryder both of Ditto
Thomas Parker resident in Plymouth & Ellen Boyse of Ditto
28 Thomas Savery & Joanna Burbank Jun[r] both of Ditto
5 Nehemiah Savery of Plymouth & Deborah Smith of Middleboro
12 John H. Rigbey resident in Plym[o] & Sarah Leonard of Plymouth
[p. 184] 1806 Publishments for Marriage
April George Donham & Polley Albertson both of Plymouth
25 Luther Ripley & Polley Simmons both of Ditto
May 3 George Fottears & Vilot Saunder People of Colour both of Plymouth
June 14 Silas Hatheway Jun[r] & Deborah Donham both of Plymouth
14 Thomas McLathley of Plymouth & Lovise Thomas of Middleboro
Joel Perkins and Lucy Barnes both of Plymouth
23 Samuel Cahoon & Mary Swift both of Plymouth
28 Barnabas Lucas & Lucy Bryant both of Plymouth
July 5 Charles Howland & Deborah Clark both of Ditto
12 Reubin Muxsom Jun[r] & Hannah King both residents in Ditto
19 M[r] William Hamnat & Miss Esther Phillips Parsons both of Ditto
19 Joshua Prat & Elen Boyse both of Plymouth

Plymouth, Mass., Vital Records

Augst 9 Solomon Faunce & Ellen Bradford both of Plymouth
30 John Mendal Nicols resident in Plymouth & Sally Lanman of Ply[mouth]
Theodore Ellenwood of Brookline & Grace Robbins of Plymouth
George Bradford & Harriot Churchell both of Plymouth
George Robbins & Betsey Churchell both of Plymouth
Sept 7 Thomas Covington & Mary Donham both of Plymouth
27 Thomas Doty of Plymouth & Mary Kempton of Frankfort
Oct 5 Laben Burt & Hannah Holmes both of Plymouth
Isaac Donham & Betsey Savery both of Plymouth
12 Josiah Finney & Salley Sylvester both of Plymouth
Josiah Clark Junr of Plymouth & Elizabeth Gifford of Sandwich
Nathaniel Cole of Middo & Betsey Bumpas of Plymouth
18 Joseph Drew & Desire Goodwin both of Plymouth
8 Abraham Raymond of Plymo & Salley Cole of Rochester
John Atwood resident in Plymouth & Hannah Richerson of Plymouth

15 Freeman Morton & Rebecca Harlow both of Plymouth
Timothey Churchell of Plymouth & Olive Curtis of Duxboro

[p. 185] Accot of Deaths

Abraham Jackson Deceasd; Decr ye 8th 1760
Job Cobb Deceasd June ye 8. 1761.
Joanna Drew, Late Widdow, of Joshua Drew, Deceased Deceased Janry 30th 1761.
Marcy Harlow Wife of Capt Samll Harlow Decd July 4. 1762
Lydia Cornish Wife of John Cornish Deceasd August 19th 1764
Thomas Spooner Deceasd Decr 19th 1762
Hannah Jackson Widdo of Jeremiah Jackson of Boston Deceasd Deceasd June 29th 1763
Mary Thomas Wife of Doctr William Thomas Decd April 13th 1749
Sarah Davee Wife of Thomas Davee Aged 41 Yrs Decd Sepr 26th 1761
Deacon Haviland Torrey Deceasd March 29th 1750
Deborah Torrey Wife of Deacon John Torrey Decesd July 22th 1744
Hannah Cobb Wife of John Cobb Deceasd Novr 30th 1765
Nathan Simmons deceased november 3. 1758. aged 27 years & 6 months.
Sarah Spooner (Widdow of Thomas Spooner Late of Plymo Deceasd) Deceasd Janry 25th 1767 aged 71 Years 9 mo & 9 Days
Mrs Elizabeth Watson wife of George: Watson Esqr Deceasd Febry 19th 1767
Mr James Shurtleff Deceasd Sept 17th 1766 aged 69 Years 9 months & 20 Days
Mr Samuel Clark Deceasd April 2nd 1763 aged 76 Years
Mrs Mary Clark Widdow of sd Samuel Clark Deceasd Sept 30th 1765 aged 74 years
Mr Joseph Rider Deceasd Decr 29th 1766 in ye 95th year of his Age
Mrs Mary Rider Wife of sd Joseph Deceasd Febry 2nd 1757
Mrs Abigail Holmes wife of Solo Holmes Deceasd Novr 15th 1766
Mr James Curtis Deceasd Janry 15th 1767 Aged 32 years & 15 Days

Plymouth, Mass., Vital Records

Mrs Faith Shurtleff . wife of James Shurtleff Above named . Deceasd March 30th 1745
Margarett Rider Wife of Ezekiel Rider Deceasd March 9th 1761
Susannah Stephens wife of Eleazr Stephens Deceasd Decr 30th 1766
Sarah Durfey Wife of Richard Durfey Deceasd Octobr ye 15th 1769
Ephraim Morton Deceasd April 27th 1758
Mercy Churchell wife of Ebenezr Churchell Deceasd Octr 28th 1769
Jerusha Harlow wife of James Harlow Deceasd 27th May 1769
Sarah Cornish wife of John Cornish Deceasd Janry 27th 1771
Lydia Hovey wife of James Hovey Esqr Deceasd Febry 23d 1771

[p. 186] Account of Deaths

James Warren Esqr Deceasd July . 1 . 1757
Remember Holmes wife of James Holmes Junr Deceasd June 10th 1772
Mrs Mary Bacon wife of the Revd Mr Jacob Bacon Deceasd Novr 17th 1772 in the 55 year of her age
Samuel Bartlett Esqr Deceasd March 25th 1769
Mr Nathaniel Goodwin Deceasd May 23d 1771
Ebenezr Tinkcom Deceasd Decembr 24th 1774
Mary Bartlett wife of Willm Bartlett deceasd July 16th 1785
Capt Samuel Harlow Deceasd June 17th 1767
James Hovey Esqr Deceasd January 2nd 1781
Mrs Mercy Davis wife of Capt Thomas Davis Deceasd Sept 20th 1779 aged 45
Capt Thomas Davis Deceasd March 7th 1785 Aged 63
Mrs Lydia Hovey 1st wife of James Hovey Esqr Deceasd*
Mrs Mary Hovey 2d wife of sd Mr Hovey Deceasd*
Mrs Margaret Hovey 3d wife of sd Mr Hovey Deceasd* at Boston*

James a Negro man died in Prisson March 13th 1798 as Mr David Bacon the Keeper thereof told me
Mr John Russell Deceasd April 2nd 1776
Capt James Russell Deceasd Sept 28th 1792
Doctr Eleazer Harlow, the Son of John Harlow, & Hannah his wife, whose birth was Octr 17th 1719 . as appears by Town Book 1st page 93rd Deceasd at Duxboro Augst 8th 1812
Mr Thomas Spooner Deceasd Decr 19th 1762 Aged 68 years
Mrs Sarah Spooner who was the wife of said Thomas Spooner Deceasd 19th † 1762 aged 72 years. Se their family recorded, book 1st for births &c page 90th
Children of John Bartlett, 3d & Eliza his wife.
1. John B. Bartlett, born Novr 20, 1831.
2. Ezra F. Bartlett, born July 3, 1836.
3d James E. Bartlett, born July 20, 1839.

(To be continued)

*These three deaths, with "at Boston" in the middle of the line below, were all entered at one time, without dates. — Editor.
† The month was not recorded.

PLYMOUTH, MASS., VITAL RECORDS

(Continued from page 115)

[p. 187] Children of Daniel Jackson & Elizabeth M Jackson his wife
Elizabeth Morton Jackson, born January 1st 1813
Daniel Lothrop Jackson born September 9th . 1817
Rebecca Jackson born July 13th 1819
Sarah Taylor Jackson born, October 1 1821
Susan Turner Jackson . born August 16 1823
Charles Jackson, born Septr 16 1825
Isaac Jackson born Octr 30 1827.

Children of John Gooding & Deborah his wife
Deborah Barnes Gooding born July 29th 1805
John Gooding born Jany 5th 1808
William Gooding born Mar: 5th 1810.
Benjamin Barnes Gooding born Jany 2d 1813.
Eliza Ann Gooding born Aug: 29 1818.
George Barnes Gooding born May 19 1822
James Bugbee Gooding born Aug 15th . 1826

Children of Daniel Goddard jr. & Mary his Wife.
1 Mary Ann Goddard, born Feby 28 . 1818.
2. Daniel Goddard,   born May 20 . 1820
3. Harriett E. Goddard   "   Augt 12 . 1823
4. Daniel F Goddard   "   Novr 29 . 1827
5. Charles Goddard   "   Jany 23. 1830.
6. Catharine L Goddard   "   Augt 16 . 1834.

Child of Henry Robbins & Margrett H. his wife
1 Francis H. Robbins, was born December 25th . 1821.

Children of Henry Robbins & Betsey B. his Wife
1. Edward L. Born . April 22d . 1836
2. Martha Churchill born Jan[*] 12th . 1839.
3 Henry H. Robbins born December 8, 1840
4 Margaret H. Robbins December 30, 1843

[p. 188] ["Children of James G. Gleason" were entered at the top of this page, but were crossed out, apparently on account of errors, and entered on page 428.—*Editor.*]

Children of Ansell Holmes jr & [†] his Wife
1. Miranda B. Holmes, born January 16 . 1835
2. Massena F. Holmes, " April 1 . 1837
3. Martha Ann " June 12, 1839 }
4. Ansell Holmes " June 12, 1839. }

* "Jany" was first written, but the "y" was erased.
† The name was not recorded. A modern hand has written "Miriam" in pencil. On original page 247 we find the marriage of "Ansel Holmes jr & Miriam C Dickson, both of Plymouth", on 30 October, 1831.—*Editor.*

Children of Benjamin Barnes 3d. & his Wife
1. Robert Hutchinson born June 28th . 1834
2. Rebecca S.   "   Ap^l 19th . 1838

Children of Atwood L. Drew & his Wife.
1. Jane Sturtevant Drew, born, August 3d . 1831
2. Atwood born, September 5th . 1833

[p. 189] Publishments for Marriage Continued from page 184
1806 Novr 22 Stephens Ellis & Betsey Churchell both of Plymouth
29 Obediah King & Hannah Clark both of Plymouth
29 John White & Salley Norcut both residents in Plymouth
Decr 3 Levi Tinkcom & Experience Hackit . both Residents in Plymouth

1807 January 3 Sewel Priest & Mary Pitsley both residents in Plymouth
Kempton* Cobb & Sukey Edwards . Both of Plymouth
John B. Bates & Mary Taylor both of Plymouth
John Richards & Lucy Hoskins both residents in Plym^o
10 Lemuel Bartlett Junr & Lucy Bartlett . both of Plymouth
Abner Burges & Deborah Wright . both of Plymouth
The Revd Caleb Holmes of Dennis & Miss Lucy Goodw^n Plymouth
17 Samuel Doten & Rebecca Bradford 2nd both of Plymouth
Barnabas Faunce of Plymouth & Zilpah Sturtev^t of Carver
25th Josiah Sears Kenrick Resident in Plymouth & Hannah Weeks of Plymouth
February 7th Joseph Bates & Hannah Bates both of Plymouth
Zenus Ripley & Lydia Simmons . both of Plymouth
14 Thomas Clark & Ellen Bartlett both of Ditto
21 Earl Donham & Jerusha Linch . both residents in Plymouth
March 21 Bartlett Holmes Junr & Elizabeth Paty Junr both of Plymouth
28 William Langford & Betsey Morton . both of Ditto
April 3 Clift Baley & Nancy Ellis both Residents in Plymouth
11 Bartlett Bradford & Lucy Bradford both of Plym^o
May 2 John White & Lydia King both Residents in Plymouth
9 William Churchell & Patty Harlow both of Plym^o
Davis† Pain resident in Plymouth & Charlotte Hatheway of Plym^o
James Bartlett ye 4th & Sarah Wethrell both of Ditto

[p. 190] 1807 Publishments for Marriage
May 8 Elias Cox of Pembrook & Patience Calderwood of Plymouth
24 Ephraim Harlow of Plymouth & Ruth Sturtevant of Carver
June 14th Ezekiel Loring Junr of Plimton & Lydia Sherman of Plymouth
26 John Nellson resident in Plym^o & Rizpah Brewer of Plymouth

* "John" has been written in the margin, before "Kempton", in a different hand and ink.—*Editor.*
† On original page 375 is the marriage, 26 May, 1807, of "David Pain & Charlotte Hatheway both of Plymouth".—*Editor.*

184   Plymouth, Mass., Vital Records

27 Ebenezer Holmes of Plymᵒ & Lusanah* Frise Resident in Plym
July 10 Joseph Bates the 3ʳᵈ & Lucy Dugless both of Plymouth
    Eleazer Crocker Tillson & Hannah Morton both of Plymouth
    Mʳ Tillson Carne from Carver about 2 years ago
18 Nathaniel Holmes yᵉ 3ʳᵈ resident in Plym & Eunice Sturtevant of Plymouth
    Edmond Sears of Plymouth & Rebecca Lucas of Carver
25 Cyrus [Hayward†] Howard a resident in Plymouth & Betsey Diman of Plymouth
Augˢᵗ 1 Ezekiel Raymond yᵉ 3ʳᵈ of Plymouth & Suke Pigslee Resident in Plymᵒ
15 Ivory Harlow & Lucy Barnes both of Plymouth
17 John Cook of Nantuckit & Lydia Raymond of Ditto‡
22 Perrey Griffen & Olive Sampson both of Plymouth
26 John Battles of Plymouth & Lydia Rickard of Plymouth
    Abraham Gifford & Ditley Norris both of Plymouth
Sepᵗ 19 Daniel Jackson Juʳ & Elizᵃ Turner both of Ditto
26 William Treeble & Betsey Bradford both of Ditto
Octob 10 Benjamin Weston & Joanna Washburn both of Ditto
    Lemuel Barnes & Lucy Covington both of Ditto
    Josiah Johnson & Hannah Bramhall both of Ditto
    Ichabod Davee & Nancy Bartlett both of Ditto
23 Ezekiel Lovell of Sandwich & Martha Cahoon of Ditto‡
24 Solomon Maynard Resident in Plymᵒ & Betsey Swift§ of Ditto
    Isaac Cole and Sarah Holmes both of Ditto
    Seth Paty & Phebe Barnes both of Ditto
31 Stephen Gibbs of Sandwich & Deborah Swift of Ditto‡
Nov. 6 James Bartlett & Hannah Morton both of Ditto
    Thomas Mayo & Lucia LeBaron both of Ditto
[p. 191] 1807 Publishments for Marriage
Novʳ 12 Thomas Soul of Duxboro & Salley MᶜCarter of Plymouth
14 William White & Francis Gibbs both of Plymouth
21 Lot Stetson of Duxboro & Hannah Ryder of Ditto
    Stephen Faunce & Sophia Eddy both of Ditto
Decʳ 5 Olever Vaughan & Salley Churchell both of Ditto
12 Benjamin Dillard & Mercy Ellis both of Ditto
19 Calvin Richmond & Salley Jackson both of Ditto
    Asa Swift of Wareham & Sarah Cornish of Ditto‡

(To be continued)

*The marriage record, on original page 375, reads "Ebenezer Holmes & Susanna Frize", 12 July, 1807.— Editor.

† "Hayward" is interlined above, apparently in the same hand and ink. On original page 284 is the marriage of "Cyrus Hayward & Betsey Diman", on 16 August, 1807, by Rev. Adoniram Judson.— Editor.

‡ "Ditto" in every case means "Plymouth".— Editor.

§ Swift.

THE MAYFLOWER DESCENDANT

A QUARTERLY MAGAZINE OF
PILGRIM GENEALOGY AND HISTORY

VOLUME XXXII

1934

PUBLISHED BY THE
MASSACHUSETTS SOCIETY OF
MAYFLOWER DESCENDANTS
BOSTON

PLYMOUTH, MASS., VITAL RECORDS

TRANSCRIBED BY THE EDITOR

(*Continued from Vol. XXXI, p. 184*)

[Vol. 2, p. 191, *continued*]
1808 January 9 Henry Casewell of Plimton & Betsey Reed of Ditto†
Ephraim Sampson of Midd°‡ & Polley Covill of Ditto†
February 13 William Hall & Lucinda Muxson both of Ditto†
America Perce & Catherine Armer people of Colour both of Plymouth
Feb'y 28 John Valler of Plymouth & Remembr Jones of Sandwich
28 William Caswell & Nancey Churchell both of Plymouth

† "Ditto" in every case means "Plymouth".—*Editor*.
‡ Middleborough, Mass

March 5 Joseph Barnes & Jane Brewster both of Plymouth
5 Obediah Covell & Mercy Collings both of Plymouth
12 Nehemiah Holmes & Eunice Morton both of Plymouth
19 Nathaniel Mayo & Hannah Bartlett both of Plymouth
26 Amaziah Churchill & Polly Harlow both of Plymouth
   William Comestock a Resident in Plym° & Hannah Faunce of Ditto
April 2 Gideon Bisbey of Plinton & Mary Williams Cuffs of Plymouth
5 John Adams resident in Plymouth & Sophia Eddy of Plymouth
May 7 Nathan Fish Resident in Plymouth & Hannah Robinson of Plym°
14 Warren Dugless & Rhoda Thrasher both of Plymouth
20 William Barrit & Ruth Wescoat both of Plymouth
28 William Stephens Junr of Plymouth & Nancey Everson of Kingston now resident in Plymouth
   Jesse Donham & Hannah Jackson Bagnall both of Plymouth
[p. 192] 1808   Publishments for Marriage
June 4 Thomas Burges of Plymouth & Jemimah Muxsom resident in Plymouth
   William Keen Jur & Abigail Barnes both of Plymouth
12th James Freeman & Abigail Sewall people of Colour now residents in Plymouth
   Wm Rogers Jur & Rebecca Lanman both of Plym^th
19 Joseph Sears of Plymouth & Hannah Robbins of Carver
   Prince Doten & Sukey Price both of Plymouth
25 Putnam Kimbal Resident in Plymouth & Eloner Donham of Plymouth
July 3rd Gideon Holbrook Jr & Elizabeth Howland both of Plymouth
9 Capt Ezra Finney & Mrs Betsey Bishop both of Plymouth
   Alanson Caswell of Plymouth & Joanna Stetson resident in Plymouth
15 Thomas Muxsom of Carver & Patience Swift of Plymouth
Augst 6 Nicholas Smith & Rebecca Sears both of Plymouth
6 Solomon Holmes & Mercy Crocker both of Plymouth
9 James Bourn of Sandwich & Cynthia Bartlett of Plymouth
13 Frederick Bartlett of Plymouth & Lydia Atwood Donham of Carver
   Joseph Bramhall Junr & Lydia Sherman both of Plymouth
22 Nathaniel Bartlett ye 3rd & Salley Lucas both of Plymouth
23 Crosbey Luce & Betsey Doten both of Plymouth
27th John Clark & Sally Rider both of Plymouth
Sept 17 Job Churchill & Hannah Turner Harlow both of Plymouth
24 Thomas Luce of Plym° & Olive Dellano of Duxboro
   Gideon Perkins & Joanna Drew both of Plymouth
28 Thomas Swift & Lowis Briggs both of Plymouth
30 Isaac Savery Junr of Rochester & Temperance Cornish of Plymouth
Octobr 1 Lewis Donham of Plymouth and Mary Rideington now resident in Plymouth
   Nathan Simmons & Nancey Simmons both of Plymouth
[p. 193] 1808   Publishments for Marriage
Octr 8 Job Ryder Junr & Salley Casseday both of Plymouth
23 Josiah Cotton Esqr & Miss Priscilla Watson both of Plymouth
   Moses Hoyet & Betsey Luce Both of Plymouth
Novembr 12th William Clark Jr & Nancy Bartlett both of Plymouth
   Lewis Drew of Duxbury & Mira Le Baron of Plymouth
19 Samuel Jackson Junr & Nancey Collings both of Plymouth
26 Benjamin Harlow Junr & Levine Shurtleff of Carver
3 Lemuel Robbins Junr & Rachel Baley both of Plymouth
10 Mr William Watson Junr of Plymouth & Miss Hulda Dellano of Duxbo
1809
Janry 14 John Lewis resident in Plymouth & Eliza Foster Donham of Plym°
   David Gray resident in Plymouth & Rebecca Drew of Plymouth
Febry 25 Daniel Vaughan of Carver and Mary Donham of Plymouth
March 11 Benjamin Chubbuck Junr & Bathsheba Harvey both of Plymouth
   Lott Chubbuck & Betsey Faunce both of Plymouth
25 Nathaniel Hewston, & Nancey Harlow ye 2nd both of Plymouth
   April Allen Cornish & Clarrissa Cornish both of Plymouth
8 Jesse Bartlett & Polley Hovey both of Plymouth
21 Jacob Donham of Plymouth & Susanna Thomas of Middleb
May 13th Branch Churchill & Sarah Holmes both of Plymouth
19 Elisha Doten & Hulda Lawrance both of Plymouth
June 4th John Harlow & Betsey Harlow both of Plymouth
11th Elisha Pope of Sandwich & Lydia Cotton of Plymouth
July 1 John Chandler & Hannah Sturtevant both of Plymouth
10 Phillip Haskins of Freetown & Lowis Chubbuck of Plymouth
   Mr Caleb Boutelle & Miss Ann Goodwin both of Plymouth
[p. 194] 1809   Publishments for Marriage
July 22 Daniel Lewis & Lucy Sampson both of Plymouth
Septr 16 Andrew Sturtevant of Savoy & Lucy Lucas of Plymouth
25 Abraham Sanders of Wareham & Anna Morie of Plymouth
30 Thomas Goodwin Junr & Abigail Thomas Torrey both of Plymouth
Octr 15 Silvanus Harlow & Hannah Weston both of Plym^th
20 Silas Valler of Plym° & Deborah Taylor Jones of Sandwich
21 Sylvester Holmes & Esther Holmes both of Plymouth
   William Bartlett ye 3rd & Abia Persons both of Plymouth
   John L Morton & Salley Bent both of Plymouth
28 Nathaniel Woods of Plymouth & Rhoda Coleburn of Deadham
Novr 11 Joseph Shurtleff Ripley & Phebe Pearsons both of Plym°
Decr 16 Branch Pierce & Rebecca Bates both of Plymouth
   Lot Weekes & Cynthia Coval both of Plymouth
   John Harlow & Anna Burges both of Ditto
30 Edward Morton & Priscilla Hewston both of Ditto
1810
January 8 Charles Peterson of Duxboro & Thankfull Clark of Ditto *
Febry 4th Capt Thos Atwood & Elizabeth Tufts of Ditto *
6th David Curtis & Sally Clarke of Ditto *

* "Ditto" here means Plymouth. — Editor.

PLYMOUTH, MASS., VITAL RECORDS

(Continued from page 24)

[p. 196] 1810   Publishments for Marriage

Octob 13 William Polden & Eunice Sturtevant both of Plymouth
24 Phineas Savery of Rochester & Hannah Cornish of Ditto*
27 James Doten & Polley Clark both of Ditto
    Benjamin Thomas of Barnestable & Deborah Bradford of Ditto
    George Bramhall & Sarah Morton both of Ditto
Novr 3 Samuel Dike of Plymouth & Diana Clark Gibbs of Wareham
10 Marshal Lane of Abington & Elizabeth Rogers of Plymouth
Decr 5 Joseph Bates of Plymouth & Abigail Chubbuck of Wareham
7 Daniel Ryder & Lydia Clark both of Plymouth
7 Phillip Taylor of Pembrook and Nancy Lebaron of Plymouth
15 Calvin Cooper & Sarah Morton both of Plymouth
22 Joshua Perkins & Betsey Morton both of Plymouth
1811 Janry 12 Capt Nathaniel Spooner Junr of Plymo & Miss Lucy Willard of Boxborough
    George Adams & Lucy Nye both of Plymouth
19th Bartlet Faunce & Lydia Holmes Savery both of Plymouth
26 Robert Hutchinson & Deborah Brewster both of Plymouth
Febry Hose Churchill & Eunice Morrey both of Plymouth
28 Joshua Thrasher & Deborah Gammons both of Ditto*
March 12 John Cunnet† & Basha Volentine people of Colour both of Ditto
May 4 Samuel West Bagnal & Lois Thomas both of Ditto
9 Benjamin Bumpas & Zilpah Chubbuck both of Ditto
11 John B. Thurston & Phebe Clark both of Ditto
18 Josiah Robbins of Plymouth & Ann Gray Cushman of Plimton
June 1 Mr Isaac LeBaron Junr & Miss Mary Doan both of Plymouth
July 13 Eleazer Holmes & Betsey Rogers both of Plymouth
Augst 3 Jacob Southworth of Duxboro and Cynthia Peterson of Plymouth
10 Elijah Sherman & Cynthia Fish both of Plymouth
[p. 197] 1811   Publishments for Marriage
Augst 17 John Hines & Lucy Donham both residents in Plymouth
31 Mr John Sampson & Miss Priscilla Bramhall both of Plymo
Sept 7 Samuel Lanman & Content Thomas both of Plymouth
14 Asa Dike & Rosannah Pearsons both of Ditto
Oct 5 John Purdy resident in Plymouth & Deborah Hatheway of Ditto

* "Ditto" in every case means Plymouth.
† The marriage record, on original page 379, gives this name as "Gurnet".— Editor.

---

24 Thomas Samson & Mercy Burges both of Plymouth
March 3d Wm Brown Jr & Sally Thomas both of Plymouth
3d Benjn Harlow of Plymouth & Betsey Vaughan of Carver
6 Nathaniel Ellis and Remember Swift both of Plymo
15 Cornelus Morey & Sarah Harlow ye 2nd both of Plymouth
31 Joseph Harris . Desire Holmes both of Ditto
    John Kempton Cobb & Polley Nellson both of Ditto
April 27 Mr James Winslow of Freetown & Mrs Ruth Clark of Ditto*
[p. 195] 1810   Publishments for Marriage
Aprl 28th Capt Wm Le Baron of Rochester & Miss Eliza Le Baron of Plymouth
May 11th Lemuel Barnes and Susanna Marshall of Plymouth
May 19th William Putnam Ripley of Plymouth & Anna Winslow of Scituate
23 Winslow Bradford of Boston & Zilliah Lucas of Plymouth
29th Revd James Kendall of Plymouth & Miss Sally Kendall of Templeton
    John Dike & Bathshea Washburn both of Plymouth
June 16 Seth Churchill & Salley Seabery Simmons both of Plymo
16 William Doten Junr & Lydia Donham both of Plymo
    Samuel Lewis & Mercy Doten both of Plymo
23 Henry Cassedy & Betsey Lewis Holmes both of Plymo
July 14 William Holmes ye 3rd & Mary Holbrook both of Plymo
21 Isaiah Smith & Dille Folied people of Colour now resident in Plymouth
Augst 4 Mr William Simmons of Boston & Miss Lucia Hammatt of Plymouth
    Mr John Roice Thomas, & Miss Mary Howland Lebaron, both of Plymo
    Mr Isaac Goodwin of Sterling & Miss Eliza Hammatt of Plymouth
    John Jackson & Martha Boston both people of Colour and resident in Plymouth
Septemr 1 Mr Jeremiah Holbrook & Miss Pegge Dyer both of Plymouth
1 Samuel Allen & Naome Leach both of Plymouth
6 William Harlow of Middo & Olive Jackson of Ditto*
29th Isaac Tribell & Lois Holbrook of Ditto*
Oct 5 Joseph Churchill of Plimton & Rebecca Morrey of Ditto*
Oct 12th Ellis Shaw of Carver & Deborah Raymond of half way pond
13 Asa Tinkham & Lucinda Hall both of Plymo

(To be continued)

* "Ditto" here means Plymouth. — Editor.

130

Novr 1 Henry Bartlett 2^d & Pruedence Straffin both of Ditto
2 Edward Nicols & Polley Rogers both of Ditto
  The Revd Adoniram Judson Junr of Plym^o & Miss Nancy Hasseltine of Bradford
16 John Nicols of Freetown & Sarah Bramhall of Plym^o
  James Robbins Doten & Betsey Robbins both of Plym^o
  Samuel Sampson of Middleboro & Abigail Bartlett of Ditto*
  Capt Lebaron Goodwin of Plymouth & Miss Sarah Thomas of Plimton
29th Calvin Holmes & Thankfull Clark both of Plymouth
Decr 6 Levi Morton & Susanna Cushman both of Plymouth
14 Abner Bartlett Esqr of Plym^o & Mrs Deborah Earl of Little Compton State of Rhode Island
1812 Jan^ry 16 Amasa Clark & Polley Morton both of Plymouth
18 Barnabas Hedge 3rd & Tryphena Covengton both of Plymouth
Feby 8 William Leonard & Abigail Bartlett both of Plymouth
15 Isaac Morton Sherman & Hope Doten both of Ditto
19 Thomas Blackman & Judith Hinds both residents in Plymouth
  Judeth Hinds forbid the bands by writing under her hand
21 George Washington Gibbs & Elener Besse both of Plymouth
22 Adam Wright of Plimton now resident in Plymouth & Rebecca Shaw of Ditto
March 10 Nathaniel Chubbuck of Plymouth & Ruth Perrey of Wareham
21 William Ripley & Cloe Thrasher both of Plym^o
28 Lewis Gray of Kingston & Judath Holmes of Plymouth
April 4 Thomas Whiteing of Plymouth & Susanna Perrey of Wareham
[p. 193] 1812   Publishments for Marriage
April 18 George Brown & Lowis Valler both of Plymouth
25 Joseph Sturtevant & Mercy Cornish both of Plymouth
May 2 John Samson Pain & Deborah Holmes both of Plymouth
6 Isaiah Raymond of Plym^o & Jane Nickerson of Dartmouth
13 Mr Charles Marcy of Plymouth & Miss Abigail Packard of Bridgew^r
16 Oliver Wood & Betsy Torrance both of Plymouth
30 Edward Savil Resident in Plymouth & Hulda Hall of Plymouth
  William Holmes the 3^d & Bathsheba Doten both of Plymouth
31 Joseph Muxsom & Cintha Hall both residents in Plymouth
12 Robert Russell & Salley Jackson People of Colour & Both Residents in Plym^o
14 Samuel Doten Holmes & Betsey Johnson both of Plymouth
20 James Reed Junr & Salley Hatheway both of Plymouth
27 Lemuel Bradford of Kingston & Bathsheba Nellson of Plymouth
  Thomas Sylvester resident in Plym^o & Mary Perse of Plym^o
  Thomas Wethrell & Lowis Robbins both of Plymouth
July 4 Enock Randall & Nancy Farmer both of Ditto
11 Eber Hall & Elizabeth Burges both of Ditto

* "Ditto" in every case means Plymouth.

131

Aug^st 1st Ebene^zr Nellson Junr & Polley Holmes both of Ditto*
1 David Hoskins & Rhoda Westgate both residents in Plymouth
19 Capt Isaac Bartlett & Miss Rebecca Bartlett both of Plymouth
22 Lothrop Conant & Salley Albertson both of Plymouth
24 Mr Winslow Watson & Miss Harriot Lothrop Goodwin both of Plymouth
29 Jacob Morton & Lydia Howard both of Plymouth
  Solomon Davie Junr & Esther Lebaron both of Plym^o
Septr 5 Levi Whiteing & Mary Barden both of Plym^o
12 Joseph Sanger & Hannah Marcy both of Plym^o
26 William Morrey & Polley Edwards both of Plym^o
  John Loring of Plimton & Abigail Thomas of Plym^o
  Barnabas Holmes Junr and Margaret Rickard both of Plym^o
[p. 199] 1812   Publishments for Marriage
Octr 17 Jeremiah Holbrook & Bethiah Dyre 2nd both of Plymouth
31 Isaac Howland & Phebe Saunders both of Plymouth
Novr 21 Joseph Burge & Salley Richmond both of Plymouth
25th Joseph Holmes 3^d & Esther Rider both of Plymouth
1813 Jan^ry 2 Nathaniel Morton of Plym^o & Salley Ransom of Carver
9 Nehemiah Burbank of Plym^o & Rebecca Soul of Plimton
30 William Thomas Appling of Carver & Deborah Barrow of Plymouth
  Nathan Burges Junr Susanna Wright both of Plymouth
  George Harlow & Lydia Ellis both of Plymouth
February 6 James Chummuck Junr of Plymouth & Alice Cunnet Resident in Plymouth both People of Colour
March 7th Mr Thomas Russell & Miss Mary Ann Goodwin both of Plym^o
13 Abraham Donham & Patience Clark both of Ditto
  Ellis Holmes the 2nd & Lois Holbrook Bartlett both of Ditto
  Charles Knap resident in Plym^o & Sibbil Dike of Plym^o
April 17 Benjamin Westgate Junr & Lucenda Tinkcom both Resident in Plymouth
24 Samuel Sherman the 3rd & Eloner Covington both of Plymouth
May 5 Joshua Hatheway & Rebecca Foster both of Plymouth
  Mr Seth F. Nye of Sandwich & Miss Salley Carver of Plymouth
July 3 Henry Howland and Susanna Leach both of Plymouth
31 Jesse Chummuck of Plym^o & Hannah Reed of Marshpee both People of Colour
Aug^st 13 John Baley & Polley Wood both of Plymouth
18 Joshua Dugless & Mary Pearce both of Plymouth
  Ezra Maxim of Carver & Polley Reed of Ditto
25 Joseph Bartlett the 4th & Grace Cornish both of Ditto
Sep^t 5 Benjamin Warren the 3rd of Plymouth & Ruth Sampson Wright of Plimton
[p. 200] 1813   Publishments for Marriage
Sep^t 8 Ansel Bartlett Junr & Abigail Ripley both of Plymouth
  Elkarah Barres & Scinthia Davis Simmons both of Plymouth

* "Ditto" in every case means Plymouth.

Plymouth, Mass., Vital Records

11 John Sherman Junr of Carver & Eloner Barnes of Plymouth
Entered See Septr 5th* Benjamin Warren the 3rd of Plymouth & Ruth Samson Wright of Plimton
18 Mr Bourn Spooner & Miss Hannah Bartlett both of Plymouth
Octobr 2 George Weston & Polley Holmes both of Plymouth
9 Jabez Swift & Eunice Thomas Donham both of Plymouth
Capt Jeremiah Rich of Orrington & Miss Jane Samson Taylor of Plymouth
16 Mr John Torrey of Boston & Miss Mercia Otis Warrin of Ditto†
Novr 6 Stephen Rogers & Polley Ripley both of Ditto
27 Mr William B Leonard of Plymouth & Miss Ruth Carver of Taunton
Decr 4 Ephraim Chandler of Kingston & Deborah Ryder of Plymouth
4 William Bartlett Junr & Susen Thacher both of Plymouth
11 Jabez Jackson Resident in Plymo & Bethiah Chummuck of Plymouth both people of Colour
Anthoney Olney resident in Plymo & Patty Crane of Canton
18 Lewis Morton of Plymouth & Elizabeth Cushman of Kingston
Clemmont Bates Junr of Hanover & Irana Sanger Burges of Plymouth
Joseph Cooper Junr & Silva Paty both of Plymouth
1814 Janry 8 Henry Swift & Mary Morton both of Plymouth
29 Josiah Gibbs of Sandwich & Jane Swift of Plymouth
Febry 12 William Roberson Resident in Plymouth & Rebecca Austen of Plymouth
22 David Thrasher & Susannah Swift both of Plymouth
March 5 Benjamin Childs of Lee & Fear Chubbuck of Plymouth
Jeremiah Holmes of Plymouth & Rhoda Lucas of Carver
Zibeon Packard of Easton & Sally Dike of Plymouth
[p. 201] 1814 Publishments for Marriage
March 19 Thomas Cooper Holmes of Plymo & Jerusha Howes Harlow of Carver
26 Ivory Hovey Bartlett & Betsey Clark both of Plymouth
April 2 Ellis Barnes & Mary Holmes both of Plymouth
16 Jesse Turner & Elizabeth Ryder both of Plymouth
Benjamin Clark Jun. & Jerusha Morrey the 2nd both of Plymouth
23 Jesse Chummuck & Hannah Reed People of Colour both of Plymouth
May 7 Amos Dean of Waltham & Nancy Robinson Kempton of Plymo
14 Nathaniel Clark 3rd & Harriot Washburn both of Plymouth
21 William Coye & Eliza Shurtleff both of Ditto
21 Alpheus Packard of Plymouth Melinde Parker of Sandwich
28 Jesse Bradford of Plymouth & Meriah Lovell of Barnstable
June 18 Samuel Gibbs & Mary Sampson both of Plymouth
Timothy Allen of Plymouth & Thankfull Snow of Rochester
22 Simeon Vallur Junr of Plymouth & Rachel Jones of Sandwich
Capt Thomas Atwood & Mrs Elizabeth Holmes both of Plymouth

*Sic.
† "Ditto" in every case means Plymouth.

July 16 Lazarus Harlow & Lucy Bradford both of Plymouth
Augst 9 Stillman Washburn of Middo & Myra Bartlett of Plymouth
31 Robert Lovell of Barnestable & Jerusha Bartlett of Plymouth
Septr 10 Lyman Josslyne of Pembrook & Betsey Dellano of Plymouth
Octr 22 Thomas Sherman Junr & Betsey Seas* both of Plymouth
29 Thomas Bartlett the 3rd & Lucenda Cornish both of Ditto
Novr 5 Jabez Burges & Salley Manter both of Ditto
Mr Michael Hodge Junr of Newberry Port & Mrs Betsey H Elliot of Plymouth
19 Otis Nicols & Sarah Clark both of Plymouth
Benjamin Wescot & Content Hall both of Ditto
Mr Josiah Diman & Miss Mary Holmes both of Ditto
26 Zacheus Harlow & Jemimah Burges both of Ditto

(To be continued)

*This is "Sears" in the marriage record on original page 379. — Editor.

THE MAYFLOWER DESCENDANT

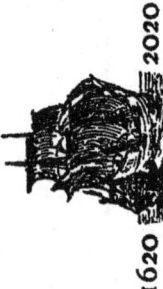

A QUARTERLY MAGAZINE OF
PILGRIM GENEALOGY AND HISTORY

VOLUME XXXIII

1935

PUBLISHED BY THE
MASSACHUSETTS SOCIETY OF
MAYFLOWER DESCENDANTS
BOSTON

PLYMOUTH, MASS., VITAL RECORDS

TRANSCRIBED BY THE EDITOR

(Continued from Vol. XXXII, p. 133)

[Vol. 2, p. 202]   Publishments for Marriage
1815 Janry 14 Alvan Sampson & Susan Crandon both of Plymouth
Febry 3 Elisha Lapum, & Polley Fish, both of Plymouth
3 Elkanah Woodward & Salley Nicols both of Plymouth
25 Merrick Ryder & Lucy Dellano both of Plymouth
March 9 Elijah Lincoln of Norton & Patience Bates of Plymouth
11 Thomas Sears Junr & Rebecca Collings both of Plymouth
14 John Howard and Eunice Burges both of Plymouth This Marriage forbidden by Thos Burges
April 8 Samuel Chapman resident in Plymouth & Nancy Churchill of Plymouth
13 John Dugless & Elizabeth Haskens both of Plymouth
22 Thomas Haskins of Plymouth & Deborah Chamberlin of Rochester
May 13 Sylvanus Stephen of Sumner District of Main & Betsey Doten of Plymouth
June 3 Clemmons Jones Resident in Plymouth & Mary Dike of Plymouth
5 Dennis Perce of Rochester & Melintha Raymond of Plymouth
16 Isaac Manchister of New bedford & Harriot Bartlett of Plymouth
Nathaniel Nye Junr of Sandwich & Deborah Clark of Plymouth
24 Mr Joseph Avery of Plymouth & Miss Sarah Thaxter of Worcester
Henry Whiteing & Grace Holmes both of Plymouth
Joseph Allen & Mary Sherman Holmes both of Plymouth
July 3 Jeremiah Bourn Swift of Wareham & Polly Lucas of Plymouth
Augst 12 Truman Cook Holmes, & Jennet Allen, both of Plymouth
19 Josiah Clark Burbank & Mary Durfey both of Plymouth

26 George Wellington now resident in Plymouth and Lucretia Bartlett of Plymouth

Sep^t 1 Joseph Muxsom & Nancy Simmons both of Plymouth
16 Caleb Fish of Plymouth & Mary Kowls* Harding of Truro
Octo^r 7 Josiah Sampson & Hannah Burges both of Plymouth
[p. 203]   Publishments for Marriage
1815 Octo^r 7 Joseph Vose of Boston & Deborah Churchil of Plymouth
Henry McCarter & Nancy Hewston both of Plymouth
Charles Goodwin & Hannah Harlow both of Plymouth
14 Cornelus Holmes & Lucy Morton both of Plymouth
21 Joshua Besse, & Betsey Berce both of Plymouth
Novr 4 Peter Hendrick Smith a resident in Plymouth, and Lydia Shearman of New Bedford
Decr 1 Rufuss Gibs of Sandwich & Abigail Whiteing of Plym^o
1 Lucas Donham of Plymouth & Metilda Lovel of Abington
9 William Cobb & Cintha Nellson both of Plymouth
9 America Perce & Vilot Sanders People of Colour both of Plymouth
16 James Mor^ton Junr of Plymouth & Betsey Coan of Truro
John Lemi Morton & Lilley Russell Torrance both of Plymouth
1816 January 6 Barneby Winslow of Freetown & Sarah Morrey of Plymouth
27 Nathaniel Bartlett the 3rd & Susan Diman both of Plymouth
31 Peter Olever, & Deborah Rafe, both people of Colour now resident in Plymouth
Feby 3 Mr William L. Gordon of the United States Navy and Miss Sophia Cotton of Plymouth
10 Israel Briggs of Wareham & Nancy Clark of Plymouth
14 William Dennis, Resident in Plym^o & Phebe Bates of Plymouth
March 2 George William Virgen & Mary Barnes the 2nd both of Plym^o
9 Reubin White of Wareham & Beulah King of Plymouth
17 Levi Maxim & Rube Hall, both of Plymouth
22 William Burges & Polley Bartlett both of Plymouth
23 John Howland of Plymouth & Nancy Saunders of Plymouth also
24 Capt John Russell & Miss Deborah Spooner both of P[lymouth]
[p. 204]   Publishments for Marriage
1816 April 1 Stephen Ellis of Plymouth & Hannah Raymond of Sandwich
1 Derias Wesgate & Orpha Hall both of Plymouth
12 Capt Josiah Carver, & Mrs Abigail Keen both of Plymouth
21 Henry Robbins, and Margaret Harper Banks, both of Plymouth
May 4 John Tribble & Mary Holmes both of Plymouth
11 Bartlett Gibbs of Wareham & Jerusha Harlow of Plymouth
11 Nathaniel Covel of Sandwich & Sarah Holmes of Plymouth
11 James Dugless resident in Plymouth & Eliza Sarah Baument of Boston
18 James Tribble & Betsey Holmes both of Plymouth
23 Israel Briggs & Patty Swift both of Plymouth
25 Willson Churchill & Sukey Lucas both of Plymouth
June 1 Alvan Vaughan of Carver & Sarah S. Ripley of Plymouth
1 Jacob Swift of Plymouth and Mary Savery of Rochester
1 Thomas Faunc & Sarah Everson Savory both of Plymouth
14 Stephen Vay resident in Plym^o & Bathsheba Hollis of Plymouth
14 Alexander Ripley, & Hannah Shaw Flemmons both of Plymouth
29 Lewis Churchell & Hannah Comninton both of Plymouth
July 27 John Nickerson & Lydia Howland both of Plymouth
Augst 11 Lemuel Savery of Plymouth and Rupah Thomas of Middleboro
17 Mr Samuel Avery Collin & Miss Esther Churchell both of Plym^o
24 Lemuel Morton Junr of Plymouth & Hannah Gibbs of Sandwich
Joshua Weeks of the Town of Gray* & Lydia Barrows of Plymouth
Spoke for ⅌ Wm Harlow of Plimton
Ezra Burbank Junr of Plymouth & Lucy Hunt of Duxboro
Isaac Davee & Rhode Perry both of Plymouth
[Da]niel Gail of Plymouth & Betsey Windsor of Duxboro Ent^d the 12th August

(*To be continued*)

---

* An error for "Knowles". So recorded in Truro Vital Records (Boston, 1933), pp. 210, 217. — *Editor.*

* Gray, Me. — *Editor.*

PLYMOUTH, MASS., VITAL RECORDS

TRANSCRIBED BY THE EDITOR

(Continued from page 35)

[Vol. 2, p. 205]   Publishments for Marriage
1816 Sept 2 Stephen Thomas & Sukey Bartlett both of Plymouth
7th William Howland & Polley Bramhall Clark both of Plymouth
28 James Glover Gleeson & Lucy T Bartlett both of Plymo
Octobr 5 Thomas Drew & Lucia Waison both of Plymouth
Isaac E. Cobb & Elizabeth Bartlett both of Plymouth
Stetson Chadler of Plimton & Elize Marston of Plymouth
19 Roswell Ballard of Plimton & Hannah Sampson of Plymouth
25 William Harlow & Sophia Holmes Both of Plymouth
William Nightingill of Sandwich & Elizabeth Cahoon of Plymouth
Zaben Olney resident in Plymouth & Rebecca Morton of Plymouth
Calvin Howland resident in Plymouth & Lydia Nickerson of Plymouth
29 Warren Bumpas of Wareham & Sarah Valler of Plymouth
30 Rowland Chubbuck of Plymo and Hannah Swift of Wareham
31 Asa Weston of Taunton & Hannah Morton Luce of Plymouth
Novr 2 Edward Besse of Plymouth & Hannah Gibbs of Wareham
2 Nathaniel Barnes & Hannah Goddard both of Plymouth
Harvey Weston & Lucy Harlow both of Plymouth
6 Benjamin Ellis & Judath Rennols both of Plymouth
Phineas Swift Junr of Plymouth & Olive Crowel of Sandwich
7 Chandler Robbins & Eloner Holmes both of Plymouth
9 Capt John Virgen & Miss Abigale Davie both of Plymouth
16 Josiah Cornish Junr of Plymo & Charlotte Wadsworth of Duxboro
Dec 14 Caleb Finney and Phebe Leonard both of Plymouth
1817 January 11 George Washburn & Margaret James Keen both of Plymouth
11 Nathaniel Cobb Lannan . & Nancey Ellis Bagnall both of Plymouth

[p. 206]   Publishments for Marriage
1817 March 15th Amasa Fuller of Attleborough & Nancy Finney of Plymouth
16 Thomas Caswell of Middo & Mary Dunber Vallur of Plymouth
22 Joseph Sampson of Plymton & Harriot Ryder of Plymouth
29 Edward Burt resident in Plymo & Betsey Donham of Plymouth
April 2 Capt Malletiah Bartlett of Plymo and Miss Salley Cushman of Kingston
4 Charles Brewster & Ellen Bradford both of Plymouth
18 Allen Raymond & Fear Chubbuck, both of Plymouth
18 Edward Miller Esqr of Quinsey & Miss Caroline Nicolson of Plymouth
26 Henry Bartlett Junr & Fanney Churchell both of Plymouth
Job E. Brewster of Duxboro & Lydia Doten of Plymouth
May 3 Nathaniel M. Davis Esqr of Plymouth & Miss Harriot Mitchell of Bridgewr
10 Lazarus Bartlett & Thankfull Bartlett both of Plymouth
17 Bartlett Ellis & Elizabeth Barnes both of Plymouth
Jeroboam Swift & Sarah Leach both of Plymouth
31 Solomon Bartlett and Clarisse Greenough I.inzey, both of Plymouth People of Colour
Caleb Ryder & Harriot Holmes both of Plymouth
June 14 Daniel Soul Junr of Plimton & Content Holmes of Plymouth
17 Mr William Goodwin of Plymouth, & Mrs Deborah Briggs, Resident in Plymouth, or Orleans
28 Rufus Skiff of Chilmark & Lowis Swift of Plymouth
28 Spooner Cornish of Plymouth & Ruth Harvey of Bath
28 Mr Charles Marcy & Miss Charlotte Warren both of Plymouth
July 5 Cannady Reed, & Dinah Edwards, People of Colour both of Plymouth
6 Leonard Snow & Meriah Holmes both of Plymouth
13 Mr Thomas J. Lobdell of Boston & Miss Hannah Sturtevant of Plymouth
Elkanah Holmes & Lowis Valler both of Plymouth

[p. 207]   Publishments in order for Marriage
1817 August 23 William Cunnet, & Clarrissa Joseph, People of Colour. both of Plymouth.
28 John Haskens & Orpah Hall both residents in Plymouth
29 Nathan Whiteing & Betsey Howland both of Plymouth
Daniel Goddard Junr & Mary Finney both of Plymouth
Sept 4 Tillden Keen & Joannah Pearsons both of Plymouth

(To be continued)

PLYMOUTH, MASS., VITAL RECORDS

(Continued from page 141)

[Vol. 2, on p. 207]
Bristol Octobr 2nd Anno: Domini 1816
This Day I the Subscriber Joind Mr Jacob Covington and Miss Patty Holbrook both of Plymouth in the Commonwealth of Massachusetts: in the bans of Marriage   Attest N. Bullock Just{e} Peace

[*The preceding marriage was entered out of place. The Intentions of September, 1817, were then continued, as follows.—Editor.*]

13 Benjamin Robbins of Plymouth and Betsey Thomas Resident in Plymouth
20 Thomas Wright of Mount Vernon State of New Hampshire — Mary Richmond Flemmons of Plymouth
27 Capt Lemuel Clark and and Miss Lydia Bartlett Finney both of Plymouth
   Samuel Bradford & Lucy Gibbs both of Plymouth
Octobr 4 Samuel Leonard & Lucy C Sepit People of Colour both of Plym{o}
[Samuel Long & Salley Holmes both of Plymouth Ent{d} by Mistake*]
18 Samuel Liscom & Elizabeth Westgate both Residents In Plymouth
25 Reuben Peterson of Duxboro & Deborah Clark of Plymouth
   Mr John Goodwin of Plymouth & Miss Dorothy Gibbs of Sandwich
Nov 23 Lemuel Rickard and Nancey Bagnell both of Plymouth
29 Joseph Sampson & Hannah Burges both of Plymouth
Decr 15 Silas Braley of Freetown & Esther Shurtleff of Plymouth
21 Thomas Green of Wareham & Abigail Holmes of Plymouth
[p. 208]   Publishments In order for Marriage
1817 Decr 26 Abraham Williams Nye of Sandwich & Abigail Clark Cornish of Plymouth
1818 Jan{ry} 10 Elisha Swift of Wareham & Betsey Clark of Plymouth
17 Bartlett Cobb and Betsey Dugless both of Plymouth

*This entry has been crossed out.

Feb_y 7th David Diman Jun_r & Abigail Bartlett Nelson of both of Plymouth
28th Samuel Fish & Ruth Rogers Goddard both of Plymouth
March 7th Nathaniel Cushing of Duxboro & Hannah J Harlow of Plymouth
Ap_l 12 Nathan Whiting Jun_r and Experience Finney both of Plym.
Ap_l 12 George Bartlett of Portland & Mary N. Delano of Plym_o
Ap_l 19 Lemuel Simmons Jun_r & Priscilla Sherman both of Plymouth
Ap_l 19 Charles Churchill of Plimpton & Abigail Russell of Plymouth
Ap_l 26 Elijah Edson of Bridgwater, & Miss Nancy Clark of Plymouth
Ap_l 26 Ira Bailey & Phoebe Bartlett Holmes, both of Plym_o
May 10 Levi Haskins of Middleborough, a resident in Plym: and Temperance Hall of Plymouth.
May 24 Sylvanus Ripley of Plympton, and Sally Sherman of Plymouth
June 21. Ellis Nightingale of Sandwich, & Hannah Swift of Plymouth
July 12. Nathaniel Holmes 3d, & Sarah Fish, both of Plymouth
July 26. George Thrasher Jun_r & Content Cornish, both of Plymouth
[p. 209] 1818. Intentions of Marriage Published
August 9. Joseph Robbins Jun_r of Carver, and Rebecca Burgess of Plymouth.
August 30. William Spooner & Hannah Otis Nicolson, both of Plymouth.
August 30. Abraham Jackson & Harriet Otis Goddard, both of Plymouth.
September 13. Joseph Pierce Drew & Ruth Rogers Bartlett, both of Plymouth.
September 13. Ichabod Weston Barstow of Pembroke & Sarah Roberts Clarke of Plymouth.
September 20. Ezekiel Harding, resident in Plymouth, & Deborah Chubbuck of Plymouth.
September 20 Lewis Weston Jun_r & Martha Bartlett Drew both of Plymouth.
Septem_r 27. Josiah Robbins & Rebecca Jackson, both of Plymouth.
October 18. Ichabod Morton Jun_r & Miss Patty Weston, both of Plymouth.
October 25. Ezra Harlow Jun_r & Rebecca Dike, both of Plymouth.
Nov_r 1. Nathan Bacon Robbins & Lucia Ryder, both of Plymouth
Nov_r 15. Benjamin Packer of Plymouth, and Molly Young, resident in Plymouth.
Nov_r 15. Amasa Morton & Deborah Morey, both of Plymouth

(To be continued)

THE
MAYFLOWER DESCENDANT

1620   2020

A QUARTERLY MAGAZINE OF
PILGRIM GENEALOGY AND HISTORY

VOLUME XXXIV

1937

PUBLISHED BY THE
MASSACHUSETTS SOCIETY OF
MAYFLOWER DESCENDANTS
BOSTON

PLYMOUTH, MASS., VITAL RECORDS

TRANSCRIBED BY THE EDITOR

(*Continued from Vol. 33, p. 180*)

[Original Vol. 2, p. 210] 1818 Intentions of Marriage published.
Novr 15. Ichabod Morey of Plymouth, & Mary Churchill of Plympton
Novr 15. Nathaniel Harlow & Margaret Bartlett both of Plymouth
Novr 15. Ephraim Lucas & Sally Loring, both of Plymouth.
Novr 29. Gideon Holbrook & Mrs Nancy Blackman, both of Plymouth.
Decr 3 Thanksgiving, Charles Raymond of Plymouth & Jerusha Clark, resident in Plymouth.
Decr 6 Charles Bramhall & Nancy, Ellis Brewster, both of Plymouth.
1819
Jany 10 Levi Whiting & Deborah Morton, both of Plymouth.
Jany 17. Elijah Macumber Junr & Deborah Thomas, both of Plymouth.
Jany 17. Lemuel Colburn & Susan Moore, residents in Plymouth.
Jany 24. John Howland & Nancy Lucas, both of Plymouth.
Feby 7. James Mcurary, foreigner & Hope Wenford, of Plymouth.

Feby 21. Samuel Andrews, a foreigner, & Jerusha Bearce of Plymouth
Feb^r 28 Thomas Oldham of Duxbury, & Miss Betsey Brewster of Plymouth.
[p. 211] 1819. Intentions of Marriage published.
March 11th Ellis Morey & Rebecca Clarke, both of Plymouth
March 11th Sylvanus Rogers Jr. & Jane Lucas, both of Plymouth.
March 4th (omitted in place) George Keen & Sarah Warren Churchill both of Plymouth
April 25th John Saunders & Betsey Sherman 2d, both of Plymouth
April 25th William Randall & Patience Churchill, both of Plymouth
May 2d Daniel Gale & Harriot Sampson, both of Plymouth
May 9th. Polycarpus Parker of Plympton & Sarah Jackson of Plymouth.
May 9th. John Smith, a resident in Plym'th & Sally Haskell of Plym'th.
May 9th. Ephraim Paty, & Patty Morton, both of Plymouth
May 16th. William Martin Brewster of Duxbury, & Sarah Warren of Plym:
May 16th. William Hall & Sarah Burgess, both of Plymouth.
May 30th. Mary Richmond Flemmons & Peter Holmes, both of Plymouth
June 20th. Zephaniah B. Lucas & Eliza I. Blackmer, both of Plymouth.
July 4th. Daniel Foster & Lucy Carver Faunce, both of Plymouth.
July 4th. Richard Bagnal & Lydia Sampson, both of Plymouth.
July 11th. Isaac Jackson Lucas & Catherine Howland, both of Plym^o
August. 1. Freeman Cahoun of Plymouth & Roxana Grunney Whareham*
August. 15. John Foster Dunham, Sarah Tufts Wiswall, both of Plymouth.
August. 22. Clarke Cornish, Plymouth, Betsey Freeman, Sandwich.
August. 22. Vinal Burgess, Esther Clarke, both of Plymouth
September 5. David Bradford Jr. Plymouth, Betsey Briggs, Freetown.
September 5. Isaac Barnes. Jr. Betsey Thomas Davee, both of Plymouth.
September 12. John Blackmer Jr. Esther Bartlett, both of Plymouth.
September. 26. Ezra Clarke, Sarah Blackmer, both of Plymouth.
September. 26. Calvin Raymond. Mary Cahoon, both of Plymouth.
October. 3. Jesse Harlow, Mary Lothrop Nelson, both of Plymouth.
October. 10. Joseph S. Reed, Boston, Sally Goodwin, Plymouth.
October. 10. Ephraim Whiting, Patience Everson, both of Plymouth
October. 17. James Bradford. Eleanor Hustons, both of Plymouth
October. 31. Samuel Battles Jr. New Hampshire, Lydia B. Holmes, P.
October. 31. Frederick Augustus Cotton, Betsey Foster, both of Plymouth.
[p. 212] 1819. Intentions of Marriage published.
November 7. Thomas Jenkins Lobdell, Boston, Mary Russell, Plym^o
November 7. Zacheus Kempton Jr. Abigail Withrell Cox, both of P.
November 7. Harvey Dunham, Plymouth, Eunice Thomas, Middleborough

* Roxanna Grunney, of Wareham, Mass.

November 7. Samuel Lewis, Mercy Sears, both of Plymouth.
November. 14. Abiathar Hawkes, Middleboro', Lydia Clarke of Plymouth
November. 14. John H. Clarke. Deborah Doten, both of Plymouth.
November. 21. Nathaniel Hodges Duxbury* . Rebecca Holmes, Plymouth.
November. 28. Sylvanus Smith, resident in, Betsey B. Robbins of, Plymouth
November. 28. Ellis Holmes Jr Plymouth, Catharine Gibbs, Sandwich.
December, 5. David Sears, Nancy Manter, both of Plymouth.
December, 19. Judah Perry, Betsey Anderson, both of Plymouth.
December, 19. James Smith, Dunbarton (New Hampshire) Sarah Finney, Plym^o
December. 26. David Maxim, Sarah Burgess, both, of Plymouth.
1820.
Jany. 23. Benjamin Westgate Jr. Abigail Haskins, both of Plymouth.
Mar. 25. William Swift & Betsey Holmes both of Plymouth
Ap^l 2. Jesse Lucas & Deborah Bagnell, both of Plymouth
Ap^l 6. John Oldam of Sumner & Sarah S. Churchill of Plym^o
Ap^l 23. Mark Cahoun of Plymouth & Isa Young of Orleans
Ap^l 23. James Wadsworth, Duxbury & Lydia Sylvester of Plymouth
Ap^l 30. William Shaw Russell & Mary Winslow Hayward both of P.
Ap^l 30. Stephen Lucas & Rebecca Holmes, both of Plymouth
May 14. Anselm Rickard & Cynthia Lucas both of Plymouth
May 14. Melvin Bailey & Maria Paty both of Plymouth
May 21. Jonas Kieth of Bridgwater & Mercy Ellis Bartlett of P
June 4. Charles Robbins of Plymouth & Emily Fuller of Kingston
June 4. Howard Nichols & Susan Clarke both of Plymouth
July 2. Ellis Skiff of Sandwich & Abigail Blackwell of P.
July, 2. Charles Bartlett & Lucinda Bartlett both of P.
July 2. John Nichols of Assonet & Hannah Johnson of P.
" 2. Samuel Powers of Philadelphia† & Hannah Scot people of Colour
July, 9. John Buckley (a foreigner) & Rebecca Long of P.
" 9. Prince Manter & Lydia Douglass both of Pth
July, 9. Phineas Norris & Susan Saunders both of P.
July, 20. Barzillaia Bumpus & Daty Cahoun both of Plymouth
Augt 20. William Lucas Jr of P. & Pamela Gross of Scituate
Augt 27. Charles Brown of Boston & Lucy C. Jackson of P.
Sep^t 17 Azbury Powers of Philadelphia & Jane Dey of P. (People of Colour)
Sept 17. Seth Benson & Lydia West Holmes both of Plymouth
Sept 17. William Swift & Mary Finney both of Plymouth

(To be continued)

* Of Duxbury, Mass.

† " of Philadelphia " is a footnote at the bottom of the original page.

VITAL RECORDS OF THE TOWN OF PLYMOUTH

A

Name	Page
ABBET, Joseph	121
ABBOT, Joseph	122
ABBOTT, Joseph	78
ABBOTT, Mercy	78
ABRAHAMS, Deliverance	69
ACQUIT, Sarah	77
ACQUIT, Sarah	120
ADAMS, Ffrances	27
ADAMS, Francis	77
ADAMS, Francis	90
ADAMS, Francis	120
ADAMS, Francis (Capt.)	90
ADAMS, George	213
ADAMS, Jemima	74
ADAMS, Jemima	127
ADAMS, Jemimah	27
ADAMS, John	27
ADAMS, John	212
ADAMS, Keziah	77
ADAMS, Keziah	90
ADAMS, Keziah	171
ADAMS, Lydia	90
ADAMS, Lyman	207
ADAMS, Mary	27
ADAMS, Mary	72
ADAMS, Mary	130
ADAMS, Richard	27
ADAMS, Saml	90
ADAMS, Samuel	90
ADAMS, Sarah	105
ADAMS, Sarah	107
ADAMS, Sarah	131
ADAMS, Thomas	27
AKEN, Sylvester	181
ALBERTSON, ----- (male)	168
ALBERTSON, Elizabeth	168
ALBERTSON, Jacob	105
ALBERTSON, Jacob	107
ALBERTSON, Jacob	168
ALBERTSON, Joseph Ryder	168
ALBERTSON, Lydia	168
ALBERTSON, Lydia Gardner	168
ALBERTSON, Margaret	107
ALBERTSON, Margaret	168
ALBERTSON, Martha	168
ALBERTSON, Martha	200
ALBERTSON, Polley	207
ALBERTSON, Rufus	168
ALBERTSON, Salley	214
ALBERTSON, William	168
ALDEN, John	197
ALEXANDER, Catharine Elizabeth	136
ALEXANDER, Charlotte	136
ALEXANDER, John Knowls	136
ALEXANDER, Samuel	136
ALEXANDER, Samuel	206
ALEXANDER, Samuel Thomas	136
ALLBERTSON, Jacob	188
ALLDEN, Gideon S. (Capt.)	206
ALLEN, Adam	177
ALLEN, Anstus	195
ALLEN, Benja.	136
ALLEN, Benjamin	136
ALLEN, Benjamin	171
ALLEN, Betsey	139
ALLEN, Beza	136
ALLEN, Eliza.	163
ALLEN, Elizabeth	66
ALLEN, Elizabeth	199
ALLEN, Esther	163
ALLEN, Esther	194
ALLEN, Esther	197
ALLEN, Ezra	116
ALLEN, Francis	73
ALLEN, Francis	80
ALLEN, Francis	130
ALLEN, James	66
ALLEN, James	206
ALLEN, Jane	73
ALLEN, Jane	80
ALLEN, Jean	175
ALLEN, Jennet	216
ALLEN, Jenny	80
ALLEN, John	163
ALLEN, John	182
ALLEN, John	200
ALLEN, John	204
ALLEN, Joseph	67
ALLEN, Joseph	69
ALLEN, Joseph	216
ALLEN, Mary	67
ALLEN, Mary	69
ALLEN, Mary	75
ALLEN, Mary	118
ALLEN, Polley	199
ALLEN, Samuel	213
ALLEN, Thomas	139
ALLEN, Thomas Jefferson	139
ALLEN, Timothy	215
ALLEN, William	163
ALLEN, William	202
ALLYN, Elizabeth	29
ALLYN, Joseph	29
ALLYN, Mary	29
AMES, Elizabeth	185
AMES, Jonathan	70
AMES, Rebeca	54
AMES, Rebeckah	70
AMOS, Nabbe	202
ANDERSON, Alexander	171
ANDERSON, Andrew	195
ANDERSON, Betsey	222
ANDERSON, Elizabeth	200
ANDERSON, John	206
ANDERSON, John	200
ANDERSON, Priscilla	190
ANDERSON, Willm.	189
ANDREWS, Samuel	222
ANDROS, Ebenazar	36
ANDROS, Joannah	36
ANDROS, John	36
ANDROS, Mary	36
ANDROS, Sarah	36
APPLING, William Thomas	214
ARMER, Catherine	211
ARMOR, George	207
ARNOLD, Gamaliel	181
ASHLEY, Elizabeth	27
ASHLEY, Joseph	27
ASHLEY, Joseph	112
ASHLEY, Thankfull	106
ASHLEY, Thomas	27
ATEQUEEN, Jeremiah	119
ATKINS, Jean	177
ATWOOD, Abigail	102
ATWOOD, Abigail	181
ATWOOD, Adoniram	148
ATWOOD, Barnabus	9
ATWOOD, Debo.	198
ATWOOD, Edward Winslow	169
ATWOOD, Elijah	102

VITAL RECORDS OF THE TOWN OF PLYMOUTH

ATWOOD, Elizabeth	9	ATWOOD, Lydia	187	AVERY, Betsey	201
ATWOOD, Elizabeth	39	ATWOOD, Lydia	197	AVERY, Joseph	216
ATWOOD, Elizabeth	174	ATWOOD, Marcy	105	AVERY, Polley	193
ATWOOD, Elizabeth	187	ATWOOD, Margerett	180		
ATWOOD, Experience	128	ATWOOD, Mary	9	**B**	
ATWOOD, Experience	39	ATWOOD, Mary	74		
ATWOOD, Experience	74	ATWOOD, Mary	102	B--ANT, Mima	120
ATWOOD, Experience	104	ATWOOD, Mary	124	BAB, Richard	183
ATWOOD, George	39	ATWOOD, Mary	190	BABB, Abigail	201
ATWOOD, George	102	ATWOOD, Micah	102	BABB, Betsey	201
ATWOOD, George	178	ATWOOD, Nancy Churchill	148	BABB, Sarah	198
ATWOOD, Hannah	143	ATWOOD, Nathaniel	189	BACON, -----	107
ATWOOD, Hannah	148	ATWOOD, Nathaniell	9	BACON, Abigail	165
ATWOOD, Hannah	163	ATWOOD, Nathanill	9	BACON, Charles	59
ATWOOD, Hannah	186	ATWOOD, Phebe	201	BACON, Charles Henry	165
ATWOOD, Hannah Tuffs	148	ATWOOD, Priscilla	173	BACON, David	59
ATWOOD, Harriet	169	ATWOOD, Rebecca	196	BACON, David	165
ATWOOD, Harriet Elizabeth	169	ATWOOD, Rebeckah	102	BACON, David	189
ATWOOD, Isaac	9	ATWOOD, Rebeckah	171	BACON, David	208
ATWOOD, Isaac	78	ATWOOD, Salley	199	BACON, Desire	70
ATWOOD, Isaac	143	ATWOOD, Sarah	74	BACON, Elisabeth	129
ATWOOD, Isaac	163	ATWOOD, Sarah	102	BACON, Elizabeth	71
ATWOOD, Isaac	184	ATWOOD, Sarah	182	BACON, Elizabeth	165
ATWOOD, Joanna	102	ATWOOD, Sarah	199	BACON, George	155
ATWOOD, Joanna	187	ATWOOD, Solomon	58	BACON, George	202
ATWOOD, Joannah	9	ATWOOD, Solomon	112	BACON, Henry Samson	165
ATWOOD, Joannah	77	ATWOOD, Solomon	115	BACON, Jacob	59
ATWOOD, John	9	ATWOOD, Solomon	187	BACON, Jacob	106
ATWOOD, John	39	ATWOOD, Susanna	201	BACON, Jacob	165
ATWOOD, John	77	ATWOOD, Thomas	143	BACON, Jacob (Rev.)	59
ATWOOD, John	102	ATWOOD, Thomas	201	BACON, Jacob (Rev.)	113
ATWOOD, John	118	ATWOOD, Thomas (Capt.)	215	BACON, Jacob (Rev.)	188
ATWOOD, John	124	ATWOOD, Thos. (Capt.)	212	BACON, Jacob (Rev.)	208
ATWOOD, John	180	ATWOOD, Wait	183	BACON, Joanna	128
ATWOOD, John	185	ATWOOD, Wait	204	BACON, John	73
ATWOOD, John	203	ATWOOD, Waite	143	BACON, John	127
ATWOOD, John	208	ATWOOD, Waite	194	BACON, John	128
ATWOOD, John	74	ATWOOD, William	102	BACON, John	131
ATWOOD, John	75	ATWOOD, William	169	BACON, John	196
ATWOOD, John	117	ATWOOD, William	190	BACON, Lucy	165
ATWOOD, John	148	ATWOOD, William	206	BACON, Mary	59
ATWOOD, John Murray	148	ATWOOD, Zacheus	143	BACON, Mary	155
ATWOOD, Keziah	77	AUSTEN, Rebecca	215	BACON, Mary	165
ATWOOD, Keziah	120	AUSTIN, Alva C.	159	BACON, Mary	188
ATWOOD, Lydia	58	AUSTIN, Bethiah	159	BACON, Mary	199
ATWOOD, Lydia	77	AUSTIN, Elizabeth Owen	159	BACON, Mary	208
ATWOOD, Lydia	78	AUSTIN, Henry Carter	159	BACON, Molley	155
ATWOOD, Lydia	112	AUSTIN, Isaac	159	BACON, Nathan	155
ATWOOD, Lydia	118	AUSTIN, Isaac L.	159	BACON, Oliver	59
ATWOOD, Lydia	143	AUSTIN, Richard	196	BACON, Rufus	165
ATWOOD, Lydia	178	AUSTIN, Selden	159	BACON, Samuel	59

VITAL RECORDS OF THE TOWN OF PLYMOUTH

Name	Page	Name	Page	Name	Page
BACON, Sarah	73	BAGNELL, Lydia	168	BARNEBE, Judeth	22
BACON, Thomas	59	BAGNELL, Nancey	219	BARNEBE, Ledia	71
BACOR, Eleanar	69	BAGNELL, Richard	61	BARNEBE, Lidiah	71
BADGER, Josiah	193	BAGNELL, Richard	168	BARNEBE, Ruth	67
BAGELET, Richard	130	BAGNELL, Richard William	168	BARNEBE, Ruth	99
BAGNAL, Benjamin	168	BAGNELL, Susan Sampson	168	BARNEBE, Stephen	22
BAGNAL, Bethiah	168	BAILEY, Ira	220	BARNEBE, Stephen	67
BAGNAL, Eliza.	195	BAILEY, Melvin	222	BARNEBE, Stephen	99
BAGNAL, Hannah	191	BAKER, Abner	189	BARNES, see BRANES	
BAGNAL, Hannah Jackson	168	BAKER, Hannah	120	BARNES, ----- (female)	58
BAGNAL, Joseph	168	BAKER, Samuell	130	BARNES, Abigail	133
BAGNAL, Lydia	200	BAKER, Thankfull	185	BARNES, Abigail	164
BAGNAL, Nancey Ellis	168	BALEY, Clift	209	BARNES, Abigail	190
BAGNAL, Richard	168	BALEY, John	214	BARNES, Abigail	212
BAGNAL, Richard	189	BALEY, Rachel	212	BARNES, Alice	93
BAGNAL, Richard	222	BALEY, Sarah	174	BARNES, Alice	177
BAGNAL, Samuel West	168	BALLARD, Roswell	218	BARNES, Alice	178
BAGNAL, Samuel West	213	BALSTON, Mary	201	BARNES, Alse	37
BAGNAL, Sarah	199	BALSTON, Joseph	198	BARNES, Benja.	123
BAGNAL, Spinks	197	BALSTON, Nanse	200	BARNES, Benjamin	37
BAGNAL, Spinks	198	BAMHALL, Joshua	70	BARNES, Benjamin	58
BAGNALD, Elizabeth	75	BAMHALL, Sarah	70	BARNES, Benjamin	78
BAGNALD, Elizabeth	117	BANKS, Isaac	201	BARNES, Benjamin	92
BAGNALL, Benjamin	55	BANKS, Lilleston	206	BARNES, Benjamin	149
BAGNALL, Benjamin	101	BANKS, Margaret Harper	217	BARNES, Benjamin	177
BAGNALL, Benjamin	105	BARDEN, Deborah	73	BARNES, Benjamin	188
BAGNALL, Benjamin	107	BARDEN, Deborah	74	BARNES, Benjamin	204
BAGNALL, Benjamin	173	BARDEN, Deborah	125	BARNES, Benjamin	209
BAGNALL, Benjamin	175	BARDEN, Mary	214	BARNES, Benjamine	37
BAGNALL, Elizabeth	55	BARDEN, Stephen	73	BARNES, Betsey	144
BAGNALL, Elizabeth	72	BARDEN, Stephen	130	BARNES, Betsey	164
BAGNALL, Hannah	55	BARKER, Beththyah	70	BARNES, Betsey	199
BAGNALL, Hannah	101	BARKER, John	125	BARNES, Betsey Davie	144
BAGNALL, Hannah	107	BARKER, Lettis	205	BARNES, Betsy Goddard	137
BAGNALL, Hannah	109	BARKER, Thomas (Capt.)	70	BARNES, Bradford	92
BAGNALL, Hannah	116	BARNABE, Elizabeth	22	BARNES, Bradford	202
BAGNALL, Hannah Jackson	212	BARNABE, Hannah	22	BARNES, Caroline F.	159
BAGNALL, Nancey Ellis	218	BARNABE, Lidiah	22	BARNES, Charles C.	159
BAGNALL, Nicholas Spinks	55	BARNABE, Ruth	22	BARNES, Charlotte	164
BAGNALL, Richard	55	BARNABE, Stephen	22	BARNES, Charlotte	200
BAGNALL, Richard	72	BARNABE, Timothy	22	BARNES, Corban	46
BAGNALL, Sarah	55	BARNABY, Lydia	105	BARNES, Corban	64
BAGNELL, -----	161	BARNABY, Lydia	107	BARNES, Corban	171
BAGNELL, Benjamin	61	BARNEB, Judith	70	BARNES, Corben	164
BAGNELL, Benjamin	161	BARNEB, Stephen	70	BARNES, Corbin	154
BAGNELL, Betsey Crocker	161	BARNEBE, Ambross	21	BARNES, Corbin	164
BAGNELL, Deborah	222	BARNEBE, Elizabeth	21	BARNES, Corbin	167
BAGNELL, Elizabeth	61	BARNEBE, Hannah	128	BARNES, Corbin	193
BAGNELL, Hannah	61	BARNEBE, James	21	BARNES, Darbey	203
BAGNELL, Lucy	161	BARNEBE, Joanah	21	BARNES, Deborah	164
BAGNELL, Lucy Emily	161	BARNEBE, Joseph	22	BARNES, Deborah	206

VITAL RECORDS OF THE TOWN OF PLYMOUTH

BARNES, Deborah	207	BARNES, James	58	BARNES, Lucy	207
BARNES, Dorcas	46	BARNES, James	105	BARNES, Lucy	210
BARNES, Dorcas	64	BARNES, James	107	BARNES, Lucy C.	144
BARNES, Dorcas	190	BARNES, James	163	BARNES, Lydia	41
BARNES, Elce	92	BARNES, James Franklin	144	BARNES, Lydia	77
BARNES, Elisabeth	122	BARNES, Jane	200	BARNES, Lydia	78
BARNES, Eliza.	78	BARNES, Jedidah	198	BARNES, Lydia	93
BARNES, Elizabeth	19	BARNES, Jerusha	156	BARNES, Lydia	118
BARNES, Elizabeth	58	BARNES, Jerusha	199	BARNES, Lydia	120
BARNES, Elizabeth	75	BARNES, Joanna	202	BARNES, Lydia	156
BARNES, Elizabeth	96	BARNES, John	19	BARNES, Lydia	172
BARNES, Elizabeth	111	BARNES, John	46	BARNES, Marcy	37
BARNES, Elizabeth	125	BARNES, John	64	BARNES, Marcy	74
BARNES, Elizabeth	132	BARNES, John	93	BARNES, Marcy	92
BARNES, Elizabeth	149	BARNES, John	101	BARNES, Marcy	128
BARNES, Elizabeth	154	BARNES, John	121	BARNES, Marcy	133
BARNES, Elizabeth	199	BARNES, John	130	BARNES, Marey	130
BARNES, Elizabeth	218	BARNES, John	185	BARNES, Margaret	81
BARNES, Elkanah	64	BARNES, John Ellis	137	BARNES, Margaret	104
BARNES, Elkanah	180	BARNES, Jonathan	19	BARNES, Margaret	128
BARNES, Elkanah	214	BARNES, Jonathan	41	BARNES, Mary	19
BARNES, Ellis	215	BARNES, Jonathan	73	BARNES, Mary	58
BARNES, Ellis D.	159	BARNES, Jonathan	80	BARNES, Mary	64
BARNES, Eloner	215	BARNES, Jonathan	81	BARNES, Mary	72
BARNES, Ester	69	BARNES, Jonathan	96	BARNES, Mary	80
BARNES, Experience	78	BARNES, Jonathan	126	BARNES, Mary	112
BARNES, Experience	92	BARNES, Jonathan	156	BARNES, Mary	113
BARNES, Experience	186	BARNES, Joseph	58	BARNES, Mary	154
BARNES, George Winslow	144	BARNES, Joseph	175	BARNES, Mary	156
BARNES, Georgianna	153	BARNES, Joseph	195	BARNES, Mary	164
BARNES, Hannah	19	BARNES, Joseph	212	BARNES, Mary	173
BARNES, Hannah	64	BARNES, Josiah	92	BARNES, Mary	217
BARNES, Hannah	70	BARNES, Lemuel	46	BARNES, Mary Frances	144
BARNES, Hannah	78	BARNES, Lemuel	64	BARNES, Mercy	133
BARNES, Hannah	93	BARNES, Lemuel	77	BARNES, Mercy	178
BARNES, Hannah	120	BARNES, Lemuel	87	BARNES, Mercy	188
BARNES, Hannah	137	BARNES, Lemuel	107	BARNES, Nancy	165
BARNES, Hannah	156	BARNES, Lemuel	118	BARNES, Nancy	195
BARNES, Hannah	176	BARNES, Lemuel	167	BARNES, Nancy	204
BARNES, Hannah	180	BARNES, Lemuel	172	BARNES, Nathanael	181
BARNES, Hannah	183	BARNES, Lemuel	190	BARNES, Nathaniel	137
BARNES, Hannah	190	BARNES, Lemuel	210	BARNES, Nathaniel	218
BARNES, Hannah	194	BARNES, Lemuel	213	BARNES, Nathll.	81
BARNES, Hannah	198	BARNES, Lemuell	37	BARNES, Nathll.	180
BARNES, Isaac	46	BARNES, Lemuell	93	BARNES, Pattey	164
BARNES, Isaac	92	BARNES, Lemuell	106	BARNES, Pattey	204
BARNES, Isaac	93	BARNES, Lidia	67	BARNES, Peter Wooden	58
BARNES, Isaac	144	BARNES, Lidiah	19	BARNES, Pheba	156
BARNES, Isaac	191	BARNES, Luce	58	BARNES, Phebe	73
BARNES, Isaac	222	BARNES, Lucy	153	BARNES, Phebe	80
BARNES, James	56	BARNES, Lucy	182	BARNES, Phebe	159

VITAL RECORDS OF THE TOWN OF PLYMOUTH

BARNES, Phebe	167	BARNES, Winslow C.	159	BARROWS, Hannah	35
BARNES, Phebe	210	BARNES, Wm.	113	BARROWS, Isaac	60
BARNES, Polley	194	BARNES, Zacheus	81	BARROWS, Isaac (Doctr.)	207
BARNES, Rachel	197	BARNES, Zacheus	156	BARROWS, Jabiz	42
BARNES, Rebecah	41	BARNS, Alce	69	BARROWS, John	35
BARNES, Rebecca	74	BARNS, Corban	180	BARROWS, John	98
BARNES, Rebecca S.	209	BARNS, Elizabeth	67	BARROWS, John	158
BARNES, Rebeccah	124	BARNS, John	67	BARROWS, John	181
BARNES, Rebeckah	164	BARNS, John	100	BARROWS, Lamuel	42
BARNES, Robert Hutchinson	209	BARNS, Johnathan	130	BARROWS, Lidiah	14
BARNES, Salley	200	BARNS, Jonathan	100	BARROWS, Luce	60
BARNES, Samuel	205	BARNS, Mary	66	BARROWS, Lurany	60
BARNES, Samuel Davis	144	BARNS, Mary	67	BARROWS, Lydia	178
BARNES, Sarah	41	BARNS, Sarah	71	BARROWS, Lydia	197
BARNES, Sarah	46	BARNS, Seth	71	BARROWS, Lydia	217
BARNES, Sarah	56	BARNS, Seth	129	BARROWS, Lydiah	14
BARNES, Sarah	58	BARNS, William	69	BARROWS, Millson	188
BARNES, Sarah	69	BARNS, William	100	BARROWS, Moses	23
BARNES, Sarah	74	BAROW, Ruth	67	BARROWS, Moses	112
BARNES, Sarah	92	BARRIT, John	195	BARROWS, Moses	115
BARNES, Sarah	107	BARRIT, William	212	BARROWS, Patience	23
BARNES, Sarah	109	BARROW, ----- (female)	59	BARROWS, Rebeckah	163
BARNES, Sarah	121	BARROW, Bethiah	70	BARROWS, Rebeckah	188
BARNES, Sarah	128	BARROW, Bethyah	70	BARROWS, Robert	14
BARNES, Sarah	163	BARROW, Elisha	59	BARROWS, Robert	42
BARNES, Seth	19	BARROW, Georg	67	BARROWS, Robert	163
BARNES, Seth	58	BARROW, John	70	BARROWS, Ruth	35
BARNES, Seth	106	BARROW, Lidiah	129	BARROWS, Saml.	116
BARNES, Seth	111	BARROW, Lidya	71	BARROWS, Samll.	60
BARNES, Seth	113	BARROW, Lydia	59	BARROWS, Samuel	23
BARNES, Seth	131	BARROW, Patience	59	BARROWS, Samuel	35
BARNES, Seth	132	BARROW, Patience	67	BARROWS, Sarah	35
BARNES, Southworth	153	BARROW, Robert	70	BARROWS, Sarah	158
BARNES, Thankfull	19	BARROW, Thankfull	59	BARROWS, Thankfull	14
BARNES, Thankfull	74	BARROW, Zacheus	59	BARROWS, Thankfull	70
BARNES, Thankfull	124	BARROWS, Asa	197	BARROWS, Thomas	14
BARNES, Thomas Davie	144	BARROWS, Bathsheba	181	BARROWS, Thomas	42
BARNES, William	19	BARROWS, Bethyah	42	BARROWS, Thomas	158
BARNES, William	37	BARROWS, Deborah	65	BARROWS, William	158
BARNES, William	58	BARROWS, Deborah	112	BARROWS, Willis	60
BARNES, William	93	BARROWS, Deborah	194	BARROWS, Zilpa	175
BARNES, William	105	BARROWS, Deborah	214	BARSE, John	129
BARNES, William	133	BARROWS, Desire	60	BARSTOW, Ichabod Weston	220
BARNES, William	156	BARROWS, Desire	71	BARTER, Margaret	115
BARNES, William	159	BARROWS, Ebenezer	198	BARTIN, John	194
BARNES, William	171	BARROWS, Ebenzr.	163	BARTLET, ----- (male)	16
BARNES, William	179	BARROWS, Elisha	14	BARTLET, Abigaiel	71
BARNES, William	191	BARROWS, Elizabeth	60	BARTLET, Abigail	78
BARNES, William	197	BARROWS, George	23	BARTLET, Benjamin	18
BARNES, William	199	BARROWS, George	71	BARTLET, Benjamin	69
BARNES, William M.	159	BARROWS, George	129	BARTLET, Benjamin	71

VITAL RECORDS OF THE TOWN OF PLYMOUTH

BARTLET, Benjamin	78	BARTLET, Saml.	77	BARTLETT, Amasa	195
BARTLET, Betty	53	BARTLET, Samuel	16	BARTLETT, Amasa S.	134
BARTLET, Ebenaz	71	BARTLET, Samuel	18	BARTLETT, Andrew	62
BARTLET, Ebenazar	16	BARTLET, Samuel	48	BARTLETT, Andrew	162
BARTLET, Elezabeth	71	BARTLET, Samuel	129	BARTLETT, Andrew	180
BARTLET, Elizabeth	16	BARTLET, Sarah	16	BARTLETT, Andrew	197
BARTLET, Elizabeth	53	BARTLET, Sarah	18	BARTLETT, Andrew	198
BARTLET, Elizabeth	70	BARTLET, Sarah	27	BARTLETT, Andrew	201
BARTLET, Elnathan	46	BARTLET, Sarah	66	BARTLETT, Anna	200
BARTLET, Elnathan	70	BARTLET, Sarah	67	BARTLETT, Ansel	204
BARTLET, Elnathan	100	BARTLET, Sarah	69	BARTLETT, Ansel	214
BARTLET, Ephraim	92	BARTLET, Sarah	71	BARTLETT, Ansell	197
BARTLET, Hanah	71	BARTLET, Sarah	97	BARTLETT, Arunah	201
BARTLET, Hanna	46	BARTLET, Sarah	129	BARTLETT, Benja.	105
BARTLET, Hanna	70	BARTLET, Sarah	130	BARTLETT, Benja.	107
BARTLET, Hannah	16	BARTLET, Silvanus	53	BARTLETT, Benja.	122
BARTLET, Hannah	46	BARTLET, Susanah	71	BARTLETT, Benjamen	66
BARTLET, Hannah	99	BARTLET, Thankfull	85	BARTLETT, Benjamin	27
BARTLET, Ichabod	71	BARTLET, Thomas	16	BARTLETT, Benjamin	34
BARTLET, Ichabod	129	BARTLET, Thomas	71	BARTLETT, Benjamin	35
BARTLET, Isaac	92	BARTLET, William	16	BARTLETT, Benjamin	64
BARTLET, Isaiah	48	BARTLET, William	53	BARTLETT, Benjamin	73
BARTLET, James	16	BARTLET, William	71	BARTLETT, Benjamin	77
BARTLET, Jerusha	53	BARTLET, Zacheus	53	BARTLETT, Benjamin	88
BARTLET, John	16	BARTLETT, ----- (Dea.)	202	BARTLETT, Benjamin	89
BARTLET, Jonathan	124	BARTLETT, ----- (female)	58	BARTLETT, Benjamin	96
BARTLET, Joseph	16	BARTLETT, ----- (female)	63	BARTLETT, Benjamin	101
BARTLET, Joseph	18	BARTLETT, ----- (female)	84	BARTLETT, Benjamin	119
BARTLET, Joseph	48	BARTLETT, ----- (female)	131	BARTLETT, Benjamin	130
BARTLET, Joseph	53	BARTLETT, ----- (female)	154	BARTLETT, Benjamin	147
BARTLET, Joseph	66	BARTLETT, ----- (male)	47	BARTLETT, Benjamin	175
BARTLET, Joseph	70	BARTLETT, Abigail	34	BARTLETT, Benjamin (Capt.)	101
BARTLET, Joseph	99	BARTLETT, Abigail	47	BARTLETT, Bethiah	178
BARTLET, Judah	64	BARTLETT, Abigail	58	BARTLETT, Betse	204
BARTLET, Lidia	66	BARTLETT, Abigail	62	BARTLETT, Betsey	193
BARTLET, Lidia	129	BARTLETT, Abigail	64	BARTLETT, Betsey Thacher	153
BARTLET, Lidiah	18	BARTLETT, Abigail	112	BARTLETT, Betsy	194
BARTLET, Lidiah	48	BARTLETT, Abigail	162	BARTLETT, Bettey	111
BARTLET, Lidiah	53	BARTLETT, Abigail	175	BARTLETT, Betty	151
BARTLET, Lidiah	69	BARTLETT, Abigail	188	BARTLETT, Betty	180
BARTLET, Lidiah	70	BARTLETT, Abigail	197	BARTLETT, Bradford	167
BARTLET, Lucretia	217	BARTLETT, Abigail	198	BARTLETT, Caleb	162
BARTLET, Mary	56	BARTLETT, Abigail	214	BARTLETT, Caleb	190
BARTLET, Mary	67	BARTLETT, Abigail	220	BARTLETT, Caleb	198
BARTLET, Mary	71	BARTLETT, Abigal	73	BARTLETT, Charles	194
BARTLET, Rebecca	92	BARTLETT, Abigail	214	BARTLETT, Charles	222
BARTLET, Rebecca	122	BARTLETT, Abner	95	BARTLETT, Chloe	84
BARTLET, Robert	16	BARTLETT, Abner	188	BARTLETT, Clarissa	198
BARTLET, Robert	66	BARTLETT, Abner	214	BARTLETT, Clark	202
BARTLET, Robert	92	BARTLETT, Amasa	131	BARTLETT, Cornelus	150
BARTLET, Robert	97	BARTLETT, Amasa	134	BARTLETT, Cynthia	212

BARTLETT, David	88	BARTLETT, Ellis	162	BARTLETT, Henry	218
BARTLETT, David	168	BARTLETT, Ellis	200	BARTLETT, Hose	201
BARTLETT, David	200	BARTLETT, Ephraim	151	BARTLETT, Hosea	162
BARTLETT, Deborah	149	BARTLETT, Ephraim	174	BARTLETT, Ichabod	30
BARTLETT, Diman	47	BARTLETT, Ephraim	188	BARTLETT, Ichabod	104
BARTLETT, Diman	197	BARTLETT, Ephraim	202	BARTLETT, Ichabod	128
BARTLETT, Diman	205	BARTLETT, Esther	134	BARTLETT, Isaac	131
BARTLETT, Dolley	159	BARTLETT, Esther	222	BARTLETT, Isaac	154
BARTLETT, Dorothy	159	BARTLETT, Eunice	149	BARTLETT, Isaac	181
BARTLETT, Ebenezer	47	BARTLETT, Eunice	194	BARTLETT, Isaac	204
BARTLETT, Ebenezer	56	BARTLETT, Euphamy	207	BARTLETT, Isaac (Capt.)	214
BARTLETT, Ebenezer	84	BARTLETT, Ezra F.	208	BARTLETT, Ivory	162
BARTLETT, Ebenezer	101	BARTLETT, Francis	96	BARTLETT, Ivory Hovey	215
BARTLETT, Ebenezer	105	BARTLETT, Francis	197	BARTLETT, Jabez	147
BARTLETT, Ebenezer	125	BARTLETT, Frederick	212	BARTLETT, James	34
BARTLETT, Ebenezr.	112	BARTLETT, Freeman	201	BARTLETT, James	64
BARTLETT, Elezabeth	71	BARTLETT, Genne	58	BARTLETT, James	84
BARTLETT, Elezebeth	117	BARTLETT, George	188	BARTLETT, James	85
BARTLETT, Elisabeth	186	BARTLETT, George	198	BARTLETT, James	92
BARTLETT, Eliza	163	BARTLETT, George	202	BARTLETT, James	168
BARTLETT, Eliza	208	BARTLETT, George	220	BARTLETT, James	178
BARTLETT, Eliza Ann	153	BARTLETT, Hannah	27	BARTLETT, James	180
BARTLETT, Eliza Ann	163	BARTLETT, Hannah	30	BARTLETT, James	193
BARTLETT, Eliza.	64	BARTLETT, Hannah	58	BARTLETT, James	199
BARTLETT, Eliza.	150	BARTLETT, Hannah	62	BARTLETT, James	209
BARTLETT, Elizabeth	63	BARTLETT, Hannah	63	BARTLETT, James	210
BARTLETT, Elizabeth	64	BARTLETT, Hannah	64	BARTLETT, James C.	151
BARTLETT, Elizabeth	71	BARTLETT, Hannah	73	BARTLETT, James E.	208
BARTLETT, Elizabeth	75	BARTLETT, Hannah	77	BARTLETT, Jane	147
BARTLETT, Elizabeth	95	BARTLETT, Hannah	89	BARTLETT, Jane	186
BARTLETT, Elizabeth	101	BARTLETT, Hannah	105	BARTLETT, Jane	193
BARTLETT, Elizabeth	112	BARTLETT, Hannah	107	BARTLETT, Jean	35
BARTLETT, Elizabeth	113	BARTLETT, Hannah	109	BARTLETT, Jean	88
BARTLETT, Elizabeth	131	BARTLETT, Hannah	111	BARTLETT, Jean	93
BARTLETT, Elizabeth	137	BARTLETT, Hannah	117	BARTLETT, Jean	107
BARTLETT, Elizabeth	147	BARTLETT, Hannah	120	BARTLETT, Jean	175
BARTLETT, Elizabeth	154	BARTLETT, Hannah	128	BARTLETT, Jemima	147
BARTLETT, Elizabeth	180	BARTLETT, Hannah	131	BARTLETT, Jenne	168
BARTLETT, Elizabeth	188	BARTLETT, Hannah	154	BARTLETT, Jerusha	30
BARTLETT, Elizabeth	194	BARTLETT, Hannah	168	BARTLETT, Jerusha	58
BARTLETT, Elizabeth	195	BARTLETT, Hannah	180	BARTLETT, Jerusha	95
BARTLETT, Elizabeth	200	BARTLETT, Hannah	182	BARTLETT, Jerusha	96
BARTLETT, Elizabeth	202	BARTLETT, Hannah	188	BARTLETT, Jerusha	111
BARTLETT, Elizabeth	204	BARTLETT, Hannah	195	BARTLETT, Jerusha	116
BARTLETT, Elizabeth	218	BARTLETT, Hannah	212	BARTLETT, Jerusha	129
BARTLETT, Elkanah	88	BARTLETT, Hannah	215	BARTLETT, Jerusha	163
BARTLETT, Elkanah	168	BARTLETT, Harriot	216	BARTLETT, Jerusha	171
BARTLETT, Elkanah	182	BARTLETT, Henery	162	BARTLETT, Jerusha	193
BARTLETT, Elkanah	199	BARTLETT, Henry	159	BARTLETT, Jerusha	197
BARTLETT, Elkanah	205	BARTLETT, Henry	197	BARTLETT, Jerusha	215
BARTLETT, Ellen	209	BARTLETT, Henry	214	BARTLETT, Jerusha H.	163

VITAL RECORDS OF THE TOWN OF PLYMOUTH

BARTLETT, Jesse	96	BARTLETT, Joseph	99	BARTLETT, Lydia	111
BARTLETT, Jesse	201	BARTLETT, Joseph	101	BARTLETT, Lydia	114
BARTLETT, Jesse	212	BARTLETT, Joseph	118	BARTLETT, Lydia	130
BARTLETT, Jo	48	BARTLETT, Joseph	127	BARTLETT, Lydia	162
BARTLETT, Jo.	69	BARTLETT, Joseph	151	BARTLETT, Lydia	194
BARTLETT, Joanna	34	BARTLETT, Joseph	167	BARTLETT, Lydia	198
BARTLETT, Joanna	88	BARTLETT, Joseph	177	BARTLETT, Lydia	201
BARTLETT, Joanna	106	BARTLETT, Joseph	183	BARTLETT, Malletiah	205
BARTLETT, Joanna	168	BARTLETT, Joseph	184	BARTLETT, Malletiah (Capt.)	218
BARTLETT, Joanna	178	BARTLETT, Joseph	194	BARTLETT, Marcy	88
BARTLETT, Joanna	201	BARTLETT, Joseph	200	BARTLETT, Marcy	121
BARTLETT, John	58	BARTLETT, Joseph	214	BARTLETT, Marcy	151
BARTLETT, John	62	BARTLETT, Joseph (Sergant)	99	BARTLETT, Marcy	177
BARTLETT, John	64	BARTLETT, Joshua	92	BARTLETT, Margaret	63
BARTLETT, John	72	BARTLETT, Joshua	186	BARTLETT, Margaret	128
BARTLETT, John	100	BARTLETT, Joshua	202	BARTLETT, Margaret	221
BARTLETT, John	117	BARTLETT, Joshua	207	BARTLETT, Margarett	137
BARTLETT, John	130	BARTLETT, Josiah	56	BARTLETT, Margerett	154
BARTLETT, John	149	BARTLETT, Josiah	89	BARTLETT, Mariah	58
BARTLETT, John	151	BARTLETT, Josiah	188	BARTLETT, Martha	89
BARTLETT, John	153	BARTLETT, Judah	131	BARTLETT, Martha	95
BARTLETT, John	159	BARTLETT, Judah	163	BARTLETT, Martha	96
BARTLETT, John	162	BARTLETT, Judah	178	BARTLETT, Martha	109
BARTLETT, John	168	BARTLETT, Judah	195	BARTLETT, Martha	189
BARTLETT, John	171	BARTLETT, Lazarus	92	BARTLETT, Martha	205
BARTLETT, John	178	BARTLETT, Lazarus	218	BARTLETT, Martha Washington	163
BARTLETT, John	182	BARTLETT, Lemuel	194	BARTLETT, Mary	58
BARTLETT, John	183	BARTLETT, Lemuel	209	BARTLETT, Mary	62
BARTLETT, John	199	BARTLETT, Lemuell	79	BARTLETT, Mary	79
BARTLETT, John	201	BARTLETT, Lemuell	93	BARTLETT, Mary	93
BARTLETT, John	203	BARTLETT, Lewis	58	BARTLETT, Mary	95
BARTLETT, John	207	BARTLETT, Lewis	159	BARTLETT, Mary	106
BARTLETT, John	208	BARTLETT, Lewis	199	BARTLETT, Mary	107
BARTLETT, John B.	208	BARTLETT, Lidiah	56	BARTLETT, Mary	131
BARTLETT, John Franklin	163	BARTLETT, Lidiah	71	BARTLETT, Mary	132
BARTLETT, John Lewis	159	BARTLETT, Lois Holbrook	214	BARTLETT, Mary	147
BARTLETT, Jonathan	27	BARTLETT, Lothrop	63	BARTLETT, Mary	183
BARTLETT, Jonathan	74	BARTLETT, Lothrop	131	BARTLETT, Mary	184
BARTLETT, Jonathan	85	BARTLETT, Lothrop	154	BARTLETT, Mary	187
BARTLETT, Jonathan	88	BARTLETT, Lowis	190	BARTLETT, Mary	188
BARTLETT, Jonathan	168	BARTLETT, Luce	85	BARTLETT, Mary	196
BARTLETT, Jonathan	179	BARTLETT, Lucey	180	BARTLETT, Mary	198
BARTLETT, Jonathan	189	BARTLETT, Lucinda	222	BARTLETT, Mary	205
BARTLETT, Joseph	27	BARTLETT, Lucy	167	BARTLETT, Mary	208
BARTLETT, Joseph	64	BARTLETT, Lucy	193	BARTLETT, Mary Ann	134
BARTLETT, Joseph	71	BARTLETT, Lucy	209	BARTLETT, Mercy	30
BARTLETT, Joseph	74	BARTLETT, Lucy T.	218	BARTLETT, Mercy	147
BARTLETT, Joseph	88	BARTLETT, Lydia	64	BARTLETT, Mercy	151
BARTLETT, Joseph	89	BARTLETT, Lydia	73	BARTLETT, Mercy	162
BARTLETT, Joseph	95	BARTLETT, Lydia	96	BARTLETT, Mercy	183
BARTLETT, Joseph	96	BARTLETT, Lydia	101	BARTLETT, Mercy	194

VITAL RECORDS OF THE TOWN OF PLYMOUTH

BARTLETT, Mercy	201	BARTLETT, Robert	92	BARTLETT, Sarah	89
BARTLETT, Mercy	202	BARTLETT, Robert	100	BARTLETT, Sarah	100
BARTLETT, Mercy	203	BARTLETT, Robert	124	BARTLETT, Sarah	105
BARTLETT, Mercy	204	BARTLETT, Robert	174	BARTLETT, Sarah	107
BARTLETT, Mercy	206	BARTLETT, Robert	183	BARTLETT, Sarah	118
BARTLETT, Mercy Ellis	222	BARTLETT, Robert	186	BARTLETT, Sarah	123
BARTLETT, Meriah	183	BARTLETT, Rocksiade	202	BARTLETT, Sarah	129
BARTLETT, Myra	215	BARTLETT, Rufus	93	BARTLETT, Sarah	131
BARTLETT, Nancy	210	BARTLETT, Rufus	195	BARTLETT, Sarah	149
BARTLETT, Nancy	212	BARTLETT, Rufus	202	BARTLETT, Sarah	168
BARTLETT, Nathal.	150	BARTLETT, Ruth Rogers	220	BARTLETT, Sarah	171
BARTLETT, Nathaniel	27	BARTLETT, Salle	198	BARTLETT, Sarah	183
BARTLETT, Nathaniel	56	BARTLETT, Salley	168	BARTLETT, Sarah	191
BARTLETT, Nathaniel	61	BARTLETT, Salley	197	BARTLETT, Sary	58
BARTLETT, Nathaniel	62	BARTLETT, Salley	203	BARTLETT, Silvanus	95
BARTLETT, Nathaniel	73	BARTLETT, Sally	201	BARTLETT, Silvanus	109
BARTLETT, Nathaniel	130	BARTLETT, Saml.	101	BARTLETT, Silvanus	115
BARTLETT, Nathaniel	132	BARTLETT, Saml.	109	BARTLETT, Silvanus	151
BARTLETT, Nathaniel	172	BARTLETT, Saml.	113	BARTLETT, Silvanus	186
BARTLETT, Nathaniel	193	BARTLETT, Saml.	115	BARTLETT, Solomon	34
BARTLETT, Nathaniel	195	BARTLETT, Samll.	63	BARTLETT, Solomon	64
BARTLETT, Nathaniel	198	BARTLETT, Samuel	38	BARTLETT, Solomon	105
BARTLETT, Nathaniel	212	BARTLETT, Samuel	56	BARTLETT, Solomon	106
BARTLETT, Nathaniel	217	BARTLETT, Samuel	63	BARTLETT, Solomon	187
BARTLETT, Nathl.	175	BARTLETT, Samuel	64	BARTLETT, Solomon	197
BARTLETT, Olive	204	BARTLETT, Samuel	71	BARTLETT, Solomon	218
BARTLETT, Pebody	198	BARTLETT, Samuel	73	BARTLETT, Sophia	96
BARTLETT, Phebe	84	BARTLETT, Samuel	75	BARTLETT, Stephen	93
BARTLETT, Phebe	137	BARTLETT, Samuel	117	BARTLETT, Stephen	162
BARTLETT, Phebe	178	BARTLETT, Samuel	130	BARTLETT, Stephen	203
BARTLETT, Phebe	194	BARTLETT, Samuel	150	BARTLETT, Stevens	89
BARTLETT, Polley	204	BARTLETT, Samuel	151	BARTLETT, Sukey	218
BARTLETT, Polley	217	BARTLETT, Samuel	154	BARTLETT, Susan	153
BARTLETT, Priscilla	64	BARTLETT, Samuel	181	BARTLETT, Susan Louisa	153
BARTLETT, Priscilla	176	BARTLETT, Samuel	193	BARTLETT, Susanna	62
BARTLETT, Rebecah	84	BARTLETT, Samuel	199	BARTLETT, Susanna	207
BARTLETT, Rebecca	147	BARTLETT, Samuel	204	BARTLETT, Susannah	92
BARTLETT, Rebecca	194	BARTLETT, Samuel	208	BARTLETT, Susannah	109
BARTLETT, Rebecca	197	BARTLETT, Samuell	63	BARTLETT, Susannah	113
BARTLETT, Rebecca	202	BARTLETT, Samuell	112	BARTLETT, Susannah	115
BARTLETT, Rebecca	214	BARTLETT, Samuell	131	BARTLETT, Susannah	151
BARTLETT, Rebecka	56	BARTLETT, Sarah	27	BARTLETT, Sussannah	112
BARTLETT, Rebeckah	56	BARTLETT, Sarah	58	BARTLETT, Sylvanus	96
BARTLETT, Rebeckah	84	BARTLETT, Sarah	64	BARTLETT, Thankfull	74
BARTLETT, Rebeckah	93	BARTLETT, Sarah	66	BARTLET, Thankfull	198
BARTLETT, Rebeckah	101	BARTLETT, Sarah	67	BARTLETT, Thankfull	218
BARTLETT, Rebeckah	174	BARTLETT, Sarah	71	BARTLETT, Thomas	47
BARTLETT, Rebeckah	182	BARTLETT, Sarah	72	BARTLETT, Thomas	61
BARTLETT, Rebeckah	191	BARTLETT, Sarah	74	BARTLETT, Thomas	84
BARTLETT, Rebekah	67	BARTLETT, Sarah	79	BARTLETT, Thomas	89
BARTLETT, Robert	56	BARTLETT, Sarah	85	BARTLETT, Thomas	131

BARTLETT, Thomas	147	BATES, Clement	163	BATES, Samuel	56
BARTLETT, Thomas	180	BATES, Clemmont	215	BATES, Samuel	69
BARTLETT, Thomas	190	BATES, Daved	41	BATES, Samuel	187
BARTLETT, Thomas	199	BATES, David	41	BATES, Sarah	88
BARTLETT, Thomas	202	BATES, David	56	BATES, Silvina	199
BARTLETT, Thomas	215	BATES, David	185	BATES, Suke	202
BARTLETT, Truman	201	BATES, Elizabeth	56	BATES, Thomas	38
BARTLETT, Waite	95	BATES, Elizabeth	163	BATES, Thomas	77
BARTLETT, William	64	BATES, Elizabeth	178	BATES, Thomas	88
BARTLETT, William	85	BATES, Hannah	202	BATES, Thomas	119
BARTLETT, William	93	BATES, Hannah	209	BATES, Thomas	193
BARTLETT, William	106	BATES, Hulda	206	BATS, Margaret	38
BARTLETT, William	131	BATES, Ira	163	BATTLES, Alise	151
BARTLETT, William	147	BATES, Irene	163	BATTLES, Benjamin	204
BARTLETT, William	151	BATES, Joannah	56	BATTLES, Caleb	201
BARTLETT, William	153	BATES, Job	38	BATTLES, Caleb	206
BARTLETT, William	168	BATES, John	38	BATTLES, Eliza.	195
BARTLETT, William	177	BATES, John	179	BATTLES, Elizabeth	151
BARTLETT, William	189	BATES, John	206	BATTLES, Experience	139
BARTLETT, William	193	BATES, John B.	209	BATTLES, Experience	204
BARTLETT, William	212	BATES, Joseph	41	BATTLES, Huldah	205
BARTLETT, William	215	BATES, Joseph	56	BATTLES, John	203
BARTLETT, Willm.	208	BATES, Joseph	122	BATTLES, John	210
BARTLETT, Wm.	107	BATES, Joseph	189	BATTLES, Joshua	139
BARTLETT, Zacheus	104	BATES, Joseph	193	BATTLES, Joshua	173
BARTLETT, Zacheus	128	BATES, Joseph	209	BATTLES, Martha	79
BARTLETT, Zacheus	137	BATES, Joseph	210	BATTLES, Martha	116
BARTLETT, Zacheus	147	BATES, Joseph	213	BATTLES, Martha	139
BARTLETT, Zacheus	168	BATES, Lidya	56	BATTLES, Martha	194
BARTLETT, Zacheus	193	BATES, Lucretia	163	BATTLES, Mary	200
BARTLETT, Zacheus (Doctr.)	200	BATES, Lydia	41	BATTLES, Polley	151
BARTLETT, Zepheniah	199	BATES, Lydia	77	BATTLES, Rebecca	197
BARTLETT, Zepheniah Holmes	167	BATES, Lydia	88	BATTLES, Saml.	177
BARTLIT, Sarah	130	BATES, Lydia	190	BATTLES, Samuel	151
BASSET, Cinthea	206	BATES, Margaret	75	BATTLES, Samuel	198
BASSETT, Abby	156	BATES, Margeret	69	BATTLES, Samuel	222
BASSETT, Angeline Stephens	156	BATES, Marget	117	BATTLES, Sarah	207
BASSETT, Jesse Thomas	156	BATES, Mary	41	BATTLES, Silvina	200
BASSETT, Thomas	156	BATES, Mercy	193	BATTLES, Timothy	139
BASSETT, William	182	BATES, Mercy	194	BAUMENT, Eliza Sarah	217
BATES, Abigail	41	BATES, Mercy	206	BAYLEY, Thomas	171
BATES, Abigail	204	BATES, Ozen	163	BEADLE, Willm.	90
BATES, Abigaill	41	BATES, Patience	188	BEAL, Mary	160
BATES, Ann	41	BATES, Patience	216	BEAL, Rhoda	109
BATES, Ann	111	BATES, Phebe	217	BEAL, Rhoda	115
BATES, Ann	172	BATES, Rebecca	212	BEAL, Simeon Rathmel	160
BATES, Augusta	163	BATES, Remember	41	BEALE, Asa	60
BATES, Barnabas	38	BATES, Remember	75	BEALE, Ase	129
BATES, Betsey	163	BATES, Remember	125	BEALE, Elizabeth	61
BATES, Betsey	199	BATES, Ruby	163	BEALE, Elizabeth	174
BATES, Charles C.	163	BATES, Samuel	38	BEALE, Elizabeth	177

VITAL RECORDS OF THE TOWN OF PLYMOUTH

Name	Page	Name	Page	Name	Page
BEALE, John	61	BENT, Joseph	174	BILLENTON, Sarah	52
BEALE, Margaret	61	BENT, Salley	212	BILLINGS, Abigail	87
BEALE, Margaret	175	BERCE, Betsey	217	BILLINGS, Abigail	115
BEALE, Mary	61	BERRY, Antoinette L.	147	BILLINGTON, Abigal	126
BEALE, Rhoda	60	BERRY, Harriet S.	147	BILLINGTON, Content	117
BEALE, Rhoda	61	BERRY, Maria	147	BILLINGTON, Marcy	74
BEALE, Sarah	61	BERRY, Maria E.	147	BILLINGTON, Marcy	128
BEALE, Sarah	112	BERRY, Mary T.	147	BILLINGTON, Sarah	72
BEALE, Sarah	175	BERRY, Timothy	147	BISBE, Lydia	106
BEALE, Susanna	60	BERRY, William T.	147	BISBE, Reuben	105
BEALE, Susanna	61	BESSE, Benjamin	65	BISBE, Reuben	106
BEALE, Susannah	111	BESSE, Benjamin	126	BISBEY, Gideon	212
BEALE, Susannah	116	BESSE, David	65	BISBEY, Jonah	183
BEALE, Susannah	123	BESSE, Ebenezer	120	BISBEY, Sylvanus	204
BEALES, Asa	71	BESSE, Ebenezr.	189	BISHOP, Betsey	212
BEALES, Rohoda	71	BESSE, Edward	218	BISHOP, Dorcas	53
BEALS, Mary	186	BESSE, Elener	214	BISHOP, Ebenezer	53
BEARCE, Experience	182	BESSE, Elizabeth	65	BISHOP, John	181
BEARCE, Ichabod	149	BESSE, Elizabeth	195	BISHOP, John	203
BEARCE, Ichabod	182	BESSE, Ephraim	199	BISHOP, Jonathan	53
BEARCE, Jerusha	222	BESSE, Hope	190	BISHOP, Jonathan	116
BEARCE, Lucy James	149	BESSE, Ichabod	199	BISHOP, Mary	53
BEARCE, Lurany	182	BESSE, Joshua	191	BISHOP, Presbury (male)	53
BEARCE, Sally	149	BESSE, Joshua	217	BISHOP, Susanna	197
BEARCE, Sarah Ann	149	BESSE, Lucy	205	BLACK, John	188
BEARD, Margaret	171	BESSE, Margaret	206	BLACK, Sarah	190
BEARSE, John	71	BESSE, Martha	65	BLACKMAN, Nancy	221
BEARSE, Robert	193	BESSE, Mary	65	BLACKMAN, Thomas	214
BEARSE, Sarah	71	BESSE, Mary	198	BLACKMER, Betsey	196
BEETEN, James	132	BESSE, Nathaniel	201	BLACKMER, Bettey	85
BELCHAR, Jonathan	186	BESSE, Nehemiah	65	BLACKMER, Betty	135
BELL, Daniel	190	BESSE, Samuel	65	BLACKMER, Branch	84
BEMIS, Joanna	165	BESSE, Tabitha	125	BLACKMER, Branch	135
BEMIS, Josiah	165	BESSE, Thankfull	65	BLACKMER, Branch	172
BEMIS, Josiah	191	BESSEE, Hannah	198	BLACKMER, Eliza I.	222
BEMON, Joshua	109	BESSEE, Mary	69	BLACKMER, Elizabeth	183
BEMON, Sarah	109	BESSEE, Robert	198	BLACKMER, Experience	85
BENIAS, Francis	115	BESSEY, Betsey	207	BLACKMER, Ivorey	135
BENNET, Joannah	117	BESSEY, Lucy	200	BLACKMER, Jerusha	85
BENNET, Mary	118	BILLENTEN, Sarah	130	BLACKMER, Jerusha	181
BENSON, Bathsheba	147	BILLENTON, Abigaiel	52	BLACKMER, Jerusha	200
BENSON, Bathsheba Thomas	147	BILLENTON, Abigaiel	67	BLACKMER, John	84
BENSON, Elias Thomas	147	BILLENTON, Abigail	52	BLACKMER, John	85
BENSON, Ellis	147	BILLENTON, Abigal	73	BLACKMER, John	135
BENSON, George	147	BILLENTON, Content	52	BLACKMER, John	197
BENSON, Lucinda Thomas	147	BILLENTON, Content	75	BLACKMER, John	222
BENSON, Lydia West	147	BILLENTON, Ffrances	52	BLACKMER, Marcy	85
BENSON, Seth	147	BILLENTON, Francis	67	BLACKMER, Mary	135
BENSON, Seth	222	BILLENTON, Jemima	52	BLACKMER, Mercy	135
BENT, Abaigaill	69	BILLENTON, Joseph	52	BLACKMER, Richard	135
BENT, Experiance	69	BILLENTON, Marcy	52	BLACKMER, Richard	204

VITAL RECORDS OF THE TOWN OF PLYMOUTH

BLACKMER, Sarah	84	BOSWORTH, Beththyah	69	BOZWORTH, Nehemiah	22
BLACKMER, Sarah	85	BOSWORTH, Betsey	134	BRACE, Eliza.	78
BLACKMER, Sarah	135	BOSWORTH, Hanah	67	BRACE, Elizabeth	112
BLACKMER, Sarah	174	BOSWORTH, Hannah Elizabeth	134	BRACE, Thomas	78
BLACKMER, Sarah	194	BOSWORTH, Helkiah	69	BRACE, Thomas	122
BLACKMER, Sarah	222	BOSWORTH, Jane	134	BRADFORD, ----- (female)	52
BLACKMER, Susanna	85	BOSWORTH, Jane Taylor	134	BRADFORD, ----- (male)	52
BLACKMER, Susannah	176	BOSWORTH, Joanah	75	BRADFORD, Abigail	98
BLACKMER, William	135	BOSWORTH, Joannah	125	BRADFORD, Abigail	170
BLACKMER, William	198	BOSWORTH, Lydia	77	BRADFORD, Abigal	11
BLACKMORE, John	75	BOSWORTH, Nathaniel	77	BRADFORD, Abigal	52
BLACKMORE, John	125	BOSWORTH, Nathaniel	118	BRADFORD, Abner	59
BLACKMORE, Sarah	75	BOSWORTH, Orrin	134	BRADFORD, Adeline Augusta	158
BLACKMUR, Phebe	67	BOSWORTH, Orrin Waterman	134	BRADFORD, Alce	69
BLACKMUR, William	98	BOTT, Elizabeth	190	BRADFORD, Alice	141
BLACKWELL, Abigail	222	BOULT, Charles	153	BRADFORD, Alice S.	141
BLACKWELL, Bathshua	116	BOULT, Charles	171	BRADFORD, Allice	70
BLACKWELL, Deborah	186	BOULT, Elizabeth	153	BRADFORD, Alse	11
BLACKWELL, Hiphzibah	198	BOULT, Lydia	153	BRADFORD, Alse	96
BLACKWELL, John	120	BOULT, Lydia	188	BRADFORD, Anna	52
BLACKWELL, Patience	121	BOULT, Lydia	189	BRADFORD, Bartlett	209
BLACKWELL, Patience	200	BOULT, William	182	BRADFORD, Bathseba	59
BLACKWELL, Sarah	183	BOURN, A.	77	BRADFORD, Bathsheba	140
BLAKMER, Experience	187	BOURN, Deborah	123	BRADFORD, Bathshua	55
BLAKMER, Mary	135	BOURN, James	212	BRADFORD, Bathshua	71
BLANCH, John	190	BOURN, Job	78	BRADFORD, Benjamin	59
BLY, Mary	198	BOURN, Job	120	BRADFORD, Benjamin Willis	165
BOISE, Sarah	202	BOURN, Lydia	78	BRADFORD, Betsey	210
BOLES, Beththyah	69	BOUTELLE, Caleb	212	BRADFORD, Betsey M.	161
BOMPO, Micah	206	BOW, Sarah	191	BRADFORD, Branch Johnson	161
BONAM, Elizabeth	66	BOWDOIN, Phebe	78	BRADFORD, Charles	48
BONAM, George	66	BOWDOIN, William	78	BRADFORD, Charles	140
BONAM, Sarah	98	BOWDOIN, William	121	BRADFORD, Charles	195
BONAN, Ann	9	BOWLAND, Michel	198	BRADFORD, Charles Coban	158
BONAN, Ebonazar	9	BOYLSTONE, Polley	206	BRADFORD, Daved	47
BONAN, Elizabeth	9	BOYSE, Elen	207	BRADFORD, David	70
BONAN, George	99	BOYSE, Ellen	207	BRADFORD, David	222
BONAN, Gorg	9	BOYSE, Sarah	200	BRADFORD, Deborah	52
BONAN, Lidiah	9	BOYSTON, Benja.	183	BRADFORD, Deborah	213
BONAN, Ruth	9	BOZWORTH, Benjamin	49	BRADFORD, Ebenezer Nelson	140
BONAN, Samuell	9	BOZWORTH, Bethyah	49	BRADFORD, Edward Winslow	165
BONAN, Sarah	9	BOZWORTH, David	22	BRADFORD, Eleanor	147
BONAN, Suzannah	9	BOZWORTH, David	67	BRADFORD, Elezabeth	47
BONNEY, Joseph	70	BOZWORTH, Hanna	49	BRADFORD, Elezebeth	52
BONNEY, Margeret	70	BOZWORTH, Hannah	22	BRADFORD, Elijah	52
BONNEY, Mary	125	BOZWORTH, Hezekiah	49	BRADFORD, Eliphalet	50
BONNEY, Mehetable	67	BOZWORTH, Joanna	49	BRADFORD, Eliphalet	106
BONNEY, William	67	BOZWORTH, Jonathan	22	BRADFORD, Elish	129
BONUM, Ann	121	BOZWORTH, Marcy	67	BRADFORD, Elisha	55
BOORNE, Hannah	66	BOZWORTH, Marsy	22	BRADFORD, Elisha	59
BOSTON, Martha	213	BOZWORTH, Nathaniel	49	BRADFORD, Elisha	71

VITAL RECORDS OF THE TOWN OF PLYMOUTH

BRADFORD, Elizabeth	18	BRADFORD, John (Maj.)	129	BRADFORD, Nathaniel Barnes	165
BRADFORD, Elizabeth	48	BRADFORD, John Howland	165	BRADFORD, Nathl.	101
BRADFORD, Elizabeth	52	BRADFORD, Jonathan	47	BRADFORD, Nathl.	123
BRADFORD, Elizabeth	70	BRADFORD, Joseph	55	BRADFORD, Nathll.	46
BRADFORD, Elizabeth	79	BRADFORD, Joseph	96	BRADFORD, Nehemiah	55
BRADFORD, Elizabeth M.	161	BRADFORD, Joseph	100	BRADFORD, Noah	79
BRADFORD, Elizabeth Richardson	158	BRADFORD, Joseph	165	BRADFORD, Noah	123
BRADFORD, Ellen	208	BRADFORD, Joseph	204	BRADFORD, Pelham	205
BRADFORD, Ellen	218	BRADFORD, Joshua	59	BRADFORD, Peris	18
BRADFORD, Ephraim	52	BRADFORD, Josiah	31	BRADFORD, Polley	203
BRADFORD, Ephraim	70	BRADFORD, Josiah	47	BRADFORD, Polley	204
BRADFORD, Ephraim	165	BRADFORD, Josiah	111	BRADFORD, Pricila	71
BRADFORD, Ephraim	207	BRADFORD, Josiah	117	BRADFORD, Pricilla	11
BRADFORD, Eudora	141	BRADFORD, Josiah	194	BRADFORD, Priscilla	129
BRADFORD, Gamaliel	18	BRADFORD, Josiah	205	BRADFORD, Priscilla	186
BRADFORD, George	208	BRADFORD, Lebaron	190	BRADFORD, Priscilla Morton	158
BRADFORD, Gideon	78	BRADFORD, Lemuel	46	BRADFORD, Rebecah	46
BRADFORD, Gideon	122	BRADFORD, Lemuel	140	BRADFORD, Rebecca	165
BRADFORD, Girshom	71	BRADFORD, Lemuel	188	BRADFORD, Rebecca	209
BRADFORD, Girshum	18	BRADFORD, Lemuel	198	BRADFORD, Rebecca Holmes	158
BRADFORD, Hanah	50	BRADFORD, Lemuel	214	BRADFORD, Rebeckah	46
BRADFORD, Hannah	18	BRADFORD, Lidiah	47	BRADFORD, Rebekah	67
BRADFORD, Hannah	31	BRADFORD, Luarama	55	BRADFORD, Robert	46
BRADFORD, Hannah	55	BRADFORD, Lucy	209	BRADFORD, Ruth	58
BRADFORD, Hannah	66	BRADFORD, Lucy	215	BRADFORD, Sally	158
BRADFORD, Hannah	70	BRADFORD, Lusanna	52	BRADFORD, Samuel	11
BRADFORD, Hannah	79	BRADFORD, Lydia	78	BRADFORD, Samuel	18
BRADFORD, Hannah	111	BRADFORD, Lydia	120	BRADFORD, Samuel	66
BRADFORD, Hannah	112	BRADFORD, Lydia	121	BRADFORD, Samuel	194
BRADFORD, Hannah Everson	140	BRADFORD, Lydia Nelson	140	BRADFORD, Samuel	219
BRADFORD, Hezekiah	70	BRADFORD, Marcy	111	BRADFORD, Samuell	50
BRADFORD, Ichabod	59	BRADFORD, Marcy	123	BRADFORD, Sarah	46
BRADFORD, Israel	58	BRADFORD, Marsey	70	BRADFORD, Sarah	48
BRADFORD, Israell	67	BRADFORD, Mary	70	BRADFORD, Sarah	58
BRADFORD, James	50	BRADFORD, Mary	96	BRADFORD, Sarah	67
BRADFORD, James	147	BRADFORD, Mary	107	BRADFORD, Sarah	78
BRADFORD, James	222	BRADFORD, Mary	185	BRADFORD, Sarah	111
BRADFORD, James M.	161	BRADFORD, Mary Ann	141	BRADFORD, Sarah	121
BRADFORD, James Madison	165	BRADFORD, Mersey	11	BRADFORD, Sarah	123
BRADFORD, Jane	78	BRADFORD, Mersy	11	BRADFORD, Sarah	165
BRADFORD, Jerusha	18	BRADFORD, Mersy	66	BRADFORD, Sarah	177
BRADFORD, Jerusha	48	BRADFORD, Nancy	141	BRADFORD, Sarah James	158
BRADFORD, Jerusha	109	BRADFORD, Nancy	165	BRADFORD, Silvanus	55
BRADFORD, Jerusha	122	BRADFORD, Nathan	47	BRADFORD, Thomas	204
BRADFORD, Jesse	215	BRADFORD, Nathaniel	46	BRADFORD, Welthe	18
BRADFORD, John	11	BRADFORD, Nathaniel	47	BRADFORD, Wiliam	11
BRADFORD, John	46	BRADFORD, Nathaniel	111	BRADFORD, William	31
BRADFORD, John	66	BRADFORD, Nathaniel	147	BRADFORD, William	48
BRADFORD, John	67	BRADFORD, Nathaniel	165	BRADFORD, William	50
BRADFORD, John	79	BRADFORD, Nathaniel	188	BRADFORD, William	70
BRADFORD, John	115	BRADFORD, Nathaniel	202	BRADFORD, William	96

VITAL RECORDS OF THE TOWN OF PLYMOUTH

Name	Page	Name	Page	Name	Page
BRADFORD, William	107	BRAMHALL, Nehemiah	27	BREWSTER, Deborah	213
BRADFORD, William	129	BRAMHALL, Priscilla	213	BREWSTER, Desire Barker	199
BRADFORD, William	141	BRAMHALL, Robert Eldridge	148	BREWSTER, Elizabeth	111
BRADFORD, William	200	BRAMHALL, Sarah	27	BREWSTER, Ellis	197
BRADFORD, William (Major)	96	BRAMHALL, Sarah	87	BREWSTER, Hannah	59
BRADFORD, Willm.	187	BRAMHALL, Sarah	109	BREWSTER, Jane	212
BRADFORD, Winslow	140	BRAMHALL, Sarah	214	BREWSTER, Job	111
BRADFORD, Winslow	213	BRAMHALL, Silvanios	40	BREWSTER, Job	131
BRADFORD, Wm.	105	BRAMHALL, Silvanus	27	BREWSTER, Job	194
BRADFORD, Zadock	50	BRAMHALL, Silvanus	27	BREWSTER, Job E.	218
BRADFORD, Zephaniah	158	BRAMHALL, Silvanus	118	BREWSTER, Mary	74
BRADSTREET, Nathaniel (Doctr.)	204	BRAMHALL, Silvanus	177	BREWSTER, Mary	125
BRALEY, Silas	219	BRAMHALL, Sylvanus	203	BREWSTER, Nancy Ellis	221
BRAMHAL, Sarah	40	BRAMHALL, William	87	BREWSTER, William	200
BRAMHALL, Albert Nelson	148	BRAMHALL, Zilpah	157	BREWSTER, William Martin	222
BRAMHALL, Benjamin	148	BRAMHALL, Zilpah	197	BREWSTER, Wrastling	59
BRAMHALL, Benjamin	195	BRANCH, Experience	55	BREWSTER, Wrastling	198
BRAMHALL, Charles	221	BRANCH, Experience	105	BRIANT, Abiah	173
BRAMHALL, Cornelios	40	BRANCH, Experience	107	BRIANT, Abigaiel	130
BRAMHALL, Cornelius	27	BRANCH, John	55	BRIANT, George	10
BRAMHALL, Cornelus	185	BRANCH, Lidiah	55	BRIANT, Jams	10
BRAMHALL, Edmond	87	BRANCH, Lidya	71	BRIANT, Joanah	10
BRAMHALL, George	27	BRANCH, Lydia	78	BRIANT, John	10
BRAMHALL, George	157	BRANCH, Lydia	121	BRIANT, Liddiah	66
BRAMHALL, George	181	BRANCH, Marcy	55	BRIANT, Ruth	10
BRAMHALL, George	204	BRANCH, Marcy	112	BRIANT, Ruth	104
BRAMHALL, George	213	BRANCH, Marcy	113	BRIANT, Samuell	173
BRAMHALL, Hannah	210	BRANCH, Thankfull	55	BRIANT, Sarah	10
BRAMHALL, Joseph	27	BRANCH, Thankfull	111	BRIANT, Susannah	176
BRAMHALL, Joseph	40	BRANCH, Thankfull	117	BRIDGETT, Sarah	130
BRAMHALL, Joseph	87	BRANCH, Thomas	55	BRIGGS, Abigail	201
BRAMHALL, Joseph	87	BRANCH, Thomas	71	BRIGGS, Betsey	222
BRAMHALL, Joseph	109	BRANCH, Thomas	129	BRIGGS, Deborah	218
BRAMHALL, Joseph	113	BRAND, James	194	BRIGGS, George	201
BRAMHALL, Joseph	182	BRANES, Sarah	58	BRIGGS, Israel	217
BRAMHALL, Joseph	185	BRATLES, Bathshuba	50	BRIGGS, Joanna	203
BRAMHALL, Joseph	187	BRATLES, Edward	50	BRIGGS, Lowis	212
BRAMHALL, Joseph	212	BRATLES, John	50	BRIGGS, Mary	207
BRAMHALL, Joshua	15	BRATLES, Jonathan	50	BRIGGS, Perez	197
BRAMHALL, Joshua	27	BRATLES, Martha	50	BRIGGS, Polley	205
BRAMHALL, Joshua	40	BRATLES, Mary	50	BRIGGS, Samuel	206
BRAMHALL, Joshua	176	BRATLES, Rebecca	50	BRIGGS, Seth	193
BRAMHALL, Lydia	27	BRATLES, Samuell	50	BRIGHAM, Antipas	156
BRAMHALL, Martha	40	BRATLES, Timothy	50	BRIGHAM, Atipas	156
BRAMHALL, Martha	112	BRECK, William	185	BRIGHAM, Mercy	156
BRAMHALL, Martha	207	BRETT, Nathaniel	187	BRIGHAM, Mercy Ann	156
BRAMHALL, Mary	27	BREWER, Rizpah	209	BRIGS, Bathsheba	68
BRAMHALL, Mary	148	BREWSTER, America	199	BRIGS, Cornelius	124
BRAMHALL, Mary	157	BREWSTER, Betsy	222	BRIGS, Ebenezer	120
BRAMHALL, Mary	189	BREWSTER, Charles	218	BRIGS, John	67
BRAMHALL, Mercy	204	BREWSTER, Debo.	194	BRIGS, Ruth	67

VITAL RECORDS OF THE TOWN OF PLYMOUTH

Name	Page	Name	Page	Name	Page
BRIMMER, Martin	190	BRYANT, James	30	BUCK, John	67
BROCK, Bathsheba	129	BRYANT, Jerusha	189	BUCK, John	98
BROCK, Bathshua	71	BRYANT, Joannah	31	BUCK, Sarah	67
BROOKS, Dorcas	199	BRYANT, John	30	BUCK, Sarah	98
BROOKS, Mary	189	BRYANT, John	67	BUCKLEY, John	222
BROOKS, Samuel	195	BRYANT, John (Lieut.)	14	BUCKLEY, Zilpa	179
BROWN, -----	126	BRYANT, Jonathan	15	BULLOCK, N. (J.P.)	219
BROWN, Charles	222	BRYANT, Jonathan	31	BULLUCK, Annah	121
BROWN, Dorcas	206	BRYANT, Jonathan	69	BUMP, Deborah	77
BROWN, George	214	BRYANT, Jonathan	71	BUMP, Deborah	121
BROWN, John	171	BRYANT, Jonathan	74	BUMPAS, ----- (male)	15
BROWN, Martha	64	BRYANT, Jonathan	127	BUMPAS, Abraham	195
BROWN, Mary	64	BRYANT, Lucy	207	BUMPAS, Benjamin	213
BROWN, Mary	109	BRYANT, Lydia	143	BUMPAS, Betsey	208
BROWN, Mary	113	BRYANT, Mahitabel	66	BUMPAS, James	193
BROWN, Nathaniel	190	BRYANT, Marcy	31	BUMPAS, Joanna	15
BROWN, Prince	198	BRYANT, Margaret	75	BUMPAS, John	202
BROWN, Priscilla	64	BRYANT, Margaret	117	BUMPAS, Joseph	205
BROWN, Priscilla	79	BRYANT, Margerey	31	BUMPAS, Lowis	193
BROWN, Priscilla	115	BRYANT, Margret	69	BUMPAS, Marcy	15
BROWN, Priscilla	206	BRYANT, Mary	14	BUMPAS, Mercy	195
BROWN, Rebecca	64	BRYANT, Mary	30	BUMPAS, Noah	195
BROWN, Rebecca	202	BRYANT, Mary	67	BUMPAS, Samuel	15
BROWN, Rebecca	204	BRYANT, Mary	71	BUMPAS, Thomas	15
BROWN, Rebeckah	190	BRYANT, Mehittabel	15	BUMPAS, Thomas	113
BROWN, Robert	64	BRYANT, Mercy	67	BUMPAS, Warren	218
BROWN, Robert	75	BRYANT, Mercy	195	BUMPASS, James	127
BROWN, Robert	104	BRYANT, Patience	207	BUMPUS, Barzillaia	222
BROWN, Robert	117	BRYANT, Polley	207	BUMPUS, Samuell	126
BROWN, Robert	126	BRYANT, Pricila	31	BUNKER, James	172
BROWN, Robert	130	BRYANT, Pricila	130	BURBANK, Abigail	147
BROWN, Robert	189	BRYANT, Rebecca	71	BURBANK, Abigail William	147
BROWN, Wm.	213	BRYANT, Rebeckah	31	BURBANK, Calvin Perkins	147
BRUSTER, Abigail	70	BRYANT, Rebekah	129	BURBANK, David	81
BRUSTER, Rasteling	129	BRYANT, Ruth	69	BURBANK, David	207
BRYANT, Abigaiel	31	BRYANT, Ruth	73	BURBANK, Elijah Walker	147
BRYANT, Abigail	14	BRYANT, Ruth	110	BURBANK, Ezra	81
BRYANT, Abigail	98	BRYANT, Ruth	130	BURBANK, Ezra	148
BRYANT, Abigaill	15	BRYANT, Saml.	143	BURBANK, Ezra	177
BRYANT, Abigaill	69	BRYANT, Samuel	15	BURBANK, Ezra	198
BRYANT, Bathsheba	68	BRYANT, Samuel	31	BURBANK, Ezra	217
BRYANT, Benjamin	15	BRYANT, Samuel	143	BURBANK, Ezra Lewis	147
BRYANT, Bethiah	15	BRYANT, Sarah	143	BURBANK, Hannah	81
BRYANT, Caleb	199	BRYANT, Stephen	15	BURBANK, Isaac	81
BRYANT, Daved	15	BRYANT, Stephen	68	BURBANK, Joanna	207
BRYANT, Ebenazar	30	BRYANT, Stephen	98	BURBANK, John	199
BRYANT, Ebenezer	124	BRYANT, Thomas	199	BURBANK, Joseph	81
BRYANT, Eleonar	143	BRYANT, Timothy	15	BURBANK, Joseph	181
BRYANT, Elizabeth	66	BRYANT, William	15	BURBANK, Joseph Clark	216
BRYANT, Hannah	15	BUCK, Abigail	66	BURBANK, Lucey	81
BRYANT, Ichabod	15	BUCK, Debrah	70	BURBANK, Lucy	181

Name	Page	Name	Page	Name	Page
BURBANK, Marcy	81	BURGES, Jabez	215	BURGESS, Vinal	222
BURBANK, Mary	74	BURGES, Jemimah	215	BURGIS, Elizabeth	181
BURBANK, Mary	105	BURGES, John	193	BURN, Elizabeth	88
BURBANK, Mary	107	BURGES, John	207	BURN, George	88
BURBANK, Mercy	188	BURGES, Lucy	206	BURN, Margaret	88
BURBANK, Nehemiah	204	BURGES, Lucy	207	BURN, Michael	88
BURBANK, Nehemiah	214	BURGES, Lydia	167	BURN, Samuel	88
BURBANK, Priscilla	195	BURGES, Lydia	204	BURN, Timasin	88
BURBANK, Priscilla Ann	147	BURGES, Marsey	27	BURNE, Michael	88
BURBANK, Prisscilla	148	BURGES, Mary	27	BURR, Mary	190
BURBANK, Rebeckah	81	BURGES, Mercy	198	BURROWS, Thomas Edward	185
BURBANK, Samuel	201	BURGES, Mercy	213	BURT, Adoniram	132
BURBANK, T.	172	BURGES, Nathan	199	BURT, Almira	132
BURBANK, Timothy	74	BURGES, Nathan	214	BURT, Benjamin Thomas	132
BURBANK, Timothy	81	BURGES, Nathaniel	27	BURT, Charity S.	132
BURBANK, William S.	147	BURGES, Patience	153	BURT, Charlotte H.	132
BURBANK, William Sherman	147	BURGES, Patience	184	BURT, Edward	132
BURBANKS, Hannah	174	BURGES, Polley	167	BURT, Edward	218
BURBANKS, Isaac	180	BURGES, Polley	204	BURT, Elizabeth	132
BURBANKS, Mary	81	BURGES, Rebecca	205	BURT, Elizabeth C.	132
BURBANKS, Rebeckah	172	BURGES, Ruth	191	BURT, Eunice D.	132
BURBANKS, Timothy	81	BURGES, Ruth	204	BURT, John E.	132
BURBANKS, Timothy	128	BURGES, Samuel	27	BURT, Laben	208
BURG, Elizabeth	130	BURGES, Thankfull	27	BURT, Silas Hathaway	132
BURGAS, Elizabeth	27	BURGES, Thankfull	124	BURT, Tamson Clark	132
BURGE, Ebenezer	121	BURGES, Thankfull	193	BURT, Thomas B.	132
BURGE, Jabez	84	BURGES, Thomas	153	BURT, William B.	132
BURGE, Jedidah	84	BURGES, Thomas	167	BURTON, Elizabeth	104
BURGE, Joseph	214	BURGES, Thomas	191	BURTON, Elizabeth	107
BURGE, Nathaniel	84	BURGES, Thomas	207	BUSHOP, Hannah	69
BURGE, Patience	108	BURGES, Thomas	212	BUTTERWORTH, John	190
BURGE, Samuel	84	BURGES, Thos.	216		
BURGE, Samuel	125	BURGES, William	167	**C**	
BURGE, Thomas	108	BURGES, William	193		
BURGE, Thomas	116	BURGES, William	217	CAHOON, Elizabeth	218
BURGE, Zacheus	118	BURGESS, Albert Thomas	144	CAHOON, Martha	210
BURGE, Zurviah	201	BURGESS, Anna	144	CAHOON, Mary	222
BURGES, Abner	209	BURGESS, Betsey	144	CAHOON, Mehitable	207
BURGES, Anna	212	BURGESS, Catharine	144	CAHOON, Samuel	207
BURGES, Benjamin	27	BURGESS, Elizabeth James	144	CAHOUN, Daty	222
BURGES, Chandler	207	BURGESS, James	144	CAHOUN, Freeman	222
BURGES, Ebenezer	27	BURGESS, John	144	CAHOUN, Mark	222
BURGES, Elizabeth	153	BURGESS, John (Capt.)	144	CALDERWOOD, John	198
BURGES, Elizabeth	214	BURGESS, Mary Ann	144	CALDERWOOD, Patience	209
BURGES, Eunice	216	BURGESS, Rebecca	220	CALDERWOOD, Priscilla	141
BURGES, George	200	BURGESS, Sally	137	CALDERWOOD, Priscilla	197
BURGES, Hannah	217	BURGESS, Sarah	222	CALDERWOOD, Saml.	141
BURGES, Hannah	219	BURGESS, Sophia	144	CALDERWOOD, Samuel	176
BURGES, Irana Sanger	215	BURGESS, Susan	144	CALDERWOOD, Samuell	141
BURGES, Jabez	27	BURGESS, Thomas	153	CALEE, Mary	73

VITAL RECORDS OF THE TOWN OF PLYMOUTH

CALEE, Peter	73	CARVER, James	190	CARVER, William	171
CALLEY, Stephen	113	CARVER, James M.	136	CASE, John	75
CAMBELL, John	149	CARVER, Jerusha	111	CASE, John	86
CAMBELL, Sarah	149	CARVER, John	18	CASE, John	125
CAMBELL, William Wallace	149	CARVER, John	35	CASE, Rebecah	86
CAMPBELL, Andrew	165	CARVER, John	61	CASE, Rebeckah	75
CAMPBELL, Andrew	188	CARVER, John	66	CASE, William	176
CAMPBELL, Bathshua	165	CARVER, John	115	CASEWELL, Henry	211
CAMPBELL, Dunking	186	CARVER, John	150	CASSADAY, William	194
CAMPBELL, John	153	CARVER, John	201	CASSEDAY, Salley	212
CAMPBELL, Mary	165	CARVER, Josiah	61	CASSEDY, Henry	213
CAMPBELL, Sarah	153	CARVER, Josiah	71	CASWELL, Alanson	212
CAMPBELL, Sarah H.	153	CARVER, Josiah	75	CASWELL, James	199
CAMPBELL, Susannah	165	CARVER, Josiah	111	CASWELL, Thomas	199
CAMPBELL, William Wallace	153	CARVER, Josiah	118	CASWELL, Thomas	218
CAMPBLE, William	182	CARVER, Josiah	123	CASWELL, William	211
CANNEDY, Annable	14	CARVER, Josiah	125	CATTO, John Mack	189
CANNEDY, Elaxander	14	CARVER, Josiah	201	CELLER, James	121
CANNEDY, Elizabeth	14	CARVER, Josiah (Capt.)	77	CEPET, Joannah	111
CANNEDY, Hannah	14	CARVER, Josiah (Capt.)	217	CEPET, Joslin	111
CANNEDY, Jean	14	CARVER, Lemuel	18	CEPIT, Joslen	123
CANNEDY, John	14	CARVER, Lucy	136	CHADLER, Stetson	218
CANNEDY, Sarah	14	CARVER, Marcy	61	CHAMBERLIN, Deborah	216
CANNEDY, William	14	CARVER, Marcy	171	CHAMBERS, William	172
CARPENTER, Mary	96	CARVER, Margarett	137	CHANDLER, David Lothrop	133
CARTE, Eliza.	123	CARVER, Mary	35	CHANDLER, Deborah	198
CARTEE, Benjamin	54	CARVER, Mary	59	CHANDLER, Ephraim	215
CARTEE, Benjamin	77	CARVER, Mary	66	CHANDLER, Everline Coleman	133
CARTEE, Benjamin	118	CARVER, Mary	71	CHANDLER, Hannah	106
CARTEE, Elizabeth	54	CARVER, Mary	197	CHANDLER, Jerusha	133
CARTEE, Elizabeth	77	CARVER, Mercy	77	CHANDLER, John	212
CARTER, Mary	204	CARVER, Mercy	197	CHANDLER, John Brown	133
CARVER, -----	61	CARVER, Nathaniel	61	CHANDLER, Mary	70
CARVER, ----- (female)	61	CARVER, Nathaniel	150	CHANDLER, Reuben	106
CARVER, Bethiah	75	CARVER, Nathaniel	156	CHANDLER, Reuben	113
CARVER, Branch	137	CARVER, Nathaniel	179	CHANDLER, Samuel	133
CARVER, Caleb	100	CARVER, Nathaniel	197	CHANDLER, Samuel Bartlett	133
CARVER, Catharine	136	CARVER, Polley	200	CHAPMAN, Samuel	216
CARVER, Chandler	136	CARVER, Robert	35	CHASE, Abigail	158
CARVER, Deborah	116	CARVER, Robert	59	CHASE, John	158
CARVER, Dorithy	71	CARVER, Robert	71	CHASE, John	163
CARVER, Dorothy	61	CARVER, Rueben	113	CHASE, John	190
CARVER, Dorothy	182	CARVER, Ruth	215	CHASE, John	205
CARVER, Elizabeth	59	CARVER, Salley	214	CHASE, Lydia	163
CARVER, Grace	18	CARVER, Sarah	18	CHASE, Lydia Allen	163
CARVER, Hannah	35	CARVER, Sarah	150	CHASE, Rebecca	195
CARVER, Hope	140	CARVER, Sarah	156	CHASE, Zenas Ripley	163
CARVER, Hope	180	CARVER, Sarah	198	CHILDS, Benjamin	215
CARVER, James	61	CARVER, Sarah Jane	150	CHIPMAN, Priscilla	58
CARVER, James	140	CARVER, Thomas	137	CHIPMAN, Seth	58
CARVER, James	171	CARVER, William	137	CHIPMAN, Seth	129

VITAL RECORDS OF THE TOWN OF PLYMOUTH

CHITMAN, Seth	129	CHURCH, Joseph	35	CHURCHELL, Amariah	32
CHITTENDEN, Mary	70	CHURCH, Joseph	39	CHURCHELL, Amariah	107
CHITTENTON, Alithea	71	CHURCH, Joseph	69	CHURCHELL, Amaziah	116
CHITTENTON, Allatheah	130	CHURCH, Joseph	99	CHURCHELL, Amaziah	188
CHUBBUCK, Abigail	213	CHURCH, Judith	70	CHURCHELL, Amaziah	212
CHUBBUCK, Alce	120	CHURCH, Juduth	35	CHURCHELL, Ansell	91
CHUBBUCK, Anna	198	CHURCH, Juduth	69	CHURCHELL, Asa	94
CHUBBUCK, Benjamin	212	CHURCH, Mary	38	CHURCHELL, Asenath	205
CHUBBUCK, Betsey	202	CHURCH, Mary	121	CHURCHELL, Barnabas	79
CHUBBUCK, Deborah	220	CHURCH, Rebeckah	39	CHURCHELL, Barnabas	102
CHUBBUCK, Elce	78	CHURCH, Richard	129	CHURCHELL, Barnabas	116
CHUBBUCK, Ephraim	198	CHURCH, Sarah	35	CHURCHELL, Barnabas	121
CHUBBUCK, Fear	215	CHURCH, Sarah	39	CHURCHELL, Barnabas	191
CHUBBUCK, Fear	218	CHURCH, Sarah	70	CHURCHELL, Barnabas	206
CHUBBUCK, Hannah	184	CHURCH, Sarah	73	CHURCHELL, Bathsheba	194
CHUBBUCK, John	193	CHURCH, Sarah	117	CHURCHELL, Bathsheba	200
CHUBBUCK, Lott	212	CHURCH, Sarah	126	CHURCHELL, Benja.	123
CHUBBUCK, Lowis	212	CHURCHEL, Abiah	50	CHURCHELL, Benjamin	82
CHUBBUCK, Margaret	193	CHURCHEL, Abigail	194	CHURCHELL, Benjamin	108
CHUBBUCK, Martha	126	CHURCHEL, Caleb	205	CHURCHELL, Benjamin	191
CHUBBUCK, Nathaniel	125	CHURCHEL, Desire	26	CHURCHELL, Bethiah	13
CHUBBUCK, Nathaniel	214	CHURCHEL, Eliza.	165	CHURCHELL, Bethiah	75
CHUBBUCK, Rowland	218	CHURCHEL, Ephraim	74	CHURCHELL, Bethiah	125
CHUBBUCK, Ruth	198	CHURCHEL, Ephraim	157	CHURCHELL, Bethiah	200
CHUBBUCK, Tabethy	201	CHURCHEL, Hannah	130	CHURCHELL, Betsey	206
CHUBBUCK, Zilpah	213	CHURCHEL, Hannah	173	CHURCHELL, Betsey	208
CHUBOCK, Mary	53	CHURCHEL, Jedidah	70	CHURCHELL, Betsey	209
CHUBUCK, Benjamine	53	CHURCHEL, John	99	CHURCHELL, Branch	13
CHUBUCK, Ealles	53	CHURCHEL, Joseph	50	CHURCHELL, Branch	190
CHUBUCK, Jonathan	53	CHURCHEL, Marcy	50	CHURCHELL, Caleb	32
CHUBUCK, Lydia	198	CHURCHEL, Margoret	50	CHURCHELL, Caleb	165
CHUBUCK, Martha	53	CHURCHEL, Mehitebel	118	CHURCHELL, Caleb	188
CHUBUCK, Mary	53	CHURCHEL, Nathaniel	100	CHURCHELL, Charles	91
CHUBUCK, Nathaniel	53	CHURCHEL, Nathaniel	117	CHURCHELL, Charles	157
CHUBUCK, Sarah	53	CHURCHEL, Patience	198	CHURCHELL, Charles	199
CHUBUCK, Susanna	53	CHURCHEL, Peleg	197	CHURCHELL, Daniel	201
CHUMMUCK, Abigail	78	CHURCHEL, Priscilla	74	CHURCHELL, David	166
CHUMMUCK, Bethiah	215	CHURCHEL, Rebeckah	99	CHURCHELL, Desire	67
CHUMMUCK, James	188	CHURCHEL, Samuel	165	CHURCHELL, Ebenezer	13
CHUMMUCK, James	206	CHURCHELL, -----	96	CHURCHELL, Ebenezer	104
CHUMMUCK, James	214	CHURCHELL, ----- (female)	94	CHURCHELL, Ebenezer	112
CHUMMUCK, Jesse	214	CHURCHELL, Abiah	77	CHURCHELL, Ebenezer	113
CHUMMUCK, Jesse	215	CHURCHELL, Abiah	118	CHURCHELL, Ebenezer	132
CHUMUCK, Abigail	121	CHURCHELL, Abigail	13	CHURCHELL, Ebenezer	171
CHURCCH, Hannah	70	CHURCHELL, Abigail	42	CHURCHELL, Ebenezr.	208
CHURCCH, Middleton	70	CHURCHELL, Abigail	107	CHURCHELL, Ebenzr	188
CHURCH, Benjamin	38	CHURCHELL, Abigail	165	CHURCHELL, Edmond	205
CHURCH, Charles	38	CHURCHELL, Abigail	166	CHURCHELL, Eleazer	13
CHURCH, Charles	39	CHURCHELL, Abigail	188	CHURCHELL, Eleazer	78
CHURCH, Deborah	38	CHURCHELL, Abigail Worchester	166	CHURCHELL, Eleazer	94
CHURCH, Hannah	129	CHURCHELL, Abner	82	CHURCHELL, Eleazer	96

VITAL RECORDS OF THE TOWN OF PLYMOUTH

CHURCHELL, Eleazer	121	CHURCHELL, Harriot	208	CHURCHELL, Josiah	78
CHURCHELL, Eleazer	188	CHURCHELL, Heman	199	CHURCHELL, Josiah	82
CHURCHELL, Elezabeth	134	CHURCHELL, Henry	165	CHURCHELL, Josiah	122
CHURCHELL, Elisabeth	32	CHURCHELL, Hose	213	CHURCHELL, Lemuel	107
CHURCHELL, Eliza.	32	CHURCHELL, Ichabod	102	CHURCHELL, Lemuel	165
CHURCHELL, Elizabeth	32	CHURCHELL, Isaac	165	CHURCHELL, Lemuell	42
CHURCHELL, Elizabeth	102	CHURCHELL, Isaac	172	CHURCHELL, Lemuell	104
CHURCHELL, Elizabeth	107	CHURCHELL, Isaac	190	CHURCHELL, Lemuell	109
CHURCHELL, Elizabeth	181	CHURCHELL, Jabez	190	CHURCHELL, Lemuell	113
CHURCHELL, Elizabeth	188	CHURCHELL, Jabez	206	CHURCHELL, Lewis	198
CHURCHELL, Elizabeth	189	CHURCHELL, James	94	CHURCHELL, Lewis	199
CHURCHELL, Elizabeth	197	CHURCHELL, James	188	CHURCHELL, Lewis	217
CHURCHELL, Elizabeth	206	CHURCHELL, Jane	194	CHURCHELL, Lucey	102
CHURCHELL, Elka.	113	CHURCHELL, Jane	199	CHURCHELL, Lucy	32
CHURCHELL, Elkanah	13	CHURCHELL, Jean	132	CHURCHELL, Lucy	165
CHURCHELL, Elkanah	30	CHURCHELL, Jedidah	13	CHURCHELL, Lucy	193
CHURCHELL, Elkanah	109	CHURCHELL, Jesse	96	CHURCHELL, Lucy	194
CHURCHELL, Elkanah	157	CHURCHELL, Jesse	165	CHURCHELL, Lucy	206
CHURCHELL, Elkanah	204	CHURCHELL, Jesse	184	CHURCHELL, Lydia	42
CHURCHELL, Ellis	91	CHURCHELL, Joanna	197	CHURCHELL, Lydia	79
CHURCHELL, Ellis	153	CHURCHELL, Joannah	13	CHURCHELL, Lydia	102
CHURCHELL, Enos	198	CHURCHELL, Job	102	CHURCHELL, Lydia	109
CHURCHELL, Ephraim	91	CHURCHELL, Job	212	CHURCHELL, Lydia	129
CHURCHELL, Ephraim	101	CHURCHELL, John	26	CHURCHELL, Lydia	131
CHURCHELL, Ephraim	124	CHURCHELL, John	48	CHURCHELL, Lydia	158
CHURCHELL, Ephraim	134	CHURCHELL, John	67	CHURCHELL, Lydia	191
CHURCHELL, Ephraim	206	CHURCHELL, John	91	CHURCHELL, Lydia	202
CHURCHELL, Esther	217	CHURCHELL, John	102	CHURCHELL, Marcy	13
CHURCHELL, Experience	87	CHURCHELL, John	112	CHURCHELL, Marcy	94
CHURCHELL, Experience	106	CHURCHELL, John	113	CHURCHELL, Marcy	95
CHURCHELL, Experience	128	CHURCHELL, John	132	CHURCHELL, Marcy	111
CHURCHELL, Ezra	42	CHURCHELL, John	172	CHURCHELL, Marcy	112
CHURCHELL, Faith	32	CHURCHELL, John	177	CHURCHELL, Marcy	174
CHURCHELL, Faith	188	CHURCHELL, John	185	CHURCHELL, Margeret	77
CHURCHELL, Fanney	218	CHURCHELL, John	189	CHURCHELL, Marget	119
CHURCHELL, Francis	96	CHURCHELL, John	204	CHURCHELL, Maria	30
CHURCHELL, Gamaliel	139	CHURCHELL, Jona.	115	CHURCHELL, Maria	111
CHURCHELL, George	13	CHURCHELL, Jonathan	13	CHURCHELL, Mariah	104
CHURCHELL, George	194	CHURCHELL, Jonathan	96	CHURCHELL, Mariah	111
CHURCHELL, Hannah	13	CHURCHELL, Jonathan	158	CHURCHELL, Mariah	117
CHURCHELL, Hannah	73	CHURCHELL, Jonathan	181	CHURCHELL, Mariah	128
CHURCHELL, Hannah	78	CHURCHELL, Joseph	94	CHURCHELL, Martha	132
CHURCHELL, Hannah	94	CHURCHELL, Joseph	102	CHURCHELL, Mary	13
CHURCHELL, Hannah	95	CHURCHELL, Joseph	111	CHURCHELL, Mary	32
CHURCHELL, Hannah	96	CHURCHELL, Joseph	116	CHURCHELL, Mary	70
CHURCHELL, Hannah	166	CHURCHELL, Joseph	157	CHURCHELL, Mary	87
CHURCHELL, Hannah	175	CHURCHELL, Joseph	166	CHURCHELL, Mary	91
CHURCHELL, Hannah	180	CHURCHELL, Joseph	206	CHURCHELL, Mary	105
CHURCHELL, Hannah	191	CHURCHELL, Joseph	213	CHURCHELL, Mary	107
CHURCHELL, Hannah	200	CHURCHELL, Joshua	50	CHURCHELL, Mary	129
CHURCHELL, Hannah	204	CHURCHELL, Josiah	13	CHURCHELL, Mary	134

VITAL RECORDS OF THE TOWN OF PLYMOUTH

CHURCHELL, Mary	139	CHURCHELL, Ruth	108	CHURCHELL, Susannah	183
CHURCHELL, Mary	158	CHURCHELL, Salley	165	CHURCHELL, Susannah	188
CHURCHELL, Mary	173	CHURCHELL, Salley	205	CHURCHELL, Sylvanus	202
CHURCHELL, Mary	190	CHURCHELL, Salley	210	CHURCHELL, Sylvanus Harlow	159
CHURCHELL, Mary	194	CHURCHELL, Saml.	102	CHURCHELL, Temperance	206
CHURCHELL, Mendal	165	CHURCHELL, Saml.	111	CHURCHELL, Thaddeus	82
CHURCHELL, Mendell	32	CHURCHELL, Samll.	113	CHURCHELL, Thaddeus	202
CHURCHELL, Mercy	195	CHURCHELL, Samuel	50	CHURCHELL, Thadeus	188
CHURCHELL, Mercy	208	CHURCHELL, Samuel	82	CHURCHELL, Thomas	139
CHURCHELL, Meriah	102	CHURCHELL, Samuel	96	CHURCHELL, Thomas	174
CHURCHELL, Meriah	201	CHURCHELL, Samuel	157	CHURCHELL, Timothey	208
CHURCHELL, Merriam	194	CHURCHELL, Samuel	165	CHURCHELL, Timothy	132
CHURCHELL, Mordica	85	CHURCHELL, Samuel	189	CHURCHELL, William	69
CHURCHELL, Nancey	211	CHURCHELL, Samuel	193	CHURCHELL, William	85
CHURCHELL, Nancy	203	CHURCHELL, Samuel	201	CHURCHELL, William	209
CHURCHELL, Nancy	216	CHURCHELL, Samuel	202	CHURCHELL, Willm.	111
CHURCHELL, Nathan	206	CHURCHELL, Samuel	205	CHURCHELL, Willm.	123
CHURCHELL, Nathaniel	42	CHURCHELL, Samuell	26	CHURCHELL, Willson	186
CHURCHELL, Nathaniel	87	CHURCHELL, Sarah	26	CHURCHELL, Willson	217
CHURCHELL, Nathaniel	201	CHURCHELL, Sarah	50	CHURCHELL, Wilson	82
CHURCHELL, Nathl.	184	CHURCHELL, Sarah	78	CHURCHELL, Zacheus	91
CHURCHELL, Nathll.	13	CHURCHELL, Sarah	94	CHURCHELL, Zacheus	129
CHURCHELL, Olive	158	CHURCHELL, Sarah	95	CHURCHELL, Zacheus	131
CHURCHELL, Patience	78	CHURCHELL, Sarah	102	CHURCHELL, Zacheus	134
CHURCHELL, Patience	82	CHURCHELL, Sarah	112	CHURCHELL, Zadock	95
CHURCHELL, Patience	153	CHURCHELL, Sarah	127	CHURCHIL, -----	46
CHURCHELL, Patience	197	CHURCHELL, Sarah	157	CHURCHIL, Benjamin	46
CHURCHELL, Patience	201	CHURCHELL, Sarah	165	CHURCHIL, Deborah	217
CHURCHELL, Peleg	95	CHURCHELL, Sarah	188	CHURCHIL, Ephraim	46
CHURCHELL, Phebe	26	CHURCHELL, Sarah	195	CHURCHIL, Mary	46
CHURCHELL, Phebe	73	CHURCHELL, Sarah	202	CHURCHIL, Nathaniel	46
CHURCHELL, Phebe	94	CHURCHELL, Sarah	207	CHURCHIL, Stephen	46
CHURCHELL, Phebe	126	CHURCHELL, Seth	102	CHURCHIL, Zacaus	46
CHURCHELL, Polley	206	CHURCHELL, Seth	193	CHURCHILL, ----- (male)	47
CHURCHELL, Priscilla	26	CHURCHELL, Seth	213	CHURCHILL, Abigaiel	67
CHURCHELL, Priscilla	91	CHURCHELL, Silvanus	94	CHURCHILL, Abigail	30
CHURCHELL, Priscilla	101	CHURCHELL, Simeon	166	CHURCHILL, Amaziah	55
CHURCHELL, Priscilla	194	CHURCHELL, Solomon	32	CHURCHILL, Amaziah	202
CHURCHELL, Rebeca	26	CHURCHELL, Stephen	13	CHURCHILL, Andrew	30
CHURCHELL, Rebecah	85	CHURCHELL, Stephen	78	CHURCHILL, Ansell	180
CHURCHELL, Rebecca	75	CHURCHELL, Stephen	95	CHURCHILL, Barnabas	29
CHURCHELL, Rebecca	194	CHURCHELL, Stephen	96	CHURCHILL, Barnabas	48
CHURCHELL, Rebeccah	125	CHURCHELL, Stephen	120	CHURCHILL, Barnabas	70
CHURCHELL, Rebeckah	13	CHURCHELL, Stephen	181	CHURCHILL, Barnabas	159
CHURCHELL, Rebeckah	183	CHURCHELL, Stephen	198	CHURCHILL, Bartlett	154
CHURCHELL, Reubin	195	CHURCHELL, Susanah	30	CHURCHILL, Bethiah	71
CHURCHELL, Ruben	96	CHURCHELL, Susanna	85	CHURCHILL, Beththya	55
CHURCHELL, Rufus	157	CHURCHELL, Susannah	30	CHURCHILL, Betsey W.	154
CHURCHELL, Rufus	200	CHURCHELL, Susannah	85	CHURCHILL, Branch	212
CHURCHELL, Ruth	69	CHURCHELL, Susannah	109	CHURCHILL, Charles	180
CHURCHELL, Ruth	82	CHURCHELL, Susannah	111	CHURCHILL, Charles	220

VITAL RECORDS OF THE TOWN OF PLYMOUTH

CHURCHILL, Cornelius Bradford	159	CHURCHILL, Lydia	180	CLARK, Anna	170
CHURCHILL, Ebenazar	55	CHURCHILL, Margeret	29	CLARK, Anna	194
CHURCHILL, Ebenezer	48	CHURCHILL, Margeret	69	CLARK, Annah	8
CHURCHILL, Ebenezer	186	CHURCHILL, Mary	65	CLARK, Annah	50
CHURCHILL, Eleazar	47	CHURCHILL, Mary	100	CLARK, Bartlett	168
CHURCHILL, Eleazar	100	CHURCHILL, Mary	190	CLARK, Benjamin	197
CHURCHILL, Eleazer	178	CHURCHILL, Mary	221	CLARK, Benjamin	215
CHURCHILL, Eliazar	47	CHURCHILL, Meriah	55	CLARK, Betsey	204
CHURCHILL, Eliazar	100	CHURCHILL, Patience	178	CLARK, Betsey	215
CHURCHILL, Elizabeth	10	CHURCHILL, Patience	222	CLARK, Betsey	219
CHURCHILL, Elizabeth	70	CHURCHILL, Picila	129	CLARK, Bettey	94
CHURCHILL, Elkana	129	CHURCHILL, Priscillah	173	CLARK, Consider	205
CHURCHILL, Elkanah	55	CHURCHILL, Prissilla	71	CLARK, Cornelius	75
CHURCHILL, Elkanah	71	CHURCHILL, Rebecca	70	CLARK, Cornelius	125
CHURCHILL, Elkanath	55	CHURCHILL, Rebeckah	10	CLARK, Daniel	207
CHURCHILL, Ellis	178	CHURCHILL, Rebekah	66	CLARK, David	168
CHURCHILL, Enos	82	CHURCHILL, Sally	159	CLARK, Deborah	94
CHURCHILL, Eunice	154	CHURCHILL, Samuel	12	CLARK, Deborah	207
CHURCHILL, Hanah	47	CHURCHILL, Sarah	10	CLARK, Deborah	216
CHURCHILL, Hanna	70	CHURCHILL, Sarah	29	CLARK, Deborah	219
CHURCHILL, Hannah	10	CHURCHILL, Sarah	179	CLARK, Edward	183
CHURCHILL, Hannah T.	159	CHURCHILL, Sarah	180	CLARK, Eliza.	203
CHURCHILL, Henery	65	CHURCHILL, Sarah S.	222	CLARK, Elizabeth	66
CHURCHILL, Henry	154	CHURCHILL, Sarah Warren	222	CLARK, Elizabeth	175
CHURCHILL, Hosea	154	CHURCHILL, Silas M.	154	CLARK, Elizabeth	191
CHURCHILL, Ichabod	48	CHURCHILL, Silvanus	82	CLARK, Experience	109
CHURCHILL, Isaac	48	CHURCHILL, Solomon	194	CLARK, Experience	198
CHURCHILL, Jabez	30	CHURCHILL, Suzana	71	CLARK, Ezra	168
CHURCHILL, James	12	CHURCHILL, Suzannah	55	CLARK, Grace	94
CHURCHILL, Job	159	CHURCHILL, Thaddeus	202	CLARK, Grace	194
CHURCHILL, John	10	CHURCHILL, Thomas	48	CLARK, Hannah	13
CHURCHILL, John	29	CHURCHILL, William	11	CLARK, Hannah	50
CHURCHILL, John	55	CHURCHILL, William	48	CLARK, Hannah	65
CHURCHILL, John	66	CHURCHILL, William	66	CLARK, Hannah	156
CHURCHILL, John	71	CHURCHILL, Zadock	186	CLARK, Hannah	209
CHURCHILL, John	129	CHURCHL, Experianc	46	CLARK, Israel	204
CHURCHILL, John	181	CHURCHL, John (Serjant)	55	CLARK, Israell	94
CHURCHILL, John (Serjant)	70	CIMBOL, Abigail	129	CLARK, James	36
CHURCHILL, John Clark	154	CLAGHORN, Mathew	175	CLARK, James	50
CHURCHILL, Jonathan	47	CLARK, Abiah	65	CLARK, James	61
CHURCHILL, Joseph	29	CLARK, Abigail	36	CLARK, James	101
CHURCHILL, Joseph	48	CLARK, Abigail	94	CLARK, James	105
CHURCHILL, Josiah	12	CLARK, Abigail	111	CLARK, James	123
CHURCHILL, Josiah	47	CLARK, Abigail	116	CLARK, James	129
CHURCHILL, Lemuel	48	CLARK, Abigail	117	CLARK, James	168
CHURCHILL, Liddiah	66	CLARK, Abigail	195	CLARK, James	170
CHURCHILL, Lidiah	11	CLARK, Abigail	202	CLARK, James	193
CHURCHILL, Lidiah	12	CLARK, Abigal	61	CLARK, Jerusha	94
CHURCHILL, Lidiah	48	CLARK, Abigall	8	CLARK, Jerusha	181
CHURCHILL, Lidiah	70	CLARK, Amasa	214	CLARK, Jerusha	221
CHURCHILL, Lydia	48	CLARK, Ann	61	CLARK, Joana	67

VITAL RECORDS OF THE TOWN OF PLYMOUTH

CLARK, Joanna	51	CLARK, Ruth	111	CLARKE, Bethiah	38
CLARK, John	36	CLARK, Ruth	213	CLARKE, Bethyah	69
CLARK, John	50	CLARK, Samuel	208	CLARKE, Elizabeth	8
CLARK, John	61	CLARK, Sarah	8	CLARKE, Elizabeth	54
CLARK, John	198	CLARK, Sarah	125	CLARKE, Elizabeth	70
CLARK, John	199	CLARK, Sarah	168	CLARKE, Elizebeth	8
CLARK, John	200	CLARK, Sarah	195	CLARKE, Esther	222
CLARK, John	212	CLARK, Sarah	215	CLARKE, Experience	93
CLARK, Jonas	181	CLARK, Seth	50	CLARKE, Experience	94
CLARK, Jonathan	168	CLARK, Seth	94	CLARKE, Ezra	222
CLARK, Joseph	156	CLARK, Seth	197	CLARKE, Hanna	71
CLARK, Josiah	156	CLARK, Susanah	8	CLARKE, Hannah	13
CLARK, Josiah	181	CLARK, Susanah	75	CLARKE, Hannah	52
CLARK, Josiah	189	CLARK, Susannah	36	CLARKE, Hannah	79
CLARK, Josiah	208	CLARK, Susannah	111	CLARKE, Hannah	97
CLARK, Lemuel (Capt.)	219	CLARK, Susannah	123	CLARKE, Hannah	121
CLARK, Lewis	168	CLARK, Susannah	189	CLARKE, HANNAH	123
CLARK, Lothrop	50	CLARK, Suzanna	129	CLARKE, Hannah	188
CLARK, Lothrop	204	CLARK, Thankfull	94	CLARKE, Israel	122
CLARK, Lucy	78	CLARK, Thankfull	168	CLARKE, Israiell	54
CLARK, Lucy	168	CLARK, Thankfull	184	CLARKE, James	20
CLARK, Lucy	207	CLARK, Thankfull	212	CLARKE, James	130
CLARK, Luranah	128	CLARK, Thankfull	214	CLARKE, Jams	71
CLARK, Lurania	94	CLARK, Thomas	8	CLARKE, Joanna	71
CLARK, Lurania	104	CLARK, Thomas	66	CLARKE, John	20
CLARK, Lurany	195	CLARK, Thomas	94	CLARKE, John	80
CLARK, Lydia	180	CLARK, Thomas	111	CLARKE, John	99
CLARK, Lydia	213	CLARK, Thomas	189	CLARKE, John	127
CLARK, Mariah	50	CLARK, Thomas	194	CLARKE, John H.	222
CLARK, Mary	50	CLARK, Thomas	199	CLARKE, Joseph	20
CLARK, Mary	178	CLARK, Thomas	209	CLARKE, Josiah	8
CLARK, Mary	208	CLARK, William	13	CLARKE, Josiah	54
CLARK, Meriah	183	CLARK, William	65	CLARKE, Josiah	93
CLARK, Meriba	61	CLARK, William	176	CLARKE, Josiah	94
CLARK, Meribah	74	CLARK, William	181	CLARKE, Josiah	98
CLARK, Nancy	217	CLARK, William	197	CLARKE, Lothrop	186
CLARK, Nancy	220	CLARK, William	212	CLARKE, Luce	121
CLARK, Nathaniel	194	CLARK, Willm.	109	CLARKE, Lucie	52
CLARK, Nathaniel	201	CLARK, Wm.	173	CLARKE, Lurany	52
CLARK, Nathaniel	215	CLARKE, -----	54	CLARKE, Lydia	51
CLARK, Olive	94	CLARKE, ----- (Deacon)	46	CLARKE, Lydia	93
CLARK, Patience	198	CLARKE, Abia	13	CLARKE, Lydia	222
CLARK, Patience	214	CLARKE, Abigail	66	CLARKE, Marriah	46
CLARK, Phebe	213	CLARKE, Abigail	94	CLARKE, Mary	20
CLARK, Polley	201	CLARKE, Abigal	73	CLARKE, Mary	46
CLARK, Polley	213	CLARKE, Abigal	130	CLARKE, Mary	52
CLARK, Polley Bramhall	218	CLARKE, Abigall	20	CLARKE, Mary	70
CLARK, Rebecca	168	CLARKE, Abigel	51	CLARKE, Matthew	38
CLARK, Rebeccah	61	CLARKE, Anna	71	CLARKE, Meriah	124
CLARK, Rebeckah	108	CLARKE, Anna	129	CLARKE, Meribah	124
CLARK, Rebeckah	117	CLARKE, Bathshabe	69	CLARKE, Nathaniel	13

CLARKE, Nathaniel	38	CLERK, Suzannah	8	COBB, Cornelius	143	
CLARKE, Nathl.	93	CLERK, Thomas	8	COBB, Cornelius	168	
CLARKE, Nathll.	94	CLERKE, Elizabeth	98	COBB, Cornelus	168	
CLARKE, Rebecaa	70	CLERKE, Thomas (Deacon)	98	COBB, Cornelus	187	
CLARKE, Rebecca	80	COAD, Hannah	146	COBB, David	143	
CLARKE, Rebecca	222	COAD, Jeams	146	COBB, Ebenazar	18	
CLARKE, Rebeck	46	COAD, Mary	146	COBB, Ebenazar	67	
CLARKE, Rebeckah	8	COAD, Sarah	146	COBB, Ebenazar	71	
CLARKE, Rebeka	20	COADE, James	178	COBB, Ebenazar	130	
CLARKE, Rebkah	97	COAN, Betsey	217	COBB, Ebenezer	74	
CLARKE, Salley	212	COB, ----- (female)	84	COBB, Ebenezer	186	
CLARKE, Samuel	13	COB, ----- (male)	84	COBB, Ebenezer	74	
CLARKE, Samuel	52	COB, Abigal	84	COBB, Ebenezor	8	
CLARKE, Samuel	70	COB, Ebenezer	57	COBB, Ebenezr.	172	
CLARKE, Sarah	13	COB, Ebenezer	127	COBB, Eleanor	184	
CLARKE, Sarah	38	COB, Ebenezer	128	COBB, Eleonar	136	
CLARKE, Sarah	46	COB, Elisha	87	COBB, Elish	34	
CLARKE, Sarah	50	COB, Elisha	118	COBB, Elisha	8	
CLARKE, Sarah	52	COB, Elizabeth	75	COBB, Elisha	15	
CLARKE, Sarah	67	COB, Elizabeth	86	COBB, Elisha	34	
CLARKE, Sarah	75	COB, Elizabeth	118	COBB, Elisha	69	
CLARKE, Sarah	117	COB, Ephraim	84	COBB, Elizabeth	18	
CLARKE, Sarah	124	COB, Fear	78	COBB, Elizabeth	77	
CLARKE, Sarah Roberts	220	COB, Jabez	105	COBB, Elizabeth	87	
CLARKE, Susan	222	COB, Jabez	107	COBB, Elizabeth	136	
CLARKE, Susanner	46	COB, Joannah	86	COBB, Elizabeth	203	
CLARKE, Suzannah	66	COB, Lemuel	78	COBB, Elizabeth	206	
CLARKE, Suzannah	71	COB, Lemuel	87	COBB, Fear	89	
CLARKE, Thankful	54	COB, Lydia	57	COBB, Fear	204	
CLARKE, Thomas	8	COB, Lydia	76	COBB, Freeman	197	
CLARKE, Thomas	46	COB, Lydia	118	COBB, Gase	168	
CLARKE, Thomas	51	COB, Marcy	74	COBB, Girshom	35	
CLARKE, Thomas	71	COB, Marcy	127	COBB, Grace	168	
CLARKE, Thomas	94	COB, Margaret	84	COBB, Hanna	35	
CLARKE, Thomas	97	COB, Mary	124	COBB, Hanna	71	
CLARKE, Thomas	98	COB, Nathan	86	COBB, Hanna	129	
CLARKE, Thomas	100	COB, Nathan	117	COBB, Hannah	18	
CLARKE, Thomas	101	COB, Priscilla	87	COBB, Hannah	57	
CLARKE, Thomas	187	COB, Rebeckah	84	COBB, Hannah	71	
CLARKE, Thos.	122	COB, Ruth	57	COBB, Hannah	77	
CLARKE, William	13	COB, Samuel	57	COBB, Hannah	120	
CLARKE, William	38	COB, Sarah	72	COBB, Hannah	136	
CLARKE, William	51	COB, Sarah	107	COBB, Hannah	140	
CLARKE, William	69	COB, Silvanus	75	COBB, Hannah	188	
CLARKE, William	93	COB, Silvanus	117	COBB, Hannah	197	
CLARKE, William	97	COB, Susannah	84	COBB, Hannah	208	
CLARKE, William	120	COB, William	86	COBB, Heman	205	
CLARKKE, Rebeckah	80	COBB, ----- (female)	92	COBB, Hust	35	
CLERK, Hannah	111	COBB, Abigail	136	COBB, Isaac	194	
CLERK, James	111	COBB, Bartlett	219	COBB, Isaac E.	168	
CLERK, Rebeckah	8	COBB, Betse	168	COBB, Isaac E.	218	

VITAL RECORDS OF THE TOWN OF PLYMOUTH

Name	Page	Name	Page	Name	Page
COBB, Isaiah	198	COBB, Lydia	143	COBB, Sarah	123
COBB, Jabez	61	COBB, Lydia	175	COBB, Sarah	130
COBB, Jabiz	35	COBB, Lydia	177	COBB, Sarah	136
COBB, James	8	COBB, Mallatiah	35	COBB, Sarah	171
COBB, James	35	COBB, Marcey	18	COBB, Sarah	172
COBB, James	69	COBB, Marcy	18	COBB, Sarah	174
COBB, James	181	COBB, Martha	8	COBB, Sarah	191
COBB, Jerusha	204	COBB, Martha	35	COBB, Sarah	199
COBB, Joanna	35	COBB, Mary	18	COBB, Scintha	202
COBB, Joannah	136	COBB, Mary	57	COBB, Seth	55
COBB, Joannah	140	COBB, Mary	71	COBB, Seth	77
COBB, Job	18	COBB, Mary	74	COBB, Seth	89
COBB, Job	115	COBB, Mary	92	COBB, Seth	100
COBB, Job	205	COBB, Mercy	18	COBB, Seth (Capt.)	101
COBB, Job	208	COBB, Mercy	67	COBB, Seth	118
COBB, Jobb	143	COBB, Nathan	18	COBB, Silvanos	35
COBB, Jobb	187	COBB, Nathan	183	COBB, Silvanus	61
COBB, John	8	COBB, Nathaniel	18	COBB, Silvanus	87
COBB, John	18	COBB, Nathaniel	57	COBB, Susannah	171
COBB, John	35	COBB, Nathaniel	71	COBB, William	136
COBB, John	61	COBB, Nathaniel	129	COBB, William	201
COBB, John	66	COBB, Nathaniel	186	COBB, William	217
COBB, John	84	COBB, Nathaniell	57	CODDING, George	173
COBB, John	92	COBB, Nehemiah	143	CODE, Joseph	199
COBB, John	100	COBB, Olive	189	CODE, Nanse	201
COBB, John	118	COBB, Patience	8	CODE, Sarah	205
COBB, John	136	COBB, Patience	35	COFFIN, Gardner	199
COBB, John	140	COBB, Patience	69	COLBURN, Lemuel	221
COBB, John	181	COBB, Patience	136	COLE, Benjamin	125
COBB, John	208	COBB, Patience	143	COLE, Elizabeth	65
COBB, John Kempton	209	COBB, Patience	191	COLE, Elizabeth	66
COBB, John Kempton	213	COBB, Pearces	136	COLE, Elizabeth	100
COBB, Joseph	71	COBB, Perces	136	COLE, Elizabeth	109
COBB, Josiah	92	COBB, Rachill	66	COLE, Elizabeth	116
COBB, Josiah	136	COBB, Rebecca	180	COLE, Ephraim	52
COBB, Kempton	209	COBB, Rebeckah	84	COLE, Ephraim	66
COBB, Lazarus	84	COBB, Rolon	18	COLE, Ephraim	81
COBB, Lemuel	35	COBB, Rowland	57	COLE, Ephraim	100
COBB, Lemuel	120	COBB, Rowland	143	COLE, Heugh	66
COBB, Lemuel	184	COBB, Rowland	193	COLE, Isaac	177
COBB, Lemuel	205	COBB, Ruth	71	COLE, Isaac	210
COBB, Lemuell	89	COBB, Ruth	136	COLE, James	81
COBB, Lemuell	101	COBB, Ruth	187	COLE, James	171
COBB, Lidiah	34	COBB, Ruthey	202	COLE, Joseph	128
COBB, Lidiah	35	COBB, Sarah	18	COLE, Lydia	181
COBB, Lidiah	69	COBB, Sarah	55	COLE, Lydia	206
COBB, Luce	57	COBB, Sarah	61	COLE, Marcy	74
COBB, Lucy	188	COBB, Sarah	77	COLE, Marcy	81
COBB, Lydia	74	COBB, Sarah	79	COLE, Marcy	124
COBB, Lydia	89	COBB, Sarah	89	COLE, Martha	186
COBB, Lydia	136	COBB, Sarah	92	COLE, Mary	129

VITAL RECORDS OF THE TOWN OF PLYMOUTH

COLE, Moses	117	CONANT, Sarah	198	COOK, William	38
COLE, Nathaniel	208	CONANT, Susannah	125	COOK, William	70
COLE, Patty	193	CONET, Charles	53	COOKE, Abigal	60
COLE, Peter	126	CONET, Elizabeth	53	COOKE, Abigal	130
COLE, Rebecka	100	CONET, George	53	COOKE, Ann	34
COLE, Rebeckah	52	CONET, Mary	53	COOKE, Anne	71
COLE, Rebeckah	105	CONETT, George	71	COOKE, Asa	52
COLE, Rebeckah	107	CONETT, Mary	71	COOKE, Caleb	130
COLE, Rebeckah	181	CONKLIN, Samuel	194	COOKE, Charles	60
COLE, Rebekah	66	CONNADAY, Elizabeth	69	COOKE, Elizabeth	59
COLE, Salley	208	CONNEL, Jeremiah	186	COOKE, Elizabeth	70
COLE, Samuel	74	CONNELL, Jeremiah	188	COOKE, Hannah	73
COLE, Samuel	81	CONNELL, Margarett	188	COOKE, Jacob	52
COLE, Samuel	128	CONNER, Eliza.	115	COOKE, Jesse	52
COLE, Samuel	206	CONNET, Josiah	120	COOKE, Joannah	75
COLE, Samuel Hermon	194	COOK, Bethiah	188	COOKE, John	59
COLE, Sarah	52	COOK, Caleb	34	COOKE, John	73
COLE, Sarah	112	COOK, Damores	22	COOKE, John	130
COLE, Sarah	113	COOK, Elisha	38	COOKE, Lidiah	22
COLEBURN, Rhoda	212	COOK, Elizabeth	34	COOKE, Lydiah	70
COLLENS, Bathshua	71	COOK, Elizabeth	66	COOKE, Marcy	59
COLLENS, John	71	COOK, Elizabeth	105	COOKE, Margret	70
COLLIN, Samuel Avery	217	COOK, Elizabeth	107	COOKE, Marsey	100
COLLINGS, Bathsheba	201	COOK, Frances	66	COOKE, Martha	65
COLLINGS, James	188	COOK, Hannah	38	COOKE, Mary	71
COLLINGS, James	193	COOK, Hulda	38	COOKE, Nathaniel	60
COLLINGS, John	201	COOK, Jacob	22	COOKE, Paul	59
COLLINGS, Mercy	212	COOK, Jacob	52	COOKE, Paul	75
COLLINGS, Nancey	212	COOK, James	34	COOKE, Paul	124
COLLINGS, Rebecca	216	COOK, Jane	34	COOKE, Phebe	52
COLLINGS, Salle	201	COOK, John	22	COOKE, Robert	59
COLLINGWOOD, Eleanor	158	COOK, John	34	COOKE, Robert	60
COLLINGWOOD, Ellen	158	COOK, John	210	COOKE, Sarah	60
COLLINGWOOD, James	158	COOK, Joseph	34	COOKE, Sarah	66
COLLINGWOOD, Jane	158	COOK, Josiah	22	COOKE, Silas	59
COLLINGWOOD, Mary	158	COOK, Lidiah	22	COOLE, Abigaiel	99
COLLINGWOOD, Robert	158	COOK, Lidiah	38	COOLE, Dorithy	71
COLLINGWOOD, Thomas	158	COOK, Marcy	34	COOLE, Dorothy	19
COLLINGWOOD, William	158	COOK, Margarett	22	COOLE, Ephraim	19
COLLONS, Elizabeth	171	COOK, Mary	34	COOLE, James	19
COLMAN, Joanna	71	COOK, Mary	52	COOLE, Martha	67
COLS, Ephraim	100	COOK, Mary	104	COOLE, Mary	19
COMBS, Elizabeth	66	COOK, Pricila	38	COOLE, Mary	71
COMESTOCK, William	212	COOK, Rebeckah	70	COOLE, Rebeckah	19
COMINGTON, Lydia	203	COOK, Rebekah	22	COOLE, Rebekah	19
COMINGTON, Nancy	205	COOK, Ruhama	79	COOLE, Samuel	19
COMMINTON, Hannah	217	COOK, Ruhami	123	COOMBS, Mary	66
CONANT, Lothrop	214	COOK, Stephen	52	COOMBS, Mary	129
CONANT, Mary	198	COOK, Tabitha	38	COOMER, William	104
CONANT, Prudence	74	COOK, Tabitha	70	COOMER, William	190
CONANT, Prudence	124	COOK, William	22	COOPER, Benjamin	199

COOPER, Calvin	213	CORNISH, Abigal	135	CORNISH, Joseph	19
COOPER, Eliza.	193	CORNISH, Allen	212	CORNISH, Joseph	126
COOPER, Elizabeth	18	CORNISH, Ann	111	CORNISH, Josiah	19
COOPER, Elizabeth	71	CORNISH, Anna	135	CORNISH, Josiah	135
COOPER, Esther	204	CORNISH, Anna	197	CORNISH, Josiah	195
COOPER, Hannah	18	CORNISH, Anne	135	CORNISH, Josiah	218
COOPER, Hannah	67	CORNISH, Benjamin	19	CORNISH, Lemuel	133
COOPER, Hannah	78	CORNISH, Benjamin	65	CORNISH, Lucenda	215
COOPER, Hannah	191	CORNISH, Benjamin	73	CORNISH, Lydia	137
COOPER, Isaac	18	CORNISH, Benjamin	105	CORNISH, Lydia	194
COOPER, John	18	CORNISH, Benjamin	131	CORNISH, Lydia	208
COOPER, John	78	CORNISH, Benjamin	133	CORNISH, Marcy	65
COOPER, John	115	CORNISH, Benjamin	197	CORNISH, Marcy	106
COOPER, John	119	CORNISH, Clark	137	CORNISH, Marcy	107
COOPER, John	183	CORNISH, Clarke	222	CORNISH, Mary	137
COOPER, John	204	CORNISH, Clarrissa	212	CORNISH, Mary	193
COOPER, Joseph	197	CORNISH, Content	220	CORNISH, Mercy	214
COOPER, Joseph	215	CORNISH, David	199	CORNISH, Meribah	74
COOPER, Nathaniel	195	CORNISH, Deborah	133	CORNISH, Meribah	84
COOPER, Pricila	96	CORNISH, Deborah	186	CORNISH, Nance	190
COOPER, Priscilla	197	CORNISH, Elizabeth	107	CORNISH, Nancey	133
COOPER, Remember	106	CORNISH, Elizabeth	135	CORNISH, Naomy	19
COOPER, Remembrance	107	CORNISH, Elizabeth	137	CORNISH, Nathaniel	181
COOPER, Richard	18	CORNISH, Elizabeth	189	CORNISH, Nathll.	65
COOPER, Richard	67	CORNISH, Experience	65	CORNISH, Pheba	137
COOPER, Richard	177	CORNISH, Experience	73	CORNISH, Phebe	137
COOPER, Samuel	188	CORNISH, Experience	173	CORNISH, Phebe	204
COOPER, Sarah	18	CORNISH, Experience	197	CORNISH, Rhoda	133
COOPER, Sarah	70	CORNISH, Freeman	137	CORNISH, Rosanna	204
COOPER, Sarah	193	CORNISH, Freeman	207	CORNISH, Samuel	19
COOPER, Sarah	200	CORNISH, George	133	CORNISH, Samuel	66
COOPER, Thomas	186	CORNISH, George	197	CORNISH, Samuel	74
COOPPER, Elizabeth	147	CORNISH, Grace	206	CORNISH, Samuel	84
COOPPER, Hannah	147	CORNISH, Grace	214	CORNISH, Samuel	124
COOPPER, Richard	147	CORNISH, Hannah	137	CORNISH, Samuel	135
COPER, Elisabeth	129	CORNISH, Hannah	197	CORNISH, Samuel	202
CORBAN, Dorcas	149	CORNISH, Hannah	213	CORNISH, Sarah	133
CORBAN, Ezra	149	CORNISH, Hannaniah	84	CORNISH, Sarah	137
CORBAN, Ezra	180	CORNISH, James	19	CORNISH, Sarah	199
CORBAN, Hannah	149	CORNISH, James	77	CORNISH, Sarah	208
CORBEN, Dorcas	130	CORNISH, James	118	CORNISH, Sarah	210
CORBIN, Elisha	186	CORNISH, Joanna	206	CORNISH, Spooner	137
CORBIN, Elkanah	187	CORNISH, John	48	CORNISH, Spooner	218
CORNISH, ----- (female)	84	CORNISH, John	65	CORNISH, Stephen	133
CORNISH, ----- (female)	137	CORNISH, John	137	CORNISH, Susanna	65
CORNISH, ----- (male)	137	CORNISH, John	171	CORNISH, Susanna	106
CORNISH, Abiah	77	CORNISH, John	183	CORNISH, Susannah	113
CORNISH, Abigail	19	CORNISH, John	186	CORNISH, Susannah	133
CORNISH, Abigail	84	CORNISH, John	191	CORNISH, Susannah	193
CORNISH, Abigail Clark	219	CORNISH, John	206	CORNISH, Suzannah	19
CORNISH, Abigal	131	CORNISH, John	208	CORNISH, Suzannah	66

VITAL RECORDS OF THE TOWN OF PLYMOUTH

Name	Page	Name	Page	Name	Page
CORNISH, Temporance	212	COTTON, Josiah	70	COTTON, Theophilus	79
CORNISH, Thomas	19	COTTON, Josiah	71	COTTON, Theophilus	95
CORNISH, Thomas	104	COTTON, Josiah	73	COTTON, Theophilus	123
CORNISH, Thomas	107	COTTON, Josiah	75	COTTON, Theophilus (Capt.)	109
CORNISH, Thomas	111	COTTON, Josiah	77	COTTON, Theophilus (Capt.)	172
CORNISH, Thomas	135	COTTON, Josiah	78	COTTON, Thomas Jackson	167
CORNISH, Thomas	172	COTTON, Josiah	95	COTTON, Ward	146
CORNISH, Thomas	201	COTTON, Josiah	110	COTTON, Ward (Rev.)	203
CORNISH, Thos.	65	COTTON, Josiah	125	COTTON, William Cushing	167
CORNISH, William	133	COTTON, Josiah	146	COTTON, Wm. Crowe	95
CORNISH, William	190	COTTON, Josiah	197	COUSINS, Sarah	106
CORPE, Abner	75	COTTON, Josiah	200	COVAL, Cynthia	212
CORPE, Abner	117	COTTON, Josiah	212	COVEL, Mary	197
CORPE, Hannah	75	COTTON, Luce	77	COVEL, Nathaniel	217
COTTON, ----- (male)	8	COTTON, Lucie	38	COVELL, Obediah	212
COTTON, ----- (male)	38	COTTON, Lucie	118	COVENGTON, Tryphena	214
COTTON, Bethia	38	COTTON, Lucy	146	COVIL, David	205
COTTON, Bethiah	75	COTTON, Lucy	197	COVIL, Ebenezer	204
COTTON, Bethiah	95	COTTON, Lucy	199	COVIL, Enos	198
COTTON, Bethiah	125	COTTON, Lydia	212	COVILL, David	206
COTTON, Bethiah	186	COTTON, Margaret	38	COVILL, Lot	206
COTTON, Bowland	8	COTTON, Margaret	110	COVILL, Polley	211
COTTON, Charles	167	COTTON, Margaret	115	COVINGTON, Catharine	150
COTTON, Edward	38	COTTON, Maria	8	COVINGTON, Edwin	160
COTTON, Edward	95	COTTON, Martha	79	COVINGTON, Elam	160
COTTON, Elizabeth	66	COTTON, Martha	95	COVINGTON, Eloner	214
COTTON, Elizabeth	146	COTTON, Mary	38	COVINGTON, Eunice	200
COTTON, Elizabeth	148	COTTON, Mary	74	COVINGTON, Harriet	160
COTTON, Elizabeth	198	COTTON, Mary	124	COVINGTON, Hellen	160
COTTON, Elzabeth	8	COTTON, Mary	146	COVINGTON, Isaac	199
COTTON, Experience	207	COTTON, Mary	190	COVINGTON, Jacob	160
COTTON, Fredc.	148	COTTON, Polley	167	COVINGTON, Jacob	219
COTTON, Frederick Augustus	222	COTTON, Priscilla	167	COVINGTON, Leonard	160
COTTON, Hanah	70	COTTON, Rosseter	145	COVINGTON, Lucy	210
COTTON, Hannah	38	COTTON, Rosseter	167	COVINGTON, Lydia	203
COTTON, Hannah	73	COTTON, Rosseter	193	COVINGTON, Martha Ann	160
COTTON, Hannah	126	COTTON, Rosseter Mather	167	COVINGTON, Mary	206
COTTON, Hannah	145	COTTON, Rowland	38	COVINGTON, Mary	207
COTTON, Hannah	146	COTTON, Rowland	95	COVINGTON, Mary Holbrook	160
COTTON, Hannah	189	COTTON, Rowland Edwin	167	COVINGTON, Nathaniel	150
COTTON, Joanna	8	COTTON, Salley	207	COVINGTON, Nathaniel C.	150
COTTON, Joanna	145	COTTON, Samuel	8	COVINGTON, Patty	160
COTTON, John	8	COTTON, Sarah	8	COVINGTON, Patty	219
COTTON, John	38	COTTON, Sarah	146	COVINGTON, Sarah	200
COTTON, John	95	COTTON, Sarah O.	148	COVINGTON, Thomas	185
COTTON, John	145	COTTON, Sophia	146	COVINGTON, Thomas	201
COTTON, John	146	COTTON, Sophia	167	COVINGTON, Thomas	208
COTTON, John	191	COTTON, Sophia	188	COVINGTON, William	150
COTTON, John Winslow	167	COTTON, Sophia	217	COWIN, Ann	160
COTTON, Josiah	8	COTTON, Theophilos	38	COWIN, Mary Ann	160
COTTON, Josiah	38	COTTON, Theophilus	8	COWIN, Robert	160

Name	Page	Name	Page	Name	Page
COWIN, Sarah Frances	160	CROAD, Priscilla	61	CRUMWEL, Bilka	71
COWIT, Eliza.	205	CROAD, Rachel	61	CRUMWEL, Toby	71
COWIT, Jesse	203	CROAD, Ruth	71	CRYMBLE, Abigal	54
COWIT, Lucy	200	CROAD, Thomas	61	CRYMBLE, Murray Holmes	54
COWIT, Mary	203	CROADE, Deborah	118	CRYMBLE, Phebe	54
COWIT, Priscilla	206	CROADE, Elizabeth	95	CRYMBLE, Phebe	112
COWIT, Sarah	202	CROADE, Nathaniel	95	CRYMBLE, Phebe	113
COX, Abigail Withrell	222	CROADE, Nathll.	95	CUFF, Mehittable	185
COX, Elias	209	CROADE, Nathll.	123	CUFFS, Hannah Wadsworth	206
COYE, Salla	201	CROCKER, Deborah	206	CUFFS, Mary Williams	212
COYE, William	186	CROCKER, Lydia	171	CUFFS, William	188
COYE, William	197	CROCKER, Mercy	212	CUNNET, Alice	214
COYE, William	202	CROMBIE, Anna	148	CUNNET, John	213
COYE, William	215	CROMBIE, Anne	148	CUNNET, Josiah	120
CRAN, Mary	130	CROMBIE, Calvin	148	CUNNET, Marcy	120
CRANDON, Benja.	146	CROMBIE, Calvin	200	CUNNET, William	121
CRANDON, Benjamin	197	CROMBIE, Kimbel	197	CUNNET, William	176
CRANDON, Grace	60	CROMBIE, Kimbell	197	CUNNET, William	218
CRANDON, Grace	115	CROMBIE, Mary	204	CUNNETT, Josiah	123
CRANDON, Grace	116	CROMBIE, Nancy	199	CUNNINGHAM, Jesse	138
CRANDON, James	60	CROMBIE, Polly	148	CUNNINGHAM, Sarah	138
CRANDON, James	86	CROMBIE, William	199	CUNNINGHAM, Sarah Elizabeth	138
CRANDON, James	106	CROOK, Alise	195	CUNNIT, Betty	178
CRANDON, James	113	CROOKER, Nancy	197	CUNNIT, William	202
CRANDON, James	146	CROOKER, Patience	197	CURCHELL, Willson	207
CRANDON, Jane	121	CROSBEY, Thomas	174	CURTES, Jacob	207
CRANDON, Jean	60	CROSMAN, Elizabeth	121	CURTICE, Benjamin	24
CRANDON, Jean	146	CROSMAN, Esther	107	CURTICE, Benjamin	69
CRANDON, John	60	CROSMAN, Nathl.	106	CURTICE, Caleb	43
CRANDON, John	86	CROSMAN, Nathl.	107	CURTICE, Eben	71
CRANDON, John	146	CROSSWELL, Andrew (Rev.)	77	CURTICE, Ebenazar	43
CRANDON, Ruth	107	CROSSWELL, Joseph	116	CURTICE, Ebenazar	70
CRANDON, Ruth	146	CROSSWELL, Rebekah	77	CURTICE, Elizabeth	34
CRANDON, Sarah	86	CROSWEL, Andrew	118	CURTICE, Elkana	42
CRANDON, Sarah	106	CROSWELL, Abigail	200	CURTICE, Ffrances	34
CRANDON, Sarah	172	CROSWELL, Andrew	178	CURTICE, Ffrances	42
CRANDON, Susan	216	CROSWELL, Andrew	188	CURTICE, Frances	67
CRANDON, Thomas	60	CROSWELL, Jerusha	111	CURTICE, Hanah	67
CRANDON, Thomas	106	CROSWELL, Joseph	111	CURTICE, Hannah	34
CRANDON, Thomas	107	CROW, Elizabeth	66	CURTICE, Hannah	42
CRANDON, Thomas	146	CROW, Hannah	109	CURTICE, Jacob	43
CRANE, Lydia	90	CROW, Saml.	109	CURTICE, Jacob	124
CRANE, Patty	215	CROW, Samll.	171	CURTICE, James	42
CRAPOO, Francis	175	CROWEL, Olive	218	CURTICE, John	34
CRIMBLE, Charles	54	CROWLEY, Mary	91	CURTICE, Lydia	42
CRIMBLE, Elizabeth	54	CROWLY, Edward	130	CURTICE, Martha	71
CRIMBLE, Elizabeth	71	CRUMBIE, Calvin	148	CURTICE, Mary	24
CRIMBLE, Holmes	54	CRUMBIE, Kimbull	148	CURTICE, Mary	43
CRIMBLE, Quinten	130	CRUMBIE, William	148	CURTICE, Mary	69
CRIMBLE, Quintin	71	CRUMBIE, William	176	CURTICE, Mary	70
CRIMBLE, Quitton	54	CRUMBIE, Zerviah	148	CURTICE, Nathaniel	42

VITAL RECORDS OF THE TOWN OF PLYMOUTH

CURTICE, Rebeckah	66	CURTIS, Mary	117	CUSHMAN, Elizabeth	66
CURTICE, Sarah	43	CURTIS, Mary	181	CUSHMAN, Elizabeth	73
CURTICE, Silvanus	42	CURTIS, Nathaniel	59	CUSHMAN, Elizabeth	96
CURTICE, Zacheus	42	CURTIS, Nathaniel	117	CUSHMAN, Elizabeth	215
CURTIS, Caleb	86	CURTIS, Noah	191	CUSHMAN, Elka.	115
CURTIS, David	79	CURTIS, Olive	208	CUSHMAN, Elkana	69
CURTIS, David	93	CURTIS, Polley	204	CUSHMAN, Elkanah	9
CURTIS, David	115	CURTIS, Sarah	86	CUSHMAN, Elkanah	65
CURTIS, David	183	CURTIS, Sarah	107	CUSHMAN, Elkanah	78
CURTIS, David	212	CURTIS, Sarah	117	CUSHMAN, Elkanah	91
CURTIS, Ebenezer	43	CURTIS, Sarah Turner	205	CUSHMAN, Elkanah	96
CURTIS, Edward	105	CURTIS, Seth	43	CUSHMAN, Elkanah	121
CURTIS, Edward	107	CURTIS, Silvanus	117	CUSHMAN, Elkanan	27
CURTIS, Elezebeth	84	CURTIS, William	160	CUSHMAN, Elkanath	27
CURTIS, Elizabeth	75	CURTIS, William	181	CUSHMAN, Elkanath	65
CURTIS, Elizabeth	86	CURTIS, Zacheus	59	CUSHMAN, Elkath	100
CURTIS, Elizabeth	93	CURTIS, Zacheus	189	CUSHMAN, Ester	69
CURTIS, Elizabeth	106	CURTISE, Hannah	127	CUSHMAN, Ester	71
CURTIS, Elizabeth	107	CURTISS, Fear	86	CUSHMAN, Eunice	179
CURTIS, Elizabeth	178	CURTISS, Jacob	86	CUSHMAN, Fear	15
CURTIS, Eunice	111	CURTISS, Zacheus	123	CUSHMAN, Feare	69
CURTIS, Eunice	117	CUSHIN, Deborah	67	CUSHMAN, Hannah	34
CURTIS, Eunis	43	CUSHING, Francis	194	CUSHMAN, Hannah	74
CURTIS, Fear	74	CUSHING, Hannah	46	CUSHMAN, Hannah	77
CURTIS, Fear	86	CUSHING, Ignatious	46	CUSHMAN, Hannah	79
CURTIS, Fear	106	CUSHING, Ignatious	70	CUSHMAN, Hannah	123
CURTIS, Fear	128	CUSHING, Ignatious	71	CUSHMAN, Hannah	124
CURTIS, Frances	84	CUSHING, James	202	CUSHMAN, Hannah	131
CURTIS, Francis	75	CUSHING, John	74	CUSHMAN, Hesther	27
CURTIS, Francis	125	CUSHING, John	124	CUSHMAN, Icabod	15
CURTIS, Hannah	59	CUSHING, Lydia	167	CUSHMAN, Ignatious	198
CURTIS, Hannah	74	CUSHING, Marcy	70	CUSHMAN, Isaac	15
CURTIS, Hannah	79	CUSHING, Marsey	46	CUSHMAN, Isaac	27
CURTIS, Hannah	86	CUSHING, Mary	74	CUSHMAN, Isaac	67
CURTIS, Hannah	93	CUSHING, Mary	181	CUSHMAN, Isaac	68
CURTIS, Hannah	160	CUSHING, Mathew	199	CUSHMAN, Jabes	9
CURTIS, Hannah	186	CUSHING, Nathaniel	220	CUSHMAN, James	27
CURTIS, Jacob	74	CUSHING, Ruth	71	CUSHMAN, James	61
CURTIS, Jacob	86	CUSHMAN, Abigaiell	34	CUSHMAN, James	72
CURTIS, James	84	CUSHMAN, Abigail	171	CUSHMAN, James	77
CURTIS, James	160	CUSHMAN, Allerton	9	CUSHMAN, James	120
CURTIS, James	208	CUSHMAN, Alse	27	CUSHMAN, James	190
CURTIS, Lydia	59	CUSHMAN, Ann Gray	213	CUSHMAN, Jams	9
CURTIS, Lydia	84	CUSHMAN, Azubah	167	CUSHMAN, Job	41
CURTIS, Lydia	171	CUSHMAN, Deborah	16	CUSHMAN, John	16
CURTIS, Lydia	180	CUSHMAN, Eliazar	15	CUSHMAN, Jonathan	34
CURTIS, Lydia	186	CUSHMAN, Eliazur	66	CUSHMAN, Joshua	34
CURTIS, Lydia	201	CUSHMAN, Elizabeth	9	CUSHMAN, Josiah	9
CURTIS, Martha	43	CUSHMAN, Elizabeth	15	CUSHMAN, Lidiah	16
CURTIS, Mary	59	CUSHMAN, Elizabeth	27	CUSHMAN, Lidiah	41
CURTIS, Mary	86	CUSHMAN, Elizabeth	65	CUSHMAN, Lydia	61

VITAL RECORDS OF THE TOWN OF PLYMOUTH

Name	Page	Name	Page	Name	Page
CUSHMAN, Lydia	78	DARLING, Jonathan	112	DAVIE, Deborah	71
CUSHMAN, Lydia	79	DARLING, Jonathan	118	DAVIE, Deborah	197
CUSHMAN, Lydia	91	DARLING, Lydia	61	DAVIE, Ebenezer	163
CUSHMAN, Lydia	112	DARLING, Lydia	186	DAVIE, Emeline	163
CUSHMAN, Lydia	115	DARLING, Martha	61	DAVIE, George	154
CUSHMAN, Martha	9	DARLING, Martha	112	DAVIE, George	195
CUSHMAN, Martha	65	DARLING, Mary	61	DAVIE, Marcia	154
CUSHMAN, Mary	15	DARLING, Sarah	61	DAVIE, Marcia Torrey	154
CUSHMAN, Mary	68	DARLING, Sarah	190	DAVIE, Mercy	163
CUSHMAN, Mary	98	DARNLEY, Betsey Ann	156	DAVIE, Mercy Ann	163
CUSHMAN, Mehittable	9	DARNLEY, Joann B.	156	DAVIE, Patience	165
CUSHMAN, Meriah	41	DARNLEY, John	156	DAVIE, Robert	71
CUSHMAN, Meriah	125	DARNLEY, William Henry	156	DAVIE, Robert	181
CUSHMAN, Perses	34	DAVE, Robert	53	DAVIE, Sarah W.	163
CUSHMAN, Phebe	27	DAVE, Thomas	53	DAVIE, Solomon	214
CUSHMAN, Rebekah	15	DAVE, William	182	DAVIE, Thomas	121
CUSHMAN, Rebekah	67	DAVEE, Betsey	205	DAVIE, Thomas	181
CUSHMAN, Robert	34	DAVEE, Betsey Thomas	222	DAVIE, William	154
CUSHMAN, Robert	130	DAVEE, Betty	96	DAVIS, ----- (female)	85
CUSHMAN, Ruth	34	DAVEE, Deborah	96	DAVIS, ----- (female)	131
CUSHMAN, Salley	218	DAVEE, Ebenezer	201	DAVIS, David	106
CUSHMAN, Sarah	15	DAVEE, Elizabeth	201	DAVIS, Elizabeth	75
CUSHMAN, Sarah	27	DAVEE, George	96	DAVIS, Elizabeth	167
CUSHMAN, Sarah	61	DAVEE, Hannah	96	DAVIS, Francis Edward	159
CUSHMAN, Sarah	67	DAVEE, Ichabod	201	DAVIS, Hannah	180
CUSHMAN, Sarah	72	DAVEE, Ichabod	210	DAVIS, Hannah Ackus	159
CUSHMAN, Susanna	214	DAVEE, Isaac	217	DAVIS, Isaac	131
CUSHMAN, Thomas	34	DAVEE, Jerusha	207	DAVIS, John	131
CUSHMAN, Thomas (Elder)	98	DAVEE, John	96	DAVIS, John	194
CUSHMANS, Elizabeth	130	DAVEE, Johnson	96	DAVIS, Joseph	159
CUSHMON, Jams	130	DAVEE, Joseph	96	DAVIS, Mary	159
CUTTLAR, Robart	66	DAVEE, Joseph	206	DAVIS, Mercy	128
CUTTLAR, Sarah	66	DAVEE, Lydia	201	DAVIS, Mercy	131
		DAVEE, Robert	96	DAVIS, Mercy	208
D		DAVEE, Robert	105	DAVIS, Nancy Rogers	159
		DAVEE, Robert	200	DAVIS, Nathaniel M.	218
DAMMON, Abigail	185	DAVEE, Sarah	96	DAVIS, Nathaniel Morton	167
DAMMON, Anna	195	DAVEE, Sarah	208	DAVIS, Nicolas	188
DAMMON, Elizabeth	188	DAVEE, Solomon	96	DAVIS, Rebecca	167
DAMOND, Hannah	125	DAVEE, Solomon	194	DAVIS, Samuel	131
DANIEL, Peter	79	DAVEE, Thomas	96	DAVIS, Sarah	107
DANIEL, Sarah	79	DAVEE, Thomas	177	DAVIS, Sarah	131
DANIELL, Peter	116	DAVEE, Thomas	199	DAVIS, Sarah	190
DANIELL, Peter	123	DAVEE, Thomas	208	DAVIS, Sarah Elizabeth	159
DARLENG, Jonathan	76	DAVEE, Thoms.	96	DAVIS, Silence	180
DARLENG, Lydia	76	DAVEE, William	96	DAVIS, Susan Nichols	159
DARLING, Benjamin	61	DAVEE, William	198	DAVIS, Thomas	104
DARLING, Eliza.	200	DAVENPORT, Deborah	171	DAVIS, Thomas	128
DARLING, Ephram	182	DAVEY, Debora	53	DAVIS, Thomas	131
DARLING, John	61	DAVIE, Abigale	218	DAVIS, Thomas	167
DARLING, Jonathan	61	DAVIE, Curtis	163	DAVIS, Thomas (Capt.)	208

VITAL RECORDS OF THE TOWN OF PLYMOUTH

DAVIS, Wendell	131	DELANO, Elkanah	74	DELLANO, Mary	182
DAVIS, William	75	DELANO, Elkanah	94	DELLANO, Olive	212
DAVIS, William	105	DELANO, Elkanah	95	DELLANO, Penelope	169
DAVIS, William	107	DELANO, Elkanah	128	DELLANO, Priscilla	169
DAVIS, William	117	DELANO, Eunice	177	DELLANO, Ruth	188
DAVIS, William	131	DELANO, Eunis	95	DELLANO, Salome	169
DAVIS, William	167	DELANO, Hannah	81	DELLANO, Welthey	207
DAVIS, William	191	DELANO, Hannah	95	DELLENO, Rebekah	66
DAVIS, Wm.	105	DELANO, Hannah	113	DENNIS, William	217
DEAN, Amos	215	DELANO, Ichabod	73	DEVERSON, Elizabeth	194
DEARSKIN, Paticience	117	DELANO, Ichabod	130	DEVERSON, George	189
DEARSKIN, Patuence	117	DELANO, Isaac	104	DEWE, Deborah	197
DEBURROUGHS, Andrew	191	DELANO, Joanna	188	DEWET, Christopher	116
DECORT, Margaret	104	DELANO, Joannah	81	DEWEY, Deborah	197
DECOST, Elizabeth	123	DELANO, Joseph	104	DEXTER, Ephraim	129
DECOSTER, Elisabeth	123	DELANO, Judah	191	DEXTER, Ephraim	171
DECOSTER, Elizabeth	109	DELANO, Mary	74	DEXTER, Martha	129
DECOSTER, Elizabeth	111	DELANO, Mary	94	DEXTER, Samuel	130
DECOSTER, Elizabeth	156	DELANO, Mary	95	DEY, Jane	222
DECOSTER, Elizbeth	113	DELANO, Mary N.	220	DICKSON, Miriam C.	209
DECOSTER, Jacob	109	DELANO, Nathan	73	DICKSON, Samuel	206
DECOSTER, Jacob	116	DELANO, Nathan	81	DIKE, Anthoney	204
DECOSTER, Jacob	184	DELANO, Nathan	126	DIKE, Asa	213
DECOSTER, Johanna	156	DELANO, Nathan (Capt.)	81	DIKE, John	213
DECOSTER, Robert	156	DELANO, Nathan (Capt.)	171	DIKE, Mary	216
DECRO, Anthony	71	DELANO, Ruth	81	DIKE, Rebecca	220
DECRO, Elizabeth	71	DELANO, Ruth	108	DIKE, Sally	215
DEERSKINS, John	77	DELANO, Ruth	123	DIKE, Samuel	213
DEERSKINS, John	120	DELANO, Sarah	81	DIKE, Sibbil	214
DEERSKINS, Kate	77	DELANO, Sarah	95	DIKE, Simeon	206
DEERSKINS, Kate	79	DELANO, Sarah	106	DILLARD, Benjamin	206
DEERSKINS, Kate	116	DELANO, Sarah	113	DILLARD, Benjamin	210
DEERSKINS, Sarah	78	DELENO, Benja.	111	DILLENO, Martha	70
DEERSKINS, Sarah	121	DELENO, Benjamin	89	DILLINGHAM, Branch	197
DELANO, ----- (male)	94	DELENO, Lydia	89	DILLINGHAM, Branch	198
DELANO, Amassa	81	DELENO, Lydia	111	DILLINGHAM, John	174
DELANO, Barzilla	95	DELLANO, ----- (female)	169	DILLINO, Martha	69
DELANO, Bathsheba	73	DELLANO, Assenath	188	DIMAN, Abby Philips	137
DELANO, Bathsheba	81	DELLANO, Avery	197	DIMAN, Betsey	210
DELANO, Bathsheba	104	DELLANO, Betsey	215	DIMAN, Daniel	48
DELANO, Bathsheba	107	DELLANO, Deborah	177	DIMAN, Daniel	106
DELANO, Bathshebah	81	DELLANO, Elizabeth	169	DIMAN, Daniel	107
DELANO, Benjamin	116	DELLANO, George	204	DIMAN, Daniel	149
DELANO, Beza	171	DELLANO, Hannah	184	DIMAN, Daniel	183
DELANO, Deborah	73	DELLANO, Henry	169	DIMAN, Daniel	186
DELANO, Deborah	95	DELLANO, Hulda	212	DIMAN, Daniel	195
DELANO, Deborah	130	DELLANO, Ichabod	81	DIMAN, Daniel	198
DELANO, Dorothy	117	DELLANO, Jonathan	188	DIMAN, David	48
DELANO, Elizabeth	73	DELLANO, Judah	169	DIMAN, David	220
DELANO, Elizabeth	74	DELLANO, Lucy	216	DIMAN, Elisabeth Fails	201
DELANO, Elizabeth	124	DELLANO, Mallicha	184	DIMAN, Eliza.	107

VITAL RECORDS OF THE TOWN OF PLYMOUTH

DIMAN, Elizabeth	48	DOGGET, Sarah	107	DONHAM, Betsey	157
DIMAN, Hannah	77	DOGGET, Seth	198	DONHAM, Betsey	207
DIMAN, James	137	DOGGETT, -----	56	DONHAM, Betsey	218
DIMAN, Jonathan	77	DOGGETT, Ebenezer	56	DONHAM, Calvin	205
DIMAN, Jonathan	118	DOGGETT, Ebenezer	112	DONHAM, Catharine	94
DIMAN, Jonathan (Deacn.)	190	DOGGETT, Elizabeth	56	DONHAM, Cornelius	184
DIMAN, Josiah	48	DOGGETT, Elizabeth	74	DONHAM, Cornelius	187
DIMAN, Josiah	198	DOGGETT, Elizabeth	77	DONHAM, Deborah	141
DIMAN, Josiah	203	DOGGETT, Elizabeth	112	DONHAM, Deborah	194
DIMAN, Josiah	215	DOGGETT, Elizabeth	120	DONHAM, Deborah	207
DIMAN, Mary Boylston	137	DOGGETT, John	56	DONHAM, Earl	209
DIMAN, Mary Harlow	137	DOGGETT, Lydia	74	DONHAM, Ebenezer	55
DIMAN, Patience	206	DOGGETT, Lydia	124	DONHAM, Ebenezer	111
DIMAN, Polly	137	DOGGETT, Samuel	56	DONHAM, Ebenezer	116
DIMAN, Rebecca	137	DOGGETT, Seth	74	DONHAM, Ebenezer	139
DIMAN, Rebecca Harlow	137	DOGGETT, Seth	124	DONHAM, Ebenezer	171
DIMAN, Rebeckah	48	DONHAM Bethiah	193	DONHAM, Ebenezr.	199
DIMAN, Rebeckah	186	DONHAM Lydia	189	DONHAM, Ebenr.	171
DIMAN, Sophia Sampson	137	DONHAM, ----- (female)	93	DONHAM, Eleazer	115
DIMAN, Susan	217	DONHAM, A.	171	DONHAM, Elener	157
DIMAN, Susannah	149	DONHAM, Abigail	94	DONHAM, Elijah	86
DIMAN, Thomas	137	DONHAM, Abigail	100	DONHAM, Elijah	141
DIMAN, Thomas	182	DONHAM, Abigail	110	DONHAM, Elisabeth	181
DIMOND, Rebekah	125	DONHAM, Abigail	112	DONHAM, Elisebeth	123
DIXON, Calvin Luther	148	DONHAM, Abigail	139	DONHAM, Elisha	58
DIXON, Jacob Washburn	148	DONHAM, Abigail	194	DONHAM, Eliza.	195
DIXON, Ruby	148	DONHAM, Abigal	55	DONHAM, Eliza. Foster	212
DIXON, Samuel	148	DONHAM, Abigal	94	DONHAM, Elizabeth	58
DIXON, Samuel Russell	148	DONHAM, Abigal	127	DONHAM, Elizabeth	81
DOAN, Mary	213	DONHAM, Abigall	73	DONHAM, Elizabeth	93
DOAN, Thomas	128	DONHAM, Abner	86	DONHAM, Elizabeth	112
DOANE, Isaiah	188	DONHAM, Abraham	214	DONHAM, Elizabeth	141
DOANE, Sarah	74	DONHAM, Amos	79	DONHAM, Elizabeth	171
DOANE, Thomas	74	DONHAM, Amos	94	DONHAM, Elizabeth	173
DOGED, Ebenazar	129	DONHAM, Amos	100	DONHAM, Elizabeth	195
DOGGET, Bathsheba	46	DONHAM, Amos	116	DONHAM, Eloner	212
DOGGET, Deborah	138	DONHAM, Amos	183	DONHAM, Ephraim	141
DOGGET, Ebenazar	71	DONHAM, Andrew	141	DONHAM, Esther	119
DOGGET, Ebenezer	46	DONHAM, Ann	75	DONHAM, Eunice	194
DOGGET, Ebenezer	112	DONHAM, Ann	79	DONHAM, Eunice Thomas	215
DOGGET, Ebenezer	123	DONHAM, Ann	86	DONHAM, Ezekiel	79
DOGGET, Ebenezr.	190	DONHAM, Ann	94	DONHAM, Ezekiel	101
DOGGET, Elizabeth	46	DONHAM, Anna	157	DONHAM, Ezekiel	116
DOGGET, Elizabeth	71	DONHAM, Anna	185	DONHAM, Fear	74
DOGGET, Elizabeth	126	DONHAM, Anne	94	DONHAM, Fear	124
DOGGET, Elizabeth	179	DONHAM, Barnabas	55	DONHAM, George	185
DOGGET, Jabez	175	DONHAM, Barnabas	181	DONHAM, George	190
DOGGET, Lydia	195	DONHAM, Barnabas	199	DONHAM, George	207
DOGGET, Samuel	138	DONHAM, Barshabah	107	DONHAM, George (Capt.)	197
DOGGET, Samuell	171	DONHAM, Bathsheba	105	DONHAM, Hannah	78
DOGGET, Sarah	105	DONHAM, Bathshua	58	DONHAM, Hannah	86

VITAL RECORDS OF THE TOWN OF PLYMOUTH

DONHAM, Hannah	93	DONHAM, Mary	141	DONHAM, Sarah	81
DONHAM, Hannah	119	DONHAM, Mary	168	DONHAM, Sarah	116
DONHAM, Hannah	121	DONHAM, Mary	188	DONHAM, Sarah	157
DONHAM, Hannah	139	DONHAM, Mary	208	DONHAM, Sarah	186
DONHAM, Hannah	188	DONHAM, Mary	212	DONHAM, Silas	93
DONHAM, Ichabod	141	DONHAM, Mercy	72	DONHAM, Silas	178
DONHAM, Ichabod	200	DONHAM, Moses	55	DONHAM, Silas	198
DONHAM, Isaac	208	DONHAM, Moses	141	DONHAM, Susanah	75
DONHAM, Jacob	212	DONHAM, Moses	194	DONHAM, Susanna	125
DONHAM, James	58	DONHAM, Nancey	199	DONHAM, Susanna	177
DONHAM, James	81	DONHAM, Nancy	199	DONHAM, Susannah	86
DONHAM, James	112	DONHAM, Nanse	198	DONHAM, Susannah	141
DONHAM, James	115	DONHAM, Nansey	141	DONHAM, Susannah	197
DONHAM, Jane	193	DONHAM, Nathaniel	73	DONHAM, Susannah	198
DONHAM, Jerusha	112	DONHAM, Nathaniel	86	DONHAM, Sylvanus	168
DONHAM, Jerusha	113	DONHAM, Nathaniel	130	DONHAM, Sylvanus	190
DONHAM, Jesse	212	DONHAM, Nathl.	93	DONHAM, Thomas	201
DONHAM, Joanna	74	DONHAM, Nathl.	104	DONHAM, William	55
DONHAM, Joanna	124	DONHAM, Nathll.	93	DONHAM, William	96
DONHAM, John	55	DONHAM, Nathll. Thomas	141	DONHAM, William	178
DONHAM, John	141	DONHAM, Pamelia	204	DONHAM, William	183
DONHAM, John	171	DONHAM, Patience	79	DONHAM, William	191
DONHAM, Joseph	124	DONHAM, Patience	101	DONHAM, William	196
DONHAM, Joseph	124	DONHAM, Phebe	111	DONHUM, Joshua	117
DONHAM, Joseph	150	DONHAM, Phebe	206	DOTE, Edward	66
DONHAM, Joshua	58	DONHAM, Polley	204	DOTE, Sarah	66
DONHAM, Joshua	75	DONHAM, Rebecca	73	DOTEN, Bathsheba	29
DONHAM, Josiah	94	DONHAM, Rebecca	130	DOTEN, Bathsheba	107
DONHAM, Josiah	157	DONHAM, Rebecca	199	DOTEN, Bathsheba	198
DONHAM, Josiah	207	DONHAM, Rebeckah	86	DOTEN, Bathsheba	214
DONHAM, Levi	58	DONHAM, Rebeckah	93	DOTEN, Betsey	189
DONHAM, Lewis	141	DONHAM, Rebeckah	190	DOTEN, Betsey	212
DONHAM, Lewis	212	DONHAM, Rebeckah	191	DOTEN, Betsey	216
DONHAM, Lucas	186	DONHAM, Robert	94	DOTEN, Betsey Warren	207
DONHAM, Lucas	217	DONHAM, Robert	157	DOTEN, Cintha	207
DONHAM, Luce	58	DONHAM, Robert	181	DOTEN, Daniel	202
DONHAM, Lucy	181	DONHAM, Robert	204	DOTEN, Deborah	185
DONHAM, Lucy	213	DONHAM, Ruth	94	DOTEN, Deborah	222
DONHAM, Lucy Tillson	202	DONHAM, Ruth	157	DOTEN, Ebenezer	105
DONHAM, Lydia	108	DONHAM, Ruth	184	DOTEN, Ebenezer	107
DONHAM, Lydia	123	DONHAM, Ruth	187	DOTEN, Edward	93
DONHAM, Lydia	157	DONHAM, Ruth	195	DOTEN, Edward	109
DONHAM, Lydia	213	DONHAM, Sally	200	DOTEN, Edward	131
DONHAM, Lydia Atwood	212	DONHAM, Salome	141	DOTEN, Edward	167
DONHAM, Marcy	58	DONHAM, Saml.	96	DOTEN, Edward	205
DONHAM, Martha	78	DONHAM, Samll.	171	DOTEN, Elisha	93
DONHAM, Martha	93	DONHAM, Samuel	55	DOTEN, Elisha	182
DONHAM, Martha	120	DONHAM, Samuel	141	DOTEN, Elisha	212
DONHAM, Mary	55	DONHAM, Samuel	191	DOTEN, Eliza.	201
DONHAM, Mary	94	DONHAM, Sarah	58	DOTEN, Elizabeth	69
DONHAM, Mary	96	DONHAM, Sarah	79	DOTEN, Elizabeth	74

VITAL RECORDS OF THE TOWN OF PLYMOUTH

DOTEN, Elizabeth	149	DOTEN, John	167	DOTEN, Phebe	150
DOTEN, Eloner	204	DOTEN, John	198	DOTEN, Phebe	155
DOTEN, Esther	167	DOTEN, John	200	DOTEN, Phebe	167
DOTEN, George Henry	150	DOTEN, Joseph	199	DOTEN, Polley	198
DOTEN, George Henry	155	DOTEN, Josiah	179	DOTEN, Prince	150
DOTEN, Hannah	43	DOTEN, Lemuel	167	DOTEN, Prince	155
DOTEN, Hannah	96	DOTEN, Lemuel	190	DOTEN, Prince	212
DOTEN, Hannah	111	DOTEN, Lemuel	197	DOTEN, Rebecca	200
DOTEN, Hannah	150	DOTEN, Lemuell	60	DOTEN, Rebeckah	88
DOTEN, Hannah	155	DOTEN, Lemuell	93	DOTEN, Rebeckah	89
DOTEN, Hannah	167	DOTEN, Lemuell	101	DOTEN, Rebeckah	137
DOTEN, Hannah	171	DOTEN, Lemuell	109	DOTEN, Rebeckah	190
DOTEN, Hannah	189	DOTEN, Lemuell	113	DOTEN, Ruth	29
DOTEN, Hannah	195	DOTEN, Lewis	167	DOTEN, Ruth	106
DOTEN, Hannah	206	DOTEN, Lois	108	DOTEN, Ruth	189
DOTEN, Hope	88	DOTEN, Lois	207	DOTEN, Samuel	104
DOTEN, Hope	149	DOTEN, Lowis	193	DOTEN, Samuel	137
DOTEN, Hope	171	DOTEN, Lowis	201	DOTEN, Samuel	167
DOTEN, Hope	197	DOTEN, Lucy	195	DOTEN, Samuel	173
DOTEN, Hope	214	DOTEN, Lucy	202	DOTEN, Samuel	191
DOTEN, Ichabod	88	DOTEN, Lydia	29	DOTEN, Samuel	209
DOTEN, Isaac	75	DOTEN, Lydia	180	DOTEN, Samuell	75
DOTEN, Isaac	88	DOTEN, Lydia	197	DOTEN, Sarah	43
DOTEN, Isaac	89	DOTEN, Lydia	218	DOTEN, Sarah	69
DOTEN, Jabez	89	DOTEN, Marcy	43	DOTEN, Sarah	110
DOTEN, Jabez	190	DOTEN, Marcy	107	DOTEN, Sarah	173
DOTEN, Jacob	174	DOTEN, Marcy	110	DOTEN, Sarah	183
DOTEN, James	88	DOTEN, Marcy	115	DOTEN, Sarah	202
DOTEN, James	93	DOTEN, Marcy	190	DOTEN, Sarah Ann	150
DOTEN, James	104	DOTEN, Martha	202	DOTEN, Sarah Ann	155
DOTEN, James	105	DOTEN, Mary	43	DOTEN, Stephen	43
DOTEN, James	106	DOTEN, Mary	75	DOTEN, Stephen	111
DOTEN, James	107	DOTEN, Mary	88	DOTEN, Stephen	117
DOTEN, James	149	DOTEN, Mary	89	DOTEN, Stephen	186
DOTEN, James	178	DOTEN, Mary	137	DOTEN, Stephen	193
DOTEN, James	197	DOTEN, Mercy	191	DOTEN, Stephen	202
DOTEN, James	213	DOTEN, Mercy	199	DOTEN, Stephen	204
DOTEN, James Robbins	214	DOTEN, Mercy	213	DOTEN, Sukey	150
DOTEN, Jane	109	DOTEN, Meriah	162	DOTEN, Susan	150
DOTEN, Jean	60	DOTEN, Nancey	205	DOTEN, Susan	155
DOTEN, Jean	88	DOTEN, Naomi	150	DOTEN, Susannah	29
DOTEN, Jean	101	DOTEN, Naomi	155	DOTEN, Thomas	69
DOTEN, Jeane	88	DOTEN, Nathaniel	205	DOTEN, Thomas	88
DOTEN, Jerusha	162	DOTEN, Nathll.	180	DOTEN, Thomas	93
DOTEN, Jerusha	199	DOTEN, Paul	29	DOTEN, Thomas	162
DOTEN, Jno. Palmer	89	DOTEN, Paul	105	DOTEN, Thomas	182
DOTEN, Joanah	75	DOTEN, Paul	106	DOTEN, Thomas	204
DOTEN, Joanna	131	DOTEN, Paul	188	DOTEN, Thomas (Capt.)	190
DOTEN, John	93	DOTEN, Paul	206	DOTEN, William	88
DOTEN, John	96	DOTEN, Phebe	93	DOTEN, William	189
DOTEN, John	116	DOTEN, Phebe	109	DOTEN, William	194

VITAL RECORDS OF THE TOWN OF PLYMOUTH

Name	Page	Name	Page	Name	Page
DOTEN, William	213	DOTY, Hannah	81	DOTY, Samuel	86
DOTEY, Desire	13	DOTY, Hannah	86	DOTY, Samuel	125
DOTEY, Elizabeth	35	DOTY, Hannah	94	DOTY, Samuel	127
DOTEY, John	13	DOTY, Isaac	10	DOTY, Samuell	10
DOTEY, Martha	67	DOTY, Isaac	88	DOTY, Samuell	94
DOTEY, Mary	69	DOTY, Isaac	117	DOTY, Sarah	9
DOTEY, Patience	13	DOTY, Jacob	10	DOTY, Sarah	23
DOTEY, Sarah	13	DOTY, Jacob	23	DOTY, Sarah	60
DOTEY, Sarah	67	DOTY, James	40	DOTY, Sarah	66
DOTEY, Thomas	35	DOTY, Jean	124	DOTY, Sarah	81
DOTTY, Eliazebeth	26	DOTY, Joannah	94	DOTY, Stephen	40
DOTTY, Hope	26	DOTY, Johanah	86	DOTY, Suzannah	23
DOTTY, Ichabd	26	DOTY, John	9	DOTY, Thomas	9
DOTTY, Isaac	26	DOTY, John	10	DOTY, Thomas	175
DOTTY, Isaac	67	DOTY, John	23	DOTY, Thomas	193
DOTTY, Jabez	26	DOTY, John	67	DOTY, Thomas	208
DOTTY, Jeane	26	DOTY, John	98	DOUGLAS, Jean	146
DOTTY, Martha	26	DOTY, Josiah	10	DOUGLAS, John	146
DOTTY, Martha	67	DOTY, Josiah	60	DOUGLAS, Mercy	146
DOTTY, Mary	26	DOTY, Lidiah	23	DOUGLASS, Lydia	222
DOTTY, Neriah	26	DOTY, Lois	40	DOUNHAM, Eliazebeth	67
DOTTY, Rebecah	26	DOTY, Mahittable	67	DOUNHAM, Mary	98
DOTY, -----	81	DOTY, Marcy	74	DOUNHAM, Micajah	67
DOTY, Abigal	60	DOTY, Marcy	81	DOW, Alexander	78
DOTY, Abigall	60	DOTY, Martha	9	DOW, Alexander	95
DOTY, Benjamin	9	DOTY, Martha	10	DOW, Alexander	181
DOTY, Desir	129	DOTY, Martha	71	DOW, Sarah	78
DOTY, Desire	71	DOTY, Mary	9	DOW, Sarah	95
DOTY, Edward	9	DOTY, Mary	65	DOWNHAM, Barshua	8
DOTY, Edward	10	DOTY, Mary	67	DOWNHAM, Bathshaba	8
DOTY, Edward	23	DOTY, Mary	79	DOWNHAM, Eliazur	8
DOTY, Edward	40	DOTY, Mary	88	DOWNHAM, Elisha	8
DOTY, Edward	98	DOTY, Mary	179	DOWNHAM, Israil	8
DOTY, Edward	121	DOTY, Mehetible	130	DOWNHAM, Joshua	8
DOTY, Eliazebeth	67	DOTY, Mehittaball	23	DOWNHAM, Josiah	8
DOTY, Elisha	10	DOTY, Mercy	9	DOWNHAM, Mercy	8
DOTY, Elisha	40	DOTY, Mercy	130	DOWNHAM, Nathannell	8
DOTY, Elisha	128	DOTY, Nathl.	94	DOWNHAM, Sarah	66
DOTY, Eliza.	123	DOTY, Patience	9	DOWNHAM, Susannah	8
DOTY, Elizabeth	9	DOTY, Patience	60	DOWNS, Joanna	205
DOTY, Elizabeth	10	DOTY, Patience	98	DRAKE, Isaac	204
DOTY, Elizabeth	94	DOTY, Patience	108	DREW, Abbet	89
DOTY, Elizabeth	98	DOTY, Patience	116	DREW, Abbit	165
DOTY, Elizabeth	108	DOTY, Paul	40	DREW, Abby	138
DOTY, Elizabeth	124	DOTY, Rebecah	121	DREW, Abigail	50
DOTY, Experience	60	DOTY, Rebekah	78	DREW, Abigail	100
DOTY, Experience	109	DOTY, Saml.	94	DREW, Abigail	182
DOTY, Experience	120	DOTY, Samuel	9	DREW, Abigal	51
DOTY, Hanna	40	DOTY, Samuel	40	DREW, Abigal	89
DOTY, Hannah	9	DOTY, Samuel	74	DREW, Ann	161
DOTY, Hannah	40	DOTY, Samuel	81	DREW, Ann	169

VITAL RECORDS OF THE TOWN OF PLYMOUTH

Name	Page	Name	Page	Name	Page
DREW, Atwood	205	DREW, Isaac	86	DREW, Lewis	212
DREW, Atwood	209	DREW, Isaac	160	DREW, Lois	89
DREW, Atwood L.	209	DREW, James	35	DREW, Lucy	151
DREW, Augusta Ann	169	DREW, James	36	DREW, Lydia	36
DREW, Augusta Winslow	138	DREW, James	51	DREW, Lydia	51
DREW, Bathsheba	89	DREW, James	105	DREW, Lydia	74
DREW, Bathsheba	155	DREW, James	107	DREW, Lydia	104
DREW, Bathsheba	201	DREW, James	151	DREW, Lydia	138
DREW, Bathshebath	77	DREW, Jane Sturtevant	209	DREW, Lydia	198
DREW, Benjamin	155	DREW, Joann	151	DREW, Lydia	199
DREW, Benjamin	179	DREW, Joanna	102	DREW, Mallechi	155
DREW, Betse Lewis	166	DREW, Joanna	138	DREW, Margaret	155
DREW, Betsey	36	DREW, Joanna	208	DREW, Margaret	171
DREW, Betsy Lewis	201	DREW, Joanna	212	DREW, Margaret	200
DREW, Charles	151	DREW, Joannah	50	DREW, Margaret James	160
DREW, Charles Lee	139	DREW, Joannah	77	DREW, Margaret James	199
DREW, Consider	181	DREW, Joannah	86	DREW, Martha Bartlett	220
DREW, David	89	DREW, Joannah	118	DREW, Mary	35
DREW, David	161	DREW, John	11	DREW, Mary	36
DREW, David	187	DREW, John Milk	138	DREW, Mary	51
DREW, David	205	DREW, Joseph	160	DREW, Mary	76
DREW, David Lewis	161	DREW, Joseph	208	DREW, Mary	107
DREW, Desire	155	DREW, Joseph Perce	165	DREW, Mary	117
DREW, Ebenezer	155	DREW, Joseph Pierce	220	DREW, Mary	138
DREW, Ebenezr.	155	DREW, Joshua	50	DREW, Mary	190
DREW, Ebenezr.	203	DREW, Joshua	86	DREW, Nicholas	51
DREW, Edward Winslow	138	DREW, Joshua	101	DREW, Nicholas	74
DREW, Eliza.	160	DREW, Joshua	113	DREW, Nicholas	77
DREW, Elizabeth	11	DREW, Joshua	117	DREW, Nicholas	89
DREW, Elizabeth	151	DREW, Joshua	208	DREW, Nicholas	118
DREW, Elizabeth	155	DREW, Josiah	50	DREW, Nicholas	124
DREW, Elizabeth	160	DREW, Josiah	86	DREW, Nicholas	165
DREW, Elizabeth	165	DREW, Josiah	89	DREW, Nicholas	183
DREW, Elizabeth	199	DREW, Josiah	148	DREW, Nicolas	89
DREW, Elizabeth	200	DREW, Josiah	186	DREW, Nicolas	171
DREW, Elizabeth	205	DREW, Lemuel	50	DREW, Nicolas	201
DREW, Ephraim	86	DREW, Lemuel	51	DREW, Nicolos	50
DREW, Eunice	166	DREW, Lemuel	70	DREW, Nicolos	70
DREW, Frederick Augustus	169	DREW, Lemuel	101	DREW, Nicolos	100
DREW, Gamaliel	151	DREW, Lemuel	106	DREW, Nicolus	11
DREW, George	160	DREW, Lemuel	107	DREW, Patience	86
DREW, George (Capt.)	207	DREW, Lemuel	119	DREW, Patience	181
DREW, George Augustus	139	DREW, Lemuel	160	DREW, Priscilla	36
DREW, Georgianna	139	DREW, Lemuel	181	DREW, Priscilla	101
DREW, Hanah	51	DREW, Lemuel	198	DREW, Priscilla	197
DREW, Hannah	11	DREW, Lemuel (Deac.)	160	DREW, Prisilla	107
DREW, Hannah	35	DREW, Lemuell	11	DREW, Rebecaa	70
DREW, Hannah	51	DREW, Levi	86	DREW, Rebecca	212
DREW, Hannah	70	DREW, Levi	138	DREW, Rebecca Ames	165
DREW, Hannah	186	DREW, Levi	172	DREW, Rebeccah	51
DREW, Harrison Warren	161	DREW, Levy	51	DREW, Rebeckah	165

Name	Page	Name	Page	Name	Page
DREW, Rebeckah	172	DUGLESS, John	194	DUNHAM, Lydia	159
DREW, Reeckah	50	DUGLESS, John	216	DUNHAM, Lydia Ann	159
DREW, Reuben	151	DUGLESS, Joshua	214	DUNHAM, Marcy	130
DREW, Ruby	139	DUGLESS, Lucy	210	DUNHAM, Marsey	69
DREW, Sally Ann	161	DUGLESS, Phebe	200	DUNHAM, Martha	39
DREW, Sam.	165	DUGLESS, Warren	212	DUNHAM, Martha	98
DREW, Samuel	11	DUNBAR, Jesse	194	DUNHAM, Mary	13
DREW, Samuel	89	DUNBER, John Danforth	199	DUNHAM, Mary	53
DREW, Samuel	165	DUNBER, William	207	DUNHAM, Mary	65
DREW, Samuel	186	DUNCAN, Sarah	78	DUNHAM, Mary	66
DREW, Sarah	35	DUNHAM, Abigaiel	34	DUNHAM, Meriam	37
DREW, Sarah	51	DUNHAM, Abigail	78	DUNHAM, Micajah	34
DREW, Sarah	112	DUNHAM, Abigail	95	DUNHAM, Nancy	153
DREW, Sarah	113	DUNHAM, Abigail	150	DUNHAM, Nathaniel	37
DREW, Sarah	151	DUNHAM, Amos	53	DUNHAM, Nathaniel	66
DREW, Sarah	160	DUNHAM, Amos	78	DUNHAM, Nathaniel	118
DREW, Sarah	193	DUNHAM, Amos	122	DUNHAM, Nathaniell	13
DREW, Sarah D.	148	DUNHAM, Ann	41	DUNHAM, Patience	41
DREW, Sarah W.	148	DUNHAM, Anna	70	DUNHAM, Rebeckah	37
DREW, Sarah Woodward	151	DUNHAM, Annah	39	DUNHAM, Robert	153
DREW, Seth	51	DUNHAM, Annah	70	DUNHAM, Ruth	53
DREW, Seth	160	DUNHAM, Bathshua	71	DUNHAM, Ruth	70
DREW, Seth	200	DUNHAM, Betsey Foster	159	DUNHAM, Sally	153
DREW, Simeon	155	DUNHAM, Charles	53	DUNHAM, Saloma Nickerson	159
DREW, Sophronia	151	DUNHAM, Ebenazar	41	DUNHAM, Samuel	13
DREW, Stephen	89	DUNHAM, Ebenazar	70	DUNHAM, Samuel	65
DREW, Stephen	151	DUNHAM, Ebenazar	129	DUNHAM, Samuel	67
DREW, Stephen	189	DUNHAM, Ebenezer	13	DUNHAM, Samuel	97
DREW, Thomas	11	DUNHAM, Eliazar	37	DUNHAM, Samuel	98
DREW, Thomas	160	DUNHAM, Elizabeth	34	DUNHAM, Samuel	99
DREW, Thomas	218	DUNHAM, Elizabeth	37	DUNHAM, Sarah	67
DREW, William	35	DUNHAM, Ester	71	DUNHAM, Seth	41
DREW, William	51	DUNHAM, Ester	78	DUNHAM, Wiliam	13
DREW, William	86	DUNHAM, Ezekell	37	DUNHAM, William	39
DREW, William	151	DUNHAM, Ezekill	37	DUNHAM, William	70
DREW, William	160	DUNHAM, Ffeare	37	DUNHAM, William	150
DREW, William	166	DUNHAM, George Foster	159	DUNHAM, William	153
DREW, William	191	DUNHAM, Hannah	53	DUNHAM, William G.	153
DREW, William	205	DUNHAM, Hannah Nickerson	159	DUNKIN, Bethyah	35
DREW, William	207	DUNHAM, Harvey	222	DUNKIN, Jabiz	35
DREW, William Warren	169	DUNHAM, Jerusha	37	DUNKIN, Jabiz	100
DREW, Winslow	138	DUNHAM, John	97	DUNKIN, Samuel	35
DREW, Wlliam	166	DUNHAM, John	98	DURFEY, Abby H.	162
DREW, Wm.	169	DUNHAM, John F.	159	DURFEY, Benjamin B.	162
DUEY, William	181	DUNHAM, John Foster	222	DURFEY, Elizabeth	146
DUFFEE, Mary	71	DUNHAM, Joseph	34	DURFEY, Hannah	146
DUFFEE, Peleg	71	DUNHAM, Joshua	34	DURFEY, Mary	116
DUGLES, Ephraim	204	DUNHAM, Joshua	130	DURFEY, Mary	146
DUGLESS, Betsey	219	DUNHAM, Josiah	53	DURFEY, Mary	216
DUGLESS, James	217	DUNHAM, Josiah	70	DURFEY, Peleg	129
DUGLESS, John	176	DUNHAM, Lydia	53	DURFEY, Rebeckah	107

VITAL RECORDS OF THE TOWN OF PLYMOUTH

DURFEY, Richard	105	**E**		EATON, Mary	111
DURFEY, Richard	107			EATON, Mersey	66
DURFEY, Richard	146	EAMES, Grace	168	EATON, Rebekah	67
DURFEY, Richard	174	EAMES, Grace	187	EATON, Sarah	21
DURFEY, Richard	184	EAMES, Isaac	53	EATON, William	21
DURFEY, Richard	198	EAMES, Jona.	115	EATTON, Benjamin	24
DURFEY, Richard	208	EAMES, Jonathan	52	EATTON, Ebenazer	24
DURFEY, Richard T.	162	EAMES, Jonathan	53	EATTON, Elisha	24
DURFEY, Sarah	208	EAMES, Lidiah	54	EATTON, Gidian	24
DURFEY, Susan T.	162	EAMES, Lydia	52	EATTON, Joanna	24
DURFY, Grace	162	EAMES, Lydia	122	EATTON, Marsey	24
DURFY, Mary	60	EAMES, Lydia	181	EAVERSON, Ebenazar	25
DURFY, Peleg	60	EAMES, Margaret	52	EAVERSON, Eliazebeth	25
DURFY, Richard	162	EAMES, Margaret	193	EAVERSON, Ephraime	25
DURPHA, Richard	146	EAMES, Rebeckah	112	EAVERSON, James	30
DURPHA, Sarah	146	EAMES, Rebeckah	113	EAVERSON, John	30
DURPHA, Thomas	146	EAMES, Rebeckah	183	EAVERSON, Marcey	30
DUTCH, Samuel	189	EAMES, Rebekah	53	EAVERSON, Richard	25
DYER, Hannah	75	EARL, Deborah	214	EDDY, Anna	148
DYER, Hannah	86	EASDELL, -----	11	EDDY, Saml.	178
DYER, John	86	EASDELL, James	11	EDDY, Samuel	148
DYER, John	117	EASDELL, Rebecca	178	EDDY, Samuel	178
DYER, John	129	EASDELL, Rebeckah	11	EDDY, Samuell	178
DYER, John	173	EASDELL, Rebeckah	105	EDDY, Seth	205
DYER, John (Capt.)	75	EASTLAND, Elizabeth	25	EDDY, Sophia	210
DYER, Pegge	213	EASTLAND, Hannah	25	EDDY, Sophia	212
DYRE, Bethiah	214	EASTLAND, Jean	25	EDSON, Elijah	220
DYRE, Charles	77	EASTLAND, John	25	EDWARDS, Dinah	218
DYRE, Charles	90	EASTLAND, John	69	EDWARDS, John	185
DYRE, Charles	118	EASTLAND, Joseph	25	EDWARDS, John	200
DYRE, Charles	186	EASTLAND, Joshuah	25	EDWARDS, Lydia	201
DYRE, Charles (Capt.)	90	EASTLAND, Marey	25	EDWARDS, Polley	214
DYRE, Hannah	74	EASTLAND, Mary	25	EDWARDS, Sarah	202
DYRE, Hannah	75	EASTLAND, Mary	69	EDWARDS, Sukey	209
DYRE, Hannah	78	EASTLAND, Mary	127	EHPRAIMS, William	185
DYRE, Hannah	82	EASTLAND, Zeruiah	25	ELDRED, Ann	70
DYRE, Hannah	122	EATON, Benja.	111	ELDREDGE, Joshua	188
DYRE, Hannah	178	EATON, Benja.	123	ELIS, Benjamin	130
DYRE, John	136	EATON, Benjamen	21	ELLECE, Abigail	54
DYRE, Luce	77	EATON, Benjamin	184	ELLECE, Ann	54
DYRE, Lucy	90	EATON, Benjamine	66	ELLECE, Ebenezer	54
DYRE, Lucy	194	EATON, Ebenazar	69	ELLECE, Elener	54
DYRE, Martha	201	EATON, Ebenezer	67	ELLECE, Elijah	54
DYRE, Mary	136	EATON, Hanah	24	ELLECE, Gedian	54
DYRE, Mary	187	EATON, Hanah	67	ELLECE, Gideon	54
DYRE, William	74	EATON, Hannah	21	ELLECE, Recka	129
DYRE, William	75	EATON, Hannah	69	ELLECE, Thomas	54
DYRE, William	82	EATON, Jabiz	21	ELLENWOOD, Theodore	208
DYRE, William	117	EATON, John	21	ELLES, Abigail	25
DYRE, William	124	EATON, Mary	21	ELLES, Barnabas	24
		EATON, Mary	66	ELLES, Benjamin	63

ELLES, Betty	29	ELLICE, Experiance	55	ELLIS, Lydia	187
ELLES, Betty	63	ELLICE, Gidion	129	ELLIS, Lydia	189
ELLES, Deborah	24	ELLICE, Joane	55	ELLIS, Lydia	198
ELLES, Deborah	25	ELLICE, Joell	36	ELLIS, Lydia	214
ELLES, Deborah	95	ELLICE, John	36	ELLIS, Marcy	61
ELLES, Deborah	178	ELLICE, Rebca	71	ELLIS, Mary	61
ELLES, Eleazer	24	ELLICE, William	55	ELLIS, Mary	82
ELLES, Eleazer	116	ELLIOT, Betsey H.	215	ELLIS, Mary	121
ELLES, Elizabeth	106	ELLIOT, Daniel Roberts	206	ELLIS, Mary	193
ELLES, Elizabeth	111	ELLIS, -----	63	ELLIS, Mary	201
ELLES, Elizabeth	131	ELLIS, Abigail	187	ELLIS, Mehitable	201
ELLES, Esther	111	ELLIS, Anna	71	ELLIS, Mercy	210
ELLES, Experience	111	ELLIS, Barnabas	183	ELLIS, Mordeca	70
ELLES, Freeman	63	ELLIS, Bartlett	218	ELLIS, Mordecai	117
ELLES, Je (Jesse?)	25	ELLIS, Benjamin	63	ELLIS, Mordecai	118
ELLES, Jean	105	ELLIS, Benjamin	73	ELLIS, Mordecai	125
ELLES, Jean	107	ELLIS, Benjamin	203	ELLIS, Mordica	195
ELLES, John	82	ELLIS, Benjamin	218	ELLIS, Nancy	204
ELLES, Jonathan (Rev.)	95	ELLIS, Betse	194	ELLIS, Nancy	209
ELLES, Jonathan (Rev.)	111	ELLIS, Betty	163	ELLIS, Nathaniel	213
ELLES, Joseph	63	ELLIS, Betty	182	ELLIS, Nathl.	193
ELLES, Luce	95	ELLIS, Debo.	198	ELLIS, Polley	201
ELLES, Lydia	29	ELLIS, Deborah	197	ELLIS, Remember	61
ELLES, Lydia	132	ELLIS, Eben.	203	ELLIS, Remembr.	194
ELLES, Marcy	111	ELLIS, Ebenezr.	200	ELLIS, Reuben	200
ELLES, Mary	29	ELLIS, Eleazer	55	ELLIS, Salley	198
ELLES, Mary	95	ELLIS, Eleazer	197	ELLIS, Samuel	61
ELLES, Mary	111	ELLIS, Eleazer	198	ELLIS, Sarah	67
ELLES, Mary	113	ELLIS, Eleazr.	200	ELLIS, Sarah	190
ELLES, Mercy	178	ELLIS, Elizabeth	70	ELLIS, Stephen	217
ELLES, Molly	25	ELLIS, Ester	123	ELLIS, Stephens	209
ELLES, Nathaniel	132	ELLIS, Esther	190	ELLIS, Susanna	206
ELLES, Nathll.	63	ELLIS, Eunice	197	ELLIS, Thomas	55
ELLES, Patience	29	ELLIS, Experience	122	ELLIS, Thomas	163
ELLES, Patience	95	ELLIS, Francis	203	ELLIS, Thomas	181
ELLES, Pelham	25	ELLIS, George	198	ELLIS, Thomas	205
ELLES, Rebeckah	112	ELLIS, George	205	ELLIS, William	163
ELLES, Rebeckah	115	ELLIS, Gidian	71	ELLIS, William	198
ELLES, Rebeckah	175	ELLIS, Hannah	63	ELLIS, William	201
ELLES, Rose	82	ELLIS, Hannah	73	ELLIS, William	205
ELLES, Saml.	104	ELLIS, Hesther	61	ELLIS, Zilpah	181
ELLES, Samuell	132	ELLIS, Jabesh	82	ELLMES, Lydia	195
ELLES, Sarah	63	ELLIS, Jean	181	EMERY, James	189
ELLES, Sarah	132	ELLIS, Jenna	207	ENGLES, Elizabeth	188
ELLES, Susannah	63	ELLIS, Jerusha	163	ENGLISH, Alse	75
ELLES, Thomas	29	ELLIS, Joel	70	ENGLISH, Peter	75
ELLES, William	25	ELLIS, John	67	ENGLISH, Peter	125
ELLES, William	29	ELLIS, John	82	ERLAND, Edwin Francis	155
ELLES, William	115	ELLIS, Jonathan (Rev.)	121	ERLAND, Henry	155
ELLES, Zilpa	24	ELLIS, Lucy	195	ERLAND, Henry Thomas	155
ELLICE, Elizabeth	36	ELLIS, Lucy	205	ERLAND, Sally C.	155

VITAL RECORDS OF THE TOWN OF PLYMOUTH

ESDELL, Mary	177	FAUNCE, Abigaill	69	FAUNCE, John	69
ESLAND, Elizabeth	69	FAUNCE, Abigal	118	FAUNCE, John	86
ESLAND, Elizabeth	98	FAUNCE, Ansell	94	FAUNCE, John	92
ESLAND, John	69	FAUNCE, Ansell	190	FAUNCE, John	94
ESLAND, Mary	69	FAUNCE, Barnabas	206	FAUNCE, John	124
EVERSON, Abigail	198	FAUNCE, Barnabas	209	FAUNCE, John	183
EVERSON, Ephraim	199	FAUNCE, Barnabe	198	FAUNCE, John	189
EVERSON, Nancey	212	FAUNCE, Barnebe	43	FAUNCE, John	207
EVERSON, Patience	222	FAUNCE, Bartlett	158	FAUNCE, Joseph	139
EWER, Abigail	183	FAUNCE, Bartlett	213	FAUNCE, Joseph	167
EWER, Eleazer	56	FAUNCE, Bathsheba	85	FAUNCE, Joseph	194
EWER, Lydia	56	FAUNCE, Benjamin	139	FAUNCE, Lediah	43
EWER, Lydia	111	FAUNCE, Betsey	197	FAUNCE, Lucy Carver	222
EWER, Mary	174	FAUNCE, Betsey	212	FAUNCE, Lydia	43
EWER, Sarah	173	FAUNCE, Caleb	204	FAUNCE, Lydia	94
EWER, Seth	178	FAUNCE, Caroline Augusta	141	FAUNCE, Lydia	105
EWER, Thomas	56	FAUNCE, Charles	168	FAUNCE, Lydia	106
EWER, Thomas	111	FAUNCE, Charles L.	158	FAUNCE, Lydia	158
EWER, Thomas	112	FAUNCE, Daniel	85	FAUNCE, Lydia	187
		FAUNCE, Daniel Wooster	141	FAUNCE, Lydia	200
F		FAUNCE, Daniel Worcester	141	FAUNCE, Marcy	118
		FAUNCE, Eleazer	73	FAUNCE, Marsey	35
FALES, Elizabeth	112	FAUNCE, Eleazer	95	FAUNCE, Martha	67
FALES, Timothy	112	FAUNCE, Eleazer	130	FAUNCE, Martha Ellen	158
FALES, Timothy	114	FAUNCE, Eleazer	139	FAUNCE, Mary	86
FARLING, Deborah	162	FAUNCE, Eleazr.	167	FAUNCE, Mary	95
FARMAR, John	91	FAUNCE, Elizabeth	95	FAUNCE, Mary	139
FARMAR, Thomas	91	FAUNCE, Elizabeth Davis	136	FAUNCE, Mary	172
FARMER, Mary	159	FAUNCE, George	94	FAUNCE, Mary	173
FARMER, Mary	205	FAUNCE, George Henry	158	FAUNCE, Mary Ann	136
FARMER, Nancy	214	FAUNCE, Hannah	43	FAUNCE, Mehittabl	70
FARMER, Susanna	195	FAUNCE, Hannah	73	FAUNCE, Mercy	77
FARMER, Susannah	159	FAUNCE, Hannah	85	FAUNCE, Mercy	167
FARMER, Thomas	159	FAUNCE, Hannah	95	FAUNCE, Nathaniel	92
FARMER, Thomas	182	FAUNCE, Hannah	104	FAUNCE, Nathaniel Brown	158
FARMER, Thomas	197	FAUNCE, Hannah	128	FAUNCE, Nathaniell	35
FARN, Sussanna	195	FAUNCE, Hannah	195	FAUNCE, Nathl. Brown	158
FARNAM, Dorcas	167	FAUNCE, Hannah	206	FAUNCE, Olive	141
FARNAM, Jonathan	167	FAUNCE, Hannah	212	FAUNCE, Patiance	112
FARNAM, Jonathan	190	FAUNCE, Jabez	87	FAUNCE, Patience	35
FARNAM, Sarah Barnes	167	FAUNCE, James	92	FAUNCE, Patience	95
FARNUM, Dorcas	167	FAUNCE, Jane	35	FAUNCE, Patience	113
FARROW, Sarah	124	FAUNCE, Jane	73	FAUNCE, Patience	188
FAUNC, Thomas	217	FAUNCE, Jane	109	FAUNCE, Pattience	67
FAUNCE, ----- (Elder)	98	FAUNCE, Jeames	43	FAUNCE, Peleg	43
FAUNCE, Abigail	77	FAUNCE, Jean	118	FAUNCE, Peleg	139
FAUNCE, Abigail	95	FAUNCE, Jean	121	FAUNCE, Peleg	141
FAUNCE, Abigail	183	FAUNCE, Jean	126	FAUNCE, Peleg	172
FAUNCE, Abigail	200	FAUNCE, Jerusha	94	FAUNCE, Peleg	191
FAUNCE, Abigail Thomas	168	FAUNCE, Jerusha	168	FAUNCE, Priscilla	94
FAUNCE, Abigaill	35	FAUNCE, John	35	FAUNCE, Priscilla	95

VITAL RECORDS OF THE TOWN OF PLYMOUTH

Name	Page	Name	Page	Name	Page
FAUNCE, Rebecca	158	FFAUNCE, John	11	FFINNEY, Mary	70
FAUNCE, Rebecca Jane	158	FFAUNCE, John	40	FFINNEY, Patience	71
FAUNCE, Rebeccah	40	FFAUNCE, John	70	FFINNEY, Phebee	14
FAUNCE, Ruth	43	FFAUNCE, Joseph	9	FFINNEY, Pricila	14
FAUNCE, Ruth	86	FFAUNCE, Juduth	9	FFINNEY, Robert	14
FAUNCE, Ruth	122	FFAUNCE, Juduth	40	FFINNEY, Robert	52
FAUNCE, Sarah	43	FFAUNCE, Lidiah	40	FFINEY, Ruth	56
FAUNCE, Sarah	66	FFAUNCE, Lidiah	71	FFINEY, Sarah	56
FAUNCE, Sarah	79	FFAUNCE, Lydiah	70	FFINNEY, Sarah	71
FAUNCE, Sarah	85	FFAUNCE, Martha	11	FFISH, Deborah	65
FAUNCE, Sarah	87	FFAUNCE, Mary	9	FFISH, Nathn	65
FAUNCE, Sarah	92	FFAUNCE, Mary	40	FFORD, Allice	71
FAUNCE, Sarah	94	FFAUNCE, Mary	69	FFORD, Peleg	71
FAUNCE, Sarah	191	FFAUNCE, Mehitabell	40	FFOSTER, Gershom	19
FAUNCE, Sarah	203	FFAUNCE, Mehittale	9	FFOSTER, Hannah	19
FAUNCE, Seth	43	FFAUNCE, Mercy	9	FFOSTER, Hannah	70
FAUNCE, Seth	92	FFAUNCE, Patience	11	FFOSTER, Ichabod	19
FAUNCE, Solomon	208	FFAUNCE, Pricilah	11	FFOSTER, John	19
FAUNCE, Stephen	94	FFAUNCE, Ruth	40	FFOSTER, Marcy	19
FAUNCE, Stephen	206	FFAUNCE, Sarah	70	FFOSTER, Marcy	71
FAUNCE, Stephen	210	FFAUNCE, Sarah	100	FFOSTER, Nathaniel	19
FAUNCE, Thaddeus	94	FFAUNCE, Thomas	9	FFOSTER, Sarah	19
FAUNCE, Thaddeus	186	FFAUNCE, Thomas	11	FFOSTER, Sarah	71
FAUNCE, Thadeus	136	FFAUNCE, Thomas	65	FFOSTER, Seth	19
FAUNCE, Thomas	43	FFAUNCE, Thomas	70	FFOSTER, Thomas	19
FAUNCE, Thomas	79	FFAUNCE, Thomas	71	FFULLAR, Abiall	27
FAUNCE, Thomas	85	FFAUNCE, Thomas	100	FFULLAR, John	27
FAUNCE, Thomas	87	FFERREN, Israiel	56	FFULLER, Abiall	69
FAUNCE, Thomas	94	FFERREN, Israill	56	FFULLER, Annis	27
FAUNCE, Thomas	123	FFERREN, Martha	56	FFULLER, Annis	69
FAUNCE, Thomas	125	FFINEY, Elizabeth	70	FFULLER, Benjamine	30
FAUNCE, Thomas	181	FFINEY, -----	56	FFULLER, Ebenazar	30
FAUNCE, Thomas	201	FFINEY, John	56	FFULLER, Elizabeth	30
FEARING, Ann	56	FFINEY, Josiah	56	FFULLER, Hannah	65
FEARING, Benjamin	56	FFINEY, Patiene	129	FFULLER, Jabez	30
FEARING, David	56	FFINEY, Phebe	56	FFULLER, James	30
FEARING, Elizabeth	56	FFINEY, Ruth	56	FFULLER, John	30
FEARING, John	56	FFINEY, Sarah	56	FFULLER, John	65
FEARING, Noah	56	FFINNEY, Ann	52	FFULLER, Marcey	30
FEARING, Polley	205	FFINNEY, Elizabeth	14	FFULLER, Nathaniel	30
FENEY, Jesiah	130	FFINNEY, Ester	69	FFULLER, Samuel	30
FERREN, Isral	130	FFINNEY, Febe	99	FFULLER, Seth	30
FFAUNCE, Benjamin	9	FFINNEY, Jerusha	52	FFULLER, William	30
FFAUNCE, Eliazar	9	FFINNEY, John	14	FFULLOUR, Mersey	66
FFAUNCE, Hannah	9	FFINNEY, John	71	FFULLOUR, Samuel	66
FFAUNCE, Hannah	40	FFINNEY, Joseph	69	FIELD, James	190
FFAUNCE, Jean	11	FFINNEY, Joshua	14	FINEY, Elizabeth	52
FFAUNCE, Jeann	65	FFINNEY, Josiah	14	FINEY, John	129
FFAUNCE, Joannah	11	FFINNEY, Josiah	52	FINEY, Mary	69
FFAUNCE, Joannah	70	FFINNEY, Lidiah	52	FINEY, Rebecca	52
FFAUNCE, John	9	FFINNEY, Mary	69	FINLEY, Rachel	190

VITAL RECORDS OF THE TOWN OF PLYMOUTH

Name	Page	Name	Page	Name	Page
FINN, Daniel	176	FINNEY, Hannah	74	FINNEY, Rebecca	74
FINNEY, ----- (Deacon)	96	FINNEY, Hannah	111	FINNEY, Rebecca	109
FINNEY, Abigaiel	71	FINNEY, Hannah	116	FINNEY, Rebecca	198
FINNEY, Abigail	105	FINNEY, Hannah	161	FINNEY, Rebeckah	156
FINNEY, Abigail	112	FINNEY, Hannah	199	FINNEY, Robert	10
FINNEY, Abigail	177	FINNEY, James	156	FINNEY, Robert	56
FINNEY, Abigail	200	FINNEY, Jane	73	FINNEY, Robert	71
FINNEY, Albert	148	FINNEY, Jerusha	10	FINNEY, Robert	101
FINNEY, Albert Thomas	148	FINNEY, Jerusha	105	FINNEY, Robert	169
FINNEY, Alice	147	FINNEY, Jerusha	106	FINNEY, Robert	180
FINNEY, Alice	199	FINNEY, John	26	FINNEY, Robert	198
FINNEY, Alse	26	FINNEY, John	56	FINNEY, Ruth	105
FINNEY, Ann	101	FINNEY, John	129	FINNEY, Ruth	106
FINNEY, Anne	71	FINNEY, John	156	FINNEY, Ruth	156
FINNEY, Benjamin C.	144	FINNEY, John	173	FINNEY, Ruth	193
FINNEY, Caleb	203	FINNEY, Joseph	26	FINNEY, Ruthe	205
FINNEY, Caleb	218	FINNEY, Joseph	67	FINNEY, Salley	199
FINNEY, Charles Harlow	148	FINNEY, Joshua	74	FINNEY, Salley	206
FINNEY, Clark	169	FINNEY, Joshua	123	FINNEY, Sarah	109
FINNEY, Clark	200	FINNEY, Joshua	127	FINNEY, Sarah	122
FINNEY, Costellow	148	FINNEY, Joshua	171	FINNEY, Sarah	156
FINNEY, Daniel	200	FINNEY, Josiah	56	FINNEY, Sarah	222
FINNEY, Ebenezer	73	FINNEY, Josiah	66	FINNEY, Seth	122
FINNEY, Ebenezer	74	FINNEY, Josiah	126	FINNEY, Seth	202
FINNEY, Ebenezer	124	FINNEY, Josiah	147	FINNEY, Silvanus	56
FINNEY, Ebenezer	126	FINNEY, Josiah	169	FINNEY, Silvanus	182
FINNEY, Eliza.	109	FINNEY, Josiah	178	FINNEY, Solomon	201
FINNEY, Eliza.	122	FINNEY, Josiah	197	FINNEY, Susannah	56
FINNEY, Elizabeth	66	FINNEY, Josiah	208	FINNEY, Susannah	194
FINNEY, Elizabeth	70	FINNEY, Lewis	206	FINNEY, Thomas	175
FINNEY, Elizabeth	144	FINNEY, Lucinda	148	FINNEY, Thomas Weston	148
FINNEY, Elizabeth	156	FINNEY, Lydia	10	FINNEY, William	56
FINNEY, Elizabeth	194	FINNEY, Lydia	169	FINNEY, William	187
FINNEY, Elizabeth	198	FINNEY, Lydia	194	FINNEY, William	207
FINNEY, Elizabeth Atwood	144	FINNEY, Lydia Bartlett	219	FINNY, John	121
FINNEY, Elkanah	169	FINNEY, Maletiah	125	FINNY, Phebe	126
FINNEY, Elkanah	202	FINNEY, Margaret	173	FINNY, Rebecah	121
FINNEY, Ephraim	56	FINNEY, Marsey	26	FISH, -----	118
FINNEY, Ephraim	188	FINNEY, Mary	26	FISH, Anna	186
FINNEY, Ephraim	206	FINNEY, Mary	194	FISH, Caleb	133
FINNEY, Eunice	204	FINNEY, Mary	218	FISH, Caleb	196
FINNEY, Experiance	169	FINNEY, Mary	222	FISH, Caleb	217
FINNEY, Experience	201	FINNEY, Mehitable	198	FISH, Cynthia	213
FINNEY, Experience	220	FINNEY, Mercy	67	FISH, Deborah	74
FINNEY, Ezra	56	FINNEY, Nancy	218	FISH, Deborah	77
FINNEY, Ezra	161	FINNEY, Olive	194	FISH, Deborah	109
FINNEY, Ezra	183	FINNEY, Olley	147	FISH, Deborah	118
FINNEY, Ezra	201	FINNEY, Phebe	73	FISH, Deborah	133
FINNEY, Ezra (Capt.)	212	FINNEY, Phebe	121	FISH, Eliza.	133
FINNEY, George	169	FINNEY, Polley	196	FISH, Hannah	111
FINNEY, George	200	FINNEY, Priscila	71	FISH, Jane	109

VITAL RECORDS OF THE TOWN OF PLYMOUTH

Name	Page	Name	Page	Name	Page
FISH, Jane	113	FOSTER, Abigail	134	FOSTER, Mary	173
FISH, Jane	133	FOSTER, Betsey	222	FOSTER, Mary	197
FISH, Jane	191	FOSTER, Betty	134	FOSTER, Mercy	190
FISH, Jean	113	FOSTER, Daniel	222	FOSTER, Nathaniel	87
FISH, Jirah	111	FOSTER, Deborah	65	FOSTER, Nathaniel	118
FISH, Jirah	116	FOSTER, Deborah	171	FOSTER, Nathaniel	134
FISH, Joanna	189	FOSTER, Elisha	65	FOSTER, Nathl.	87
FISH, Joanna	191	FOSTER, Elizabeth	56	FOSTER, Nathl.	115
FISH, Joannah	133	FOSTER, Elizabeth	158	FOSTER, Peter	87
FISH, Joannah	187	FOSTER, Elizabeth	182	FOSTER, Peter Thatcher	158
FISH, Johannah	133	FOSTER, Elizabeth	196	FOSTER, Philemon	56
FISH, John	190	FOSTER, Eunice	56	FOSTER, Priscilla	38
FISH, Lemuel	74	FOSTER, Eunice	191	FOSTER, Rebecca	214
FISH, Lemuel	125	FOSTER, George	38	FOSTER, Salome	56
FISH, Lemuel	131	FOSTER, Gershom	65	FOSTER, Salome	182
FISH, Lemuel	133	FOSTER, Gershom	134	FOSTER, Samuel	60
FISH, Lucy	133	FOSTER, Hannah	38	FOSTER, Samuel	130
FISH, Lucy	196	FOSTER, Hannah	65	FOSTER, Sarah	134
FISH, Marcy	111	FOSTER, Hannah	67	FOSTER, Seth	56
FISH, Mary	133	FOSTER, Hannah	73	FOSTER, Susana	56
FISH, Mehetabel	106	FOSTER, Hannah	87	FOSTER, Thomas	38
FISH, Nathan	212	FOSTER, Hannah	134	FOSTER, Thomas	56
FISH, Polley	216	FOSTER, Joanna	59	FOSTER, Thomas	65
FISH, Samuel	133	FOSTER, Joanna	128	FOSTER, Thomas	74
FISH, Samuel	220	FOSTER, Joanna	131	FOSTER, Thomas	79
FISH, Sarah	185	FOSTER, Joannah	112	FOSTER, Thomas	101
FISH, Sarah	206	FOSTER, Job	56	FOSTER, Thomas	110
FISH, Sarah	220	FOSTER, John	60	FOSTER, Thomas	113
FISH, Thomas	207	FOSTER, John	65	FOSTER, Thomas	116
FISH, William	111	FOSTER, John	67	FOSTER, Thomas	125
FISH, William	116	FOSTER, John	74	FOSTER, Thomas	126
FISHER, Abijah	106	FOSTER, John	87	FOSTER, Thomas	173
FISHER, Abijah	128	FOSTER, John	124	FOSTER, Ths.	112
FISHER, Archibold	123	FOSTER, John	158	FOSTER, William	59
FISHER, Jean	171	FOSTER, John	181	FOSTER, William	73
FISHER, Mary	128	FOSTER, John (Deacon)	101	FOSTER, William	112
FISHER, Mary	173	FOSTER, John (Deacon)	125	FOSTER, William	126
FITZGERALD, John	202	FOSTER, Lois	65	FOSTER, William	158
FLANEGA, Catherine	113	FOSTER, Lois	101	FOTTEARS, George	207
FLEMMONS, Hannah Shaw	217	FOSTER, Lois	110	FOUNTAIN, Barnabas	172
FLEMMONS, Mary Richmond	219	FOSTER, Lois	173	FOWLER, George P.	139
FLEMMONS, Mary Richmond	222	FOSTER, Lucey	38	FOWLER, Harriet Frankson	139
FLING, Rebeccah	86	FOSTER, Marcy	38	FOWLER, Margarett	139
FOLIED, Dille	213	FOSTER, Marcy	87	FOWLER, Margarett Elizabeth	139
FORD, Annah	70	FOSTER, Marcy	112	FOWLER, Sophia Hersey	139
FORD, Bethiah	70	FOSTER, Marcy	173	FOWLER, Thomas Baretlett	139
FORD, Hannah	69	FOSTER, Margett	60	FOX, Fanny	154
FORD, Marsey	70	FOSTER, Marsy	129	FREEMAN, Betsey	222
FORD, Sarah	70	FOSTER, Mary	56	FREEMAN, Bradford	117
FORD, Theodotious	174	FOSTER, Mary	79	FREEMAN, Edward	206
FOSTER, ----- (Dea.)	46	FOSTER, Mary	87	FREEMAN, Hanna	124

FREEMAN, James	212	FULLER, Joanna	60	GARDNER, Susan Gear	136
FREEMAN, Jonathan	74	FULLER, John	181	GARDNER, Thomas	75
FREEMAN, Jonathan	128	FULLER, Josiah	60	GARDNER, Thomas	89
FREEMAN, Joshua	128	FULLER, Lois	126	GARDNER, Thomas	117
FREEMAN, Martha	78	FULLER, Lowis	136	GARDNER, Thomas	120
FREEMAN, Nathaniel	78	FULLER, Mariah	128	GARDNER, William	136
FREEMAN, Nathaniel	120	FULLER, Mercy	202	GARLU, Daniel	195
FREEMAN, Sarah	74	FULLER, Rebecca	200	GARNER, Nathaniel	11
FREEMAN, Sarah	105	FULLER, Rebeccah	60	GARNER, Nathaniel	70
FREEMAN, Sarah	107	FULLER, Samuel	60	GARNER, Samuel	11
FREMAN, Jonathan	70	FULLER, Seth	171	GARNER, Samuel	98
FREMAN, Marsey	70			GARNER, Sarah	70
FRENCH, John	172	**G**		GARNER, Suzannah	11
FRINK, Isabella	102			GARNER, Suzannah	66
FRINK, Peter	102	GAIL, Daniel	217	GAULT, Deborah	202
FRINK, Thomas (Rev.)	102	GALE, Daniel	222	GENNEY, Elizabeth	69
FRINK, Thomas (Rev.)	107	GALE, Noah	195	GIBBS, Ansel	187
FRINK, Thos (Rev.)	109	GAMBLE, George	160	GIBBS, Anselm (Capt.)	203
FRISE, Lusanah	210	GAMBLE, Mary	160	GIBBS, Bartlett	217
FRIZE, Susanna	210	GAMBLE, Mary	190	GIBBS, Benjamin	195
FROBERRY, Phebe	199	GAMBLE, Rebeckah	160	GIBBS, Bettey	53
FULSHAM, Charles	137	GAMBLE, Rebeckah	182	GIBBS, Betty	122
FULSHAM, Charles	149	GAMBLE, Robert	160	GIBBS, Catharine	222
FULSHAM, Hannah	149	GAMBLE, Robert	175	GIBBS, Catherine	206
FULSHAM, Joseph	79	GAMMON, Hannah	77	GIBBS, Deborah	116
FULSHAM, Joseph	104	GAMMON, William	77	GIBBS, Diana Clark	213
FULSHAM, Joseph	128	GAMMONS, Benjamin	186	GIBBS, Dorothy	219
FULSHAM, Joseph	137	GAMMONS, Deborah	213	GIBBS, Eliza Ann	164
FULSHAM, Joseph	149	GAMMONS, Fear	128	GIBBS, Elizabeth	35
FULSHAM, Joseph (Capt.)	149	GAMMONS, Fear	136	GIBBS, Elizabeth	183
FULSHAM, Josiah	116	GAMMONS, Nancey	205	GIBBS, Elizabeth	204
FULSHAM, Luranah	128	GAMMONS, Rebeckah	136	GIBBS, Exsperiance	29
FULSHAM, Lurania	149	GAMMONS, Stephen	205	GIBBS, Francis	210
FULSHAM, Mercy	149	GAMMONS, Thankful	201	GIBBS, George Washington	214
FULSHAM, Rebackah	137	GAMMONS, William	106	GIBBS, Hannah	29
FULSHAM, Rebeckah	79	GAMMONS, William	119	GIBBS, Hannah	217
FULSHAM, Rebeckah	149	GAMMONS, William	128	GIBBS, Hannah	218
FULLER, Abiel	171	GAMMONS, Willm.	136	GIBBS, Henry	164
FULLER, Allden	193	GARDNER, Andrew Gear	136	GIBBS, Hesther	29
FULLER, Amasa	218	GARDNER, Ann	136	GIBBS, Jabez	106
FULLER, Anna	177	GARDNER, Ann Maria	136	GIBBS, Jabez	113
FULLER, Archippus	104	GARDNER, Candis	196	GIBBS, Jane	29
FULLER, Archipus	128	GARDNER, Dorothy	109	GIBBS, Jerusha	198
FULLER, Betsey	206	GARDNER, Elizabeth	124	GIBBS, Jobe	35
FULLER, Deborah	189	GARDNER, Hannah	89	GIBBS, John	29
FULLER, Eben	129	GARDNER, Haywood	204	GIBBS, Jonathan	188
FULLER, Ebenezar	177	GARDNER, John	136	GIBBS, Joshua	29
FULLER, Ebenezer	60	GARDNER, Margaret	75	GIBBS, Joshua	53
FULLER, Ebenezer	136	GARDNER, Mary	89	GIBBS, Josiah	106
FULLER, Ebenezer	172	GARDNER, Mary Clark	136	GIBBS, Josiah	107
FULLER, Emily	222	GARDNER, Mehitable	207	GIBBS, Josiah	215

VITAL RECORDS OF THE TOWN OF PLYMOUTH

Name	Page	Name	Page	Name	Page
GIBBS, Juduth	35	GILBERT, Peter	190	GODDARD, Nancey	154
GIBBS, Lucy	219	GILMAN, Benjamin Ives	197	GODDARD, Rufus	204
GIBBS, Marcey	29	GLEASON, James G.	209	GODDARD, Ruth Rogers	220
GIBBS, Marcey	53	GLEESON, James Glover	218	GODDARD, Sarah	96
GIBBS, Marcy	107	GLOVER, Fanny	207	GODDARD, Sarah	154
GIBBS, Martha	130	GLOVER, George	137	GODDARD, Sarah	175
GIBBS, Martha Bourne	164	GLOVER, George	173	GODDARD, Sarah	204
GIBBS, Mary	206	GLOVER, Margaret	137	GODDARD, Sarah Elizabeth	165
GIBBS, Patience	115	GLOVER, Margaret	195	GODDARD, William	200
GIBBS, Ruth	53	GLOVER, Mary	137	GOODING, Benjamin Barnes	209
GIBBS, Samuel	187	GLOVER, Mary	186	GOODING, Deborah	209
GIBBS, Samuel	215	GLOVER, Saml.	137	GOODING, Deborah Barnes	209
GIBBS, Sarah	67	GNASH, Giles	75	GOODING, Eliza Ann	209
GIBBS, Silva	205	GNASH, Remembrance	75	GOODING, George Barnes	209
GIBBS, Stephen	210	GODDARD, -----	104	GOODING, James Bugbee	209
GIBBS, Susanna	106	GODDARD, Benja.	96	GOODING, John	207
GIBBS, Temperance	118	GODDARD, Benjamin	181	GOODING, John	209
GIBBS, Temperence	53	GODDARD, Benjamin	198	GOODING, Mary Ann	162
GIBBS, Thomas	187	GODDARD, Caroline	165	GOODING, William	162
GIBS, Betty	120	GODDARD, Caroline Frances	165	GOODING, William	209
GIBS, Experience	73	GODDARD, Catharine L.	209	GOODING, William Putnam	162
GIBS, Experience	131	GODDARD, Charles	209	GOODWIN, ----- (male)	167
GIBS, Hannah	73	GODDARD, Daniel	199	GOODWIN, Ann	212
GIBS, Hannah	130	GODDARD, Daniel	209	GOODWIN, Anna	143
GIBS, Jedidah	125	GODDARD, Daniel	218	GOODWIN, Benjamin	110
GIBS, John	53	GODDARD, Daniel F.	209	GOODWIN, Benjamin	173
GIBS, Joshua	53	GODDARD, Elizabeth	194	GOODWIN, Charles	217
GIBS, Marcy	120	GODDARD, Elizabeth	207	GOODWIN, Desire	208
GIBS, Mica	84	GODDARD, Francis	165	GOODWIN, Elizabeth	207
GIBS, Micah	125	GODDARD, Francis J.	165	GOODWIN, Eunice	200
GIBS, Phebe	53	GODDARD, Hannah	218	GOODWIN, Francis Lebaron	143
GIBS, Rufuss	217	GODDARD, Harriet E.	209	GOODWIN, Francs. LeBaron	195
GIBS, Ruth	118	GODDARD, Harriet Otis	220	GOODWIN, George	143
GIBS, Sarah	84	GODDARD, John	77	GOODWIN, George	197
GIBS, Thankfull	84	GODDARD, John	96	GOODWIN, Hannah	110
GIFFORD, Abraham	210	GODDARD, John	118	GOODWIN, Hannah	203
GIFFORD, Benjamin	125	GODDARD, John	163	GOODWIN, Harriet Lothrop	214
GIFFORD, Daniel	181	GODDARD, John	173	GOODWIN, Isaac	167
GIFFORD, Desire	174	GODDARD, John	200	GOODWIN, Isaac	213
GIFFORD, Elizabeth	118	GODDARD, Lemuel	154	GOODWIN, John	143
GIFFORD, Elizabeth	149	GODDARD, Lemuell	96	GOODWIN, John	187
GIFFORD, Elizabeth	151	GODDARD, Lemuell	177	GOODWIN, John	190
GIFFORD, Elizabeth	208	GODDARD, Lydia	77	GOODWIN, John	219
GIFFORD, Gideon	109	GODDARD, Lydia	96	GOODWIN, Lazarus	143
GIFFORD, Gideon	123	GODDARD, Lydia	163	GOODWIN, Lebaron (Capt.)	214
GIFFORD, Joseph	120	GODDARD, Lydia	175	GOODWIN, Lewis	206
GIFFORD, Joseph	149	GODDARD, Mary	163	GOODWIN, Lydia	111
GIFFORD, Joseph	151	GODDARD, Mary	209	GOODWIN, Lydia	143
GIFFORD, Lois	109	GODDARD, Mary Ann	209	GOODWIN, Lydia	167
GIFFORD, Mary	66	GODDARD, Mary James	165	GOODWIN, Lydia	186
GILBERT, Lydia	181	GODDARD, Mercy	163	GOODWIN, Lydia	206

GOODWIN, Mary Ann	214	GRAFTON, Ruth	109	GREENE, Mary	38
GOODWIN, Mary Jackson	199	GRAY, Ann	10	GREENE, William	38
GOODWIN, Mercy	143	GRAY, Anna	70	GREENE, William	70
GOODWIN, Mercy	191	GRAY, David	212	GREENE, William	96
GOODWIN, Mercy	206	GRAY, Desire	10	GREENLEAF, John	79
GOODWIN, Nathaniel	111	GRAY, Edward	10	GREENLEAF, John	115
GOODWIN, Nathaniel	183	GRAY, Elizabeth	198	GREENLEAF, Mary	109
GOODWIN, Nathaniel	191	GRAY, Joanah	10	GREENLEAF, Priscilla	79
GOODWIN, Nathaniel	208	GRAY, Joanna	129	GREENLEAF, Will	113
GOODWIN, Nathl.	123	GRAY, Joannah	10	GREENLEAF, William	109
GOODWIN, Nathll.	143	GRAY, Joannah	66	GREN, Elizabeth	11
GOODWIN, Nathll.	143	GRAY, John	10	GREN, William	11
GOODWIN, Prince	205	GRAY, John	66	GRENE, Desire	38
GOODWIN, Roby	143	GRAY, John	207	GRENNOLDS, Lydia	205
GOODWIN, Salley	204	GRAY, Katherine	74	GREY, Lidiah	67
GOODWIN, Sally	222	GRAY, Katherine	82	GRIFFEN, Elizabeth	171
GOODWIN, Simeon Samson	167	GRAY, Lewis	214	GRIFFEN, Perrey	210
GOODWIN, Thomas	143	GRAY, Marcey	10	GRIFFIN, George	136
GOODWIN, Thomas	190	GRAY, Mary	10	GRIFFIN, George Henry	136
GOODWIN, Thomas	200	GRAY, Rebekah	66	GRIFFIN, Hannah Elizabeth	136
GOODWIN, Thomas	212	GRAY, Saml.	177	GRIFFIN, Henry	136
GOODWIN, Timothy	188	GRAY, Samuel	10	GRIFFIN, Marcia	136
GOODWIN, William	143	GRAY, Sarah	117	GRIFFIN, Sarah Williams	136
GOODWIN, William	167	GRAY, Sukey	198	GRIFFING, William	117
GOODWIN, William	191	GRAY, Thorton	74	GRISWELL, Hannah	65
GOODWIN, William	218	GRAY, Thorton	82	GRISWOLD, Lydia	48
GOODWN., Lucy	209	GRAY, Thorton	128	GRIZWEL, Lidia	66
GOOLD, Elisabeth	129	GREEN, Charles G.	133	GROSS, Pamela	222
GOOLE, Elezabeth	71	GREEN, Edward Everett	133	GRUNNEY, Roxanna	222
GOOLE, John	129	GREEN, Elizabeth	132	GUARDNA, Jacob	190
GORDON, William L.	217	GREEN, George Franklin	133	GULLIFER, Mary	205
GOREHAM, Abigell	46	GREEN, Harriet Elizabeth	132	GUNDERSON, Christopher	188
GOREHAM, David	46	GREEN, Henry T.	132	GURNET, John	213
GOREHAM, Jabez	105	GREEN, Henry W.	132		
GOREHAM, Jabez	107	GREEN, John	202	**H**	
GOREHAM, Mary	46	GREEN, Marcia	133		
GOREHAM, Mary	107	GREEN, Marcia Ann	133	HACKET, Susannah	200
GOREHAM, Mercy	186	GREEN, Mary	38	HACKIT, Experience	209
GOREHAM, Penelope	46	GREEN, Mary Jane	133	HACKIT, Susanna	206
GOREHAM, Sarah	190	GREEN, Mary T.	133	HACKMAN, Thomas	185
GORHAM, Abigail	107	GREEN, Nathaniel Holmes	133	HALL, Betsey	167
GORHAM, David	106	GREEN, Rachel T.	133	HALL, Cintha	214
GORHAM, David	107	GREEN, Richard	133	HALL, Content	215
GORHAM, Ebenezer	180	GREEN, Richard F.	133	HALL, Eber	214
GORHAM, Jabez	88	GREEN, Thomas	219	HALL, Huldah	214
GORHAM, Jabez	89	GREEN, William	11	HALL, Ichabod	206
GORHAM, James	88	GREEN, William	38	HALL, Isaac Thomas	141
GORHAM, Mary	88	GREEN, William C.	133	HALL, James	141
GOULD, John (Capt.)	125	GREEN, William Henry	133	HALL, Jasper	193
GOULD, Sarah	200	GREENE, Desire	38	HALL, Jasper	194
GRAFTON, Ruth	104	GREENE, Desire	70	HALL, John	177

VITAL RECORDS OF THE TOWN OF PLYMOUTH

HALL, John	207	HAMMOND, Brittan	177	HARLOW, Ansell	183
HALL, John Atwood	167	HAMMOND, Elizabeth	201	HARLOW, Asa	157
HALL, John Frederick	141	HAMMOND, Faunce	177	HARLOW, Benjamin	48
HALL, Joseph	70	HAMMOND, Hannah	79	HARLOW, Benjamin	57
HALL, Judah	47	HAMMOND, Hannah	105	HARLOW, Benjamin	78
HALL, Judah	70	HAMMOND, Hannah	113	HARLOW, Benjamin	92
HALL, Lucinda	213	HAMMOND, Hannah	198	HARLOW, Benjamin	120
HALL, Mary	70	HAMMOND, Jabez	77	HARLOW, Benjamin	148
HALL, Mary	141	HAMMOND, Job	79	HARLOW, Benjamin	212
HALL, Mary Ann	167	HAMMOND, Job	123	HARLOW, Benjn.	213
HALL, Mary Wendal	167	HAMMOND, Jona.	116	HARLOW, Betsey	145
HALL, Mehittabel	47	HAMMOND, Rebecca	207	HARLOW, Betsey	163
HALL, Mehittabl	70	HAMMOND, Zoeth	188	HARLOW, Betsey	205
HALL, Nathan	137	HAMOND, Jabez	118	HARLOW, Betsy	212
HALL, Nathan Thomas	137	HAMSHERE, Mary	125	HARLOW, Bette	21
HALL, Orpah	218	HANKS, Abigal	61	HARLOW, Betty	161
HALL, Orpha	217	HANKS, Benjamin	61	HARLOW, Bradford	162
HALL, Patty	205	HANKS, Isaac	61	HARLOW, Charles Goodwin	145
HALL, Prince	195	HANKS, John	61	HARLOW, Clarissa	92
HALL, Rube	217	HANKS, Mary	61	HARLOW, Clarrassa	197
HALL, Sally	137	HANKS, Richard White	61	HARLOW, Clarrisse	206
HALL, Sarah	201	HANKS, Silas	61	HARLOW, David	159
HALL, Silvanus	126	HANKS, Uriah	61	HARLOW, David L.	159
HALL, Susan	141	HANKS, William	61	HARLOW, Deborah	21
HALL, Susan Williams	141	HANMUR, William	98	HARLOW, Deborah	60
HALL, Tabitha	70	HARDEN, Phebe	125	HARLOW, Deborah	157
HALL, Temperance	220	HARDIN, Phebe	75	HARLOW, Deborah	193
HALL, Wendal	167	HARDING, Ezekiel	220	HARLOW, Deborah	202
HALL, William	211	HARDING, Mary Knowles	217	HARLOW, Desire	147
HALL, William	222	HARDING, Mary Kowls	217	HARLOW, Desire	196
HALL, William Curtis	141	HARLO, Jedida	43	HARLOW, Ebenezer	60
HALL, Wm.	141	HARLOW, -----	57	HARLOW, Ebenezer	84
HAMBLEN, Elkanah	75	HARLOW, -----	159	HARLOW, Ebenezer	111
HAMBLEN, Isaac	120	HARLOW, ----- (female)	13	HARLOW, Ebenezer	121
HAMBLEN, Margaret	75	HARLOW, ----- (male)	58	HARLOW, Ebenezer	150
HAMBLEN, Thomas	118	HARLOW, Abigail	66	HARLOW, Ebenezer	157
HAMBLETON, Elizabeth	74	HARLOW, Abigail	90	HARLOW, Ebenezer	174
HAMBLETON, John	74	HARLOW, Abigal	17	HARLOW, Ebenezer	180
HAMBLETON, John	124	HARLOW, Abigall	17	HARLOW, Ebenezr.	157
HAMBLETON, Mary	79	HARLOW, Amariah	27	HARLOW, Eleazar	53
HAMBLETON, Mary	123	HARLOW, Amaziah	38	HARLOW, Eleazar	129
HAMLEN, Elkanah	117	HARLOW, Amaziah	108	HARLOW, Eleazer	43
HAMMATT, Abraham	115	HARLOW, Amaziah	156	HARLOW, Eleazer	53
HAMMAT, Bathsheba	190	HARLOW, Amaziah	195	HARLOW, Eleazr.	116
HAMMAT, William	207	HARLOW, Amaziah	200	HARLOW, Eleazr.	161
HAMMATT, Eliza	213	HARLOW, Andrew	60	HARLOW, Eleazr. (Doctr.)	208
HAMMATT, Lucia	213	HARLOW, Andrew	157	HARLOW, Elen	163
HAMMET, Abraham	188	HARLOW, Ann Eliza	159	HARLOW, Elephas	53
HAMMET, Lucy	205	HARLOW, Ansel	198	HARLOW, Eliazer	18
HAMMOND, Abigail	77	HARLOW, Ansell	92	HARLOW, Elieazar	53
HAMMOND, Antipas	119	HARLOW, Ansell	161	HARLOW, Elijah	90

HARLOW, Elijah	181	HARLOW, Hannah	121	HARLOW, Jedidah	161
HARLOW, Eliza.	92	HARLOW, Hannah	124	HARLOW, Jedidah	190
HARLOW, Eliza.	193	HARLOW, Hannah	159	HARLOW, Jedidah	206
HARLOW, Elizabeth	13	HARLOW, Hannah	161	HARLOW, Jenna	198
HARLOW, Elizabeth	38	HARLOW, Hannah	181	HARLOW, Jerusha	21
HARLOW, Elizabeth	43	HARLOW, Hannah	187	HARLOW, Jerusha	42
HARLOW, Elizabeth	53	HARLOW, Hannah	205	HARLOW, Jerusha	106
HARLOW, Elizabeth	58	HARLOW, Hannah	208	HARLOW, Jerusha	138
HARLOW, Elizabeth	69	HARLOW, Hannah	217	HARLOW, Jerusha	183
HARLOW, Elizabeth	78	HARLOW, Hannah J.	220	HARLOW, Jerusha	193
HARLOW, Elizabeth	90	HARLOW, Hannah Turner	212	HARLOW, Jerusha	208
HARLOW, Elizabeth	92	HARLOW, Henry M.	159	HARLOW, Jerusha	217
HARLOW, Elizabeth	109	HARLOW, Hose	157	HARLOW, Jerusha Howes	215
HARLOW, Elizabeth	164	HARLOW, Ichabod	205	HARLOW, Jesse	84
HARLOW, Elizabeth	175	HARLOW, Isaac	21	HARLOW, Jesse	147
HARLOW, Elizabeth	177	HARLOW, Isaac	46	HARLOW, Jesse	164
HARLOW, Elizabeth	188	HARLOW, Isaac	57	HARLOW, Jesse	177
HARLOW, Elizabeth	194	HARLOW, Isaac	93	HARLOW, Jesse	194
HARLOW, Elizabeth	201	HARLOW, Isaac	105	HARLOW, Jesse	222
HARLOW, Elizabeth Frances	145	HARLOW, Isaac	106	HARLOW, Jesse (Capt.)	207
HARLOW, Ellis	194	HARLOW, Isaac	162	HARLOW, Jno.	176
HARLOW, Ephraim	147	HARLOW, Isaac	183	HARLOW, Joanna	46
HARLOW, Ephraim	199	HARLOW, Isaac N.	159	HARLOW, Joanna	70
HARLOW, Ephraim	209	HARLOW, Ivorey	161	HARLOW, Joanna	78
HARLOW, Esther	154	HARLOW, Ivory	210	HARLOW, John	17
HARLOW, Experience	80	HARLOW, Jabez	80	HARLOW, John	38
HARLOW, Experience	128	HARLOW, Jabez	84	HARLOW, John	69
HARLOW, Ezra	84	HARLOW, Jabez	106	HARLOW, John	70
HARLOW, Ezra	159	HARLOW, Jabez	128	HARLOW, John	75
HARLOW, Ezra	181	HARLOW, Jabez	188	HARLOW, John	80
HARLOW, Ezra	182	HARLOW, James	17	HARLOW, John	84
HARLOW, Ezra	201	HARLOW, James	42	HARLOW, John	101
HARLOW, Ezra	220	HARLOW, James	57	HARLOW, John	104
HARLOW, Freeman	163	HARLOW, James	93	HARLOW, John	112
HARLOW, George	42	HARLOW, James	138	HARLOW, John	125
HARLOW, George	154	HARLOW, James	139	HARLOW, John	161
HARLOW, George	157	HARLOW, James	157	HARLOW, John	207
HARLOW, George	214	HARLOW, James	169	HARLOW, John	208
HARLOW, George Henry	154	HARLOW, James	173	HARLOW, John	212
HARLOW, Hanah	78	HARLOW, James	184	HARLOW, Jonathan	43
HARLOW, Hanna	40	HARLOW, James	191	HARLOW, Jonathan	92
HARLOW, Hannah	17	HARLOW, James	194	HARLOW, Jonathan	111
HARLOW, Hannah	46	HARLOW, James	208	HARLOW, Jonathan	161
HARLOW, Hannah	48	HARLOW, James William	156	HARLOW, Jonathan	183
HARLOW, Hannah	53	HARLOW, Jean	15	HARLOW, Joseph	162
HARLOW, Hannah	74	HARLOW, Jean	106	HARLOW, Josiah	42
HARLOW, Hannah	78	HARLOW, Jedediah	92	HARLOW, Josiah	163
HARLOW, Hannah	93	HARLOW, Jedidah	43	HARLOW, Juduth	69
HARLOW, Hannah	98	HARLOW, Jedidah	70	HARLOW, Keziah	48
HARLOW, Hannah	101	HARLOW, Jedidah	111	HARLOW, Keziah	92
HARLOW, Hannah	109	HARLOW, Jedidah	115	HARLOW, Lazarus	84

VITAL RECORDS OF THE TOWN OF PLYMOUTH

HARLOW, Lazarus	190	HARLOW, Martha	177	HARLOW, Polly	212
HARLOW, Lazarus	215	HARLOW, Martha	197	HARLOW, Pricilah	98
HARLOW, Lemuel	21	HARLOW, Martha Dandridge Washington	156	HARLOW, Pricillia	18
HARLOW, Lemuel	53	HARLOW, Mary	38	HARLOW, Priscilla	17
HARLOW, Lemuel	78	HARLOW, Mary	46	HARLOW, Rebecah	48
HARLOW, Lemuel	121	HARLOW, Mary	58	HARLOW, Rebecca	74
HARLOW, Lemuel	161	HARLOW, Mary	65	HARLOW, Rebecca	124
HARLOW, Lemuel	181	HARLOW, Mary	66	HARLOW, Rebecca	150
HARLOW, Lemuel	195	HARLOW, Mary	75	HARLOW, Rebecca	194
HARLOW, Levi	188	HARLOW, Mary	84	HARLOW, Rebecca	197
HARLOW, Lewis	145	HARLOW, Mary	90	HARLOW, Rebecca	200
HARLOW, Lewis	161	HARLOW, Mary	100	HARLOW, Rebecca	208
HARLOW, Lewis	162	HARLOW, Mary	122	HARLOW, Rebeckah	21
HARLOW, Lewis	200	HARLOW, Mary	150	HARLOW, Rebeckah	38
HARLOW, Lewis Otis	145	HARLOW, Mary	161	HARLOW, Rebeckah	80
HARLOW, Lidiah	13	HARLOW, Mary	185	HARLOW, Rebeckah	104
HARLOW, Lidiah	43	HARLOW, Mary	186	HARLOW, Rebeckah	128
HARLOW, Lidiah	70	HARLOW, Mary	190	HARLOW, Rebeckah	161
HARLOW, Lois	27	HARLOW, Mercy	78	HARLOW, Rebeckah	193
HARLOW, Lois	108	HARLOW, Mercy	161	HARLOW, Rebekah	17
HARLOW, Lois	181	HARLOW, Mercy	182	HARLOW, Rebekah	67
HARLOW, Lot (Deacn.)	206	HARLOW, Mercy	205	HARLOW, Rebekah	125
HARLOW, Lucy	92	HARLOW, Meriah	60	HARLOW, Remember	58
HARLOW, Lucy	191	HARLOW, Meriah	111	HARLOW, Remembrance	111
HARLOW, Lucy	197	HARLOW, Meriah	197	HARLOW, Reubin	139
HARLOW, Lucy	218	HARLOW, Nancey	212	HARLOW, Reubin	197
HARLOW, Lucy James	145	HARLOW, Nathaniel	17	HARLOW, Robert	15
HARLOW, Lydia	46	HARLOW, Nathaniel	43	HARLOW, Robert	57
HARLOW, Lydia	58	HARLOW, Nathaniel	66	HARLOW, Robert	58
HARLOW, Lydia	84	HARLOW, Nathaniel	71	HARLOW, Robert	101
HARLOW, Lydia	111	HARLOW, Nathaniel	80	HARLOW, Robert	105
HARLOW, Lydia	112	HARLOW, Nathaniel	138	HARLOW, Robert	106
HARLOW, Lydia	154	HARLOW, Nathaniel	193	HARLOW, Robert	111
HARLOW, Lydia	157	HARLOW, Nathaniel	200	HARLOW, Robert	113
HARLOW, Lydia	182	HARLOW, Nathaniel	221	HARLOW, Ruben	57
HARLOW, Lydia	189	HARLOW, Nathaniel Ellis	154	HARLOW, Ruben	104
HARLOW, Lydia Ellis	154	HARLOW, Patience	53	HARLOW, Ruth	156
HARLOW, Maray	92	HARLOW, Patience	71	HARLOW, Ruth T.	156
HARLOW, Marcy	41	HARLOW, Patience	78	HARLOW, Salley	205
HARLOW, Marcy	48	HARLOW, Patience	90	HARLOW, Sally	201
HARLOW, Marcy	93	HARLOW, Patience	101	HARLOW, Saml.	123
HARLOW, Marcy	111	HARLOW, Patience	122	HARLOW, Samll.	41
HARLOW, Marcy	208	HARLOW, Patience	163	HARLOW, Samll. (Capt.)	208
HARLOW, Marsey	48	HARLOW, Patience	199	HARLOW, Samuel	17
HARLOW, Marsey	70	HARLOW, Patty	207	HARLOW, Samuel	48
HARLOW, Martha	38	HARLOW, Patty	209	HARLOW, Samuel	98
HARLOW, Martha	69	HARLOW, Phebe	48	HARLOW, Samuel	181
HARLOW, Martha	70	HARLOW, Phebe	112	HARLOW, Samuel (Capt.)	208
HARLOW, Martha	84	HARLOW, Phebe	113	HARLOW, Samuell	41
HARLOW, Martha	101	HARLOW, Philemon	60	HARLOW, Samuell	101
HARLOW, Martha	162	HARLOW, Philemon	157	HARLOW, Samuell	111

HARLOW, Samuell	178	HARLOW, Thomas	90	HASKEL, Lot	198
HARLOW, Sarah	15	HARLOW, Thomas	101	HASKELL, Abraham (Doctr.)	207
HARLOW, Sarah	46	HARLOW, Thomas	119	HASKELL, Sally	222
HARLOW, Sarah	48	HARLOW, Thomas	177	HASKENS, Elizabeth	216
HARLOW, Sarah	78	HARLOW, Thomas (Deacon)	96	HASKENS, John	218
HARLOW, Sarah	92	HARLOW, Timothy	162	HASKINS, Abigail	222
HARLOW, Sarah	111	HARLOW, William	13	HASKINS, George Henry	149
HARLOW, Sarah	121	HARLOW, William	17	HASKINS, George Henry	150
HARLOW, Sarah	148	HARLOW, William	46	HASKINS, Keziah	149
HARLOW, Sarah	157	HARLOW, William	48	HASKINS, Keziah	150
HARLOW, Sarah	161	HARLOW, William	70	HASKINS, Keziah Davis	149
HARLOW, Sarah	169	HARLOW, William	78	HASKINS, Keziah Davis	150
HARLOW, Sarah	178	HARLOW, William	93	HASKINS, Lathley	207
HARLOW, Sarah	187	HARLOW, William	99	HASKINS, Levi	220
HARLOW, Sarah	194	HARLOW, William	109	HASKINS, Nathan	149
HARLOW, Sarah	202	HARLOW, William	120	HASKINS, Nathan	150
HARLOW, Sarah	213	HARLOW, William	122	HASKINS, Nathan Thomas	149
HARLOW, Seth	48	HARLOW, William	157	HASKINS, Nathan Thomas	150
HARLOW, Seth	148	HARLOW, William	178	HASKINS, Philip	212
HARLOW, Seth	174	HARLOW, William	190	HASKINS, Sarah Royal	149
HARLOW, Seth	178	HARLOW, William	201	HASKINS, Sarah Royal	150
HARLOW, Seth	199	HARLOW, William	213	HASKINS, Thomas	216
HARLOW, Silvanus	84	HARLOW, William	218	HASSELTINE, Nancy	214
HARLOW, Silvanus	147	HARLOW, William (Serjant)	98	HATCH, -----	127
HARLOW, Silvanus	174	HARLOW, Willm.	21	HATCH, Abigal	76
HARLOW, Silvanus	212	HARLOW, Wm.	217	HATCH, Abigal	118
HARLOW, Simeon	93	HARLOW, Zacheus	84	HATCH, Asa	78
HARLOW, Simeon	188	HARLOW, Zacheus	190	HATCH, Asa	122
HARLOW, Southworth	157	HARLOW, Zacheus	205	HATCH, Esther	74
HARLOW, Stephen	92	HARLOW, Zacheus	215	HATCH, Esther	106
HARLOW, Stephen	161	HARLOW, Zebulon	157	HATCH, Esther	107
HARLOW, Stephen	162	HARLOW, Zephaniah	93	HATCH, Jedediah	127
HARLOW, Stephen	200	HARLOW, Zepheniah	163	HATCH, Mary	78
HARLOW, Submit	58	HARLOW, Zepheniah	186	HATCH, Mary	79
HARLOW, Submitt	188	HARLOW, Zepheniah	200	HATCH, Mary	112
HARLOW, Susanna	57	HAROW, Daniel	200	HATCH, Mary	113
HARLOW, Susanna	139	HARREY, Martha	198	HATCH, Mary	115
HARLOW, Susanna	190	HARREY, Susannah	175	HATCH, Mary	153
HARLOW, Susanna	198	HARRINGTON, Joseph	206	HATCH, Mary	178
HARLOW, Susanna	201	HARRIS, Betsey	196	HATCH, Nathaniel	153
HARLOW, Susannah	58	HARRIS, Joseph	213	HATCH, Nathl.	117
HARLOW, Susannah	101	HARRIS, Martha	201	HATCH, Nathll.	108
HARLOW, Susannah	184	HARRIS, Owin	198	HATCH, Redolphus	74
HARLOW, Sussanna	57	HART, ----- (Mris.)	98	HATCH, Redolphus	128
HARLOW, Sylvanus	162	HARVEY, Bathsheba	212	HATCH, Rodolphus	101
HARLOW, Sylvanus	196	HARVEY, Jonathan	202	HATCH, Ruth	108
HARLOW, Thankfull	38	HARVEY, Joseph	106	HATCH, Ruth	153
HARLOW, Thankfull	60	HARVEY, Ruth	218	HATCH, Ruth	172
HARLOW, Thomas	13	HASCALL, Mary	70	HATCH, Ruth	181
HARLOW, Thomas	43	HASCOLL, Susanna	105	HATCH, Sarah	70
HARLOW, Thomas	70	HASKEL, Hunnewell	205	HATCH, Sarah	72

VITAL RECORDS OF THE TOWN OF PLYMOUTH

HATCH, Sarah	130	HEDGE, Hannah	146	HIGHTON, Eliza.	159
HATCH, Thomas	70	HEDGE, Hannah	177	HIGHTON, Hennery	159
HATHAWAY, Abby Seaver	165	HEDGE, Isaac Lothrop	146	HIGHTON, Hennery	182
HATHAWAY, Betsey W.	147	HEDGE, James Goreham	146	HIGHTON, Margaret	159
HATHAWAY, Charles F.	147	HEDGE, John Sloss Hobert	146	HILL, Abigail	78
HATHAWAY, Edward Emerson	147	HEDGE, Jube	199	HILL, Abigal	122
HATHAWAY, Frederick C.	147	HEDGE, Judath	206	HILL, Andrew	181
HATHAWAY, George A.	147	HEDGE, Lemuel	85	HILL, Bathsheba	73
HATHAWAY, George A.	165	HEDGE, Lemuell	85	HILL, Bathsheba	126
HATHAWAY, John A.	147	HEDGE, Lothrop	85	HILL, Daniel	178
HATHAWAY, Joshua	147	HEDGE, Lydia G.	147	HILL, Jonathan	193
HATHAWAY, Joshua T.	147	HEDGE, Lydia Goodwin	147	HILL, Jonathan	204
HATHAWAY, Lamson	197	HEDGE, Marcy	85	HINCKLEY, Phebe	128
HATHAWAY, Patience	165	HEDGE, Marcy	104	HINCKLEY, Thomas	128
HATHAWAY, Rebeca	147	HEDGE, Mary Ellen	147	HINDS, Judith	214
HATHAWAY, Rebecca	127	HEDGE, Mercy	90	HINES, John	213
HATHAWAY, Samuel G.	147	HEDGE, Mercy	128	HINES, Mary	204
HATHAWAY, Sarah Ann	147	HEDGE, Priscilla Lothrop	146	HINKLEY, Elizabeth	109
HATHAWAY, Sarah Carver	147	HEDGE, Sarah	85	HINKLEY, Ruth	207
HATHEWAY, Charlotte	209	HEDGE, Sarah Thomas	146	HINKLEY, Thomas	109
HATHEWAY, Deborah	213	HEDGE, Thomas	146	HINKLEY, Thomas	113
HATHEWAY, Fanney	205	HEDGE, Thomas	147	HINKLEY, Thos.	104
HATHEWAY, Joshua	214	HEDGE, Thomas B.	147	HOBART, Noah (Rev.)	174
HATHEWAY, Salley	214	HEDGE, Tryphena	146	HODGE, Michael	215
HATHEWAY, Silas	207	HEDGE, Vilot	202	HODGES, Nathaniel	222
HAWKES, Abiathar	222	HEDGE, William	146	HOLBROOK, Elizabeth	203
HAWS, Jedidah	199	HEDGE, Wm.	147	HOLBROOK, Gideon	195
HAYSES, Bethiah	73	HEELEY, Alice	84	HOLBROOK, Gideon	212
HAYSES, John	73	HEELEY, Benja.	84	HOLBROOK, Gideon	221
HAYWARD, ----- (Doctr.)	200	HEELEY, Timothy	84	HOLBROOK, Huldah	201
HAYWARD, Beza	204	HELEY, Timothy	120	HOLBROOK, Jeremiah	213
HAYWARD, Cyrus	210	HELY, Elce	78	HOLBROOK, Jeremiah	214
HAYWARD, Mary Winslow	222	HELY, Timothy	78	HOLBROOK, Lois	213
HAYWARD, Susannah	194	HERSEY, Elizabeth	177	HOLBROOK, Mary	213
HAYWAYD, ----- (Doctr.)	201	HERSEY, Gideon	174	HOLBROOK, Naaman	199
HEDGE, ----- (female)	146	HEWSTON, Elizabeth	201	HOLBROOK, Patty	219
HEDGE, Abby Burr	147	HEWSTON, Mary	205	HOLBROOK, Rachel	197
HEDGE, Abigail	85	HEWSTON, Nancy	217	HOLBROOK, Ruth	198
HEDGE, Abigail	90	HEWSTON, Nathaniel	212	HOLBROOK, Sarah	197
HEDGE, Abigail	146	HEWSTON, Priscilla	212	HOLBROOK, Sarah	198
HEDGE, Albert Goodwin	147	HEWSTON, William	190	HOLBROOK, Sarah	200
HEDGE, Barnabas	85	HEWSTON, William	205	HOLLAND, Joanna	194
HEDGE, Barnabas	90	HICKS, Abraham	51	HOLLAND, William	187
HEDGE, Barnabas	177	HICKS, Abraham	101	HOLLAND, William	203
HEDGE, Barnabas	214	HICKS, Abraham	105	HOLLIS, Bathsheba	217
HEDGE, Barnebas	124	HICKS, Abraham	107	HOLLIS, Esther	201
HEDGE, Barnabus	146	HICKS, Barshabah	107	HOLLIS, Esther	205
HEDGE, Edward Goodwin	147	HICKS, Bathsheba	51	HOLLIS, Samuel	182
HEDGE, Elizabeth	146	HICKS, Bathsheba	101	HOLME, Charles	50
HEDGE, Ellen Hobert	146	HICKS, John	51	HOLME, Elisha	34
HEDGE, Eunice Dennie	146	HICKST, Margarret	66	HOLME, Nathaniel	34

VITAL RECORDS OF THE TOWN OF PLYMOUTH

Name	Page	Name	Page	Name	Page
HOLME, Rebecka	34	HOLMES, Barnabas	159	HOLMES, Charles	197
HOLME, Sarah	43	HOLMES, Barnabas	183	HOLMES, Content	46
HOLME, Suanna	34	HOLMES, Barnabas	190	HOLMES, Content	74
HOLMES, -----	43	HOLMES, Barnabas	194	HOLMES, Content	82
HOLMES, -----	65	HOLMES, Barnabas	195	HOLMES, Content	188
HOLMES, -----	93	HOLMES, Barnabas	201	HOLMES, Content	218
HOLMES, ----- (female)	50	HOLMES, Barnabas	214	HOLMES, Cornelious	39
HOLMES, ----- (female)	56	HOLMES, Barter	168	HOLMES, Cornelis	56
HOLMES, ----- (female)	82	HOLMES, Bartlett	85	HOLMES, Cornelius	56
HOLMES, ----- (male)	47	HOLMES, Bartlett	159	HOLMES, Cornelius	104
HOLMES, ----- (male)	56	HOLMES, Bartlett	180	HOLMES, Cornelius	110
HOLMES, ----- (male)	93	HOLMES, Bartlett	209	HOLMES, Cornelius	115
HOLMES, ----- (male)	146	HOLMES, Bathshabe	22	HOLMES, Cornelius	140
HOLMES, Abigail	50	HOLMES, Bathsheba	73	HOLMES, Cornelus	168
HOLMES, Abigail	53	HOLMES, Bathsheba	89	HOLMES, Cornelus	191
HOLMES, Abigail	111	HOLMES, Bathsheba	92	HOLMES, Cornelus	198
HOLMES, Abigail	141	HOLMES, Bathsheba	93	HOLMES, Cornelus	217
HOLMES, Abigail	181	HOLMES, Bathsheba	126	HOLMES, David	89
HOLMES, Abigail	195	HOLMES, Bathsheba	177	HOLMES, David	186
HOLMES, Abigail	197	HOLMES, Bathsheba	206	HOLMES, David	201
HOLMES, Abigail	202	HOLMES, Bathsheba J.	150	HOLMES, David Cobb	138
HOLMES, Abigail	208	HOLMES, Bathshebeth	78	HOLMES, David Winsor	138
HOLMES, Abigail	219	HOLMES, Benja.	104	HOLMES, Deborah	43
HOLMES, Abigall	60	HOLMES, Benjaman	56	HOLMES, Deborah	47
HOLMES, Abigall	75	HOLMES, Benjamin	24	HOLMES, Deborah	93
HOLMES, Abner	29	HOLMES, Benjamin	39	HOLMES, Deborah	153
HOLMES, Abner	78	HOLMES, Benjamin	140	HOLMES, Deborah	188
HOLMES, Abner	89	HOLMES, Benjamin	172	HOLMES, Deborah	189
HOLMES, Abner	92	HOLMES, Benjamin	201	HOLMES, Deborah	193
HOLMES, Abner	120	HOLMES, Bethiah	180	HOLMES, Deborah	214
HOLMES, Abner	203	HOLMES, Betsey	50	HOLMES, Desire	43
HOLMES, Abigail	154	HOLMES, Betsey	150	HOLMES, Desire	64
HOLMES, Albert	138	HOLMES, Betsey	160	HOLMES, Desire	67
HOLMES, Amasa	154	HOLMES, Betsey	199	HOLMES, Desire	105
HOLMES, Amasa	202	HOLMES, Betsey	200	HOLMES, Desire	106
HOLMES, Amelia Anne	137	HOLMES, Betsey	201	HOLMES, Desire	213
HOLMES, Andrew	50	HOLMES, Betsey	202	HOLMES, Ebenazar	53
HOLMES, Andrew	138	HOLMES, Betsey	217	HOLMES, Ebenazar	71
HOLMES, Andrew	198	HOLMES, Betsey	222	HOLMES, Ebenazar	129
HOLMES, Anna	207	HOLMES, Betsey Lewis	213	HOLMES, Ebenezer	21
HOLMES, Ansel	150	HOLMES, Bettey	93	HOLMES, Ebenez.	203
HOLMES, Ansel	185	HOLMES, Betty	56	HOLMES, Ebenazar	67
HOLMES, Ansel	203	HOLMES, Betty	131	HOLMES, Ebenezer	21
HOLMES, Ansell	168	HOLMES, Bradford	93	HOLMES, Ebenezer	56
HOLMES, Ansell	204	HOLMES, Caleb	82	HOLMES, Ebenezer	92
HOLMES, Ansell	209	HOLMES, Caleb	154	HOLMES, Ebenezer	111
HOLMES, Barhsheba	93	HOLMES, Caleb (Rev.)	209	HOLMES, Ebenezer	172
HOLMES, Barnabas	22	HOLMES, Calvin	214	HOLMES, Ebenezer	201
HOLMES, Barnabas	75	HOLMES, Chandler	47	HOLMES, Ebenezer	210
HOLMES, Barnabas	82	HOLMES, Chandler	201	HOLMES, Ebenezr.	116
HOLMES, Barnabas	125	HOLMES, Charles	50	HOLMES, Ebnazar	53

VITAL RECORDS OF THE TOWN OF PLYMOUTH

HOLMES, Eleanar	69	HOLMES, Elizabeth	194	HOLMES, Fear	120
HOLMES, Eleazer	46	HOLMES, Elizabeth	215	HOLMES, Ffeare	48
HOLMES, Eleazer	93	HOLMES, Elizabeth Mason	160	HOLMES, Frederick	165
HOLMES, Eleazer	96	HOLMES, Elkanah	65	HOLMES, George	54
HOLMES, Eleazer	111	HOLMES, Elkanah	218	HOLMES, George	71
HOLMES, Eleazer	168	HOLMES, Ellinor	24	HOLMES, George	78
HOLMES, Eleazer	194	HOLMES, Ellis	47	HOLMES, George	92
HOLMES, Eleazer	213	HOLMES, Ellis	182	HOLMES, George	104
HOLMES, Eleazer (Capt.)	201	HOLMES, Ellis	197	HOLMES, George	118
HOLMES, Eleazr.	123	HOLMES, Ellis	214	HOLMES, George	122
HOLMES, Elener	24	HOLMES, Ellis	222	HOLMES, George	179
HOLMES, Eliazer	46	HOLMES, Elnathan	34	HOLMES, Gershom	77
HOLMES, Eliazur	11	HOLMES, Elnathan	75	HOLMES, Gershom	89
HOLMES, Eliezor	70	HOLMES, Elnathan	85	HOLMES, Gershom	118
HOLMES, Elish	129	HOLMES, Elnathan	125	HOLMES, Gershom	177
HOLMES, Elisha	11	HOLMES, Elnathan	177	HOLMES, Gershom	195
HOLMES, Elisha	34	HOLMES, Elnathan	194	HOLMES, Gilbert	53
HOLMES, Elisha	55	HOLMES, Elnethan	85	HOLMES, Gilbert	182
HOLMES, Elisha	67	HOLMES, Eloner	195	HOLMES, Girshom	43
HOLMES, Elisha	71	HOLMES, Eloner	199	HOLMES, Grace	200
HOLMES, Elisha	85	HOLMES, Eloner	201	HOLMES, Grace	216
HOLMES, Elisha	100	HOLMES, Eloner	218	HOLMES, Hannah	46
HOLMES, Elisha	101	HOLMES, Emeline Frances	150	HOLMES, Hannah	60
HOLMES, Elisha	121	HOLMES, Emeline Frances	160	HOLMES, Hannah	64
HOLMES, Elisha	129	HOLMES, Ephraim	60	HOLMES, Hannah	70
HOLMES, Elisha	173	HOLMES, Ephraim	93	HOLMES, Hannah	78
HOLMES, Eliza.	194	HOLMES, Ephraim	182	HOLMES, Hannah	93
HOLMES, Eliza.	195	HOLMES, Ephraim	204	HOLMES, Hannah	122
HOLMES, Elizabeth	11	HOLMES, Ephram	22	HOLMES, Hannah	136
HOLMES, Elizabeth	21	HOLMES, Ephrm.	122	HOLMES, Hannah	184
HOLMES, Elizabeth	34	HOLMES, Epm.	109	HOLMES, Hannah	187
HOLMES, Elizabeth	46	HOLMES, Ester	47	HOLMES, Hannah	195
HOLMES, Elizabeth	47	HOLMES, Ester	70	HOLMES, Hannah	208
HOLMES, Elizabeth	53	HOLMES, Esther	53	HOLMES, Harriet	160
HOLMES, Elizabeth	71	HOLMES, Esther	74	HOLMES, Harriot	218
HOLMES, Elizabeth	73	HOLMES, Esther	93	HOLMES, Henry B.	150
HOLMES, Elizabeth	77	HOLMES, Esther	96	HOLMES, Hester	43
HOLMES, Elizabeth	79	HOLMES, Esther	111	HOLMES, Hulda	183
HOLMES, Elizabeth	91	HOLMES, Esther	128	HOLMES, Ichabod	46
HOLMES, Elizabeth	93	HOLMES, Esther	168	HOLMES, Ichabod	47
HOLMES, Elizabeth	98	HOLMES, Esther	182	HOLMES, Ichabod	112
HOLMES, Elizabeth	115	HOLMES, Esther	203	HOLMES, Ichabod	115
HOLMES, Elizabeth	130	HOLMES, Esther	212	HOLMES, Ichabod	194
HOLMES, Elizabeth	133	HOLMES, Experiance	26	HOLMES, Isaac	60
HOLMES, Elizabeth	136	HOLMES, Experience	186	HOLMES, Isaac	89
HOLMES, Elizabeth	165	HOLMES, Exsperiance	39	HOLMES, Isaac	182
HOLMES, Elizabeth	168	HOLMES, Ezra	82	HOLMES, Isaac	193
HOLMES, Elizabeth	177	HOLMES, Ezra	186	HOLMES, Isaac	197
HOLMES, Elizabeth	178	HOLMES, Ezra	191	HOLMES, Jabez	74
HOLMES, Elizabeth	186	HOLMES, Fanny Winsor	137	HOLMES, Jabez	75
HOLMES, Elizabeth	190	HOLMES, Fear	78	HOLMES, Jabez	89

HOLMES, Jabez	100	HOLMES, Job	106	HOLMES, Joshua	46
HOLMES, Jabez	101	HOLMES, John	11	HOLMES, Joshua	136
HOLMES, Jabez	117	HOLMES, John	26	HOLMES, Joshua	171
HOLMES, Jabez	124	HOLMES, John	34	HOLMES, Joshua	193
HOLMES, Jabiz	34	HOLMES, John	39	HOLMES, Josiah	43
HOLMES, James	22	HOLMES, John	43	HOLMES, Judath	214
HOLMES, James	74	HOLMES, John	53	HOLMES, Keziah	60
HOLMES, James	82	HOLMES, John	70	HOLMES, King John	43
HOLMES, James	128	HOLMES, John	86	HOLMES, Lathrop	82
HOLMES, James	146	HOLMES, John	90	HOLMES, Lemuel	46
HOLMES, James	178	HOLMES, John	98	HOLMES, Lemuel	191
HOLMES, James	186	HOLMES, John	101	HOLMES, Lemuel	199
HOLMES, James	208	HOLMES, John	117	HOLMES, Lemuel D.	134
HOLMES, James Avery	168	HOLMES, John	154	HOLMES, Lemuell	111
HOLMES, Jane	64	HOLMES, John	177	HOLMES, Lemuell	117
HOLMES, Jane	93	HOLMES, John	188	HOLMES, Lewis	197
HOLMES, Jemima	29	HOLMES, John	205	HOLMES, Lidia	56
HOLMES, Jemima	73	HOLMES, John	206	HOLMES, Lidiah	46
HOLMES, Jemima	91	HOLMES, Jonathan	43	HOLMES, Lidiah	48
HOLMES, Jemima	127	HOLMES, Jonathan	46	HOLMES, Lidiah	54
HOLMES, Jemimah	175	HOLMES, Jonathan	48	HOLMES, Lidiah	69
HOLMES, Jenne	181	HOLMES, Jonathan	60	HOLMES, Lidiah	71
HOLMES, Jeremiah	50	HOLMES, Jonathan	64	HOLMES, Lois	86
HOLMES, Jeremiah	53	HOLMES, Jonathan	106	HOLMES, Lois	90
HOLMES, Jeremiah	112	HOLMES, Josep	48	HOLMES, Lothrop	183
HOLMES, Jeremiah	113	HOLMES, Joseph	24	HOLMES, Louisa	138
HOLMES, Jeremiah	191	HOLMES, Joseph	34	HOLMES, Louisa	138
HOLMES, Jeremiah	201	HOLMES, Joseph	48	HOLMES, Luce	47
HOLMES, Jeremiah	215	HOLMES, Joseph	53	HOLMES, Luce	93
HOLMES, Jerusha	85	HOLMES, Joseph	60	HOLMES, Lucy	159
HOLMES, Jerusha	154	HOLMES, Joseph	64	HOLMES, Lucy	183
HOLMES, Jerusha	173	HOLMES, Joseph	65	HOLMES, Lucy	195
HOLMES, Jerusha	201	HOLMES, Joseph	69	HOLMES, Lucy	201
HOLMES, Jerusha	207	HOLMES, Joseph	73	HOLMES, Lucy	202
HOLMES, Jesse	154	HOLMES, Joseph	78	HOLMES, Lucy	207
HOLMES, Jesse	205	HOLMES, Joseph	89	HOLMES, Lydia	48
HOLMES, Jo.	18	HOLMES, Joseph	96	HOLMES, Lydia	56
HOLMES, Joana	22	HOLMES, Joseph	101	HOLMES, Lydia	77
HOLMES, Joana	67	HOLMES, Joseph	120	HOLMES, Lydia	78
HOLMES, Joanna	22	HOLMES, Joseph	121	HOLMES, Lydia	79
HOLMES, Joanna	67	HOLMES, Joseph	126	HOLMES, Lydia	89
HOLMES, Joanna	93	HOLMES, Joseph	168	HOLMES, Lydia	92
HOLMES, Joanna	105	HOLMES, Joseph	178	HOLMES, Lydia	101
HOLMES, Joanna	106	HOLMES, Joseph	183	HOLMES, Lydia	104
HOLMES, Joanna	181	HOLMES, Joseph	187	HOLMES, Lydia	112
HOLMES, Joannah	29	HOLMES, Joseph	196	HOLMES, Lydia	116
HOLMES, Joannah	47	HOLMES, Joseph	200	HOLMES, Lydia	129
HOLMES, Joannah	75	HOLMES, Joseph	201	HOLMES, Lydia	132
HOLMES, Joannah	124	HOLMES, Joseph	214	HOLMES, Lydia	133
HOLMES, Job	46	HOLMES, Joseph Johnson	160	HOLMES, Lydia	140
HOLMES, Job	48	HOLMES, Joshua	24	HOLMES, Lydia	150

VITAL RECORDS OF THE TOWN OF PLYMOUTH

HOLMES, Lydia	178	HOLMES, Mary	217	HOLMES, Nathaniel	199
HOLMES, Lydia	180	HOLMES, Mary Antoinette	134	HOLMES, Nathaniel	200
HOLMES, Lydia	181	HOLMES, Mary Sherman	216	HOLMES, Nathaniel	210
HOLMES, Lydia	185	HOLMES, Mary Smith	138	HOLMES, Nathaniel	220
HOLMES, Lydia	190	HOLMES, Massena F.	209	HOLMES, Nathaniell	132
HOLMES, Lydia	194	HOLMES, Mehetable	48	HOLMES, Nathl.	55
HOLMES, Lydia	195	HOLMES, Mehetable Pain	137	HOLMES, Nathl.	131
HOLMES, Lydia	198	HOLMES, Mehittabl	70	HOLMES, Nathll.	53
HOLMES, Lydia B.	222	HOLMES, Melatiah	24	HOLMES, Nathll.	56
HOLMES, Lydia Mason	150	HOLMES, Melatiah	181	HOLMES, Nathll.	172
HOLMES, Lydia Morton	149	HOLMES, Mercy	67	HOLMES, Nehemiah	86
HOLMES, Lydia West	222	HOLMES, Mercy	78	HOLMES, Nehemiah	90
HOLMES, Malletiah	206	HOLMES, Mercy	129	HOLMES, Nehemiah	185
HOLMES, Marcy	34	HOLMES, Mercy	133	HOLMES, Nehemiah	212
HOLMES, Marcy	43	HOLMES, Mercy	150	HOLMES, Oliver	137
HOLMES, Marcy	71	HOLMES, Mercy	159	HOLMES, Pamela	137
HOLMES, Marcy	73	HOLMES, Mercy	182	HOLMES, Patience	24
HOLMES, Marcy	86	HOLMES, Mercy	183	HOLMES, Patience	39
HOLMES, Marcy	91	HOLMES, Mercy	189	HOLMES, Patience	53
HOLMES, Marcy	93	HOLMES, Mercy	198	HOLMES, Patience	56
HOLMES, Marcy	110	HOLMES, Mercy	199	HOLMES, Patience	69
HOLMES, Marcy	130	HOLMES, Mercy Johnson	160	HOLMES, Patience	71
HOLMES, Margaret	86	HOLMES, Meriah	64	HOLMES, Patience	79
HOLMES, Margaret	186	HOLMES, Meriah	65	HOLMES, Patience	115
HOLMES, Maria Thomas	137	HOLMES, Meriah	181	HOLMES, Patience	116
HOLMES, Mariah	89	HOLMES, Meriah	218	HOLMES, Patience	198
HOLMES, Marsey	24	HOLMES, Mersey	11	HOLMES, Patience	201
HOLMES, Marsey	43	HOLMES, Mersy	11	HOLMES, Patience	205
HOLMES, Marsey	70	HOLMES, Micah	60	HOLMES, Peleg	43
HOLMES, Martha	188	HOLMES, Miranda B.	209	HOLMES, Peter	50
HOLMES, Martha Ann	209	HOLMES, Miriam	209	HOLMES, Peter	53
HOLMES, Mary	43	HOLMES, Nancy	197	HOLMES, Peter	189
HOLMES, Mary	46	HOLMES, Nath.	129	HOLMES, Peter	205
HOLMES, Mary	47	HOLMES, Nathan	154	HOLMES, Peter	222
HOLMES, Mary	60	HOLMES, Nathan	165	HOLMES, Pheba	64
HOLMES, Mary	74	HOLMES, Nathan	202	HOLMES, Phebe	21
HOLMES, Mary	85	HOLMES, Nathan	207	HOLMES, Phebe	50
HOLMES, Mary	89	HOLMES, Nathaniel	11	HOLMES, Phebe	53
HOLMES, Mary	98	HOLMES, Nathaniel	22	HOLMES, Phebe	64
HOLMES, Mary	125	HOLMES, Nathaniel	24	HOLMES, Phebe	65
HOLMES, Mary	150	HOLMES, Nathaniel	39	HOLMES, Phebe	67
HOLMES, Mary	153	HOLMES, Nathaniel	67	HOLMES, Phebe	73
HOLMES, Mary	165	HOLMES, Nathaniel	69	HOLMES, Phebe	104
HOLMES, Mary	168	HOLMES, Nathaniel	71	HOLMES, Phebe	109
HOLMES, Mary	176	HOLMES, Nathaniel	82	HOLMES, Phebe	112
HOLMES, Mary	177	HOLMES, Nathaniel	93	HOLMES, Phebe	113
HOLMES, Mary	178	HOLMES, Nathaniel	120	HOLMES, Phebe	128
HOLMES, Mary	193	HOLMES, Nathaniel	129	HOLMES, Phebe	193
HOLMES, Mary	194	HOLMES, Nathaniel	141	HOLMES, Phebe	197
HOLMES, Mary	198	HOLMES, Nathaniel	175	HOLMES, Phebe	200
HOLMES, Mary	215	HOLMES, Nathaniel	197	HOLMES, Phebe Bartlett	220

HOLMES, Polley	133	HOLMES, Richard	70	HOLMES, Sarah	78
HOLMES, Polley	168	HOLMES, Richard	89	HOLMES, Sarah	85
HOLMES, Polley	199	HOLMES, Richard	92	HOLMES, Sarah	89
HOLMES, Polley	201	HOLMES, Richard	133	HOLMES, Sarah	91
HOLMES, Polley	204	HOLMES, Richard	178	HOLMES, Sarah	93
HOLMES, Polley	206	HOLMES, Richard	185	HOLMES, Sarah	98
HOLMES, Polley	214	HOLMES, Richard	195	HOLMES, Sarah	100
HOLMES, Polley	215	HOLMES, Richard	207	HOLMES, Sarah	101
HOLMES, Polley Samson	204	HOLMES, Robert	146	HOLMES, Sarah	105
HOLMES, Polly	134	HOLMES, Robert	202	HOLMES, Sarah	107
HOLMES, Polly	165	HOLMES, Rowland	200	HOLMES, Sarah	109
HOLMES, Priscilla	56	HOLMES, Rufus	146	HOLMES, Sarah	111
HOLMES, Priscilla	71	HOLMES, Rufus	198	HOLMES, Sarah	125
HOLMES, Priscilla	190	HOLMES, Ruth	46	HOLMES, Sarah	129
HOLMES, Priscilla	195	HOLMES, Ruth	47	HOLMES, Sarah	130
HOLMES, Priscilla	196	HOLMES, Ruth	78	HOLMES, Sarah	149
HOLMES, Priscilla	206	HOLMES, Ruth	86	HOLMES, Sarah	178
HOLMES, Rachel	194	HOLMES, Ruth	110	HOLMES, Sarah	181
HOLMES, Rebecah	89	HOLMES, Ruth	181	HOLMES, Sarah	186
HOLMES, Rebecca	47	HOLMES, Ruth	185	HOLMES, Sarah	188
HOLMES, Rebecca	74	HOLMES, Ruth	191	HOLMES, Sarah	189
HOLMES, Rebecca	75	HOLMES, Salley	207	HOLMES, Sarah	190
HOLMES, Rebecca	150	HOLMES, Salley	219	HOLMES, Sarah	198
HOLMES, Rebecca	168	HOLMES, Sally	200	HOLMES, Sarah	210
HOLMES, Rebecca	198	HOLMES, Sally	201	HOLMES, Sarah	212
HOLMES, Rebecca	199	HOLMES, Saloma	149	HOLMES, Sarah	217
HOLMES, Rebecca	203	HOLMES, Saloma N.	149	HOLMES, Sarah Elizabeth	149
HOLMES, Rebecca	222	HOLMES, Saml. Doten	160	HOLMES, Sary	89
HOLMES, Rebecca W.	149	HOLMES, Samuel	26	HOLMES, Seth	82
HOLMES, Rebeckah	47	HOLMES, Samuel	39	HOLMES, Seth	153
HOLMES, Rebeckah	85	HOLMES, Samuel	47	HOLMES, Seth	154
HOLMES, Rebeckah	100	HOLMES, Samuel	55	HOLMES, Seth	178
HOLMES, Rebeckah	101	HOLMES, Samuel	64	HOLMES, Seth	200
HOLMES, Rebeckah	111	HOLMES, Samuel	124	HOLMES, Seth Luce	149
HOLMES, Rebeckah	112	HOLMES, Samuel	194	HOLMES, Silva.	122
HOLMES, Rebeckah	116	HOLMES, Samuel	200	HOLMES, Silvanos	43
HOLMES, Rebeckah	118	HOLMES, Samuel	205	HOLMES, Silvanus	78
HOLMES, Rebeckah	173	HOLMES, Samuel Doten	160	HOLMES, Silvanus	150
HOLMES, Rebeckah	188	HOLMES, Samuel Doten	214	HOLMES, Silvanus	183
HOLMES, Rebekah	77	HOLMES, Sarah	11	HOLMES, Silvester	46
HOLMES, Rebekah	153	HOLMES, Sarah	22	HOLMES, Silvina	154
HOLMES, Rebekah	160	HOLMES, Sarah	34	HOLMES, Silvinay	198
HOLMES, Rebekah	181	HOLMES, Sarah	39	HOLMES, Sintha	206
HOLMES, Remember	47	HOLMES, Sarah	46	HOLMES, Solo.	208
HOLMES, Remember	146	HOLMES, Sarah	55	HOLMES, Solomon	82
HOLMES, Remember	181	HOLMES, Sarah	60	HOLMES, Solomon	141
HOLMES, Remember	208	HOLMES, Sarah	67	HOLMES, Solomon	175
HOLMES, Rememberance	201	HOLMES, Sarah	70	HOLMES, Solomon	182
HOLMES, Richard	24	HOLMES, Sarah	71	HOLMES, Solomon	212
HOLMES, Richard	43	HOLMES, Sarah	72	HOLMES, Sophia	205
HOLMES, Richard	54	HOLMES, Sarah	75	HOLMES, Sophia	218

VITAL RECORDS OF THE TOWN OF PLYMOUTH

HOLMES, Stephen	89	HOLMES, Zacheus	110	HOWARD, Ebenezer	207
HOLMES, Stephen	154	HOLMES, Zacheus	194	HOWARD, Elizabeth	65
HOLMES, Stephen	202	HOLMES, Zacheus	205	HOWARD, Elizabeth	107
HOLMES, Susanna	139	HOLMES, Zeffaniah	22	HOWARD, Eloner	201
HOLMES, Susanna	206	HOLMES, Zephaniah	93	HOWARD, Enice	48
HOLMES, Susannah	55	HOLMES, Zephaniah	121	HOWARD, Eunice	111
HOLMES, Susannah	56	HOLMES, Zephaniah	178	HOWARD, Eunice	190
HOLMES, Susannah	60	HOLMES, Zepheniah	78	HOWARD, Eunice	191
HOLMES, Susannah	65	HOLMES, Zepheniah	146	HOWARD, Ezra	203
HOLMES, Susannah	92	HOLMES, Zepheniah	200	HOWARD, Fear	180
HOLMES, Susannah	104	HOLMES, Zeruiah	60	HOWARD, Francis	60
HOLMES, Susannah	111	HOLMES. Jenna	202	HOWARD, Francis	65
HOLMES, Susannah	116	HOMES, Thankfull	178	HOWARD, Francis	106
HOLMES, Suzanah	39	HOOPER, Deborah	191	HOWARD, Francis	107
HOLMES, Suzannah	71	HOPKINS, Peter	129	HOWARD, Francis	188
HOLMES, Sylvester	194	HORTON, Samuel	189	HOWARD, James	48
HOLMES, Sylvester	212	HOSE, Daniel	182	HOWARD, James	60
HOLMES, Thankful	181	HOSE, Hannah	197	HOWARD, James	72
HOLMES, Thankfull	89	HOSEE, Robert	173	HOWARD, James	101
HOLMES, Thankfull	184	HOSKINS, David	214	HOWARD, James	106
HOLMES, Thomas	29	HOSKINS, Deborah	204	HOWARD, James	111
HOLMES, Thomas	39	HOSKINS, Jeremiah	200	HOWARD, James	117
HOLMES, Thomas	67	HOSKINS, Job	206	HOWARD, James	128
HOLMES, Thomas	77	HOSKINS, John	195	HOWARD, James	130
HOLMES, Thomas	91	HOSKINS, Lucy	209	HOWARD, James	186
HOLMES, Thomas	118	HOSKINS, William	98	HOWARD, James	204
HOLMES, Thomas	121	HOULAND, Martha	67	HOWARD, John	48
HOLMES, Thomas	141	HOULAND, Nathaniel	67	HOWARD, John	60
HOLMES, Thomas	177	HOVEY, Abial	185	HOWARD, John	111
HOLMES, Thomas	186	HOVEY, Anna	188	HOWARD, John	117
HOLMES, Thomas	197	HOVEY, Dominnicus	203	HOWARD, John	184
HOLMES, Thomas	207	HOVEY, Gideon	204	HOWARD, John	216
HOLMES, Thomas Cooper	215	HOVEY, James	77	HOWARD, Lydia	214
HOLMES, Truman Cook	216	HOVEY, James	118	HOWARD, Marcy	128
HOLMES, William	47	HOVEY, James	177	HOWARD, Margaret	201
HOLMES, William	50	HOVEY, James	185	HOWARD, Margaret	205
HOLMES, William	53	HOVEY, James	188	HOWARD, Martha	48
HOLMES, William	78	HOVEY, James	208	HOWARD, Martha	185
HOLMES, William	122	HOVEY, Jane	202	HOWARD, Mary	48
HOLMES, William	133	HOVEY, Jas.	39	HOWARD, Mary	60
HOLMES, William	193	HOVEY, Lydia	77	HOWARD, Mary	79
HOLMES, William	195	HOVEY, Lydia	208	HOWARD, Mary	116
HOLMES, William	197	HOVEY, Margaret	208	HOWARD, Melatiah	206
HOLMES, William	204	HOVEY, Mary	208	HOWARD, Permela	199
HOLMES, William	213	HOVEY, Polley	212	HOWARD, Sarah	48
HOLMES, William	214	HOVEY, Ruth	199	HOWARD, Sarah	60
HOLMES, Winslow (Capt.)	150	HOVEY, Sarah	197	HOWARD, Sarah	72
HOLMES, Winslow S.	150	HOWARD, Charles	201	HOWARD, Sarah	101
HOLMES, Zacheus	46	HOWARD, Cyrus	210	HOWARD, Sarah	105
HOLMES, Zacheus	82	HOWARD, Ebenez.	189	HOWARD, Sarah	107
HOLMES, Zacheus	104	HOWARD, Ebenezer	48	HOWARD, Sarah	181

VITAL RECORDS OF THE TOWN OF PLYMOUTH

HOWARD, Sarah	195	HOWLAND, Elizabeth	212	HOWLAND, Mary	62
HOWARD, Thankfull	60	HOWLAND, Experiance	35	HOWLAND, Mary	71
HOWARD, Thankfull	111	HOWLAND, Experiance	74	HOWLAND, Mary	72
HOWARD, Thomas	60	HOWLAND, Experience	62	HOWLAND, Mary	130
HOWARD, Thomas	181	HOWLAND, Experience	128	HOWLAND, Mary	185
HOWARD, Unice	48	HOWLAND, Experience	181	HOWLAND, Mary	198
HOWARD, William	60	HOWLAND, Fortune	193	HOWLAND, Nathaniel	22
HOWARD, Zadock	182	HOWLAND, Hanna	129	HOWLAND, Nathaniel	73
HOWES, Amos	113	HOWLAND, Hannah	34	HOWLAND, Nathaniel	124
HOWES, Deborah	71	HOWLAND, Hannah	35	HOWLAND, Nathll.	126
HOWES, Ebenr.	86	HOWLAND, Hannah	62	HOWLAND, Pamelia	195
HOWES, Hannah	144	HOWLAND, Hannah	71	HOWLAND, Patience	49
HOWES, Jeremiah	75	HOWLAND, Hannah	75	HOWLAND, Patience	50
HOWES, Jeremiah	117	HOWLAND, Hannah	82	HOWLAND, Patience	78
HOWES, Jeremiah	144	HOWLAND, Hannah	117	HOWLAND, Patience	188
HOWES, Jeremiah	175	HOWLAND, Hannah	202	HOWLAND, Ruth	62
HOWES, Jerusha	86	HOWLAND, Henry	214	HOWLAND, Ruth	73
HOWES, Jerusha	182	HOWLAND, Ichabod	206	HOWLAND, Ruth	106
HOWES, Mariah	75	HOWLAND, Isaac	81	HOWLAND, Ruth	107
HOWES, Meriah	86	HOWLAND, Isaac	183	HOWLAND, Sarah	201
HOWES, Meriah	144	HOWLAND, Isaac	202	HOWLAND, Susannah	113
HOWES, Rebecca	86	HOWLAND, Isaac	214	HOWLAND, Thankfull	34
HOWES, Rebeckah	176	HOWLAND, Issacher	194	HOWLAND, Thomas	35
HOWES, Sarah	86	HOWLAND, Jacob	189	HOWLAND, Thomas	82
HOWES, Silvanus	109	HOWLAND, Jacob	202	HOWLAND, Thomas	100
HOWES, Silvanus	174	HOWLAND, James	34	HOWLAND, Thomas Southworth	62
HOWES, Thankfull	109	HOWLAND, Jno.	122	HOWLAND, Thomas Southworth	185
HOWLAND, ----- (male)	49	HOWLAND, Joanna	35	HOWLAND, William	81
HOWLAND, Abigaiel	34	HOWLAND, Joanna	62	HOWLAND, William	218
HOWLAND, Abigaill	130	HOWLAND, Joanna	100	HOWS, Hanah	70
HOWLAND, Abigal	73	HOWLAND, Joannah	35	HOWS, Jeremiah	86
HOWLAND, Abraham	198	HOWLAND, Joannah	79	HOWS, Joseph	70
HOWLAND, Benjamine	98	HOWLAND, Joannah	116	HOWS, Meriah	86
HOWLAND, Bethiah	62	HOWLAND, John	34	HOWS, Silvanus	86
HOWLAND, Betsey	218	HOWLAND, John	49	HOYE, Benjamin	188
HOWLAND, Caleb	194	HOWLAND, John	62	HOYET, Jacob	206
HOWLAND, Calvin	218	HOWLAND, John	78	HOYET, Moses	206
HOWLAND, Catherine	222	HOWLAND, John	217	HOYET, Moses	212
HOWLAND, Charles	207	HOWLAND, John	221	HOYET, Susanna	206
HOWLAND, Consider	35	HOWLAND, Joseph	22	HOYET, Susanna	207
HOWLAND, Consider	62	HOWLAND, Joseph	35	HOYT, Israel	194
HOWLAND, Consider	73	HOWLAND, Joseph	62	HUBBARD, Catherine	207
HOWLAND, Consider	130	HOWLAND, Joseph	98	HUBBARD, Hannah	75
HOWLAND, Conten	182	HOWLAND, Luce	62	HUBBARD, Hannah	77
HOWLAND, Content	182	HOWLAND, Luce	115	HUBBARD, Hannah	119
HOWLAND, Elizabeth	34	HOWLAND, Lydia	217	HUBBARD, Samuel	75
HOWLAND, Elizabeth	35	HOWLAND, Martha	22	HUBBARD, Thankfull	145
HOWLAND, Elizabeth	62	HOWLAND, Martha	62	HUBBARD, Thankfull	176
HOWLAND, Elizabeth	81	HOWLAND, Martha	188	HUBBERD, Samuel	124
HOWLAND, Elizabeth	98	HOWLAND, Mary	22	HUCKINS, Lowis	202
HOWLAND, Elizabeth	129	HOWLAND, Mary	34	HUMPHRYS, John	172

VITAL RECORDS OF THE TOWN OF PLYMOUTH

HUMPRY, John	175	JACKSON, Charles	209	JACKSON, Hosea	148
HUNT, ----- (male)	50	JACKSON, Daniel	102	JACKSON, Isaac	41
HUNT, Asa	50	JACKSON, Daniel	168	JACKSON, Isaac	130
HUNT, Asa	101	JACKSON, Daniel	194	JACKSON, Isaac	148
HUNT, Buzi	50	JACKSON, Daniel	209	JACKSON, Isaac	178
HUNT, Deborah	199	JACKSON, Daniel	210	JACKSON, Isaac	209
HUNT, Judeth	73	JACKSON, Daniel Lothrop	209	JACKSON, Isaac C.	150
HUNT, Judeth	126	JACKSON, David	87	JACKSON, Isaac Carver	168
HUNT, Lucy	217	JACKSON, Deborah	197	JACKSON, Isaac W.	150
HUNT, Sarah	50	JACKSON, Deborah	199	JACKSON, Israel	72
HUNT, Ziba	50	JACKSON, Edward H.	150	JACKSON, Israel	130
HUSTON, Elizabeth	135	JACKSON, Elisabeth	162	JACKSON, Jabez	215
HUSTON, William	135	JACKSON, Elisabeth	181	JACKSON, Jacob	86
HUSTON, William	171	JACKSON, Eliza.	194	JACKSON, Jacob	168
HUSTONS, Eleanor	222	JACKSON, Eliza.	195	JACKSON, Jane	200
HUTCHENSON, John	190	JACKSON, Elizabeth	46	JACKSON, Jeane	46
HUTCHINSON, Adeline	154	JACKSON, Elizabeth	73	JACKSON, Jeremiah	208
HUTCHINSON, Betsey E.	154	JACKSON, Elizabeth	126	JACKSON, Joanna	70
HUTCHINSON, Deborah	154	JACKSON, Elizabeth	186	JACKSON, John	213
HUTCHINSON, Deborah B.	154	JACKSON, Elizabeth	201	JACKSON, John G.	150
HUTCHINSON, Emeline	154	JACKSON, Elizabeth M.	209	JACKSON, Joseph	61
HUTCHINSON, Joshua B.	154	JACKSON, Elizabeth Morton	209	JACKSON, Joseph	73
HUTCHINSON, Lydia D.	154	JACKSON, Ester	71	JACKSON, Joseph	95
HUTCHINSON, Robert	154	JACKSON, Ester	77	JACKSON, Joseph	130
HUTCHINSON, Robert	213	JACKSON, Esther	86	JACKSON, Lemuel	48
HUTCHINSON, Susan A.	154	JACKSON, Esther	89	JACKSON, Lemuel	77
		JACKSON, Eunice	171	JACKSON, Lemuel	86
I		JACKSON, Experiance	128	JACKSON, Lemuel	87
		JACKSON, Experience	191	JACKSON, Lemuel	89
IRISH, Content	120	JACKSON, Faith	117	JACKSON, Lemuel	118
		JACKSON, George	205	JACKSON, Lemuell	87
J		JACKSON, George H.	150	JACKSON, Lois	109
		JACKSON, Hannah	64	JACKSON, Lois	123
JACK-, Jere.	15	JACKSON, Hannah	102	JACKSON, Lucy	102
JACKSON, Abigail	48	JACKSON, Hannah	105	JACKSON, Lucy	193
JACKSON, Abigail	106	JACKSON, Hannah	107	JACKSON, Lucy C.	222
JACKSON, Abigail	107	JACKSON, Hannah	148	JACKSON, Lydia	48
JACKSON, Abraham	41	JACKSON, Hannah	185	JACKSON, Lydia	102
JACKSON, Abraham	100	JACKSON, Hannah	187	JACKSON, Lydia	111
JACKSON, Abraham	116	JACKSON, Hannah	199	JACKSON, Lydia	116
JACKSON, Abraham	122	JACKSON, Hannah	200	JACKSON, Lydia	148
JACKSON, Abraham	148	JACKSON, Hannah	208	JACKSON, Lydia	204
JACKSON, Abraham	150	JACKSON, Harriet	150	JACKSON, Margaret	41
JACKSON, Abraham	168	JACKSON, Harriet O.	150	JACKSON, Mary	41
JACKSON, Abraham	195	JACKSON, Henry	201	JACKSON, Mary	75
JACKSON, Abraham	208	JACKSON, Hezekiah	64	JACKSON, Mary	95
JACKSON, Abraham	220	JACKSON, Hezekiah	162	JACKSON, Mary	100
JACKSON, Bethiah	41	JACKSON, Hezekiah	180	JACKSON, Mary	125
JACKSON, Bethiah	190	JACKSON, Hezekiah	198	JACKSON, Mercy	72
JACKSON, Charles	102	JACKSON, Hezekiah	201	JACKSON, Moley	64
JACKSON, Charles	199	JACKSON, Horace	150	JACKSON, Molley	183

JACKSON, Morton Spenser	143	JACKSON, Sarah	222	JACSON, Joannah	32
JACKSON, Nancy	148	JACKSON, Sarah Taylor	209	JACSON, John	32
JACKSON, Nancy	204	JACKSON, Seth	71	JACSON, John	67
JACKSON, Naoma	200	JACKSON, Seth	176	JACSON, Lidia	9
JACKSON, Nathaiel	64	JACKSON, Susan Turner	209	JACSON, Marcey	32
JACKSON, Nathaniel	48	JACKSON, Sylvina	143	JACSON, Margareat	9
JACKSON, Nathaniel	129	JACKSON, Sylvina Augusta	143	JACSON, Margarret	66
JACKSON, Nathaniel	182	JACKSON, Thomas	64	JACSON, Mary	32
JACKSON, Nathaniel	189	JACKSON, Thomas	102	JACSON, Nathaniell	66
JACKSON, Nathaniel	202	JACKSON, Thomas	106	JACSON, Ransom	33
JACKSON, Olive	148	JACKSON, Thomas	107	JACSON, Remember	99
JACKSON, Olive	213	JACKSON, Thomas	130	JACSON, Ruth	66
JACKSON, Polley	194	JACKSON, Thomas	188	JACSON, Ruth	129
JACKSON, Priscilla	102	JACKSON, Thomas	193	JACSON, Samuel	9
JACKSON, Priscilla	193	JACKSON, Thomas	195	JACSON, Sarah	9
JACKSON, Ransom	148	JACKSON, Thomas	207	JACSON, Seth	9
JACKSON, Ransom	203	JACKSON, Thomas O.	150	JACSON, Suzannah	33
JACKSON, Rebecca	103	JACKSON, Thomas Taylor	168	JACSON, Thomas	26
JACKSON, Rebecca	168	JACKSON, Thos.	176	JARVIS, Thomas	206
JACKSON, Rebecca	209	JACKSON, William	102	JEFERY, Amos	178
JACKSON, Rebecca	220	JACKSON, William	195	JEFFERY, Deborah	200
JACKSON, Rebeckah	104	JACKSON, William	200	JEFFRY, Accalabe	118
JACKSON, Rebeckah	113	JACKSON, William	207	JEFFRY, Lydia	125
JACKSON, Rebeckah	128	JACKSON, William Hall	64	JEFFRY, Rachel	127
JACKSON, Rebeckah	203	JACKSON, William Hall	190	JENKINS, Caleb	197
JACKSON, Remembrance	61	JACKSON, William Morton	168	JENNA, Elizabeth	186
JACKSON, Remembrance	73	JACKSON, William Spenser	143	JENNES, Experiance	130
JACKSON, Remembrance	75	JACKSON, Wm. M.	143	JENNEY, Elizabeth	66
JACKSON, Remembrance	95	JACKSON, Woodworth	103	JENNEY, Experiance	130
JACKSON, Remembrance	125	JACKSON, Woodworth	203	JENNINGS, Joseph	190
JACKSON, Remembrance	130	JACOB, Hannah	126	JENNINGS, Joseph	200
JACKSON, Robert	148	JACSON, Abigail	67	JENY, Ruth	66
JACKSON, Ruth	64	JACSON, Abigall	32	JERMAN, Eleonar	37
JACKSON, Ruth	71	JACSON, Abraham	9	JERMAN, Eleoner	111
JACKSON, Ruth	129	JACSON, Abraham	66	JERMAN, Mary	38
JACKSON, Ruth	131	JACSON, Abraham	99	JERMAN, William	37
JACKSON, Salley	148	JACSON, Abraham	100	JERMAN, William	111
JACKSON, Salley	210	JACSON, Benjamin	33	JERMAN, Willm.	123
JACKSON, Salley	214	JACSON, Content	33	JOB, Hasadiah	176
JACKSON, Salsberry	204	JACSON, Deborah	33	JOHNSON, Abigail	144
JACKSON, Saml.	104	JACSON, Eliazar	32	JOHNSON, Bethiah	202
JACKSON, Samuel	46	JACSON, Eliazar	66	JOHNSON, Betsey	214
JACKSON, Samuel	64	JACSON, Ephraim	33	JOHNSON, Caleb	59
JACKSON, Samuel	191	JACSON, Exsperiance	33	JOHNSON, Clark	205
JACKSON, Samuel	212	JACSON, Hanah	26	JOHNSON, Eleazer	37
JACKSON, Samuell	128	JACSON, Hannah	32	JOHNSON, Elizabeth	59
JACKSON, Sarah	46	JACSON, Hannah	66	JOHNSON, Hannah	144
JACKSON, Sarah	70	JACSON, Hannah	69	JOHNSON, Hannah	197
JACKSON, Sarah	102	JACSON, Israel	9	JOHNSON, Hannah	222
JACKSON, Sarah	107	JACSON, Jeremiah	26	JOHNSON, Jacob	84
JACKSON, Sarah	190	JACSON, Jeremiah	69	JOHNSON, Jacob	124

VITAL RECORDS OF THE TOWN OF PLYMOUTH

Name	Page	Name	Page	Name	Page
JOHNSON, Jacob	144	JONES, Marcey	27	KEEN, William	123
JOHNSON, Jacob	175	JONES, Marcy	130	KEEN, William	171
JOHNSON, Jacob	179	JONES, Mary	27	KEEN, William	194
JOHNSON, Jacob	199	JONES, Rachel	215	KEEN, William	212
JOHNSON, Jacob	204	JONES, Remember	27	KEEN, Willm.	95
JOHNSON, Jane	59	JONES, Remembr.	211	KEEYS, Oliver	200
JOHNSON, Jean	118	JONES, Robert	130	KEITH, Abiah	118
JOHNSON, John	129	JONES, Sarah	102	KEMBER, Susannah	183
JOHNSON, Joseph	59	JONES, Sarah	109	KEMPTON, -----	94
JOHNSON, Joseph	144	JONES, Sarah	116	KEMPTON, ----- (male)	45
JOHNSON, Joseph	196	JONES, Sarah	180	KEMPTON, Abigail	21
JOHNSON, Josiah	37	JONES, Sarah	185	KEMPTON, Bathshebah	118
JOHNSON, Josiah	84	JONES, Thomas	102	KEMPTON, Bathshebath	77
JOHNSON, Josiah	112	JONSON, Anne	71	KEMPTON, Bathshua	45
JOHNSON, Josiah	113	JONSON, Elezabeth	71	KEMPTON, Charles	153
JOHNSON, Josiah	181	JONSON, Elizabeth	70	KEMPTON, Deborah	94
JOHNSON, Josiah	186	JONSON, George	130	KEMPTON, Elizabeth	94
JOHNSON, Josiah	210	JONSON, Hanna	130	KEMPTON, Elizabeth	178
JOHNSON, Mason	144	JONSON, James	71	KEMPTON, Elizabeth	188
JOHNSON, Patiance	112	JONSON, John	71	KEMPTON, Ephm.	11
JOHNSON, Patience	37	JONSON, Robert	70	KEMPTON, Ephraim	86
JOHNSON, Patience	186	JORDAN, Baruch	65	KEMPTON, Ephraime	24
JOHNSON, Priscilla	130	JORDAN, Esther	98	KEMPTON, Ephraime	67
JOHNSON, Richard Francis	197	JORDAN, Estur	97	KEMPTON, Hannah	94
JOHNSON, Robert	59	JORDAN, Mary	65	KEMPTON, Hannah	184
JOHNSON, Sarah	59	JORDEN, John	98	KEMPTON, Jerusha	94
JOHNSON, Sarah	84	JOSEPH, Clarrisa	218	KEMPTON, Jerusha	172
JOHNSON, Sarah	106	JOSEPH, Lemuel	194	KEMPTON, Jerusha	173
JOHNSON, Sarah	109	JOSSELYN, Isaac	201	KEMPTON, Joanna	24
JOHNSON, Sarah	206	JOSSELYN, Jacob	200	KEMPTON, Joannah	94
JOHNSON, Thomas	84	JOSSLYNE, Lyman	215	KEMPTON, John	45
JOHNSON, Thomas	144	JOURDAINE, Barak	98	KEMPTON, John	94
JOHNSON, Thomas	197	JOYCE, Elizabeth	172	KEMPTON, John	118
JONAS, Hannah	118	JUDSON, Adoniram (Rev.)	214	KEMPTON, John	153
JONES, Adam	27			KEMPTON, John	178
JONES, Addam	130	**K**		KEMPTON, Joseph	153
JONES, Ann	124			KEMPTON, Joseph	175
JONES, Annah	67	KANEDY, Hannah	67	KEMPTON, Juana	117
JONES, Benjamin	137	KEEN, Abigail	217	KEMPTON, Lemuel	153
JONES, Clemmons	216	KEEN, Bethiah	71	KEMPTON, Loes	45
JONES, Deborah Taylor	212	KEEN, Elizabeth	95	KEMPTON, Lois	117
JONES, Ebenezr.	137	KEEN, George	222	KEMPTON, Lydia	94
JONES, Elizabeth	74	KEEN, Grace	95	KEMPTON, Mabel	77
JONES, Elizabeth	124	KEEN, Lydia	109	KEMPTON, Mabell	94
JONES, James	102	KEEN, Margaret James	218	KEMPTON, Mabell	104
JONES, John	102	KEEN, Peggy	188	KEMPTON, Manasseh	47
JONES, John	109	KEEN, Ruth	79	KEMPTON, Manassh	47
JONES, John	121	KEEN, Ruth	95	KEMPTON, Manassieh	70
JONES, John	137	KEEN, Snow	172	KEMPTON, Marcy	45
JONES, John	172	KEEN, Tillden	218	KEMPTON, Marcy	121
JONES, Lydia	137	KEEN, William	79	KEMPTON, Marey	45

KEMPTON, Margaret	171	KEMPTON, William	24	KING, Eliazar	38
KEMPTON, Margret	81	KEMPTON, William	74	KING, Eliza	142
KEMPTON, Marsey	45	KEMPTON, William	86	KING, Eliza Ann	142
KEMPTON, Mary	74	KEMPTON, William	125	KING, Elizabeth	66
KEMPTON, Mary	81	KEMPTON, Zacheus	94	KING, Elizabeth	86
KEMPTON, Mary	86	KEMPTON, Zacheus	153	KING, Elizabeth	124
KEMPTON, Mary	94	KEMPTON, Zacheus	193	KING, Elizabeth	187
KEMPTON, Mary	100	KEMPTON, Zacheus	222	KING, Hannah	10
KEMPTON, Mary	128	KEMTON, Marsey	69	KING, Hannah	74
KEMPTON, Mary	153	KEMTON, Samuel	69	KING, Hannah	104
KEMPTON, Mary	186	KENDALL, James (Rev.)	204	KING, Hannah	107
KEMPTON, Mary	208	KENDALL, James (Rev.)	213	KING, Hannah	207
KEMPTON, Mehitabl	47	KENDALL, Sally	213	KING, Hannah Lewis	142
KEMPTON, Mehittabl	70	KENDRICK, Asa	144	KING, Isaac	38
KEMPTON, Mercy	78	KENDRICK, Charlotte	144	KING, Isaac	55
KEMPTON, Mercy	122	KENDRICK, Reuben	144	KING, Isaac	66
KEMPTON, Nancy Robinson	215	KENRICK, Josiah Sears	209	KING, Isaac	70
KEMPTON, Nathl. Hatch	153	KENT, Desire	101	KING, Isaac	74
KEMPTON, Nathll.	94	KENT, Desire Barker	102	KING, Isaac	124
KEMPTON, Olever	202	KENT, Hannah	102	KING, Joanah	26
KEMPTON, Oliver	94	KENT, Hulda	102	KING, Joannah	38
KEMPTON, Oliver	181	KENT, Ichabod	102	KING, Joannah	116
KEMPTON, Pattience	24	KENT, John	102	KING, Johannah	111
KEMPTON, Pattience	67	KENT, Nathl.	102	KING, John	10
KEMPTON, Rebakah	185	KENT, Samuel	101	KING, John	38
KEMPTON, Rebeccah	45	KENT, Samuell	101	KING, John	105
KEMPTON, Richard	81	KENT, Sarah	102	KING, John	107
KEMPTON, Ruth	47	KEYS, Benjamin	201	KING, John	178
KEMPTON, Ruth	70	KIETH, Jonas	222	KING, John	188
KEMPTON, Ruth	79	KIMBAL, Putnam	212	KING, John	205
KEMPTON, Ruth	122	KIMBALL, see CIMBAL		KING, Jonathan	55
KEMPTON, Saml.	94	KIMBALL, Zerviah	176	KING, Jonathan	59
KEMPTON, Samuel	45	KIMBELL, Richard	177	KING, Jonathan	116
KEMPTON, Samuel	75	KIMBER, Peter	190	KING, Joseph	38
KEMPTON, Samuel	77	KING, Abigail	59	KING, Joseph	66
KEMPTON, Samuel	94	KING, Amariah	10	KING, Joseph	69
KEMPTON, Samuel	119	KING, An	97	KING, Joseph	71
KEMPTON, Samuel	153	KING, Anna	113	KING, Joseph	101
KEMPTON, Samuel	177	KING, Annah	101	KING, Joseph	129
KEMPTON, Sarah	21	KING, Benjamin	27	KING, Joseph	195
KEMPTON, Sarah	45	KING, Benjamin	105	KING, Lidiah	55
KEMPTON, Sarah	94	KING, Benjamin	107	KING, Luce	59
KEMPTON, Seth	153	KING, Benjamin	189	KING, Lydia	59
KEMPTON, Stephen	153	KING, Bethia	26	KING, Lydia	77
KEMPTON, Thomas	24	KING, Bethyah	38	KING, Lydia	118
KEMPTON, Thomas	74	KING, Bethyah	70	KING, Lydia	183
KEMPTON, Thomas	81	KING, Bettey	27	KING, Lydia	201
KEMPTON, Thomas	124	KING, Betty	107	KING, Lydia	206
KEMPTON, Thomas	125	KING, Beulah	217	KING, Lydia	209
KEMPTON, Thos.	100	KING, Deborah	59	KING, Mahitabel	66
KEMPTON, Viza	94	KING, Eleazer	101	KING, Marcy	86

VITAL RECORDS OF THE TOWN OF PLYMOUTH

KING, Marcy	101	KING, William	161	LANMAN, George F.	138
KING, Marey	55	KING, William	184	LANMAN, George Francis	138
KING, Marsey	38	KING, William	205	LANMAN, George Francis	149
KING, Marsey	69	KINGSTON, Nancy	177	LANMAN, George Francis	153
KING, Martha	38	KIRK, Jane	73	LANMAN, Joannah	112
KING, Martha	55	KIRK, Jane	130	LANMAN, Lucy	207
KING, Martha	115	KIRK, Jane	190	LANMAN, Mary	75
KING, Mary	59	KITRIDGE, Thomas	195	LANMAN, Mary	117
KING, Mary	76	KNAP, Charles	214	LANMAN, Mary	207
KING, Mary	86	KNOWLTON, Zerviah	180	LANMAN, Nathaniel Cobb	218
KING, Mehetable	67			LANMAN, Peter	93
KING, Mehittab	38	**L**		LANMAN, Peter	193
KING, Mercy	59			LANMAN, Polley	204
KING, Mercy	71	LABARON, Ffrances	129	LANMAN, Rebecca	202
KING, Mercy	195	LABARON, Joseph	55	LANMAN, Rebecca	212
KING, Nathaniel	38	LABARON, Lazaros	54	LANMAN, Rebeckah	93
KING, Nathl.	59	LABARON, Lazaros	71	LANMAN, Sally	208
KING, Obediah	209	LABARON, Lazaros	129	LANMAN, Saml.	106
KING, Olive	202	LABARON, Lazarus	54	LANMAN, Samll.	93
KING, Rebecca	73	LABARON, Lidiah	54	LANMAN, Samuel	149
KING, Rebeccah	130	LABARON, Lidiah	71	LANMAN, Samuel	153
KING, Rebeckah	27	LABARON, Lydia	55	LANMAN, Samuel	191
KING, Rebeckah	189	LABARRON, Mary	70	LANMAN, Samuel	213
KING, Rebekah	26	LAKEY, James	171	LANMAN, Samuel Ellis	138
KING, Robert	142	LANDERS, John	188	LANMAN, Samuel Ellis	149
KING, Robert	206	LANDMAN, Edward	88	LANMAN, Samuel Ellis	153
KING, Robert Williams	142	LANDMAN, James	88	LANMAN, Samuell	93
KING, Samll	26	LANDMAN, Joannah	88	LANMAN, Sarah Holmes	149
KING, Samuel	26	LANDMAN, Thomas	88	LANMAN, Sarah Holmes	153
KING, Samuel	38	LANDMAN, William	88	LANMAN, Temperance	149
KING, Samuel	55	LANE, Archelaus	123	LANMAN, Temperance	153
KING, Samuel	76	LANE, Marshal	213	LANMAN, Thomas	93
KING, Samuel	86	LANGERELL, Joseph	71	LANMAN, Thomas	185
KING, Samuel	97	LANGERELL, Mary	71	LANMAN, William	138
KING, Samuel	118	LANGFORD, William	209	LAPUM, Elisha	216
KING, Sara	38	LANGLEE, Sarah	171	LARANCE, Joshua	127
KING, Sarah	26	LANMAN, Abby	138	LASSELL, Martha	68
KING, Sarah	38	LANMAN, Abiah	138	LATHEROP, Elizabeth	129
KING, Sarah	67	LANMAN, Betsy	202	LATHLE, Rhoda	129
KING, Sarah	100	LANMAN, Content	149	LATHLE, Rohoda	71
KING, Sarah	199	LANMAN, Content	153	LATHROP, Elizabeth	67
KING, Seth	86	LANMAN, Edward	131	LATHROP, Elizabeth	71
KING, Susanna	199	LANMAN, Edward	138	LATHROP, Isaac	67
KING, Susanna	202	LANMAN, Edward	173	LAWRANCE, Abigail	159
KING, Susannah	27	LANMAN, Edward	201	LAWRANCE, Benjamin	206
KING, Susannah	86	LANMAN, Eliza.	191	LAWRANCE, Daniel	194
KING, Susannah	161	LANMAN, Elizabeth	93	LAWRANCE, Hulda	212
KING, Sussannah	161	LANMAN, Elizabeth	149	LAWRANCE, James	159
KING, Thankfull	55	LANMAN, Elizabeth	153	LAWRANCE, James	183
KING, Thankfull	70	LANMAN, Ellis Thomas	149	LAWRANCE, Joseph	159
KING, Thankfull	104	LANMAN, Ellis Thomas	153	LAWRANCE, Seth	185

VITAL RECORDS OF THE TOWN OF PLYMOUTH

LAWTON, Mary	125	LEBARON, Mary Howland	213	LEBARRON, Sarah	81
LAYTHUM, Elizabeth	66	LEBARON, Mira	212	LEBARRON, Sarah	106
LAZEL, Margaret	50	LEBARON, Nancy	213	LEBARRON, Sarah	107
LAZEL, Margret	70	LEBARON, Priscilla	141	LEBARRON, Sarah	112
LAZEL, Simon	70	LEBARON, Priscilla	188	LEBARRON, William	92
LAZELL, Eliazabeth	67	LEBARON, Priscilla	206	LEE, Abigail	182
LAZELL, Elizabeth	13	LEBARON, Sarah	71	LEE, Deborah Farling	162
LAZELL, Hannah	13	LEBARON, Sarah	77	LEE, Elizabeth	73
LAZELL, John	13	LEBARON, Sarah	119	LEE, Phillip	73
LAZELL, Joshua	13	LEBARON, Sarah	141	LEE, Phillip	126
LAZELL, Joshua	50	LEBARON, Sarah	207	LEE, Susannah	162
LAZELL, Lydia	50	LEBARON, Terress	55	LEE, Susannah	177
LAZELL, Mary	13	LEBARON, William	141	LEECHFEILD, Bathshabe	69
LAZELL, Sarah	13	LEBARON, William	188	LEECHFEILD, Nicklos	69
LAZELL, Simon	50	LEBARON, Wm. (Capt.)	213	LEMOAT, Mercy	198
LAZELL, Thomas	13	LEBARRON, ----- (female)	64	LEMOAT, Thankfull	207
LEACH, David	106	LEBARRON, Bartlett	177	LEMONT, Catherine	154
LEACH, Finney	203	LEBARRON, Elizabeth	92	LEMONT, Francis	154
LEACH, Lemuel	181	LEBARRON, Elizabeth	177	LEMONT, George	154
LEACH, Lemuel	198	LEBARRON, Francis	64	LEMONT, George	188
LEACH, Lydia	197	LEBARRON, Francis	92	LEMONT, Mary	175
LEACH, Marcy	177	LEBARRON, Hannah	110	LEMONT, Mercy	154
LEACH, Naome	213	LEBARRON, Hannah	173	LEMOTE, Abigail	81
LEACH, Sarah	198	LEBARRON, Isaac	64	LEMOTE, Abigal	81
LEACH, Sarah	218	LEBARRON, Isaac	92	LEMOTE, George	81
LEACH, Susanna	214	LEBARRON, Joseph	81	LEMOTE, George	178
LEBARON, Bartlett	55	LEBARRON, Joseph	112	LEMOTE, Joseph	81
LEBARON, Bartlett	148	LEBARRON, Joseph	123	LEMOTE, Marcy	74
LEBARON, Bartlett	195	LEBARRON, Lazarus	172	LEMOTE, Marcy	81
LEBARON, Eliza	141	LEBARRON, Lazarus (Doctor)	101	LEMOTE, Marcy	171
LEBARON, Eliza	213	LEBARRON, Lazarus (Doctor)	109	LEMOTE, Mary	81
LEBARON, Esther	214	LEBARRON, Lazarus (Doctr.)	92	LEMOTE, Mathew	74
LEBARON, Ffrances	21	LEBARRON, Lazarus (Doctr.)	96	LEMOTE, Mathew	81
LEBARON, Ffrances	71	LEBARRON, Lazarus (Doctr.)	112	LEMOTE, Mathew	128
LEBARON, Frances	21	LEBARRON, Lazarus (Doctr.)	115	LEMOTE, Susannah	81
LEBARON, Frances	67	LEBARRON, Lazarus (Doctr.)	172	LEMOTE, Susannah	172
LEBARON, Hannah	55	LEBARRON, Lazarus (Dr.)	79	LEONARD, -----	107
LEBARON, Hannah	148	LEBARRON, Lazs. (Doctr.)	113	LEONARD, Abiel	63
LEBARON, Isaac	188	LEBARRON, Lemuel	92	LEONARD, Abigail	175
LEBARON, Isaac	213	LEBARRON, Lydia	79	LEONARD, Anna	63
LEBARON, James	21	LEBARRON, Lydia	92	LEONARD, Anna	124
LEBARON, Lazaros	21	LEBARRON, Lydia	96	LEONARD, Anne	112
LEBARON, Lucia	210	LEBARRON, Lydia	101	LEONARD, Anne	113
LEBARON, Lucy	141	LEBARRON, Lydia	111	LEONARD, Bethiah	162
LEBARON, Lucy	203	LEBARRON, Lydia	123	LEONARD, Daniel	63
LEBARON, Martha	204	LEBARRON, Margaret	92	LEONARD, Elizabeth	63
LEBARON, Mary	21	LEBARRON, Mary	64	LEONARD, Ephraim	63
LEBARON, Mary	55	LEBARRON, Mary	105	LEONARD, Ephraim	206
LEBARON, Mary	67	LEBARRON, Mary	107	LEONARD, George	65
LEBARON, Mary	141	LEBARRON, Priscilla	92	LEONARD, Hannah	159
LEBARON, Mary	148	LEBARRON, Sarah	64	LEONARD, Hannah	203

VITAL RECORDS OF THE TOWN OF PLYMOUTH

Name	Page	Name	Page	Name	Page
LEONARD, Margaret	65	LEWEN, John	107	LITTLE, Hanna	100
LEONARD, Mary	63	LEWEN, Joseph	65	LITTLE, Isaac	26
LEONARD, Nath. Warrin	200	LEWEN, Joseph	125	LITTLE, Isaac	73
LEONARD, Nathanel (Rev.)	73	LEWEN, Mariah	113	LITTLE, Isaac	80
LEONARD, Nathaniel	63	LEWEN, Meriah	112	LITTLE, Isaac	104
LEONARD, Nathaniel	162	LEWEN, Moriah	65	LITTLE, Isaac	106
LEONARD, Nathaniel	177	LEWEN, Sarah	107	LITTLE, Isaac	123
LEONARD, Nathaniel (Rev.)	73	LEWES, Jacob	130	LITTLE, Isaac	126
LEONARD, Nathaniel (Rev.)	74	LEWING, Hannah	72	LITTLE, Joseph	80
LEONARD, Nathaniel (Rev.)	75	LEWING, Joseph	72	LITTLE, Lucie	44
LEONARD, Nathaniel (Rev.)	77	LEWING, Joseph	130	LITTLE, Lucy	191
LEONARD, Nathaniel (Rev.)	78	LEWIS, Albert	139	LITTLE, Mary	26
LEONARD, Nathaniel (Rev.)	111	LEWIS, Bathsheba	74	LITTLE, Mary	71
LEONARD, Nathaniel (Rev.)	112	LEWIS, Daniel	71	LITTLE, Mary	126
LEONARD, Nathaniel (Rev.)	113	LEWIS, Daniel	212	LITTLE, Mayhew	26
LEONARD, Nathaniel (Rev.)	130	LEWIS, Daniel J.	139	LITTLE, Nathaniell	171
LEONARD, Nathaniel Warrin	159	LEWIS, Jacob	74	LITTLE, Sarah	43
LEONARD, Nathaniell (Rev.)	63	LEWIS, Jacob	128	LITTLE, Sarah	44
LEONARD, Nathaniell (Rev.)	79	LEWIS, James Augustus	139	LITTLE, Sarah	67
LEONARD, Nathl. (Rev.)	107	LEWIS, John	212	LITTLE, Sarah	73
LEONARD, Nathl. (Rev.)	128	LEWIS, Mary	124	LITTLE, Sarah	80
LEONARD, Nathll. (Rev.)	65	LEWIS, Nathaniel	186	LITTLE, Sarah	171
LEONARD, Nathll. (Rev.)	78	LEWIS, Nathaniel	198	LITTLE, Sarah	172
LEONARD, Paul	174	LEWIS, Samuel	213	LITTLE, Thomas	26
LEONARD, Phebe	65	LEWIS, Samuel	222	LITTLE, Thomas (Docter)	99
LEONARD, Phebe	218	LEWIS, Sarah	139	LITTLE, William	100
LEONARD, Philip	180	LEWIS, Sarah	162	LITTLEJOHN, Hannah	65
LEONARD, Phillip	159	LEWIS, Sarah	197	LITTLEJOHN, Hannah	78
LEONARD, Priscilla	63	LEWIS, Thomas	162	LITTLEJOHN, Hannah	122
LEONARD, Priscilla	65	LEWIS, William	139	LITTLEJOHN, Henery	71
LEONARD, Samuel	219	LIBERTY, Francis	197	LITTLEJOHN, Henry	65
LEONARD, Sarah	63	LINCH, Jerusha	209	LITTLEJOHN, Henry	71
LEONARD, Sarah	112	LINCOLN, Benjamin	171	LITTLEJOHN, James	65
LEONARD, Sarah	123	LINCOLN, Elijah	216	LITTLEJOHN, Mary	71
LEONARD, Sarah	207	LING, Elizabeth	107	LITTLEJOHN, Sarah	65
LEONARD, Thomas	65	LING, Thomas	107	LITTLEJOHN, Sarah	71
LEONARD, Thomas	162	LING, Thomas	116	LITTLEJOHN, Sarah	109
LEONARD, Thomas	198	LINZEY, Clarisse Greenough	218	LITTLEJOHN, Sarah	120
LEONARD, William	162	LISCOM, Samuel	219	LITTLEJOHN, William	65
LEONARD, William	197	LITTLE, Sarah	100	LITTLES, Charles	100
LEONARD, William	207	LITTLE, ----- (male)	71	LITTLES, Sarah	70
LEONARD, William	214	LITTLE, Bethia	44	LOBDEL, Eunice	199
LEONARD, William B.	215	LITTLE, Beththyah	70	LOBDELL, ----- (female)	10
LESTER, Sarah	153	LITTLE, Charles	43	LOBDELL, Isaak	10
LESTER, Sarah	183	LITTLE, Charles	44	LOBDELL, Lydia	104
LESTER, Territ	153	LITTLE, Charles	70	LOBDELL, Martha	10
LESTER, Territ	172	LITTLE, Ephraim	71	LOBDELL, Samuell	10
LETTES, ----- (widow)	96	LITTLE, Ephrame	67	LOBDELL, Sarah	10
LEWEN, Hannah	65	LITTLE, George	26	LOBDELL, Thomas J.	218
LEWEN, John	65	LITTLE, George	80	LOBDELL, Thomas Jenkins	222
LEWEN, John	105	LITTLE, George	171	LOCK, Joseph	206

VITAL RECORDS OF THE TOWN OF PLYMOUTH

LOCKE, John	203	LOTHROP, Elizabeth	101	LOVIL, Phebe	195
LOGAN, Marcy	105	LOTHROP, Elizabeth	120	LUCAS, Abigail	75
LONG, Betsey	198	LOTHROP, Experiance	74	LUCAS, Abigail	136
LONG, Miles	184	LOTHROP, Experience	84	LUCAS, Abigail	193
LONG, Rebecca	222	LOTHROP, Freeman	81	LUCAS, Allden	206
LONG, Samuel	219	LOTHROP, Hannah	81	LUCAS, Anna	206
LONG, Thankfull	191	LOTHROP, Hannah	84	LUCAS, Ansel	198
LONG, Thomas	200	LOTHROP, Harriet	199	LUCAS, Ansell	150
LOREIN, Caleb	22	LOTHROP, Isaac	24	LUCAS, Barnabas	207
LOREIN, Deborah	23	LOTHROP, Isaac	73	LUCAS, Bazaliel	198
LOREIN, Deborah	67	LOTHROP, Isaac	74	LUCAS, Bela	136
LOREIN, Hanah	22	LOTHROP, Isaac	75	LUCAS, Bela	191
LOREIN, Ignatious	22	LOTHROP, Isaac	78	LUCAS, Benjamin	59
LOREIN, John	22	LOTHROP, Isaac	81	LUCAS, Benjamin	136
LOREIN, Lidiah	22	LOTHROP, Isaac	96	LUCAS, Benjamin	150
LOREIN, Policarpos	22	LOTHROP, Isaac	100	LUCAS, Benjamin	171
LOREIN, Thomas	22	LOTHROP, Isaac	101	LUCAS, Benjamin	207
LOREIN, Thomas	23	LOTHROP, Isaac	117	LUCAS, Cynthia	222
LOREIN, Thomas	67	LOTHROP, Isaac	124	LUCAS, Eliza	162
LOREING, Elizabeth	117	LOTHROP, Isaac	125	LUCAS, Elkanah	181
LORING, Caleb	67	LOTHROP, Isaac	129	LUCAS, Elnathan	150
LORING, Ezekiel	209	LOTHROP, John	84	LUCAS, Elnathan	194
LORING, John	214	LOTHROP, John	106	LUCAS, Emely H.	162
LORING, Lidiah	67	LOTHROP, John	186	LUCAS, Ephraim	221
LORING, Sally	221	LOTHROP, Joseph	84	LUCAS, Ezra	136
LORING, Sarah	186	LOTHROP, Joseph	88	LUCAS, Hannah	191
LORING, William	181	LOTHROP, Joseph	90	LUCAS, Isaac	59
LOTHROP, ----- (female)	24	LOTHROP, Lydia	90	LUCAS, Isaac	136
LOTHROP, ----- (female)	163	LOTHROP, Maltiah	24	LUCAS, Isaac Jackson	222
LOTHROP, Ansell	90	LOTHROP, Mary	77	LUCAS, Ivory B.	162
LOTHROP, Anselm	77	LOTHROP, Mary	88	LUCAS, Jane	222
LOTHROP, Anselm	118	LOTHROP, Mary	90	LUCAS, Jesse	222
LOTHROP, Anslem	88	LOTHROP, Mary	172	LUCAS, Joseph	59
LOTHROP, Bathsheba	163	LOTHROP, Mary	175	LUCAS, Joseph	104
LOTHROP, Bathsheba May	198	LOTHROP, Nathaniel	81	LUCAS, Joseph	150
LOTHROP, Bathshebah May	163	LOTHROP, Nathaniel (Doctr.)	205	LUCAS, Lazarus	201
LOTHROP, Benja.	84	LOTHROP, Nathll.	84	LUCAS, Levi	199
LOTHROP, Benjamin	74	LOTHROP, Priscilla	75	LUCAS, Levi	205
LOTHROP, Benjamin	84	LOTHROP, Priscilla	81	LUCAS, Lovisa	150
LOTHROP, Benjamin	112	LOTHROP, Priscilla	174	LUCAS, Lovisa	190
LOTHROP, Benjamin	114	LOTHROP, Thomas	81	LUCAS, Lucey	136
LOTHROP, Benjamin	128	LOTHROP, Thomas	84	LUCAS, Lucy	212
LOTHROP, Betty	90	LOTHROP, Thomas Howland	84	LUCAS, Lydia	136
LOTHROP, Caleb	81	LOTHROP, William	90	LUCAS, Lydia	201
LOTHROP, Colln.	77	LOVEL, Metilda	217	LUCAS, Mary	150
LOTHROP, David	163	LOVELL, Betty	105	LUCAS, Mary	201
LOTHROP, David	184	LOVELL, Betty	107	LUCAS, Mehetabel	59
LOTHROP, Deborah	104	LOVELL, Ezekiel	210	LUCAS, Mehetabell	59
LOTHROP, Deborah	112	LOVELL, Joseph	177	LUCAS, Mehitable	181
LOTHROP, Elizabeth	24	LOVELL, Meriah	215	LUCAS, Molle	150
LOTHROP, Elizabeth	96	LOVELL, Robert	215	LUCAS, Nancy	221

VITAL RECORDS OF THE TOWN OF PLYMOUTH

LUCAS, Naomi	136	LUCE, Seth	183	MACOMBER, Emeline	160
LUCAS, Perces	207	LUCE, Seth	198	MACOMBER, John	160
LUCAS, Persis	181	LUCE, Thomas	212	MACOMBER, John Alfred	160
LUCAS, Pheba	190	LUCES, Patience	66	MACUMBER, Elijah	221
LUCAS, Phebe	59	LUCES, Phebe	111	MACUMBER, Elisha	205
LUCAS, Phebe	116	LUCES, Samuel	66	MAGOUN, Abigail	113
LUCAS, Phebe	150	LUCOS, Benoney	35	MAHOMMAN, Phebe	110
LUCAS, Polly	216	LUCOS, Bethyah	35	MAHOMMAN, Simon	110
LUCAS, Priscilla	59	LUCOS, Elisha	35	MAHOMON, Simon	131
LUCAS, Rebecca	210	LUCOS, Joanna	35	MALLIS, Bathsheba	74
LUCAS, Rhoda	215	LUCOS, John	13	MALLIS, Bathsheba	128
LUCAS, Ruth	171	LUCOS, Joseph	13	MALLISE, Allexander	73
LUCAS, Salley	212	LUCOS, Marey	35	MALLISE, Allexander	126
LUCAS, Samuel	75	LUCOS, Patience	13	MALLISE, Bathsheba	73
LUCAS, Stephen	222	LUCOS, Patience	66	MANCHESTER, Priscilla	74
LUCAS, Sukey	217	LUCOS, Patience	71	MANCHESTER, Priscilla	124
LUCAS, Warren	197	LUCOS, Repentance	35	MANCHESTER, Suzana	71
LUCAS, William	59	LUCOS, Samuel	13	MANCHESTER, Suzanah	129
LUCAS, William	222	LUCOS, Samuel	35	MANCHISTER, Isaac	216
LUCAS, Zephaniah B.	162	LUCOS, Samuel	100	MANDO, Dolphin	195
LUCAS, Zephaniah B.	222	LUCOS, Samuell	66	MANNING, Sarah	181
LUCAS, Zilliah	213	LUCOS, Sarah	35	MANSFEILD, Hanna	70
LUCE, Ann	30	LUCOS, William	13	MANTE, Belcher	203
LUCE, Betsey	212	LUCUST, William	130	MANTER, George	198
LUCE, Crosbe	188	LUMBERT, Bathshaba	70	MANTER, Graften	197
LUCE, Crosbey	30			MANTER, Katharine	196
LUCE, Crosbey	212	**M**		MANTER, Mehitable	206
LUCE, Deborah	30			MANTER, Nancy	222
LUCE, Deborah	191	MACKEE, Isaac	151	MANTER, Prince	200
LUCE, Ebenezer	30	MACKEE, Sarah	151	MANTER, Prince	222
LUCE, Ebenezr.	189	MACKEEL, Abigail	143	MANTER, Rebecca	199
LUCE, Ebenzr.	190	MACKEEL, John	143	MANTER, Salley	215
LUCE, Eliza.	187	MACKEEL, John	172	MANTER, Sarah	198
LUCE, Elizabeth	30	MACKEEL, Susanah	143	MANTER, William	201
LUCE, Elizabeth	187	MACKELROY, Ann	79	MARBLE, Mary	180
LUCE, Ephraim	30	MACKELROY, Ann	116	MARCY, Abigail	154
LUCE, Ephraim	162	MACKEY, Hannah	151	MARCY, Abigail	162
LUCE, Ephraim	183	MACKEY, Isaac	178	MARCY, Charles	154
LUCE, Hannah	30	MACKEY, Martha	151	MARCY, Charles	162
LUCE, Hannah	78	MACKEY, Mary	151	MARCY, Charles	214
LUCE, Hannah	162	MACKEY, Patty	197	MARCY, Charles	218
LUCE, Hannah	183	MACKEY, William	151	MARCY, Charlotte	162
LUCE, Hannah	198	MACKFARLING, Hannah	182	MARCY, Hannah	214
LUCE, Hannah Morton	218	MACKFUN, Elizabeth	107	MARCY, James Warren	162
LUCE, Joanna	206	MACKFUN, Elizabeth	116	MARCY, Mary Ann	162
LUCE, Lydia	206	MACKIE, Andrew	141	MARCY, Stephen	193
LUCE, Ruth	162	MACKIE, Hitty	141	MARCY, Susan Packard	154
LUCE, Salley	205	MACKIE, John Howel	141	MARCY, Susan Packard	162
LUCE, Seth	30	MACOMBER, Augusta Jane	160	MARRENER, Anthoney Coast	129
LUCE, Seth	78	MACOMBER, Betsy Ann	160	MARRIFIELD, Margaret	178
LUCE, Seth	121	MACOMBER, Eleanor	160	MARSH, Thomas	204

VITAL RECORDS OF THE TOWN OF PLYMOUTH

Name	Page	Name	Page	Name	Page
MARSHAL, Bartlett	198	MAY, Anna	26	McKEEL, Abigail	193
MARSHAL, Elizabeth	118	MAY, Anna	182	McKEEL, Susannah	186
MARSHALL, Elizabeth	77	MAY, Anne	70	McLATHLEY, Deborah	200
MARSHALL, John	171	MAY, Bathsheba	184	McLATHLEY, Jedidah	201
MARSHALL, Mary	73	MAY, Bathshua	26	McLATHLEY, Thomas	207
MARSHALL, Mary	78	MAY, Cordelia	160	McLATHLEY, William	187
MARSHALL, Mary	122	MAY, Cordelia Frances	160	McLATHLY, William	187
MARSHALL, Mary	126	MAY, Edward	98	McLAUGHLIN, Freeman Thomas	148
MARSHALL, Priscila	71	MAY, John	26	McLAUGHLIN, Lovisa	148
MARSHALL, Saml.	115	MAY, John	48	McLAUGHLIN, Lovisa Thomas	148
MARSHALL, Samll.	112	MAY, John	70	McLAUGHLIN, Mercy Warren	148
MARSHALL, Samuel	71	MAY, John	113	McLAUGHLIN, Seth	148
MARSHALL, Susanna	213	MAY, John	116	McLAUGHLIN, Thomas	148
MARSHALL, Sussannah	112	MAY, John	190	MEGOUNDS, Edward	197
MARSHEL, Elizabeth	193	MAY, Mary	48	MEHURIN, -----	202
MARSHELL, Bartlett	167	MAY, Mary	124	MEHURIN, Josiah	202
MARSHELL, Bartlett	189	MAY, Nicolos	100	MELECK, John	203
MARSHELL, Priscilla	188	MAY, Sarah	48	MENDAL, Ellis	198
MARSHELL, Ruth	167	MAY, Sarah	195	MENDAL, Jabez	111
MARSHELL, Ruth	203	MAY, Thomas	160	MENDAL, John	193
MARSHELL, Samuel	167	MAYFIELD, Thomas	188	MENDAL, Maria	111
MARSHELL, Susannah	183	MAYHEW, Anna	138	MENDAL, Phebe	193
MARSTON, Elize	218	MAYHEW, Anna	186	MENDAL, Samuell	55
MARSTON, Luca	183	MAYHEW, Bethyah	69	MENDALL, Jabez	55
MARSTON, Nimphas	193	MAYHEW, Betty	138	MENDALL, Jabez	117
MARSTON, Patience	171	MAYHEW, Elizabeth	138	MENDALL, Mary	111
MARTEN, Stephen	188	MAYHEW, Lucy	138	MENDALL, Meriah	55
MARTIN, Eleazer	130	MAYHEW, Mary	78	MENDALL, Ruth	183
MARTIN, John Charles	198	MAYHEW, Mary	138	MENDALL, Zacheus	111
MASHALL, ----- (male)	52	MAYHEW, Sarah	138	MENDALL, Zacheus	113
MASHALL, Elizabeth	52	MAYHEW, Sarah	185	MERIFEILD, Francis	117
MASHALL, John	52	MAYHEW, Tho	45	MERIFIELD, Content	75
MASHALL, Mary	52	MAYHEW, Thomas	78	MERIFIELD, Francis	75
MASHALL, Pricila	52	MAYHEW, Thomas	121	MEROP, John Michael	200
MASHALL, Samuel	52	MAYHEW, Thomas	138	MEROP, John Michael	201
MASON, Hannah	175	MAYHEW, William	138	MERREY, Ralph	188
MASON, Lydia	158	MAYNARD, Solomon	210	MERRICK, Prissilla	118
MASON, Lydia	199	MAYO, Daniel	196	MERRYFIELD, Content	104
MASON, Polley	202	MAYO, Nathaniel	212	MERRYFIELD, Content	109
MASON, Polly	158	MAYO, Thomas	210	MEVAS, John	202
MASON, Stevens	158	McCABE, Bridget	86	MICHEL, Mary	26
MASON, Stevens	181	McCARTER, Henry	217	MICHEL, Seth	26
MASON, Susanna	158	McCARTER, Polley	207	MICHELL, Elizabeth	26
MASTON, Elizabeth	172	McCARTER, Salley	210	MICHELL, Isaac	26
MATTHEWS, Thomas	174	McCARTER, Sally	204	MICHELL, Jacob	26
MAXIM, David	222	McFARLING, Abigail	188	MICHELL, Jacob	67
MAXIM, Ezra	214	McFARLING, Mary	182	MICHELL, Lidia	26
MAXIM, Levi	217	McFERSON, Paul	191	MICHELL, Noah	26
MAY, Abigaiell	70	McHURIN, Nancy	156	MICHELL, Rebeckah	26
MAY, Ann	48	McHURIN, Seth	156	MICHELL, Rebekah	26
MAY, Ann	176	McHURIN, Susan Maria	156	MICHELL, Rebekah	67

MICHELL, Sarah	26	MORDO, John	65	MORREY, Mercy	144
MICHELL, Suzanah	26	MORDO, Lidia	65	MORREY, Mercy	183
MILK, Mary	172	MORDO, Robert	45	MORREY, Rebecca	147
MILLAR, Deborah	69	MORDO, Ruth	45	MORREY, Rebecca	213
MILLER, Edward	218	MORDOCH, John	56	MORREY, Salley	206
MILLER, Stephen (Coll.)	178	MORDOCH, John	71	MORREY, Sarah	109
MILLIGEN, William	190	MORDOCH, Joseph	56	MORREY, Sarah	144
MINGO, Rosanna	195	MORDOCH, Phebe	56	MORREY, Sarah	169
MIRICK, Susanna	205	MORDOCH, Phebe	71	MORREY, Sarah	190
MITCHEL, Alce	42	MORDOW, James	11	MORREY, Sarah	217
MITCHEL, Bathshaba	70	MORDOW, John	11	MORREY, Silas	147
MITCHEL, Bathsheba	42	MORDOW, John	129	MORREY, Silas	194
MITCHEL, Bathshua	42	MORDOW, Jonat	11	MORREY, Silvanus	144
MITCHEL, Benjamin	42	MORDOW, Lidiah	11	MORREY, Sylvanus	198
MITCHEL, Hanna	42	MORDOW, Robert	11	MORREY, William	169
MITCHEL, John	42	MORDOW, Thomas	11	MORREY, William	214
MITCHEL, John	198	MOREY, Cornelus	213	MORRIS, James	137
MITCHEL, Joseph	42	MOREY, Deborah	220	MORRIS, John	137
MITCHEL, Joseph	70	MOREY, Elisha	88	MORRIS, Mary	137
MITCHEL, Martha	42	MOREY, Ellis	222	MORRIS, Patrick	137
MITCHEL, Mary	42	MOREY, Hannah	88	MORRIS, Patrick	176
MITCHEL, Mary	194	MOREY, Ichabod	221	MORS, Abigail	23
MITCHEL, Nancey	198	MOREY, Mary	88	MORS, Edward	23
MITCHEL, Rebecca	200	MOREY, Mary	100	MORS, Eliazebeth	23
MITCHEL, Ruth	42	MOREY, Meriah	111	MORS, Eliazebeth	67
MITCHEL, Sarah	42	MOREY, Meriah	129	MORS, Elizabeth	23
MITCHEL, Susaner	130	MOREY, Philemon	88	MORS, Joseph	23
MITCHEL, Thomas	171	MOREY, Sarah	144	MORS, Joshua	23
MITCHELL, Allice	70	MORIE, Anna	212	MORS, Joshua	67
MITCHELL, Betty	175	MORONG, John	199	MORS, Newberrey	23
MITCHELL, Ebenezer	150	MORREY, Cornelius	106	MORS, Theodoros	23
MITCHELL, Ebenezer	201	MORREY, Cornelius	109	MORSE, Edward	207
MITCHELL, Edward	70	MORREY, Cornelius	144	MORSE, Isaac	181
MITCHELL, Elizabeth	176	MORREY, Cornelus	169	MORSE, Isaac	198
MITCHELL, Elizabeth	198	MORREY, Cornelus	185	MORSE, Melatiah	196
MITCHELL, Harriot	218	MORREY, Cornelus	193	MORSE, Noah	207
MITCHELL, James	150	MORREY, Elijah	144	MORTON, ----- (Decon)	57
MITCHELL, Joseph	150	MORREY, Elijah	147	MORTON, ----- (female)	40
MITCHELL, Joseph	175	MORREY, Elijah	169	MORTON, ----- (female)	41
MITCHELL, Mary	150	MORREY, Elijah	178	MORTON, ----- (female)	43
MITCHELL, Priscilla	200	MORREY, Elijah	206	MORTON, ----- (male)	41
MITCHELL, Thomas	171	MORREY, Eunice	213	MORTON, ----- (male)	62
MITCHELL, Thomas	173	MORREY, Jerusha	109	MORTON, ----- (male)	159
MOORE, John	73	MORREY, Jerusha	169	MORTON, Abigail	52
MOORE, John	126	MORREY, Jerusha	215	MORTON, Abigail	78
MOORE, Margaret	109	MORREY, John	106	MORTON, Abigail	108
MOORE, Margaret	116	MORREY, John	109	MORTON, Abigail	112
MOORE, Mary	73	MORREY, Josiah	144	MORTON, Abigail	117
MOORE, Susan	221	MORREY, Josiah	169	MORTON, Abigail	122
MORDO, Jennet	45	MORREY, Marcy	111	MORTON, Abigail	132
MORDO, John	45	MORREY, Marcy	116	MORTON, Abigail	194

VITAL RECORDS OF THE TOWN OF PLYMOUTH

MORTON, Abigaill	72	MORTON, Deborah	73	MORTON, Ephraim	61
MORTON, Abigal	43	MORTON, Deborah	75	MORTON, Ephraim	62
MORTON, Abigal	57	MORTON, Deborah	125	MORTON, Ephraim	98
MORTON, Abigiel	57	MORTON, Deborah	221	MORTON, Ephraim	150
MORTON, Abner	52	MORTON, Ebenazar	14	MORTON, Ephraim	159
MORTON, Amasa	102	MORTON, Ebenazar	29	MORTON, Ephraim	201
MORTON, Amasa	195	MORTON, Ebenazar	71	MORTON, Ephraim	206
MORTON, Amasa	220	MORTON, Ebenazar	129	MORTON, Ephraim	208
MORTON, Ambros	64	MORTON, Ebenezar	46	MORTON, Ephraim (Capt.)	43
MORTON, Andrew	133	MORTON, Ebenezur	11	MORTON, Ephraim (Capt.)	70
MORTON, Ann	98	MORTON, Edmond	46	MORTON, Ephraim (Capt.)	101
MORTON, Anna	90	MORTON, Edward	159	MORTON, Ephraim (Left.)	66
MORTON, Anna	178	MORTON, Edward	190	MORTON, Ephraim (Left.)	98
MORTON, Anne	71	MORTON, Edward	212	MORTON, Eunice	207
MORTON, Azubah	167	MORTON, Eleazer	27	MORTON, Eunice	212
MORTON, Barnaba	45	MORTON, Eleazer	58	MORTON, Experience	102
MORTON, Barneby	61	MORTON, Eleazer	64	MORTON, Experience	111
MORTON, Barneby	201	MORTON, Eleazer	73	MORTON, Experience	207
MORTON, Bartlett	46	MORTON, Eleazer	188	MORTON, Ezekel	41
MORTON, Bathsheba	65	MORTON, Elisha	29	MORTON, Ezekiel	52
MORTON, Bathshua	112	MORTON, Elisha	61	MORTON, Ezekiel	108
MORTON, Bathshua	114	MORTON, Elisha	62	MORTON, Ezekiel	117
MORTON, Benja.	104	MORTON, Elisha	153	MORTON, Ezekiel	188
MORTON, Benjamin	29	MORTON, Elisha	176	MORTON, Ezra	29
MORTON, Benjamin	44	MORTON, Elisha	198	MORTON, Ezra	199
MORTON, Benjamin	45	MORTON, Eliza.	107	MORTON, Freeman	208
MORTON, Benjamin	46	MORTON, Eliza.	191	MORTON, George	27
MORTON, Benjamin	61	MORTON, Elizabeth	29	MORTON, George	37
MORTON, Benjamin	128	MORTON, Elizabeth	37	MORTON, George	47
MORTON, Benjamin	194	MORTON, Elizabeth	41	MORTON, George	70
MORTON, Betsey	152	MORTON, Elizabeth	46	MORTON, George	96
MORTON, Betsey	209	MORTON, Elizabeth	58	MORTON, George	133
MORTON, Betsey	213	MORTON, Elizabeth	62	MORTON, George	204
MORTON, Betty	59	MORTON, Elizabeth	70	MORTON, Hanah	46
MORTON, Betty	62	MORTON, Elizabeth	73	MORTON, Hanna	41
MORTON, Caleb	194	MORTON, Elizabeth	102	MORTON, Hannah	11
MORTON, Caleb	203	MORTON, Elizabeth	106	MORTON, Hannah	14
MORTON, Caroline	153	MORTON, Elizabeth	150	MORTON, Hannah	29
MORTON, Cary Harris	133	MORTON, Elizabeth	153	MORTON, Hannah	37
MORTON, Cary Harris	202	MORTON, Elizabeth	187	MORTON, Hannah	43
MORTON, Charles	46	MORTON, Elizabeth	193	MORTON, Hannah	45
MORTON, Charles	77	MORTON, Elizabeth	204	MORTON, Hannah	52
MORTON, Charles	119	MORTON, Elizabeth Cushman	167	MORTON, Hannah	57
MORTON, Cornelius	118	MORTON, Elkanah	29	MORTON, Hannah	61
MORTON, Curnelios	29	MORTON, Elkanah	62	MORTON, Hannah	65
MORTON, David	40	MORTON, Elkanah	73	MORTON, Hannah	67
MORTON, David	109	MORTON, Elkanah	130	MORTON, Hannah	73
MORTON, David	121	MORTON, Ephraim	11	MORTON, Hannah	75
MORTON, David	186	MORTON, Ephraim	29	MORTON, Hannah	77
MORTON, Deborah	14	MORTON, Ephraim	37	MORTON, Hannah	78
MORTON, Deborah	64	MORTON, Ephraim	43	MORTON, Hannah	117

VITAL RECORDS OF THE TOWN OF PLYMOUTH

Name	Page	Name	Page	Name	Page
MORTON, Hannah	118	MORTON, John	41	MORTON, Lydia	61
MORTON, Hannah	121	MORTON, John	44	MORTON, Lydia	73
MORTON, Hannah	128	MORTON, John	46	MORTON, Lydia	106
MORTON, Hannah	130	MORTON, John	66	MORTON, Lydia	109
MORTON, Hannah	150	MORTON, John	96	MORTON, Lydia	115
MORTON, Hannah	171	MORTON, John	101	MORTON, Lydia	130
MORTON, Hannah	174	MORTON, John L.	212	MORTON, Lydia	171
MORTON, Hannah	184	MORTON, John Lemi	217	MORTON, Maletiah	88
MORTON, Hannah	189	MORTON, Jonathan	57	MORTON, Manasseh	37
MORTON, Hannah	195	MORTON, Jonathan	112	MORTON, Manasses	29
MORTON, Hannah	207	MORTON, Jonathan	113	MORTON, Marcy	71
MORTON, Hannah	210	MORTON, Jonathan	133	MORTON, Marcy	105
MORTON, Harriet	152	MORTON, Jonothan	40	MORTON, Margaret	193
MORTON, Henery	10	MORTON, Joseph	11	MORTON, Margaret	194
MORTON, Henery	41	MORTON, Joseph	41	MORTON, Mariah	52
MORTON, Henry	152	MORTON, Joseph	70	MORTON, Mariah	75
MORTON, Ichabod	43	MORTON, Joseph	77	MORTON, Mariah	90
MORTON, Ichabod	58	MORTON, Joseph	90	MORTON, Marsey	70
MORTON, Ichabod	150	MORTON, Joseph	118	MORTON, Martha	29
MORTON, Ichabod	159	MORTON, Joseph	121	MORTON, Martha	44
MORTON, Ichabod	174	MORTON, Josiah	10	MORTON, Martha	65
MORTON, Ichabod	195	MORTON, Josiah	40	MORTON, Martha	67
MORTON, Ichabod	220	MORTON, Josiah	41	MORTON, Martha	112
MORTON, Isaac	52	MORTON, Josiah	44	MORTON, Martha	115
MORTON, Isaac	57	MORTON, Josiah	66	MORTON, Martha	133
MORTON, Isaac	112	MORTON, Josiah	70	MORTON, Martha	188
MORTON, Isaac	113	MORTON, Josiah	88	MORTON, Mary	14
MORTON, Isaac	181	MORTON, Josiah	98	MORTON, Mary	29
MORTON, Jacob	214	MORTON, Josiah	102	MORTON, Mary	38
MORTON, James	40	MORTON, Josiah	111	MORTON, Mary	41
MORTON, James	118	MORTON, Josiah	122	MORTON, Mary	44
MORTON, James	132	MORTON, Josiah	125	MORTON, Mary	46
MORTON, James	152	MORTON, Josiah	190	MORTON, Mary	47
MORTON, James	217	MORTON, Josiah	205	MORTON, Mary	52
MORTON, Jane	207	MORTON, Josiah	206	MORTON, Mary	66
MORTON, Jerusha	27	MORTON, Lazarus	62	MORTON, Mary	69
MORTON, Jerusha	112	MORTON, Lazarus	204	MORTON, Mary	70
MORTON, Jerusha	183	MORTON, Lemuel	29	MORTON, Mary	77
MORTON, Jesse	133	MORTON, Lemuel	141	MORTON, Mary	79
MORTON, Joanna	37	MORTON, Lemuel	167	MORTON, Mary	86
MORTON, Joanna	67	MORTON, Lemuel	193	MORTON, Mary	101
MORTON, Joannah	14	MORTON, Lemuel	197	MORTON, Mary	107
MORTON, Joannah	66	MORTON, Lemuel	217	MORTON, Mary	111
MORTON, Job	29	MORTON, Lemuell	29	MORTON, Mary	112
MORTON, Job	46	MORTON, Levi	214	MORTON, Mary	115
MORTON, Job	112	MORTON, Lewis	215	MORTON, Mary	116
MORTON, Job	113	MORTON, Lidiah	29	MORTON, Mary	125
MORTON, Job	197	MORTON, Lucy	202	MORTON, Mary	128
MORTON, John	11	MORTON, Lucy	204	MORTON, Mary	131
MORTON, John	14	MORTON, Lucy	217	MORTON, Mary	132
MORTON, John	40	MORTON, Lydia	45	MORTON, Mary	133

MORTON, Mary	141	MORTON, Peres	90	MORTON, Ruth	122
MORTON, Mary	178	MORTON, Persis	14	MORTON, Ruth	183
MORTON, Mary	181	MORTON, Phebe	14	MORTON, Ruth	204
MORTON, Mary	182	MORTON, Phebe	62	MORTON, Samll.	45
MORTON, Mary	199	MORTON, Phebe	71	MORTON, Samll.	113
MORTON, Mary	215	MORTON, Phebe	96	MORTON, Samuel	29
MORTON, Mary Ellis	167	MORTON, Phebe	129	MORTON, Samuel	61
MORTON, Melatiah	44	MORTON, Polley	205	MORTON, Samuel	73
MORTON, Mercy	150	MORTON, Polley	214	MORTON, Samuel	130
MORTON, Mercy	152	MORTON, Polly	207	MORTON, Samuel	185
MORTON, Mercy	190	MORTON, Priscilla	195	MORTON, Samuel	195
MORTON, Mercy	191	MORTON, Priscilla	199	MORTON, Samuell	45
MORTON, Mercy S.	156	MORTON, Priscille	45	MORTON, Samuell	112
MORTON, Meriah	59	MORTON, Rebca	71	MORTON, Sarah	27
MORTON, Meriah	112	MORTON, Rebecaa	70	MORTON, Sarah	29
MORTON, Meriah	117	MORTON, Rebecca	27	MORTON, Sarah	43
MORTON, Meriah	189	MORTON, Rebecca	47	MORTON, Sarah	44
MORTON, Nahaniel	124	MORTON, Rebecca	50	MORTON, Sarah	45
MORTON, Nancy	167	MORTON, Rebecca	58	MORTON, Sarah	52
MORTON, Nathanel	129	MORTON, Rebecca	59	MORTON, Sarah	61
MORTON, Nathaniel	29	MORTON, Rebecca	90	MORTON, Sarah	74
MORTON, Nathaniel	38	MORTON, Rebecca	194	MORTON, Sarah	75
MORTON, Nathaniel	58	MORTON, Rebecca	200	MORTON, Sarah	102
MORTON, Nathaniel	59	MORTON, Rebecca	205	MORTON, Sarah	117
MORTON, Nathaniel	64	MORTON, Rebecca	218	MORTON, Sarah	127
MORTON, Nathaniel	71	MORTON, Rebeccah	125	MORTON, Sarah	159
MORTON, Nathaniel	86	MORTON, Rebeckah	37	MORTON, Sarah	188
MORTON, Nathaniel	90	MORTON, Rebeckah	45	MORTON, Sarah	190
MORTON, Nathaniel	96	MORTON, Rebeckah	59	MORTON, Sarah	197
MORTON, Nathaniel	111	MORTON, Rebeckah	96	MORTON, Sarah	198
MORTON, Nathaniel	121	MORTON, Rebeckah	109	MORTON, Sarah	213
MORTON, Nathaniel	128	MORTON, Rebeckah	112	MORTON, Seth	44
MORTON, Nathaniel	133	MORTON, Rebeckah	128	MORTON, Seth	88
MORTON, Nathaniel	141	MORTON, Rebeckah	133	MORTON, Seth	150
MORTON, Nathaniel	167	MORTON, Rebeckah	186	MORTON, Seth	152
MORTON, Nathaniel	188	MORTON, Rebeckah	190	MORTON, Seth	173
MORTON, Nathaniel	214	MORTON, Rebeckah	191	MORTON, Seth	177
MORTON, Nathaniel (Leftenant)	99	MORTON, Rebekah	47	MORTON, Seth	200
MORTON, Nathaniel (Lieut.)	69	MORTON, Reliance	40	MORTON, Silas	29
MORTON, Nathl.	59	MORTON, Reliance	44	MORTON, Silas	46
MORTON, Nathl.	104	MORTON, Reliance	101	MORTON, Silas	112
MORTON, Nathl.	131	MORTON, Roas	96	MORTON, Silas	115
MORTON, Nathll.	90	MORTON, Ruth	37	MORTON, Silvanus	57
MORTON, Nathll.	116	MORTON, Ruth	41	MORTON, Silvanus	104
MORTON, Nathll.	117	MORTON, Ruth	45	MORTON, Silvanus	128
MORTON, Olever	29	MORTON, Ruth	57	MORTON, Silvanus	132
MORTON, Osborn	159	MORTON, Ruth	67	MORTON, Silvanus	183
MORTON, Osborn	191	MORTON, Ruth	78	MORTON, Simeon	102
MORTON, Patience	46	MORTON, Ruth	102	MORTON, Solomon	46
MORTON, Patience	67	MORTON, Ruth	111	MORTON, Susannah	201
MORTON, Patty	222	MORTON, Ruth	112	MORTON, Suzanna	43

MORTON, Suzannah	10	MORTTON, Nathaniel	32	MURDOCH, Thomas	77	
MORTON, Suzannah	66	MORTTON, Rebekah	32	MURDOCH, Thomas	120	
MORTON, Suzannah	70	MORY, ----- (female)	88	MURFEE, James	182	
MORTON, Tabor	133	MORY, Abigal	88	MUXSOM, Jemimah	212	
MORTON, Thomas	29	MORY, Benjamin	18	MUXSOM, Jesse	201	
MORTON, Thomas	37	MORY, Benjamin	50	MUXSOM, Joseph	214	
MORTON, Thomas	57	MORY, Curnelios	18	MUXSOM, Joseph	217	
MORTON, Thomas	65	MORY, Elizabeth	85	MUXSOM, Thomas	212	
MORTON, Thomas	67	MORY, Hannah	18	MUXSON, Lucinda	211	
MORTON, Thomas	72	MORY, Hannah	66	MUXSON, Reubin	207	
MORTON, Thomas	73	MORY, John	50			
MORTON, Thomas	96	MORY, Jonathan	18	**N**		
MORTON, Thomas	98	MORY, Jonathan	66			
MORTON, Thomas	102	MORY, Jonathan	85	NASH, Bridget	173	
MORTON, Thomas	126	MORY, Jonathan	98	NASH, Gyles	125	
MORTON, Thomas	130	MORY, Jonathan	100	NASH, Remembrance	119	
MORTON, Thomas	131	MORY, Jonathan	128	NASH, Sarah	105	
MORTON, Thomas	133	MORY, Jonathan (Left.)	99	NASH, Sarah	107	
MORTON, Thomas	188	MORY, Josep	18	NED, Esther Lawrance	120	
MORTON, Thomas	191	MORY, Joseph	88	NED, Jo Titus	120	
MORTON, Thomas	205	MORY, Joseph	117	NELLSON, Alathea	102	
MORTON, Timothey	29	MORY, Maria	18	NELLSON, Bathsheba	214	
MORTON, Timothy	37	MORY, Marsy	50	NELLSON, Betsey	197	
MORTON, Timothy	46	MORY, Mary	18	NELLSON, Betty	102	
MORTON, Timothy	70	MORY, Mary	50	NELLSON, Cintha	217	
MORTON, Timothy	101	MORY, Mary	77	NELLSON, Eben.	195	
MORTON, Timothy	120	MORY, Mary	88	NELLSON, Ebenezer	129	
MORTON, William	27	MORY, Mary	98	NELLSON, Ebenezr.	214	
MORTON, William	47	MORY, Mary	120	NELLSON, Hannah	172	
MORTON, William	96	MORY, Meriah	50	NELLSON, Hezekiah	195	
MORTON, William	102	MORY, Moriah	121	NELLSON, Jacob Warren	102	
MORTON, William	107	MORY, Relyance	18	NELLSON, John	189	
MORTON, William	133	MORY, Thankful	71	NELLSON, John	209	
MORTON, William	152	MORY, Thankfull	18	NELLSON, Joseph Warren	198	
MORTON, William	194	MORY, Thankfull	50	NELLSON, Lemuel	202	
MORTON, William	195	MORY, Thomas	85	NELLSON, Lucy	205	
MORTON, William	199	MOSES, David	202	NELLSON, Patiance	102	
MORTON, William	206	MOSES, Sarah	107	NELLSON, Patience	188	
MORTON, Wm.	105	MOSES, Sarah	207	NELLSON, Polley	213	
MORTON, Zacheas	46	MOSES, Simon	105	NELLSON, Priscilla	102	
MORTON, Zacheus	181	MOSES, Simon	107	NELLSON, Priscilla	199	
MORTON, Zeffaniah	29	MOURARY, James	221	NELLSON, Ruth	129	
MORTON, Zeffaniah	47	MOYSES, John	97	NELLSON, Samuel	195	
MORTON, Zephaniah	27	MURDOCH, Elizabeth	77	NELLSON, Sarah	102	
MORTON, Zephaniah	112	MURDOCH, Elizabeth	104	NELLSON, Thomas	197	
MORTON, Zephaniah	113	MURDOCH, Elizabeth	171	NELLSON, William	198	
MORTON, Zepheniah	186	MURDOCH, John	77	NELSON, Abigail	140	
MORTON, Zilpah	199	MURDOCH, John	125	NELSON, Alathea	102	
MORTON, Zilph	150	MURDOCH, John	172	NELSON, Bathsbaba	49	
MORTTON, Ann	32	MURDOCH, Phebe	78	NELSON, Bathsheba	120	
MORTTON, Eliazer	32	MURDOCH, Phebe	121	NELSON, Bathshebe	69	

NELSON, Bathshebeth	78	NELSON, Sarah	77	NICOLSON, Carroline	163
NELSON, Charles	140	NELSON, Sarah	118	NICOLSON, Catherine	178
NELSON, Ebenezer	49	NELSON, Thomas	86	NICOLSON, Daniel	163
NELSON, Ebenezer	131	NERO, Elizabeth	185	NICOLSON, Eliza.	163
NELSON, Elisha	140	NESON, Bathsheba	49	NICOLSON, Hannah	163
NELSON, Elizabeth	102	NEWBERRY, James	186	NICOLSON, Hannah	199
NELSON, Elizabeth	107	NEWBURY, James	165	NICOLSON, Hannah Otis	163
NELSON, George William	140	NEWBURY, Lemuel	165	NICOLSON, Hannah Otis	220
NELSON, Hannah	49	NEWBURY, Susannah	165	NICOLSON, James	163
NELSON, Hannah	69	NEWCOM, Margaret	173	NICOLSON, Lucy	163
NELSON, Hannah	73	NEWCOMB, Hannah	43	NICOLSON, Margaret	109
NELSON, Hannah	86	NEWCOMB, Hannah	106	NICOLSON, Nancey	163
NELSON, Hannah	126	NEWCOMB, Joseph	43	NICOLSON, Polley	163
NELSON, Hannah Thomas	140	NEWCOMB, Joshua	43	NICOLSON, Polley	204
NELSON, Harriet	140	NEWCOMB, Joshua	122	NICOLSON, Samuel	163
NELSON, Jeann	65	NEWCOMB, Matha	201	NICOLSON, Sarah	163
NELSON, Joanah	15	NEWCOMB, Ruth	43	NICOLSON, Sarah	198
NELSON, John	15	NEWCOMB, Sarah	43	NICOLSON, Seth	197
NELSON, John	49	NEWPORT, Sarah	197	NICOLSON, Thomas	102
NELSON, John	67	NEY, Zerviah	121	NICOLSON, Thomas	163
NELSON, John	86	NICHOLS, Howard	222	NICOLSON, Thomas (Capt.)	196
NELSON, John	98	NICHOLS, John	222	NIGHTINGALE, Ellis	220
NELSON, John	125	NICHOLSON, Elizabeth	102	NIGHTINGILL, William	218
NELSON, Liddiah	15	NICHOLSON, Elizabeth	186	NILES, Nathaniel	195
NELSON, Lidiah	15	NICHOLSON, Hannah	102	NORCUT, Ebenezer	21
NELSON, Lidiah	70	NICHOLSON, James	102	NORCUT, Elizabeth	21
NELSON, Lidiah	98	NICHOLSON, Lydia	161	NORCUT, Salley	209
NELSON, Lucy	140	NICHOLSON, Magaret	89	NORCUT, Susanna	21
NELSON, Lydia	86	NICHOLSON, Margaret	105	NORCUTT, Anna	70
NELSON, Mahittable	67	NICHOLSON, Margaret	107	NORRICE, Abigal	56
NELSON, Mary	86	NICHOLSON, Seth	89	NORRICE, Benjamin	56
NELSON, Mary Lothrop	222	NICHOLSON, Seth	109	NORRICE, Elizabeth	56
NELSON, Mehitabel	8	NICHOLSON, Seth	116	NORRICE, Mary	56
NELSON, Patience	15	NICHOLSON, Seth	161	NORRICE, Olliver	56
NELSON, Patience	49	NICHOLSON, Seth	181	NORRICE, Samuel	56
NELSON, Patience	67	NICHOLSON, Thomas	185	NORRICE, Samuel	130
NELSON, Patience	100	NICKERSON, Jane	214	NORRICE, Sarah	56
NELSON, Saml.	102	NICKERSON, John	217	NORRIS, Benjamin	207
NELSON, Saml. Nicholls	107	NICKERSON, Lydia	218	NORRIS, Dilley	210
NELSON, Saml. Nicholls	116	NICKOLSON, Lydia	188	NORRIS, John	117
NELSON, Saml. Nichols	102	NICOLDS, Bathshebe	69	NORRIS, Marjery	127
NELSON, Samuel	15	NICOLS, Edward	214	NORRIS, Mercy	197
NELSON, Samuel	49	NICOLS, Eleazr.	195	NORRIS, Phineas	222
NELSON, Samuel	69	NICOLS, Hanah	71	NORRIS, Polley	201
NELSON, Samuel	71	NICOLS, John	214	NORRIS, Samuel	186
NELSON, Samuel	86	NICOLS, John Mendal	208	NORRIS, Sarah	120
NELSON, Samuel Nicols	49	NICOLS, Otis	215	NORTON, Salley	206
NELSON, Sarah	15	NICOLS, Polley	206	NOYSE, Sarah	118
NELSON, Sarah	49	NICOLS, Price	71	NUMMOCK, Sarah	106
NELSON, Sarah	52	NICOLS, Salley	216	NUMMOCK, Sarah	107
NELSON, Sarah	71	NICOLSON, Caroline	218	NUMMUCK, Ame	191

VITAL RECORDS OF THE TOWN OF PLYMOUTH

Name	Page
NUMMUCK, Moses	78
NUMMUCK, Moses	121
NUMMUCK, Sarah	78
NUMUCK, Ama	193
NUTE, Samuel	206
NUTING, Richard	164
NUTTING, Benjamin	164
NUTTING, John	164
NUTTING, Joseph	164
NUTTING, Mehitable	164
NUTTING, Richard	164
NYE, Abigail	198
NYE, Abraham Williams	219
NYE, Ebenezr.	189
NYE, Elias	194
NYE, Elisha	190
NYE, Lucy	213
NYE, Mercy	200
NYE, Nathaniel	216
NYE, Polley	203
NYE, Seth F.	214
NYE, William	207

O

Name	Page
OBRIAN, Joseph	202
OLDAM, John	222
OLDHAM, Thomas	222
OLEVER, Jonathan	181
OLEVER, Mehetable	188
OLEVER, Peter	217
OLIVE, Elizabeth	104
OLNEY, Anthoney	215
OLNEY, Zaben	218
ORKET, Hannah	69
OSBERN, Obediah	172
OTIS, Barnabas	163
OTIS, Barnabas	191
OTIS, Betsey	144
OTIS, Grace Hayman	200
OTIS, Hannah	156
OTIS, Hannah	196
OTIS, Henry	163
OTIS, John	156
OTIS, John	180
OTIS, Marcy	170
OTIS, Mary	163
OTIS, Temperance	194
OTIS, Temporance	156
OTIS, Vilot	193
OZMENT, William	173

P

Name	Page
PACKARD, Abigail	132
PACKARD, Abigail	206
PACKARD, Abigail	214
PACKARD, Alpheus	215
PACKARD, Elijah (Rev.)	110
PACKARD, Elijah (Rev.)	128
PACKARD, Elijah (Rev.)	131
PACKARD, Elijah (Rev.)	132
PACKARD, Mary	128
PACKARD, Mary	132
PACKARD, Zadock	204
PACKARD, Zibeon	215
PACKER, Benjamin	220
PADDOCK, Ephrm.	123
PADDOCK, Jane	78
PADDOCK, Jane	122
PADDOCK, Jenne	183
PADDOCK, Joanna	78
PADDOCK, Joanna	121
PADDOCK, Priscilla	126
PADDUCK, Ichabod	70
PADDUCK, Joannah	70
PAIN, David	209
PAIN, Davis	209
PAIN, John Samson	214
PAIN, Mary	198
PAIN, Mehitable	204
PAIN, Seth	182
PAIN, Stephen	202
PAINE, Sarah	196
PAINE, Stephen	195
PALMER, John	124
PALMER, Sarah	188
PALMER, Yetmercy	124
PAPILLON, Mary	90
PAPPOON, Daniel	175
PARKER, Annis	69
PARKER, Jonathan	111
PARKER, Jonathan (Rev.)	114
PARKER, Lydia	111
PARKER, Melinde	215
PARKER, Polycarpus	222
PARKER, Seth	188
PARKER, Thomas	207
PARSONS, Boston	205
PARSONS, Esther	207
PARSONS, Esther Phillips	207
PARSONS, Susannah	190
PATE, John	205
PATE, Levi	194
PATE, Margaret	197
PATE, Sylvanus	194
PATEE, Ann	143
PATEE, Ephraim	143
PATEE, John	118
PATEE, John	143
PATEE, John	173
PATEE, Levi	143
PATEE, Margaret	143
PATEE, Silvenus	143
PATISON, Susannah	111
PATISON, Thomas	111
PATTISON, Thomas	123
PATY, Deborah	206
PATY, Elizabeth	209
PATY, Ephraim	206
PATY, Ephraim	222
PATY, Hannah	199
PATY, Maria	222
PATY, Nancy	205
PATY, Seth	210
PATY, Silva	215
PATY, Thomas	199
PATYEE, Hannah	143
PATYEE, Thomas	143
PAUL, Mary	175
PAYNE, Deborah	168
PAYNE, Hannah Sherman	168
PAYNE, John S.	168
PAYNE, John Sampson	168
PAYNE, Reuben Church'll	168
PAYNE, Stephen	168
PAYNE, Susan	168
PEACH, Joseph	125
PEACKEN, Lydia	122
PEAK, Daniel	109
PEAK, Daniell	115
PEAK, Rhoda	109
PEARCE, Elezabeth	57
PEARCE, Elizabeth	149
PEARCE, Elizabeth	186
PEARCE, Experience	149
PEARCE, Hannah	57
PEARCE, Hannah	105
PEARCE, Jesse	202
PEARCE, Joseph	57
PEARCE, Joseph	113
PEARCE, Joseph	112
PEARCE, Joseph	129

VITAL RECORDS OF THE TOWN OF PLYMOUTH

PEARCE, Mary	214	PENISS, Noah	121	PETERSON, Joseph	69
PEARCE, Rebeckah	112	PENNIMON, Joseph (Rev.)	185	PETERSON, Lurania	186
PEARCE, Rebeckah	186	PEPIT, Betty	176	PETERSON, Perez	197
PEARCE, Richard	190	PERCE, America	211	PETERSON, Reuben	219
PEARCE, Saml.	149	PERCE, America	217	PETERSON, Sarah	69
PEARCE, Samuel	149	PERCE, Benjamin	204	PETINGELL, Betty	195
PEARCE, Sarah	149	PERCE, Dennis	216	PHILIPS, Rebeca	72
PEARSE, Elizabeth	142	PERCE, Desire	202	PHILIPS, Rebeckah	130
PEARSE, Joseph	142	PERCE, Ignatious	207	PHILIPS, Thomas	130
PEARSE, Rebeckah	142	PERCE, John	207	PHILLIPS, -----	73
PEARSON, Phebe	109	PERCE, Patience Burges	202	PHILLIPS, Bethiah	130
PEARSON, William Bundick	104	PERKINS, Beza	205	PHILLIPS, Bleaney	43
PEARSON, William Bundick	109	PERKINS, George	204	PHILLIPS, Elizabeth	46
PEARSONS, Joannah	218	PERKINS, Gideon	212	PHILLIPS, Hannah	73
PEARSONS, Phebe	212	PERKINS, Joel	207	PHILLIPS, Hannah	74
PEARSONS, Rosannah	213	PERKINS, Joshua	213	PHILLIPS, Hannah	80
PECK, Esther	118	PERKINS, Noah	202	PHILLIPS, Hannah	82
PECK, Mary	185	PERKINS, Sarah	190	PHILLIPS, Hannah	124
PECK, Rhoda	172	PERKINS, Susannah	194	PHILLIPS, John	43
PECKHAM, George	129	PERKINS, Timothey	199	PHILLIPS, John	46
PECKHAM, George	171	PERREY, Elisha	195	PHILLIPS, John	106
PECKHAM, Jerusha	129	PERREY, Henerey	69	PHILLIPS, John	109
PEIRCE, Abraham	8	PERREY, James	193	PHILLIPS, John	178
PEIRCE, Amanda Stephens	168	PERREY, Ledia	71	PHILLIPS, John	189
PEIRCE, Asa	168	PERREY, Mary	69	PHILLIPS, Lamuel	43
PEIRCE, Benjamin	164	PERREY, Ruth	214	PHILLIPS, Lydia	109
PEIRCE, Eliza	168	PERREY, Salathiel	199	PHILLIPS, Margeret	70
PEIRCE, Experience	74	PERREY, Susanna	214	PHILLIPS, Rebecca	204
PEIRCE, Experience	124	PERREY, William	71	PHILLIPS, Rebeckah	43
PEIRCE, Hannah	107	PERRIGO, Robert	104	PHILLIPS, Rebeckah	106
PEIRCE, John	73	PERRY, Abner	84	PHILLIPS, Saml.	46
PEIRCE, John	130	PERRY, Benjamin	84	PHILLIPS, Thomas	43
PEIRCE, Judith	164	PERRY, Daniel	194	PHILLIPS, Timothy	202
PEIRCE, Lucy	164	PERRY, Elisha	126	PHILLIPS, Tompson	73
PEIRCE, Mary	164	PERRY, Joaanah	84	PHILLIPS, Tomson	80
PEIRCE, Melzar	164	PERRY, Jonathan	100	PHILLIPS, Tomson	126
PEIRCE, Mendall	164	PERRY, Joseph	84	PHINNEY, Mary	180
PEIRCE, Rebecah	125	PERRY, Judah	222	PHINNEY, Phebe	109
PEIRCE, Rebecca	73	PERRY, Rhode	217	PIERCE, Branch	212
PEIRCE, Rebeckah	8	PERRY, Susannah	186	PIERCE, Dorcas M.	153
PEIRCE, Rebeckah	75	PERSE, Mary	214	PIERCE, Phineas	153
PEIRCE, Saml.	177	PERSONS, Abia	212	PIGSLEE, Benjamin	203
PEMBERTON, Hephzibah	177	PERSONS, Phebe	190	PIGSLEE, Elizabeth	203
PENES, Mercy	188	PERSONS, William	193	PIGSLEE, Mary	207
PENES, Noah	131	PETER, Amos	188	PIGSLEE, Suke	210
PENIAS, Francis	79	PETERS, Sarah	124	PIGSLEE, Temperance	200
PENIAS, Mary	79	PETERS, Thomas	129	PITSLEY, Mary	209
PENIS, Sarrah	117	PETERSON, Anna	118	PITTS, ----- (female)	42
PENISS, Abigail	78	PETERSON, Charles	212	PITTS, Mary	42
PENISS, Mercy	123	PETERSON, Cynthia	213	PITTS, Mary	79
PENISS, Noah	78	PETERSON, Ichabod	206	PITTS, Thomas	42

VITAL RECORDS OF THE TOWN OF PLYMOUTH

PITTS, Thomas	79	POLDEN, Thomas	201	PRAT, Joshua	171		
PITTS, Thomas	116	POLDEN, William	32	PRAT, Joshua	200		
PIXLY, Temporence	200	POLDEN, William	85	PRAT, Joshua	207		
POAQUENETT, Betty	119	POLDEN, William	144	PRAT, Lydia	140		
POCKNOT, Joshua	131	POLDEN, William	177	PRAT, Mary	21		
POLAND, Elizabeth	72	POLDEN, William	213	PRAT, Pricilla	129		
POLAND, Lidia	32	POLEN, Mary	73	PRAT, Priscilla	129		
POLDEN, Benjamin	32	POLLAND, Eliazebeth	32	PRAT, Ruth	21		
POLDEN, Catharine B.	138	POLLAND, John	32	PRAT, Ruth	140		
POLDEN, Deborah	85	POLLAND, John	32	PRAT, Susanna	121		
POLDEN, Eliza.	182	POLON, Elizabeth	130	PRAT, William	21		
POLDEN, Elizabeth	85	POOL, David Vining	165	PRAT, William Cobb	140		
POLDEN, Elizabeth	144	POOL, John	175	PRATT, ----- (female)	16		
POLDEN, Elizabeth	194	POOL, Lydia	165	PRATT, Abigaiel	130		
POLDEN, Francis	138	POOL, Perez	165	PRATT, Abigail	38		
POLDEN, George	155	POOR, Mary	197	PRATT, Abigaill	72		
POLDEN, George	201	POOR, Michael	186	PRATT, Asenath	195		
POLDEN, Hannah	32	POOR, Sarah	204	PRATT, Benejah	120		
POLDEN, Hannah	75	POPE, Deborah	122	PRATT, Benijah	16		
POLDEN, Hannah	85	POPE, Deborah	195	PRATT, Benijah	98		
POLDEN, Hannah	124	POPE, Elisabeth	123	PRATT, Bennijah	38		
POLDEN, Hannah	144	POPE, Elisha	212	PRATT, Daniel	67		
POLDEN, Harriet Thomas	138	POPE, Elizabeth	69	PRATT, Danniel	69		
POLDEN, James	85	POPE, Eunice	148	PRATT, David	30		
POLDEN, James	144	POPE, Lucy Ann	148	PRATT, Debora	38		
POLDEN, James	177	POPE, Lydia Covington	148	PRATT, Deborah	73		
POLDEN, James	193	POPE, Phebe	186	PRATT, Ebenazar	16		
POLDEN, James	207	POPE, Richard	148	PRATT, Eliazar	30		
POLDEN, Jonathan	85	POPE, Richard Thomas	148	PRATT, Esther	67		
POLDEN, Jonathan	154	POPE, Rufus H.	148	PRATT, Hannah	30		
POLDEN, Jonathan	180	POPE, Thomas	198	PRATT, Hannah	67		
POLDEN, Jonathan	201	POPE, Thomas	200	PRATT, Hannah	129		
POLDEN, Jonathan	202	POPE, William Wallace	148	PRATT, Jane	77		
POLDEN, Lydia	32	PORTER, John	204	PRATT, Jeane	119		
POLDEN, Lydia	77	PORTER, Olever	205	PRATT, Jemima	181		
POLDEN, Lydia	85	POTTER, Levi	112	PRATT, Joannah	16		
POLDEN, Lydia	118	POULDAND, John	68	PRATT, John	16		
POLDEN, Lydia	180	POULDAND, Lidiah	68	PRATT, John	98		
POLDEN, Lydia	198	POWERS, Azbury	222	PRATT, John	130		
POLDEN, Mary	32	POWERS, Samuel	222	PRATT, Joseph	32		
POLDEN, Mary	154	POWIN, Reeckah	129	PRATT, Joseph	68		
POLDEN, Mary	173	PRAAT, Joshua	98	PRATT, Joshua	143		
POLDEN, Rebeckah	85	PRAT, Daniel	128	PRATT, Margaret	16		
POLDEN, Rebeckah	175	PRAT, Daniel	140	PRATT, Margeret	16		
POLDEN, Thankfull	32	PRAT, Daniel	175	PRATT, Martha	32		
POLDEN, Thankfull	106	PRAT, Deborah	130	PRATT, Martha	68		
POLDEN, Thankfull	128	PRAT, Eleazar	67	PRATT, Mary	38		
POLDEN, Thomas	32	PRAT, Esther	128	PRATT, Mary	69		
POLDEN, Thomas	85	PRAT, Hannah	67	PRATT, Mary	71		
POLDEN, Thomas	124	PRAT, Hopefull	140	PRATT, Mary Ann	143		
POLDEN, Thomas	155	PRAT, Joshua	140	PRATT, Mary Ann Goodwin	143		

VITAL RECORDS OF THE TOWN OF PLYMOUTH

PRATT, Mehitabell	66	QUONDA, Cate	195	RANSOM, Hannah	66
PRATT, Mehittable	16	QUOY, Ephraim	123	RANSOM, Hannah	75
PRATT, Patience	16	QUOY, Hanah	123	RANSOM, Hannah	117
PRATT, Patience	126	QUOY, Hannah	79	RANSOM, Joanna	198
PRATT, Pirses	32	QUOY, Hannah	123	RANSOM, Joshua	66
PRATT, Priscilla	71			RANSOM, Joshua	98
PRATT, Priscilla	177	**R**		RANSOM, Lidiah	15
PRATT, Prisilla	38			RANSOM, Lidiah	32
PRATT, Rebeckah	123	RAFE, Deborah	217	RANSOM, Mary	15
PRATT, Samuel	16	RAFE, Joshua	77	RANSOM, Mary	32
PRATT, Sarah	38	RAFE, Joshua	119	RANSOM, Mary	66
PRATT, Sarah	71	RAFE, Nab	77	RANSOM, Mary	98
PRATT, Sarah	130	RALPH, Abigail	116	RANSOM, Rebeckah	128
PRATT, Sarah	181	RAMOND, Barnabas	190	RANSOM, Robert	15
PRATT, Thomas	16	RAMSDEN, Benjamin	30	RANSOM, Robert	32
PRICE, George	186	RAMSDEN, Daniel	30	RANSOM, Robertt	32
PRICE, John	128	RAMSDEN, Hannah	30	RANSOM, Ruth	182
PRICE, Mary	69	RAMSDEN, Joseph	30	RANSOM, Salley	214
PRICE, Sukey	212	RAMSDEN, Samuel	30	RANSOM, Saml.	104
PRIEST, Sewel	209	RAMSDEN, Sarah	30	RANSOM, Samuel	109
PRINCE, Eunice	138	RAND, Samuel	201	RANSOM, Suzannah	66
PRINCE, Hannah	106	RANDAL, Enoch	165	RATHMEL, Simeon	160
PRINCE, James	138	RANDAL, Enoch	195	RAYMOND, Abraham	208
PRINCE, James	191	RANDAL, Lucy	165	RAYMOND, Allen	218
PRINCE, Jane	177	RANDAL, Mercy	165	RAYMOND, Anna	202
PRINCE, Job	129	RANDAL, Phebe	165	RAYMOND, Asa	197
PRINCE, Lydia	138	RANDAL, Phebe	191	RAYMOND, Caleb	193
PRINCE, Lydia	171	RANDAL, William	165	RAYMOND, Caleb	206
PRINCE, Polley	138	RANDAL, William	204	RAYMOND, Calvin	222
PRINCE, Thomas	96	RANDALL, Bethiah	73	RAYMOND, Celia	156
PRINCE, Thomas	138	RANDALL, Doughty	108	RAYMOND, Charles	221
PRISE, Abigail	164	RANDALL, Dowty	123	RAYMOND, Clark	201
PRISE, George	164	RANDALL, Elizabeth	108	RAYMOND, Cordelia Ann	156
PRISE, George	195	RANDALL, Enoch	181	RAYMOND, Deborah	213
PRISE, Jenna	164	RANDALL, Enock	214	RAYMOND, Eliza.	195
PRISE, Sarah	164	RANDALL, John	182	RAYMOND, Ezekiel	190
PRYOR, Jabez	201	RANDALL, William	222	RAYMOND, Ezekiel	210
PULCEFER, Abiel	118	RANDEL, Alce	125	RAYMOND, George	206
PULCIFER, Abiel	85	RANDEL, Elizabeth	118	RAYMOND, Hannah	217
PULCIFER, Abiel	125	RANDEL, Jean	124	RAYMOND, Isaiah	214
PULCIFER, Bethiah	85	RANDELL, Alse	75	RAYMOND, Joseph Newell	156
PULCIFER, Joseph	85	RANSOM, Abigaill	15	RAYMOND, Lydia	201
PULSIFUR, Abiall	75	RANSOM, Ann	15	RAYMOND, Lydia	210
PULSIFUR, Bethiah	75	RANSOM, Anna	32	RAYMOND, Mary	193
PUMROYE, Ebenezr.	198	RANSOM, Benjamin	198	RAYMOND, Melintha	216
PURDY, John	213	RANSOM, Content	109	RAYMOND, Mercy	183
		RANSOM, Deborah	203	RAYMOND, Nathaniel	185
		RANSOM, Eben.	128	RAYMOND, Newell	156
Q		RANSOM, Ebenazar	15	RAYMOND, Perkins	205
QUACOM, Samuel	118	RANSOM, Ebenezer	32	RAYMOND, Salley	206
QUACUM, Phillis	202	RANSOM, Ebenezer	104	RAYMOND, Sarah	197

VITAL RECORDS OF THE TOWN OF PLYMOUTH

RAYMOND, Stephen	194	REED, Richard Williams	163	RICKARD, Bathsheba	65
RAYMOND, Stephen	198	REED, Ruth	169	RICKARD, Bathshebah	188
RAYMOND, Susannah	205	REED, Salley	169	RICKARD, Bathshua	112
RAYMOND, Tabitha	185	REED, Samuel	169	RICKARD, Benjamin	30
READING, Mosses	180	REED, Sarah	207	RICKARD, Benjamin	55
REAVIS, Sarah	130	RENNOLS, Judath	218	RICKARD, Benjamin	65
RECARD, Hannah	15	RENOFF, Charles	190	RICKARD, Bethyah	30
RECARD, Rebekah	15	REVES, Deliverance	69	RICKARD, Deborah	69
RECARD, Samuel	15	REVES, James	69	RICKARD, Desire	123
REDING, ----- (female)	157	REVIS, Ann	75	RICKARD, Eleazer	115
REDING, Bennet	157	REVIS, Ann	117	RICKARD, Eliazar	29
REDING, Bruse	157	REYNOLDS, Elizabeth	116	RICKARD, Elizabeth	71
REDING, Fear	185	REYNOLDS, James	173	RICKARD, Elizabeth	129
REDING, Moses	157	RHODES, Sarah	202	RICKARD, Elkanan	30
REDING, Moses	189	RICH, Ann	85	RICKARD, Ester	10
REDING, Sarah	104	RICH, Anne	179	RICKARD, Esther	100
REDING, Sarah	157	RICH, Ebenezer	85	RICKARD, Giles	29
REED, Benjamin	198	RICH, Eleazer	85	RICKARD, Giles	66
REED, Betsey	169	RICH, Elizabeth	85	RICKARD, Giles	99
REED, Betsey	211	RICH, Elizabeth	104	RICKARD, Hanah	67
REED, Cannadey	207	RICH, Experance	107	RICKARD, Hanah	70
REED, Cannady	218	RICH, Jane	130	RICKARD, Hanh	55
REED, Cordelia Green	163	RICH, Jeremiah (Capt.)	215	RICKARD, Hannah	55
REED, Deborah	78	RICH, John	195	RICKARD, Hannah	66
REED, Deborah	122	RICH, Nathaniel	85	RICKARD, Hannah	69
REED, Eunice	163	RICH, Rebecca	85	RICKARD, Hannah	71
REED, Hannah	214	RICH, Rebeckah	85	RICKARD, Hannah	98
REED, Hannah	215	RICH, Rebeckah	175	RICKARD, Hannah	99
REED, Henry	169	RICH, W.	171	RICKARD, Henery	30
REED, Henry Holmes	163	RICH, Walter	85	RICKARD, Henery	70
REED, Hezekiah B.	149	RICH, Walter	106	RICKARD, James	10
REED, Hezekiah Bryant	169	RICH, Walter	107	RICKARD, James	36
REED, James	169	RICH, Walter	125	RICKARD, James	55
REED, James	196	RICHARDS, John	209	RICKARD, James	71
REED, James	214	RICHERSON, Hannah	208	RICKARD, James	129
REED, Jean	112	RICHMOND, Alpheus	207	RICKARD, Joannah	18
REED, Jean	113	RICHMOND, Calvin	210	RICKARD, John	10
REED, Joanna	197	RICHMOND, Eliab	187	RICKARD, John	18
REED, John	191	RICHMOND, Henry	200	RICKARD, John	36
REED, Joseph S.	222	RICHMOND, Nancey	198	RICKARD, John	55
REED, Lemuel Fish	163	RICHMOND, Penelope	199	RICKARD, John	65
REED, Lemuel Fish	169	RICHMOND, Rhoda	198	RICKARD, John	99
REED, Levi	202	RICHMOND, Salle	214	RICKARD, John	112
REED, Lucy	169	RICHMOND, Sarah	193	RICKARD, John	114
REED, Lucy Ann	163	RICHMOND, Simon	203	RICKARD, John	119
REED, Mary	149	RICHMOND, Zilpah	181	RICKARD, John	183
REED, Mary Freeman	149	RICKARD, Abigaiel	18	RICKARD, John Howland	65
REED, Nathan	198	RICKARD, Abner	201	RICKARD, Joseph	18
REED, Nathan	200	RICKARD, Anselm	200	RICKARD, Joseph	69
REED, Polley	169	RICKARD, Anselm	222	RICKARD, Josiah	29
REED, Polley	214	RICKARD, Azubah Cushman	197	RICKARD, Josiah	30

RICKARD, Josiah	67	RIDER, Abigail	107	RIDER, Elizabeth	15
RICKARD, Juduth	29	RIDER, Abigail	111	RIDER, Elizabeth	49
RICKARD, Lemuel	206	RIDER, Abigail	117	RIDER, Elizabeth	59
RICKARD, Lemuel	219	RIDER, Abigail	136	RIDER, Elizabeth	75
RICKARD, Lidiah	18	RIDER, Abigail	158	RIDER, Elizabeth	111
RICKARD, Lidiah	29	RIDER, Abigal	59	RIDER, Elizabeth	117
RICKARD, Lidiah	69	RIDER, Abigall	57	RIDER, Elizabeth	131
RICKARD, Lothrop	55	RIDER, Amos	59	RIDER, Elizabeth	155
RICKARD, Lydia	210	RIDER, Amos	93	RIDER, Elizabeth	160
RICKARD, Marcy	18	RIDER, Amos	188	RIDER, Elizabeth	181
RICKARD, Marcy	70	RIDER, An	98	RIDER, Esther	214
RICKARD, Margaret	214	RIDER, Ann	45	RIDER, Experience	58
RICKARD, Marsey	70	RIDER, Ann	70	RIDER, Experience	78
RICKARD, Martha	181	RIDER, Anna	71	RIDER, Experience	123
RICKARD, Mary	10	RIDER, Anna	129	RIDER, Ezekel	88
RICKARD, Mary	18	RIDER, Bathsheba	155	RIDER, Ezekiel	77
RICKARD, Mary	30	RIDER, Bathsheba	186	RIDER, Ezekiel	88
RICKARD, Mary	65	RIDER, Benjam	129	RIDER, Ezekiel	89
RICKARD, Mary	70	RIDER, Benjamin	57	RIDER, Ezekiel	119
RICKARD, Mary	99	RIDER, Benjamin	59	RIDER, Ezekiel	156
RICKARD, Mary	104	RIDER, Benjamin	103	RIDER, Ezekiel	158
RICKARD, Mary	191	RIDER, Benjamin	111	RIDER, Ezekiel	186
RICKARD, Mercy	10	RIDER, Benjamin	113	RIDER, Ezekiel	208
RICKARD, Mersey	99	RIDER, Benjamin	185	RIDER, Ezekill	45
RICKARD, Rebecah	29	RIDER, Benjamin	188	RIDER, Ezra	89
RICKARD, Rebeckah	18	RIDER, Benjamine	15	RIDER, Ezra	156
RICKARD, Rebeckah	30	RIDER, Bethiah	133	RIDER, Ezra	156
RICKARD, Rebekah	15	RIDER, Bethiah	177	RIDER, Hallet	143
RICKARD, Rebekah	66	RIDER, Bethiah	186	RIDER, Hannah	15
RICKARD, Rebekah	67	RIDER, Betsey	151	RIDER, Hannah	49
RICKARD, Samuel	30	RIDER, Bettey	103	RIDER, Hannah	57
RICKARD, Samuel	66	RIDER, Bettey	111	RIDER, Hannah	59
RICKARD, Samuel	195	RIDER, Bettey	184	RIDER, Hannah	69
RICKARD, Sarah	29	RIDER, Betty	143	RIDER, Hannah	73
RICKARD, Sarah	36	RIDER, Caleb	58	RIDER, Hannah	78
RICKARD, Sarah	190	RIDER, Caleb	182	RIDER, Hannah	84
RICKARD, Thomas	65	RIDER, Cesiah	45	RIDER, Hannah	98
RICKARD, William	55	RIDER, Charles	49	RIDER, Hannah	109
RICKARD, William	178	RIDER, Charles	57	RIDER, Hannah	111
RICORD, Hannah	70	RIDER, Charles	122	RIDER, Hannah	117
RIDE, Ezekiel	178	RIDER, Charles	186	RIDER, Hannah	119
RIDEINGTON, Mary	212	RIDER, Deborah	84	RIDER, Hannah	126
RIDER, -----	84	RIDER, Deborah	88	RIDER, Hannah	136
RIDER, -----	88	RIDER, Deborah	179	RIDER, Hannah	155
RIDER, ----- (female)	57	RIDER, Desiah	155	RIDER, Hannah	171
RIDER, ----- (female)	136	RIDER, Ebenazar	49	RIDER, Hannah	175
RIDER, ----- (male)	93	RIDER, Ebenezer	73	RIDER, Hannah	177
RIDER, Abigaiel	15	RIDER, Ebenezer	82	RIDER, Henry Cassady	151
RIDER, Abigaiel	71	RIDER, Ebenezer	126	RIDER, Huldah	155
RIDER, Abigaiel	130	RIDER, Ebenezer	172	RIDER, Isaac	58
RIDER, Abigail	104	RIDER, Elezabeth	71	RIDER, Isaac	173

RIDER, James	133	RIDER, Luce	57	RIDER, Pheba	155
RIDER, Jane	178	RIDER, Lucy	181	RIDER, Phebe	49
RIDER, Jean	57	RIDER, Lydia	58	RIDER, Phebe	188
RIDER, Jemima	75	RIDER, Lydia	59	RIDER, Phillippe	79
RIDER, Jemima	117	RIDER, Lydia	82	RIDER, Phillippe	116
RIDER, Jerusha	111	RIDER, Lydia	105	RIDER, Priscilla	103
RIDER, Jerusha	117	RIDER, Lydia	107	RIDER, Priscilla	189
RIDER, Jesse	59	RIDER, Lydia	111	RIDER, Rebecca	57
RIDER, Jesse	103	RIDER, Lydia	156	RIDER, Rebeckah	57
RIDER, Jesse	133	RIDER, Lydia	183	RIDER, Rebeckah	116
RIDER, Jesse	170	RIDER, Lydia	188	RIDER, Rebeckah	184
RIDER, Jo.	9	RIDER, Lydia William	151	RIDER, Ruth	58
RIDER, Joanna	136	RIDER, Margaret	88	RIDER, Ruth	93
RIDER, Job	151	RIDER, Margaret	185	RIDER, Ruth	105
RIDER, Job	155	RIDER, Margarett	89	RIDER, Ruth	106
RIDER, Job	186	RIDER, Margarett	208	RIDER, Ruth	108
RIDER, John	49	RIDER, Margeret	77	RIDER, Ruth	117
RIDER, John	82	RIDER, Margeret	88	RIDER, Sally	151
RIDER, John	98	RIDER, Marsey	70	RIDER, Sally	212
RIDER, John	101	RIDER, Marsy	49	RIDER, Saml.	84
RIDER, John	117	RIDER, Martha	84	RIDER, Samuel	15
RIDER, John	173	RIDER, Mary	15	RIDER, Samuel	45
RIDER, John	176	RIDER, Mary	49	RIDER, Samuel	49
RIDER, Joseph	15	RIDER, Mary	56	RIDER, Samuel	70
RIDER, Joseph	57	RIDER, Mary	58	RIDER, Samuel	72
RIDER, Joseph	70	RIDER, Mary	59	RIDER, Samuel	84
RIDER, Joseph	71	RIDER, Mary	70	RIDER, Samuel	88
RIDER, Joseph	88	RIDER, Mary	71	RIDER, Samuel	98
RIDER, Joseph	106	RIDER, Mary	72	RIDER, Samuel	100
RIDER, Joseph	121	RIDER, Mary	84	RIDER, Samuel	130
RIDER, Joseph	128	RIDER, Mary	103	RIDER, Samuel	136
RIDER, Joseph	130	RIDER, Mary	105	RIDER, Samuel	181
RIDER, Joseph	136	RIDER, Mary	106	RIDER, Samuel	188
RIDER, Joseph	151	RIDER, Mary	125	RIDER, Sarah	15
RIDER, Joseph	155	RIDER, Mary	128	RIDER, Sarah	49
RIDER, Joseph	158	RIDER, Mary	131	RIDER, Sarah	58
RIDER, Joseph	181	RIDER, Mary	155	RIDER, Sarah	59
RIDER, Joseph	208	RIDER, Mary	172	RIDER, Sarah	70
RIDER, Joseph 3d	136	RIDER, Mary	174	RIDER, Sarah	74
RIDER, Joshua	89	RIDER, Mary	179	RIDER, Sarah	84
RIDER, Josiah	15	RIDER, Mary	186	RIDER, Sarah	88
RIDER, Josiah	58	RIDER, Mary	208	RIDER, Sarah	128
RIDER, Josiah	130	RIDER, Mercy	58	RIDER, Sarah	155
RIDER, Kesia	88	RIDER, Mercy	180	RIDER, Sarah	172
RIDER, Kezia	117	RIDER, Meriah	116	RIDER, Sarah	190
RIDER, Lemuel	58	RIDER, Micah	49	RIDER, Seth	49
RIDER, Lemuell	88	RIDER, Moriah	84	RIDER, Seth	156
RIDER, Lidiah	15	RIDER, Nathaniel	49	RIDER, Stephen	103
RIDER, Lidiah	69	RIDER, Nathaniel	186	RIDER, Stevens	59
RIDER, Lois	84	RIDER, Nathl.	155	RIDER, Thankfull	73
RIDER, Lowis	172	RIDER, Patience	88	RIDER, Thankfull	82

RIDER, Thankfull	109	RIPLEY, David	206	ROBBINS, Chandler	218
RIDER, Thankfull	128	RIPLEY, Elizabeth	201	ROBBINS, Chandler (Rev.)	145
RIDER, Thankfull	136	RIPLEY, Experience	81	ROBBINS, Chandler (Rev.)	176
RIDER, Thankfull	174	RIPLEY, Experience	181	ROBBINS, Chandler (Rev.)	177
RIDER, Thomas	58	RIPLEY, John	195	ROBBINS, Chandler (Rev.)	197
RIDER, Thomas	93	RIPLEY, Joseph Shurtleff	212	ROBBINS, Charles	199
RIDER, Thomas	151	RIPLEY, Levi	207	ROBBINS, Charles	222
RIDER, Tilden	57	RIPLEY, Lucy	202	ROBBINS, Charles Frederick	164
RIDER, William	15	RIPLEY, Luther	207	ROBBINS, Charles Henry	156
RIDER, William	49	RIPLEY, Nathanel	180	ROBBINS, Consider	162
RIDER, William	57	RIPLEY, Nathaniel (Capt.)	64	ROBBINS, Consider	198
RIDER, William	59	RIPLEY, Nathll.	81	ROBBINS, Curtis Holmes	159
RIDER, William	143	RIPLEY, Nehemiah	81	ROBBINS, Ebenezer	204
RIDER, Willm.	175	RIPLEY, Polley	215	ROBBINS, Ebenezr.	191
RIGBEY, John H.	207	RIPLEY, Rufus	178	ROBBINS, Ebenzr.	162
RING, Andrew	13	RIPLEY, Sarah	113	ROBBINS, Ebenzr.	162
RING, Andrew	14	RIPLEY, Sarah S.	217	ROBBINS, Edward L.	209
RING, Andrew	98	RIPLEY, Sylvanus	220	ROBBINS, Eliza	159
RING, Anna	70	RIPLEY, Thaddeus	195	ROBBINS, Eliza.	167
RING, Deborah	14	RIPLEY, Uriah	199	ROBBINS, Elizabeth	24
RING, Deborah	21	RIPLEY, William	214	ROBBINS, Elizabeth Fuller	133
RING, Deborah	77	RIPLEY, William Putnam	207	ROBBINS, Eunice	162
RING, Deborah	119	RIPLEY, William Putnam	213	ROBBINS, Eunice	191
RING, Eleazar	13	RIPLEY, Zenus	209	ROBBINS, Francis H.	209
RING, Elezebeth	129	RIPLY, Nehemiah	74	ROBBINS, Frederick	164
RING, Eliazar	21	RIPLY, Nehemiah	81	ROBBINS, George	145
RING, Eliazar	70	RIPLY, Nehemiah	127	ROBBINS, George	208
RING, Eliazur	66	RIPLY, Peter	81	ROBBINS, Grace	208
RING, Elizabeth	21	RIPLY, Sarah	74	ROBBINS, Hannah	24
RING, Elkanan	14	RIPLY, Sarah	81	ROBBINS, Hannah	67
RING, Hanah	21	ROBARDS, Robert	183	ROBBINS, Hannah	145
RING, Hanah	100	ROBBENS, Benjamin	171	ROBBINS, Hannah	197
RING, Hanna	100	ROBBENS, Eleazer	113	ROBBINS, Hannah	212
RING, Hannah	67	ROBBENS, Phebe	110	ROBBINS, Hannah Tilden	133
RING, Hannah	96	ROBBERTSON, Nanny	153	ROBBINS, Harriet Newell	146
RING, John	118	ROBBIN, Daniel	116	ROBBINS, Harriett	146
RING, Jonathan	14	ROBBIN, Phebe	131	ROBBINS, Heman	156
RING, Lettis	98	ROBBINS, Abigail	24	ROBBINS, Henry	209
RING, Mary	13	ROBBINS, Almira F.	156	ROBBINS, Henry	217
RING, Mary	14	ROBBINS, Ammi-Ruhamah (Rev.)	177	ROBBINS, Henry H.	209
RING, Mary	66	ROBBINS, Ansel	197	ROBBINS, Hesther	24
RING, Phebe	14	ROBBINS, Ansell	162	ROBBINS, Isaac	145
RING, Phebe	129	ROBBINS, Benjamin	197	ROBBINS, Isaac	159
RING, Samuel	14	ROBBINS, Benjamin	219	ROBBINS, Isaac Marshal	159
RING, Suzannah	14	ROBBINS, Betsey	167	ROBBINS, Isabella Grayham	164
RING, William	21	ROBBINS, Betsey	214	ROBBINS, James	162
RING, William	67	ROBBINS, Betsey B.	209	ROBBINS, James	202
RING, William	96	ROBBINS, Betsey B.	222	ROBBINS, James Hewit	159
RING, William	100	ROBBINS, Caroline A.	156	ROBBINS, Jane	145
RIPLEY, Abigail	214	ROBBINS, Chandler	145	ROBBINS, Jane	164
RIPLEY, Alexander	217	ROBBINS, Chandler	199	ROBBINS, Jane	195

Name	Page	Name	Page	Name	Page
ROBBINS, Jeduthan	24	ROBBINS, Ruth	203	ROGERS, Benjamin	86
ROBBINS, Jeduthan	67	ROBBINS, Sally	200	ROGERS, Benjamin	125
ROBBINS, Jenney	145	ROBBINS, Samuel	188	ROGERS, Bethiah	158
ROBBINS, Jesse	205	ROBBINS, Samuel	204	ROGERS, Bethiah	189
ROBBINS, Jesse	206	ROBBINS, Samuel Prince	145	ROGERS, Betse	213
ROBBINS, John	24	ROBBINS, Sarah	186	ROGERS, Desier	62
ROBBINS, Joseph	167	ROBBINS, Sarah Elizabeth	159	ROGERS, Desire	116
ROBBINS, Joseph	220	ROBBINS, Seth	200	ROGERS, Eleazer	62
ROBBINS, Josiah	207	ROGERS, Sylvanus	222	ROGERS, Eleazer	172
ROBBINS, Josiah	213	ROBBINS, Temperance	200	ROGERS, Eleazr.	158
ROBBINS, Josiah	220	ROBBINS, Thaddeus	162	ROGERS, Eliza	138
ROBBINS, Leavitt T.	133	ROBBINS, William	193	ROGERS, Eliza.	185
ROBBINS, Leavitt Taylor	133	ROBERSON, Abigail	132	ROGERS, Elizabeth	107
ROBBINS, Lemuel	24	ROBERSON, Alexander	132	ROGERS, Elizabeth	172
ROBBINS, Lemuel	190	ROBERSON, Alezander	132	ROGERS, Elizabeth	213
ROBBINS, Lemuel	212	ROBERSON, Micah	132	ROGERS, Experiance	74
ROBBINS, Lemuel Fuller	133	ROBERSON, Thomas	171	ROGERS, Experience	127
ROBBINS, Lemuel Stephens	167	ROBERSON, William	215	ROGERS, George	201
ROBBINS, Levi	146	ROBERTS, Eliza.	203	ROGERS, Hanna	130
ROBBINS, Levi	162	ROBERTS, John	133	ROGERS, Hannah	48
ROBBINS, Lois	188	ROBERTS, Margaret	133	ROGERS, Hannah	62
ROBBINS, Lowis	214	ROBERTS, Mary	160	ROGERS, Hannah	66
ROBBINS, Lucia	133	ROBERTS, Polly	200	ROGERS, Hannah	72
ROBBINS, Lucia Rider	133	ROBERTS, R.	171	ROGERS, Hannah	86
ROBBINS, Lydia	133	ROBERTS, Robert	104	ROGERS, Hannah	104
ROBBINS, Lydia	195	ROBERTS, Robert	133	ROGERS, Hannah	107
ROBBINS, Lydia Johson	133	ROBERTS, Robert	160	ROGERS, Hannah	128
ROBBINS, Margaret H.	209	ROBERTS, Robert	183	ROGERS, Hannah	173
ROBBINS, Margrett H.	209	ROBERTS, Robert (Capt.)	201	ROGERS, Hannah	177
ROBBINS, Maria	146	ROBERTS, Sarah	160	ROGERS, Hannah	187
ROBBINS, Martha Churchill	209	ROBERTSON, Ruth	153	ROGERS, Joanna	201
ROBBINS, Mary Ann	156	ROBERTSON, Sarah	153	ROGERS, John	62
ROBBINS, Mary Bacon	133	ROBERTSON, Thomas	153	ROGERS, John	86
ROBBINS, Mary Elizabeth	156	ROBIN, Daniel	107	ROGERS, John	152
ROBBINS, Mary Jane	164	ROBIN, Daniel	116	ROGERS, John	177
ROBBINS, Mehitabel	24	ROBIN, Sarah	107	ROGERS, John	207
ROBBINS, Mercy	167	ROBINS, Daniel	117	ROGERS, Lydia Holmes	138
ROBBINS, Nathan Bacon	133	ROBINS, Ester	78	ROGERS, Margaret	73
ROBBINS, Nathan Bacon	220	ROBINS, Lemuel	78	ROGERS, Margaret	127
ROBBINS, Nathaniel	203	ROBINS, Lemuel	119	ROGERS, Mary	152
ROBBINS, Nicolos	24	ROBINS, Mehetibel	121	ROGERS, Patience	128
ROBBINS, Patience	178	ROBINSON, Anna	191	ROGERS, Phebe	86
ROBBINS, Patience	195	ROBINSON, Hannah	124	ROGERS, Polley	214
ROBBINS, Perses	24	ROBINSON, Hannah	212	ROGERS, Priscilla	48
ROBBINS, Peter Gilman	145	ROBINSON, John	131	ROGERS, Priscilla	62
ROBBINS, Philemon	145	ROBINSON, Sarah	193	ROGERS, Priscilla	130
ROBBINS, Polley	205	ROBINSON, Thomas	172	ROGERS, Priscilla	158
ROBBINS, Rebeckah	181	ROGER, Abijah	121	ROGERS, Priscilla	184
ROBBINS, Remembr.	185	ROGERS, Abigail	205	ROGERS, Prissilla	71
ROBBINS, Rufus	194	ROGERS, Abijah	78	ROGERS, Ruth	62
ROBBINS, Rufus	205	ROGERS, America	138	ROGERS, Ruth	112

VITAL RECORDS OF THE TOWN OF PLYMOUTH

Name	Page	Name	Page	Name	Page
ROGERS, Ruth	113	RUSSEL, Nancy	197	RYDER, Hariot	218
ROGERS, Ruth	202	RUSSELL, Abigail	138	RYDER, Jane	201
ROGERS, Saml.	107	RUSSELL, Abigail	220	RYDER, Joanna	158
ROGERS, Samll.	48	RUSSELL, Charles	138	RYDER, Job	212
ROGERS, Samll.	105	RUSSELL, Experience	204	RYDER, John	76
ROGERS, Samuel	62	RUSSELL, George	138	RYDER, John	169
ROGERS, Samuel	158	RUSSELL, James	138	RYDER, Joseph	57
ROGERS, Samuel	188	RUSSELL, James (Capt.)	194	RYDER, Joseph	200
ROGERS, Samuel	197	RUSSELL, James (Capt.)	208	RYDER, Joshua	202
ROGERS, Samuel	201	RUSSELL, Jane	138	RYDER, Lucia	220
ROGERS, Samuell	48	RUSSELL, Jane	200	RYDER, Lucy	206
ROGERS, Sarah	48	RUSSELL, John	138	RYDER, Lydia	123
ROGERS, Sarah	202	RUSSELL, John	173	RYDER, Lydia	205
ROGERS, Stephen	215	RUSSELL, John	194	RYDER, Margaret	158
ROGERS, Sylvanus	199	RUSSELL, John	208	RYDER, Mariah	111
ROGERS, Sylvanus	202	RUSSELL, John (Capt.)	217	RYDER, Mary	75
ROGERS, Thomas	62	RUSSELL, Jonathan	194	RYDER, Mary	76
ROGERS, Thomas	71	RUSSELL, Marcy	138	RYDER, Mary	169
ROGERS, Thomas	106	RUSSELL, Mary	138	RYDER, Merrick	216
ROGERS, Thomas	107	RUSSELL, Mary	222	RYDER, Michael	158
ROGERS, Thomas	129	RUSSELL, Mercy	138	RYDER, Nathaniel	169
ROGERS, Thomas	158	RUSSELL, Mercy	200	RYDER, Patience	162
ROGERS, Thomas	199	RUSSELL, Mercy	202	RYDER, Patience	200
ROGERS, William	138	RUSSELL, Nancey	138	RYDER, Polley	207
ROGERS, William	195	RUSSELL, Nathaniel	138	RYDER, Rebecca	203
ROGERS, Willis	62	RUSSELL, Nathaniel (Capt.)	204	RYDER, Rebeckah	111
ROGERS, Wm.	212	RUSSELL, Robert	214	RYDER, Samuel	199
ROGGERS, Abijah	32	RUSSELL, Thomas	138	RYDER, Sarah	122
ROGGERS, Benjn.	75	RUSSELL, Thomas	196	RYDER, Sarah	123
ROGGERS, Eleazar	32	RUSSELL, Thomas	214	RYDER, Sarah	190
ROGGERS, Eliazar	32	RUSSELL, William Shaw	222	RYDER, Seth	169
ROGGERS, Elizabeth	32	RYDER, Abigail	57	RYDER, Seth	195
ROGGERS, Experience	32	RYDER, Abigail	158	RYDER, Seth	197
ROGGERS, Hannah	32	RYDER, Abigail	162	RYDER, William	158
ROGGERS, Moriah	32	RYDER, Abigail	200	RYDER, William	191
ROGGERS, Phebe	75	RYDER, Amos	122		
ROGGERS, Ruhamah	32	RYDER, Benjamin (Maj.)	162	**S**	
ROGGERS, Ruth	32	RYDER, Betsey	202		
ROGGERS, Sarah	70	RYDER, Caleb	218	SACHAMUS, Kate	79
ROGGERS, Sarrah	126	RYDER, Daniel	213	SACHAMUS, Moses	79
ROGGERS, Thomas	32	RYDER, Deborah	215	SACHAMUS, Moses	106
ROGGERS, Willis	32	RYDER, Desire	190	SACHAMUS, Moses	107
ROOS, Mary	70	RYDER, Elizabeth	215	SACHAMUS, Moses	116
ROSE, Lucrecy	128	RYDER, Elkanah	57	SACHAMUS, Moses	175
ROSE, Lucretia	74	RYDER, Esther	169	SACHAMUS, Sarah	107
ROSE, Mary	76	RYDER, Ezekiel	206	SACHAMUS, Susannah	177
ROSE, Mary	118	RYDER, George	198	SACHEMAS, Ruth	194
ROSE, Permelia	199	RYDER, Hanah	123	SACHEMUS, Joseph	122
RUGGLES, Hannah	79	RYDER, Hannah	169	SACHEMUS, Phillip	118
RUGGLES, Joseph	79	RYDER, Hannah	195	SALTONSTALL, Abigail	80
RUGGLES, Joseph	123	RYDER, Hannah	210	SALTONSTALL, Abigail	114

VITAL RECORDS OF THE TOWN OF PLYMOUTH

SAMPSON, ----- (male)	162	SAMSON, Charles	121	SAMSON, Joseph	198
SAMPSON, Alvan	216	SAMSON, Clarrissa	205	SAMSON, Josiah	32
SAMPSON, Deborah	162	SAMSON, Deborah	79	SAMSON, Lazarus	82
SAMPSON, Ebenezer	78	SAMSON, Deborah	200	SAMSON, Lazarus	96
SAMPSON, Ebenezer	91	SAMSON, Deiser	87	SAMSON, Lazerus	73
SAMPSON, Elizabeth	91	SAMSON, Desire	87	SAMSON, Lazerus	82
SAMPSON, Elizabeth	177	SAMSON, Desire	174	SAMSON, Lazerus	124
SAMPSON, Ephraim	211	SAMSON, Ebenezer	121	SAMSON, Lazerus	127
SAMPSON, George Washington	162	SAMSON, Ebenezer	144	SAMSON, Lidiah	32
SAMPSON, Hanah	78	SAMSON, Ebenezer	177	SAMSON, Lydia	92
SAMPSON, Hannah	91	SAMSON, Ebenezr.	194	SAMSON, Lydia	185
SAMPSON, Hannah	218	SAMSON, Elizabeth	87	SAMSON, Lydia	201
SAMPSON, Harriot	222	SAMSON, Elizabeth	199	SAMSON, Lydia Cushing	162
SAMPSON, Isaac	162	SAMSON, Elnathan	95	SAMSON, Lydia Cushing	191
SAMPSON, John	213	SAMSON, Enoch	50	SAMSON, Marcy	75
SAMPSON, Joseph	201	SAMSON, Ephraim	32	SAMSON, Marcy	86
SAMPSON, Joseph	218	SAMSON, Ephraim	74	SAMSON, Marcy	95
SAMPSON, Joseph	219	SAMSON, Ephraim	82	SAMSON, Martha Washington	162
SAMPSON, Josiah	217	SAMSON, Ephraim	128	SAMSON, Mary	82
SAMPSON, Lucy	193	SAMSON, Esther	95	SAMSON, Mary	92
SAMPSON, Lucy	212	SAMSON, George	92	SAMSON, Mary	176
SAMPSON, Lydia	77	SAMSON, George	186	SAMSON, Mary	188
SAMPSON, Lydia	162	SAMSON, George	191	SAMSON, Mary	189
SAMPSON, Lydia	222	SAMSON, George	200	SAMSON, Mary	193
SAMPSON, Marah	162	SAMSON, Hannah	92	SAMSON, Mary	199
SAMPSON, Marcy	177	SAMSON, Hannah	144	SAMSON, Mercy	162
SAMPSON, Mary	162	SAMSON, Hannah	177	SAMSON, Noah	75
SAMPSON, Mary	215	SAMSON, Hannah	195	SAMSON, Noah	87
SAMPSON, Meriah	162	SAMSON, Hannah	207	SAMSON, Noah	117
SAMPSON, Olive	210	SAMSON, Hennery	50	SAMSON, Peleg	32
SAMPSON, Polley	204	SAMSON, Icabod	86	SAMSON, Penelope	50
SAMPSON, Ruth	32	SAMSON, Ichabod	75	SAMSON, Penelope	191
SAMPSON, Samuel	214	SAMSON, Ichabod	95	SAMSON, Pricila	32
SAMPSON, Sarah	205	SAMSON, Ichabod	124	SAMSON, Rebeckah	70
SAMPSON, Simeon	162	SAMSON, Isaac	32	SAMSON, Rufus	50
SAMPSON, Simeon (Capt.)	162	SAMSON, James	50	SAMSON, Ruth	69
SAMPSON, Sylvanus	204	SAMSON, James	188	SAMSON, Ruth	74
SAMSEN, Lydia	118	SAMSON, Jemima	73	SAMSON, Ruth	124
SAMSON, Abaigaill	69	SAMSON, Jemima	75	SAMSON, Saml.	95
SAMSON, Abigail	50	SAMSON, Jemima	82	SAMSON, Samuel	195
SAMSON, Abigail	112	SAMSON, Jemima	87	SAMSON, Sarah	92
SAMSON, Abigail	189	SAMSON, Jemima	96	SAMSON, Sarah	101
SAMSON, Abigall	82	SAMSON, Jemimah	171	SAMSON, Sarah	112
SAMSON, Abner	191	SAMSON, Joanna	197	SAMSON, Sarah	183
SAMSON, Ann	69	SAMSON, John	92	SAMSON, Sophia	203
SAMSON, Barnabas	32	SAMSON, John	181	SAMSON, Southworth	87
SAMSON, Benjamin	70	SAMSON, Jonathan	32	SAMSON, Stephen	50
SAMSON, Benjamin	92	SAMSON, Jonathan	101	SAMSON, Stephen	112
SAMSON, Benjamin	121	SAMSON, Jonathan	112	SAMSON, Stephen	191
SAMSON, Benjamin	194	SAMSON, Jonathan	113	SAMSON, Susanna	207
SAMSON, Caleb	144	SAMSON, Joseph	69	SAMSON, Susannah	82

VITAL RECORDS OF THE TOWN OF PLYMOUTH

Name	Page	Name	Page	Name	Page
SAMSON, Susannah	172	SAVERY, Lemuel	194	SCARRET, Alse	74
SAMSON, Thomas	86	SAVERY, Lemuel	217	SCARRET, Alse	81
SAMSON, Thomas	213	SAVERY, Lydia	60	SCARRET, Joanna	106
SAMSON, William	50	SAVERY, Lydia	190	SCARRET, Johanna	128
SAMSON, William	82	SAVERY, Lydia Holmes	213	SCARRET, Thomas	74
SANDER, Vilot	217	SAVERY, Marcy	60	SCARRET, Thomas	81
SANDERS, Abigaiel	27	SAVERY, Marcy	75	SCARROT, Thomas	128
SANDERS, Abraham	212	SAVERY, Mary	217	SCHACHEMUS, Joshua	119
SANDERS, Ann	27	SAVERY, Mehetibell	60	SCOKE, Joanna	78
SANDERS, Anna	126	SAVERY, Mercy	200	SCOKE, Joanna	121
SANDERS, Annah	27	SAVERY, Nehemiah	199	SCOKE, Mary	111
SANDERS, Deborah	120	SAVERY, Nehemiah	207	SCOKE, Mary	115
SANDERS, Ebenezer	124	SAVERY, Phineas	213	SCOT, Hannah	222
SANDERS, Eliza.	109	SAVERY, Priscilla	86	SCOT, Phebe	191
SANDERS, Elizabeth	93	SAVERY, Samuel	60	SEABERRY, Hopestill	186
SANDERS, Henery	27	SAVERY, Thomas	60	SEABERRY, Sarah	183
SANDERS, Henry	123	SAVERY, Thomas	86	SEABURY, Barnabas	130
SANDERS, Jonathan	27	SAVERY, Thomas	126	SEAKINS, Ezekiel	202
SANDERS, Jonathan	93	SAVERY, Thomas	198	SEARS, Bartlett	201
SANDERS, Jonathan	109	SAVERY, Thomas	207	SEARS, Betsey	215
SANDERS, Martha	123	SAVERY, Uriah	60	SEARS, Betty	177
SANDERS, Mary	74	SAVERY, Uriah	207	SEARS, Cloe	175
SANDERS, Mary	93	SAVERY, William	181	SEARS, David	222
SANDERS, Mary	128	SAVIL, Edward	214	SEARS, Edmond	207
SANDERS, Sarah	27	SAVORY, ----- (female)	159	SEARS, Edmond	210
SANDERS, Sarah	107	SAVORY, Deborah	77	SEARS, Eleazer	207
SANDERS, Sarah	116	SAVORY, Esther	86	SEARS, Elizabeth	75
SANDERS, Sarah	125	SAVORY, Esther	182	SEARS, Joseph	212
SANGER, Joseph	214	SAVORY, James	86	SEARS, Marcy	50
SANGERELE, Joseph	129	SAVORY, James	163	SEARS, Mary	50
SARJANT, Ruth	79	SAVORY, James	188	SEARS, Mehetabel	50
SAUNDER, Vilot	207	SAVORY, Lemuel	86	SEARS, Mercy	222
SAUNDERS, Billey	200	SAVORY, Lydia	77	SEARS, Rebecca	212
SAUNDERS, Henry	79	SAVORY, Lydia	119	SEARS, Rebeckah	176
SAUNDERS, John	222	SAVORY, Lydia	159	SEARS, Sara	198
SAUNDERS, Martha	79	SAVORY, Marcy	124	SEARS, Sarah	182
SAUNDERS, Mary	79	SAVORY, Mercy	163	SEARS, Thomas	50
SAUNDERS, Nancy	217	SAVORY, Priscilla	177	SEARS, Thomas	75
SAUNDERS, Phebe	214	SAVORY, Ruth	86	SEARS, Thomas	101
SAUNDERS, Susan	222	SAVORY, Ruth	186	SEARS, Thomas	106
SAVARY, Augusta S.	156	SAVORY, Sarah Everson	217	SEARS, Thomas	117
SAVARY, Ester	77	SAVORY, Thomas	86	SEARS, Thomas	184
SAVARY, Ruth Ann	156	SAVORY, Thomas	175	SEARS, Thomas	201
SAVARY, Wm.	156	SAVORY, Uriah	77	SEARS, Thomas	216
SAVERY, Bethiah	86	SAVORY, Uriah	121	SEARS, Willard	186
SAVERY, Bethiah	172	SAVORY, William	86	SEAS, Betsey	215
SAVERY, Betsey	208	SAVORY, William	159	SEAVER, James (Capt.)	200
SAVERY, Esther	60	SAWYER, Margaret	110	SEERS, James	21
SAVERY, Esther	118	SAWYER, Thomas	110	SEERS, John	21
SAVERY, George	207	SAWYER, Thos.	115	SEERS, Mary	21
SAVERY, Isaac	212	SCARRET, -----	81	SEERS, Richard	21

SEERS, Seth	21	SHANKS, Kate	120	SHAW, Elizabeth	32
SEERS, Silas	21	SHANKS, Nab	77	SHAW, Elizabeth	162
SEKINS, Aaron	185	SHANKS, Nab	119	SHAW, Elkanah	111
SELLER, James	180	SHAREMAN, -----	100	SHAW, Elkanah	116
SELLER, Jean	171	SHAREMAN, Caleb	29	SHAW, Elkanah	131
SEPIT, Benjamin	195	SHAREMAN, Caleb	77	SHAW, Elknath	32
SEPIT, Betty	194	SHAREMAN, Caleb	100	SHAW, Ellis	213
SEPIT, Hannah	206	SHAREMAN, Caleb	116	SHAW, Experience	133
SEPIT, Joannah	116	SHAREMAN, Caleb	119	SHAW, Experience	194
SEPIT, Josselyn	116	SHAREMAN, Deborah	77	SHAW, Hannah	32
SEPIT, Lucy C.	219	SHAREMAN, Deborah	87	SHAW, Hannah	162
SEPIT, Mary	172	SHAREMAN, Debro	100	SHAW, Ichabod	47
SEPIT, Micah	172	SHAREMAN, Elizabeth	29	SHAW, Ichabod	133
SEPIT, Mosis	200	SHAREMAN, Experience	107	SHAW, Ichabod	173
SEPIT, Phebe	178	SHAREMAN, Hannah	29	SHAW, Ichabod	199
SEPIT, Sarah	194	SHAREMAN, Hannah	116	SHAW, Ichabod	203
SEPIT, Solomon	124	SHAREMAN, Hannah	181	SHAW, James	32
SEPITT, David	78	SHAREMAN, Joshua	87	SHAW, Johannah	111
SEPITT, David	121	SHAREMAN, Joshua	118	SHAW, John	32
SEPITT, Joanna	78	SHAREMAN, Nathl.	87	SHAW, John Atwood	134
SEPITT, Saml.	122	SHAREMAN, Rebeckah	29	SHAW, Jonathan	32
SERJANT, Eliza.	198	SHAREMAN, Ring	29	SHAW, Jonathan	66
SERJANT, Elizabeth	136	SHAREMAN, Saml.	107	SHAW, Jonathan	201
SERJANT, Experience	135	SHAREMAN, Samuel	183	SHAW, Joshua	162
SERJANT, Experience	186	SHAREMAN, Samuell	105	SHAW, Joshua	180
SERJANT, Hannah	136	SHAREMAN, Sarah	29	SHAW, Lidiah	32
SERJANT, Lydia	136	SHAREMAN, Sarah	186	SHAW, Lucas	206
SERJANT, Lydia	187	SHAREMAN, Young	29	SHAW, Lucy	133
SERJANT, Mary	135	SHARMON, Caleb	111	SHAW, Lucy	198
SERJANT, Mary	136	SHARMON, Rebeckah	111	SHAW, Lydia	133
SERJANT, Mary	193	SHATTUCK, Mary	59	SHAW, Margaret	162
SERJANT, Ruth	135	SHATTUCK, Mary	71	SHAW, Margarett	32
SERJANT, Ruth	186	SHATTUCK, Mary	73	SHAW, Mary	32
SERJANT, Sarah	136	SHATTUCK, Mary	77	SHAW, Mary	66
SERJANT, William	135	SHATTUCK, Mary	119	SHAW, Mary	117
SERJANT, William	200	SHATTUCK, Mary	126	SHAW, Mary	133
SERJEANT, Mary	106	SHATTUCK, Randel	59	SHAW, Mary	193
SERJEANT, Ruth	123	SHATTUCK, Robert	59	SHAW, Mehitabell	66
SERJEANT, William	105	SHATTUCK, Robert	71	SHAW, Mehitable	201
SERJEANT, William	106	SHATTUCK, Robert	79	SHAW, Mehittabel	32
SERS, Bathshua	21	SHATTUCK, Robt.	123	SHAW, Mehittabel	32
SEVER, John	197	SHATTUCK, Ruhama	79	SHAW, Mercy	200
SEVER, William	171	SHAW, Abigaiel	32	SHAW, Mosses	32
SEVER, William	202	SHAW, Abigail	75	SHAW, Nancy	201
SEWALL, Abigail	212	SHAW, Bennoni	164	SHAW, Nansey	134
SEYMOUR, Henry	149	SHAW, Bennony	32	SHAW, Perces	32
SEYMOUR, Margarett Augusta	149	SHAW, Benoni	186	SHAW, Phebe	32
SEYMOUR, Nancy	149	SHAW, Desire	133	SHAW, Pricila	32
SEYMOUR, Nancy Seely	149	SHAW, Desire	197	SHAW, Priscilla	133
SHANKS, Kate	77	SHAW, Egerthy	199	SHAW, Priscilla	191
SHANKS, Kate	118	SHAW, Elias	200	SHAW, Priscilla	206

SHAW, Rebecca	214	SHERMAN, Leander Lovell	144	SHURTLEFF, Barnabas	74
SHAW, Ruth	164	SHERMAN, Lydia	132	SHURTLEFF, Barnabas	127
SHAW, Ruth	191	SHERMAN, Lydia	209	SHURTLEFF, Bathshua	55
SHAW, Ruth	201	SHERMAN, Lydia	212	SHURTLEFF, Benjamin (Doctr.)	206
SHAW, Salley	206	SHERMAN, Mary D.	144	SHURTLEFF, Betsey	206
SHAW, Samuel	134	SHERMAN, Priscilla	220	SHURTLEFF, Clark	102
SHAW, Sarah	134	SHERMAN, Rufus	188	SHURTLEFF, Eliza	215
SHAW, Southworth	133	SHERMAN, Ruth	183	SHURTLEFF, Elizabeth	132
SHAW, Southworth	201	SHERMAN, Sally	144	SHURTLEFF, Elizabeth	178
SHAW, Sylvanus	191	SHERMAN, Sally	220	SHURTLEFF, Elizebeth	48
SHEARMAN, Lydia	217	SHERMAN, Samuel	132	SHURTLEFF, Eloner	199
SHEARMAN, Nathaniel	183	SHERMAN, Samuel	153	SHURTLEFF, Esther	219
SHEPARD, -----	100	SHERMAN, Samuel	197	SHURTLEFF, Faith	48
SHEPARD, ----- (male)	24	SHERMAN, Samuel	214	SHURTLEFF, Faith	132
SHEPARD, Abigal	24	SHERMAN, Samuell	177	SHURTLEFF, Faith	177
SHEPARD, Abigall	75	SHERMAN, Thomas	153	SHURTLEFF, Faith	208
SHEPARD, Daved	100	SHERMAN, Thomas	197	SHURTLEFF, Hannah	48
SHEPARD, David	24	SHERMAN, Thomas	215	SHURTLEFF, Hannah	132
SHEPARD, David	66	SHERMAN, William	153	SHURTLEFF, Hannah	172
SHEPARD, Prudence	24	SHERMAN, William	199	SHURTLEFF, Ichabod	195
SHEPARD, Rebecah	24	SHERMAN, Winslow B.	144	SHURTLEFF, James	48
SHEPARD, Rebecca	71	SHIRMON, Hannah	67	SHURTLEFF, James	57
SHEPARD, Rebecka	129	SHIRTLEF, Abiall	21	SHURTLEFF, James	79
SHEPARD, Rebeckah	66	SHIRTLEF, Benjamin	21	SHURTLEFF, James	116
SHEPARD, Rebecker	130	SHIRTLEF, David	21	SHURTLEFF, James	117
SHEPARD, Rebekah	24	SHIRTLEF, Elizabeth	21	SHURTLEFF, James	132
SHEPARD, Ruth	24	SHIRTLEF, Hannah	21	SHURTLEFF, James	187
SHEPHERD, Abigal	125	SHIRTLEF, James	21	SHURTLEFF, James	208
SHEPHERD, Arthur	128	SHIRTLEF, John	21	SHURTLEFF, Joanna	57
SHEPHERD, Arthur	131	SHIRTLEF, Joseph	21	SHURTLEFF, Joannah	79
SHEPHERD, Mary	128	SHIRTLEF, Lidiah	21	SHURTLEFF, Joseph	55
SHEPHERD, Ruth	74	SHIRTLEF, Wiliam	21	SHURTLEFF, Joseph	79
SHEPHERD, Ruth	127	SHIRTLEFF, Lydia	89	SHURTLEFF, Joseph	123
SHEPHERD, Ruth	128	SHIRTLEFF, Nathaniel	89	SHURTLEFF, Joseph	200
SHERMAN, Abby L.	144	SHIRTLIF, Barnabas	14	SHURTLEFF, Levi	102
SHERMAN, Andrew	153	SHIRTLIF, Elizabeth	14	SHURTLEFF, Levine	212
SHERMAN, Betsey	197	SHIRTLIF, Ichabod	14	SHURTLEFF, Luce	102
SHERMAN, Betsey	222	SHIRTLIF, Jabiz	14	SHURTLEFF, Lucy	78
SHERMAN, Betsey D.	144	SHIRTLIF, John	14	SHURTLEFF, Lucy	90
SHERMAN, Betty	153	SHIRTLIF, Mary	14	SHURTLEFF, Lucy	102
SHERMAN, Elijah	132	SHIRTLIF, Sarah	14	SHURTLEFF, Lydia	48
SHERMAN, Elijah	194	SHIRTLIF, Suzannah	14	SHURTLEFF, Lydia	78
SHERMAN, Elijah	213	SHIRTLIF, Thomas	14	SHURTLEFF, Lydia	89
SHERMAN, Elizabeth	187	SHIRTLIF, William	14	SHURTLEFF, Lydia	132
SHERMAN, Experiance	132	SHURTLEF, Lucy	188	SHURTLEFF, Lydia	171
SHERMAN, George	144	SHURTLEFF, Abial	102	SHURTLEFF, Marcy	89
SHERMAN, Hannah	144	SHURTLEFF, Abiel	78	SHURTLEFF, Mary	48
SHERMAN, Hope	144	SHURTLEFF, Abiel	90	SHURTLEFF, Mary	55
SHERMAN, Isaac M.	144	SHURTLEFF, Abiel	121	SHURTLEFF, Mary	89
SHERMAN, Isaac Morton	214	SHURTLEFF, Abigail	206	SHURTLEFF, Mary	178
SHERMAN, John	215	SHURTLEFF, Abigal	124	SHURTLEFF, Mary	195

SHURTLEFF, Molley	132	SILVESTER, Hannah	53	SILVESTER, Thomas	132
SHURTLEFF, Nathaniel	78	SILVESTER, Hannah	70	SIMMONS, Abigail	194
SHURTLEFF, Nathaniel	89	SILVESTER, Hannah	132	SIMMONS, Abigail	207
SHURTLEFF, Nathaniel	121	SILVESTER, Hannah	138	SIMMONS, Bennet	136
SHURTLEFF, Noah	102	SILVESTER, Hannah	179	SIMMONS, Bennet	193
SHURTLEFF, Paticience	89	SILVESTER, Jedidah	24	SIMMONS, Bulah	199
SHURTLEFF, Peter	181	SILVESTER, Jedidah	111	SIMMONS, Chloe	204
SHURTLEFF, Rebecca	204	SILVESTER, Joseph	29	SIMMONS, Eunice T.	160
SHURTLEFF, Samuel	102	SILVESTER, Joseph	53	SIMMONS, Fanny	154
SHURTLEFF, Sarah	55	SILVESTER, Joseph	64	SIMMONS, Fanny Wilkins	154
SHURTLEFF, Sarah	79	SILVESTER, Joseph	71	SIMMONS, Ferdinand Augustus	161
SHURTLEFF, Sarah	89	SILVESTER, Joseph	129	SIMMONS, George	154
SHURTLEFF, Sarah	109	SILVESTER, Joseph	131	SIMMONS, George	206
SHURTLEFF, Sarah	175	SILVESTER, Joseph	132	SIMMONS, George Augustus	154
SHURTLEFF, Silvina	201	SILVESTER, Joseph	171	SIMMONS, Hannah	69
SHURTLEFF, Sylvanus	201	SILVESTER, Lemuel	132	SIMMONS, Harriet	160
SHURTLEFF, Thankfull	89	SILVESTER, Lucy	138	SIMMONS, Harriet Louisa	161
SHURTLEFF, Thomas	121	SILVESTER, Lydia	53	SIMMONS, Ichabod	145
SHURTLEFF, Thomas Branch	89	SILVESTER, Lydia	109	SIMMONS, Isabella	154
SHURTLEFF, Waite	207	SILVESTER, Lydia	113	SIMMONS, Joann Adelaide	145
SHURTLEFF, William	89	SILVESTER, Marcy	64	SIMMONS, Job	69
SHURTLEIF, Abiall	67	SILVESTER, Marcy	71	SIMMONS, Lemuel	160
SHURTLEIF, Lidia	67	SILVESTER, Marcy	74	SIMMONS, Lemuel	220
SHURTLETT, Jemima	74	SILVESTER, Marcy	128	SIMMONS, Lorenzo Frederick	154
SHURTLIF, Elezabeth	71	SILVESTER, Marey	130	SIMMONS, Lydia	136
SHURTLIF, Elizabeth	129	SILVESTER, Marsey	29	SIMMONS, Lydia	181
SHURTLIF, Jabiz	50	SILVESTER, Martha	106	SIMMONS, Lydia	209
SHURTLIF, Jabiz	70	SILVESTER, Martha	132	SIMMONS, Lydia Anderson	203
SHURTLIF, Martha	70	SILVESTER, Mary	72	SIMMONS, Marcia	145
SHURTLIF, Mary	50	SILVESTER, Mary	84	SIMMONS, Marcia Ann Bates	145
SILVESTER, -----	53	SILVESTER, Mary	132	SIMMONS, Mary	200
SILVESTER, Abigail	24	SILVESTER, Nathaniell	53	SIMMONS, Mary S.	160
SILVESTER, Abner	24	SILVESTER, Nathll.	24	SIMMONS, Moses	154
SILVESTER, Abner	53	SILVESTER, Ruben	53	SIMMONS, Nancey	207
SILVESTER, Abner	111	SILVESTER, Sarah	64	SIMMONS, Nancey	212
SILVESTER, Abner	115	SILVESTER, Sarah	112	SIMMONS, Nancy	217
SILVESTER, Bartlet	53	SILVESTER, Sarah	123	SIMMONS, Nathan	104
SILVESTER, Caleb	24	SILVESTER, Sarah	132	SIMMONS, Nathan	136
SILVESTER, Caleb	53	SILVESTER, Sollomon	29	SIMMONS, Nathan	208
SILVESTER, Caleb	132	SILVESTER, Soloman	53	SIMMONS, Nathan	212
SILVESTER, Content	74	SILVESTER, Solomon	71	SIMMONS, Polley	207
SILVESTER, Content	128	SILVESTER, Solomon	132	SIMMONS, Priscilla	160
SILVESTER, Ebenezer	53	SILVESTER, Solomon	138	SIMMONS, Priscilla C.	160
SILVESTER, Ebenezer	132	SILVESTER, Solomon	173	SIMMONS, Salley Seabery	213
SILVESTER, Elezabeth	71	SILVESTER, Susannah	131	SIMMONS, Scinthia Davis	214
SILVESTER, Elezebeth	53	SILVESTER, Susannah	180	SIMMONS, Victorine Annette	145
SILVESTER, Elizabeth	53	SILVESTER, Thankfull	29	SIMMONS, William	213
SILVESTER, Elizabeth	116	SILVESTER, Thankfull	73	SIMMONS, William D.	160
SILVESTER, Elizabeth	138	SILVESTER, Thankfull	126	SIMONS, Betty	118
SILVESTER, George	138	SILVESTER, Thomas	105	SIMONS, Mary	120
SILVESTER, Hannah	29	SILVESTER, Thomas	106	SIMONS, Mol	117

VITAL RECORDS OF THE TOWN OF PLYMOUTH

SIMONS, Moll	119	SOUL, Daniel	218	SPINNEY, Sophia	157
SIMSON, Joseph	196	SOUL, Josiah	191	SPONER, Bethiah	71
SKIFF, Ebenezr.	198	SOUL, Mabel	77	SPONER, Bethya	129
SKIFF, Ellis	222	SOUL, Rachill	66	SPONER, Eben	70
SKIFF, Rufus	218	SOUL, Rebecca	214	SPONER, Mary	70
SLOCOMB, Robert	177	SOUL, Rebekah	66	SPONER, Susanah	71
SMALE, John	128	SOUL, Thomas	210	SPONER, Suzanna	129
SMITH, Abiather	207	SOUL, Zachere	198	SPOON-, Thos.	15
SMITH, Abigaiel	129	SOULE, Beniamin	35	SPOONER, ----- (female)	149
SMITH, Benjamin	105	SOULE, Deborah	35	SPOONER, ----- (male)	149
SMITH, Benjamin	106	SOULE, Hanah	35	SPOONER, Anna	21
SMITH, Benjamin	110	SOULE, Hannah	104	SPOONER, Anna	156
SMITH, Benjamin	173	SOULE, Samuel	172	SPOONER, Benjamin	52
SMITH, Deborah	207	SOULE, Sarah	35	SPOONER, Bourn	134
SMITH, Hannah	198	SOULE, Zachariah	35	SPOONER, Bourn	215
SMITH, Isaiah	213	SOUTHWICK, William	204	SPOONER, Caleb Alexander	207
SMITH, James	222	SOUTHWORTH, Constant	9	SPOONER, Charles Walter	134
SMITH, John	222	SOUTHWORTH, Desier	9	SPOONER, Deborah	21
SMITH, Joseph	78	SOUTHWORTH, Desire	98	SPOONER, Deborah	124
SMITH, Joseph	89	SOUTHWORTH, Edward	153	SPOONER, Deborah	156
SMITH, Joseph	120	SOUTHWORTH, Hannah	191	SPOONER, Deborah	217
SMITH, Lydia	78	SOUTHWORTH, Ichabod	9	SPOONER, Ebenezar	52
SMITH, Lydia	89	SOUTHWORTH, Jacob	213	SPOONER, Ebenezr.	115
SMITH, Mary	188	SOUTHWORTH, Jacob William	153	SPOONER, Ebenezr.	149
SMITH, Mary	195	SOUTHWORTH, Marcia Ellen	153	SPOONER, Edward Amasa	134
SMITH, Meriah	200	SOUTHWORTH, Mary	9	SPOONER, Eliza.	149
SMITH, Nicholas	183	SOUTHWORTH, Mary	70	SPOONER, Elizabeth	149
SMITH, Nicholas	212	SOUTHWORTH, Nathaniel	98	SPOONER, Ephraim	52
SMITH, Pera	194	SOUTHWORTH, Nathaniell	9	SPOONER, Ephraim	149
SMITH, Peter Hendrick	217	SOUTHWORTH, Ruth	153	SPOONER, Ephraim	178
SMITH, Saml.	116	SOUTHWORTH, Susannah	183	SPOONER, Hannah	134
SMITH, Samuel	119	SOUTHWORTH, Thomas	96	SPOONER, Horatio	137
SMITH, Samuel	197	SOUTHWORTH, Thomas	104	SPOONER, James	149
SMITH, Sarah	89	SPARHAWK, Hannah	64	SPOONER, James	204
SMITH, Sarah	106	SPARHAWK, John	64	SPOONER, Jean	52
SMITH, Sarah	110	SPARHAWK, John	126	SPOONER, Jenna	183
SMITH, Sarah	188	SPARHAWK, Sarah	64	SPOONER, John	156
SMITH, Stephen	178	SPARROW, Edward	59	SPOONER, John Adams	134
SMITH, Sylvanus	222	SPARROW, Edward	122	SPOONER, Joseph	52
SMITH, Thomas	177	SPARROW, Edwd.	109	SPOONER, Marcy	129
SMITH, William	183	SPARROW, Jerusha	59	SPOONER, Marmion	134
SMMONS, Patience [sic]	67	SPARROW, Jerusha	109	SPOONER, Mercy	71
SNELL, Abigail	100	SPARROW, Jerusha	111	SPOONER, Nathaniel	21
SNELL, Thomas	100	SPARROW, Jerusha	123	SPOONER, Nathaniel	156
SNOW, Hannah	66	SPEAR, Thomas	206	SPOONER, Nathaniel	194
SNOW, Leonard	218	SPINK, Mary	75	SPOONER, Nathaniel (Capt.)	213
SNOW, Mercy	207	SPINK, Nicolas	125	SPOONER, Nathaniel Bourn	134
SNOW, Rebekah	66	SPINK, Nicolis	75	SPOONER, Nathl.	156
SNOW, Thankfull	215	SPINKS, Nicholas	175	SPOONER, Patience	52
SOLE, Mabel	119	SPINNEY, Daniel Jackson	157	SPOONER, Patience	78
SOUL, Abigail	171	SPINNEY, John	157	SPOONER, Patience	122

SPOONER, Sarah	52	STEPHENS, Eleazer	112	STETSON, Abigail	134
SPOONER, Sarah	71	STEPHENS, Eleazer	123	STETSON, Abisha	58
SPOONER, Sarah	111	STEPHENS, Eleazer	186	STETSON, Barzilla	58
SPOONER, Sarah	123	STEPHENS, Eleazr.	159	STETSON, Barzilla	92
SPOONER, Sarah	149	STEPHENS, Eleazr.	208	STETSON, Barzilla	122
SPOONER, Sarah	156	STEPHENS, Elizabeth	48	STETSON, Barzillia	79
SPOONER, Sarah	165	STEPHENS, Elizabeth	78	STETSON, Barzillia	122
SPOONER, Sarah	208	STEPHENS, Elizabeth	159	STETSON, Bradford	134
SPOONER, Thomas	21	STEPHENS, George	171	STETSON, Caleb	58
SPOONER, Thomas	52	STEPHENS, Hannah	48	STETSON, Caleb	75
SPOONER, Thomas	71	STEPHENS, Hannah	77	STETSON, Caleb	125
SPOONER, Thomas	149	STEPHENS, Hannah	129	STETSON, Caleb	134
SPOONER, Thomas	156	STEPHENS, John	195	STETSON, Caleb	170
SPOONER, Thomas	184	STEPHENS, Lemuel	48	STETSON, Deborah	75
SPOONER, Thomas	208	STEPHENS, Levi	78	STETSON, Elizabeth	58
SPOONER, Thos.	52	STEPHENS, Levi	122	STETSON, Experience	198
SPOONER, Thos.	123	STEPHENS, Lydia	74	STETSON, Ezra	172
SPOONER, William	220	STEPHENS, Mary	48	STETSON, Jedediah	92
SPOONER, William Thomas	134	STEPHENS, Mary	78	STETSON, Jedidiah	58
SPRAGUE, Elizabeth	127	STEPHENS, Mary	104	STETSON, Jerusha	58
SPRAGUE, Love	178	STEPHENS, Mary	128	STETSON, Joanna	212
SPRAGUE, Ruth	207	STEPHENS, Nabbe	206	STETSON, John	58
SQUIB, Jeremiah	111	STEPHENS, Peleg	160	STETSON, Joshua	58
SQUIB, Mary	111	STEPHENS, Phebe	35	STETSON, Lot	210
SQUIB, Mary	176	STEPHENS, Phebe	112	STETSON, Lucy	205
SQUIBB, Jeremiah	115	STEPHENS, Salley	201	STETSON, Mehitable	181
STACE, Joseph	129	STEPHENS, Sarah	48	STETSON, Mehittable	92
STACE, Patience	56	STEPHENS, Sarah	112	STETSON, Ruth	79
STACEY, Hanna	56	STEPHENS, Sarah	159	STETSON, Ruth	92
STACEY, Joseph	56	STEPHENS, Sarah	160	STETSON, Ruth	194
STACY, Joseph	71	STEPHENS, Susanna	197	STETSON, Sarah	58
STACY, Patience	71	STEPHENS, Susannah	159	STETSON, Sarah	92
STAFF, John	78	STEPHENS, Susannah	208	STETSON, Sarah	183
STAFF, John	120	STEPHENS, William	160	STEVENS, Edward	70
STAFF, Rebekah	78	STEPHENS, William	194	STEVENS, Edward	74
STANDFORD, Rebecka	70	STEPHENS, William	212	STEVENS, Eleazer	180
STANDISH, Ichabod	129	STEPHENSON, Elizabeth	136	STEVENS, Elizabeth	120
STANDISH, Miles	121	STEPHENSON, Elizabeth	186	STEVENS, Hannah	119
STANDISH, Phebe	189	STEPHENSON, Elizabeth	189	STEVENS, Lydia	127
STEELL, Samuel	70	STEPHENSON, Jasper Hall	136	STEVENS, Marcy	74
STEELL, Sarah	70	STEPHENSON, Jasper Hall	197	STEVENS, Mary	70
STEHENS, Samuel	196	STEPHENSON, John	136	STEVENS, Mary	128
STEPHEN, Sylvanus	216	STEPHENSON, Rebecca	205	STEVENS, Peleg	175
STEPHENS, Asa	160	STEPHENSON, Willm.	136	STEVENSON, Isabella	195
STEPHENS, Edward	35	STERMY, Denniss	60	STEWART, Marcy	113
STEPHENS, Edward	48	STERMY, Rebecah	120	STEWART, Mehetabell	106
STEPHENS, Edward	112	STERMY, Rebeckah	118	STIRTEVAN, John	99
STEPHENS, Edward	128	STERMY, Rebekah	78	STIRTEVANT, Anna	21
STEPHENS, Edward	205	STERMY, Thomas	60	STIRTEVANT, Annah	21
STEPHENS, Edwd.	113	STERNY, Rebeca	72	STIRTEVANT, Annah	67
STEPHENS, Eleazer	48	STERNY, Thomas	72	STIRTEVANT, Charles	54

VITAL RECORDS OF THE TOWN OF PLYMOUTH

Name	Page	Name	Page	Name	Page
STIRTEVANT, David	21	STUDSON, Elisha	42	STURTEVANT, Ruth	209
STIRTEVANT, David	130	STUDSON, Elisha	70	STURTEVANT, Samuel	199
STIRTEVANT, Ephraim	21	STUDSON, Hannah	67	STURTEVANT, Sarah	60
STIRTEVANT, Feare	69	STUDSON, Hopstill	42	STURTEVANT, Sarah	62
STIRTEVANT, Hannah	10	STUDSON, Sarah	42	STURTEVANT, Sarah	72
STIRTEVANT, Hannah	54	STUDSON, Zeresh	42	STURTEVANT, Sarah	203
STIRTEVANT, Hannah	99	STURDEFUNT, Josiah	129	STURTEVANT, William	54
STIRTEVANT, John	70	STURGES, Thomas (Capt.)	194	STURTEVANT, William	198
STIRTEVANT, John	130	STURMEY, Denis	105	STURTEVANT, Zadok	54
STIRTEVANT, Jonathan	21	STURMEY, Dennis	36	STURTEVANT, Zenas	198
STIRTEVANT, Joseph	21	STURMEY, Dennis	107	STURTEVT., Sylvanus	195
STIRTEVANT, Joseph	67	STURMEY, Elizabeth	36	STURTEVT., Zilpah	209
STIRTEVANT, Josiah	54	STURMEY, Elizabeth	107	STUTSON, Ruth	122
STIRTEVANT, Mary	21	STURMEY, Elizabeth	188	SULLIVEN, Jane	186
STIRTEVANT, Mary	69	STURMEY, Rebeckah	36	SULLIVIN, James	197
STIRTEVANT, Mary	70	STURMEY, Thomas	36	SUTTON, Abigail	66
STIRTEVANT, Nehemiah	32	STURMY, Rebecah	60	SUTTON, Elizabeth	188
STIRTEVANT, Nehemiah	69	STURMY, Thomas	60	SUTTON, John	66
STIRTEVANT, Ruth	32	STURTAVANT, John	130	SUTTON, Lydia	107
STIRTEVANT, Ruth	69	STURTEVANT, -----	129	SUTTON, Lydia	185
STIRTEVANT, Samuel	69	STURTEVANT, Abigail	206	SUTTON, William	105
STIRTEVANT, William	69	STURTEVANT, Andrew	212	SUTTON, William	107
STIRTIVANT, Marcy	67	STURTEVANT, Church	54	SWIF, Thankful	53
STIRTVENT, Anna	129	STURTEVANT, Cornelios	32	SWIFIT, Betsey	210
STOCKBRIDGE, David	112	STURTEVANT, David	60	SWIFT, -----	95
STOCKBRIDGE, David	113	STURTEVANT, David	72	SWIFT, Abia	86
STOCKBRIDGE, Jean	112	STURTEVANT, Elijah	187	SWIFT, Abiah	16
STOOPS, David	178	STURTEVANT, Eunice	210	SWIFT, Abiah	187
STOORMY, Thomas	130	STURTEVANT, Eunice	213	SWIFT, Abigail	95
STRAFFEN, Susannah	189	STURTEVANT, Hanah	70	SWIFT, Abigail	175
STRAFFEN, William	183	STURTEVANT, Hannah	10	SWIFT, Abigail	181
STRAFFIN, George	169	STURTEVANT, Hannah	54	SWIFT, Abigal	59
STRAFFIN, George	200	STURTEVANT, Hannah	212	SWIFT, Abigal	119
STRAFFIN, Lucy	169	STURTEVANT, Hannah	218	SWIFT, Alce	80
STRAFFIN, Pruedence	214	STURTEVANT, Heman	193	SWIFT, Asa	210
STRAFFIN, Sophia	143	STURTEVANT, Isaac	200	SWIFT, Benjamin	197
STRAFFIN, Sophia Bartlett	143	STURTEVANT, Jane	178	SWIFT, Betsey	210
STRAFFIN, Susannah	169	STURTEVANT, John	10	SWIFT, Deborah	52
STRAFFIN, William	143	STURTEVANT, John	54	SWIFT, Deborah	111
STRAFFIN, William	169	STURTEVANT, John	62	SWIFT, Deborah	121
STRAFFIN, William	199	STURTEVANT, John	72	SWIFT, Deborah	210
STRAFFIN, William Turner	143	STURTEVANT, John	101	SWIFT, Desire	106
STUARD, Mary	130	STURTEVANT, Joseph	214	SWIFT, Desire	109
STUDLEY, Eliab	131	STURTEVANT, Josiah	129	SWIFT, Ebenezer	64
STUDLEY, Elizabeth	131	STURTEVANT, Josiah	207	SWIFT, Elisha	219
STUDLY, Elizabeth	74	STURTEVANT, Josiah (Capt.)	110	SWIFT, Elizabeth	53
STUDLY, John	74	STURTEVANT, Josiah (Capt.)	173	SWIFT, Elizabeth	59
STUDLY, John	124	STURTEVANT, Lois	110	SWIFT, Elizabeth	64
STUDSON, Abigaiel	42	STURTEVANT, Lucy	193	SWIFT, Elizabeth	112
STUDSON, Abigail	70	STURTEVANT, Marcy	54	SWIFT, Elizabeth	122
STUDSON, Eglah	42	STURTEVANT, Polley	205	SWIFT, Elizabeth	128

VITAL RECORDS OF THE TOWN OF PLYMOUTH

Name	Page	Name	Page	Name	Page
SWIFT, Enoch	64	SWIFT, Lidiah	50	SWIFT, Thankfull	53
SWIFT, Hannah	59	SWIFT, Lidiah	52	SWIFT, Thomas	51
SWIFT, Hannah	111	SWIFT, Lowis	218	SWIFT, Thomas	52
SWIFT, Hannah	123	SWIFT, Lusanna	95	SWIFT, Thomas	53
SWIFT, Hannah	218	SWIFT, Lydia	78	SWIFT, Thomas	71
SWIFT, Hannah	220	SWIFT, Lydia	80	SWIFT, Thomas	108
SWIFT, Henry	215	SWIFT, Lydia	120	SWIFT, Thomas	117
SWIFT, Jabez	215	SWIFT, Lydia	195	SWIFT, Thomas	212
SWIFT, Jacob	194	SWIFT, Maria	59	SWIFT, Wiliam	117
SWIFT, Jacob	217	SWIFT, Mary	59	SWIFT, William	50
SWIFT, James	59	SWIFT, Mary	64	SWIFT, William	222
SWIFT, James	117	SWIFT, Mary	65	SWIFT, Zephaniah	80
SWIFT, Jane	95	SWIFT, Mary	77	SWINBORN, Jane Johnson	149
SWIFT, Jane	109	SWIFT, Mary	111	SWINBORN, Jane Johnson	150
SWIFT, Jane	181	SWIFT, Mary	113	SWINBORN, Keziah	149
SWIFT, Jane	215	SWIFT, Mary	117	SWINBORN, Keziah	150
SWIFT, Jean	95	SWIFT, Mary	190	SWINBORN, Robert	149
SWIFT, Jean	118	SWIFT, Mary	207	SWINBORN, Robert	150
SWIFT, Jedidah	16	SWIFT, Micah	64	SWINERTON, Timothy	186
SWIFT, Jedidah	186	SWIFT, Micah	175	SWINNERTON, James	41
SWIFT, Jeremiah Bourn	216	SWIFT, Nanse	194	SWINNERTON, James	79
SWIFT, Jeroboam	218	SWIFT, Nathaniel	86	SWINNERTON, James	116
SWIFT, Jerusha	53	SWIFT, Nathll.	194	SWINNERTON, Martha	41
SWIFT, Jerusha	106	SWIFT, Patience	212	SWINNERTON, Martha	79
SWIFT, Jerusha	109	SWIFT, Patty	217	SWINNERTON, Martha	183
SWIFT, Joanna	196	SWIFT, Phineas	16	SWINNERTON, William	41
SWIFT, Job	64	SWIFT, Phineas	53	SYLVESTER, Abigail	189
SWIFT, John	95	SWIFT, Phineas	190	SYLVESTER, Abner	104
SWIFT, John	106	SWIFT, Phineas	218	SYLVESTER, Bartlett	191
SWIFT, John	109	SWIFT, Phinehas	106	SYLVESTER, Elizabeth	107
SWIFT, John	183	SWIFT, Rebecca	194	SYLVESTER, Elizabeth	186
SWIFT, John	199	SWIFT, Rebecka	51	SYLVESTER, Elizabeth	206
SWIFT, John	206	SWIFT, Rebeckah	16	SYLVESTER, Elizabith	193
SWIFT, Jonathan	51	SWIFT, Rebeckah	108	SYLVESTER, Hannah	190
SWIFT, Joseph	65	SWIFT, Remember	213	SYLVESTER, Jedidah	194
SWIFT, Joseph	77	SWIFT, Rhoda	53	SYLVESTER, John	201
SWIFT, Joseph	95	SWIFT, Rhoda	105	SYLVESTER, Joseph	183
SWIFT, Joseph	119	SWIFT, Rufus	86	SYLVESTER, Lucy	207
SWIFT, Joseph	195	SWIFT, Saml.	106	SYLVESTER, Lydia	194
SWIFT, Joseph	204	SWIFT, Samuel	59	SYLVESTER, Lydia	222
SWIFT, Joshua	95	SWIFT, Sarah	65	SYLVESTER, Mary	188
SWIFT, Joshua	109	SWIFT, Sarah	77	SYLVESTER, Mary	194
SWIFT, Joshua	121	SWIFT, Seth	59	SYLVESTER, Mercy	195
SWIFT, Joshua	190	SWIFT, Seth	105	SYLVESTER, Nathaniel	199
SWIFT, Josiah	77	SWIFT, Seth	106	SYLVESTER, Salley	208
SWIFT, Josiah	120	SWIFT, Seth	129	SYLVESTER, Susannah	197
SWIFT, Josiah	201	SWIFT, Solomon	50	SYLVESTER, Thomas	181
SWIFT, Judah	64	SWIFT, Stephen	193	SYLVESTER, Thomas	214
SWIFT, Keziah	173	SWIFT, Susannah	215	SYMMES, Hannah	153
SWIFT, Lemuel	53	SWIFT, Thankful	71	SYMMS, Grace	197
SWIFT, Lemuell	172	SWIFT, Thankfull	52	SYMMS, Isaac	153

VITAL RECORDS OF THE TOWN OF PLYMOUTH

SYMMS, Isaac	180	TAYLOR, Mary	193	THOMAS, Dorothy	153
SYMMS, Isaac	188	TAYLOR, Mary	209	THOMAS, Eleazer	139
SYMMS, Isaac	194	TAYLOR, Nancy	153	THOMAS, Eleonar	123
SYMMS, Isaac	201	TAYLOR, Nancy Catharine	153	THOMAS, Eleoner	111
SYMMS, Lazarus	205	TAYLOR, Philip	213	THOMAS, Elizabeth	60
SYMMS, Margaret	204	TAYLOR, Sarah	107	THOMAS, Elizabeth	90
SYMMS, Martha	198	TAYLOR, Sarah	156	THOMAS, Elizabeth	112
SYVESTER, Mary	197	TAYLOR, Sarah	195	THOMAS, Elizabeth	114
		TAYLOR, Sarah Jane	156	THOMAS, Ephraim	95
T		TENTER, Dorothy	205	THOMAS, Eunice	222
		TESSIER, John Mitchell	207	THOMAS, Eunice Burr	141
TABER, Lemuel	186	TEWE, ----- (Capt.)	99	THOMAS, Ezra	139
TABOR, Rebekah	67	THACHER, Betsey Hayward	206	THOMAS, Ezra	193
TABOR, Thomas	67	THACHER, Elizabeth	180	THOMAS, Fanny	139
TACK, Job	185	THACHER, James (Doctr.)	194	THOMAS, Frederick	165
TAYLER, -----	81	THACHER, John	70	THOMAS, Gamaliel	139
TAYLER, Edward	132	THACHER, Mary	178	THOMAS, Hannah	60
TAYLER, Elizabeth	132	THACHER, Susen	215	THOMAS, Hannah	129
TAYLER, Jacob	74	THARE, Zilpah	174	THOMAS, Hannah	141
TAYLER, Jacob	81	THATCHER, Fear	190	THOMAS, Hannah	146
TAYLER, Jacob	124	THATCHER, Marcy	118	THOMAS, Hannah	191
TAYLER, Jacob	132	THAXTER, Sarah	216	THOMAS, Hannah	193
TAYLER, Jacob	171	THOMAS, -----	139	THOMAS, Hannah	194
TAYLER, Jemimah	132	THOMAS, ----- (female)	102	THOMAS, Hannah	204
TAYLER, Joannah	132	THOMAS, ----- (female)	153	THOMAS, Hope	60
TAYLER, Leavitt	81	THOMAS, ----- (male)	95	THOMAS, Hope	71
TAYLER, Lucy	132	THOMAS, Abigail	21	THOMAS, Ichabod	95
TAYLER, Mary	74	THOMAS, Abigail	27	THOMAS, Ichabod	184
TAYLER, Mary	81	THOMAS, Abigail	95	THOMAS, Isaac	102
TAYLER, Mary	132	THOMAS, Abigail	102	THOMAS, Isaac	112
TAYLER, Priscilla	81	THOMAS, Abigail	111	THOMAS, Isaac	113
TAYLER, Rebeckah	81	THOMAS, Abigail	113	THOMAS, Isaac	146
TAYLER, Sarah	81	THOMAS, Abigail	178	THOMAS, Isaac	198
TAYLER, Sarah	106	THOMAS, Abigail	186	THOMAS, Isabela	169
TAYLER, Sarah	132	THOMAS, Abigail	214	THOMAS, Isabella	169
TAYLOR, Edward	81	THOMAS, Abraham	199	THOMAS, James	27
TAYLOR, Edward	197	THOMAS, Alanson	139	THOMAS, James	95
TAYLOR, Elizabeth	200	THOMAS, Ann	90	THOMAS, James	105
TAYLOR, Frances Elizabeth	156	THOMAS, Anna	165	THOMAS, James	146
TAYLOR, George Washington	156	THOMAS, Asa	139	THOMAS, James	176
TAYLOR, Jane Samson	215	THOMAS, Benjamin	187	THOMAS, Joab	207
TAYLOR, Jemima	188	THOMAS, Benjamin	213	THOMAS, John	19
TAYLOR, Joanna	193	THOMAS, Bethiah	133	THOMAS, John	60
TAYLOR, John	153	THOMAS, Bethiah	170	THOMAS, John	95
TAYLOR, John	195	THOMAS, Betsey	144	THOMAS, John	96
TAYLOR, John	198	THOMAS, Betsey	219	THOMAS, John	102
TAYLOR, John	203	THOMAS, Charles	147	THOMAS, John	111
TAYLOR, Joseph	156	THOMAS, Content	213	THOMAS, John	141
TAYLOR, Lucy	197	THOMAS, Deborah	112	THOMAS, John	153
TAYLOR, Lydia	81	THOMAS, Deborah	114	THOMAS, John	165
TAYLOR, Mary	81	THOMAS, Deborah	221	THOMAS, John	186

Name	Page	Name	Page	Name	Page
THOMAS, John Boice	213	THOMAS, Nathaniel	75	THOMSON, Charles	200
THOMAS, John Boies	169	THOMAS, Nathaniel	118	THRASHER, Azariah	189
THOMAS, John Boyse	169	THOMAS, Nathaniel	124	THRASHER, Cloe	214
THOMAS, Jonathan	27	THOMAS, Nathaniel	125	THRASHER, Daniel	190
THOMAS, Jonathan	95	THOMAS, Nathaniel	130	THRASHER, David	195
THOMAS, Jonathan	102	THOMAS, Nathaniel	173	THRASHER, David	215
THOMAS, Joseph	19	THOMAS, Nathaniel	191	THRASHER, George	194
THOMAS, Joseph	153	THOMAS, Nathaniel	200	THRASHER, George	220
THOMAS, Joshua	102	THOMAS, Nathl.	95	THRASHER, Jonathan	194
THOMAS, Joshua	153	THOMAS, Nathl.	96	THRASHER, Joshua	213
THOMAS, Joshua	169	THOMAS, Nathl.	101	THRASHER, Rhoda	212
THOMAS, Joshua	195	THOMAS, Nathl.	153	THRASHER, Thankfull	184
THOMAS, Joshua	197	THOMAS, Nathl. Gardner	165	THROOP, Billings	174
THOMAS, Josiah	193	THOMAS, Peter	90	THROOP, Esther	124
THOMAS, Justus	147	THOMAS, Peter	181	THURSTON, David	188
THOMAS, Keziah	182	THOMAS, Priscilla	27	THURSTON, John B.	213
THOMAS, Lemuel	195	THOMAS, Priscilla	74	TILDEN, Margeret	130
THOMAS, Levi	204	THOMAS, Priscilla	128	TILLEY, Martha	178
THOMAS, Lois	213	THOMAS, Ranson	194	TILLEY, Mary	106
THOMAS, Lovise	207	THOMAS, Rebeccah	153	TILLSON, Eleazer Crocker	210
THOMAS, Lydia	123	THOMAS, Rupah	217	TILLSON, Elizabeth	197
THOMAS, Lydia	204	THOMAS, Salley	200	TILLSON, Sarah	109
THOMAS, Marcy	126	THOMAS, Sally	213	TILSEN, Edmond	64
THOMAS, Margaret	185	THOMAS, Sarah	71	TILSEN, Elizabeth	64
THOMAS, Margeret	153	THOMAS, Sarah	102	TILSEN, Hanah	64
THOMAS, Mary	19	THOMAS, Sarah	147	TILSEN, Peres	64
THOMAS, Mary	71	THOMAS, Sarah	193	TILSON, -----	18
THOMAS, Mary	74	THOMAS, Sarah	214	TILSON, An	18
THOMAS, Mary	75	THOMAS, Sarah Ann	147	TILSON, Ann	69
THOMAS, Mary	79	THOMAS, Solomon	187	TILSON, Edmond	66
THOMAS, Mary	90	THOMAS, Stephen	147	TILSON, Edmond	69
THOMAS, Mary	95	THOMAS, Stephen	218	TILSON, Edmond	71
THOMAS, Mary	102	THOMAS, Susan Frances	147	TILSON, Edmond	129
THOMAS, Mary	112	THOMAS, Susanna	212	TILSON, Edmund	18
THOMAS, Mary	115	THOMAS, Susannah	95	TILSON, Eliazebeth	18
THOMAS, Mary	118	THOMAS, Susannah	171	TILSON, Eliza.	123
THOMAS, Mary	128	THOMAS, Waterman	146	TILSON, Elizabeth	18
THOMAS, Mary	129	THOMAS, William	90	TILSON, Elizabeth	66
THOMAS, Mary	171	THOMAS, William	95	TILSON, Elizabeth	71
THOMAS, Mary	200	THOMAS, William	105	TILSON, Elizabeth	108
THOMAS, Mary	208	THOMAS, William	153	TILSON, Hannah	69
THOMAS, Mary-Anna	165	THOMAS, William	169	TILSON, Hannah	106
THOMAS, Mercy	153	THOMAS, William	185	TILSON, Hannah	113
THOMAS, Meriah	201	THOMAS, William (Docter)	153	TILSON, Joanna	18
THOMAS, Micah	185	THOMAS, William (Doctr.)	90	TILSON, John	18
THOMAS, Nancy Everson	147	THOMAS, William (Doctr.)	208	TILSON, John	69
THOMAS, Nathan	71	THOMAS, Wm.	113	TILSON, John	197
THOMAS, Nathaniel	19	THOMAS. John	117	TILSON, Lidiah	68
THOMAS, Nathaniel	60	THOMAS. Mary	77	TILSON, Lidiah	69
THOMAS, Nathaniel	71	THOMSON, Andrew	171	TILSON, Marsy	68
THOMAS, Nathaniel	74	THOMSON, Betty	194	TILSON, Mary	18

TILSON, Mary	66	TINCOM, Ruth	40	TINKCOM, Mary	111
TILSON, Patience	119	TINCOM, Sarah	34	TINKCOM, Mary	123
TILSON, Peres	108	TINCOM, Sarah	39	TINKCOM, Mary	163
TILSON, Peres	123	TINCOM, Sarah	67	TINKCOM, Mary	175
TILSON, Ruth	18	TINCOM, Zedekiah	39	TINKCOM, Mercy	158
TILSON, Sarah	113	TINKAM, Ann	52	TINKCOM, Peter	34
TILSSON, Perez	178	TINKAM, Edward	123	TINKCOM, Peter	50
TIMBERLAKE, James	188	TINKCOM, Arthur	50	TINKCOM, Peter	119
TIMBERLECK, James	137	TINKCOM, Briggs	102	TINKCOM, Phebe	89
TIMBERLECK, Lydia	137	TINKCOM, Caleb	73	TINKCOM, Phebe	181
TIMBERLECK, Sarah	137	TINKCOM, Caleb	130	TINKCOM, Priscilla	89
TINCKAM, Edward	52	TINKCOM, Ebenezer	89	TINKCOM, Priscilla	189
TINCKAM, John	52	TINKCOM, Ebenezer	119	TINKCOM, Remembrance	107
TINCKAM, Mary	52	TINKCOM, Ebenezer	125	TINKCOM, Sarah	105
TINCKAM, Mary	70	TINKCOM, Ebenezr.	208	TINKCOM, Sarah	106
TINCKCOM, Ebenezer	89	TINKCOM, Edwd.	111	TINKCOM, Sarah	158
TINCKCOM, Isaac	121	TINKCOM, Eleoner	173	TINKCOM, Sarah	186
TINCKCOM, Mary	89	TINKCOM, Eliza.	109	TINKCOM, Susanna	182
TINCKCOM, Sarah	89	TINKCOM, Elizabeth	102	TINKCOM, Susannah	89
TINCKHAM, Caleb	89	TINKCOM, Fear	172	TINKCOM, Zedekiah	104
TINCKHAM, Caleb	90	TINKCOM, Hannah	34	TINKCOM, Zedekiah	158
TINCKHAM, Fear	90	TINKCOM, Hannah	181	TINKHAM, Anna	70
TINCKHAM, Hanna	56	TINKCOM, Ichabod	163	TINKHAM, Asa	213
TINCKHAM, Jacob	56	TINKCOM, Ichabod	186	TINKHAM, Ebenezar	77
TINCKHAM, Jacob	129	TINKCOM, Isaac	102	TINKHAM, Edward	123
TINCKHAM, Marcy	56	TINKCOM, Isaac	106	TINKHAM, Hannah	71
TINCKHAM, Mercy	89	TINKCOM, Isaac	107	TINKHAM, Jacob	71
TINCKHAM, Nathaniel	90	TINKCOM, Isaac	183	TINKHAM, Jacob	73
TINCKHAM, Patience	90	TINKCOM, Jacob	34	TINKHAM, Jane	77
TINCKHAM, Ruth	71	TINKCOM, Jacob	50	TINKHAM, John	70
TINCKHAM, Ruth	130	TINKCOM, Jacob	108	TINKHAM, Judeth	73
TINCKHAM, Sarah	90	TINKCOM, Jacob	123	TINKHAM, Ruth	181
TINCKOM, Sarah	100	TINKCOM, Jacob	126	TISDALL, Abraham	159
TINCOM, Caleb	34	TINKCOM, Jacob	205	TISDALL, Experience	159
TINCOM, Ebenazar	34	TINKCOM, James	89	TISDALL, Isaac	159
TINCOM, Ebenezer	40	TINKCOM, Jean	89	TISDALL, Samuel	159
TINCOM, Elizabeth	39	TINKCOM, Kezia	102	TISDELL, Abraham	180
TINCOM, Hannah	39	TINKCOM, Levi	205	TOBE, Jonathan	121
TINCOM, Helkiah	34	TINKCOM, Levi	209	TOBEY, Deborah	111
TINCOM, Helkiah	39	TINKCOM, Lucenda	214	TOBEY, Joan	131
TINCOM, Isaac	39	TINKCOM, Lydia	34	TOBEY, Jonathan	111
TINCOM, Isaac	67	TINKCOM, Lydia	108	TOBEY, Thomas	122
TINCOM, Jacob	34	TINKCOM, Lydia	111	TOMMAS, Abigall	73
TINCOM, John	34	TINKCOM, Lydia	172	TOMMAS, John	73
TINCOM, John	39	TINKCOM, Marcy	73	TOMMAS, John	127
TINCOM, Lydia	40	TINKCOM, Marcy	104	TOMMAS, Richard	120
TINCOM, Martha	39	TINKCOM, Marcy	105	TOMPOM, Leah	125
TINCOM, Martha	105	TINKCOM, Martha	106	TOMSON, Isaac	117
TINCOM, Mary	34	TINKCOM, Mary	34	TOMSON, James	34
TINCOM, Mary	39	TINKCOM, Mary	50	TOMSON, Joseph	34
TINCOM, Ruth	34	TINKCOM, Mary	89	TOMSON, Peter	34

Name	Page	Name	Page	Name	Page
TOMSON, Sarah	34	TORREY, Lucy	195	TOTMAN, Elizabeth	188
TOREY, Heveland	47	TORREY, Lucy Haviland	154	TOTMAN, Elizabeth	202
TOREY, Heverland	47	TORREY, Lydia	154	TOTMAN, Elizh.	156
TOREY, John	47	TORREY, Lydia Ann	154	TOTMAN, Elkanah	65
TOREY, Joseph	48	TORREY, Marcy	24	TOTMAN, Elkanah	101
TOREY, Josiah	48	TORREY, Mary	27	TOTMAN, Elkanah	123
TOREY, Nathaniel	48	TORREY, Mary	35	TOTMAN, Elkanah	127
TOREY, Thomas	48	TORREY, Mary	153	TOTMAN, Elkanah	132
TOREY, William	48	TORREY, Mercy	178	TOTMAN, Elkanan	29
TORRANCE, Betsy	214	TORREY, Mercy	185	TOTMAN, Experance	107
TORRANCE, Lilley Russell	217	TORREY, Meriah Morton	203	TOTMAN, Experiance	74
TORRANCE, Thomas	196	TORREY, Nathaniel	137	TOTMAN, Experience	32
TORREY, ----- (Deacon)	112	TORREY, Nathl.	113	TOTMAN, Experience	106
TORREY, Abigail	187	TORREY, Nathll.	112	TOTMAN, Experience	180
TORREY, Abigail Thomas	212	TORREY, Patty	197	TOTMAN, Experience	189
TORREY, Anna	35	TORREY, Priscilla	137	TOTMAN, Hannah	32
TORREY, Anna	137	TORREY, Priscilla	187	TOTMAN, Hannah	156
TORREY, Annah	137	TORREY, Saml.	131	TOTMAN, Joanna	132
TORREY, Anne	112	TORREY, Samuel	128	TOTMAN, Joanna	185
TORREY, Betsey Harlow	207	TORREY, Sarah	137	TOTMAN, Johanna	128
TORREY, Daniel	137	TORREY, Thomas	113	TOTMAN, John	82
TORREY, Deborah	78	TORREY, Thomas	154	TOTMAN, John	109
TORREY, Deborah	128	TORREY, Thomas	194	TOTMAN, John	140
TORREY, Deborah	131	TORREY, William	35	TOTMAN, John	175
TORREY, Deborah	208	TORREY, William	115	TOTMAN, John	188
TORREY, Elizabeth	137	TORRY, ----- (Decon)	75	TOTMAN, Joseph	65
TORREY, Elizabeth	153	TORRY, Elizabeth	150	TOTMAN, Joseph	156
TORREY, Elizabeth Thomas	154	TORRY, Elizabeth Harlow	150	TOTMAN, Joseph	178
TORREY, George	153	TORRY, George Washington	150	TOTMAN, Joshua	32
TORREY, Hannah	190	TORRY, Haviland	74	TOTMAN, Joshua	65
TORREY, Hannah	204	TORRY, Haviland	125	TOTMAN, Joshua	106
TORREY, Haviland	27	TORRY, Jesse Harlow	150	TOTMAN, Joshua	128
TORREY, Haviland	153	TORRY, John	150	TOTMAN, Joshua	132
TORREY, Haviland (Deacon)	113	TORRY, Meriah	150	TOTMAN, Joshua	172
TORREY, Haviland (Deacon)	208	TORRY, Meriah Morton	150	TOTMAN, Joshua	188
TORREY, John	27	TORY, Elizabeth	47	TOTMAN, Lidiah	29
TORREY, John	78	TOTMAN, Abial	65	TOTMAN, Lucretia	74
TORREY, John	106	TOTMAN, Asaph	140	TOTMAN, Lucretia	82
TORREY, John	122	TOTMAN, Betty	132	TOTMAN, Mary	82
TORREY, John	137	TOTMAN, Deborah	32	TOTMAN, Priscilla	65
TORREY, John	153	TOTMAN, Deborah	48	TOTMAN, Reubin	140
TORREY, John	189	TOTMAN, Deborah	112	TOTMAN, Sam	70
TORREY, John	193	TOTMAN, Deborah	115	TOTMAN, Saml.	104
TORREY, John	215	TOTMAN, Debrah	70	TOTMAN, Samll.	32
TORREY, John (Deacon)	153	TOTMAN, Dorithy	29	TOTMAN, Samuel	48
TORREY, John (Deacon)	208	TOTMAN, Dorothy	65	TOTMAN, Samuel	74
TORREY, Joseph	24	TOTMAN, Ebenezer	82	TOTMAN, Samuel	127
TORREY, Joseph	35	TOTMAN, Elizabeth	65	TOTMAN, Samuell	32
TORREY, Joshua	202	TOTMAN, Elizabeth	109	TOTMAN, Sarah	65
TORREY, Josiah	24	TOTMAN, Elizabeth	140	TOTMAN, Sarah	109
TORREY, Josiah	105	TOTMAN, Elizabeth	171	TOTMAN, Sarah	156

VITAL RECORDS OF THE TOWN OF PLYMOUTH

Name	Page	Name	Page	Name	Page	Name	Page
TOTMAN, Sarah	173	TRIBBLE, John	217	TURNER, Joseph	41
TOTMAN, Simeon	109	TRIBELL, Isaac	213	TURNER, Lothrop	193
TOTMAN, Simeon	120	TRIBLE, Joseph	107	TURNER, Lothrop	197
TOTMAN, Simmion	48	TRIBLE, Sarah	107	TURNER, Lucy	198
TOTMAN, Stephen	29	TUBS, Deborah	128	TURNER, Lydia D.	156
TOTMAN, Thomas	29	TUCKER, Lemuel	190	TURNER, Martha Thomas	156
TOTMAN, Thomas	74	TUCKER, Stephen Hill	205	TURNER, Mary	41
TOTMAN, Thomas	82	TUCKERMAN, Polley	203	TURNER, Mary	115
TOTMAN, Thomas	128	TUFFTS, Jonathan	197	TURNER, Mary	197
TOTMAN, Thomas	132	TUFTS, Elizabeth	212	TURNER, Mary Ann	156
TOTO, George	179	TUFTS, Jonathan	186	TURNER, Pricila	41
TOXE, Robert	121	TUNER, David	104	TURNER, Prudence	199
TRASHER, Abiah	193	TUNER, Judah	199	TURNER, Rebecca	194
TRASK, Abigail	18	TUPER, Meriba	130	TURNER, Ruth	65
TRASK, Abigal	18	TUPPER, -----	92	TURNER, Ruth	71
TRASK, Elias	18	TUPPER, Charles	92	TURNER, Ruth	101
TRASK, Jerusha	138	TUPPER, Eliakim	92	TURNER, Ruth	190
TRASK, Jerusha	200	TUPPER, Enoch	194	TURNER, Sally	156
TRASK, John	18	TUPPER, Joannah	79	TURNER, Sarah	65
TRASK, Joseph	138	TUPPER, Joannah	116	TURNER, Sarah	70
TRASK, Joseph	172	TUPPER, Joannah	121	TURNER, Stephen	156
TRASK, Joseph	173	TUPPER, Martha	78	TWINEY, Jabez	120
TRASK, Mary	129	TUPPER, Martha	116		
TRASK, Mary	131	TUPPER, Martha	120	**U**	
TRASK, Priscilla	138	TUPPER, Mary	92		
TRASK, Rebeckah	177	TUPPER, Mary	117	UNQUIT, Mathew	77
TRASK, Samuel	18	TUPPER, Mary	197	UNQUIT, Mathew	120
TRASK, Thomas	138	TUPPER, Nathaniel	176	UNQUIT, Sarah	77
TRASK, Thomas	177	TUPPER, Ruth	92		
TRASK, William	138	TUPPER, Susannah	183	**V**	
TREBLE, Joseph	105	TURNER, Benjamin Franklin	156		
TREEBLE, Anna	103	TURNER, Bethiah	41	VAHAN, Joseph	129
TREEBLE, Anna	193	TURNER, Daved	71	VALLAR, Silas	183
TREEBLE, Betsey	103	TURNER, David	65	VALLER, Ann	88
TREEBLE, Elizabeth	195	TURNER, David	101	VALLER, Anne	88
TREEBLE, James	206	TURNER, David	104	VALLER, John	88
TREEBLE, John	206	TURNER, David	129	VALLER, John	124
TREEBLE, Joseph	103	TURNER, David	172	VALLER, John	211
TREEBLE, Joseph	124	TURNER, David	198	VALLER, Lois	88
TREEBLE, Joseph	186	TURNER, Deborah	65	VALLER, Lowis	188
TREEBLE, Joseph	199	TURNER, Deborah	104	VALLER, Lowis	214
TREEBLE, Lydia	103	TURNER, Deborah	189	VALLER, Lowis	218
TREEBLE, Lydia	191	TURNER, Deborah	191	VALLER, Mary	88
TREEBLE, Polley	204	TURNER, Eliza.	210	VALLER, Sarah	88
TREEBLE, Sarah	103	TURNER, Emeline Frances	156	VALLER, Sarah	218
TREEBLE, Sarah	185	TURNER, Ephraim	41	VALLER, Silas	88
TREEBLE, Sarah	199	TURNER, Hannah	194	VALLER, Silas	212
TREEBLE, William	210	TURNER, Humphray	41	VALLER, Silvanus	88
TREEBLES, Mary	190	TURNER, Humphry	41	VALLER, Simeon	88
TRENT, James	202	TURNER, Jesse	215	VALLER, Simeon	191
TRIBBLE, James	217	TURNER, John	200	VALLUR, Mary Dunber	218

VITAL RECORDS OF THE TOWN OF PLYMOUTH

VALLUR, Sarah	181	WAITE, Mary	78	WARD, Robart (Rev.)	73		
VALLUR, Simeon	215	WAITE, Return	101	WARD, Sarah	79		
VAUGHAN, Alvan	217	WAITE, Richard	61	WARD, Sarah	82		
VAUGHAN, Betsey	213	WAITE, Richard	72	WARD, Sarah	104		
VAUGHAN, Daniel	212	WAITE, Sarah	61	WARD, Thomas	45		
VAUGHAN, Elezabeth	71	WAITE, Sarah	172	WARD, Thomas	74		
VAUGHAN, Hosea	206	WAITE, Thomas	61	WARD, Thomas	82		
VAUGHAN, Joseph	71	WALKER, Antionette A.	149	WARD, Thomas	156		
VAUGHAN, Levi	206	WALKER, Elijah	149	WAREN, Hanah	21		
VAUGHAN, Olever	210	WALKER, Elizabeth B.	149	WAREN, Pricila	26		
VAUGHAN, Saml.	115	WALKER, Hannah	149	WARREN, -----	35		
VAY, Stephen	217	WALKER, Paulina Ross	149	WARREN, Abigaiel	71		
VEAZIE, Deborah	79	WALKER, Remembrance	115	WARREN, Abigail	35		
VEAZIE, Samuell (Rev.)	79	WALL, John	171	WARREN, Abigial	21		
VINCENT, Mary	106	WAMPUM, Joseph	117	WARREN, Alatheah	156		
VINCENT, Mary	176	WANFOR, John	201	WARREN, Alethear	198		
VINCENT, Philip	116	WARD, Alse	45	WARREN, Alithea	71		
VINCENT, Phillip	79	WARD, Alse	74	WARREN, Alletheah	58		
VINCENT, Phillippe	79	WARD, Benjamin	45	WARREN, Allice	71		
VIRGEN, George William	217	WARD, Benjamin	82	WARREN, Alse	14		
VIRGEN, John (Capt.)	218	WARD, Ebenezer	82	WARREN, Ann	64		
VIRGEN, Samuel	204	WARD, Ebenezer	180	WARREN, Anne	70		
VOLENTINE, Basha	213	WARD, Ebenezr.	156	WARREN, Benjamin	21		
VOLENTINE, Simeon	206	WARD, Elizabeth	45	WARREN, Beniamin	21		
VOSE, Joseph	217	WARD, Elizabeth	69	WARREN, Benjamin	67		
		WARD, Elizabeth	82	WARREN, Benjamin	78		
W		WARD, Elizabeth	106	WARREN, Benjamin	90		
		WARD, Elizabeth	107	WARREN, Benjamin	100		
WADE, James	170	WARD, Ephraim	45	WARREN, Benjamin	149		
WADSWORTH, Charlotte	218	WARD, Ephraim	79	WARREN, Benjamin	178		
WADSWORTH, Christopher	204	WARD, Ephraim	82	WARREN, Benjamin	197		
WADSWORTH, James	222	WARD, Ephraim	116	WARREN, Benjamin	206		
WADSWORTH, Mercy	201	WARD, Hannah	45	WARREN, Benjamin	214		
WADSWORTH, Peleg	186	WARD, Hannah	79	WARREN, Benjamin	215		
WADSWORTH, Prince	181	WARD, Hannah	82	WARREN, Benjamin (Capt.)	21		
WADSWORTH, Zilpah	204	WARD, Hannah	115	WARREN, Benjamin (Capt.)	71		
WAIT, Martha	78	WARD, Hannah	178	WARREN, Benjamin (Capt.)	101		
WAIT, Return	78	WARD, Joanna	74	WARREN, Benjamin (Capt.)	201		
WAITE, Abigal	61	WARD, Joanna	82	WARREN, Charles	141		
WAITE, Elizabeth	61	WARD, Joanna	176	WARREN, Charles Henry	141		
WAITE, Elizabeth	171	WARD, Johanna	182	WARREN, Charlotte	218		
WAITE, Hannah	61	WARD, John	45	WARREN, Cornelius	75		
WAITE, Hannah	181	WARD, Jonathan	82	WARREN, David	200		
WAITE, Lydia	61	WARD, Lydia	156	WARREN, Edward	14		
WAITE, Lydia	78	WARD, Marcy	45	WARREN, Elizabeth	14		
WAITE, Martha	61	WARD, Margaret	73	WARREN, Elizabeth	58		
WAITE, Martha	109	WARD, Mary	82	WARREN, Elizabeth	66		
WAITE, Martha	115	WARD, Mary	180	WARREN, Elizabeth	107		
WAITE, Martha	171	WARD, Mercy	75	WARREN, Elizabeth	116		
WAITE, Mary	61	WARD, Nathan	45	WARREN, Ester	71		
WAITE, Mary	72	WARD, Nathan	69	WARREN, Esther	21		

VITAL RECORDS OF THE TOWN OF PLYMOUTH

WARREN, George	141	WARREN, Mehittabel	67	WARREN, William	156
WARREN, Hanna	100	WARREN, Mehittabl	26	WARREN, William	178
WARREN, Hannah	21	WARREN, Mercy	75	WARREN, William	187
WARREN, Hannah	35	WARREN, Mercy	154	WARREN, Winslow	64
WARREN, Hannah	67	WARREN, Mersy	66	WARREN, Winslow	141
WARREN, Hannah	73	WARREN, Nathaniel	21	WARRIN, Edward	141
WARREN, Hannah	180	WARREN, Nathaniel	35	WARRIN, Mercia Otis	215
WARREN, Henry	141	WARREN, Nathaniel	75	WARRIN, Rebecca	197
WARREN, Henry	198	WARREN, Nathaniel	99	WASHBN., Abial	194
WARREN, Hope	14	WARREN, Nathaniel	117	WASHBN., Ruth	198
WARREN, Hope	71	WARREN, Nathl.	35	WASHBON, Mary	69
WARREN, Jabiz	98	WARREN, Patience	14	WASHBOND, Josiah	68
WARREN, James	14	WARREN, Patience	21	WASHBOND, Marsy	68
WARREN, James	64	WARREN, Patience	66	WASHBORN, Ephraim	73
WARREN, James	99	WARREN, Patience	71	WASHBORN, Mary	73
WARREN, James	141	WARREN, Pelham Winslow	141	WASHBURN, Abial	194
WARREN, James	170	WARREN, Penelope	64	WASHBURN, Abial	201
WARREN, James	208	WARREN, Pricila	21	WASHBURN, Abigail	104
WARREN, James (Capt.)	100	WARREN, Pricila	99	WASHBURN, Abigal	82
WARREN, Jams	66	WARREN, Priscilla	58	WASHBURN, Bathshea	213
WARREN, Jane	149	WARREN, Priscilla	106	WASHBURN, Benjamin	194
WARREN, Jesse L.	156	WARREN, Prisilla	107	WASHBURN, Benjamin	198
WARREN, John	14	WARREN, Rebecca	90	WASHBURN, George	139
WARREN, John	35	WARREN, Rebecca	194	WASHBURN, George	218
WARREN, Joseph	21	WARREN, Rebeckah	149	WASHBURN, Harriot	215
WARREN, Joseph	26	WARREN, Rebeckah	156	WASHBURN, Israel	160
WARREN, Joseph	58	WARREN, Rebeckah	172	WASHBURN, Joanna	210
WARREN, Joseph	67	WARREN, Rebekah	78	WASHBURN, John	82
WARREN, Joseph	71	WARREN, Richard	98	WASHBURN, John	171
WARREN, Joseph	98	WARREN, Richard	99	WASHBURN, John	189
WARREN, Joseph	105	WARREN, Richard	141	WASHBURN, John	194
WARREN, Joseph	106	WARREN, Ruth	35	WASHBURN, Levi	160
WARREN, Joseph	107	WARREN, Ruth	188	WASHBURN, Lydia	198
WARREN, Joseph	116	WARREN, Salle	198	WASHBURN, Marcy	82
WARREN, Joseph	154	WARREN, Salley	149	WASHBURN, Mary	82
WARREN, Joseph	178	WARREN, Sarah	14	WASHBURN, Mary	106
WARREN, Josiah	64	WARREN, Sarah	35	WASHBURN, Mary	137
WARREN, Lydia	107	WARREN, Sarah	64	WASHBURN, Mary	195
WARREN, Marcia Otis	141	WARREN, Sarah	66	WASHBURN, Nathaniel	137
WARREN, Marcy	14	WARREN, Sarah	70	WASHBURN, Nathaniel	172
WARREN, Marcy	21	WARREN, Sarah	73	WASHBURN, Nathl.	137
WARREN, Marcy	106	WARREN, Sarah	75	WASHBURN, Pearce	200
WARREN, Marcy	141	WARREN, Sarah	98	WASHBURN, Perces	200
WARREN, Marcy	177	WARREN, Sarah	171	WASHBURN, Phillip	82
WARREN, Mary	14	WARREN, Sarah	178	WASHBURN, Phillip	160
WARREN, Mary	58	WARREN, Sarah	222	WASHBURN, Phillips	180
WARREN, Mary	105	WARREN, Susannah	35	WASHBURN, Prince	194
WARREN, Mary	107	WARREN, Susannah	181	WASHBURN, Priscilla	139
WARREN, Mary	141	WARREN, Thomas	105	WASHBURN, Priscilla	205
WARREN, Mary	200	WARREN, Thomas	107	WASHBURN, Priscilla D.	139
WARREN, Mary Ann	141	WARREN, William	58	WASHBURN, Reubin	181

VITAL RECORDS OF THE TOWN OF PLYMOUTH

WASHBURN, Sarah	160	WATERMAN, Samuel	18	WATSON, Mary	38
WASHBURN, Seth	82	WATERMAN, Samuel	98	WATSON, Mercy	38
WASHBURN, Seth	180	WATERMAN, Samuell	18	WATSON, Phebe	38
WASHBURN, Silence	160	WATERMAN, Sarah	79	WATSON, Priscilla	49
WASHBURN, Stillman	215	WATERMAN, Sarah	116	WATSON, Priscilla	74
WASHBURN, Thankfull	191	WATKINS, James	111	WATSON, Priscilla	75
WASHBURN, Thomas	198	WATKINS, James	117	WATSON, Priscilla	212
WASHBURNE, Thankfull	82	WATKINS, Jerusha	111	WATSON, Salley	190
WASHINGTON, Henry	136	WATKINS, Jerusha	171	WATSON, Sarah	67
WAST, Elizabeth	69	WATKINS, Jonathan	181	WATSON, Sarah	101
WAST, Rebecca	178	WATSON, ----- (male)	80	WATSON, Thomas	183
WAST, Richard	69	WATSON, Abigail	80	WATSON, William	49
WATE, Abigail	160	WATSON, Abigail	101	WATSON, William	136
WATE, Amasa	160	WATSON, Benjamin	136	WATSON, William	172
WATERMAN, Abigail	105	WATSON, Daniel	80	WATSON, William	212
WATERMAN, Annah	18	WATSON, Eliza.	196	WATSON, Winslow	214
WATERMAN, Bethiah	18	WATSON, Elizabeth	38	WEBBER, Priscilla	90
WATERMAN, Elizabeth	66	WATSON, Elizabeth	80	WEBBER, Richard	90
WATERMAN, Elizabeth	85	WATSON, Elizabeth	101	WEBQUIST, Mary	193
WATERMAN, Elizabeth	174	WATSON, Elizabeth	136	WEEKES, Lot	212
WATERMAN, Elkanah	85	WATSON, Elizabeth	183	WEEKS, Benjamin	58
WATERMAN, Elkanah	137	WATSON, Elizabeth	195	WEEKS, Elizabeth	58
WATERMAN, Fear	145	WATSON, Elizabeth	208	WEEKS, Hannah	209
WATERMAN, Hannah	18	WATSON, Elkanah	38	WEEKS, Isaac	58
WATERMAN, Hannah	74	WATSON, Elkanah	49	WEEKS, Jabesh	58
WATERMAN, Hannah	85	WATSON, Elkanah	98	WEEKS, Joshua	217
WATERMAN, Hannah	177	WATSON, Elkanah	171	WEEKS, Mary	58
WATERMAN, Ichabod	173	WATSON, Elkanah	177	WEEKS, Mehittable	206
WATERMAN, Isaac	27	WATSON, Ellen	136	WEIGHT, Martha	70
WATERMAN, James	85	WATSON, Ellen	194	WEIGHT, Mary	70
WATERMAN, James	183	WATSON, Georg	97	WEIGHT, Retorne	70
WATERMAN, Jerusha	145	WATSON, George	80	WELLINGTON, George	217
WATERMAN, Joanna	193	WATSON, George	101	WENTFORD, Hope	221
WATERMAN, John	18	WATSON, George	104	WESCOAT, Ruth	212
WATERMAN, John	74	WATSON, George	114	WESCOT, Benjamin	215
WATERMAN, John	85	WATSON, George	173	WESGATE, Derias	217
WATERMAN, Joshua	145	WATSON, George	181	WEST, Bethiah	71
WATERMAN, Josiah	27	WATSON, George	191	WEST, Bethiah	85
WATERMAN, Josiah	145	WATSON, George	208	WEST, Bethiah	101
WATERMAN, Josiah	172	WATSON, John	38	WEST, Bethiah	189
WATERMAN, Marsey	18	WATSON, John	49	WEST, Beththya	55
WATERMAN, Mary	27	WATSON, John	74	WEST, Bethya	55
WATERMAN, Mary	67	WATSON, John	80	WEST, Charles	55
WATERMAN, Mary	71	WATSON, John	101	WEST, Charles	85
WATERMAN, Mary	98	WATSON, John	116	WEST, David	55
WATERMAN, Mary	137	WATSON, John	183	WEST, Elizabeth	55
WATERMAN, Mercy	137	WATSON, John	199	WEST, Elizabeth	184
WATERMAN, Noah	190	WATSON, John	200	WEST, Ester	69
WATERMAN, Robert	27	WATSON, Lucia	203	WEST, Jean	85
WATERMAN, Robertt	68	WATSON, Lucia	218	WEST, Jean	105
WATERMAN, Samel	18	WATSON, Marsey	38	WEST, Jean	106

WEST, John	85	WESTON, John	22	WETHERHEAD, Remembrance	111	
WEST, Joshua	55	WESTON, Lewis	137	WETHERHEAD, Saml.	90	
WEST, Josiah	55	WESTON, Lewis	159	WETHERHEAD, Saml.	101	
WEST, Josiah	171	WESTON, Lewis	193	WETHERHEAD, Samuel	41	
WEST, Juda	55	WESTON, Lewis	202	WETHERHEAD, Submit	163	
WEST, Juda	71	WESTON, Lewis	220	WETHERHEAD, Submit	200	
WEST, Judah	55	WESTON, Martha	159	WETHRED, Remember	113	
WEST, Judah	101	WESTON, Mary	72	WETHREL, Hannah	45	
WEST, Lydia	55	WESTON, Mary	137	WETHREL, Lemuel	45	
WEST, Lydia	78	WESTON, Mary	205	WETHREL, Mary	78	
WEST, Lydia	109	WESTON, Mary	206	WETHREL, Thomas	75	
WEST, Margret	69	WESTON, Nathan	22	WETHRELL, Anna May	200	
WEST, Mary	67	WESTON, Patty	220	WETHRELL, Anne	160	
WEST, Mary	85	WESTON, Prudence	95	WETHRELL, Anne May	160	
WEST, Peter	109	WESTON, Rebeckah	22	WETHRELL, Elizabeth	43	
WEST, Saml.	104	WESTON, Rebekah	66	WETHRELL, Elizabeth	112	
WEST, Samuel	55	WESTON, Sarah	95	WETHRELL, Elizabeth	115	
WEST, Samuel (Rev.)	181	WESTON, Sarah	183	WETHRELL, Elizabeth	160	
WEST, Sarah	85	WESTON, Sophia	159	WETHRELL, Hannah	43	
WEST, Silas	85	WESTON, Sylvanus Bartlett	159	WETHRELL, Hannah	85	
WEST, Silas	175	WESTON, Thomas	72	WETHRELL, Hannah	87	
WEST, William	55	WESTON, William	104	WETHRELL, Hariot	160	
WEST, William	85	WESTON, William	137	WETHRELL, Isaac	160	
WESTERN, Mary	62	WESTON, William	190	WETHRELL, James	101	
WESTERN, Thomas	62	WESTON, William	204	WETHRELL, John	45	
WESTGATE, Benjamin	214	WESTON, Zabdial	202	WETHRELL, John	172	
WESTGATE, Benjamin	222	WESTON, Zachariah	22	WETHRELL, Lemuell	43	
WESTGATE, Charles	136	WESTRON, Mary	104	WETHRELL, Lucia	160	
WESTGATE, Charles Howard	136	WESTRON, Prudence	74	WETHRELL, Marcy	45	
WESTGATE, Elizabeth	219	WESTRON, Sarah	183	WETHRELL, Marcy	113	
WESTGATE, Lydia	136	WESTRON, Thomas	74	WETHRELL, Rebeckah	85	
WESTGATE, Nancy Polden	136	WESWALL, Pricila	71	WETHRELL, Rebeckah	87	
WESTGATE, Rhoda	214	WETHEREL, James	45	WETHRELL, Rebeckah	112	
WESTGATE, Susan Polden	136	WETHEREL, Mary	45	WETHRELL, Rebeckah	113	
WESTGATE, Tryphona	201	WETHEREL, Rebeah	45	WETHRELL, Sarah	160	
WESTON, Abigail	110	WETHEREL, Thomas	45	WETHRELL, Sarah	178	
WESTON, Asa	218	WETHEREL, William	45	WETHRELL, Sarah	194	
WESTON, Benjamin	210	WETHERELL, Marcy	112	WETHRELL, Sarah	209	
WESTON, Comer	137	WETHERHEAD, Abigaill	41	WETHRELL, Thomas	43	
WESTON, Coomer	193	WETHERHEAD, John	41	WETHRELL, Thomas	101	
WESTON, Coomer	206	WETHERHEAD, John	75	WETHRELL, Thomas	160	
WESTON, Edmon	66	WETHERHEAD, John	90	WETHRELL, Thomas	182	
WESTON, Edmond	22	WETHERHEAD, John	163	WETHRELL, Thomas	190	
WESTON, Edward L.	159	WETHERHEAD, John	188	WETHRELL, Thomas	201	
WESTON, Elizabeth	206	WETHERHEAD, Mary	163	WETHRELL, Thomas	214	
WESTON, George	215	WETHERHEAD, Mary	189	WETHRELL, William	85	
WESTON, Hannah	212	WETHERHEAD, Polley	200	WETHRELL, William	101	
WESTON, Harvey	218	WETHERHEAD, Rebeckah	90	WETHRELL, William	160	
WESTON, Horace	159	WETHERHEAD, Rebekah	41	WETHRELL, Wm.	87	
WESTON, James	110	WETHERHEAD, Remember	75	WHARTON, Robert	190	
WESTON, James	112	WETHERHEAD, Remember	178	WHITE, Gideon	79	

Name	Page	Name	Page	Name	Page	Name	Page
WHITE, Gideon	116	WHITTEN, Azariah	111	WINSLOW, James	24		
WHITE, Joanna	184	WHITTEN, Marcy	105	WINSLOW, James	213		
WHITE, Joannah	79	WHITTEN, Marcy	107	WINSLOW, Joanna	163		
WHITE, John	209	WHITTEN, Rebeckah	111	WINSLOW, John	82		
WHITE, Katherine	74	WHITTENEY, ----- (female)	98	WINSLOW, John	90		
WHITE, Mehetabel	172	WHITTING, Levi	193	WINSLOW, John	177		
WHITE, Reubin	217	WHOOD, Mary	117	WINSLOW, Josiah	82		
WHITE, William	210	WICKET, Bathsheba	206	WINSLOW, Mary	24		
WHITEHORN, John	181	WICKET, Beck	172	WINSLOW, Mary	82		
WHITEING, Abigail	217	WICKIT, Obediah	190	WINSLOW, Mary	163		
WHITEING, Abraham	200	WILDER, Abiah	65	WINSLOW, Mary	198		
WHITEING, Amos	206	WILDER, Anna	70	WINSLOW, Pelham	163		
WHITEING, Ephraim	200	WILDER, Mary	65	WINSLOW, Pelham	184		
WHITEING, Henry	216	WILDER, Mary	67	WINSLOW, Penelope	90		
WHITEING, Joseph	205	WILDER, Mehittabel	67	WINSLOW, Sarah	90		
WHITEING, Levi	214	WILLARD, Jacob	37	WINSLOW, Seth	24		
WHITEING, Melzer	207	WILLARD, Lucy	213	WINSLOW, Thomas	190		
WHITEING, Nathan	200	WILLARD, Sarah	37	WISWALL, Sarah Tufts	222		
WHITEING, Nathan	218	WILLARD, Simon	37	WISWELL, -----	137		
WHITEING, Thomas	214	WILLARD, Susan	205	WISWELL, John	137		
WHITEMORE, Abigal	76	WILLIAMS, Hannah	106	WISWELL, John Bradford	137		
WHITEMORE, Joseph	76	WILLIAMS, Hannah	109	WISWELL, Priscilla Thomas	137		
WHITEMORE, Joseph	118	WILLIAMS, John	175	WITHERED, Abigail	101		
WHITFIELD, Rebecca	172	WILLIAMS, Nathl.	106	WITHERED, Mercy	178		
WHITING, Benjamin	197	WILLIAMS, Thomas	109	WITHERED, Rebeckah	175		
WHITING, Ephraim	222	WILLIAMS, Thomas	116	WITHERHEAD, Abigaiell	70		
WHITING, Joseph	197	WILLIAMS, Thomas	207	WITHERHEAD, John	90		
WHITING, Levi	221	WILLIAMS, William	184	WITHERHEAD, Mary	90		
WHITING, Mary	190	WILLIS, Benj. (Judge)	165	WITHERHEAD, Marcy	90		
WHITING, Nathan	220	WILLIS, Benjamin	177	WITHERHEAD, Rebecca	90		
WHITMAN, Daniel	160	WINDSOR, Abigail	205	WITHERHEAD, Remember	90		
WHITMAN, John	160	WINDSOR, Betsey	217	WITHERHEAD, Sam	70		
WHITMAN, Mary	160	WING, Charlotte	205	WITON, Alpheus	104		
WHITMAN, Mary	201	WING, Jedediah	118	WITON, Alpheus	109		
WHITMARSH, Betsey	205	WING, Mary	183	WITON, Azariah	116		
WHITMARSH, Dorothy	109	WING, Salley	206	WITON, Bethiah	116		
WHITMARSH, Ezra	109	WING, Susannah	199	WITON, Ruth	109		
WHITMARSH, Thomas	204	WING, Vaspasian	206	WOLLINS, James	184		
WHITMARSH, William	205	WINGFORD, Lydia	205	WOMPUS, Jacob	177		
WHITNEY, Mary	188	WINSLOW Hannah	78	WOOD, Amos	188		
WHITTEMORE, Joannah	95	WINSLOW, ----- (male)	90	WOOD, Azuba	201		
WHITTEMORE, Josiah	79	WINSLOW, Anna	213	WOOD, Betty	200		
WHITTEMORE, Josiah	95	WINSLOW, Barneby	217	WOOD, Deborah	77		
WHITTEMORE, Josiah	115	WINSLOW, Edward	78	WOOD, Deborah	109		
WHITTEMORE, Josiah	186	WINSLOW, Edward	90	WOOD, Eliza.	109		
WHITTEMORE, Mary	79	WINSLOW, Edward	109	WOOD, Elizabeth	10		
WHITTEMORE, Mary	95	WINSLOW, Edward	163	WOOD, Elizabeth	92		
WHITTEMORE, Mehitable	95	WINSLOW, Edward	177	WOOD, Elizabeth	112		
WHITTEMORE, Thankfull	188	WINSLOW, Edward	200	WOOD, Elizabeth	115		
WHITTEMORE, Thomas Hatch	95	WINSLOW, Edwd.	163	WOOD, Elydia	39		
WHITTEMORE, Thomas Hatch	184	WINSLOW, Hannah	90	WOOD, Experience	39		

VITAL RECORDS OF THE TOWN OF PLYMOUTH

WOOD, Hannah	39	WOTSON, John	70	YOUNG, James	71
WOOD, Hannah	67	WOTSON, Sarah	49	YOUNG, James	130
WOOD, Isaac	39	WOTSON, Sarah	70	YOUNG, Mary	56
WOOD, James	77	WRIGHT, ----- (male)	26	YOUNG, Molly	220
WOOD, James	109	WRIGHT, Abijah	78	YOUNG, Rebecca	71
WOOD, James	118	WRIGHT, Abijah	93	YOUNG, Rebeckah	56
WOOD, Johanna	183	WRIGHT, Adam	214	YOUNG, Rebeckah	79
WOOD, John	39	WRIGHT, Benjamin	200	YOUNG, Rebeckah	116
WOOD, Keziah	39	WRIGHT, Caleb	199		
WOOD, Lidiah	71	WRIGHT, Deborah	202	**NEGROES**	
WOOD, Lydia	197	WRIGHT, Deborah	209	**NO SURNAME**	
WOOD, Marey	39	WRIGHT, Edward	111		
WOOD, Marsy	98	WRIGHT, Elizabeth	93	Barberry	194
WOOD, Mary	10	WRIGHT, Elizabeth	111	Barberry	196
WOOD, Mary	72	WRIGHT, Esther	67	Bess	75
WOOD, Mary	113	WRIGHT, Hannah	204	Bilka	71
WOOD, Nathaniel	72	WRIGHT, James	200	Billa	129
WOOD, Oliver	214	WRIGHT, Joseph	26	Boston	105
WOOD, Polley	214	WRIGHT, Joseph	137	Boston	113
WOOD, Rebeckah	186	WRIGHT, Joseph	207	Cato	74
WOOD, Sarah	39	WRIGHT, Joshua	190	Cato	125
WOOD, Soloman	39	WRIGHT, Lydia	190	Ceasor	163
WOOD, Suzannah	66	WRIGHT, Martin	26	Cesar	177
WOOD, William	92	WRIGHT, Martin	112	Cipio	119
WOOD, William	109	WRIGHT, Mehittable	189	Cuff	181
WOODEN, Sarah	71	WRIGHT, Mercy	207	Cuffe	75
WOODORTH, Abigail	67	WRIGHT, Perez	190	Cuffe	117
WOODS, Nathaniel	212	WRIGHT, Phebe	206	Dick	75
WOODWARD, Elkanah	216	WRIGHT, Polly	200	Dick	125
WOODWARD, James	204	WRIGHT, Ruth Sampson	214	Dolphin	75
WOODWORTH, Lucey	174	WRIGHT, Ruth Samson	215	Dolphin	125
WOOLSTON, Mary	116	WRIGHT, Sally	137	Dutch	124
WOOTTEN, John	187	WRIGHT, Samuel	193	Dutchess	73
WORCESTER, Abigail	184	WRIGHT, Sarah	26	Easter	163
WORMWOLL, Ester	70	WRIGHT, Sarah	112	Ebed	178
WORSTER, Hannah	115	WRIGHT, Sarah	175	Eseck	173
WOSHBON, -----	100	WRIGHT, Sarah	188	Esther	177
WOSHBON, Desre	100	WRIGHT, Sarah	203	Eunice	163
WOSHBON, John	100	WRIGHT, Sarah Robbins	137	Flora	75
WOSHBORN, Barnabas	24	WRIGHT, Susanna	214	Flora	125
WOSHBORN, Eben	24	WRIGHT, Thomas	78	Ginney	113
WOSHBORN, Elisha	24	WRIGHT, Thomas	93	Guiney	112
WOSHBORN, Ephraim	24	WRIGHT, Thomas	219	Hagar	112
WOSHBORN, Ichabod	24	WRIGHT, William	93	Hagar	113
WOSHBORN, Jabiz	24	WRITE, Richard	98	Hager	112
WOSHBORN, John	24			Hager	113
WOSHBORN, Lidiah	24	**Y**		Hannah	119
WOSHBORN, Marsey	24			Hannah	172
WOSHBORN, Thankfull	24	YONG, Lidia	65	Hannah	177
WOTSON, George	49	YOUNG, Isa	222	Hester	163
WOTSON, John	49	YOUNG, James	56	Jack	74

VITAL RECORDS OF THE TOWN OF PLYMOUTH

Jack	75
Jack	121
James	75
James	77
James	117
James	176
James	208
Jenne	74
Jenne	125
Jo	74
Joseph	130
Kate	77
Kate	125
Margeret	130
Mariah	74
Marth	130
Mary	130
Mingo	130
Nanne	75
Nanne	117
Nanne	181
Patience	121
Pebe	75
Pero	172
Phebe	74
Phebe	125
Phillip	163
Phillis	109
Phillis	172
Pompe	196
Prince	194
Quomeny	125
Quominy	73
Quosh	109
Quosh	172
Richard	130
Rose	173
Rose	176
Scipio	112
Scipio	113
Silas	186
Tobe	124
Tobe	129
Venis	186

www.ingramcontent.com/pod-product-compliance
Lightning Source LLC
Chambersburg PA
CBHW081150290426
44108CB00018B/2496